Department for Economic and Social Information
and Policy Analysis

ST/ESA/SER.R/127

Internal Migration of Women in Developing Countries

Proceedings of the United Nations
Expert Meeting on the Feminization
of Internal Migration
Aguascalientes, Mexico, 22-25 October 1991

 New York, 1993

NOTE

The designations employed and the presentation of the material in the present publication do not imply the expression of any opinion whatsoever on the part of the Secretariat of the United Nations concerning the legal status of any country, territory, city or area or of its authorities, or concerning the delimitation of its frontiers or boundaries.

The term "country" as used in the text of this publication also refers, as appropriate, to territories or areas.

In some tables, the designations "developed" and "developing" economies are intended for statistical convenience and do not necessarily express a judgement about the stage reached by a particular country or area in the development process.

The views expressed in signed papers are those of the individual authors and do not imply the expression of any opinion on the part of the United Nations Secretariat.

Papers have been edited and consolidated in accordance with United Nations practice and requirements.

ST/ESA/SER.R/127

UNITED NATIONS PUBLICATION
Sales No. E.94.XIII.3

ISBN 92-1-151260-3

Copyright © United Nations 1993
All rights reserved
Manufactured in the United States of America

PREFACE

Despite their deficiencies, statistics on internal migration suggest that women constitute about half of all internal migrants in the world. Furthermore, as the forces of modernization contribute to expand the choices open to women, many of them have been opting for migration as a means of improving their well-being and that of their families. Migration has thus become closely interrelated with the changing roles and status of women. In order to elucidate such interrelations, the Population Division of the Department of International Economic and Social Affairs,* in collaboration with the Instituto Nacional de Estadística, Geografía e Informática (INEGI) of Mexico and with the financial support of the United Nations Population Fund (UNFPA), convened an Expert Group Meeting on the Feminization of Internal Migration. The meeting was held at the headquarters of INEGI at Aguascalientes, Mexico, from 22 to 25 October 1991. Contained in this volume are the report and recommendations of the meeting as well as a selection of the papers presented to it.

The United Nations acknowledges with appreciation the support provided by Carlos Jarque, President of INEGI, whose staff handled the organizational aspects of the meeting and greatly contributed to its success. Special thanks are also due to Richard E. Bilsborrow, Carolina Population Center of the University of North Carolina, who served as the scientific editor of this volume. In addition, full recognition is due to the experts who prepared invited papers and who graciously made the necessary revisions of those papers, as well as to other participants in the meeting, who contributed significantly and constructively to the deliberations. Lastly, the financial support of UNFPA, which made this publication possible, is gratefully acknowledged.

---

*Now the Department for Economic and Social Information and Policy Analysis.

CONTENTS

	Page
Preface	iii
Explanatory notes	xi

INTERNAL FEMALE MIGRATION AND DEVELOPMENT: AN OVERVIEW
   Richard E. Bilsborrow and United Nations Secretariat 1

PART ONE. REPORT AND RECOMMENDATIONS OF THE MEETING

Chapter

I. REPORT OF THE MEETING 21
   A. The main issues relating to female migration 21
   B. The scale and scope of female migration 22
   C. Selectivity of female migrants 24
   D. Determinants of female migration 26
   E. The consequences of female migration 29
   F. Labour-market aspects of female migration 31
   G. Policy issues relevant to the migration of women and their role in development 33

II. RECOMMENDATIONS TO IMPROVE THE STATUS OF FEMALE MIGRANTS 35
   A. General measures 35
   B. Measures directed to rural areas 36
   C. Measures directed to urban areas 36
   D. Research and data needs 37

ANNEXES

I. Agenda 39
II. List of participants 40
III. List of documents 42

PART TWO. BACKGROUND AND STATEMENT ISSUES

III. MIGRANT WOMEN IN DEVELOPING COUNTRIES
   Graeme J. Hugo 47

PART THREE. DATA-COLLECTION AND MEASUREMENT ISSUES

IV. LEVELS AND TRENDS OF FEMALE INTERNAL MIGRATION IN DEVELOPING COUNTRIES, 1960-1980
   Joachim Singelmann 77

V. TYPES OF FEMALE MIGRATION
   United Nations Secretariat 94

| Chapter | Page |

VI. ISSUES IN THE MEASUREMENT OF FEMALE MIGRATION IN DEVELOPING COUNTRIES
Richard E. Bilsborrow 116

PART FOUR. CHARACTERISTICS OF FEMALE MIGRANTS AND SELECTIVITY

VII. CHARACTERISTICS OF FEMALE MIGRANTS ACCORDING TO THE 1990 CENSUS OF MEXICO
María de la Paz López, Haydea Izazola and José Gómez de León 133

VIII. FEMALE MIGRATION AND LABOUR FORCE PARTICIPATION IN A MEDIUM-SIZED CITY OF A HIGHLY URBANIZED COUNTRY
Zulma Recchini de Lattes and Sonia María Mychaszula 154

IX. THE LABOUR MARKET ASPECTS OF FEMALE MIGRATION TO BANGKOK
Pasuk Phongpaichit 178

PART FIVE. DETERMINANTS OF FEMALE MIGRATION

X. MIGRATION DECISIONS: THE ROLE OF GENDER
Nancy E. Riley and Robert W. Gardner 195

XI. THE STRUCTURAL DETERMINANTS OF FEMALE MIGRATION
Lin Lean Lim 207

XII. THE DETERMINANTS OF FEMALE MIGRATION FROM A MULTILEVEL PERSPECTIVE
Philip Guest 223

XIII. SOCIAL APPEARANCES AND ECONOMIC REALITIES OF FEMALE MIGRATION IN RURAL MALI
Sally E. Findley and Assitan Diallo 244
Annex. Variables used in the analysis and their means and standard deviations 256

XIV. THE ROLE OF WAGE DIFFERENTIALS IN DETERMINING MIGRATION SELECTIVITY BY SEX: THE CASE OF BRAZIL
Alicia Puente Cackley 259

PART SIX. CONSEQUENCES OF MIGRATION FOR WOMEN

XV. EMANCIPATION OR SUBORDINATION? CONSEQUENCES OF FEMALE MIGRATION FOR MIGRANTS AND THEIR FAMILIES
Janet Rodenburg 273

XVI. INCOME ASPIRATIONS AND MIGRANT WOMEN'S LABOUR FORCE ACTIVITY IN MALAYSIA
Kanta Alvi and Rebeca Wong 290

XVII. THE CONSEQUENCES OF TEMPORARY OUT-MIGRATION FOR THE FAMILIES LEFT BEHIND: THE CASE OF JEQUITINHONHA VALLEY, BRAZIL
Franklin W. Goza, Eduardo Rios-Neto and Paula Vieira 301

Chapter	Page

PART SEVEN. FEMALE MIGRATION, DEVELOPMENT AND POLICY ISSUES

XVIII. THE ROLE OF FEMALE MIGRATION IN DEVELOPMENT
 Gavin Jones 325

XIX. GOVERNMENT POLICIES, WOMEN AND MIGRATION: A REVIEW OF RESEARCH FINDINGS AND POLICY OPTIONS IN DEVELOPING COUNTRIES
 Alan B. Simmons 345

TABLES

No.

1. Interrelations of level of development, patterns of internal migration and share of women in migration 6
2. Number of workers in export-processing zones and other offshore manufacturing facilities, 1975 and 1986 8
3. Percentage of women among workers in export-processing zones and in manufacturing outside those zones in selected countries, early 1980s 9
4. Sex ratios of metropolitan populations and net migration, selected metropolitan centres, 1960-1970 50
5. Selected countries of Africa: estimated net rural-urban migration in recent intercensal periods .. 51
6. Selected countries of Asia: estimated net rural-urban migration in recent intercensal periods ... 52
7. Selected countries of Latin America and the Caribbean: estimated net rural-urban migration in recent intercensal periods 53
8. Urban population growth, natural increase and internal migration, selected countries in major areas by region, 1960-1980 79
9. Percentage of women in rural-urban migration and sex-specific rural-urban migration rates, selected countries in major areas by region, 1960s and 1970s 82
10. Age-specific net in-migration rates to urban areas, by sex, selected countries in major areas by region, 1960-1980 85
11. Percentage of women in net rural-urban migration, by age, selected countries in major areas by region, 1960-1980 90
12. Intrastate and interstate migrants by sex, selected developing countries 96
13. Migrants by sex and type of flow, according to urban or rural origin and destination 98
14. Migrants by sex and duration of stay at place of current residence recorded by censuses of selected developing countries 103
15. Migrants by sex and reason for migration, selected developing countries 110
16. Distribution of the population aged five years or over by migration status, sex and state of origin or destination, Mexico, 1990 135
17. Distribution of the population aged five years or over by migration status, sex, and age group, selected states of origin and destination, Mexico, 1990 137
18. Distribution of the population aged five years or over by relationship to head of household, migration status and sex, selected states of origin and destination, Mexico, 1990 139
19. Distribution of the population aged 12 years or over by marital status, migration status and sex, selected states of origin and destination, Mexico, 1990 142
20. Distribution of the population aged 12 years or over by educational attainment, migration status and sex, selected states of origin and destination, Mexico, 1990 143

No.		Page
21.	Distribution of the population aged 12 years or over by labour force participation status, migration status and sex, selected states of origin and destination, Mexico, 1990	145
22.	Distribution of the employed population by manual or non-manual occupation, migration status and sex, selected states of origin and destination, Mexico, 1990	147
23.	Distribution of the employed population by sector or economic activity, migration status and sex, selected states of origin and destination, Mexico, 1990	148
24.	Distribution of the employed population by level of income, migration status and sex, selected states of origin and destination, Mexico, 1990	151
25.	Level of urbanization and distribution of women by educational attainment, regions of Argentina, 1980	157
26.	Indicators of urbanization and urban structure, Argentina, 1950-1980	158
27.	Demographic indicators of Neuquén City, 1950-1980	159
28.	Distribution of women aged 14 or over by age group, marital status and educational attainment, according to migration status and region of origin, Neuquén City, 1980	160
29.	Sex ratio by migration status and distribution of women aged 14 or over by migration status and region of origin, according to age group, marital status and educational attainment, Neuquén City, 1980	162
30.	Gross number of years of working life for women aged 14-69, by age group, migration status and region of origin, Neuquén City, 1980	164
31.	Gross number of years of working life for women aged 14-69, by migration status, age group and marital status, Neuquén City, 1980	165
32.	Gross number of years of working life for single migrant women aged 14-24 and married migrant women aged 25-44, by region of origin, Neuquén City, 1980	165
33.	Comparison of observed and age-standardized proportions of single and married women in the labour force, by selected regions of residence or origin	166
34.	Gross number of years of working life, by age group, educational attainment and migration status of women aged 14-69, Neuquén City, 1980	167
35.	Gross number years of working life for migrant women aged 25-44, by educational attainment, Neuquén City, 1980	168
36.	Distribution of women aged 14-69 in the labour force, by occupational group, migration status and region of origin, Neuquén City, 1980	169
37.	Distribution of women aged 14-69 in the labour force, by occupational group and migration status, Neuquén City, 1980	170
38.	Observed and standardized distributions of women aged 14-69 in the labour force, by occupational group and region of origin	171
39.	Distribution of the male and female labour force by sector, migration status, age group and region of origin, Neuquén City, 1980	173
40.	Structure of production and the labour force, Republic of Korea and Thailand, 1965-1985	179
41.	Per capita income by region and sector, at current prices, Thailand, 1975/76-1985/86	182
42.	Number of migrants during the five years preceding each census, Thailand, 1970-1990	183
43.	Percentage distribution of migrants, by type of migration, Thailand, 1982-1989	183
44.	Characteristics of migrants to Bangkok Metropolis, 1986-1988	184
45.	Number of migrants to Bangkok Metropolis and percentage female, by period of arrival and place of previous residence	185
46.	Labour force participation rates, by migration status, aged group and sex, Bangkok Metropolis	185
47.	Unemployment rates, by migration status, age group and sex, Bangkok Metropolis	186
48.	Previous and current occupation of employed migrants, by sex, Bangkok Metropolis, 1988	186
49.	Employed rural migrants as a percentage of non-professional workers, by region and sex, Thailand, 1988	187

No.		Page
50.	Methods used by migrants to seek work, by sex, Bangkok Metropolis, 1986-1988	188
51.	Average wages, by sex, years of education and migration status, central region of Thailand, 1988	189
52.	Employed migrants, by sex, amount of remittances sent home per annum and frequency of remittances, Bangkok Metropolis, 1988	189
53.	Distribution of prospective migrants according to how they took the decision to migrate, by sex and type of destination, Philippine Migration Study	198
54.	Female and male migration from the Senegal River Valley, Mali, 1982-1989	248
55.	Female and male migrants by duration, Senegal River Valley, Mali, 1982-1989	248
56.	Female and male migrants by destination, Senegal River Valley, Mali, 1982-1989	249
57.	Characteristics of female migrants and non-migrants, Senegal River Valley, Mali, 1982-1989	249
58.	Motives attributed to female migration, Senegal River Valley, Mali, 1982-1989	250
59.	Status, family and community variables expected to affect female migration, Senegal River Valley, Mali, 1982-1989	250
60.	Logistic regression coefficients for factors affecting female migration, from a complete model, Senegal River Valley, Mali, 1982-1989	251
61.	Logistic regression coefficients for factors affecting female migration, model excluding prior migration, Senegal River Valley, Mali, 1982-1989	253
62.	Residents of the north-eastern region of Brazil in 1970, by sex and marital status in 1970 and by migrant and wage-earning status in 1976	266
63.	Results from a probit model of the individual probability of migrating from the north-eastern region of Brazil to the extended south-eastern region	267
64.	Results from a probit model of a married-couple's probability of migrating from the north-eastern region of Brazil to the extended south-eastern region	268
65.	Results from probit models of the probability of individual women and married couples migrating from the north-eastern region of Brazil to the extended south-eastern region	269
66.	Distribution of wives of heads of household by migration status and ethnicity, Malaysia	294
67.	Migration status in relation to relative income, Malaysia	295
68.	Results of fitting Model I for women's hours of work, Malaysia	296
69.	Results of fitting Model II for women's hours of work, Malaysia	296
70.	Results of fitting models for migrant and non-migrant women's hours of work, Malaysia	297
71.	Economic and domestic activities performed by male heads of household, according to time-budget data, Jequitinhonha Valley, Brazil	309
72.	Economic and domestic activities performed by wives of heads of household, according to time-budget data, Jequitinhonha Valley, Brazil	310
73.	Economic and domestic activities performed by wives of non-migrant heads of household, according to time-budget data, Jequitinhonha Valley, Brazil	312
74.	Economic and domestic activities performed by wives of migrant heads of household, according to time-budget data, Jequitinhonha Valley	313
75.	Results of probit regression of the effects of socio-economic and life-cycle characteristics on the labour force participation of wives, as measured by the census-type question	315
76.	Results of probit regression of the effects of socio-economic and life-cycle variables on the economic activity of wives, as measured by the time-budget method	315
77.	Literacy rates by municipality and urban or rural location, 1970 and 1980	318

Figures

No.		Page
I.	The multilevel approach to the study of determinants of internal migration of women in developing countries	11
II.	Thailand: age-specific and sex-specific interprovincial migration rates, 1975-1980	58

Map

Argentina: location of Neuquén City and of the main regions of origin of internal migrants ... 155

Explanatory notes

Symbols of United Nations documents are composed of capital letters combined with figures.

The following symbols have been used in the tables throughout this report:

Two dots (..) indicate that data are not available or are not separately reported.
An em dash (—) indicates that the amount is nil or negligible.
A hyphen (-) indicates that the item is not applicable.
A minus sign (−) before a number indicates a decrease.
A point (.) is used to indicate decimals.
A slash (/) indicates a crop year or financial year, e.g., 1988/89.
Use of a hyphen (-) between dates representing years (e.g., 1985-1985), signifies the full period involved, including the beginning and end years.

Details and percentages in table do not necessarily add to totals because of rounding.

Reference to "dollars" ($) indicates United States dollars, unless otherwise stated.

The term "billion" signifies a thousand million.

The following abbreviations have been used in this report:

AIDS	acquired immunodeficiency syndrome
ASEAN	Association of South-East Asian Nations
BAMA	Buenos Aires Metropolitan Area
CAPA	Canadian-Caribbean-Central America Policy Alternate
CASA	Centre for Asian Studies Amsterdam
CEDEPLAR	Centro de Desenvolvimento e Planejamento Regional
CEDES	Centro de Estudios de Estado y Sociedad
CELADE	Centro Latinoamericano de Demografía
CENEP	Centro Nacional de Población
CERLAC	Centre for Research on Latin America and the Caribbean
CERPOD	Centre d'études et de recherche sur la population et pour le développement
CEUR	Centro de Estudios Urbanos y Regionales
CONADE	Consejo Nacional de Desarrollo (Ecuador)
CONAPO	Consejo Nacional de Población (Mexico)
ECLAC	Economic Commission for Latin America and the Caribbean (United Nations)
ESCAP	Economic and Social Commission for Asia and the Pacific (United Nations)
FELDA	Federal Land Development Agency (Malaysia)
GATT	General Agreement on Tariffs and Trade
GDP	gross domestic product
GNP	gross national product
HIV	human immunodeficiency virus
IBGE	Instituto Brasileiro de Geografia e Estatística
ICDDR,B	International Centre for Diarrhoeal Diseases, Bangladesh
IDB	Inter-American Development Bank
IDRC	International Development Research Centre (Canada)
ILO	International Labour Organisation
INEGI	Instituto Nacional de Estadística e Informática (Mexico)
INSTRAW	International Research and Training Institute for the Advancement of Women
ISH	Institut de sciences humaines
LAPTAP	Labour and Population Team for Asia and the Pacific
MFLS	Malaysian and Family Life Survey
OECD	Organisation for Economic Co-operation and Development

OMVS	Organisation pour la mise en valeur du fleuve Sénégal
ORSTOM	Office de la recherche scientifique et technique d'outre-mer
PNAD	Pesquisa Nacional de Amostra de Domicilios (Brazil)
PREALC	Programa Regional del Empleo para América Latina y el Caribe (ILO)
PROLAP	Programa Latinoamericano de Actividades en Población
UAPS	Union for African Population Studies
UNFPA	United Nations Population Fund

INTERNAL FEMALE MIGRATION AND DEVELOPMENT: AN OVERVIEW

Richard E. Bilsborrow* and United Nations Secretariat**

The world is changing. Development is change. Migration is an intrinsic part of development and so are the changes that development brings about in the roles and status of women. In general, women that migrate experience significant changes in their lives and migration is a means of enhancing their status and increasing their involvement in the development process. There is no guarantee, however, that the changes brought about by migration will, on balance, be positive for all the women concerned.

The issue of when and in what circumstances migration has positive effects on the status of women was considered by the Expert Group Meeting on the Feminization of Internal Migration, organized by the Population Division of the Department of International Economic and Social Affairs[1] of the United Nations Secretariat, in collaboration with the Instituto de Estadística, Geografía e Informática of Mexico, and held at Aguascalientes, Mexico, from 22 to 25 October 1991. The Meeting represented the collective efforts of a group of scholars, including many prominent women, to address the interrelations between the internal migration of women and development and to derive, to the extent possible, implications for policy and further research. In the process, several methodological issues, as well as substantive issues, were addressed, including problems concerning the definition of female migration, inadequacies of existing sources of data, biased conceptual approaches and their resultant shortcomings in characterizing female migrants and guiding the analysis of the determinants and consequences of female migration.

A. WHO IS A MIGRANT?

Migration is a complex phenomenon, more so than those associated with the other two demographic fields, namely, fertility and mortality. There are several reasons for that complexity. First, migration must be defined in terms of both spatial and temporal dimensions. As concerns the spatial dimension, migration involves a movement across a political or an administrative boundary which, being determined for political or administrative purposes, need not remain the same forever. Indeed, both borders between countries and internal or subnational political jurisdictions can change and have changed over time, thus introducing confounding effects into the measurement of migration. In addition, the size and characteristics of administrative units vary considerably between countries and often compromise the validity of international comparisons. Some of the provinces of China or India, for instance, are larger in terms of population size than many countries in the world.

Migration is generally defined as a "change of residence", where residence is an ill-defined concept with both legal and temporal connotations. In countries where there are legal restrictions on changes of residence, a person can conceivably be present in a place for a long time before being granted permission to establish residence there. Even where legal restrictions on residence do not apply, it may be difficult to identify the place of residence of people that move regularly, albeit at relatively lengthy intervals, between two places. For demographic purposes, residence is often defined in terms of length of stay, whether actual or intended. That approach poses the problem of setting limits on the length of stay beyond which a person becomes a migrant rather than a sojourner. Yet, as the study of migration advances, it has become increasingly clear that setting such temporal limits may distort the view of migration by eliminating from the universe considered various types of temporary movements that have important social and economic implications.

The general problems involved in defining migration are further compounded in the case of female migration. Although it would not seem, a priori, that spatial and timing considerations could have differential effects on the measurement of male and female migration, reality proves otherwise. Thus, the practice of defining internal

---

*Carolina Population Center, University of North Carolina at Chapel Hill, North Carolina, United States of America.

**Population Division of the Department of International Economic and Social Affairs (now the Department for Economic and Social Information and Policy Analysis).

migration only as changes of residence between relatively large geographical units, such as states or provinces, may lead to an underrepresentation of female migrants, because the proportion of women among migrants between smaller geographical units (such as districts or *municipios*) tends to be higher than that among migrants between larger geographical units (see United Nations Secretariat and Bilsborrow, chapters V and VI in this volume). Similarly, because in many contexts the share of women in temporary migration is less than their share in long-term migration, researchers focusing only on one type of movement may misrepresent the extent of women's participation in migration.

There are two main sources of information on internal migration in developing countries: population censuses and specialized surveys. Censuses have the advantage of gathering information on migration at the national level, so that problems of sample representativity do not arise. However, they are crude instruments that can include only a handful of questions and thus at best produce static pictures coloured by a limited range of brush strokes. Nevertheless, as mentioned by Singelmann and the United Nations Secretariat (chapters IV and V), the most comprehensive measures of migration by sex available to date are derived from censuses; and the data they produce, although certainly not free from error, provide the basis for stating that, at the global level, the number of women migrating within their countries is comparable to that of men and that in some regions women outnumber men in internal migration flows. One must understand, however, that such assertions are based on rather narrow definitions of migration that usually involve a long-term change of residence between different and relatively large geographical areas. Indeed, censuses are generally not able to capture temporary migration and they tend to miss most return migration.

Surveys are considerably more flexible instruments for the study of migration. However, most tend to provide only a partial view of the phenomenon, mainly because few are nationally representative and because the definitions, criteria or procedures that they use to identify migrants often eliminate, either implicitly or explicitly, important subsets of the potential universe of interest. When that happens, women are likely to be selectively omitted. Thus, surveys that focus only on the migration of heads of household automatically eliminate most women from the universe of migrants. Similarly, surveys that focus only on economically active women or on women that migrate for economic reasons (usually related to employment at the time of the move) are almost certain to misrepresent female migration. Sex-related biases in coverage may even result from less obviously unbalanced procedures. For instance, surveys that investigate out-migration from a certain area, that is, conceptualize that area exclusively as an "area of origin", are very likely to miss entire families that have left the area and may therefore underrepresent the migration of women if they are, as is often the case, more likely than men to migrate as part of a family group than on their own. The choice of respondent may further exacerbate such a bias, if information is obtained from heads of household, who tend to be men, and they selectively omit or distort reports about female household members that out-migrated (see Bilsborrow, chapter VI).

The study of female migration must therefore take special precautions to avoid biases in coverage. To do so, it is important to understand and unmask the possible sources of bias in existing data sources (see Bilsborrow, chapter VI). The question as to who is a migrant should therefore be the first that every researcher should answer. For far too long, researchers have answered that question with a single image: a man moving in search of a job. The image is slowly changing to incorporate a woman moving in search of a job. Neither image, however, makes adequate allowance for the variety and richness of human motivation, and even the two taken together still fail to encompass a large proportion of the persons considered migrants according to the typical census merely because they changed their place of residence from one state to another during a certain period.

B. WHY HAS THE MIGRATION OF WOMEN BEEN PARTICULARLY NEGLECTED?

Despite calls for a change, Hugo reports that the study of female migration continues to be neglected (see chapter III in this volume), even though women constitute roughly half of all internal migrants in developing countries. In India alone, 29 million women changed their place of residence at least once during the period 1976-1981. One may ask why the movement of so many millions of persons has failed to attract more attention from the research community. To answer this question, one needs only to pause for a moment and consider the situation of women in most societies. In the home, women typically own few assets and earn no income; and economically active women tend to be concentrated in low-paying occupations with little prestige. In many countries, women's education still lags behind that of men. Few women are entrepreneurs, investors, lawyers, journalists, physicians, high-level government officials or politicians. Although the situation is changing, women still lack a voice in decision-making, especially in the most important areas of economic, civil or political life. Is it then surprising that they attract little attention when they migrate by the millions to make a new life for themselves and their families?

In terms of disciplines, the field of economics with its conceptualization of what constitutes work has had an important influence in marginalizing women in general and female migrants in particular as subjects of study. As Waring (1988) notes, many of the activities in which women play a dominant role are not considered work because they do not produce a monetary income. Consequently, although women contribute directly and substantially to the socio-economic welfare of their families, their contributions are institutionally ignored, both in macroeconomic accounting (national accounts only measure the value of activities paid for in the marketplace) and in most microeconomic studies (even the category "unpaid family workers" fails to reflect the many women whose activities within the home, having no easily imputable monetary value, are disregarded). Although it can be argued that in countries where a high proportion of women are in the labour force, the cost of the tasks that they used to perform as part of their household duties is becoming measurable because it is increasingly carried out by paid workers, in most developing countries that is not yet the case. Thus, the time and effort that women put into such activities as buying and processing food for home consumption, cooking for the family; fetching fuelwood or water, growing vegetables or raising small animals for family consumption; making, repairing and washing clothes; and especially caring for children generally go unrecognized and unrecorded. That women may migrate because they want to improve the conditions under which they carry out those activities has rarely been considered in the literature. Instead, by focusing mainly on the traditional economic aspects of migration, migration theory and research have greatly contributed to the invisibility of migrant women or, as several of the chapters in this volume illustrate, have prompted researchers to highlight only those aspects of female migration which are more easily amenable to fit the traditional economic mould.

There is no denying, however, that although more women are migrating for ostensibly economic reasons, the vast majority do so for reasons that researchers have categorized as "associational", that is, non-economic. The investigation of the reasons for migration is fraught with difficulties, especially because they are normally recorded only after migration has taken place and there is much room for rationalization. In addition, reasons that may be fairly complex in terms of the factors involved are usually partitioned by data gatherers into a few neat categories that are supposed to be mutually exclusive. According to Findley and Diallo (chapter XIII in this volume), respondent error is very likely to affect the answers obtained not only because of rationalization but because the women involved are often not the respondents and even when they are societal norms may prevent them from acknowledging their true reasons for moving. Yet, given the limited economic opportunities open to women in many societies, it seems acceptable and realistic, if not perfectly accurate, that women are generally reported to migrate to get married, join or accompany their husbands, leave their husbands, join or accompany their families and so on. It is less acceptable, however, that even when significant proportions of men are also reported to move for similar reasons (see United Nations Secretariat, chapter V), researchers feel bound to assume that men migrate for economic reasons—and are hence worthy of investigation—whereas women are just passive followers of men or migrate for various personal reasons that do not warrant serious consideration. The analysis of a large-scale survey of internal migration in Pakistan is illustrative of such researcher bias. The brief summary of the National Migration Survey of 1984, which covered 14,000 households and was carried out by the Federal Bureau of Statistics, introduces the results by stating that "females who usually are the accompanying members" were disregarded and proceeds to discuss only the results pertaining to men (Pakistan, 1990).

A group of migrant women that has been particularly neglected on the basis of such preconceived notions about the relative importance of their roles as migrants are all those migrating because of marriage. There are a number of variants of marriage migration, but most of them imply that the main motivation of the women involved is to begin a family through the mechanism normally sanctioned by society, marriage. Although in those terms marriage migration appears to have mainly social implications, to the extent that in many societies marriage represents the main avenue open for women to ensure that they shall have a means of support, its economic implications are not far-fetched. In societies where marriage is sealed by an exchange of assets, its economic value is even more obvious. Yet, only recently have researchers begun to consider the economic aspects of marriage in relation to migration (Thadani and Todaro, 1984). As an attempt to validate the importance of marriage migration, those efforts are important, but it must nevertheless be stressed that when that type of migration involves millions of women, as it does in Southern Asia (see United Nations Secretariat, chapter V), its implications, whether economic, social or cultural, should not be as generally disregarded as they have been to date.

Given that in most countries women usually have fewer economic options than men and are less likely than men to obtain an education, to be in the labour force, to be employed if in the labour force and to have a decent occupation or earnings if working, requiring them to be economic actors similar to men in order to be considered worthy subjects of study as migrants means that most of them will be relegated to the back-burner for a long time to come. That is not to deny the importance of the economic aspects of migration but rather to stress that neither the practice of imputing to women only non-economic motivations nor that of assuming that they are male surrogates is adequate. As several papers in this volume point out, women are subject to greater social and cultural constraints than men and it is important to take those constraints into account in understanding under what conditions women engage in migration and what they can get out of it. The issue, therefore, should not be whether they are worthy of study if they migrate on their own or in the company of relatives but rather whether they have more options or opportunities as a result of migration and whether they take advantage of them.

C. How significant is female migration?

The simple answer to this question is that, in terms of the number of persons involved, female migration is almost certainly just as significant as that of men at the world level. Yet, the data available provide only incomplete and indirect evidence to validate that claim. Census data constitute the best basis for estimating general levels of female migration at the world and regional levels, but only a relatively small number of countries gather and disseminate the necessary information. Thus, the estimation of rural-urban migration by sex during 1960s and 1970s from two consecutive censuses was possible only for 45 countries (see table 9). At the time of writing, the 1990 census results were not yet available for a sufficient number of countries to make a similar exercise possible for the 1980s.

The estimates of net rural-urban migration presented by Singelmann (chapter IV) indicate that for the 32 developing countries with data available for the 1970s, the distribution of the proportion of women in net rural-urban flows had a median value of 50.7 per cent and that half of the countries fell within the range of 47-52 per cent. As is well known, women tended to outnumber men among net rural-urban migrants in Latin America; they were generally outnumbered by men in the few African countries with data available; and the situation varied considerably within Asia, where women tended to account for over half of all net rural-urban migrants in Eastern and South-eastern Asian countries and for less than half of those migrants in Southern and Western Asian countries.

Singelmann also presents estimates of net rural-urban migration rates for the 1960s and 1970s for a number of countries (see table 9). They indicate that for the majority of countries with data available, the intercensal net rural-urban migration rates of women, as well as those of men, tended to decline slightly from the 1960s to the 1970s. Thus, out of the 25 countries with data for those two intercensal periods, 15 experienced declines in the rural-urban migration rates of women, 9 experienced increases and for 1 the rates remained unchanged. On a population-weighted basis, however, the data available, though scarcely representative of all developing countries, would imply an increase in women's net rural-urban migration rates, because significant increases were estimated in the three largest Asian countries—India, Indonesia and Bangladesh. That is, the limited data available indicate that there is considerable variation in the experiences of different developing countries. Generalizations are therefore unwarranted.

The estimates discussed so far relate only to one type of flow, rural-urban migration. Data on the other types, rural-rural, urban-rural and urban-urban, are even scarcer (see table 13). However, they indicate that the prevailing belief that rural-urban migration is the dominant type in terms of the number of persons it involves in developing countries is generally a misperception. Only in three of the nine countries with the necessary data did rural-urban migration account for the highest percentage of all internal migrants, and in none of those three did that type of migration involve as many as half of all internal migrants. In general, the flow involving the largest proportion of migrants was associated with the level of urbanization already reached in a country. Thus, rural-rural migration tended to be dominant in countries that were still mainly rural, such as India and Thailand, whereas urban-urban migration dominated in highly urbanized countries, such as Brazil. Rural-urban flows were the most important in countries that could still be described as being in a stage of transition, such as the Philippines or the Republic of Korea in the 1960s and 1970s.

The proportion of women in each of the four types of migration flows identified above also belies some common perceptions.[2] First, women constitute over half of all rural-rural migrants only in the Indian subcontinent (Bangladesh, India and Pakistan) and in Egypt, probably because of the practice of marrying women to men from other villages and sending them to live in the husband's paternal home. In the other countries considered, women tend to be underrepresented in rural-rural flows, probably because there are fewer wage-earning opportunities for women than for men in rural areas. Because of its potential to change the lives of migrant women, rural-urban migration has generally been given greater attention. The data on the number of migrants declaring to have moved from rural to urban areas indicate that only in two of the nine countries considered, Egypt and India, is the share of women in rural-urban migration lower than their share in total migration, while in five countries it is higher. In the remaining two, Malaysia and Pakistan, women's share in rural-urban migration is about the same as in all flows together. Furthermore, contrary to what the estimates of rural-urban migration presented by Singelmann imply, reports by census respondents indicate that even in India women account for slightly over half of all rural-urban migrants. That is, women are important participants in rural-urban migration even in societies where their migration is subject to considerable socio-cultural constraints. Such a change of environment is likely to have major effects on their prospects, activities and status.

Although the data reviewed so far provide a weak basis for generalization, they nevertheless suggest that some patterns of change in the relative participation of women in the different types of migration flows may repeat themselves. Table 1 presents a view of the way in which overall patterns of migration and the relative participation of women in them tend to evolve over time. As countries develop, their level of urbanization increases and internal migration shifts from being predominantly rural-rural to being more concentrated in rural-urban movements until it eventually becomes dominated by urban-urban flows. As those changes take place, the distribution of internal migrants by sex tends to become more balanced, whether it began with a highly unbalanced situation favouring men or one favouring women. Thus, in countries like India, where village exogamy combined with patrilocal residence leads to a female-dominated rural-rural migration and therefore to a high proportion of women in all internal migration flows considered together, that proportion would decline and come closer to 50 per cent as development proceeds and the dominant flows change from rural-rural to rural-urban and then to urban-urban. In contrast, in countries where rural-rural migration flows are dominant and involve greater numbers of men than women, the evolution towards the dominance of urban-urban migration would lead to an increase in the proportion of women in overall internal migration so that it would eventually oscillate around the 50 per cent mark. That is, in both cases, development would lead to a more balanced distribution of internal migrants by sex.

TABLE 1. INTERRELATIONS OF LEVEL OF DEVELOPMENT, PATTERNS OF INTERNAL MIGRATION AND
SHARE OF WOMEN IN MIGRATION

	Level of development and urbanization		
	Low	Transitional	High
Relative importance of different migratory flows	Rural-rural predominant, incipient rural-urban	Rural-urban becoming dominant; rural-rural still important; incipient urban-urban and urban-rural	Urban-urban dominant; low urban-rural and rural-urban; trivial rural-rural
Share of women in internal migration	Low and mostly associational	Rising or declining, depending on whether it was low or high, respectively, to start with, but still less than representative of the proportion of women in the overall population; increasing share of autonomous migration	Converging towards the proportion of women in the population

D. WHICH WOMEN MIGRATE?

To understand why women move, as well as the consequences of their migration, it is necessary first to determine which women move. It is well known that migrants are not randomly selected from the population in the areas of origin. In general, migrants tend to be younger, to have higher levels of educational attainment and to be less likely to be currently married than the population from which they originate. Female migrants are no exception. Thus, data from the 1990 census of Mexico indicate that, for the country as a whole, migrant women are more likely to be younger, single and better educated than non-migrant women (see López, Izazola and Gómez de León, chapter VII in this volume). Although migrant men are selected in similar ways, the age and marital status selectivity of female migrants is generally stronger than that among their male counterparts. Thus, the female migrants enumerated in Mexico in 1990 were more highly concentrated in age group 15-29 than were the male migrants. One must note, however, that in most censuses and surveys the characteristics of interest often refer only to the time of interview and, consequently, do not necessarily represent those at the time of migration.

It is important not to misinterpret the usual selectivity of migration to mean that all or even most migrant women are young and single. In fact, women migrating at age 15 or over are more likely to be married than single at the time of migration. Furthermore, selectivity varies depending upon the perspective used to assess it, so that in certain cases migrants may be older and more likely to be married than the reference population. The experience of Neuquén City, a medium-sized city in Argentina that has grown in large part because of migration, illustrates that point. In 1980, female migrants constituted 77 per cent of the total female population of Neuquén City; and whereas 74 per cent of them were aged 25 or over, only about half of the native-born female population was in that age group (see table 29). Even among recent female migrants (those who had migrated during 1975-1980), the proportion aged 25 or over was 63 per cent, making them considerably older, on average, than the native population of the place of destination. Because the female migrants were older, a higher proportion of them were married: over 61 per cent of recent migrants were still married in 1980, compared with 50 per cent of natives, but standardization by age reduced the difference between those proportions to only 2.2 per cent. Thus, in 1980, recent female migrant women in Neuquén City were typically older and married, but their tendency to be married was not very different from that of natives once the differences in age between the two subpopulations were controlled for.

The data for Neuquén City illustrate why migrant women that are still single are generally the focus of attention: their propensity to be in the labour force was between two and three times higher than that of married migrants and they also had a higher propensity to work than single native women (see table 31). In contrast, migrant women at Neuquén City who were still married had a slightly lower propensity to be in the labour force than married native women.

Selectivity in terms of labour force participation or occupation with respect to the population in the area of origin could be assessed for out-migrants from selected states of Mexico and for female in-migrants to Neuquén City. In Mexico, the experience of female out-migrants varied considerably from one state of origin to another. According to the 1990 census, female out-migrants from the northern state of Baja California and from the southern state of Quintana Roo were less likely to be in the labour force or to be employed than women that had stayed in those states of origin, but the reverse was true for female out-migrants from the states of Mexico and Zacatecas (see table 21). In terms of occupation, female out-migrants showed a tendency to be more concentrated in service occupations than their non-migrant counterparts in the states of origin, although there were exceptions. At the country level, however, the distributions by occupation of both female migrants and non-migrants were remarkably similar and showed that the majority of working women were concentrated in the service sector: 71 and 72 per cent of non-migrant and migrant women, respectively, worked in that sector, which includes, among other occupations, that of domestic servant. It is well known that in many countries domestic service is one of the major employment outlets for women and that many women migrate to perform such work, especially in Latin America. However, the service sector also includes a number of other "female" occupations that require skilled personnel, such as teaching, nursing, clerical work and some of the professions. The data on Neuquén City, which differentiate between occupations requiring highly skilled workers, those with medium-level skills and the unskilled, indicate that migration is highly selective at both the upper and the lower end of the skills scale. They also show that, at least in the case of Neuquén City, female in-migrants originating in neighbouring regions tended to be selected from the lower end of the skills scale, whereas those originating in provinces that were farther away tended to be selected from the upper end of that scale (see tables 38 and 39).

In a number of developing countries, the expansion of export-oriented manufacturing has led to the expansion of employment opportunities for unskilled women in the industrial sector. As of 1986, 47 developing countries had established export-processing zones, that is, industrial sites operating under special legislation allowing the duty-free import of raw materials for the assembly and manufacture of goods destined primarily for exportation (Zlotnik, 1993). According to table 2, the number of workers employed in export-processing zones and other offshore manufacturing facilities increased from about 800,000 in 1975 to nearly 2,000,000 in 1986. In general, the proportion of women among workers of export-processing zones has been high (see table 3), higher than in overall manufacturing; and the partial evidence available suggests that many can be classified as migrants, even if they are not recent migrants or did not migrate specifically to obtain a job in export-processing zones (Zlotnik, 1993). Several authors, however, see a direct link between the expansion of export-led industrialization and the increase of female migration to industrial centres of developing countries, particularly those in South-eastern Asia (see Phongpaichit, Lim, Rodenburg and Jones, chapters IX, XI, XV and XVIII in this volume). In the case of Mexico, it has also been suggested that the growth of the *maquiladora* industry has helped increase migration towards the northern states and has been a source of employment for women. The 1990 census data for the northern state of Baja California do indicate that a relatively high proportion of working women are employed in the industrial sector (27 per cent) and that the relative concentration of female in-migrants in that sector is strong—about 42 per cent (see table 23). In Thailand as well, the proportion of female migrants employed as production workers in Bangkok Metropolis reached 35 per cent (see table 48), and although it did not surpass the proportion employed in the service sector (50 per cent), it nevertheless constituted the second most important occupational group among working migrant women.

These examples suggest that it is not possible to provide general characterizations of female migrants. Even though many tend to be young, older women are disproportionately involved in certain types of flows. The higher propensity of single women to migrate does not generally counterbalance the fact that most women aged 15 or over are in the ever-married category and, consequently, tend to outnumber never-married women in migration flows. In terms of labour force participation, however, single women, whether migrant or not, are more likely to be in the economically active category

TABLE 2. NUMBER OF WORKERS IN EXPORT-PROCESSING ZONES AND OTHER OFFSHORE MANUFACTURING FACILITIES, 1975 AND 1986

Major area and country or area	Export-processing zones		Other offshore facilities		Total	
	1975	1986	1975	1986	1975	1986
Africa	34.1	131.2	5.3	37.6	39.4	168.8
Botswana	—	—	—	1.8	—	1.8
Côte d'Ivoire	—	—	2.8	3.2	2.8	3.2
Egypt	..	25.0	—	—	..	25.0
Ghana	—	2.6	—	—	—	2.6
Lesotho	—	—	—	1.0	—	1.0
Liberia	—	0.7	—	—	—	0.7
Mauritius	10.0	61.7	—	—	10.0	61.7
Morocco	—	..	..	10.0	..	10.0
Namibia	—	—	—	1.6	—	1.6
Senegal	0.2	1.2	—	—	0.2	1.2
South Africa	—	—	—	20.0	—	20.0
Swaziland	—	—	2.5	..	2.5	..
Tunisia	24.0	40.0	..	..	24.0	40.0
Asia and the Pacific	391.9	787.7	29.5	198.8	421.4	986.5
Bahrain	2.8	..	..	4.6	2.8	4.6
Bangladesh	—	4.5	—	—	—	4.5
Hong Kong	59.6	89.0	..	..	59.6	89.0
India	1.2	17.0	..	60.0	1.2	77.0
Indonesia	—	13.0	11.2	—	11.2	13.0
Macau	—	62.5	—	..	—	62.5
Malaysia	40.5	81.7	..	16.0	40.5	97.7
Pakistan	—	1.5	—	12.0	—	13.5
Philippines	8.2	39.0	1.7	50.0	9.8	89.0
Qatar	—	—	—	1.2	—	1.2
Republic of Korea	112.3	140.0	..	..	112.3	140.0
Singapore	105.0	217.0	..	..	105.0	217.0
Sri Lanka	—	35.0	—	27.0	—	62.0
Syrian Arab Republic	0.2	..	—	—	0.2	..
Taiwan Province of China	62.1	80.5	..	..	62.1	80.5
Thailand	—	4.7	16.7	28.0	16.7	32.7
Tonga	—	1.0	—	—	—	1.0
United Arab Emirates	—	1.3	—	—	—	1.3
Latin America and the Caribbean	122.4	381.3	243.5	385.2	365.8	766.4
Barbados	—	—	3.0	6.9	3.0	6.9
Belize	—	—	—	0.2	—	0.2
Brazil	27.7	63.0	100.0	200.0	127.7	263.0
Chile	—	2.0	—	—	—	2.0
Colombia	5.6	6.7	—	—	5.6	6.7
Costa Rica	—	..	..	8.6	..	8.6
Dominica	—	—	—	0.2	—	0.2
Dominican Republic	6.5	36.0	—	—	6.5	36.0
El Salvador	6.1	2.1	—	—	6.1	2.1
Haiti	—	5.0	25.0	38.0	25.0	43.0
Honduras	—	2.6	—	..	—	2.6
Jamaica	—	8.0	6.1	..	6.1	8.0
Mexico	74.7	250.0	9.6	..	84.3	250.0

TABLE 2 (continued)

Major area and country or area	Export-processing zones		Other offshore facilities		Total	
	1975	1986	1975	1986	1975	1986
Montserrat	—	—	—	0.2	—	0.2
Netherlands Antilles	—	0.4	..	—	..	0.4
Panama	1.3	2.1	—	—	1.3	2.1
Puerto Rico	0.5	0.7	96.2	130.2	96.7	131.0
Saint Lucia	—	..	3.5	—	3.5	..
Saint Vincent and the Grenadines	—	—	—	0.8	—	0.8
Trinidad and Tobago	—	2.7	..	—	..	2.7
TOTAL	548.3	1 300.2	278.3	621.6	826.7	1 921.8

Source: Hania Zlotnik, "Women as migrants and workers in developing countries", in "Sociology and social development in a time of economic adversity", James Midgley and Joachim Singelmann, eds., *International Journal of Contemporary Sociology* (Joensuu, Finland), vol. 30, No. 1, special issue (1993), pp. 39-62.

TABLE 3. PERCENTAGE OF WOMEN AMONG WORKERS IN EXPORT-PROCESSING ZONES AND IN MANUFACTURING OUTSIDE THOSE ZONES IN SELECTED COUNTRIES, EARLY 1980s

	Percentage of women in	
Major area and country or area	Export-processing zones	Other manufacturing
Africa		
Egypt	68	17
Mauritius	79	10
Tunisia	90	48
Asia		
Hong Kong	60	49
India	80	10
Indonesia	90	48
Macau	74	48
Malaysia	85	33
Philippines	74	48
Republic of Korea	75	38
Singapore	60	44[a]
Sri Lanka	88	17
Latin America and the Caribbean		
Caribbean		
Barbados	90	12
Dominican Republic	68	18
Jamaica	95	19
Trinidad and Tobago	10	28
Other Latin America		
Brazil	48	25
Mexico	77	25

Source: Hania Zlotnik, "Women as migrants and workers in developing countries", in "Sociology and social development in a time of economic adversity", James Midgley and Joachim Singelmann, eds., *International Journal of Contemporary Sociology* (Joensuu, Finland), vol. 30, No. 1, special issue (1993), pp. 39-62.

[a] Figure based on total manufacturing employment.

and as migrants they are better able than their married counterparts to respond to available job opportunities (see Cackley, chapter XIV in this volume). Hence the growing interest in the "young single female migrant" who is increasingly likely to be working in manufacturing in a number of developing countries. Unfortunately, few of those countries have the data needed to assess whether the linkages between migration and the promotion of export-led growth are as direct as is sometimes suggested. Indeed, one must keep in mind that even in rapidly growing economies, the majority of migrant women are still working in the service sector, where they remain concentrated at the lower end of the skills scale.

E. WHY DO WOMEN MIGRATE?

The answer to the question concerning why women migrate can be addressed at different levels. The first and most immediate level is that of the women themselves, whose motives for migration can be explored. Mention of those motives has already been made in discussing whether women migrate for economic or associational reasons. Because women, like men, can and usually do have a variety of motives for migrating, the dichotomy imposed by the economic versus non-economic taxonomy of reasons may be unenlightening. Furthermore, societal constraints may prevent women from acknowledging that their decisions or actions are based on economic motives (see Findley and Diallo, chapter XIII). Consequently, in terms of the reasons that respondents tend to acknowledge as important in determining the migration of women, the understanding of the process has hardly advanced.

A more promising avenue of inquiry is to try to ascertain whether the decision to migrate is made mostly by the woman involved, with her active participation or largely by someone else. Riley and Gardner (chapter X in this volume) discuss various facets of the participation of women in the decision-making process leading to migration. Although little hard information is available, they suggest that the degree of a woman's involvement in the decision to migrate will vary according to the type of migration involved (whether it is that of the woman herself or of some other family member, whether it is that of herself on her own or in the company of other family members etc.), according to the position of the woman within the family or household and according to prevailing norms and values with regard to the general status of women in society. Determining whether women have some say on whether they themselves migrate is important because several authors have suggested that, to the extent that women are able to make migration decisions on their own, they are more likely to benefit from migration and, to the extent that women are compelled to obey the decisions of others, they are less likely to reap many rewards from migration.

The issue also arises in trying to ascertain whether the increasing numbers of women reporting that they migrate on their own for economic reasons are doing so to improve their own economic situation or because of the need to assure the survival of their families of origin. It is assumed, rightly or wrongly, that in the latter case migrant women are simply complying with decisions made by others, usually their close family members, without having much say on how those decisions are made. Since it is argued that women who engage in migration to assure family survival are not likely to benefit personally from migration, it is important to determine who makes the migration decision, an issue that is scarcely explored in the course of data collection.

At another level, the question can be investigated on the basis of their individual characteristics and abilities, and the interaction of these factors with societal factors that may condition an individual's response to the migration option. Thus, research on the determinants of migration has come to recognize the importance of considering not only the individual characteristics of the migrant—her age, marital status, level of education, number of children, employment experience, current or most recent job, earnings, whether unemployed etc.—but also those of her household, including her husband's or parents' status in terms of occupation, level of education and earnings or assets, their attitudes towards her participation in the labour force, her status within the household, the household's size and composition, ownership by herself or her immediate family of a dwelling, land and other fixed assets, their likely liquidity, other household income etc. Furthermore, the fundamental importance of structural factors in the community of residence, which a rational migrant is expected to compare, either explicitly or implicitly, with those of possible places of destination, is generally acknowledged. Such structural factors are particularly important in determining the migration propensity of women because they include not only economic factors but also the norms, values and cultural mores determining gender relations and gender roles (see Lim, chapter XI). The analytical advantages of taking explicit account of factors at the individual or household level, the community level and a more encompassing geographical level, such as the province or even the country as a whole, are discussed by Guest (chapter XII in this volume). Although the need to use a multilevel approach in examining the forces leading to migration has been suggested by a number of authors,[3] it has only recently begun to be used in the examination of the determinants of female migration (see Findley and Diallo, chapter XIII) and much remains to be done to incorporate in that approach the normative factors suggested by Lim and Guest (chapters XI and XII). Nevertheless, Guest provides a useful first step to link the multilevel approach with the more general considerations raised by Lim and discusses some of the analytical difficulties that need to be confronted by users of the new approach (see also Bilsborrow and Guilkey, 1987).

Figure I illustrates how factors at different levels interact to influence the migration decision of individuals, particularly women. At the far left, under the label "overall society and community", are the factors operating at levels above the community, that is, regional, national or even international factors that include the Government's economic or development policies and that affect, directly or indirectly, the socio-economic situation and value systems at the level of the local community. The local context therefore acts as a filter through which factors beyond the community may differentially influence households and individuals. The policies of local government, the degree of linkages of the community to other communities, the economic situation of the community etc. all condition the types of influences that persons receive from the wider society and also determine whether individuals or households have the means to respond to the options available. Thus, household factors that affect migration decisions are influenced by community factors and in turn filter community influences to the individual level. Consequently, a person's decision to migrate is influenced by his or her characteristics, by how those characteristics have been conditioned by household and community factors and by the broader community situation that includes labour-market opportunities and norms with regard to the appropriate roles and behaviour of women.

An example of the multilevel approach to study the factors influencing the out-migration of women in a strongly patriarchal society, the Islamic Soninke of Mali, is provided by Findley and Diallo (chapter XIII). Their analysis, based on a household survey of 309 households interviewed in both 1982 and 1989, is one of the rare studies using longitudinal data. Although in the population under study women had traditionally had modest economic roles restricted to the family compound, a series of droughts prompted them to engage in migration to towns in Mali. Thus, by 1989, 26 per cent of all women interviewed in the survey had migrated at some time. Using multivariate analysis, it was found that women were more likely to migrate if they had migrated in the past, if they were single, if other family members in the household had migrated, if there were relatively few children in the family compound, if the family's cash income was low and if there were few cash-earning opportunities for women in the village.

Figure I. The multilevel approach to the study of determinants of
internal migration of women in developing countries

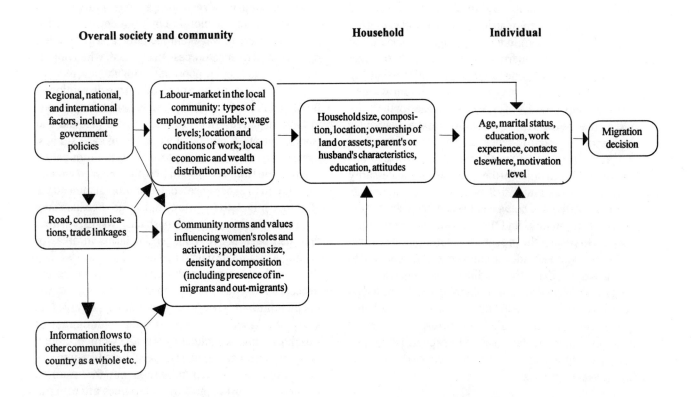

The last-named factor was measured by a variable indicating whether sheep or goats were raised in the village, since that activity was mainly carried out by women and provided them with some economic opportunities. Except for sheep and goat raising, which was measured only at the community level, none of the other community-level factors considered proved to have significant effects on the probability of female out-migration. In particular, neither the existence of development projects in the village nor the relative vulnerability of the village to drought was found to be significant. The authors interpreted such results as meaning that existing development projects did not increase the local economic opportunities for women and hence did not affect their migration prospects. They suggested that projects directed specifically to improving the cash-earning opportunities of women in the village were likely to reduce the pressures for female out-migration.

Using data on persons that migrated from the north-eastern to the south-eastern region of Brazil between 1970 and 1976, Cackley (chapter XIV) investigated whether it is appropriate to model the probability of migrating in the same way for single as for married women or for single as married men. She argues that the utility function determining when migration takes place is not the same for married couples as for two single persons acting independently. In particular, the utility function of a couple may reach a maximum without maximizing the utility of either the husband or the wife. Given that gender roles and relations make it easier for husbands to respond to better wage opportunities, wives are more likely to be "tied" migrants, moving to improve the overall utility of the couple but not necessarily their own. By assuming that the utility function depends upon the difference between the expected wages at the place of destination and those at the place of origin, models to predict the probability of migration are proposed for both individuals and couples. When fitted to the Brazilian data, they indicate that whereas both single and married men, as well as single women, tended to migrate in response to better expected wages in the place of destination, married women responded instead to improvements in their husband's expected wages but did not migrate in response to their own expected improvement in wages.

Although Cackley's results are important in indicating the limitations of the individualistic approach to the economic study of migration, especially where women are concerned, they are also, to a great extent, based on such an approach, since in deriving them no allowance is made for community-level factors that are likely to influence both the probability of migration and the choice of destination. Only a single variable indicating rural or urban residence is used to indicate the contextual environment in which the decision to migrate is made. It is clear that much remains to be done to expand and improve the use of community-level factors in the study of the determinants of migration in general and that of women in particular.

F. CONSEQUENCES OF MIGRATION FOR WOMEN

A recent assessment of the consequences of migration concludes: "Because of the diverse factors that condition and mediate the effects of migration on women's position, and because these circumstances vary across societies, there is no consensus about whether migration improves or erodes women's position *vis-à-vis* men" (Tienda and Booth, 1988, p. 295). The authors further state that the status of migrant women tends to improve when migration involves a change from a more to a less oppressive socio-economic environment or when it provides access to wage remuneration that gives them some control over resources. In contrast, when migration leads to fewer job opportunities for women, reduces their control over income or results in the disruption of family relations through separation or divorce, it tends to have negative effects on their status (Tienda and Booth, 1988). A review of a number of case-studies, particularly those referring to Africa, is illuminating (Tienda and Booth, 1988). In Lesotho, married women were found to experience a deterioration in their status after they migrated to the city of Maseru because they became dependent upon their husbands' wages, whereas they had been active managers of farms in areas of origin. At Kampala, Uganda, married migrant women living in a low-income neighbourhood had better access to economic opportunities than in their areas of origin, but their husbands restricted their market activities. A study of migrant women in squatter communities of Lusaka, Zambia, concluded that single women, though poor and uneducated, were nevertheless likely to improve their status after migration but that married women often lost control over resources after migration. In contrast, single Yoruba women who migrated to the small city of Ilorin, Nigeria were reported to benefit economically by marrying urban men, whereas married migrant women maintained control over the agricultural income produced by their plots in the area of origin. According to Tienda and Booth (1988), such a review, though selective, illustrates the difficulty of drawing general inferences without specifying the cultural context in which decisions were made as well as the family and employment situation of women prior to migration. Their review suggests that migration usually maintains gender asymmetries although certain aspects of gender relations are modified. However, in the absence of information about the timing of migration with respect to other events, such as marriage, divorce, the birth of a child or entry into the labour force, it is difficult to distinguish the effects of migration from those of other events. The papers in this volume further confirm the difficulty of drawing generalizations (see Rodenburg, chapter XV).

It is important to stress that an assessment of the consequences of migration is far more complex methodologically than is usually recognized. First, consequences must be assessed by taking into account the conditions under which migration took place. In the case of women, it is important to know at what stage of the life cycle they migrated (as children, as single adults, as married women, as widows etc.), whether they moved on their own or as part of a family group and the geography of the move (by type of origin or destination, distance etc). Secondly, it is necessary to establish whether the consequences are to be assessed with respect to the woman herself, her family of origin, her family of procreation, the community of origin, that of destination or even the country as a whole. Consequences that are positive for a certain unit of analysis need not be so for another. Thus, as Cackley (chapter XIV) shows, migration may have positive effects on the joint income of a married couple without necessarily improving that of the wife.

As suggested above, women that migrate as a result of their own decision are expected to be more successful, because they will be more committed to achieving whatever goals they have set for themselves. The likelihood of positive consequences is deemed to diminish when women are not major actors in making the decision to migrate and especially when, in societies where women's roles are circumscribed, they are compelled to migrate because of family need.

In the latter case, however, their migration may be deemed successful because it assures family survival.

A woman's relative success will also depend upon the goals that she has set or that others have set for her. Women may want to find a job, support themselves or their families, study, find a husband, improve their children's opportunities etc. Achievement of those goals is influenced by the woman's own characteristics and background. For instance, success in the labour-market will depend upon a woman's age, her educational attainment, her prior work experience, her contacts, her motivation to work and succeed, and the constraints to which she may be subject because of her family responsibilities. In addition, community-level factors will exert an important influence in determining the opportunities open for women. Those factors include labour-market conditions, which are closely associated with the urban or rural nature of the place of destination, and the norms and values that determine the roles of women in society and within the household. Community-level factors are particularly important in determining the consequences of migration for married women, because they are more likely to see their roles and options constrained by being part of a larger unit (the couple or family). Thus, examining the consequences of migration for women would also benefit from a multilevel approach, similar to that described in analysing the determinants of migration.

The nature of the areas of origin and destination—whether urban or rural—is important in determining whether a migrant's characteristics match those needed for success in the area of destination. In societies experiencing sustained economic growth, where urbanization and industrialization are expanding rapidly, rural-urban migration is more likely to lead to positive outcomes for female migrants, as documented in this volume for several countries, particularly those of Southeastern Asia. Rural-rural migration, on the other hand, has less potential to increase either the employment or the social opportunities open for female migrants, especially for those who are married. Improvements in educational attainment, particularly in rural areas, are highly likely to lead to out-migration when better educated women are unable to find suitable jobs in their rural communities of origin.

Although the consequences of migration may be appraised at the level of the individual woman, her family, her community of origin or that of destination, little has been done so far to assess them beyond the level of the migrant herself or her family.[4] One problem in assessing the consequences of migration at the community level is that data are required not only on migrant and non-migrant households in the areas of origin and destination at the time of interview but also over time. That is, because non-migrants are affected indirectly by the migration of others, information on their situation before and after migration is necessary to assess the impact of migration on them.

In the case of female migrants, changes in their status can be assessed by comparing their situation before and after migration or by comparing their situation after migration with that of non-migrant women remaining in the area of origin, with that of non-migrant women in the place of destination or with that of migrant men in the place of destination. Comparisons can be carried out in terms of a variety of characteristics indicative of status, including marital status, educational attainment, employment status, individual earnings, household income, ownership of land or assets etc. Improvements may be experienced over time with respect to some characteristics but not others, further complicating the assessment of the impact of migration.

In general, if a woman's own status improves after migration with respect to her previous status, it is assumed that migration was beneficial. That interpretation, however, fails to take account of the possibility that women who did not migrate may have experienced similar or better improvements. Since it is not possible to know with certainty what status a woman would have had had she not migrated, a more common approach to assess change is to make a static comparison of the situation of migrant women with that of non-migrants in the place of origin, preferably controlling for key characteristics, such as age and education. A less adequate comparison, but one that is often carried out in practice because it requires only data for the area of destination, is that between migrant and non-migrant women in the place of destination. Strictly speaking, however, such a comparison does not show what the consequences of migration have been for female migrants but rather how quickly they are adapting to the area of destination by becoming similar to non-migrants. Lastly, the situation of female migrants can be compared with that of male migrants to determine whether women benefit as much from migration as men.

Despite their shortcomings, comparisons commonly carried out indicate that in-migrants often have higher participation rates than non-migrants in the place of destination. However, that differential can be explained by the tendency of migrants to have a lower reservation wage, that is, the minimum wage at which they are willing to work (Standing, 1978), and is therefore not by itself indicative of a better labour-market situation for in-migrants. Yet, if in-migrants also have higher wages than equivalent non-migrants (meaning persons of the same sex and similar age, educational attainment and employment experience), it would follow that in-migrants would indeed be better off that non-migrants in labour-market terms. Data for Thailand indicate that, for both males and females, labour force participation rates in Bangkok Metropolis were higher for migrants than for non-migrants in most age groups. For females, the differences were largest for those under age 25 (see table 46). Furthermore, unemployment rates were lower for migrant than for non-migrant women in Bangkok Metropolis and there were indications that the wages of migrant women were also lower than those of non-migrants (see tables 47 and 51). These data therefore suggest that female migrants to Bangkok Metropolis were not necessarily better off in terms of employment than were non-migrant women in the area of destination. They provide no basis, however, for assessing changes in the status of the migrants themselves.

In the case of Mexico, data from the 1990 census permit a comparison between the labour force characteristics of male and female migrants. Female migrants exhibit lower labour force participation rates than their male counterparts and earn considerably lower wages, implying that they benefit less from migration than men (see table 24). However, given that in Mexico the earnings of working women in general are considerably lower than those of working men, the difference observed between the earnings of female and male migrants was to be expected. To validate the conclusion reached above, it is therefore necessary to compare the male/female earnings differential of migrants with that of non-migrants. Such a comparison indicates that whereas male migrants are considerably better off in terms of earnings than male non-migrants, the difference in earnings between migrant and non-migrant women is trivial. Thus, the conclusion reached above stands and this example illustrates how critical it is to consider both earnings and employment information in comparing the status of migrants with that of other groups.

One important issue related to the more general consequences of migration is how the temporary out-migration of men affects the women, especially the wives, that have been left behind. Several studies on the topic have focused on the consequences of male labour out-migration to South Africa from neighbouring countries, but male temporary out-migration is so common in the rural areas of many developing countries that the issue requires broader attention. In this volume, Goza, Rios-Neto and Vieira (chapter XVII) investigate the effects of male out-migration from the Jequitinhonha Valley of Brazil on the labour force participation of the women left behind. A crucial part of their research is the utilization of a time-budget to elicit better information on women's economic activities. Their data indicate not only that women married to migrant men were slightly less likely to work for wages than women married to non-migrant men but that the former were more likely to undertake work on the farm (harvesting, weeding and seeding) and other tasks that the absent husbands would have probably done if they had been there. Lack of detailed information on such activities would have produced a misleading view of the effects of male out-migration.

G. Development and policy implications of the internal migration of women

Before considering specific policy implications relating to the migration of women, it is important to review the relevance of studies on the determinants or consequences of migration for policy assessment or formulation. Strictly speaking, studies on the consequences of migration can only provide information about whether those consequences for individual migrants, their families, the communities of origin or destination or the country as a whole are such as to warrant policy intervention to ameliorate them. In themselves, such studies say nothing about the types of policies that should be adopted or about their likely effectiveness. In contrast, studies of the determinants of migration, especially if they are appropriately designed and incorporate a multilevel approach, indicate the factors that affect migration and, consequently, offer policy guidance about how to influence migration flows. Those studies say nothing, however, about the necessity of policies to alter migration flows. That is, both types of studies are needed—studies of the determinants to identify and studies of the consequences to justify the policies selected to modify migration flows. The latter studies also have some inherent policy value if they determine that a certain group of migrants is particularly vulnerable to negative outcomes from migration. In such a case, policies specifically designed to change those outcomes would be appropriate.

Like men, women contribute directly to development by means of their economic activities regardless of whether this is reflected in the usual labour force measures (Buvinic, Lycette and McGreevey, 1983). Migration is a major mechanism for improving the spatial allocation of labour, whether provided by men or women, by redistributing it from areas of relative labour surplus (or from those with low labour productivity and low wages) to areas of labour shortage (or to those of high labour productivity and wages). Therefore, women's contribution to development is directly linked both to their economic activities and to their participation in internal migration. In most cases, the two are also closely linked with and dependent upon a variety of sociocultural and normative factors that determine women's roles and status in different societies. Those factors, which tend to restrict women's economic and social activities in traditional societies, are likely to change over the course of development in ways that facilitate a fuller participation of women in economic and social life, including their increased participation in migration. Consequently, migration can act as a feedback mechanism promoting development in positive, synergistic ways and fostering relaxation of the normative values that limit women's roles and activities, particularly outside the home (see Jones and Simmons, chapters XVIII and XIX in this volume).

Several of the papers in this volume consider the linkages between the development process and changes in the internal migration of women. Thus, the study of female migration to Bangkok Metropolis describes the relation between increasing female migration and the dynamic processes of structural change and economic expansion that have been taking place in Thailand in general, but mostly in Bangkok and its surrounding areas (see Phongpaichit, chapter IX). Annual migration to Bangkok Metropolis increased by over 50 per cent between the mid-1970s and the mid-1980s, with the percentage of females rising from 53 to 63. During that period, Thailand experienced an economic boom, which both contributed to the increase in female migration and benefited from it. Even in Thailand, however, government policies do not seem to have dealt directly with the issues posed by increasing female migration or by the conditions that female migrants face when they become part of the labour force of the place of destination.

Indeed, the Governments of developing countries, generally dominated by male élites, have often paid little more than lip-service to the potential economic contributions and special needs of women, including migrant women. Thus, few development plans have explicitly tackled the issue of incorporating women into development and some have even continued to stress the traditional roles of women as homemakers and dependants of men (see Jones and Simmons, chapters XVIII and XIX). Policies intended to affect migration directly have, in general, not shown special concern about the sex distribution of migration and few have appeared to be effective in modifying overall migration patterns. In contrast, policies intended to promote development, whether in the economic, the social or the cultural sphere, have often had important indirect effects on migration that have not been gender-neutral. Therefore, in considering the types of policies that can improve the prospects of female migrants, one must look beyond migration-oriented policies to broader policies directed to affecting economic development and general welfare.

Given the Government's responsibility to promote society's collective welfare and the generally inferior status of women, particular attention should be given to policies that improve the options open to women. In many countries, policies are sensitive to the needs of women only in the health sector, where the promotion of maternal and child health programmes and family planning have been major goals. Although such programmes do help increase women's choices with regard to their reproductive lives and the well-being of their children, they do not necessarily have an impact on the broader societal roles of women. A more promising and broader area of policy action is education. A commitment to improve the educational attainment of females can potentially both give women the tools to improve their status and significantly increase their productivity. Countries need a skilled labour force to compete effectively in the global market. Women must be given greater opportunities to become part of that labour force as highly productive workers by being able to obtain an education at least equal to that of men. Access to education is likely to increase the spatial mobility of women by, among other things, changing their attitudes and aspirations, facilitating their access to information and increasing their potential earnings in the market-place. A number of other development policies likely to have important impacts on female migration are reviewed by Jones (chapter XVIII).

Ensuring that women shall have equal rights as men, particularly with respect to employment, divorce and remarriage, and ownership of land and other property, is essential. Because female migrants are often separated from the network of relatives and friends from whom they traditionally derived support in the areas of origin, the existence of effective institutional protection in the places of destination is especially important for them. In addition, special measures are needed to ensure that female migrants in vulnerable situations, such as those in domestic service, those doing piece-work at home, those working in other areas of the informal sector or those in the so-called "sex industry", shall be protected from exploitation and shall have some means of improving their situation. Some of the measures suggested in this volume include the provision of job-placement facilities for migrant women, facilitation of their access to credit and support for the formation of women's cooperatives to promote self-help schemes (see chapter II).

In sum, no matter which policies a Government adopts to promote development, the crucial point is that both their formulation and their implementation should take account of women as development actors and particularly of those who, by migrating, have made a personal commitment to change. Indeed, if development is to be successful it must make the best use possible of women's potential, and migration must be seen as one of the most effective mechanisms for realizing that potential.

NOTES

[1] Currently called the Department for Economic and Social Information and Policy Analysis.
[2] Some studies even fail to recognize that four possible types of flows exist. For example, Orlansky and Dubrovsky (1983) list three types of

migration: rural-rural, rural-urban and urban-urban; they then state that the rural-urban and urban-urban types compete with each other for supremacy, as if the process were random, independent of the level of urbanization or development of the country.

[3]See, for instance, Bilsborrow (1981), Findley (1981), Wood (1982), Bilsborrow, Oberai and Standing (1984), Lee (1985) and Massey (1990).

[4]A study by Singh, based on a survey of 200 families in five villages of the district of Madhubani in the northern Bihar plain of India, concludes that "the process of out-migration has transformed the economy and social status of the families of the out-migrants considerably" (1989, p. vii), noting, in particular, the positive effects on social attitudes, increased use of family planning and higher age at marriage among those families. Despite its title, however, the book considers only the effects of out-migration on the families of migrants and not on families without migrants. There is therefore not an assessment of the consequences of migration for the villages of origin as a whole.

REFERENCES

Bilsborrow, Richard E. (1981). *Surveys of Internal Migration in Low-income Countries: The Need for and Content of Community-level Variables*. Population and Labour Policies Programme, Working Paper No. 98. Geneva: International Labour Office.

_____ (1993). Issues in the measurement of female migration in developing countries. Chapter VI in the present volume.

_____, and David K. Guilkey (1987). *Community and Institutional Influences on Fertility: Analytical Issues*. Population and Labour Policies Programme, Working Paper No. 157. Geneva: International Labour Office.

Bilsborrow, Richard E., A. S. Oberai and Guy Standing (1984). *Migration Surveys in Low-income Countries: Guidelines for Survey and Questionnaire Design*. Beckenham, United Kingdom; and Sydney, Australia: Croom Helm.

Buvinic, Mayra, Margaret A. Lycette and William Paul McGreevey, eds. (1983). *Women and Poverty in the Third World*. Baltimore: The Johns Hopkins University Press.

Cackley, Alicia Puente (1993). The role of wage differentials in determining migration selectivity by sex: the case of Brazil. Chapter XIV in the present volume.

Findley, Sally E. (1981). Methods for linking community-level variables with migration survey data. Paper presented at the United Nations Economic and Social Commission for Asia and the Pacific, Technical Working Group on Migration and Urbanization, Bangkok, 1-3 December.

_____, and Assitan Diallo (1993). Social appearances and economic realities of female migration in rural Mali. Chapter XIII in the present volume.

Goza, Franklin W., Eduardo Rios-Neto and Paula Vieira (1993). The consequences of temporary out-migration for the families left behind: the case of Jequitinhonha Valley, Brazil. Chapter XVII in the present volume.

Guest, Philip (1993). The determinants of female migration from a multilevel perspective. Chapter XII in the present volume.

Hugo, Graeme J. (1993). Migrant women in developing countries. Chapter III in the present volume.

Jones, Gavin W. (1993). The role of female migration in development. Chapter XVIII in the present volume.

Lee, Sun-hee (1985). *Why People Intend to Move: Individual and Community-level Factors of Out-migration in the Philippines*. Boulder, Colorado; and London: Westview Press.

Lim, Lin Lean (1993). The structural determinants of female migration. Chapter XI in the present volume.

López, María de la Paz, Haydea Izazola and José Gómez de León (1993). Characteristics of female migrants according to the 1990 census of Mexico. Chapter VII in the present volume.

Massey, Douglas S. (1990). Social structure, household strategies, and the cumulative causation of migration. *Population Index* (Princeton, New Jersey), vol. 56, No. 1 (Spring), pp. 3-25.

Orlansky, Dora, and Silvia Dubrovsky (1983). *The Effects of Rural-urban Migration on Women's Role and Status in Latin America*. Reports and Papers in the Social Sciences, No. 41. Paris: United Nations Educational, Scientific and Cultural Organization.

Pakistan (1990). *National Migration Survey, 1984*. Karachi: Federal Bureau of Statistics.

Phongpaichit, Pasuk (1993). The labour-market aspects of female migration to Bangkok. Chapter IX in the present volume.

Recchini de Lattes, Zulma, and Sonia María Mychaszula (1993). Female migration and labour force participation in a medium-sized city of a highly urbanized country. Chapter VIII in the present volume.

Riley, Nancy E., and Robert W. Gardner (1993). Migration decisions: the role of gender. Chapter X in the present volume.

Rodenburg, Janet (1993). Emancipation or subordination? Consequences of female migration for migrants and their families. Chapter XV in the present volume.

Simmons, Alan B. (1993). Government policies, women and migration: a review of research findings and policy options in developing countries. Chapter XIX in the present volume.

Singelmann, Joachim (1993). Levels and trends of female internal migration in developing countries, 1960-1980. Chapter IV in the present volume.

Singh, Ram Nath (1989). *Impact of Out-migration on Socio-economic Conditions: A Case Study of Khutouno Block*. Delhi: Amar Prarashan.

Standing, Guy (1978). Aspiration wages, migration and urban unemployment. *Journal of Development Studies* (London), vol. 14, No. 2 (January), pp. 232-248.

Thadani, Veena N., and Michael P. Todaro (1984). Female migration: A conceptual framework. In *Women in the Cities of Asia: Migration and Urban Adaptation*, James T. Fawcett, Siew-Ean Khoo and Peter C. Smith, eds. Boulder, Colorado: Westview Press.

Tienda, Marta, and Karen Booth (1988). Migration, gender and social change: a review and reformulation. *Conference on Women's Position and Demographic Change in the Course of Development, Oslo, 15-18 June: Solicited papers*. Liège: International Union for the Scientific Study of Population.

United Nations Secretariat (1993). Types of female migration. Chapter V in the present volume.

Waring, Marilyn (1988). *If Women Counted: A New Feminist Economics*. San Francisco, California: Harper Collins.

Wood, Charles H. (1982). Equilibrium and historical-structural perspectives on migration. *International Migration Review* (Staten Island, New York), vol. 16, No. 2 (Summer), pp. 298-319.

Zlotnik, Hania (1993). Women as migrants and workers in developing countries. In "Sociology and social development in a time of economic adversity", James Midgley and Joachim Singelmann, eds. *International Journal of Contemporary Sociology* (Joensuu, Finland), vol. 30, No. 1, special issue, pp. 39-62.

Part One

REPORT AND RECOMMENDATIONS OF THE MEETING

I. REPORT OF THE MEETING

Migration, a process affecting the lives of millions of women in the developing world, is closely interrelated to the changing roles and status of women. The task of elucidating in which circumstances migration leads to improvements of the status of women was undertaken by those participating in the Expert Group Meeting on the Feminization of Internal Migration, organized by the Department of International Economic and Social Affairs of the United Nations Secretariat, in collaboration with the Instituto Nacional de Estadística, Geografía e Informática of Mexico. The Meeting took place at INEGI headquarters at Aguascalientes, Mexico from 22 to 25 October 1991. It was made possible by the financial support of the UNFPA.

The Meeting was attended by over 20 international experts and by representatives of both Mexican institutions and international organizations, including the INEGI, Colegio de la Frontera Norte, the Consejo Nacional de Población (CONAPO), the Ministry of Foreign Affairs and the Ministry of Labour among the former; and the International Labour Organisation (ILO) and the International Research and Training Institute for the Advancement of Women (INSTRAW) among the latter.

Opening statements were made by Shunichi Inoue, Director of the Population Division, and Carlos M. Jarque, President of INEGI. Both stressed the importance of understanding the determinants and consequences of migration from a gender-specific perspective. Mr. Jarque underscored the need for better data on female migration and made a brief sociodemographic characterization of migrant women in Mexico. Mr. Inoue took note that the results and recommendations emanating from the Meeting would be used in preparing for the International Conference on Population and Development to be held in 1994.

The bureau for the Meeting consisted of Clara Jusidman as Chairperson, Lin Lean Lim as Vice-Chairperson and Richard E. Bilsborrow as Rapporteur.

The deliberations of the Meeting were organized around the following topics: (*a*) an overview of the main issues relating to female migration; (*b*) the scale and scope of female internal migration; (*c*) the selectivity of internal migration; (*d*) the determinants of female migration; (*e*) its consequences; (*f*) the labour-market aspects of female migration; and (*g*) policy issues relevant to the migration of women and their role in development. Each topic is treated separately below.

A. THE MAIN ISSUES RELATING TO FEMALE MIGRATION

Recognizing that not all the changes deriving from migration would necessarily result in positive changes of status for the women concerned, participants underscored the need to determine the conditions under which migration would result in improvements of the status of women. It was recognized, however, that the task of disentangling the effects of migration *per se* from those of other processes that affected women's status was far from straightforward.

Among the factors that complicated such a task, defects that affected available data sources and resulted in inadequate coverage of female migrants were highlighted. The practices of gathering migration information only about household heads or of identifying migrants only in terms of fairly large administrative units (e.g., states) were mentioned as important sources of bias, because women were less likely than men to be perceived as the household head by interviewers or to move over long distances. The need to adopt data-collection procedures that would minimize such biases was stressed, together with the need to investigate possible sources of bias in existing data sources so as to make appropriate use of them.

The systematic evaluation and use of existing data sources to document trends and patterns of female migration was strongly recommended. The potential uses of census data remained largely to be tapped, although the 1970 and 1980 rounds of censuses were used at the Meeting to examine worldwide trends during the 1970s for the first time. Unfortunately, data from the 1990 round, which would allow the examination of trends during the 1980s, were generally not available. The data for earlier periods showed that female migration, especially rural-urban migration, had increased. There was also evidence suggesting that the complexity and types of female migration were growing, although existing data sets still reflected only a small part of female mobility.

The problem of viewing women that moved mostly as associational migrants (i.e., as passive companions of other family members), while assuming that males were generally autonomous migrants or active decision makers, was recognized as a serious obstacle to advancement of the understanding of the causes and consequences of female migration. The need to develop new ways of categorizing or describing female migration was stressed, especially because women were often motivated by economic factors. Marriage migration, for instance, might not be devoid of economic motives, including the possibility of upward mobility; and its effects on the women concerned had to be further investigated.

Emphasis was placed on the need to examine the processes that shaped the selectivity of female migration in order to determine if they differed from those which gave rise to male migration. In studying selectivity, migrant women should be compared not only with migrant men but with non-migrant women both at origin and at destination. Female migrants were said to be highly selected in terms of such characteristics as age, education or marital status.

With regard to the causes of female migration, the need to investigate not only household factors but broader societal causes was stressed. It was noted that economic factors were gaining importance in inducing female migration and that sociocultural factors had played major roles in both stimulating and constraining the migration of women. With respect to the consequences of migration, the importance of distinguishing its effects on women from those on their families was stressed, especially when women migrated alone as part of a family-survival strategy. Mention was made of situations where migration might result in a higher income for the family as a whole but might not necessarily entail an improved economic status for the women concerned. Migration was recognized as having the potential to improve the status of women, both within their families and in society at large, particularly by providing women with opportunities to earn their own income and by weakening traditional patriarchal authority. Such positive effects could accrue even when women moved together with other family members and were not the main decision makers.

Although policies directed to influencing migration had had an impact on female mobility, the effects of broader socio-economic development policies had usually been dominant. Migration policies were characterized as a blunt instrument to affect the status of women. More direct policy measures, such as raising the level of education of women, providing them with equal access to employment and equal pay for equal work or ensuring their equality of rights with regard to property ownership, marriage and divorce, were judged to be more effective means to enhance women's status.

B. THE SCALE AND SCOPE OF FEMALE MIGRATION

Using data from censuses up to the 1980 round, estimates of net rural-urban migration were obtained for the 1960s and 1970s. Female participation in net rural-urban migration varied considerably from region to region, although within regions the differences detected between the 1960s and 1970s were generally small. Only in Asia was there a clear trend towards the increasing feminization of net rural-urban migration. Females predominated in net rural-urban migration in most countries of Latin America and the Caribbean, while males did so in Africa and Asia. With respect to specific age groups, females tended to predominate over males in terms of net migration in the younger age groups (5-19) and at older ages (35 or over).

Mention was made of the varied definitions of rural and urban areas and of the increasing importance of flows other than rural-urban in countries where urbanization was fairly advanced. Note was taken that the estimates of rural-urban migration depended upon assumptions about differences in natural increase between rural and urban areas. Although varying those assumptions did entail changes in the estimated level of net rural-urban migration, the distribution by sex was not greatly affected.

Census data on other types of migration flows, namely, rural-rural, urban-urban and urban-rural, showed that the participation of women differed considerably from one type to another and that there was also significant variation between countries. In India, for instance, women accounted for 79 per cent of rural-rural migration, whereas only 51 per cent of rural-urban migration involved women. In Thailand, in contrast, women accounted for only 45 per cent of rural-rural migration and for 54 per cent of rural-urban flows. In both countries, rural-rural migration predominated in internal migration flows. In fact, rural-urban migration was not the predominant type in most of the countries with the necessary data available. Consequently, it was pointed out that the results of studies concerning exclusively rural-urban migration, which had predominated in the literature, might not be representative of the true impact of migration on women as a whole.

With regard to migrant types defined on the basis of duration of stay, note was taken that women were said to participate less than men in so-called "circulation", that is, in temporary movements that did not involve a change of residence. The term "circulation", however, was not well defined and different authors conceptualized it in different and sometimes conflicting ways. In addition, the term often carried economic connotations which were likely to lead to the exclusion of women. Consequently, it could not be concluded that, in terms purely of duration of stay, women were less likely than men to participate in circulation.

The consideration of temporary movements that did involve a change of residence showed that women were indeed less well represented among migrants having short durations of stay (less than one year) than among longer term migrants. The data used to examine this point were derived from census information on duration of stay at the place of residence at the time of enumeration.

Data on the reasons for migrating indicated that women were far more likely than men to move in order to accompany or join other family members or because of marriage (that is, because of non-economic reasons). Men, on the other hand, predominated among migrants moving for economic reasons (finding a job, being transferred, working etc.). In all countries, however, a significant proportion of men also cited non-economic reasons for moving; and in some countries, a significant proportion of female migrants were reported to have moved for economic reasons. Consequently, the practice of characterizing female migration as generally "associational" appeared to be unwarranted.

There was little evidence concerning the relative participation of women in short- and long-distance migration. Among the four countries that had data on intrastate and interstate flows, only in Brazil did the proportion of women in interstate migration exceed that in intrastate flows. The differences in female participation in intrastate and interstate flows were generally small, but in India the participation of women rose sharply as the level of disaggregation increased. Such differentials were said to be associated with the generalized practice of village exogamy combined with patrilocal residence. Little had been done, however, to understand the effects of that type of marriage migration on women.

To the extent that women did indeed participate more in short-distance migration than in moves over longer distances, the practice of censuses to record migration or to tabulate it only at the interstate or, at most, at the interdistrict level would underrepresent female migration. Censuses carried out on a *de jure* basis were also likely to undercount migrants among persons whose place of residence was not clear or among those that desired to hide it. Thus, the homeless, those engaged in illegal activities or even persons that worked in domestic service and had only temporary accommodation might not be recorded. Since women tended to predominate in the latter groups, they would not be adequately represented.

One of the most important sources of bias in the recording of migration by sex was judged to be the determination of migration status on the basis of economic activity. Censuses significantly understated the extent of female labour force participation, in part because the methods of measurement used were fairly crude. An adequate measurement of female labour force participation demanded the use of detailed surveys employing special data-collection methods, such as a time-budget that would list specific economic activities, to elicit the information from those interviewed.

One of the most common sources of bias in reporting either female labour force participation or female migration was said to be the choice of respondent. When information was obtained from household heads, most of whom were male, both women's work and their movement tended to be omitted. Thus, a survey carried out in the rural areas of Ecuador that asked the head of household about the migration of sons and daughters showed that men predominated among out-migrants, a result judged to derive from the selective omission of daughters because it was inconsistent with the census data, which indicated that women constituted a majority of rural-urban migrants in Ecuador.

Important biases could also be related to the attitude and characteristics of interviewers and, perhaps more importantly, of the investigators themselves. Thus, preconceived notions about appropriate female activities or behaviour could lead to biased questions or analytical frameworks that disregarded the extent and importance of female migration.

Given that the above-mentioned sources of bias in the measurement of female migration were likely to be selective according to the characteristics of female migrants, including their motives for migration, such biases could have serious consequences for analysis of the selectivity, determinants and consequences of female migration.

In studying either the determinants or the consequences of migration, the importance of selecting the appropriate comparison group was stressed. Thus, the practice of comparing migrants with non-migrants at the place of destination shed more light on the adaptation process than on the consequences of migration *per se*. The appropriate comparison group to study as concerned consequences would be non-migrants at the place of origin. Surveys that focused only on areas of destination were therefore inappropriate for the study of the consequences of migration.

The need to design and carry out specialized migration surveys to better understand the determinants and consequences of female migration was emphasized. The special value of questionnaires relating migration to other events in a woman's life through a life-history approach was mentioned. In the study of migration, particularly the migration of women, it was important to consider the effects of migration when it marked the transition from the family of orientation to the family of procreation (as when migration occurred at the time of marriage). Of equal interest were the interrelations between migration and fertility or between migration and other aspects of the family life cycle, including widowhood or divorce. The study of migration in relation to the life cycle was considered a useful strategy to take account of the dynamic aspects of the process.

Fostering a dialogue between data producers and data users was judged to be essential in promoting both the gathering of adequate information and its in-depth analysis. Researchers were urged to develop clear and practical data-collection guidelines with regard to migration. In doing so, special care should be taken to prevent common preconceptions or stereotypes from biasing the data. In addition, data-collection procedures should take account of the cultural and social factors that might prevent women from being interviewed or from providing the information being sought.

C. SELECTIVITY OF FEMALE MIGRANTS

To understand the process of female migration and its interrelations with socio-economic development, consideration of the selectivity of female migrants—their characteristics and differences with respect to female non-migrants and male migrants—and of the forces that led to such selectivity was a first step. Three studies, based on the cases of Colombia, Mali and Mexico, were presented. Each was based on a different type of data with specific advantages and limitations.

In the study of Mexico, results from the 1990 population census were used to examine migration selectivity by sex. Attention was focused on migrant flows to four quite different states, in order to illustrate how the context and characteristics of the areas of destination affected the characteristics of migration movements. The state of Baja California, for instance, was described as an area of high economic and population growth that was especially attractive to migrants because it bordered the United States of America. Its capital, Tijuana, had grown rapidly, mainly as a result of the expansion of tourism and the *maquiladora* industry. Migrants to Baja California tended to be relatively well educated. The state of Quintana Roo in the Yucatan Peninsula had grown even faster because of the development of the tourist industry and had experienced the highest rate of in-migration in the country.

Zacatecas, in contrast, was one of the poorest and most agricultural states, located in the north-central highlands. It had experienced more out- than in-migration during the late 1980s, some of the latter being return migration. Lastly, the state of Mexico, being contiguous to and partially surrounding the Distrito Federal, had a large number of in-migrants to the Mexico City metropolitan area.

The 1990 census of Mexico allowed migrants to be identified as persons that had, in 1985, lived in a state different from that of enumeration. For the country as a whole, women constituted a majority of all internal migrants (51.4 per cent) and they also predominated among in-migrants to the states of Mexico and Zacatecas. Migrants in general tended to be concentrated in age group 15-29, but such concentration was even greater among females. The proportion of female heads of household in Mexico was slightly lower among migrants than among non-migrants (6.7 versus 7.5 per cent). Migrant women were slightly more likely than non-migrants to be either in a consensual union or married and less likely to be single or widowed.

A comparison of female migrants with female non-migrants, on the one hand, and with male migrants and non-migrants, on the other, in the four states selected disclosed a number of both expected and striking differences. In general, the differences between the sexes were greater than those between migrants and non-migrants of either sex. Both female and male migrants were positively selected according to education and were also more likely than non-migrants to be in the labour force, although the overall levels of female labour force participation were less than half those of males (under 30 versus over 70 per cent). Among working women, the proportion in manual occupations was higher among migrants, which indicated employment of lower status, although both groups of women were more likely than men to engage in non-manual occupations. In addition, working women tended to be heavily concentrated in the service sector, except in Baja California, where 42 per cent were engaged in industry. Migrant women were more likely than non-migrants to work in the personal services sector (especially in domestic service) and less likely to be in commerce. Despite the inevitable shortcomings of census data on income, a comparison of earnings levels showed major differences in all four states, with female in-migrants earning far less than their male counterparts. Women in general reported earnings of between one fourth and one half of those reported by men; the striking exception was Baja California, where the gap between male and female earnings was less than 25 per cent.

The case-study on Colombia was unusual in that it compared two different birth cohorts, one born before and the other after a period of sharp fertility decline and massive population redistribution (the share of the urban population had more than doubled between 1937 and 1973, to reach 62 per cent). The aim was to examine the extent to which the experiences of the two cohorts, aged 25-29 and 45-49 in 1984, differed. The data used were a subset of a national longitudinal survey that had been carried out in 1984. Comparisons were made between migrant women at Bogotá and non-migrant women both there and in two areas of origin of rural-urban migrants to the city, namely, Boyacá and Cundinamarca. Life-history data, including all changes of residence of at least six months, were examined.

The results showed that over three quarters of migrants in the younger cohort and two thirds of those in the older cohort moved directly from rural areas to Bogotá. A larger proportion of the young cohort than of the older cohort had been single at the time of migration. Selectivity by education and occupation was high for both cohorts, but among those that worked after migration few had worked before: 94 per cent of the young cohort and 88 per cent of the older one had found their first job at Bogotá. A comparison of the occupational status of rural-urban migrants and that of non-migrants at Bogotá was undertaken to examine the process of migrant adaptation. The fact that migrants were far more likely than non-migrants to be engaged in domestic service (29 versus 9 per cent) was taken as evidence of little upward mobility, although mobility appeared to be greater for the younger cohort, whose proportion of migrants in clerical and professional occupations was larger. The general lack of upward occupational mobility among female migrants in Colombia was attributed, at least in part, to the Government's policy of promoting urbanization during the 1970s. That policy, by attracting migrants to Bogotá faster than new jobs were being created in the formal sector of the economy, had left few avenues open for female employment aside from domestic service.

The study of Mali differed from those on Latin America with respect both to the macroeconomic conditions prevailing in the country and to the type of data used. Whereas Colombia and Mexico, which had experienced considerable economic growth during the periods considered, were mainly characterized by "mobility migration" due to pull factors attracting migrants to areas of destination, Mali had been struck by a series of droughts during the 1980s that had led primarily to "survival migration" stimulated by push factors in areas of origin. The data used to examine the migration process were obtained from an intensive migration survey of 309 households in 39 villages of the upper Senegal River Valley, an area that had experienced severe drought during the period 1983-1985 and had subsequently been affected by a deepening economic crisis. Households had been interviewed both in 1982 and in 1989. In addition, information from an in-depth survey of 71 families in seven villages was used to interpret the quantitative data obtained from the larger survey. The survey in 1982 had focused mainly on the emigration of males (generally heads of household) to France; note was taken that both heads of household and the women themselves rarely reported that women migrated. The survey in 1989 had been based on the premise that the drought would have compelled even women to migrate in order to ensure family survival.

Sex roles in the strongly patriarchal and Islamic Soninke society, characterized by large compounds of up to 100 persons belonging to an extended family, were clearly defined, and women had lower status both within the household and in the community. Men were responsible for providing income and shelter for the family, whereas women fed and took care of children, grew certain vegetables and cared for small livestock. Women did, therefore, have economic responsibilities even if unacknowledged by society. Although women often engaged in migration, even they themselves seldom reported economic motives; but such motives did exist and had probably become more important during the 1980s because of the economic crisis. Thus, in the follow-up survey in 1989 it had been found that women constituted 41 per cent of all recent migrants (most of whom had migrated since 1982) and that 28 per cent of all women had migrated at least once, compared with 46 per cent of men.

Factors that had influenced the migration decisions of female migrants aged 15 or over in 1982 were examined using a multivariate logistic model. Female migrants tended to be young, single, with low fertility if married, with previous migration experience (interpreted as reflecting the availability of contacts at destination) and from the lower economic strata. The effects of a number of community-level factors were also examined; and it was found that while the overall level of economic development and the existence of village development projects were not associated with out-migration, the existence of local economic activities for women was. Unfortunately, most of the agricultural development programmes in Mali had failed to involve women. It was therefore suggested that projects to promote vegetable production and small livestock raising or the creation of local savings clubs for women could reduce the need for them to migrate. In addition, delayed marriage and the promotion of lower fertility through family planning would give women more time to become economically active and thus increase the likelihood that they would migrate autonomously. Policies to promote women's organizations and to provide low-cost housing at destination were considered important. Equally central was the need to promote a realistic image of migrant women in Malian society and to combat common stereotypes, such as the view that migrant women tended to engage in prostitution.

Analytical problems in assessing the impact of migration on the status of women were stressed, including the need to use appropriate comparison groups and to collect information on the status of women both before and after the move. It was recognized that data on the characteristics of migrants at the time of interview were more likely to reflect the consequences of migration than its causes.

D. DETERMINANTS OF FEMALE MIGRATION

The existing body of knowledge concerning female migration was considered to be particularly deficient with respect to the determinants of migration. Existing gender asymmetries in all spheres of life—sociocultural, economic and political—were said both to constrain and to create opportunities that differed for males and females. Many of the underlying societal forces that influenced women's roles also influenced women's migration. The general structural determinants of female migration were categorized as: *(a)* those which were related to the economic development context and derived mostly from government policies that influenced gender-based economic opportunities and constraints in areas of origin and destination; *(b)* those which were related to institutional factors that, by maintaining gender inequalities, either facilitated or hindered migration; and *(c)* those which arose from the sociocultural system of gender roles and relations that operated in accordance with prevalent norms, values and expectations. It was suggested that any framework developed to investigate the causes of female migration had to distinguish between the proximate and the less proximate determinants of the phenomenon. The family could be taken as the mediating structure between the two. In addition, at least four types of intervening variables were identified: *(a)* information about opportunities at different destinations, usually obtained from kinship and other types of networks; *(b)* the potential migrant's own socio-economic characteristics (e.g., age, education and occupation); *(c)* the social norms with regard to gender relations and women's roles at both origin and destination; and *(d)* the actual roles and status of women within their own families.

It was stated that factors related to the economic development context were the easiest to change, whereas those related to the system of sociocultural norms and values determining gender roles were more resistant to change. Traditional systems of sex stratification might either promote or constrain female migration. Thus, in Southern Asia, a patriarchal system combined with the practice of village exogamy and patrilocal residence led to very high levels of rural-rural migration among women that had to move to the husband's home at the time of marriage. However, such practices were not conducive to an improvement of the status of the women concerned. Similarly, lower class women that had to migrate to work for their own or their family's survival, or women that migrated as female heads of household or upon becoming widowed were unlikely to see their status improved as a result of migration.

With regard to the impact of economic development, in several countries of Eastern and, in particular, Southeastern Asia, economic growth and structural changes that had occurred since the 1960s had led to major increases in employment opportunities for women and hence to the migration of women from rural to urban areas in order to work in factories. Such spatial mobility, however, had had little impact on social mobility, because the women concerned usually had low-wage employment with few fringe benefits and poor working conditions. In fact, women were selected to fill those jobs mainly because of their "feminine" qualities, including their submission to authority, acceptance of low wages, manual dexterity, low boredom level and low likelihood of forming a labour union. Furthermore, women had often been hard hit by the consequences of structural adjustment policies pursued by some Governments.

The importance of social networks in facilitating female migration was stressed, particularly because women, who were generally less educated and subject to greater social constraints than men, were more likely to rely upon friends or relatives for help, information and guidance at destination. Social networks were also deemed responsible for reducing the resistance to female migration among families at origin.

Among the structural factors amenable to policy manipulation, the enhancement of women as a human resource through the provision of better education and training services or the improvement of the conditions of women's participation in the labour-market was highlighted. It was stressed, however, that better educational opportunities would not, by themselves, be sufficient to ensure upward mobility. The promotion of equal employment opportunities for men and women was needed. It was important to prevent the perpetuation of segmented labour-markets for males and females to the detriment of the latter.

The potential value of multilevel models to investigate the determinants of female migration was considered. Those models attempted to take into account the effects of factors measured at different levels (e.g., individual, household or community) and their interactions. At the household level, migration could be treated as part of a household strategy of risk diversification wherein a member of the household was encouraged or helped to migrate so as to send back remittances. Assuming that the household adopted a rational accumulation strategy, it should select for migration the person having the highest expected earnings, which usually was a young educated male. Since in at least some contexts, such as South-eastern Asia, daughters were more likely than sons to send back remittances, a rational survival strategy was for daughters to migrate. Moreover, because migrant women often had less stable and lower paid jobs than men, they had a greater stake in sending remittances so as to maintain the option of returning to their family of origin in case of necessity.

Community-level factors affecting migration were usually measured at relatively high levels of aggregation, such as the district level (the district being the lowest administrative unit used). A wide range of community or areal factors could affect migration rates by sex, including the economic structure of the community, the types of facilities available, overall demographic characteristics, transport linkages and existing social norms with regard to appropriate behaviour and roles by sex. In general, those factors would operate through the differential creation of opportunities by sex. Thus, the commercialization and mechanization of agriculture might generate increased demand for farm labour while at the same time it reduced the demand for female labour. The effects of community-level factors could vary according to the different macro-contexts and also over time. For instance, better transport systems, by increasing interchanges between communities, would reduce the differences between them and, consequently, the need to migrate. The operation of social networks was considered crucial to foster female migration, although their effects varied according to the prevailing socio-economic context. In general, social networks, by reducing the economic and social risks of female migration, helped promote such movement; and as networks developed, migration tended to become less selective.

Given that the process of policy formulation would benefit from better information on the effects that community-level factors had on the migration of women, more research on multilevel analysis was thought warranted. In particular, it was important to clarify the seemingly contradictory results obtained with respect to certain factors, such as the impact of educational facilities and electrification on female out-migration. Compared with a purely macrolevel approach, multilevel analysis had the advantage of incorporating existing microlevel theory and thus having a better theoretical foundation. It also allowed for the explicit interaction of factors operating at different levels. It was clear that policies directed at individual women were unlikely to be effective unless they took into account the larger community context and the social norms that shaped the roles and status of women. Unfortunately, the task of developing operational measures of social norms and values was far from simple, especially on the basis of the data gathered by the typical demographic survey. The investigation of the causes of migration required that data be gathered in the areas of origin. Other useful data-collection approaches included the use of retrospective questionnaires, longitudinal surveys and in-depth qualitative interviews. The need to foster cooperation between migration specialists and those interested in gender issues was noted.

The roles that men and women played in arriving at the decision to migrate were discussed next. In general, the literature on the decision-making process that led to migration made no explicit mention of differences by sex. Decisions could be made at the individual level or at the group level. Individual views largely depended upon a person's characteristics and socialization with regard to sex roles. Decisions that involved several persons usually entailed a process of negotiation, although the final decision could also be taken by fiat, being determined solely by a person in a position of authority, be it the head of household, another family member, a community leader or the Government. Labour recruiters were also known to play important roles in prompting migration decisions. Collective decision-making depended upon the relative power of the persons involved, which derived from their access to and control over resources, including their relative economic contributions and employment status; their relevant personal characteristics, such as age and education; their access to information and connections through networks and their gender, in the context of societal norms and values.

Given the lack of information on the roles women actually play in decision-making relating to migration, the need for in-depth anthropological-type studies and family narratives was stressed. Among the scanty evidence available, a study of internal migrants in the Philippines undertaken about a decade earlier, indicated that 81 per cent of men and 61 per cent of women said that the decision to migrate had been entirely or mostly their own, whereas 8 and 14 per cent, respectively, said it had been largely that of others. Thus, although differences by sex did exist, they did not indicate that women were mostly passive in the decision-making process. Moreover, the active participation of women in taking the decision to migrate was even greater when international migration was involved.

E. THE CONSEQUENCES OF FEMALE MIGRATION

An overview of research on the consequences of female migration showed that few generalizations could be made concerning the impact of migration on the status of women. A crucial problem was the lack of a general definition of female status. The variety of indicators of status used in the literature made comparisons difficult. In addition, the scope and methods of the studies available varied widely. Consequently, the main conclusion arrived at was that the outcome of migration for women varied considerably according to the sociocultural and family contexts in which migration took place. Thus, in some contexts, migration contributed to the emancipation of women from patriarchal control by opening new opportunities for them and providing them with their own income. In others, however, migration did not seem to free women from patriarchal control. That was the case, for instance, when women moved in order to work and contribute to the sustenance of the families that they had left behind. Often, a woman in such circumstances would put most of her income at the disposal of her family and would thus remain financially dependent and subject to their control. Emancipation was often further hindered by the nature of the work in which migrant women were engaged. When that work was low-paid and involved poor working conditions with little prospect of upward mobility, it was unlikely to lead to an improvement of the status of women either within the household or in society at large.

Even when women managed to acquire greater decision-making power inside the household as a result of migration, their position in society might remain unchanged. Evidence was cited showing that women who moved from a rural to an urban environment sometimes passed from the patriarchy of the home to that of society, exercised through state policies or through social norms or structures that prevented true emancipation.

The consequences of migration could not be discussed without taking account of the forces that mobilized women and the determinants of their move. Thus, migrant women with little or no education would be likely to hold low-paid, low-status jobs that would rarely lead to an improvement in status. Many migrant women worked in the informal sector, including domestic service, so that they were engaged in activities that were a direct extension of their traditional household duties (sewing, food preparation, petty trade etc.). Both within and outside the informal sector, female migrants usually earned lower wages than migrant men. In such circumstances, the mere earning of an independent income was not conducive to greater freedom or decision-making power within the home.

Women that migrated in the company of family members or to join other family members were not necessarily less likely to improve their status than women that migrated alone. In Southern Asia, for instance, the migration of women from rural to urban areas in order to accompany or join their husbands might enhance their independence by separating them from the extended family. However, loss of the rural social network might lead them to remain more confined to the home than they would have been in the rural environment.

Mention was made of the need to differentiate migration undertaken as a survival strategy (that is, determined mostly by push factors at origin) and mobility migration (that which resulted mainly from pull factors). Although it was recognized that the difference between the two would not always be clear cut, the distinction was useful in considering the consequences of migration for women. Thus, it was judged that survival migration was less likely to lead to an improvement in the status of women than mobility migration. It was also mentioned that, according to historical studies of Europe, at the early stages of urbanization the growing employment of women and their capacity to earn an income did not lead immediately to their emancipation from patriarchal control within the family. In the long run, however, such societal changes did provide the basis for improvement in the status of women.

The case-study of Malaysia investigated the role of married women in attaining the economic status desired by migrant families. It was suggested that those families determined their economic position by comparing their income with that of a particular reference group in the urban area of destination and aspired to a similar income. The participation of women in income-generating activities was an important strategy used by migrant families to improve their economic status. By identifying migrant families as those in which the wife of the head of household had migrated after the most recent marriage but at most 15 years prior to the survey and by estimating the aspired income for each migrant family as the average of those earned by men with similar socio-economic characteristics (age, occupation etc.) as those of the head of the migrant household, two hypotheses were tested. The first stated that the lower the ratio between the observed husband's income and the aspired household income, the longer the hours migrant women would work; the second postulated that migrant women would work longer hours than non-migrant women in families where observed income was less than aspired income. The use of a multivariate model controlling for various factors that determined female labour force participation provided evidence to validate the second hypothesis. The evidence was weaker in favour of the first, but it nevertheless suggested that the number of hours worked by migrant women was directly related to the gap between observed and aspired income. It was also concluded that the economic position of women usually improved with migration because of their increased income-earning activities and that such position was directly related to their relative contribution to household income.

A study of rural-urban female migrants in a *gecekondu* (squatter area) of Istanbul showed that the property owned by migrant women or their immediate families (mostly in the areas of origin) tended to diminish as the proportion of their lives spent at Istanbul increased, whereas the number of consumer goods in migrant households increased. Women reported that they had more decision-making power within the household, and they were more likely to be living in nuclear families or to be working for wages as the proportion of their life spent in the city rose. Despite these indicators of positive changes over time in the status of migrant women, decision-making power in the community studied remained in the hands of men, who were not responsive to the needs of women even when the latter took action to have a health-service facility reinstated in their neighbourhood.

The effects of male rural-rural migration on the married women left behind were considered for the region of the Jequitinhonha Valley near São Paulo, Brazil. That region was characterized as an economically stagnant area populated mostly by small producers (*minifundistas*), where men engaged in circular migration to raise the cash needed to supplement the incomes generated by their small properties. Men usually left the valley for periods of from three to nine months every year to work as sugar-cane cutters in the state of São Paulo. During those periods, their wives remained behind as the de facto heads of household. Although it was anticipated that the effects of migration on the women left behind would be positive in terms of changes in their status, no significant differences were detected between women with migrant husbands and those with non-migrant husbands as concerned participation in market activities. Differences were significant, however, with respect to domestic activities, indicating that the wives of migrant men tended to devote more time to such chores as gathering wood or hauling water than did the wives of non-migrants. In addition, migration, by exposing husbands to some modernizing experiences, left their non-migrant wives in an even weaker position inside the home.

An important finding with regard to the broader socio-economic effects of male circular migration on the families left behind concerned the education of children. It was found that children of migrants achieved, at every age, a lower educational attainment than children of non-migrants. This outcome was explained in terms of the nature of the migration being considered: because circular migration was mainly a survival strategy, the resources accumulated were too meagre to promote the development of human capital. In fact, the absence of fathers probably made it necessary for children to take on added responsibilities that conflicted with normal school attendance.

The difficulty of disentangling the effects of migration and poverty on the status of women was noted. It was suggested that programmes to provide women with viable income-generating activities in rural areas, such as craft production and other non-agricultural activities, were urgently needed. It was also necessary to provide agricultural extension services directed specifically to the needs of women and to increase their access to both formal education and vocational training. The dependence of women and families left behind upon remittances from absent husbands was seen as potentially destabilizing, because migrants that stayed away for long periods were prone to start new families at destination and abandon those left behind.

F. LABOUR MARKET ASPECTS OF FEMALE MIGRATION

In considering the labour-market aspects of female migration, it was important to determine the extent to which married and unmarried women differed in their ability to respond to economic opportunities. The case of migration between the poverty-stricken north-eastern region of Brazil and the prosperous south-eastern region was used to investigate how women responded to wage differentials. The probability of migrating was estimated separately for single and married men and for women and was related to the expected wage differentials between origin and destination while controlling for certain other factors thought to influence migration (e.g., rural or urban location and household size). It was found that the expected wage differential had the anticipated positive and significant effect on the probability of migrating for all persons except married women. For the latter group, however, the husband's expected wage differential was significant. These results implied that married women who migrated were making suboptimal decisions as to their economic prospects. As tied movers, they could not take full advantage of the opportunities open to them. The model used, however, assumed that single women were not tied movers and made their migration decisions independently. Since single women often moved in conjunction with their families, such an assumption might not have been realistic.

The issue of how the characteristics of labour-markets at destination influenced the migration of women was considered in the context of three countries, namely, Argentina, Mexico and Thailand. In the case of Argentina, attention was centred on Neuquén, a medium-sized city of some 90,000 inhabitants in 1980, that had experienced very sizeable migrant inflows, particularly during the 1960s. The census of 1980 showed that more than three quarters of the women aged 14 or over at Neuquén had been born outside the city. Five different flows of migrant women to Neuquén were distinguished on the basis of place of origin: those from neighbouring areas; those from the Buenos Aires metropolitan area; those from other parts of the Province of Buenos Aires; those from other parts of Argentina; and those from foreign countries. Women originating in both the Buenos Aires metropolitan area and the Province of Buenos Aires tended to be older and better educated and to work in higher status jobs at Neuquén. They included a high proportion that worked in professional activities. In contrast, women that had originated in neighbouring areas tended to be younger, single and less well educated. As a result, they were concentrated in the informal sector and mainly worked in domestic service.

The labour-market of Neuquén was thus characterized by segmentation of the formal and informal sectors. Female migrants tended to be more concentrated in the informal sector than their male counterparts. Participation in that sector was highest among the youngest and oldest migrant women, particularly those who had arrived recently (since 1975), which indicated that they constituted the most vulnerable group of migrants

In the case of Mexico, the labour-market aspects of female migration to the cities of León, Mérida, Monterrey and Tijuana were considered. Tijuana, located on the border between Mexico and the United States, was characterized as a major location of *maquiladora* industries, which were important employers of unskilled female labour. Monterrey, an old industrial centre, was the site of heavy industry, while León and Mérida were smaller cities where textile industries predominated. At Mérida, tourist services were also important. In all cities except Mérida, labour force participation was lower among migrant women than among non-migrants. The types of activities in which migrant women engaged were determined by the employment structure of each city: at Monterrey and Mérida migrant women were mostly concentrated in "other services" (generally domestic service), followed by commerce, education and medical services (nurses). At Tijuana, in contrast, commerce attracted the largest group of migrant women, followed by heavy industry and the education and medical fields.

The study of Thailand indicated that the important structural changes in the country had derived from the different development strategies followed since the 1950s. During the 1960s, agricultural exports had been promoted, but during the 1970s, policies had shifted to promote export-oriented manufacturing, and by the

1980s, tourism had been added. The availability of surplus labour in rural areas, particularly among women, constituted a crucial factor that allowed the successful pursuit of those policies. The growth recorded in the secondary and tertiary sectors of the economy was closely linked to increases in rural-urban migration, particularly of women. Migration to Bangkok, which in 1980 contained over 60 per cent of the urban population of the entire country, had increased from 35,000 to 63,000 persons per annum between 1975 and 1985, while the proportion of women had risen from 53 to 63 per cent. The share of female migrants among teenagers living at Bangkok had risen from 16 to 43 per cent between 1974 and 1987. Job-related reasons for migration were those most often reported by both male and female migrants. Unemployment was fairly low among all migrants but was particularly low among teenage female migrants. A majority of both male and female migrants had at most completed elementary education, and females were less likely to have higher educational levels than males. Both migrant men and women tended to rely upon informal social networks to secure a job at Bangkok, but networks were more important for females than for males. With respect to wages, migrants were better off than non-migrants at origin but worse off than non-migrants at destination, and women generally had lower wages than men. In addition, whereas migrant men were more likely to work in the secondary sector, migrant women usually found work in the service sector or in sales.

The Thai mode of development was said to have fostered entreprises that took advantage of the "feminine" qualities of female labour—its low cost, docility and expendability. High labour turnover was a common practice, which make it unlikely for women to derive long-term beneficial effects from such an employment experience. In such circumstances, the conditions of employment were far from liberating, because patriarchal control was effectively transferred from the home to the workplace, owned and managed by men. Even when migration opened new opportunities for women and afforded them the freedom to earn and spend their own income, such changes did not guarantee positive effects on their sex roles, which tended to change more slowly.

The case-studies considered indicated that women did migrate in order to respond to the economic opportunities open to them, though their situation within the home and the characteristics of the labour-market that they entered imposed considerable constraints on their labour force participation. Thus, married women were less likely than single women to participate in the labour force in the areas of destination, and married women that migrated with their husbands were not as likely as the latter to reap the benefits from migration. In addition, the segmentation of the urban labour-market typical of developing countries precluded competition between men and women. Women were segregated to certain sectors of the economy, particularly those involving low-status, low-paid jobs with little prospect for advancement.

The tendency of female migrants to work in the informal sector was noted. Two types of activities could be identified in that sector: those where the supply of female labour created its own demand (as in the case of domestic servants); and those where women had, in some sense, to create their own jobs through individual entrepreneurship. The second possibility was said to be responsible for the relatively low unemployment rates registered among migrants. The informal sector provided conditions of work where women were better able to cope with both their productive and reproductive responsibilities. However, note was taken that most jobs in the informal sector provided few opportunities for advancement and thus were unlikely to have positive effects on the status of women.

In highly segmented labour-markets, where job opportunities for women were restricted, women often worked only when they had to. As the family income improved, women dropped out from the labour force altogether and devoted themselves solely to family responsibilities. The availability of domestic servants could, however, relieve other women from such responsibilities and thus free them for market employment. That process was probably taking place in the urban areas of many developing countries, though it was hampered by the dearth of attractive economic opportunities for educated women.

Although the studies discussed concerned only women that migrated to urban areas, mention was made of the importance of rural-rural migration in many contexts. In Thailand itself, rural-rural flows were dominant and little was known about the labour-market aspects of that migration for women. In addition, given the growing urbanization of many developing countries, rural-urban migration was expected to decrease in importance, being replaced by urban-urban flows that were likely to involve better educated women. The need to look at how those processes evolved was stressed.

G. POLICY ISSUES RELEVANT TO THE MIGRATION OF WOMEN AND THEIR ROLE IN DEVELOPMENT

The discussion of policies that affected internal migration flows and their impact on women was complicated by the fact that a wide range of policies could have indirect effects on population mobility by increasing or decreasing inequalities between regions, urban and rural areas, social classes or the sexes. At the most general level, countries could be distinguished according to the types of development policies that they had pursued. Such policies, by affecting socio-economic conditions differently across regions or population groups, differentially influenced opportunities for men and women and, consequently, had an impact on migration patterns and migration outcomes for women.

If one of the goals of policies intended to influence migration was to improve the well-being and status of women, it was not sufficient to focus solely on female migrants, because women were affected by migration even when they themselves did not move. On the other hand, policies to improve the well-being of women in general would also be beneficial to female migrants. Although the economic well-being of women could improve without changing their status, changes in women's status were likely to enhance their well-being through empowerment.

Successful development policies that improved socio-economic conditions and therefore increased the resources available for society in general might not necessarily have a positive effect on the status of women. It was essential to ensure that women themselves should have both more resources and the power to use them. From that perspective, policies or programmes that focused directly on women were likely to be more effective in improving their status, though policies directed to influencing migration could ensure that migrant women should be treated fairly in terms of access to employment, wages and conditions of work.

The difficulty of making generalizations about the outcomes of policies and, therefore, about their desirability was recognized. Significant variations existed not only between world regions but between countries within the same region. In addition, information on policies that related to migration or to women was scanty in many countries. Consideration of the development plans adopted by various countries showed that most disregarded women's issues. The most recent plans of Bangladesh and Pakistan were seen as an exception. It was stated, moreover, that the general trend throughout the world was towards the elimination or reduction of government planning. In particular, most countries that were undergoing structural adjustment had to reduce the size of the government sector and were therefore unlikely to devote sufficient attention to the migration implications of public or private investment.

It was suggested that three broad types of policies should be distinguished: *(a)* non-migration directed policies, those which were not explicitly directed to affecting migration but that affected it nevertheless; *(b)* migration-directed policies, those explicitly intended to affect migration; and *(c)* migration-responsive policies, those intended to respond to the consequences of migration. In suggesting possible avenues for policy formulation, the deficiencies of current knowledge about both the determinants and consequences of migration were stressed. Indeed, it was noted that accurate information about the determinants and consequences of internal migration was needed to formulate effective policies. The dearth of information on migration was contrasted with the efforts made to gather relevant data on fertility: over 100 fertility surveys had been carried in some 60 developing countries during the past 20 years.

When the outcomes of migration were not seen as unequivocally beneficial, Governments might rightly be hesitant to promote migration. In addition, policies designed to prevent migration might not have the desired outcomes. In Ecuador, for instance, efforts to improve living conditions in rural areas through integrated rural development had been successful but had not reduced rural-urban migration significantly: the broader societal effects of modernization and increasing aspirations could not be counterbalanced by the socio-economic changes achieved by local policies. Consequently,

Governments were more likely to adopt migration-responsive policies. Given the expected growth of urban areas in the developing world, policies to provide migrant women with better opportunities in an urban environment were thought necessary.

Among the migration-responsive policies considered, efforts to make the participation of women in the informal sector more productive were highlighted. It was noted that there was no universal definition of what constituted the informal sector but that it often encompassed a large number of salaried workers whose conditions of work did not meet legal standards. Although the prevention of exploitation was judged to be necessary, it was recognized that efforts to impose minimum standards of work either in the informal sector or even in the free trade zones established by certain countries might lead to a reduction of the economic opportunities open for women, particularly those who were migrants. It was thus acknowledged that greater regulation of informal sector activities might not necessarily lead to better outcomes for the women concerned.

The need for policies that would improve the status of women in general and of migrant women in particular was stressed, especially those policies intended to improve the educational attainment and skills of women. Although it was recognized that the occupational opportunities for educated women were still not equivalent to those of men, education was thought to improve the income-earning prospects of women in general. Improved access to health and family planning services, particularly in rural areas, was also recommended, especially in the light of the connection between human mobility and the spread of certain communicable diseases, notably human immunodeficiency virus (HIV) infection.

Given the high level of poverty that prevailed in rural areas, programmes to improve the situation of rural women were strongly recommended. Many women still moved from one rural area to another, often as a result of the labour displacement brought about by the introduction of modern labour-saving technology or the substitution of subsistence food production by cash crops. The need to create alternative employment opportunities for women in rural areas was therefore stressed. In addition, a better understanding of the environmental causes and consequences of rural-rural migration and of measures that Governments might take to involve women in environmental protection was thought necessary.

The formulation of policies intended to affect migration either directly or indirectly had to take into account the heterogeneity of female migration and the fact that the timing and nature of the migration of women was subject to greater social and cultural constraints than those of men. Consequently, women were likely to respond to different sets of incentives and disincentives for migration.

Lastly, it was suggested that the organization of women at the grass-roots level had to be fostered so as to provide them with mechanisms to make their views and needs known to policy makers. Women's organizations could also work towards improving the perception that society had of migrant women. The use of educational programmes and of the mass media to disseminate positive information about women and migration was suggested. Only by making people in general aware of the many positive roles that migrant women played in society would their opportunities for improving their status remain viable.

II. RECOMMENDATIONS TO IMPROVE THE STATUS OF FEMALE MIGRANTS

Given the extensive participation of women in migration flows within developing countries and the obstacles that women often face in achieving the potential benefits of migration, measures that would aid them in maximizing those benefits are needed. Recognizing that some women would not engage in migration if suitable economic, social and educational opportunities were open to them at their place of origin, measures that would increase those opportunities and that would improve access to them are both necessary. Noting that all measures directed to improving the status of women in general will also benefit female migrants, and taking account of the principles and objectives of relevant international instruments[1] and of all those plans of action[2] intended to improve the situation of women and to ensure their full integration in society on an equal basis with men, the following recommendations suggest strategies to achieve all the above-mentioned goals. Because most of the strategies identified differ according to whether they involve women in rural or in urban areas, they are presented under different headings.

A. GENERAL MEASURES

Recommendation 1. In formulating general development policies, including those related to structural adjustments, industrialization and agricultural development, education and health, Governments should take into account their impact on the opportunity and constraint structures in different areas and the differential effects that those structures have on the mobility of men and women.

Recommendation 2. In formulating policies designed to influence migration flows, Governments are urged to take account of the fact that men and women may react differently to incentives meant to prevent or to stimulate migration. In this context, regional development plans should make specific provisions directed to offering appropriate incentives and adequate opportunities for women.

Recommendation 3. Governments, as well as the private sector and non-governmental organizations, are urged to expand the income-earning opportunities for women in both the formal and informal sectors and to disseminate gender-sensitive information about those opportunities among the appropriate target populations in regions where potential migrants live. Dissemination of information on educational opportunities, available health services, transport, housing and cost of living in different localities would also be desirable to aid potential migrants in making migration-related decisions. This information should be disseminated in terms appropriate for women.

Recommendation 4. Governments, as well as governmental and non-governmental organizations, should make efforts to eliminate negative stereotyped perceptions about migrant women, including the view that they are only passive followers of men. Efforts should also be made to highlight the contributions that migrant women make to socio-economic development and the well-being of their family.

Recommendation 5. Governments are encouraged to facilitate the creation of voluntary organizations by and for women affected by migration, particularly among groups, such as women left behind, urban squatters, domestic servants, young female migrants in export-processing zones and others living in precarious situations. Such organizations should, among other things, promote the dissemination of information among migrants, provide counselling and other social and legal services and identify problems and make them known to decision makers.

Recommendation 6. Governments should take appropriate steps to protect the rights of all migrant women, especially women in vulnerable groups, such as those in the informal sector, those in domestic service, those engaging in outwork, those who are victims of trafficking and involuntary prostitution and any others in potentially exploitable circumstances.

Recommendation 7. There is a need for education, including vocational education, and retraining for adult women, particularly migrant women and women left behind. Such training should be directed to extending employment opportunities in occupations that are non-traditional or new to women and facilitating their adaptation to new technologies. Provision of adequate child-care services in conjunction to such training programmes is needed for women with child-rearing responsibilities.

Recommendation 8. Recognizing that the migration of women is increasingly arranged by labour recruiters, Governments are urged to introduce appropriate legislative or administrative measures to regulate and control the activities of these recruiters.

Recommendation 9. Recognizing that seasonal migrants, including women, engage in economic activities and are provided accommodations that expose them to high health and safety hazards, Governments and non-governmental organizations are urged to adopt effective measures to protect the workers concerned.

Recommendation 10. Governments and international organizations are urged to accord priority to the provision of adequate health services and health education in regions where the risk of exposure to various diseases is increasing because of the temporary migration of men and women. Particular attention should be given to the spread of venereal diseases and of HIV infection along migrant paths.

Recommendation 11. Given that women and children are particularly vulnerable as internally displaced persons, Governments and the international community are urged to take special measures to assist them.

B. MEASURES DIRECTED TO RURAL AREAS

Recommendation 12. Given that rural women are often compelled to migrate in search of employment because their access to productive resources is limited, Governments should take measures to ensure that women shall have equal access as men to land, credit, agricultural extension training and other means of agricultural production. Governments and the private sector should also promote local off-farm employment opportunities for women as an alternative to migration. In addition, agricultural extension workers must be sensitized to the special needs of female farmers and efforts should be made to hire and train more women as extension workers. Since women are often engaged in food production for household consumption, programmes to increase their productivity should be given priority.

Recommendation 13. In many cases, female out-migration from rural areas results from labour-displacing agricultural technology or the switch to cash crops. Therefore, in formulating agricultural modernization strategies, Governments should take into account the labour-displacement effects by gender of such strategies and should take measures to create employment opportunities for displaced workers, particularly women.

Recommendation 14. In order to help create alternatives to out-migration from rural areas, Governments are encouraged to facilitate the establishment of credit and production cooperatives and other grass-roots organizations that would give women control over resources and improve their welfare in rural areas.

Recommendation 15. Since the employment prospects of rural women that migrate are often restricted to unskilled work because of their lack of education, efforts to reduce the high levels of illiteracy and low educational attainment still prevalent among rural women in many countries should be given priority. Educational programmes geared to the rural environment should not only promote functional literacy but should place special emphasis on health, family planning, nutrition and the promotion of viable economic skills, particularly among women.

C. MEASURES DIRECTED TO URBAN AREAS

Recommendation 16. Given that the economic motive dominates for both male and female migrants, Governments, the private sector and non-governmental organizations should increase their efforts to expand employment opportunities for women, especially migrant women, in the modern sectors of the economy. In doing so, minimum standards, equal to those for men, should be ensured with regard to remuneration, safe working conditions, hours of work and the right to join trade unions.

Recommendation 17. Given that a substantial number of migrant women engage in economic activities within the informal sector of the economy, efforts should be made to improve their income-earning capabilities by facilitating their access to fair credit, vocational training, a place to ply their trade, transport, child-care services and health services. Because self-help cooperatives provide an effective means to raise needed capital, their creation should be facilitated and measures should be taken to make them eligible for financial assistance.

Recommendation 18. Because migrant women, particularly those who are the household head, are often at a disadvantage as concerns access to adequate housing in urban areas, government planners are urged to ensure that women shall have equal access to housing as men in any public housing projects or housing credit schemes developed by government authorities. In addition, Governments should ensure that existing legislation and administrative practices shall grant equal ownership and tenancy rights to women as to men.

Recommendation 19. Efforts should be made to ensure that both migrant families and single migrant women shall have access to health services, including family planning and health and sex education. Of special importance is the provision of adequate counselling and health services to women involved in prostitution, who are subject to a greater risk of contracting HIV as well as spreading it.

Recommendation 20. Governments, the private sector and non-governmental organizations are urged to provide adequate support services to first-time migrants in urban areas, including job-placement services and accommodation for migrant women.

D. RESEARCH AND DATA NEEDS

Recommendation 21. Given that adequate and detailed information on the extent and characteristics of female migration is sorely needed, Governments are urged to facilitate the collection and dissemination of adequate information on the topic by, *inter alia*: *(a)* publishing census data on migration by sex and by greater levels of disaggregation; *(b)* carrying out specialized surveys and using any other appropriate data-collection methods that take account of sociocultural contexts to gather detailed information on migration, especially female migration; and *(c)* promoting the further exploitation of existing data sources, such as census samples and migration surveys, by making machine-readable versions available to the research community and to local-level planners.

Recommendation 22. Respondent biases are common in existing procedures for collecting data on women's migration and economic activities, including the custom of obtaining data from the household head, who is presumed to be a male adult. Therefore, measures should be taken to obtain information directly from the women themselves and when this is not possible, from the most knowledgeable women available.

Recommendation 23. Among the many aspects of female migration that demand further research, four deserve particular attention: *(a)* the measurement and conceptualization from a gender-specific perspective of female migration; *(b)* the formulation and application of improved methods for assessing the determinants of female migration; *(c)* the study of the consequences of migration for both the women themselves and their families; and *(d)* methods to measure the contribution of migrant and non-migrant women to development.

Recommendation 24. Recognizing that the informed formulation of policy requires the understanding of both the determinants and consequences of female migration, Governments are encouraged to conduct and support studies into both of these dimensions and their relationship to development. Research to establish the conditions under which migration would result in an improvement of the status of women is crucial for the formulation of policy.

NOTES

[1] Including the Universal Declaration of Human Rights (General Assembly resolution 217 A(III)); the International Covenant on Economic, Social and Cultural Rights (General Assembly resolution 2200 A(XXI), annex); the Declaration on the Elimination of Discrimination against Women (General Assembly resolution 2263 (XXII)); the Convention on the Elimination of All Forms of Discrimination against Women (General Assembly resolution 34/180, annex); the Declaration on the Participation of Women in Promoting International Peace and Co-operation (General Assembly resolution 37/63, annex).

[2] In particular, the World Plan of Action for the Implementation of the Objectives of the International Woman's Year, adopted at Mexico City in 1975 and endorsed by the General Assembly in its resolution 3520 (XXX); the Programme of Action for the Second Half of the United Nations Decade for Women, adopted at the 1980 Copenhagen World Conference and endorsed by the General Assembly in its resolution 35/136; and the Nairobi Forward-looking Strategies for the Advancement of Women, endorsed by the General Assembly in its resolution 40/108.

ANNEXES

ANNEX I

Agenda

1. Opening of the meeting:

    (*a*) Opening statements;
    (*b*) Election of officers.

2. Adoption of the agenda.

3. Overview.

4. The scale and scope of female internal migration:

    (*a*) Global assessment of levels and trends of female internal migration;
    (*b*) Types of female migration;
    (*c*) Issues in the measurement of female migration in developing countries.

5. Explanation of the selectivity of female migrants:

    (*a*) The characteristics of female migrants according to the 1990 census of Mexico;
    (*b*) Rural-urban female migrant selection and adaptation: evidence from longitudinal data for Colombia;
    (*c*) Social appearances and economic realities of female migration in rural Mali.

6. Determinants of female migration:

    (*a*) The structural determinants of female migration;
    (*b*) The determinants of female migration from a multi-level perspective;
    (*c*) Migration decisions: the role of gender.

7. Consequences of migration:

    (*a*) Emancipation or subordination? Consequences of female migration for migrants and their families;
    (*b*) Women's role in female migration;
    (*c*) The consequences of migration for women migrating to Istanbul. Gockent: a case-study;
    (*d*) The consequences of migration for the families left behind: the case of Jequitinhonha Valley, Brazil.

8. The labour-market consequences of female migration:

    (*a*) The labour-market aspects of female migration in Thailand;
    (*b*) The role of wage differentials in determining migration selectivity by sex: the case of Brazil;
    (*c*) Female migration and labour force participation in a medium-sized city of a highly urbanized country.

9. Policy issues relevant for the migration of women:

    (*a*) State policies, women and migration: a review of research findings and policy options;
    (*b*) The role of female migration in development.

10. Adoption of recommendations.

11. Closing of the Meeting.

ANNEX II

List of participants

EXPERTS

Kanta Alvi, Urban Volunteer, International Centre for Diarrhoeal Diseases Research, Bangladesh (ICDDR,B), Dhaka, Bangladesh

Richard E. Bilsborrow, Research Professor of Biostatistics, Economist/Demographer, Carolina Population Center, Chapel Hill, North Carolina, United States of America

Alicia Puente Cackley, Economist, United States General Accounting Office, Washington, D.C., United States of America

Assitan Diallo, Sociology Department, Brown University, Providence, Rhode Island, United States of America

Sally E. Findley, Associate Clinical Professor of Public Health, Center for Population and Health, Columbia University, New York, New York, United States of America

Carmen Elisa Florez, Facultad de Economía, Universidad de los Andes, Bogotá, Colombia

Robert W. Gardner, Research Associate and Assistant Director for Graduate Study, East-West Population Institute, Honolulu, Hawaii, United States of America

Franklin W. Goza, Assistant Professor of Sociology, Department of Sociology, Bowling Green State University, Bowling Green, Ohio, United States of America

Philip Guest, Researcher, Division of Sociology and Demography, The Australian National University, Canberra, Australia

Akile R. Gürsoy-Tezcan, Visiting Associate Professor, Center for Middle Eastern Studies, University of Texas at Austin, Austin, Texas, United States of America

Graeme J. Hugo, Reader, School of Social Sciences, The Flinders University of South Australia, Adelaide, Australia

Haydea Izazola, Coordinador Administrativo de la Oficina de la Secretaría de Trabajo y Seguridad Social, México, D.F., Mexico

Gavin W. Jones, Professor of Demography and Coordinator, Demography Program, Division of Demography, Research School of Social Sciences, The Australian National University, Canberra, Australia

Lin Lean Lim, Regional Adviser on Women, Population and Development for Asia and the Pacific, Labour and Population Team for Asia and the Pacific (LAPTAP), International Labour Organisation, Regional Office for Asia and the Pacific, Bangkok, Thailand

María de la Paz López, Directora, Investigación Censal, Dirección de Estadística, México, D.F., Mexico

Zulma Recchini de Lattes, Director, Centro Nacional de Estudios de Población (CENEP), Buenos Aires, Argentina

Janet Rodenburg, Researcher, Anthropological-Sociological Centre, Department of South and Southeast Asia Studies, University of Amsterdam, Amsterdam, The Netherlands

Alan B. Simmons, Associate Professor of Sociology, Director, Centre for Research on Latin America and the Caribbean (CERLAC), York University, Toronto, Ontario, Canada

Joachim Singelmann, Professor of Sociology and Rural Sociology, Department of Sociology, Louisiana State University, Baton Rouge, Louisiana, United States of America

Rensje Teerink, Centre for Asian Studies Amsterdam (CASA), Amsterdam, The Netherlands

UNITED NATIONS SECRETARIAT

Population Division of the Department of International Economic and Social Affairs
Shunichi Inoue, Director
Birgitta Bucht, Chief, Population Trends and Structure Section
Hania Zlotnik, Population Affairs Officer

United Nations Population Fund (UNFPA)
Graciela Duce, United Nations Population Fund Country Director in Mexico

International Research and Training Institute for the Advancement of Women (INSTRAW)
Mercedes Pedrero, Consultant

SPECIALIZED AGENCIES

International Labour Organisation (ILO)
Lin Lean Lim, Regional Adviser

GOVERNMENTAL ORGANIZATIONS

Instituto Nacional de Estadística, Geografía e Informática (INEGI)

Presidencia
Carlos M. Jarque, Presidente

Coordinación Administrativa
Raúl Alvarez Ramírez
Arcelia Breceda Solis
Elda Estañol
Daniel García Agoitia
Pilar García Velázquez
Mario Palma Rojo
Lourdes Rodríguez Orenday
Arturo Sánchez Martínez

Dirección General de Estadística
Eunice Bañuelos Flores, Seguimiento Censal

Jesús Castañeda, Adjunto Regional Norte
María de los Angeles Valdez, Estadísticas Demográficas y Sociales
Marcela Eternod Aramburu, Investigación y Diseño Conceptual
Patricia Fernández Ham, Investigación Censal
Ricardo García Palacios, Adjunto Regional Occidente
Arturo González Morales, Análisis Demográfico y Proyecciones de Población
Elvia Gutiérrez Morales, Departamento de Desarrollo Metodológico y Coordinación Regional
Patricia Maldonado Opereza, Evaluación Censal
Hortensia Medina Uribe, Departamento de Análisis de Información Regional
Gerardo Medrano, Adjunto Regional Noreste
Tomás Ramírez Reynoso, Estadísticas Demográficas
Atilia Ramírez Suárez, Investigación Demográfica
Gabriela Vázquez Benítez, Evaluación Demográfica

OBSERVERS

Mexico

Consejo Nacional de Población (CONAPO)
Reina Corona Cuapio, Jefa, Departamento de Migración Interna
Constanza Rodríguez Hernández, Jefa, Departamento de Modelos, Demográficos y Socioeconómicos

Secretaría de Programación y Presupuesto
José Gómez de León, Asesor del Secretario de Programación y Presupuesto

Secretaría de Relaciones Exteriores
Aída González Martínez, Asesora del Sr. Secretario de Relaciones

Secretaría el Trabajo y Previsión Social
Sergio Sierra Romero, Subdirector de Estudios de Políticas de Empleo

Other observers

Child Study Centre, Ottawa, Canada
Jean Turner

Colegio de la Frontera Norte, Tijuana, Mexico
Norma Ojeda, Directora, Departamento de Estudios de Población

Columbia University, New York, New York, United States of America
María de los Angeles Crummett, Department of Economics

The Johns Hopkins University, Baltimore, Maryland, United States of America
Rebeca Wong, Assistant Professor, School of Hygiene and Public Health

Universidad de Guadalajara, Mexico
Fermina Robles Sotelo

ANNEX III

List of documents

Document No.	Agenda item	Title and author
IESA/P/AC.35/1	2	Provisional agenda
IESA/P/AC.35/2	3	Migrant women in developing countries Graeme J. Hugo
IESA/P/AC.35/3	4	Global assessment of levels and trends of female internal migration Joachim Singelmann
IESA/P/AC.35/4	4	Types of female migration Population Division
IESA/P/AC.35/5	4	Issues in the measurement of female migration in developing countries Richard E. Bilsborrow
IESA/P/AC.35/6	5	The characteristics of female migrants according to the 1990 census of Mexico María de la Paz López, Haydea Izazola and José Gómez de León
IESA/P/AC.35/7	5	Rural-urban female migrant selection and adaptation: evidence from longitudinal data for Colombia Carmen Elisa Florez
IESA/P/AC.35/8	5	Social appearances and economic realities of female migration in rural Mali Sally E. Findley and Assitan Diallo
IESA/P/AC.35/9	6	The structural determinants of female migration Lin Lean Lim
IESA/P/AC.35/10	6	The determinants of female migration from a multilevel perspective Philip Guest
IESA/P/AC.35/11	6	Migration decisions: the role of gender Robert W. Gardner and Nancy E. Riley
IESA/P/AC.35/12	7	Emancipation or subordination? Consequences of female migration for migrants and their families Janet Rodenburg
IESA/P/AC.35/13	7	Women's role in female migration Kanta Alvi

Document No.	Agenda item	Title and author
IESA/P/AC.35/14	7	The consequences of migration for women migrating to Istanbul. Gockent: a case study Akile R. Gürsoy-Tezcan
IESA/P/AC.35/15	7	The consequences of migration for the families left behind: the case of Jequitinhonha Valley, Brazil Franklin W. Goza and Eduardo Rios-Neto
IESA/P/AC.35/16	8	The labour-market aspects of female migration in Thailand Pasuk Phongpaichit
IESA/P/AC.35/17	8	The role of wage differentials in determining migration selectivity by sex: the case of Brazil Alicia Puente Cackley
IESA/P/AC.35/18	8	Female migration and labour force participation in a medium-sized city of a highly urbanized country Zulma Recchini de Lattes and Sonia María Mychaszula
IESA/P/AC.35/19	9	State policies, women and migration: a review of research findings and policy options Alan B. Simmons
IESA/P/AC.35/20	9	The role of female migration in development Gavin W. Jones
IESA/P/AC.35/INF.1	-	Provisional list of documents
IESA/P/AC.35/INF.2	-	Provisional list of participants
IESA/P/AC.35/INF.4	-	Provisional organization of work

Part Two

BACKGROUND AND STATEMENT OF ISSUES

III. MIGRANT WOMEN IN DEVELOPING COUNTRIES

*Graeme J. Hugo**

Among the processes that have reshaped the world in the second half of the twentieth century, few have been so far-reaching or profound in their impact as those associated with the changes taking place in the roles and status of women. Such changes have rightfully become a major focus of social science research and population studies are no exception. The relation between the changing roles and status of women, on the one hand, and demographic dynamics, on the other, is complex, because women's roles and status both determine and are determined by demographic change. Up to now, however, both population research and the attention of policy makers have been focused mainly on the interrelations between fertility or mortality and the changing status of women. Consideration of the third major demographic process—migration—has, as is often the case, been largely neglected. Such neglect is regrettable, not only because female migration is occurring on a scale comparable to that of men in most regions but because there are important interrelations between female migration and the wider socio-economic transformations taking place in developing countries.

This paper is not intended to be a comprehensive review of existing literature and knowledge concerning female migration in developing countries; a number of reviews and anthologies already serve that purpose.[1] The objective here is to raise a number of issues related to female migration in developing countries which are considered to be of major significance from a policy perspective, especially taking into account that gender is a socially constructed rather than a biologically determined category (Benería and Roldán, 1987) and that the roles and status of women are the result of historical and social processes, of which migration is a part.

The economic and social transformations that have swept across developing countries during the past two decades have had profound effects on the distribution of institutional and economic power between the sexes. Not all these changes have been positive with respect to the status of women. The study of how such changes have impinged upon and, in turn, been influenced by the spatial mobility of women provides a window from which to view the highly complex interrelations between economic development, social change and the status of women. Given that migration has considerable potential to reshape gender relations, it is important to establish in which circumstances it can benefit women and in which it may have detrimental effects for the women involved.

Although the trends and patterns of female migration cannot be ascertained with perfect accuracy in many contexts, attempts to quantify them are needed in order to clarify and understand the nature of the processes shaping them. In particular, it is necessary to identify the differences and similarities between the processes leading to female migration and those impinging upon males. Although migration research is typically hindered by failure of the available data to reflect the full extent of population mobility or the full range of forces leading to migration, the study of female migration has to cope with even greater constraints. Thus, as Morokvasic (1984b) states, migrant women are often "invisible" as a result of data-collection practices and procedures that tend to conceal or distort systematically the migration of women. Accordingly, before considering any of the substantive issues related to female migration it is desirable to focus on the data issues relating to the migration of women.

A. DATA AND MEASUREMENT ISSUES

The fact that knowledge is determined by the nature of the information available is all too often overlooked in migration research. Almost any data set on persons that move excludes significant numbers of mobile individuals because of the specific criteria used to define "migration". This outcome is inevitable, given

---

*Reader, School of Social Sciences, The Flinders University of South Australia, Adelaide, Australia.

the complexity and frequency of population movement as compared with discrete and definite events, such as births and deaths. It becomes problematic, however, when researchers fail to acknowledge the systematic exclusion of particular groups of movers and assume that their findings are relevant to all movers. For more than a decade, there have been references to a male bias in migration research. Indeed, as Morokvasic points out: "Acknowledgement that female migrants have been neglected by research and policy makers or that they have been represented in a stereotypical manner as 'passive dependents', while migration has been treated as a phenomenon involving males only, has become part of the conventional wisdom in the field" (1984c, p. 899). Yet, a male bias has persisted, in part because of the biases characteristic of the standard data-collection systems. It is therefore important to establish how those biases arise and their effects on the results obtained.

The most obvious bias arises when surveys seek to interview only male migrants or "heads of household". As Morokvasic states:

"The term *migrant* covers a wide range of subtypes and subcategories. But when used, as it often is, with the phrase 'and their families', the term inevitably acquires a male gender and 'family' is understood to mean dependent women and children. Whether this is a genuine or only ascribed dependency, the division into migrants (male) and dependants has served as a basic guideline in recording statistics and determining policy, and has had an impact on research. It has contributed largely to creating, as well as perpetuating, the invisibility of migrant women." (1984b, p. 111)

Given such preconceptions, it is hardly surprising that migration studies often report female migration as being limited in scale or predominantly "associated" with male migration. Even when women are interviewed in migration surveys, it is often in a context that leads them to emphasize (sometimes incorrectly) their dependent status. For example, when women are interviewed in the presence of male relatives, they are likely to give culturally or socially sanctioned responses rather than the real reasons. Thus, Bryant (1977) found that women at Gaborone (Botswana) tended to report economic motives for their migration more frequently when interviewed alone than when interviewed by men in front of the entire household.

Not only do women need to be properly represented as migrants in the data-collection process, it is also necessary to evaluate critically the types of questions posed to them. Here the discrimination is subtler. The concepts and actual questions used when inquiring about motives and other aspects of the migration experience are often based on male experience (see Bilsborrow, 1993). For instance, special care must be taken to capture appropriately the labour force participation of female migrants. As is well known, standard data-collection systems generally underestimate the participation of women in the labour force, especially in developing countries. As Youssef, Buvinic and Kudat point out:

"This largely untested attribution of 'marriage only' motives to the migration of women is in part due to the invisibility of (or lack of data on) women as economic producers and an overemphasis on their roles as reproducers and homemakers. It naturally led scholars and development experts to overlook any socio-economic significance of female migration. ..." (1979, pp. 82-83)

Hence, not only are surveys failing to detect significant groups of female migrants, many are not even asking the relevant questions. It is a source of some frustration that among the more than 100 major fertility surveys that have been carried out in developing countries during the past two decades, only a handful gathered some information on the migration experience of women. Consequently, an important opportunity to advance the understanding of how migration interacts with other demographic processes has been missed.

Serious biases are of special concern when they affect the most widely used sources of migration information, namely, population censuses. There is an urgent need to assess the types of biases that affect those data and to establish the distortions that those biases introduce in the analysis of female migration. Such understanding is essential to develop appropriate data collection and analytical methods to ensure that migrant women shall be properly represented in data-collection efforts and that biases shall be reduced. In particular, it is important for researchers to guard against sampling strategies or questionnaire designs that either overtly or covertly bypass female migrants.

B. CHANGING SCALE AND SCOPE OF FEMALE MIGRATION: REGIONAL DIFFERENCES

Despite the limitations of existing data, it is clear that female mobility has grown both in size and in complexity over the past 20 years. There is a need, however, to make a comprehensive assessment of the extent of female migration using the 1980 round of censuses (many of which included specific questions on migration). At the time of writing, however, available international comparisons were based largely on the 1970 round of censuses and did not include estimates for earlier periods. Thus, Youssef, Buvinic and Kudat (1979) used a technique based on the comparison of expected and observed sex ratios in the rural areas of 46 developing countries to infer the extent of female rural-urban migration. This approach assumes that differences in sex ratios brought about by differential mortality can be disregarded. On the basis of their analysis, Youssef, Buvinic and Kudat conclude that:

(a) Among the four major areas of the developing world, male dominance in rural-urban migration flows was greatest in the African countries included in the analysis. One interesting exception, however, was that among those over age 50, where females dominated in all but three countries;

(b) In Eastern, South-eastern and Southern Asia, there were generally very low sex differentials in rural-urban migration. In half the countries considered, females dominated among migrants aged 15-19, while in all countries, males were more numerous over age range 25-34. Only in the Philippines did women dominate over most of the age range;

(c) Females also tended to be more numerous among rural-urban migrants in Central America and in most of the Caribbean countries considered. In South America, the pattern was similar, although there was greater variability between countries;

(d) In Western Asia, Turkey had heavily male-dominated out-migration from rural areas, whereas the other countries studied displayed relatively low differentials by sex.

Despite the limitations of this analysis, the regional differences identified are generally confirmed by case-studies carried out in the various regions.

Using intercensal survival techniques, the United Nations (1985) produced a comparative study of migration to metropolitan areas based on the 1960 and 1970 rounds of censuses. Twenty-six metropolitan areas in developing countries were considered. Table 4 gives the overall sex ratios of the population in each metropolitan area for 1960 and 1970, together with the gains attributable to net migration or reclassification over the intercensal period. Those data largely confirm the trends identified by Youssef, Buvinic and Kudat (1979):

(a) The male dominance in both the net migration component and the resident populations of the small number of African cities considered. However, disregarding South Africa, the data given in table 4 suggest that the feminization of net migration to cities in low-income countries of Africa increased;

(b) The existence of diverse patterns in Asia, where some cities or areas show female dominance (Bangkok and Metropolitan Manila), others male dominance (Hong Kong) and yet others (Jakarta) relatively balanced sex ratios with respect to both net migration and the overall population;

(c) The typical female dominance in both net migration and resident populations in Latin American cities.

Estimates of net migration by age indicate that, in the 1960s, net migration contributed, on average, nearly 54 per cent of the growth of the female population aged 15-29 in the cities and two thirds of the growth of males in the same cohorts. If the entire population of working age (15-64) is considered, the equivalent proportions are somewhat lower—37 and 35.4 per cent, respectively—but still indicate that more than one third of the population growth in the cities was attributable to net migration and reclassification.

TABLE 4. SEX RATIOS OF METROPOLITAN POPULATIONS AND NET MIGRATION, SELECTED METROPOLITAN CENTRES, 1960-1970

Major area and city or area	Metropolitan population About 1960	Metropolitan population About 1970	Net migration and reclassification
Africa			
Accra	114	106	115
Algiers	99	101	112
Cape Town	99	100	201
East Rand	148	122	a
Johannesburg	108	106	b
Asia			
Bangkok	104	98	70
Damascus	106	106	118
Hong Kong	105	103	116
Jakarta	104	102	101
Manila	94	93	84
Seoul	100	100	98
Singapore	113	103	a
Teheran	110	111	127
Latin America			
Belo Horizonte	93	93	89
Bogotá	87	87	79
Buenos Aires	94	94	88
Caracas	101	95	78
Guadalajara	93	94	92
Lima	100	100	99
Mexico City	92	95	92
Monterrey	99	99	94
Porto Alegre	95	94	81
Recife	88	89	66
Rio de Janeiro	96	95	78
Santiago	84	88	94
São Paulo	99	99	97

Source: *Migration, Population Growth and Employment in Metropolitan Areas of Selected Developing Countries* (United Nations publication, ST/ESA/SER.R/57).

NOTE: Figures indicate the number of males per 100 females.

a East Rand and Singapore had male net out-migration and female net in-migration.

b Johannesburg had female net out-migration and male net in-migration.

Recently, the Population Division of the Department for Economic and Social Information and Policy Analysis of the United Nations Secretariat estimated net rural-urban migration using intercensal survival techniques applied to the 1960, 1970 and 1980 rounds of censuses. The data for rural-urban migration in Africa corroborate the fact that males tend to outnumber females in net migration flows (see table 5). The fact that in some countries, male dominance is slightly less pronounced in relation to migration rates (not shown) than in terms of numbers of migrants suggests that the tempo of migration of women with respect to that of men is increasing.

The estimates for Asian countries or areas confirm the "mixed" patterns already documented above (see table 6). In Hong Kong, Japan and the Republic of Korea, the relative participation of women in rural-urban migration has been increasing, although in Hong Kong, males still outnumber females among migrants. In most of the South-eastern Asian countries with data available, women outnumber men among rural-urban migrants, the only exceptions being Brunei Darussalam and the "frontier" area of Sabah in Malaysia. During the 1970s, the dominance of women among migrants was especially pronounced in the Philippines and in Thailand. A totally different situation prevails in Southern Asia, where all countries display a clear majority of men in net rural-urban migration. In the four countries of Western Asia with the requisite data, male migrants tend to outnumber female migrants, with Israel being the only exception. However, in the Syrian Arab Republic and in Turkey, the sex ratios of migrants have been decreasing over time.

In Latin America and the Caribbean, a remarkably consistent pattern is in evidence: in most countries women outnumber men in net rural-urban migration (the only exception being Argentina during the period 1947-1960). Few countries, however, display a consistent trend of increasing female dominance over time. Problems related to differential census coverage or the use of different definitions of urban areas over time may be affecting the comparability of the estimates for some of the countries presented here (see table 7).

Smith, Khoo and Go (1984) present international comparisons of female migration levels in nine Asian countries, using data from the 1970 round of censuses for the age groups of peak mobility, 15-24. Their analysis is based on migration rates by sex. It highlights general female dominance in the Philippines, greater female selectivity in age group 15-19 in Indonesia and Thailand and in age group 20-24 in the Republic of Korea; and differing degrees of male dominance in India, the Islamic Republic of Iran,

TABLE 5. SELECTED COUNTRIES OF AFRICA: ESTIMATED NET RURAL-URBAN MIGRATION IN RECENT INTERCENSAL PERIODS
(Thousands)

Region and country	Intercensal period	Migrants (on 10-year basis)		Sex ratio (3)=(1) x 100 (2)
		Male (1)	Female (2)	
Eastern Africa				
Kenya	1969-1979	443	344	129
United Republic of Tanzania	1967-1978	629	578	109
Zimbabwe	1969-1982	237	218	109
Northern Africa				
Egypt	1960-1976	708	613	116
Libyan Arab Jamahiriya	1964-1973	358	309	116
Morocco	1952-1960	381	355	107
	1960-1971	303	387	78
	1971-1982	769	640	120
Tunisia	1966-1975	258	294	88
	1975-1984	146	135	108
Southern Africa				
Botswana	1964-1971	21	21	103
	1971-1981	30	24	128
South Africa	1960-1970	517	261	198
Western Africa				
Ghana	1960-1970	195	195	100
Togo	1959-1970	25	22	115

Source: Unpublished estimates produced by the Population Division of the Department for Economic and Social Information and Policy Analysis of the United Nations Secretariat.

Malaysia and Singapore. Unfortunately, as in any attempt at making international comparisons, the data used vary greatly in terms of the underlying definitions of migration. For example, in the Indonesian census, a person had to move permanently across the borders of any two of the 27 provinces to be counted as a migrant, whereas in Malaysia, all permanent changes of residence were recorded as migration. Even within the same country, different censuses sometimes use different definitions of migration.

Despite their shortcomings, census data still represent the richest source of information on internal migration. It is therefore essential that an effort be made to promote the comprehensive and systematic analysis of migration data from the 1990 round of censuses, taking care to give appropriate attention to gender issues.

C. TYPES OF FEMALE MIGRATION

Not only is the magnitude of female migration on the increase but, as the growing literature on female migrants indicates, the types of movements in which women engage are also growing in complexity. However, existing data are not well suited to show that growing complexity. Hence, researchers have only examined the "tip of the iceberg" of spatial mobility among women and the hidden part is likely to be significant. Indeed, it may be argued that any analysis of migration should indicate not only the types of

TABLE 6. SELECTED COUNTRIES OF ASIA: ESTIMATED NET RURAL-URBAN MIGRATION IN RECENT INTERCENSAL PERIODS
(Thousands)

Region and country or area	Intercensal period	Migrants (on 10-year basis)		
		Male (1)	Female (2)	Sex ratio (3)=(1)/(2) x 100

Region and country or area	Intercensal period	Male (1)	Female (2)	Sex ratio (3)=(1)/(2) x 100
Eastern Asia				
Hong Kong	1961-1971	59	55	109
	1971-1981	91	89	103
Japan	1955-1965	5 424	5 358	101
	1960-1970	3 824	3 870	99
	1965-1975	3 492	3 700	94
	1970-1980	1 758	2 054	86
	1975-1985	190	347	55
Macau	1960-1970	2	2	114
Republic of Korea	1960-1970	1 874	1 867	100
	1970-1980	2 373	2 507	95
	1975-1985	2 758	2 857	97
South-eastern Asia				
Brunei Darussalam	1960-1971	11	10	106
Indonesia	1961-1971	965	1 006	96
	1971-1980	3 379	3 508	96
Malaysia				
Peninsular Malaysia	1970-1980	428	433	99
Sabah	1960-1970	8	6	130
	1970-1980	39	39	100
Sarawak	1960-1970	3	4	78
	1970-1980	47	49	96
Philippines	1970-1980	1 144	1 416	81
Thailand	1970-1980	852	967	88
Southern Asia				
Bangladesh	1961-1974	1 050	793	132
	1974-1981	3 560	2 655	134
India	1951-1961	3 785	2 161	175
	1961-1971	5 125	4 324	119
	1971-1981	11 789	10 388	114
Iran (Islamic Republic of)	1966-1976	1 505	1 167	129
Maldives	1967-1977	7	4	164
Nepal	1961-1971	27	15	178
	1971-1981	162	146	111
Pakistan	1972-1981	817	627	131
Sri Lanka	1953-1963	199	192	104
	1963-1971	258	233	111
	1971-1981	-39	-26	151
Western Asia				
Iraq	1957-1965	462	475	97
	1965-1977	561	486	116
Israel	1972-1983	77	79	97
Syrian Arab Republic	1960-1970	181	154	118
	1970-1982	140	128	109
Turkey	1950-1960	921	524	176
	1960-1970	1 846	1 581	117
	1970-1980	2 032	2 032	100

Source: Unpublished estimates produced by the Population Division of the Department for Economic and Social Information and Policy Analysis of the United Nations Secretariat.

TABLE 7. SELECTED COUNTRIES OF LATIN AMERICA AND THE CARIBBEAN: ESTIMATED NET
RURAL-URBAN MIGRATION IN RECENT INTERCENSAL PERIODS
(Thousands)

Region and country or area	Intercensal period	Migrants (on 10-year basis)		
		Male (1)	Female (2)	Sex ratio (3)=(1) x 100 (2)
Caribbean				
Cuba	1953-1970	114	124	92
	1970-1981	386	412	94
Dominican Republic	1950-1960	79	106	75
	1960-1970	159	185	86
	1970-1981	251	307	82
Haiti	1950-1971	55	104	53
Jamaica	1953-1960	101	103	98
Puerto Rico	1960-1970	168	179	94
	1970-1980	118	135	87
Central America				
Costa Rica	1950-1963	10	21	48
	1963-1973	59	70	85
El Salvador	1950-1961	24	39	61
	1961-1971	39	57	67
Guatemala	1950-1964	120	143	84
	1964-1973	77	105	74
Honduras	1961-1974	74	91	81
Mexico	1960-1970	1 720	1 844	93
Nicaragua	1950-1971	49	64	77
Panama	1950-1960	21	29	72
	1960-1970	45	56	81
	1970-1980	26	36	73
South America				
Argentina	1947-1960	902	896	101
	1960-1980	672	748	90
Brazil	1950-1960	3 289	3 721	88
	1960-1970	4 302	4 668	92
	1970-1980	6 532	6 853	95
Chile	1952-1960	282	339	83
	1960-1970	286	315	91
	1970-1982	278	327	85
Colombia	1951-1964	662	798	83
	1964-1973	284	584	49
	1973-1985	1 321	1 412	94
Ecuador	1950-1962	103	130	79
	1962-1974	143	178	80
	1974-1982	365	369	99
Guyana	1960-1970	46	48	95
Paraguay	1962-1972	33	48	68
	1972-1982	94	103	91
Peru	1961-1972	662	678	98
	1972-1981	522	547	95
Uruguay	1975-1981	45	59	76
Venezuela	1950-1961	430	452	95
	1961-1971	237	322	74
	1971-1981	461	479	89

Source: Unpublished estimates produced by the Population Division of the Department for Economic and Social Information and Policy Analysis of the United Nations Secretariat.

moves reflected in the data used but also those excluded from the analysis. Therefore, it is important to develop comprehensive typologies of population mobility, not as an end in themselves but to avoid the blind adoption of typologies determined almost exclusively by the characteristics of the particular data set at hand.

In conceptualizing population mobility, a number of parameters can be taken into account, such as the direction of the move (rural-urban, urban-urban etc.), the distance covered, the timing of the move, its long-term or short-term nature, its periodicity (when the move is repetitive) and the factors that give rise to it. Different combinations of such parameters can lead to different types of moves. The challenge is to identify those where women play a special role and to establish the relative tendency of men and women to engage in different types of mobility.

The classic typologies of migration make no distinction between males and females in classifying population movements, perhaps because they reflect a male bias in approaching the study of migration.[2] The literature on female migration, however, includes few typologies and even fewer attempts to assess comprehensively the significance of different types of mobility. Herold (1979), for instance, while examining the socio-economic characteristics of female migrants in Chile, uses information on place of birth and on place of residence five years prior to the 1970 census to distinguish settled migrants (those whose province of residence in 1965 was the same as that at the time of the census but was different from their province of birth) from recent migrants (those whose province of residence in 1965 was different from that in 1970). Among the latter group, she further distinguishes first migrants (those living in the province of birth in 1965 but outside it in 1970), chronic migrants (those whose provinces of birth and of residence in 1965 and 1970 all differ) and return migrants (those whose province of birth and of residence in 1970 coincide). It is clear that Herold's migrant categories are largely determined by the type of data available; she makes no attempt to elucidate the types of mobility that are not adequately covered by the data at hand.

A crucial issue is the relevance of existing typologies for the study of female migration. Is it just a matter of exploring the relative weight of men and women in the different categories of movers or should a typology be developed expressly as a tool for furthering the understanding of female migration as a process? Abadan-Unat (1984), for instance, developed a specific typology for women migrating internationally. She took into account mainly two characteristics of migrating women: their residential background (rural, urban by birth and urban by migration); and the nature of their departure (accompanying the male head of household, induced by a previous move of a male relative or autonomous). Although developed for the study of international migration, such a typology has elements useful for understanding the internal migration of women.

Time is undoubtedly the second most important dimension to be considered in identifying different types of population mobility. At the very least, permanent versus temporary changes of residence must be distinguished. There are, however, important methodological problems in distinguishing between "permanent" or "temporary" moves which are compounded by the necessity of making their definitions operational. When censuses are conducted on a *de jure* basis, people are assigned to their usual place of residence. As a result, the majority of short-term migrants, be they seasonal migrants, circular migrants or sojourners, are not detected by censuses (Hugo, 1975 and 1983; Standing, 1984a). Yet, the incidence of short-term movements is increasing rapidly as better communication and transport systems in developing countries reduce the friction associated with distance (Goldstein, 1978; Hugo, 1982; Standing, 1984b; Prothero and Chapman, 1984). Lack of information on place of work that would permit an analysis of both temporary migration and commuting patterns in relation to place of usual residence is a drawback. It is clear that the mobility involved in travelling periodically from residence to workplace has considerable economic and social significance and its impacts (on movers and their communities of origin and destination) differ substantially from those of more permanent displacements (Hugo, 1987b).

Although current knowledge of temporary migration patterns in developing countries is still limited, substantial differences between males and females are apparent in many contexts. For instance, early studies of mobility in West Java, Indonesia (Hugo, 1975 and

1978) indicated a strong male dominance in temporary migration to Jakarta. More recent studies, however, have shown that the tempo of female temporary migration to large Indonesian cities has been increasing (Jellinek, 1978; Lerman, 1983; Hetler, 1989). In addition, substantial differences in the economic activities of male and female migrants in urban areas have been documented. More needs to be done, however, to ascertain the extent of women's involvement in circulation to the urban centres of the developing world and to document their distinctive roles as circular migrants.

Another dimension along which female migration can be differentiated is the direction of movement, especially in terms of the areas of origin and destination (rural-rural, rural-urban etc.). Within countries, migration streams can have special distributions by sex. For instance, in India men tended to outnumber women in flows from rural to urban areas, whereas women were dominant in flows between rural areas (Libbee and Sopher, 1975; Singh, 1984; Zachariah, 1964). By comparing census data for 1961, 1971 and 1981, Premi (1989) shows that the character of rural-urban flows in India has been changing: by 1981, females outnumbered males in those streams. Males, however, were still dominant in interstate moves involving a rural-urban change of residence and usually longer distances.

The census data for India allow migrants to be differentiated according to whether they move within a district, between districts or between states. Such categories can be taken as proxies for the distance involved in the move. In India, women have traditionally constituted the majority of migrants moving over short distances (intradistrict migrants), whereas men are generally more numerous in long-distance moves (interstate), thus confirming the observation made by Ravenstein (1885) about the tendency of women to move mostly over short distances. The dominance of Indian women in migration over short distances has been ascribed to marriage migration associated with the preference in most parts of the country for village exogamy and patrilocal residence (Premi, 1979). Thus, with few exceptions (Singh, 1980 and 1984), female migration in India has generally been dismissed as being associated almost entirely with marriage or with the movement of a male relative. This tendency is widespread in the literature, with "marriage migration" and "associational migration" being considered a priori as the dominant categories for female migrants. Such an approach persists despite a growing and convincing body of empirical evidence suggesting that significant numbers of women migrate independently (see, for instance, Singh, 1980 and 1984; Bilsborrow and others, 1987). Even "objective" analysis in the 1980s is highly coloured by the preconceptions of the researcher, as exemplified by the following assessment of migration in India:

"As migration distance increases, sex ratio improves sharply in all the four migration streams. Among interstate migrants, the sex ratio was favourable to males up to 1971, but in 1981, females outnumbered males. This probably reflected a greater tendency in recent years towards family migration in long distance moves, wives moving in of those married males who came earlier, and, probably, a certain amount of independent female migration as well." (Premi, 1989, p. 280)

The causes of migration have also been used to identify different migrant categories. One basic distinction is that between forced and voluntary movements. In the international arena, the category of refugees encompasses most migrants that have been forced to leave their country of citizenship. The equivalent category, often identified by the term "displaced persons", exists in the context of internal movements. The involuntary uprooting of populations caused by civil strife, war, famine, natural disasters or environmental degradation has led to a growing number of displaced persons in a number of developing countries (Hugo, 1984, 1986, 1987a and 1990; Hugo and Chan, 1990; Jacobson, 1989). The forced displacement of population groups is more likely in developing countries as these States are more prone to political instability and have fewer resources to devote to environmental protection (Hugo, 1986). As Olson (1979) notes, the exogenous forces compelling people to move can be classified as: *(a)* physical dangers (floods, volcanic eruptions etc.); *(b)* economic insufficiency (drought, famine); *(c)* religious persecution; *(d)* ethnic persecution; and *(e)* ideological persecution.

Although it would superficially appear that most processes leading to forced migrations should affect men and women equally, specific situations show that that is often not the case (Hugo, 1984 and 1991). Particularly when armed conflict is involved, the situation of women is often more vulnerable. Yet, not enough is known about the extent to which women are forced to move or about the consequences of their forced migration. In particular, it is necessary to understand better the strategies that displaced women develop to secure their survival and that of their families.

With respect to voluntary migration, the movement of women has traditionally been categorized as either "associational" or "autonomous". Such a distinction should in fact be made regarding all migrants by distinguishing the active decision makers from those moving mainly as a result of the decisions taken by others (usually relatives). When applied exclusively to female migrants, however, such a distinction has unfortunately taken on additional meanings. Thus, it has generally been assumed that if a woman moves with her husband, father or other adult male, she is a passive follower. Even when women move alone, their migration is often assumed to be "associational" because it is attributed to the prospects of getting married or to the desire to join family members already established at the place of destination. Increasing evidence about the active involvement of women in the decision-making process leading to migration is challenging the view that they are usually dependent on the decisions made by males (Youssef, Buvinic and Kudat, 1979; Findley and Williams, 1991). In addition, the growing number of women moving alone is challenging the stereotypes prevalent in female migration research. However, there are still strong cultural and normative pressures that lead even the migrant women themselves to misrepresent their motives for migration when questioned about them. Hence, there is a need for new approaches and concepts to study the forces mobilizing women, approaches that must be sensitive to the constraints that specific cultural and social environments impose on women and that limit or otherwise condition the choices that they can make, as well as their own interpetration of decisions taken.

Such sensitivity is particularly necessary in considering the category of women engaged in the so-called "marriage migration". Typically, large proportions of migrant women in developing countries are assumed to belong to that category. Yet, the processes leading to migration associated with marriage are complex. As Thadani and Todaro state, marriage may be conceptualized as a utilitarian decision leading to social mobility:

> "The importance of marriage as a means of upward social mobility for women, in both developed and developing societies, has been generally acknowledged. ... It has been suggested that whereas males rely largely on occupational achievement for social mobility, women can acquire social status through marriage. Implicit in this idea is an 'exchange theory' of marriage that posits a marriage market...not dissimilar to the market in which economic goods and services are exchanged—females offer the characteristics sought after by males in exchange for the characteristics and status they desire from males. Implicit also is the idea that rational, status-seeking considerations are important in the marital choices of females." (1984, p. 47)

In such countries as Pakistan (Shah, 1984 and 1986) and India (Premi, 1989), where marriage has been deemed to be a major cause of migration among women, a more in-depth investigation of what mobility in relation to marriage means to women is necessary. In particular, it is important to consider the effects on migration of changes in marriage patterns and in the power or autonomy that women have in deciding whom to marry and when. In doing so, one must dintinguish between the effects of migration on marriage patterns when, for instance, single women migrate in order to gain autonomy and to improve their marriage prospects, from those of marriage on migration associated with the customary migration of brides following arranged marriages. In the latter case, women may well lose autonomy by becoming separated from their family of origin and other potential sources of support in their home community.

In the category of autonomous or independent migrants, various subgroups may be identified. The growing number of women migrating to work in offshore factories located in developing countries represents a distinctive flow (*Southeast Asia Chronicle*, 1979; Ariffin, 1984). Similarly, the large number of women migrating to cities to work in domestic service constitutes another (Hugo, 1975; Jelin, 1977), although their experience has probably not been studied in as much detail as that of the considerably smaller international movement of domestic workers (Asia and Pacific Development Centre, 1989). Women moving because of economic considerations can further be categorized according to whether they are likely to join the formal or the informal sector at destination. Their relative vulnerability to exploitation may be another factor to consider, especially when economic need forces migrant women into prostitution (Lerman, 1983; Gaidzanwa, 1985; United Nations, ESCAP, 1986).

To conclude, it should be noted that Thadani and Todaro (1984), in proposing a model to explain the female propensity to migrate from rural to urban areas, distinguished several types of female migrants: *(a)* married women migrating in search of urban employment and induced to do so by perceived urban/rural wage differentials; *(b)* unmarried women seeking urban employment and induced to migrate for economic or marital reasons; *(c)* unmarried women induced to migrate solely for marriage reasons; and *(d)* married women engaged in associational migration with no thought of employment (see also United Nations Secretariat, 1993).

D. THE SELECTIVITY OF FEMALE MIGRATION

Female migrants can be characterized by specific demographic, economic and social attributes amply documented in the literature (e.g., Findley and Williams, 1991; Youssef, Buvinic and Kudat, 1979; Fawcett, Khoo and Smith, 1984). It is useful to distil general patterns with regard to the selectivity of female migration so as to facilitate the study of the processes shaping those patterns. Because migrants are not selected at random from the populations at origin, the task of disentangling the interrelations between female migration and the roles and status of women requires a grasp of the attributes that characterize women that migrate in different contexts. Moreover, the characteristics of migrants are crucial determinants of the impact of migration at both origin and destination.

Despite the significance of migration selectivity, the study of the processes that give rise to it remains a relatively undeveloped area of migration research.

With respect to female migrants, it is crucial to determine how and why their characteristics differ from those of at least three other groups: *(a)* non-migrant women in the community of origin; *(b)* non-migrant women in the community of destination; and *(c)* migrant men in the same migration stream. It is also important to consider whether the characteristics of migrant women differ significantly according to the type of migration, whether that type be distinguished in terms of the degree of permanence, spatial direction or causation, as discussed above.

The selectivity of female migration in relation to that of males is in part a function of gender inequality and the differentiation of male and female roles in each society. However, the processes shaping migration differentials by sex have not yet attracted the attention they deserve. As with all migration, women that move are highly selected with respect to age. The studies reviewed by Findley and Williams (1991), Youssef, Buvinic and Kudat, (1979); and Smith, Khoo and Go (1984) lead to the following generalizations:

(a) The age distribution of female migrants peaks in age group 15-24 and the largest differentials between the non-migrant and migrant populations are found in those ages;

(b) The distribution of female migrants at the peak ages tends to be similar to that of males, although it is slightly skewed to the left, suggesting that young women migrate at younger ages than men;

(c) The concentration of female migrants in age group 15-24 is generally greater than that of males;

(d) The extent of the age concentration of female migrants in age group 15-24 increases according to whether the destination is rural areas, urban areas in general or metropolitan areas; and

(e) There is a second, although much less pronounced, peak in the age distribution of migrant women at older ages (over age 50).

Such typical characteristics of the age distribution of female migrants are reflected in other measures of migration, such as age-specific migration rates. Figure II, for instance, shows the interprovincial migration rates for Thailand during the period 1975-1980. It is apparent that although both men and women are most likely to migrate when they are young (aged 20-24), during most of the age span the probabilities of migrating are significantly lower among women. Interestingly, only at ages under 20 and at older ages (65 or over) do women appear to be equally or more likely to migrate than men.

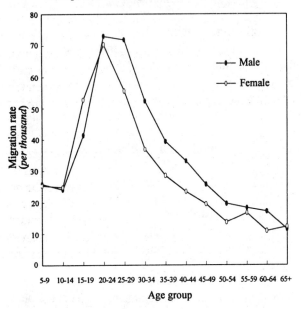

Figure II. Thailand: age-specific and sex-specific interprovincial migration rates, 1975-1980

Source: Thailand, *1980 Population and Housing Census, Subject Report No. 2: Migration* (Bangkok, Office of the Prime Minister, National Statistical Office, 1984).

One aspect of the age selectivity of female migration that deserves greater attention is the relatively high proportions of older female migrants (over age 50) observed in some developing countries. Indeed, the predominance of women aged 50 or over among migrants is especially striking in rural-urban migration flows (Youssef, Buvinic and Kudat, 1979; Findley and Williams, 1991). In urban areas of the member countries of the Association of South-East Asia Nations (ASEAN), for instance, the proportion of women aged 60 or over is significantly higher than that of males. Such a differential is often associated with the effects of female migration since, as Neysmith and Edwardh state:

"The limited data suggest that a considerable proportion of these women live in slums and squatter communities where they are engaged in roles as house and/or child caretakers. It appears that the urban areas attract and retain more older females than males. Unlike widowers, widows remain in or migrate towards urban areas." (1984, p. 25)

The latter pattern has been observed in an analysis of migration to and from the larger urban centres in Indonesia, where, following the death of their husbands, many older women migrate from rural to urban areas to join their children or to take advantage of greater access to amenities and services (Hugo, 1981a and 1981b).

Despite these general observations, important gaps remain in the knowledge of age selectivity of female migration. First, because data on migration flows are difficult to obtain, the age selectivity of migration can often be studied only from data on stocks. Even when allowance can be made for the time at which migration occurred, relying upon information obtained at a particular time, reflecting mainly the cumulative effects of net flows, may hide their distinctive and most recent characteristics. Furthermore, cross-sectional data generally do not allow the analysis of changes over time. Consequently, the suggestion that migration streams become either less age-selective or less sex-selective over time remains untested. There is thus a need for data on migrant flows by age and sex over time to permit a longitudinal analysis in developing countries.

There is a general lack of information on the age selectivity of temporary migration, whether of men or of women. A study in Indonesia showed that age selectivity among circular migrants and commuters was substantially less marked than among permanent migrants, with those migrating temporarily being more evenly spread over the working ages (Hugo, 1987b). Although most of the temporary migrants in that study were male, subsequent studies concerning female circular migration suggest that similar patterns may apply (Lerman, 1983; Hetler, 1989). At least in the case of Indonesia, the repetitive and cyclical movement of persons known as "circulation" is an integral component of the exercise of economic activity and is therefore often practised over most of a person's working life.

It is generally agreed that one of the major causes of rapid social change in developing countries in recent decades has been the rapid expansion of formal educational systems. High levels of educational selectivity of migrants have been documented in various reviews of migration in developing countries (Connell and others, 1976; Goldstein, 1973; Lipton, 1980; Hugo, 1981a). Only a few studies, however, present data classified by sex. Findley and Williams (1991) argue that education is not as strong a factor in the selection of female migrants as it is in that of male migrants. Youssef, Buvinic and Kudat (1979) also conclude that, in the case of female migrants, the data available do not support the assumption that the level of migration is directly related to the level of education. The relative homogeneity of the female population with respect to educational attainment, especially in rural areas, coupled with the low average levels of education reached by women in most settings, probably contributes to that outcome. There are, however, significant differences between the average educational attainment of male and female migrants. Whereas male migrants in urban areas have educational levels similar to those of urban male residents, the educational levels of female migrants are significantly lower than those of their non-migrant counterparts. In addition, the extent and nature of the educational selectivity in female migration may vary considerably between different migration streams in the same country (Herold, 1979).

Occupational selectivity is another important aspect of migration. Yet, the occupational selectivity of migrants is often difficult to apprehend because information on the occupation exercised prior to migration is necessary. In the case of female migrants, Findley and Williams (1991) point out that migration is often associated with their first employment experience outside the home or with their incorporation into the wage economy. In addition, unemployment prior to migration among those who are in the labour force appears to be higher among women than among men. The actual occupational distribution of migrants, either prior to or after migration, also tends to be different for men and women, often because certain occupations are virtually closed to women (Recchini de Lattes, 1989).

One of the most interesting and important areas in the study of migration selectivity among women relates to their marital and family situation. As indicated earlier, much of the literature categorizes female migration as primarily associational or marriage-related. Yet, the situation of a woman within her own family prior to migration and its effect on the decision to migrate have, in general, not been investigated. At the very least, marriage prospects and marital status appear to be more crucial determinants of female than of male migration (Bilsborrow and others, 1987). To examine this issue, it would be useful to gather information on marital status at the time of migration as well as other information about the circumstances in which migration took place, including whether a person moved alone; with part of the nuclear family, the entire nuclear family, other family members or other unrelated persons (friends, for instance); or to join family members already settled in the place of destination. Innovative data-collection methods may be necessary to link migrants to their families and thus to understand how family dynamics shape migration. This may be done by tracing the family and community of origin of in-migrants interviewed in their current place of residence or by tracing out-migrants in their place of destination through reports provided by family members interviewed in the place of origin.

Some consistent patterns with regard to the selectivity of migration with respect to marital status have been documented. For example, according to Findley and Williams (1991), an almost universal finding is that women engaging in autonomous migration tend to be those not living in marital unions. Indeed, in many contexts female migrants are more likely to be single than their male counterparts (Smith, 1981).

The role of widowhood and divorce in initiating migration is little understood, and as Youssef, Buvinic and Kudat (1979) point out, the topic is difficult to study because censuses generally report widowed, divorced and separated women as a single category. Although widowhood is clearly a major factor leading to the relatively high mobility rates displayed by older women, the role of divorce is less well established. In developed countries, the increase in divorce rates has been influential in increasing and reshaping female migration patterns in the past two decades (Grundy,

1985), but the picture for developing countries remains blurred. The necessity to examine differentials from a dynamic perspective again becomes apparent. There have been major changes in the structure and functioning of the family in developing countries during the past two decades, yet little is known of how they have impinged upon the migration of women. Thus, it would be important to explore how the transition from extended to nuclear families has reshaped migration patterns or the extent to which different patterns of marriage, partner selection, family formation and dissolution, divorce and child-bearing have influenced the types and numbers of women migrating.

The differentials relevant to the examination of female migration vary from place to place. In some contexts, ethnic, religious and cultural differences are important. Among some groups, sanctions against the migration of women may be strong, whereas in others female mobility may be either expected or encouraged. Cultural and social differences of this type need to be documented.

The analysis of the selectivity of migration should not be static or purely descriptive. The processes leading to selectivity ought to be explored and, to the extent possible, the directions in which selectivity may be changing should be established. A thorough and informed analysis of selectivity can contribute to further the understanding of the determinants of mobility. Moreover, the distinctive characteristics of migrants significantly influence the consequences of migration in both areas of origin and areas of destination; consequently, they deserve careful consideration. In particular, it is necessary to identify the situations in which migration selectivity has positive impacts for women.

E. APPROACHES TO EXPLAIN FEMALE MIGRATION

A comprehensive examination of the causes of female migration needs to take into account not only the decision-making processes of individual women and their families but the wider contextual forces which impinge upon and shape those decisions. While structural forces, on the one hand, and individual decisions, on the other, are inextricably connected, it is useful to distinguish macro-forces from the microlevel decision-making process.

With respect to macrolevel approaches, a number of theories have been advanced to explain internal migration, although few, if any, are gender-specific. There are two main competing perspectives, that of neoclassical economics and that based on a historical-structuralist perspective. The former perspective sees population movement as a "natural" response to interregional differences in social and economic opportunities. People move from areas where labour is relatively plentiful and capital relatively scarce to those with labour shortages and capital surpluses. Hence, the levels of development in the various regions of a country determine the magnitude and direction of migration streams. This approach implies that migration is beneficial to development, in that it acts as an equilibrating mechanism. Thus, in areas of out-migration, regional development and welfare are enhanced by increased labour productivity and reduced pressure on wages and on the local labour-market, and by the subsequent influx of remittances. In areas of destination, a larger labour force and market allows economies of scale and more efficient use of capital and resources. In this "equilibrium" approach, the usual gains experienced by the migrants themselves are matched by the benefits which accrue to the entire society as a result of their migration.

The historical-structuralist view claims that the neoclassical approach places too much emphasis on the free choice of individuals and neglects the structural forces underlying the regional disparities to which migrants respond. It therefore seeks the causes of migration in the factors or forces that create or underlie the unequal spatial distribution of opportunities. As Wood states:

"Structuralist approaches to the study of internal and international migration have stressed a wide range of phenomena. These include the emergence and expansion of the capitalist mode of production; the style of development that is pursued; a country's role in the international division of labor; the unequal development within and between countries; the articulation of capitalist and non-capitalist formations as it affects the distribution of the maintenance and reproduction costs of labor, and the cost-lowering anticyclical functions of a migrant labor force." (1983, p. 303)

The structuralist approach sees the consequences of migration for development as being generally negative. Migration to the core regions increases dependency and inequality by draining the periphery of its economic surplus and of its most talented residents. Consequently, the disparities between core and periphery tend to increase. By facilitating the disproportionate concentration of talented people, resources, power and capital in core areas, migration exacerbates interregional inequalities and contributes to social and economic problems at both origin and destination.

These two perspectives have quite different policy implications for development. According to the neoclassical approach, migration is beneficial; consequently, interventions, if used at all, should enhance existing patterns of mobility so as to speed up positive developmental processes. Policies to be considered might include: improvement of transport means, including expansion of road systems; better provision of information on jobs available; assistance to migrants in obtaining housing in areas of destination; and reduction of barriers to movement in general. In contrast, according to the structuralist approach, migration should be diverted or, at least, slowed by means of measures to attain a more spatially balanced or integrated regional development by enhancing social and economic opportunities in peripheral regions.

Most researchers espousing either approach have ignored gender considerations, and yet gender is a crucial dimension whatever the theoretical perspective. A neoclassical perspective, for example, would indicate that women accompanying male migrants tend to benefit along with men (see Cackley, 1993). But as long as women have less education than men or participate less in the labour force (for whatever reasons), they are less likely to be able to take advantage of employment or income-earning opportunities in alternative places of destination and are therefore less likely to migrate. One can also draw a parallel between the core versus periphery analysis of the structuralist perspective and male versus female status in society. If migration is a form of exploitation of the periphery by the core, in a male-dominated environment, migrant women are more likely to be exploited than migrant men. Thus, recent changes in the international division of labour that have led to the widespread establishment of export-processing zones in developing countries have had selective effects on the migration of women, mostly because women are deemed to be more docile and cheaper workers than men. In Malaysia, for example, female migrants are concentrated in production jobs in factories operated mainly by multinational corporations. According to Hugo, Lim and Narayan (1989), who summarize the findings of various studies on female factory workers in industrial estates and free trade zones in Peninsular Malaysia, those women are the victims of a new form of exploitation, being subject to a battery of methods developed to manipulate and control them. Grossman reports:

"[Employers] exploit the traditionally defined attributes of femininity: passivity, submissiveness, sentimentality, sexual desirability...to make workers more immediately productive and to inculcate into them a long-term sense of identity with the company. At the same time, emphasis on passive and ornamental femininity is intended to forestall the rise of any sense of independence or unified strength among the workers." (1979, pp. 3-4)

Unionization is discouraged and women are often kept in insecure or unstable jobs. It is also in the interest of employers not to engage female workers for long periods, to prevent them from demanding higher wages or greater job security. Periodically renewing the stock of female labour, largely through migration, facilitates such a strategy. Hence, both theories offer plausible and parallel (if dissimilar) explanations about why women are less likely to benefit from migration than men.

The increasing commercialization of agricultural production and processing that has taken place in many developing countries has contributed to the proletarianization of the agricultural workforce with detrimental effects for women. In Java, for instance, during the 1970s, traditional hand-pounding was replaced by the introduction of mechanical hullers in rice milling, thus displacing a large number of female workers (Collier and others, 1974). It was estimated that in Western Java, some 3,700 labourers, on average, were displaced by each mechanical huller (Collier, 1981), implying that in 1971 alone some 7.7 million part-time workers in Java, mostly women, lost that source of wages. Similarly, other innovations in the planting, maintenance and harvesting of rice in Java have disproportionately affected female workers in rural areas (Hugo, 1985). The differential impact of such changes on men and women and on their subsequent tendency to migrate remains to be studied.

A broader issue is the effect that the roles and status of women have on female mobility. How do existing norms impinge upon the choices that women can make with regard to migration? How do religious or cultural forces, through their influence on the status of women, constrain or promote female mobility? Comparative studies would be useful to establish the structural conditions or types of context that are conducive to female migration and those which constrain the mobility of women.

At the microlevel, the decision-making process needs to be examined from a family rather than from an individual perspective. When women migrate, do they make the decision to move on their own? What is the role of other family members? Would the family have had a similar role if men were migrating? To what extent is female migration the result of family decisions on the allocation of labour resources? In answering those questions, one needs to take into account the type of migration considered. The decisions leading to the autonomous migration of women are likely to be different from those resulting in the migration of family groups. Care must be taken to consider the different circumstances in which associational migration may arise. Given the tendency to assign the majority of migrant women to that category under the assumption that they are passive followers of another migrant, it is important not to disregard the roles they play in making the decision to migrate. In the case of migration for marriage, the complex motives leading to it, especially in terms of the social and economic mobility that marriage may provide, need to be explored.

According to Findley and Williams (1991), decisions on migration are influenced primarily by family welfare issues, often survival itself. With respect to female migration, Hetler (1990) found that much of the mobility from a village in Java could be understood as part of a household survival strategy. Yet, the existing literature on this subject largely neglects any differentiation by gender, although it seems likely that the pressures leading to the migration of women in developing countries are increasing.

In assessing motives for migration, the reasons reported by the migrants themselves often provide only a partial picture. Germani (1965), Speare (1969), Elizaga (1972) and Caldwell (1976) demonstrate the importance of making a comprehensive examination of the context in which the decision to migrate is made. Frequently, only the events that triggered the move are reported and the complex set of factors leading to those events are ignored. Problems with partial or misleading responses are exacerbated when information is not obtained directly from the migrant or when it is obtained retrospectively and relates to events that took place several years in the past. In the case of female migrants, interviews conducted in the presence of relatives, particularly husbands, may result in socially acceptable answers that do not reflect reality.

In summarizing the results of a large number of studies on the reasons for female migration in developing countries, Findley and Williams (1991) found that in the majority of cases (56 per cent of 241 studies), economic reasons were cited for the move, including searching for a job, better education, occupational mobility, improved economic well-being or the need to support children. Economic motives were slightly more common in studies conducted in Latin America and the Caribbean (66 per cent) than in Africa or Asia (52 per cent in each). With respect to "associational" reasons (to get married or to accompany husband or family), only 18 per cent of the studies for Latin America reported them as primary factors, in contrast to 31-32 per cent for Africa and Asia. According to the authors, these findings "run counter to the arguments of those who suggest that women's moves tend to be more highly social or personal, than economic in nature" (Findley and Williams, 1991, p. 12).

The role of education in shaping female migration patterns needs to be investigated in more detail, especially in the light of the increasing educational attainment of women throughout the developing world. In examining the migration decisions of sons and daughters of families in the Ecuadorian Sierra, Bilsborrow and his colleagues found that although for men migration was associated with higher educational levels as expected, "the least educated daughters were most likely to move, the opposite of what one would expect from the human capital model" (1987, p. 201). This outcome is attributed in part to the fact that "urban employment opportunities for women are concentrated at the lower end of the services sector (e.g. domestic services or household servants)" (Bilsborrow and others, 1987, p. 201), leading the authors to conclude that since education did not have the expected positive effects on rural-urban migration, there is a need to re-examine the applicability of the human capital model in developing countries, particularly for women.

Bilsborrow and his colleagues (1987) also found that marriage had no effect on the out-migration of sons but that it had a significant negative effect on that of daughters, confirming that marriage and marital status have a greater influence on the migration of women than that of men. The processes through which those factors determine the propensity to move remain, however, to be elucidated.

A thorough investigation of the causes of migration needs to consider also the determinants of non-migration. Considerable light may be shed on the migration process by examining why people do not move despite the existence of seemingly strong pressures to do so. It is important to determine which factors constrain and which facilitate female migration, and the extent to which they differ from those which operate on the mobility of men. Examination of the changes necessary to counterbalance the forces constraining female migration, including policy measures, would also be useful.

The importance of social networks in initiating, sustaining and channelling migration in developing countries is well established. However, little has been done to examine how networks either facilitate or hinder female migration. Since an analysis of the operation of networks requires information from both areas of origin and those of destination, a thorough examination of the effects of networks has not been carried out except for very small populations. In addition, little has been done to elucidate their differential impacts on men and women.

F. INTERACTIONS BETWEEN FEMALE MIGRATION AND CHANGING FAMILY STRUCTURE AND FUNCTIONING

It is crucial that the causes and consequences of female migration be considered in a family context and that attention be paid to the interrelations between the roles and status of women within the family and their migration. Major changes have been occurring in the structure and functioning of families in developing countries, especially as the extended family gives way to the nuclear one. Such changes have important implications for the roles, status and behaviour of women. Their effects on population mobility and particularly on that of women remain to be addressed. Migration may also have significant effects on the changing structure of the family and the roles of women. The seven roles of women identified by Oppong and Abu (1985)—namely, parental, occupational, conjugal, domestic, kin, community and individual—could be used as a basis to explore the linkages between their changes over time and female mobility. An important issue is the extent to which the mobility of women can be accommodated within existing patterns of family structure and to what extent it requires a break with the past.

Hetler (1990) documents how migration, especially that of a temporary nature, reshaped family structures in a Javanese village. Migrants from the village included married women moving independently of their husbands, married men leaving their wives behind and both husband and wife migrating together and leaving someone else in charge of the household at origin (often a female relative). Consequently, the village was left with many households that were headed by women, at least during part of the year. Among the 903 households studied, 14 per cent had a *de jure* female head of household under the standard definitions used in national censuses and 21 per cent had a de facto female head at one time or another.

Because migration often entails the separation of family members, it not only results in changes in family structure but may also lead to modifications in the roles of family members. Thus, migration often produces changes in the division of labour within the family and in the way labour is used in both the community of origin and that of destination. Gonzalez (1961) shows how types of migration differentiated according to degree of permanency have different impacts on family structure. Permanent migration is often associated with a separation of the nuclear family from other kin and consequently leads to stronger obligations and a tighter relationship within the nuclear family and to a concomitant weakening of wider kinship relationships and obligations. In such circumstances, members of the nuclear family, and especially women, tend to take on new roles (Gonzalez, 1961). Such changes are of particular significance for fertility decline in the light of Caldwell's (1976) conclusion that the emotional nucleation of the family is critical in initiating the transition from high to decreasing fertility levels.

In urban areas of developing countries, the proportion of migrant women living in families with non-traditional structures tends to be greater than in their villages of origin. Households often tend to be larger in urban areas than in villages because of urban housing shortages caused by rapid population growth and the in-migration of relatives from rural areas. According to the 1980 census of Indonesia, for instance, the proportion of households with nine or more members was almost twice as large in urban (11.8 per cent) as in rural areas (6.1 per cent). That is, rural-urban migration may not lead to the nucleation of the family structure.

G. IMPACT OF MIGRATION ON THE WOMEN WHO MOVE

Research on female mobility has tended to neglect the consequences of migration. However, the role of migration as a determinant of economic development and social change at the macrolevel should be addressed directly. Of central importance are changes in the roles and status of women at the microlevel resulting from migration. The migration of women in developing countries has often been associated with changes in their roles within and outside the family (especially in the economy) and with changes in their own attitudes through exposure to new or different ideas and ways of doing things. Yet, some types of migration (rural-rural, for instance) and certain contexts in which migration occurs may lead to a retention or even an enhancement of the traditionally established roles of women. There is a need to establish in what circumstances migration may lead to the increased independence and enhanced status of women.

Women migrating from rural to urban areas of developing countries often experience not only a transition from living in an extended family to living in a nuclear family but also an important change in the nature of their economic activity, from working as unpaid family members to working for wages in the formal or the informal sector of the economy. Such changes are likely to enhance the independence of women and to strengthen their role in decision-making. Thus, Williams (1990) reports that in Java, residential mobility after marriage increased women's decision-making power.

A consistent element in most explanations of the demographic transition from high to low fertility is the social and economic change associated with increasing levels of urbanization. In Asian countries, fertility in urban areas tends to be between 20 and 60 per cent lower than in rural areas. According to Stolnitz (n.d.), women in rural areas of developing countries have at least one more child, on average, than those in urban areas. The linkages between urbanization and fertility, however, are complex and it is impossible to separate the effects of urbanization *per se* on fertility decline from those of wider social and economic forces. Nevertheless, aspects of urban living that are known to exert a direct or indirect effect on fertility behaviour include: more extensive formal and informal communication networks than exist in rural areas; enhanced educational and employment opportunities, particularly for women; inducements to marry later; greater access to public health and family planning; and an increase in the costs in relation to the benefits of child-bearing and child-rearing (Stolnitz, n.d.; Findley and Orr, 1978).

Data linking fertility and migration in developing countries are limited (Goldstein and Goldstein, 1982; Stolnitz, n.d.), but suggest that the fertility of rural-urban migrants generally falls between the overall levels of the areas of origin and destination and in some cases is as low as that of native city-dwellers (Goldstein and Goldstein, 1982). Three types of theories have been put forward to explain the lower fertility of rural-urban migrants compared with that of rural non-migrants (Stolnitz, n.d.):

(a) *Adaptation theories*. These theories suggest that, as migrants from rural areas settle into new urban surroundings, their fertility moves towards the lower urban levels, as new family-size norms and new cost/benefit considerations begin to affect child-bearing decisions. Some variants of this theory suggest that this change takes place only in the second and later generations of migrants;

(b) *Selectivity theories*. In these theories, it is suggested that migrants are disproportionately drawn from rural-dwellers that had lower than average fertility goals even before they migrated. The propensity to migrate and to have small-family norms may both be indicative of an orientation towards modernity;

(c) *Disruption theories*. These theories suggest that the act of migration itself interrupts normal childbearing patterns by delaying marriage, promoting the separation of spouses or temporarily increasing psychological stress.

A simplistic interpretation of the theory of adaptation would suggest that policies encouraging population mobility from rural to urban areas would reduce overall fertility levels in a country. Yet, the fertility of migrant women depends not only upon the move itself but upon the context of that move. Contextual factors, such as the availability of work for women at the place of destination (usually greater in urban destinations), the absence of an extended kin network and greater access to family planning services, can all influence fertility behaviour. It is clear that more needs to be known about the processes linking fertility and mobility.

Another important consequence of migration on women is the extent to which their vulnerability is affected by the move. Mention has already been made of the experience of migrant women working in export-processing zones. When migration leads to economic activity in either the worst-paid or unregulated sectors of the economy (such as domestic service, the informal sector or prostitution), the potential for exploitation is high. Because of the limited job opportunities open for women in the formal economy, they are more likely than men to be working in those sectors. A better understanding of the processes that make female migrants more vulnerable to poverty or exploitation than their male counterparts is necessary to devise policy measures that would reduce or prevent such negative migration outcomes.

To sum up, it is crucial to devote more attention to the consequences of migration for women and, in particular, to its effects on gender roles both within the family (in terms of authority, influence in decision-making, control over resources etc.) and in the wider society.

There is a need to establish in what circumstances migration has different effects on women than on men, whether and under what conditions the participation of women in associational migration increases their dependence upon men, whether becoming a wage-earner in the place of destination enhances the status of women, and whether and under what conditions migration contributes to undermine patriarchy and to modify the structure and functioning of the family.

H. THE LABOUR-MARKET CONSEQUENCES OF FEMALE MIGRATION

Although there are many case-studies on the employment experience of female migrants and a great deal of analysis of census data relating to the female labour force in developing countries, there are few studies on the larger role of migrant female labour in the economy. The literature suggests that migrant women differ markedly from migrant men in both their underemployment and unemployment, in their prospects for occupational mobility, in the incomes they earn, in the occupations they perform, in their participation in the informal sector and in their tendency to send remittances home. These differences, however, need to be documented systematically and analysed in terms of the processes leading to them.

There is considerable scope for study of the differences in the labour force participation of migrants and non-migrants, using census and labour force survey data from developing countries. Comparative analysis across countries would be useful in identifying general patterns. The comparison of the labour force experience of female and male migrants, as well as that between migrants and non-migrants by sex, is likely to be illuminating. In most countries, women generally earn lower salaries than men and migrant women earn even less than non-migrant women (Findley and Williams, 1991; López, Izazola and Gómez de León, 1993).

There is a need to understand how the labour-market functions with respect to gender in different societies. Labour-market segmentation along gender lines generally confines women to jobs on the lowest rung, with few prospects for promotion or advancement. Given that a large number of women go into domestic service, it is important to establish whether that type of employment represents a beachhead for advancement in the urban labour-market, while recognizing that even if it involves no prospects for advancement, domestic service may be attractive for women wishing to leave rural areas that offer no opportunities for advancement. On the other hand, better-educated women in rural areas or those with some resources may be dissuaded from out-migrating by the low prospects of obtaining attractive employment in the formal sector of the urban economy. The extent to which gender segregation in urban labour-markets prevents women from improving their status through migration is consequently an important issue (see Lim, 1993; and Rodenburg, 1993).

The processes by which migrant women enter the labour-market in the areas of destination also need to be explored. The role of social networks is often likely to be crucial. Of equal importance may be the activities of formal or informal recruiters working on behalf of large factories. The profitability of overseas investments by multinational corporations is affected by their access to cheap labour. Migration can play an important role in maintaining that pool, especially where women are concerned. Urgent measures are needed to prevent the exploitation of working women in general and of female migrants in particular.

I. Consequences for Women Left Behind

In considering the impact of migration on women, it is important to look not only at the women who move but also at the women who are left behind when their husbands, fathers, brothers or even daughters or mothers move (see Goza, Rios-Neto and Vieira, 1993). As already mentioned, the separation of families brought about by migration often produces female-headed households where, at least on a temporary basis, women must assume a series of new economic and social responsibilities. Although interest in the women left behind has been criticized as a manifestation of the long-standing tradition whereby migration researchers have considered women's roles only in terms of the migration of men (Morokvasic, 1984c), it is nevertheless important to assess whether the changed family situation brought about by migration has a significant effect on the roles and status of those women. The migration of close relatives who exercise authority can have both negative and positive effects, since it often entails extra responsibilities and burdens on the women left behind, but it may also enhance their decision-making power and influence and force them into new roles within the family (Colfer, 1985). Identification of the adjustments made by women must be complemented by an understanding of the processes leading to such adjustments in order to assess whether the results are likely to be permanent or temporary.

It has been suggested that male migration increases the vulnerability of women left behind. The extent of such vulnerability, its nature (e.g., through increasing poverty) and its implications need to be explored. The structure of female-headed households and their way of functioning remains to be examined, especially in the context of the different processes that can give rise to it. Because the effects of migration on the roles and status of the women left behind are likely to vary with the context and the type of migration involved, it would be useful to identify the contexts and types leading to positive outcomes concerning their status and to distinguish them from those leading to negative outcomes.

Families of migrants at the place of origin must adjust not only to the permanent or temporary absence of family members but also to the influences of any newly acquired money, goods, ideas, attitudes, behaviour and innovations transmitted back to them by the migrants. The type of adjustments needed will depend upon which family members move, the length of their absence and the sociocultural system at the place of origin, especially the family structure and the degree of flexibility within that structure. Some studies suggest that kinship linkages and family residence patterns influence the family's adaptation to migration, patrilocal societies being more adaptable than matrilocal, as are those in which the extended family dominates over the nuclear family (Connell and others, 1976). Where temporary rather than permanent absence from the village is the norm, migration is usually highly selective of economically active men, and separation from their wives and children requires adjustments both within the nuclear family and within the community at large.

Female headship of incomplete nuclear families is common in areas where temporary mobility occurs. In such circumstances, women and children must perform tasks traditionally done by men. Siegel (1969), for example, found that the out-migration of Acehnese men in Indonesia, usually for periods of almost a year, led women to undertake additional agricultural tasks. The extent to which this substitution occurs depends in part upon the periodicity of male mobility. Whereas on the Indonesian island of Bawean absences may last several years (Vredenbregt, 1964), in Western Java, most movement is over relatively short distances, so that movers can return to their villages more frequently, especially at times of peak labour demand (Hugo, 1975). Another important factor in the family's adaptation to migration is whether an extended family and kinship structure exists to allow other male family members to fill roles normally assigned to the absent male. Lineton (1975) reports that in southern Sulawesi, Bugis women have little difficulty in coping with their husbands' absence because members of the extended family move in and provide companionship and other support. On the other hand, Naim (1974) found that the extended absences of Minangkabau migrant men from their western Sumatran homes created strains within the family.

The effects of population mobility on women's traditional roles in rural areas needs more systematic study. Research should encompass changes affecting the women that migrate and those remaining in villages where men are absent for long periods. In southern Sulawesi, for example, some women in areas of heavy out-migration were appointed to head their villages, although traditionally that role was reserved for men. One of the few detailed studies of the impact of heavy male circular migration from rural areas in Indonesia (Colfer, 1985) found that in eastern Kalimantan, women's involvement in rice and vegetable production increased as a direct result of male out-movement. More than half of the women Colfer interviewed reported that life was "difficult" during their husbands' absence, and most of the difficulties they mentioned related to agricultural labour—especially tree-felling and fence and field-hut construction. Colfer stresses, however, that such comments tell only part of the story. What impressed her most during her fieldwork was the women's competence in providing for the family during the husband's absence and the women's pride in their autonomy and competence. Their efforts to cope also received support from other members of the community. As another example, a study of a village of central Java categorizes a woman whose husband was absent for long periods as the de facto household head and shows how such women frequently assumed the roles of a *de jure* head by paying taxes, providing labour and household representatives for village activities and attending meetings (Hetler, 1984).

As with most aspects of the impact of rural-urban migration, studies of fertility have concentrated on the effects of permanent migration and have virtually ignored the effects of temporary mobility. Only a few studies have examined the fertility effects of temporary separation of spouses caused by mobility (Addo, 1975; Findley and Orr, 1978; Myntti, 1978). In an Indian study, it was found that the total marital fertility rate for couples separated by migration for 9-11 months of the year was 6.4, compared with 7.5 for those not separated (Singh, Yadava and Yadava, 1981). In a study of eastern Kalimantan, several women respondents mentioned the fertility-regulating effect of male circular migration; and in one village where migrants' absences averaged 9.4 months, fertility was substantially lower than in another village, where the average absence was 2.8 months (Colfer, 1985). It appears that for migration-enforced abstinence to have any significant influence on fertility levels, a continuous absence of at least four months is necessary and even then the effects are far less than proportionate. As Kols and Lewison (1983) point out, however, that is only one of the possible effects of temporary migration on fertility. The adoption of modern ideas favouring contraception is another, and it has not been analytically separated from the effect of separation.

The influence of rural-urban mobility on marriage has also been studied. Gonzalez (1961) suggests that migration-induced imbalances in sex ratios have led to a lower incidence of arranged marriage and to higher ages at marriage. In Indonesia, researchers have taken note of the strains created by difficulties in finding a spouse, such as inflation of dowries (Naim, 1974) and the ability of migrants to marry women of higher status or caste than would normally be the case (Lineton, 1975).

Evidence of the impact of temporary migration on divorce is mixed. Hathaway (1934) suggests that mobility-induced separation of family members, even for short periods, leads to marital instability and the permanent breakup of the family unit, whereas Gonzalez (1961) cites several studies of societies in which the temporary separation of husband and wife has not led to such instability. In western Java, a substantially larger incidence of divorce was documented among households with movers than among those without movers, especially in households experiencing prolonged separations (Hugo, 1975). A high incidence of divorce among the Minangkabau of western Sumatra has been attributed to high rates of male out-migration (Naim, 1974), whereas Lineton (1975) suggests that the incidence of divorce among the Bugis is low partially because nuclear families migrate together.

A particular group of women left behind which is often overlooked consists of the elderly parents of migrants. Since female life expectancy is usually higher than that of males and women are usually younger than their husbands, widows significantly outnumber widowers in most countries. Hence, when young families migrate it is often the older women who are left behind. Several studies document the contribution of rural-urban migration to the reduced status and increased neglect of the aged population. In Malaysia, for example, Chan (1983) found that in depressed states, such as Kelantan, age-selective out-migration leads to the neglect of elderly persons who, for various reasons, are much less mobile and consequently are left behind.

J. Some policy implications

In order to discuss policy implications, one needs to establish first the extent to which policies currently impinge upon the migration of women. In doing so, it is important to consider not only interventions that directly seek to influence the scale, composition and spatial patterns of female movement but also the indirect effects of a wide range of policies which have largely unintended impacts on that movement (see Simmons, 1993). In many contexts, the indirect effects of such policies are more influential than those of migration-directed policies and thus may more than counteract the latter. The literature addressing these policy issues is sparse. In addition, there does not appear to be much gender specificity in the goals of migration-directed policies and programmes. Differential effects by gender are thus largely the result of policies and programmes that shape internal migration only indirectly. For example, differences in the provision of education to males and females may lead to differences in the propensity to migrate by sex. Government controls on the recruitment of labour for development projects or settlement in certain parts of the country may specify the age and sex characteristics of those to be recruited. Thus, a great deal of scope exists for assessment of government policies in such areas as education, recruitment for government service, the building of infrastructure, social welfare, employment, occupational licensing, training, land-ownership, land settlement, access to government housing and legal rights, in order to establish whether they differ by sex and whether those differences have differential migration effects on men and women.

It is also important to consider whether particular types of female migration have favourable consequences for the well-being of the women involved, their families, the community and the country. Such findings would provide a basis for the formulation of policies to promote certain types of female migration or, at the very least, to remove or reduce existing obstacles. Alternatively, research that establishes the negative effects of certain flows could guide policy makers in devising measures to reduce such flows or to channel them in other directions. A better understanding of whether and if so, how female migration contributes to the reduction of inequalities, be it by gender, class or region, could also be of critical policy relevance. However, migration may well be a rather blunt tool to improve the status of women. Strategies that address the issue more directly are likely to achieve greater success (see Jones, 1993).

Lastly, it is important to develop policies and programmes that address the problems encountered by female migrants and by the families left behind. These measures would include the protection of especially vulnerable groups, easy access to recourse procedures against employers that exploit female workers, the establishment of minimum wages and secure working conditions, the provision of cheap and safe housing, the establishment of cooperative self-help groups and unions etc. Undoubtedly, in many developing countries, the proportion of female migrants that are in vulnerable situations is greater than that of male migrants, in part because of the institutionalization of gender inequality in local customary law and practice. An important factor is that considerable numbers of female migrants work in situations prone to exploitation. Many go into domestic service, for example, where establishing minimum working standards or reasonable working hours is very difficult. The presence of large multinational corporations in developing countries has led to the increased recruitment of young women to work in assembly-type occupations. In this context, the potential for exploitation is considerable, although effective government control seems feasible. The involvement of migrant women in prostitution also puts them in very vulnerable situations, especially in this era of the acquired immunodeficiency syndrome (AIDS). To protect the most vulnerable groups, the appropriate targets for policy intervention must be identified—such as the migrants themselves, their families and their employers—and any measures adopted must be implemented effectively. Protection of migrant women should be part of a concerted plan of action to reduce the widespread gender inequities prevailing in most societies.

K. Conclusion

Few areas of migration research have been as neglected as the migration of women, especially in developing countries. This neglect is related to the fact that data-collection systems have tended to understate the degree to which women participate in internal migration, partially because the concepts used are too narrow and partially because both interviewers and interviewees have tended to disregard the mobility of women. A similar attitude has pervaded researchers, who have tended to dismiss female migration as being mostly "associational", that is, as occurring mainly as a result of male initiative. The evidence suggests, however, that not only is female migration greater in volume and complexity than generally believed but also that the migration of women is often autonomous and economically motivated, even though it differs in many important and significant ways from that of men, particularly in its patterns, composition, causes and consequences. It is therefore crucial that gender be regarded as a basic dimension of migration research in developing countries. To do so, it is necessary to develop both better theoretical approaches that explicitly take gender into account and data-collection procedures that combat the invisibility of women.

Although the scale and complexity of female migration have increased in recent years, the understanding of its causes and consequences is still very limited. There is a pressing need to elucidate the complex interrelations between the changing patterns, levels and types of female migration in developing countries, on the one hand, and the wider processes of economic development and social change, on the other. The unravelling of such interrelations is essential to provide guidance to policy makers and planners in developing countries, because the measures directed to improving the lives of migrant women, one of the most dynamic groups in society, are also likely to contribute significantly to improving the well-being of society as a whole.

Notes

[1] See Youssef, Buvinic and Kudat (1979); International Geographical Union (1983); Fawcett, Khoo and Smith (1984); Morokvasic (1984a), UNESCO (1984), Recchini de Lattes (1989), Findley and Williams (1991) and Chant (1992).

[2] See Fairchild (1925), Jerome (1926), Hobbs (1942), United Nations (1953), Rossi (1955), Petersen (1958); Mills, Senior and Goldsen (1960); Beshers and Nishiura (1962), Touraine and Ragazzi (1961), Mayer (1961), Wenthold (1961), Kant (1962), Lee (1966), Mangalam (1968), Taylor (1969), George (1970), Zelinsky (1971), Pryor (1971, 1975), Goldscheider (1971), Cerase (1974), Swindell and Ford (1975), Eichenbaum (1975), Gould and Prothero (1975), Lewis and Maund (1976) and Roseman (1977).

References

Abadan-Unat, Nermin (1984). International labour migration and its effect upon women's occupation and family roles: a Turkish view. In *Women on the Move: Contemporary Changes in Family and Society*. Paris: United Nations Educational, Scientific and Cultural Organization.

Addo, N. O. (1975). Internal migration differentials and their effects on sociodemographic change. In *Population Growth and Socioeconomic Change in West Africa*, John C. Caldwell and others, eds. New York: Columbia University Press.

Ariffin, Jamilah (1984). Industrial development and rural-urban migration of Malay women in the Peninsular Malaysia. Unpublished doctoral dissertation. St. Lucia: University of Queensland.

Asia and Pacific Development Centre (1989). *Trade in Domestic Helpers: Causes, Mechanisms and Consequences*. Kuala Lumpur.

Benería, Lourdes, and Martha Roldán (1987). *The Crossroads of Class and Gender: Industrial Homework, Subcontracting and Household Dynamics in Mexico City*. Chicago, Illinois: The University of Chicago Press.

Beshers, James M., and Eleanor N. Nishiura (1961). A theory of internal migration differentials. *Social Forces* (Chapel Hill, North Carolina), vol. 39, No. 3 (March), pp. 214-218.

Bilsborrow, Richard E. (1993). Issues in the measurement of female migration in developing countries. Chapter VI in the present volume.

_____, and others (1987). The impact of origin community characteristics on rural-urban out-migration in a developing country. *Demography* (Washington, D.C.), vol. 24, No. 2 (May), pp. 191-210.

Bryant, C. (1977). Women migrants, urbanization and social change: the Botswana case. Paper presented at the annual meeting of the American Political Science Association, Washington D. C.

Cackley, Alicia Puente (1993). The role of wage differentials in determining migration selectivity by sex: the case of Brazil. Chapter XIV in the present volume.

Caldwell, John C. (1976). Toward a restatement of demographic transition theory. *Population and Development Review* (New York), vol. 2, No. 3-4 (September/December), pp. 321-366.

Cerase, Francesco P. (1974). Expectations and reality: case study of return migration from the United States to Southern Italy. *International Migration Review* (Staten Island, New York), vol. 8, No. 2 (Summer), pp. 245-262.

Chan, K. E. (1983). Socio-economic implications of population ageing in a developing country: the Malaysian case. Kuala Lumpur: University of Malaya, Population Studies Programme. Mimeographed.

Chant, Sylvia, ed. (1992). *Gender and Migration in Developing Countries*. London: Pinter.

Colfer, Carol (1985). On circular migration: from the distaff side. In *Labour Circulation and the Labour Process*, Guy Standing, ed. Beckenham, United Kingdom; and Sydney, Australia: Croom Helm.

Collier, William L. (1981). Agricultural evolution in Java. In *Agricultural and Rural Development in Indonesia*, Gary E. Hansen, ed. Boulder, Colorado: Westview Press.

_____, and others (1974). Choice of technique in rice milling: a comment. *Bulletin of Indonesian Economic Studies* (Jakarta), vol. 10, No. 1, pp. 106-120.

Connell, John, and others (1976). *Migration From Rural Areas: The Evidence From Village Studies*. New Delhi: Oxford University Press.

Eichenbaum, Jacob (1975). A matrix of human movement. *International Migration* (Geneva), vol. 13, No. 1/2, pp. 21-41.

Elizaga, Juan C. (1972). Internal migration: an overview. *International Migration Review* (Staten Island, New York), vol. 6, No. 2 (Summer), pp. 121-146.

Fairchild, Henry Pratt (1925). *Immigration: A World Movement and its American Significance*. Rev. ed. New York: Macmillan.

Fawcett, James T., Siew-Ean Khoo and Peter C. Smith, eds. (1984). *Women in the Cities of Asia: Migration and Urban Adaptation*. Boulder, Colorado: Westview Press.

Findley, Sally E., and Ann C. Orr (1978). Patterns of urban-rural fertility differentials in developing countries: a suggested framework. Washington, D.C.: United States Agency for International Development.

Findley, Sally E., and Linda Williams (1991). *Women Who Go and Women Who Stay: Reflections of Family Migration Processes in a Changing World*. Population and Labour Policies Programme, Working Paper No. 176. Geneva: International Labour Office.

Gaidzanwa, R. D. (1985). Rural migration and prostitution. Paper presented at the International Meeting on the Social and Cultural Causes of Prostitution and Strategies Against Procuring and Sexual Exploitation of Women, Madrid. SH5-85/CONF 608/7. Paris: United Nations Educational, Scientific and Cultural Organization.

George, M. V. (1970). *Internal Migration in Canada: Demographic Analyses*. 1961 Census Monograph Series. Ottawa: Dominion Bureau of Statistics.

Germani, Gino (1965). Migration and acculturation. In *Handbook for Social Research in Urban Areas*, Philip M. Hauser, ed. Technology and Society Series, No. 13. Paris: United Nations Educational, Scientific and Cultural Organization.

Goldsheider, Calvin (1971). *Population, Modernization, and Social Structure*. Boston: Little, Brown.

Goldstein, Sidney (1973). Interrelations between migration and fertility in Thailand. *Demography* (Washington, D.C.), vol. 10, No. 2 (May), pp. 225-241.

_____ (1978). *Circulation in the Context of Total Mobility in Southeast Asia*. Papers of the East West Population Institute, No. 53. Honolulu, Hawaii: East-West Center.

_____, and Alice Goldstein (1982). *Techniques for Analysis of the Interrelations between Migration and Fertility*. Rand Paper P-6844. Santa Monica, California: Rand Corporation.

Gonzalez, Nancie L. Soliende (1961). Family organization in five types of migratory wage labour. *American Anthropologist* (Washington, D.C.), vol. 63, No. 6 (December), pp. 1264-1280.

Gould, W. T. S., and R. M. Prothero (1975). Space and time in African population mobility. In *People on the Move: Studies in Internal Migration*, Leszek A. Kosinski and R. Mansell Prothero, eds. London: Methuen.

Goza, Franklin W., Eduardo Rios-Neto and Paula Vieira (1993). The consequences of temporary out-migration for the families left behind: the case of Jequitinhonha Valley, Brazil. Chapter XVII in the present volume.

Grossman, R. (1979). Women's place in the integrated circuit. *Southeast Asia Chronicle* (Berkeley, California), vol. 66 (January-February), pp. 2-17.

Grundy, Emily (1985). Divorce, widowhood, remarriage and geographical mobility among women. *Journal of Biosocial Science* (Cambridge, United Kingdom), vol. 17, No. 4 (October), pp. 415-435.

Hathaway, Marion (1934). *The Migratory Worker and Family Life*. Chicago, Illinois: The University of Chicago Press.

Herold, Joan M. (1979). Female migration in Chile: types of movers and socioeconomic characteristics. *Demography* (Washington, D.C.), vol. 16, No. 2 (May), pp. 257-278.

Hetler, Carol B. (1984). Rural and urban female-headed households in Java: results of a village study in Central Java. Seminar paper presented at the Department of Demography of the Australian National University, Canberra.

_____ (1989). The impact of circular migration on a village economy. *Bulletin of Indonesian Economic Studies* (Jakarta), vol. 25, No. 1 (April), pp. 53-75.

_____ (1990). Survival strategies, migration and household headship. In *Structures and Strategies: Women, Work and Family*, Leela Dube and Rajni Palriwala, eds. New Delhi: Sage.

Hobbs, A. H. (1942). Specificity and selective migration. *American Sociological Review* (Washington, D.C.), vol. 7, No. 6 (December), pp. 772-781.

Hugo, Graeme J. (1975). Population mobility in West Java, Indonesia. Doctoral dissertation. Canberra: The Australian National University, Department of Demography.

_____ (1978). *Population Mobility in West Java*. Yogyakarta, Indonesia: Gadjah Mada University Press.

_____ (1981a). Characteristics of interprovincial migrants. In *Migration, Urbanization and Development in Indonesia*. Bangkok: United Nations Economic and Social Commission for Asia and the Pacific.

_____ (1981b). Implications of the imbalance in age and sex composition of sub-areas as a consequence of migration: the case of a rural developing nation: Indonesia. In *International Population*

Conference, Manila, 1981, vol. 2. Liège: International Union for the Scientific Study of Population.

_____ (1982). Circular migration in Indonesia. *Population and Development Review* (New York), vol. 8, No. 1 (March), pp. 59-84.

_____ (1983). New conceptual approaches to migration in the context of urbanization: a discussion based on the Indonesian experience. In *Population Movements: Their Forms and Functions in Urbanization and Development*, Peter A. Morrison, ed. Liège: Ordina Editions.

_____ (1984). The demographic impact of famine. In *Famine as a Geographical Phenomenon*, Bruce Currey and Graeme Hugo, eds. Dordrecht, The Netherlands: D. Reidel.

_____ (1985). Some policy aspects of the relationships between internal migration and regional development in less developed countries with particular reference to Indonesia. Centre for Development Studies, Discussion Paper No. 9. Adelaide: The Flinders University of South Australia.

_____ (1986). Differences and similarities between forced and voluntary migrations in Asia and some policy implications. Paper presented at the International Seminar on People Affected by Uprootedness, organized by the United Nations Research Institute for Social Development, Palais des Nations, Geneva, 5-7 May.

_____ (1987a). Forgotten refugees: postwar forced migration within Southeast Asian countries. In *Refugees: A Third World Dilemma*, John R. Rogge, ed. Totowa, New Jersey: Rowman and Littlefield.

_____ (1987b). Demographic and welfare implications of urbanization: direct and indirect effects on sending and receiving areas. In *Urbanization and Urban Policies in Pacific Asia*, Roland J. Fuchs, Gavin W. Jones and Ernesto M. Pernia, eds. Boulder, Colorado: Westview Press.

_____ (1990). The changing urban situation in South-east Asia and Australia: some implications for the elderly. In *Ageing and Urbanization*. Proceedings of the United Nations International Conference on Aging Populations in the Context of Urbanization, Sendai (Japan), 12-16 September 1988. Sales No. E.91.XIII.12. New York: United Nations.

_____ (1991). Changing famine coping strategies under the impact of population pressure and urbanisation: the case of population mobility. In *Famine and Food Security in Africa and Asia: Indigenous Response and External Intervention to Avoid Hunger*, Hans G. Bohle and others, eds. Bayreuth, Germany: Naturwissenschaftliehe Gesellaschaft Bayreuther.

_____, and Chan Kwok Bun (1990). Conceptualizing and defining refugee and other forced migrations in Asia. *Southeast Asian Journal of Social Science* (Singapore), vol. 18, No. 1, pp. 19-42.

Hugo, Graeme J., Lin Lean Lim and S. Narayan (1989). Malaysian Human Resources Development Planning Project Module II: labour supply and processes. Study No. 4, Labour Mobility. First draft of final report. Adelaide: The Flinders University of South Australia, School of Social Sciences.

International Geographical Union, Commission on Population Geography, eds. (1983). The role of women in the redistribution of population. *Population Geography* (Chandigarh, India), Special Issue, vol. 5, No. 1-2.

Jacobson, Jodi L. (1989). Environmental refugees: nature's warning system. *POPULI* (New York), vol. 16, No. 1 (March), pp. 29-41.

Jelin, Elizabeth (1977). Migration and labor force participation of Latin American women: the domestic servants in the cities. *Signs* (Chicago, Illinois), vol. 13, No. 1 (Autumn), pp. 129-141.

Jellinek, Lea (1978). The pondok system and circular migration. In *The Life of the Poor in Indonesian Cities*, Lea Jellinek, Chris Manning and Gavin Jones, eds. Melbourne, Australia: Monash University, Centre of Southeast Asian Studies.

Jerome, Harry (1926). *Migration and Business Cycles*. New York: National Bureau of Economic Research.

Jones, Gavin W. (1993). The role of female migration in development. Chapter XVIII in the present volume.

Kant, Edgar (1962). Classification and problems in migration. In *Readings in Cultural Geography*, Philip L. Wagner and Marvin W. Mikesell, eds. Chicago, Illinois: The University of Chicago Press.

Kols, Adrienne, and Dana Lewison (1983). *Migration, Population Growth and Development*. Population Reports, Series M, No. 7. Baltimore, Maryland: The Johns Hopkins University, Population Information Program.

Lee, Everett S. (1966). A theory of migration. *Demography* (Washington, D.C.), vol. 3, No. 1 (March), pp. 47-57.

Lerman, Charles (1983). Sex-differential patterns of circular migration: a case study of Semarang Indonesia. *Peasant Studies* (Salt Lake City, Utah), vol. 10, No. 4 (Summer), pp. 251-269.

Lewis, G. J., and D. J. Maund (1976). The urbanization of the countryside: a framework for analysis. *Geografiska Annaler, Series B, Human Geography* (Stockholm, Sweden), vol. 58, No. 1, pp. 17-27.

Libbee, M. J., and D. E. Sopher (1975). Marriage migration in rural India. In *People on the Move: Studies on Internal Migration*, Leszek A. Kosinski and R. Mansell Prothero, eds. London: Methuen.

Lim, Lin Lean (1993). The structural determinants of female migration. Chapter XI in the present volume.

Lineton, J. A. (1975). An Indonesian society and its universe: a study of the Bugis of South Sulawesi and their role in a wider social and economic system. Doctoral dissertation. London: University of London, School of Oriental and African Studies.

Lipton, Michael (1980). Migration from rural areas of poor countries: the impact on rural productivity and income distribution. *World Development* (Oxford and New York), vol. 8, pp. 1-24.

López, María de la Paz, Haydea Izazola and José Gómez de León (1993). Characteristics of female migrants according to the 1990 census of Mexico. Chapter VII in the present volume.

Mangalam, J. J., and Cornelia Morgan (1968). *Human Migration: A Guide to Migration Literature in English, 1955-1962*. Lexington: University of Kentucky Press.

Mayer, Philip (1961). *Townsmen or Tribesmen: Urbanisation in a Divided Society*. Oxford, United Kingdom: Oxford University Press.

Mills, C. Wright, Clarence Senior and Rose Kohn Goldsen (1960). *The Puerto Rican Journey: New York's New Migrants*. New York: Russell and Russell.

Morokvasic, Mirjana, ed. (1984a). Women in migration. *International Migration Review* (Staten Island, New York), Special Issue, vol. 18, No. 4 (Winter), pp. 885-1314.

_____ (1984b). Migrant women in Europe: a comparative perspective. In *Women on the Move: Contemporary Changes in Family and Society*. Paris: United Nations Educational, Scientific and Cultural Organization.

_____ (1984c). Birds of passage are also women... *International Migration Review* (Staten Island, New York), vol. 18, No. 4 (Winter), pp. 886-907.

Myntti, Cynthia (1978). *The Effects of Breastfeeding: Temporary Emigration and Contraceptive Use on the Fertility of the Yemen Arab Republic*. Cairo: The Population Council.

Naim, M. (1974). Merantau, Mingangkabau voluntary migration. Doctoral dissertation. Singapore: University of Singapore.

Neysmith, Sheila M., and Joey Edwardh (1984). Economic dependency in the 1980s: its impact on Third World elderly. *Ageing and Society* (New York; and Cambridge, United Kingdom), vol. 4, No. 1 (March), pp. 21-44.

Olson, Maxine E. (1979). Refugees as a special case of population redistribution. In *Population Redistribution: Patterns, Policies and Prospects*, L. A. Peter Gosling and Linda Yeun Ching Lim, eds. Policy Development Studies, No. 2. New York: United Nations Fund for Population Activities.

Oppong, Christine, and Katharine Abu (1985). *A Handbook for Data Collection and Analysis on Seven Roles and Statuses of Women*. Geneva: International Labour Office.

Petersen, William (1958). A general typology of migration. *American Sociological Review* (Washington, D.C.), vol. 23, No. 2 (June), pp. 256-265.

Premi, M. K. (1979). Pattern of internal migration of females in India. New Delhi: Indian Council of Social Sciences. Mimeographed.

_____ (1989). Pattern of internal migration in India: some new dimensions. In *Population Transition in India*, vol. 2, S. N. Singh and others, eds. Delhi: BR Publishing Corporation.

Prothero, R. Mansell, and Murray Chapman, eds. (1985). *Circulation in Third World Countries*. London; and Boston, Massachusetts: Routledge and Kegan Paul.

Pryor, Robin J. (1971). *Internal Migration and Urbanization*. Geography Department Monograph Series, No. 2. Townsville: James Cook University of North Queensland.

_____ (1975). Migration and the process of modernization. In *People on the Move: Studies in Internal Migration*, Leszek A. Kosinski and R. Mansell Prothero, eds. London: Methuen.

Ravenstein, E. G. (1885). The laws of migration. *Journal of the Royal Statistical Society* (London), vol. 48, No. 2 (June), pp. 167-235.

Recchini de Lattes, Zulma (1989). Women in internal and international migration, with special reference to Latin America. *Population Bulletin of the United Nations* (New York), No. 27, pp. 95-107. Sales No. E.89.XIII.7.

Rodenburg, Janet (1993). Emancipation or subordination? Consequences of female migration for migrants and their families. Chapter XV in the present volume.

Roseman, Curtis C. (1977). *Changing Migration Patterns Within the United States*. Resource Papers for College Geography, No. 77-2. Washington, D.C.: Association of American Geographers.

Rossi, Peter H. (1955). *Why Families Move: A Study of the Social Psychology of Urban Residential Mobility*. Glencoe, Illinois: Free Press.

Shah, Nasra M. (1984). The female migrant in Pakistan. In *Women in the Cities of Asia: Migration and Urban Adaptation*, James T. Fawcett, Siew-Ean Khoo and Peter C. Smith, eds. Boulder, Colorado: Westview Press.

_____ (1986). Internal migration: patterns and migrant characteristics. In *Pakistani Women: A Socioeconomic and Demographic Profile*, Nasra M. Shah, ed. Islamabad: Pakistan Institute of Development Economics; and Honolulu, Hawaii: East-West Center.

Siegel, James T. (1969). *The Rope of God*. Berkeley: University of California Press.

Simmons, Alan B. (1993). Government policies, women and migration: a review of research findings and policy options in developing countries. Chapter XIX in the present volume.

Singh, Andrea Menefee (1980). The impact of migration on women and the family: research policy and programme issues in developing countries. *Social Action* (New Delhi, India), vol. 30, Nos. 4-5 (April-June), pp. 181-200.

_____ (1984). Rural-to-urban migration of women in India: patterns and implications. In *Women in the Cities of Asia: Migration and Urban Adaptation*, James T. Fawcett, Siew-Ean Khoo and Peter C. Smith, eds. Boulder, Colorado: Westview Press.

Singh, S. N., R. C. Yadava and K. N. S. Yadava (1981). A study on the fertility of migrants. *Health and Population: Perspectives and Issues* (New Delhi, India), vol. 4, No. 1 (January-March), pp. 59-65.

Smith, Peter C. (1981). Migration, sex and occupations in urban Indonesia and Thailand. In *International Population Conference Manila, 1981*, vol. 3. Liège: International Union for the Scientific Study of Population.

Smith, Peter C., Siew-Ean Khoo and Stella P. Go (1984). The migration of women to cities: a comparative perspective. In *Women in the Cities of Asia: Migration and Urban Adaptation*, James T. Fawcett, Siew-Ean Khoo and Peter C. Smith, eds. Boulder, Colorado: Westview Press.

Southeast Asia Chronicle (1979). Volume 66.

Speare, Alden (1969). The determinants of rural to urban migration in Taiwan. Doctoral dissertation. Ann Arbor, Michigan: University of Michigan. This paper refers to Taiwan Province of China.

Standing, Guy (1984a). Conceptualising territorial mobility. In *Migration Surveys in Low Income Countries: Guidelines for Survey and Questionnaire Design*, Richard E. Bilsborrow, A. S. Oberai and Guy Standing, eds. Beckenham, United Kingdom; and Sydney, Australia: Croom Helm.

_____, ed. (1984b). *Labour Circulation: Short Term Migration and the Labour Process*. London: Croom Helm.

Stolnitz, G. J. (n.d.). Urbanization and rural-to-urban migration in relation to LDC fertility. Project paper prepared for the Fertility Determinants Group. Bloomington: Indiana University.

Swindell, Kenneth, and Robert G. Ford (1975). Places, migrants and organisation: some observations on population mobility. *Geografiska Annaler, Series B, Human Geography* (Stockholm, Sweden), vol. 57, No. 1, pp. 68-76.

Taylor, R. C. (1969). Migration and motivation: a study of determinants and types. In *Migration*, John A. Jackson, ed. Cambridge, United Kingdom: Cambridge University Press.

Thadani, Veena N., and Michael P. Todaro (1984). Female migration: a conceptual framework. In *Women in the Cities of Asia: Migration and Urban Adaptation*, James T. Fawcett, Siew-Ean Khoo and Peter C. Smith, eds. Boulder, Colorado: Westview Press.

Thailand (1984). *1980 Population and Housing Census: Subject Report No. 2: Migration*. Bangkok: Office of the Prime Minister, National Statistical Office.

Touraine, Alain, and Orietta Ragazzi (1961). *Ouvriers d'origine agricole*. Paris: Aux éditions du Seuil.

United Nations (1953). *The Determinants and Consequences of Population Trends: A Summary of Findings of Studies on the Relationships between Population Changes and Economic and Social Conditions*. Population Studies, No. 17. Sales No. 1953.XIII.3.

_____ (1985). *Migration, Population Growth and Employment in Metropolitan Areas of Selected Developing Countries*. ST/ESA/SER.R/57.

United Nations Secretariat (1993). Types of female migration. Chapter V in the present volume.

United Nations, Economic and Social Commission for Asia and the Pacific (1986). *Women in the Economy: Employment*. Bangkok.

United Nations Educational, Scientific and Cultural Organization (1984). *Women on the Move: Contemporary Changes in Family and Society*, Paris: UNESCO.

Vredenbregt, J. (1964). Bawean migrations. *Bijdragen Tot de Taal-Land-En Volkenkunde* ('s-Gravenhage), vol. 120, pp. 109-139.

Wentholt, R. (1961). The characteristics of Dutch emigrants. In *Characteristics of Overseas Migrants*, G. Beijer and others, eds. The Hague: Government Printing and Publishing Office.

Williams, Linda B. (1990). *Development, Demography and Family Decision-Making: The Status of Women in Rural Java*. Boulder, Colorado: Westview Press.

Wood, Charles H. (1982). Equilibrium and historical-structural perspectives on migration. *International Migration Review* (Staten Island, New York), vol. 16, No. 2 (Summer), pp. 298-319.

Youssef, Nadia, Mayra Buvinic and Ayse Kudat (1979). *Women in Migration: A Third World Focus*. Report of the International Center for the Advancement of Women. Washington, D.C.: United States Agency for International Development.

Zachariah, K. C. (1964). *A Historical Study of Internal Migration in the Indian Sub-continent, 1901-1931*. Bombay: Asia Publishing House.

Zelinsky, Wilbur (1971). The hypothesis of the mobility transition. *Geographical Review* (New York), vol. 61, No. 2 (April), pp. 219-249.

Part Three

DATA-COLLECTION AND MEASUREMENT ISSUES

IV. LEVELS AND TRENDS OF FEMALE INTERNAL MIGRATION IN DEVELOPING COUNTRIES, 1960-1980

Joachim Singelmann*

As the twentieth century draws to a close, two major issues of policy relevance are the role of women in society and population distribution. Although rates of population growth are still high in a number of developing countries, the declining fertility rates recorded during the past two decades in many of them will ensure the eventual deceleration of population growth. It is thus generally thought that at the world level the rate of population growth is likely to have already peaked. Yet, despite the prospect of declining growth rates, population distribution within countries remains an important concern. Policy makers have recognized that even as the pressures resulting from rapid population growth abate, the concentration of population in selected areas of a country can pose challenges similar to those of overall population growth. Given that migration is a major component of the growth or decline of regions within a country and that the growth of cities is often attributable as much to internal migration as to natural increase, the former will remain a key demographic issue for policy makers even as overall rates of population growth continue to fall.

With respect to the role of women in society, there is as yet no country in which women have the same status and power as men. Even where existing legislation explicitly outlaws sex discrimination, past gender-typing and female disadvantages continue to cast shadows on the position of women in the family, household, the labour-market and society at large.

One specific concern linking the issues of migration and the role of women in society is the participation of women in internal migration and the consequences of migration for women. This concern was viewed as sufficiently urgent by the International Conference on Population held at Mexico City in 1984, to merit a special recommendation. Thus, recommendation 44 states:

"Governments should adopt effective policies to assist women migrants, especially those who are agricultural workers, as well as women, children and the elderly left behind unsupported in rural areas. Governments are also urged to pay special attention to the difficulties of adaptation encountered in urban areas by migrant women of rural origin and to take appropriate measures to overcome these difficulties." (United Nations, 1986, pp. 157-158)

The emphasis put on female rural-urban migration justifies a closer look at women's participation in that type of flow. This paper presents an assessment of levels and trends of such migration in all those developing countries having the necessary data.

A. METHODS AND DATA

Research on internal migration in developing countries continues to be limited by inadequate data. The two major sources of information on migration are demographic surveys and population censuses. Although demographic surveys can yield detailed information on migrants, they are often not representative of the total population of a country or have sample sizes too small to permit adequate estimates of internal migration flows. For this reason, census data are usually the main source of comprehensive statistics on these flows. Migrants are normally identified by obtaining information on the place of residence of the enumerated population at some time prior to enumeration (five years before the census, for instance). Some censuses record instead the length of time a person has resided in the current place of residence. Both types of question permit a temporal specification of the migratory move and make possible the calculation of migration rates. Unfortunately, many censuses only include a question on place of birth; and although that question yields information about who is a migrant, it does not indicate when migration took place and therefore yields only rough indicators of migration.

---

*Professor of Sociology and Rural Sociology, Department of Sociology, Louisiana State University, Baton Rouge, Louisiana, United States of America.

There had been some hope of overcoming the lack of timing specificity associated with data on place of birth in countries which included a question on place of birth in two consecutive censuses. Because each census would permit the estimation of lifetime migration, intercensal migration could be estimated as the difference between the two populations of lifetime migrants. Such an estimation procedure, however, has not been successful. In the Republic of Korea, for instance, the 1970 and 1980 censuses gathered information on both place of birth and place of residence five years before the census. Estimates of internal migration between 1970 and 1980 based on information on place of birth for the two census years were compared with those based on information on place of residence five years before the 1980 census. The comparison showed that the estimates derived from data on place of birth underestimated intercensal migration substantially (Singelmann and Li, 1992). More importantly, although the underestimation affected all ages, it was particularly marked for age group 15-29, which typically exhibits the highest migration rates. Varying the assumptions made about mortality differentials and return migration did not substantially improve the intercensal migration estimates based on information on place of birth.

Consequently, the present analysis is based on estimates of rural-urban migration obtained by the census survival ratio method. This method has been used in several United Nations publications concerned with urban population growth and migration (United Nations, 1980, 1983, 1985). Since the method is generally well known and is extensively described in the United Nations publications listed above, a brief summary of the estimation procedure will suffice. In essence, the method projects the number of urban-dwellers by sex from one census to the next using age- and sex-specific census survival ratios. The difference between the projected urban population and that observed age group by age group is attributed to net rural-urban migration and to the reclassification of rural areas into urban areas.[1] However, the estimates thus obtained represent the net number of migrants surviving to the second census. To obtain an estimate of the number of net migrants for the intercensal period, those surviving to the second census are reverse-projected to the mid-point of the intercensal period (usually located five years before the most recent census used). This procedure assumes that migration and the deaths of migrants are equally distributed over the intercensal period. Because intercensal periods are usually 10 years, the method outlined thus far cannot produce an estimate of net migrants aged 0-4 years. Their number is therefore estimated by applying to the intercensal number of net female migrants aged 15-49 the same child/woman ratio as that of the native urban population.

Once a complete set of estimates of net intercensal migration by sex and age group is available, their sum provides an estimate of total net rural-urban migration and reclassification by sex. Subtracting that number from the total population growth of urban areas during the intercensal period yields an estimate of natural increase.

Application of the census survival ratio method requires as input the distribution by age group and sex of the urban and rural populations of a country for two consecutive censuses. Although censuses normally yield the distribution by age group and sex of the total population, many do not produce or publish those of the urban and rural populations separately.[2] For this reason, the present analysis is limited to 36 developing countries having data for the 1960s and 34 developing countries with data for the 1970s. For 25 of these countries, net rural-urban migration could be estimated for both decades.[3] The data for these countries were collected by the Population Division[4] as part of its ongoing global estimation and projection of urban and rural population growth.[5]

B. GENDER AND NET RURAL-URBAN MIGRATION

In 1980, the Population Division prepared a major study identifying the sources of urban population growth (United Nations, 1980; see also Preston, 1979). This study shows that during the 1960s, on average, natural increase accounted for 60 per cent of urban population growth in developing countries (see table 8). However, the study also shows that there was substantial variation among countries in the relative contributions of natural increase and net migration to urban population growth. Net migration in a number of developing countries accounted for over half of urban growth and its contribution was over 60 per cent in the Republic of

TABLE 8. URBAN POPULATION GROWTH, NATURAL INCREASE AND INTERNAL MIGRATION,
SELECTED COUNTRIES IN MAJOR AREAS BY REGION, 1960-1980

Region and country	Annual intercensal population growth rate of urban areas		Estimated annual urban rate of natural increase		Estimated annual rate of urban growth from internal migration and reclassification		Estimated percentage of growth attributable to internal migration reclassification	
	1960s	1970s	1960s	1970s	1960s	1970s	1960s	1970s

A. *Africa*

Region and country	1960s	1970s	1960s	1970s	1960s	1970s	1960s	1970s
Eastern Africa								
Kenya	..	7.9	..	3.4	..	4.5	..	57.4
United Republic of Tanzania	..	12.6	..	4.8	..	7.8	..	61.9
Zimbabwe	..	5.4	..	2.2	..	3.3	..	60.0
Northern Africa								
Egypt	3.0	..	2.1	..	0.9	..	31.5	..
Libya Arab Jamahiriya	13.9	..	5.9	..	8.0	..	57.2	..
Morocco	4.1	4.4	2.6	2.4	1.6	2.0	37.8	44.6
Tunisia	4.7	3.2	2.3	2.3	2.4	0.9	52.0	27.9
Southern Africa								
Botswana	15.7	9.6	3.6	4.4	12.2	5.2	77.4	53.7
Western Africa								
Ghana	4.7	..	2.7	..	1.9	..	41.5	..
Togo	5.8	..	3.4	..	2.4	..	40.7	..

B. *Asia*

Region and country	1960s	1970s	1960s	1970s	1960s	1970s	1960s	1970s
Eastern and South-eastern Asia								
Republic of Korea	6.2	5.0	2.5	2.2	3.7	2.8	60.3	56.4
Indonesia	3.5	5.1	2.5	2.5	1.1	2.6	31.5	50.6
Malaysia	..	4.8	..	2.3	..	2.5	..	52.1
Philippines	..	4.3	..	2.6	..	1.7	..	40.2
Thailand	..	5.1	..	2.1	..	3.0	..	57.8
Southern Asia								
Bangladesh	6.6	10.6	2.7	3.7	3.9	6.9	58.6	65.7
India	3.2	3.7	2.2	2.1	1.0	1.7	31.3	44.8
Iran (Islamic Republic of)	..	4.8	..	2.7	..	2.1	..	43.2
Nepal	3.2	7.3	2.1	2.9	1.1	4.3	33.6	59.7
Pakistan	..	4.3	..	3.6	..	0.7	..	17.1
Sri Lanka	4.2	1.2	2.1	1.4	2.1	-0.2	49.8	-18.0
Western Asia								
Iraq	6.4	5.1	3.5	3.4	2.9	1.7	45.8	33.7
Israel	..	2.7	..	2.2	..	0.5	..	18.2
Syrian Arab Republic	4.9	3.9	3.3	3.2	1.5	0.7	31.1	18.5
Turkey	5.5	4.7	2.1	2.2	3.4	2.5	61.7	52.3

C. *Latin America and the Caribbean*

Region and country	1960s	1970s	1960s	1970s	1960s	1970s	1960s	1970s
Caribbean and Central America								
Costa Rica	4.9	..	2.8	..	2.1	..	42.9	..
El Salvador	3.7	..	2.9	..	0.8	..	21.8	..
Guatemala	3.0	0.7	1.8	1.7	1.0	-1.0	37.6	-150.5
Honduras	5.0	..	2.5	..	2.5	..	49.5	..
Mexico	4.9	..	3.3	..	1.6	..	32.0	..
Nicaragua	4.2	..	2.7	..	1.5	..	36.0	..

TABLE 8 (continued)

Region and country	Annual intercensal population growth rate of urban areas		Estimated annual urban rate of natural increase		Estimated annual rate of urban growth from internal migration and reclassification		Estimated percentage of growth attributable to internal migration reclassification	
	1960s	1970s	1960s	1970s	1960s	1970s	1960s	1970s
Panama	4.5	2.8	2.7	2.0	1.8	0.8	40.5	28.8
Cuba	2.5	2.4	2.0	1.0	0.5	1.3	20.7	56.0
Dominican Republic	5.8	5.3	3.0	2.9	2.8	2.4	47.8	44.9
Haiti	4.0	..	1.9	..	2.2	..	53.6	..
South America								
Argentina[a]	2.3	2.3	1.6	1.6	0.7	0.7	30.1	30.1
Brazil	4.7	4.3	2.6	2.3	2.1	2.0	44.9	46.5
Chile	3.0	2.8	2.0	2.0	1.0	0.7	34.3	26.6
Colombia	3.4	3.4	2.6	1.7	0.8	1.7	24.0	50.2
Ecuador	4.5	4.6	3.0	2.4	1.4	2.2	32.5	48.4
Guyana	8.8	..	2.5	..	6.3	..	71.6	..
Paraguay	3.1	3.8	2.1	2.0	1.0	1.8	33.8	47.3
Peru	4.9	3.5	2.9	2.4	2.1	1.1	41.8	32.2
Uruguay	0.7	1.0	0.6	0.6	0.0	0.4	8.8	40.8
Venezuela	4.1	3.9	3.2	3.0	0.9	1.0	21.1	24.5

[a]The data for Argentina refer to the 1960-1980 intercensal period.

Korea. A later study on the sources of metropolitan population growth (United Nations, 1985) found that migration was usually an even more important contributor to that growth than it was for urban areas as a whole.

The results of the present analysis indicate that during the 1970s there was still considerable variation between countries with regard to the relative contribution of internal migration and reclassification to urban population growth. As table 8 shows, of the 25 countries having the relevant data for both the 1960s and the 1970s, 12 recorded an increase in the contribution of internal migration to urban population growth; and in two the estimated net rural-urban migration was negative during the 1970s, that is, it contributed to a reduction of the rate of growth of the urban population. Among the 36 countries having data for the 1960s, the median proportion of urban population growth accounted for by migration was 39 per cent, whereas among the 32 countries where migration made a positive contribution to urban population growth during the 1970s, the median proportion of that growth accounted for by migration was 47 per cent. That is, in terms of central values it would appear that internal migration tended to make a greater contribution to urban population growth during the 1970s than during the 1960s. Such results, however, must be interpreted with caution because the range of variation of the contribution of migration to population growth was fairly wide (from nearly 9 to over 77 per cent during the 1960s and from 18 to 66 per cent during the 1970s), and countries with very different population sizes were given equal weight in the calculation of central indices. It is worth noting, nevertheless, that countries with a large population, such as Bangladesh, Brazil, India and Indonesia, all recorded increases in the proportion of urban population growth attributable to migration.

With respect to the estimated degree of female participation in rural-urban migration, table 9 presents data on the percentage of women in net intercensal rural-urban migration flows as well as net in-migration rates to urban areas by sex. The data indicate that, on average, net rural-urban migration during the 1960s was slightly more female than male. For all the developing countries considered, women accounted, on average, for 52.1 per cent of all net rural-urban migration. During the 1970s, however, the average proportion of women in net rural-urban migration flows declined to 49.8 per cent. That is, in terms both of averages and of the experience of at least half of the countries with estimates available, women constituted about half of all net rural-urban migrants.

There were, however, considerable regional variations in the participation of women in net rural-urban migration. In Latin American and Caribbean countries, women tended to outnumber men among net rural-urban migrants, especially during the 1960s. Thus, among the 19 countries with data available for the 1960s, net migration to urban areas was dominated by women in all of them. Although net rural-urban migration in most Latin American and Caribbean countries became less dominated by women during the 1970s, women still accounted for over half the total net rural-urban migration in every country with data available for the 1970s. In the case of Guatemala, net rural-urban migration was estimated to be negative for both sexes during the 1970s. However, women accounted for only 45.7 per cent of the negative outflow, meaning that, in net terms, fewer women than men left urban areas. Excluding Guatemala, among the other 11 countries that had the required data from three consecutive censuses (permitting comparisons for two intercensal periods), the percentage of women in net rural-urban migration rose slightly in four and fell by wider margins in six, especially in Colombia, a country that has experienced considerable international emigration, which may be biasing the estimates of net rural-urban migration. The same may hold true for Uruguay.

In the other less developed regions, net rural-urban migration tended to be either gender-balanced or male-dominated. However, this conclusion is based on the experience of the relatively few countries with data available. For Africa, in particular, data for only seven countries were available for the 1960s. Their average indicates that net rural-urban migration involved almost equal numbers of men and women. Yet, in terms of specific countries, women were underrepresented in the net rural-urban flows of four countries and overrepresented only in Morocco and Tunisia (in Ghana, women accounted for about half of all net rural-urban migrants). Estimates for the three countries of Africa with information for two intercensal periods indicate that the proportion of women in net rural-urban migration declined from the 1960s to the 1970s, but the number of countries is evidently too small to make any generalization. However, in all African countries with data available for the 1970s, women were underrepresented in net rural-urban migration.

Although during the 1960s, Asian countries tended to have, on average, the lowest proportion of women among net rural-urban migrants (46.2 per cent), they were the only group of countries that experienced an increase in that average proportion between the 1960s and the 1970s. During the 1960s, women outnumbered men in net rural-urban migration only in two Asian countries (Indonesia and Iraq), whereas they were outnumbered by men in the other seven with data available. Although net rural migration to urban areas in Asia became more feminized during the 1970s, males continued to dominate (the average proportion of women rose only to 48.6 per cent). Yet, during the 1970s, women equalled or slightly outnumbered men in net rural-urban migration in 7 of the 15 countries with data available. Among the eight Asian countries with data from three consecutive censuses, the percentage of women in net rural-urban migration rose in five (India, Nepal, the Republic of Korea, the Syrian Arab Republic and Turkey) and fell by more than a half a percentage point only in Iraq. In Bangladesh and Indonesia, the proportion female remained almost unchanged; and in Sri Lanka, the estimated net rural-urban migration during the 1970s was negative, with a majority of men, implying that women had represented lower net losses to urban areas.

Table 9 also shows the net in-migration rates to urban areas by sex. The sex differentials exhibited by those rates are generally consistent with the differences in the sex distribution of the net rural-urban migration flows discussed above. However, the migration rates by sex also reflect the effect of the sex distribution of the urban population during the intercensal period. That is, the longer there is a sex imbalance in net rural-urban migration, the more likely it is that the net in-migration rates of men and women will be equal. Table 9 shows that during the 1960s, for all the developing countries considered, the average net in-migration rate to urban areas for women was slightly higher than for men (2.4 versus 2.3 per cent). By the 1970s, both rates were equal (2.0 per cent), suggesting that net in-migration to urban areas was tending to reproduce the sex imbalances already present in the urban population.

TABLE 9. PERCENTAGE OF WOMEN IN RURAL-URBAN MIGRATION AND SEX-SPECIFIC RURAL-URBAN MIGRATION RATES, SELECTED COUNTRIES IN MAJOR AREA BY REGIONS, 1960s AND 1970s

Region and country	Percentage female of rural-urban migration		Rural-urban migration rate					
			Total		Male		Female	
	1960s	1970s	1960s	1970s	1960s	1970s	1960s	1970s

A. *Africa*

Eastern Africa								
Kenya	..	43.7	..	4.5	..	4.6	..	4.5
United Republic of Tanzania	..	47.9	..	7.8	..	7.8	..	7.8
Zimbabwe	..	47.9	..	3.3	..	3.1	..	3.5
Northern Africa								
Egypt	46.4	..	0.9	..	1.0	..	0.9	..
Libyan Arab Jamahiriya	46.4	..	7.9	..	8.0	..	7.9	..
Morocco	56.1	45.4	1.5	2.0	1.4	2.2	1.7	1.8
Tunisia	53.3	48.0	2.4	0.9	2.2	0.9	2.7	0.9
Southern Africa								
Botswana	49.3	44.0	12.2	5.2	12.4	5.7	12.0	4.6
Western Africa								
Ghana	50.1	..	1.9	..	1.9	..	2.0	..
Togo	46.6	..	2.4	..	2.6	..	2.1	..

B. *Asia*

Eastern and South-eastern Asia								
Republic of Korea	49.9	51.4	3.8	2.8	3.8	2.8	3.8	2.9
Indonesia	51.0	50.9	1.1	2.6	1.1	2.6	1.2	2.7
Malaysia	..	50.7	..	2.5	..	2.5	..	2.5
Philippines	..	55.3	..	1.7	..	1.6	..	1.9
Thailand	..	53.1	..	3.0	..	2.8	..	3.1
Southern Asia								
Bangladesh	43.0	42.7	3.9	7.0	3.9	7.2	3.9	6.8
India	45.8	46.8	1.0	1.7	1.0	1.7	1.0	1.7
Iran (Islamic Republic of)	..	43.7	..	2.1	..	2.2	..	1.9
Nepal	36.0	47.5	1.1	4.3	1.3	4.3	0.8	4.5
Pakistan	..	43.4	..	0.7	..	0.8	..	0.7
Sri Lanka	47.5	a	2.1	-0.2	2.0	-0.2	2.1	-0.2
Western Asia								
Iraq	50.7	46.4	2.9	1.7	2.8	1.8	3.1	1.6
Israel	..	50.7	..	0.5	..	0.5	..	0.5
Syrian Arab Republic	46.0	47.8	1.5	0.7	1.6	0.7	1.4	0.7
Turkey	46.1	50.0	3.4	2.5	3.4	2.3	3.4	2.6

C. *Latin America and the Caribbean*

Caribbean and Central America								
Costa Rica	54.0	..	2.1	..	2.1	..	2.2	..
El Salvador	59.7	..	0.8	..	0.7	..	0.9	..
Guatemala	57.5	a	1.1	-1.0	1.0	-1.1	1.2	-0.9
Honduras	55.2	..	2.5	..	2.3	..	2.6	..
Mexico	51.7	..	1.6	..	1.5	..	1.6	..
Nicaragua	56.5	..	1.5	..	1.4	..	1.6	..
Panama	55.1	57.8	1.8	0.8	1.7	0.7	1.9	0.9
Cuba	52.2	51.6	0.5	1.3	0.5	1.3	0.5	1.4
Dominican Republic	53.8	55.0	2.8	2.4	2.7	2.3	2.8	2.5
Haiti	65.4	..	2.2	..	1.7	..	2.5	..

TABLE 9 (continued)

Region and country	Percentage female of rural-urban migration		Rural-urban migration rate					
			Total		Male		Female	
	1960s	1970s	1960s	1970s	1960s	1970s	1960s	1970s
South America								
Argentina[b]	52.7	52.7	0.7	0.7	0.7	0.7	0.7	0.7
Brazil	52.0	51.2	2.1	2.0	2.1	2.0	2.1	2.0
Chile	52.4	54.1	1.0	0.7	1.0	0.7	1.0	0.8
Colombia	67.3	51.7	0.8	1.7	0.6	1.7	1.0	1.7
Ecuador	55.5	50.3	1.5	2.3	1.3	2.3	1.5	2.2
Guyana	51.3	..	6.3	..	6.5	..	6.2	..
Paraguay	59.5	52.4	1.1	1.8	0.9	1.8	1.2	1.8
Peru	50.6	51.2	2.1	1.1	2.0	1.1	2.1	1.2
Uruguay	[a]	56.8	0.1	0.4	-0.0	0.4	0.2	0.5
Venezuela	57.6	52.8	0.9	1.0	0.7	1.0	1.0	1.0
All countries								
Africa	49.7	46.2	4.2	4.0	4.2	4.1	4.2	3.8
Asia	46.2	48.6	2.3	2.2	2.2	2.2	2.3	2.3
Latin America	55.8	53.1	1.7	1.2	1.6	1.1	1.7	1.2
TOTAL	52.1	49.8	2.3	2.1	2.3	2.1	2.4	2.0
Countries with three censuses								
Africa	52.9	45.8	5.4	2.7	5.3	2.9	5.5	2.4
Asia	46.1	47.9	2.3	2.6	2.3	2.6	2.3	2.6
Latin America	55.3	52.8	1.3	1.2	1.2	1.1	1.3	1.2
TOTAL	51.6	50.1	2.2	1.9	2.1	1.9	2.2	1.9

[a]In the cases of Guatemala and Sri Lanka, net rural-urban migration for the 1970s was negative for both men and women; and the proportion of women amounted to 45.7 and 39.9 per cent, respectively, meaning that in net terms fewer women than men left urban areas in both cases. For Uruguay in the 1960s, net rural-urban migration was negative for men and positive for women.

[b]The data for Argentina refer to the 1960-1980 intercensal period.

At the regional level, among countries of Africa, male in-migration rates to urban areas tended to be higher than the equivalent female rates during the 1960s, but during the 1970s, only two countries, Botswana and Kenya, exhibited higher male than female net in-migration rates to urban areas. In Latin America and the Caribbean, male net in-migration rates tended to be lower or at most equal to those of women during the 1960s (only in Guyana did the male rate surpass that for females) and the same held true during the 1970s. Among Asian countries also, the male net in-migration rates tended to be below or at most equal to those of females in both periods. Exceptions included Nepal and the Syrian Arab Republic during the 1960s; and Bangladesh, the Islamic Republic of Iran, Iraq and Pakistan during the 1970s. That is, in both of those major areas, women were contributing more to the growth of the urban population through migration than men in relative terms.

C. SEX DIFFERENTIALS IN NET IN-MIGRATION RATES TO URBAN AREAS BY AGE

Age selectivity is a universal characteristic of migration. The typical migrant tends to be between 15 and 34 years of age. Although such age selectivity characterizes most internal migration streams, there are exceptions. Persons displaced by natural disasters or internal conflict, for instance, are not likely to be selected in terms of age. There are also migration streams where migrants are overrepresented in age groups other than ages 15-34. Urban-rural migration in developing countries, for example, often involves older persons, because many are returning migrants. In Ghana, migration from the capital to the poorest regions had about the same age structure as that of the general population (Singelmann, 1988). However, such types of migration streams usually constitute only a small proportion of internal migration in developing countries.

Given that the estimates available refer only to net rural-urban migration, it is not possible to differentiate the age selectivity of in-migrants from that of out-migrants. It can be assumed, however, that most rural-urban migrants who return do so either relatively soon (within, say, from three to five years after arrival in urban areas) or wait until late in life. If that is the case, net rural-urban migration is likely to approximate the age pattern of rural-urban migration. Nevertheless, it is important to stress that the present analysis concerns only the age and sex patterns of net rural-urban migration and not those of migration streams from rural to urban areas. Moreover, given the possibility that the sex selectivity of rural-urban and urban-rural migration differs by gender, it is important to bear in mind that sex differentials refer here only to the age profile of net migration.

Table 10 presents estimates of the age-specific net in-migration rates to urban areas for men and women separately. Since the method of estimation used yields a predetermined sex composition for age group 0-4, that group is not considered in this analysis. In general, the data presented in table 10 display the typical age selectivity of migration, although there is considerable variation between countries and over time. Migration rates tend to be higher at younger (under 30) than at older ages for both men and women, and they tend to reach a maximum fairly early in life. In 6 of the 10 countries of Africa with data available, for instance, male migration rates reached their highest value at ages 20-24, whereas those for females peaked at ages 15-19. In the remaining four, female net rural-urban migration rates reached their maximum at ages 10-14, whereas those for men peaked either in that group or in age group 15-19. In most countries of South America, female net migration rates also tended to reach a maximum in age group 10-14 or 15-19, whereas those of men displayed greater variability in terms of the age groups registering the highest migration rate. Thus, in Colombia and Uruguay during the first intercental period considered, the highest net migration rate among males corresponded to age group 5-9 and male migration rates were considerably lower than female migration rates for almost all age groups. That outcome may be the result of the underestimation of male rural-urban migration brought about by a failure of the estimation method used to take account of the effects of international migration. Disregarding those deviant cases, male migration rates in most of the other South American countries tended to peak somewhere over the range 15-24 years.

The countries in Central America and in the Caribbean region display more consistency in terms of the age group at which migration rates peaked for each sex: in 8 of those 10 countries, female migration rates reached a maximum in age group 10-14, whereas in 7 of the 10, male rates reached their highest level in age group 15-19. A similar pattern tended to prevail in Southern Asia, whereas in Eastern and South-eastern Asia, both male and female migration rates tended to reach a maximum at ages 15-19. The countries of Western Asia failed to display a consistent pattern.

In sum, in most countries, male net rural-urban migration rates tended to peak somewhere over ages 10-24, whereas those for women tended to reach a maximum over age range 10-19. Usually, female migration rates tended to exceed those of men over the range below and including the female maximum, that is, from age 5 to age 14 or 19. From then on, there was usually a range over which the female migration rates were lower than those for men; and at a certain age, which varied considerably from region to region, a switch-over took place, so that at older ages female net migration rates again tended to exceed those of men. Among the countries of Africa the switch-over tended to occur over age 35, so that between ages 15 and 34 male migration rates were usually higher than those for women. In the countries of Latin America and the Caribbean, in contrast, the range over which male migration rates were higher was considerably shorter, often encompassing at most one or two five-year age groups (20-24 and 25-29 in a number of cases). A similar pattern was evident in some countries of South-eastern Asia, such as Indonesia, the Philippines and Thailand. In certain countries of Southern Asia, such

TABLE 10. AGE-SPECIFIC NET IN-MIGRATION RATES TO URBAN AREAS, BY SEX, SELECTED COUNTRIES IN MAJOR AREAS BY REGION, 1960-1980

Region, country and period	Sex	Age-specific rural-urban net migration rates											
		5-9	10-14	15-19	20-24	25-29	30-34	35-39	40-44	45-49	50-54	55-59	60-64
A. Africa													
Eastern Africa													
Kenya													
1969-1979	M	2.7	7.9	23.9	27.0	12.0	4.5	2.3	1.1	-0.1	-1.4	-1.2	-0.5
	F	4.0	9.9	15.1	10.8	2.7	1.8	2.2	1.7	2.5	2.2	3.1	2.5
Tanzania, United Republic of													
1968-1978	M	6.3	13.0	19.5	23.4	10.4	10.2	6.9	7.4	3.6	5.0	4.5	2.7
	F	7.5	13.8	14.7	12.1	6.1	6.8	4.9	5.5	4.5	4.4	7.5	4.5
Zimbabwe													
1972-1982	M	2.4	9.0	31.8	40.8	14.8	1.7	-1.1	-0.0	-1.2	-1.9	-1.7	-4.1
	F	4.8	12.1	23.2	17.6	6.8	5.4	1.8	0.1	-1.0	0.0	-3.7	-3.0
Northern Africa													
Egypt													
1966-1976	M	3.5	9.4	14.4	15.7	13.1	10.5	3.7	7.1	4.0	6.7	0.1	2.8
	F	7.2	11.9	14.9	9.6	3.4	2.9	5.9	4.0	8.0	1.6	2.8	0.3
Libyan Arab Jamahiriya													
1963-1973	M	5.6	6.1	8.5	8.3	7.8	8.8	7.5	7.4	5.8	4.7	4.5	3.5
	F	5.6	6.9	8.4	7.2	5.2	7.0	5.5	5.3	4.8	4.2	5.3	4.3
Morocco													
1961-1971	M	8.4	14.5	10.7	3.1	5.7	10.3	7.2	6.2	-0.8	1.4	-0.7	-4.1
	F	16.7	23.0	6.4	-2.1	5.7	11.6	6.4	4.6	9.2	2.9	12.9	-3.3
1971-1981	M	10.8	18.9	30.9	25.1	21.5	17.1	14.5	10.0	7.7	3.2	9.3	0.2
	F	15.0	21.5	18.9	10.4	10.1	12.9	12.6	7.0	10.4	3.9	10.7	-1.1
Tunisia													
1965-1975	M	28.2	23.5	23.7	10.0	7.0	21.4	21.5	19.8	15.3	15.5	11.9	12.1
	F	31.1	27.1	26.4	19.9	18.7	24.9	20.1	22.4	18.3	17.6	15.4	18.0
1974-1984	M	11.9	13.4	12.0	14.7	19.1	10.6	7.9	7.2	3.8	5.0	2.6	2.5
	F	14.3	15.4	9.8	8.1	8.5	8.7	3.9	6.0	8.2	6.4	5.4	5.4
Southern Africa													
Botswana													
1961-1971	M	3.1	6.2	13.4	20.7	17.9	17.7	13.6	13.1	8.3	6.2	4.5	2.5
	F	6.1	10.5	12.7	11.8	9.8	9.2	6.2	6.5	4.1	3.2	3.1	1.9
1971-1981	M	0.6	10.3	35.6	44.9	20.6	12.4	8.2	4.6	0.8	0.6	-1.4	-2.1
	F	3.4	13.3	20.4	13.7	7.4	4.1	2.1	0.3	-0.5	-0.3	-0.5	-0.5
Western Africa													
Ghana													
1960-1970	M	5.6	15.6	24.7	18.2	3.1	-0.5	0.0	1.2	-0.1	0.8	-0.3	-0.5
	F	12.9	15.8	11.6	6.1	2.8	4.0	2.2	2.7	4.8	2.3	2.5	2.0
Togo													
1960-1970	M	4.0	13.8	12.7	0.1	2.1	0.8	0.5	0.7	1.2	0.3	0.8	-0.6
	F	7.2	11.4	2.5	0.1	1.6	0.4	0.7	1.2	1.7	0.9	1.5	0.6
B. Asia													
Eastern and South-eastern Asia													
Republic of Korea													
1960-1970	M	19.6	30.3	33.1	29.9	39.9	27.4	15.4	10.9	6.1	3.7	1.7	1.5
	F	20.3	34.3	43.5	31.8	27.5	17.2	11.5	9.9	8.7	9.8	9.7	7.9

TABLE 10 (continued)

Region, country and period	Sex	Age-specific rural-urban net migration rates											
		5-9	10-14	15-19	20-24	25-29	30-34	35-39	40-44	45-49	50-54	55-59	60-64
1970-1980	M	23.7	44.0	54.1	35.0	47.6	26.6	20.8	15.1	7.9	5.6	2.9	3.1
	F	21.2	48.3	82.8	43.2	28.7	20.7	19.2	14.7	11.2	12.7	12.6	14.6
Indonesia													
1961-1971	M	2.9	9.5	7.5	0.5	-2.3	-0.4	1.1	0.5	0.6	1.6	-0.4	-0.4
	F	4.2	10.8	3.4	-1.3	-0.5	1.4	0.9	1.0	0.7	1.5	0.8	0.6
1970-1980	M	5.7	13.6	15.2	7.3	0.8	4.4	4.3	4.7	4.3	4.4	3.3	1.5
	F	7.0	16.2	10.8	4.1	2.4	6.1	5.0	4.7	5.4	3.8	5.1	2.6
Malaysia													
1970-1980	M	9.7	16.9	19.8	14.5	11.5	9.4	10.1	6.9	6.3	4.4	4.2	4.4
	F	9.9	17.5	20.5	15.3	10.6	8.1	8.4	6.5	6.7	6.9	8.3	7.4
Philippines													
1970-1980	M	6.9	11.7	16.4	13.5	8.0	5.5	5.1	5.0	4.1	3.4	1.4	1.5
	F	8.6	20.4	23.1	9.4	5.9	6.3	7.2	7.4	7.0	6.6	5.2	6.6
Thailand													
1970-1980	M	4.2	7.8	10.6	7.4	4.4	3.5	3.6	3.2	3.2	2.6	2.7	2.1
	F	5.0	9.9	11.0	8.2	4.4	3.9	4.0	3.7	3.8	3.3	3.7	3.0
Southern Asia													
Bangladesh													
1964-1974	M	3.6	5.8	8.0	6.7	1.7	2.3	2.8	1.9	2.4	0.8	2.0	0.4
	F	3.8	5.0	2.5	3.3	2.5	2.1	2.2	1.7	1.9	0.8	2.9	0.9
1971-1981	M	9.3	11.6	18.5	18.5	10.4	10.3	9.5	8.1	9.1	5.3	10.4	4.1
	F	9.2	10.4	10.5	8.1	6.7	7.0	7.1	6.0	10.0	4.3	12.1	3.7
India													
1961-1971	M	3.9	6.3	10.3	3.9	-0.4	1.3	0.7	0.3	-1.6	-1.2	-3.1	-1.4
	F	4.2	5.0	4.8	2.5	0.5	1.5	0.5	0.6	0.7	0.2	0.9	0.5
1971-1981	M	5.7	9.0	13.3	7.1	1.7	4.1	3.6	2.5	0.9	0.2	-0.9	0.1
	F	6.0	8.4	8.9	5.0	2.2	3.7	2.9	2.1	2.9	1.4	3.2	2.0
Iran (Islamic Republic of)													
1966-1976	M	21.9	36.3	34.1	21.7	6.4	15.6	16.2	10.7	13.2	7.0	6.8	4.1
	F	18.1	24.6	16.8	13.1	11.6	14.8	14.2	10.2	16.8	9.0	5.5	6.3
Nepal													
1961-1971	M	0.7	1.8	2.6	0.9	-0.6	-0.2	0.1	0.7	-0.2	-0.3	-0.7	-0.0
	F	0.8	1.1	0.8	0.0	-0.2	0.2	0.3	0.1	0.1	-0.2	-0.2	0.2
1971-1981	M	2.7	3.9	4.5	2.7	1.2	2.1	1.9	2.2	1.7	0.9	1.7	1.6
	F	2.6	3.6	3.3	2.4	2.1	2.3	2.0	1.9	1.9	1.2	1.8	1.3
Pakistan													
1971-1981	M	3.3	7.9	10.6	4.4	-0.1	1.9	2.9	1.3	-1.6	-1.7	-2.2	-0.6
	F	5.7	8.8	2.2	-0.3	-1.1	2.7	2.1	0.4	1.0	-0.2	2.1	0.4
Sri Lanka													
1961-1971	M	6.9	9.2	13.0	7.0	3.3	2.3	3.0	4.3	3.1	2.4	1.0	1.1
	F	6.6	6.7	6.9	4.5	5.0	5.5	4.4	5.6	4.4	4.8	4.7	4.8
1971-1981	M	1.2	3.5	4.6	0.5	-4.5	-5.2	-4.0	-3.3	-3.1	-2.8	-4.4	-3.4
	F	1.1	1.3	0.6	-0.2	-1.2	-2.1	-2.2	-1.9	-0.9	-0.9	-1.4	-0.1
Western Asia													
Iraq													
1955-1965	M	29.2	41.0	41.2	23.0	15.4	16.5	15.4	19.0	25.5	23.5	14.8	7.8
	F	30.3	38.3	35.6	22.5	13.6	20.4	20.6	24.3	23.0	24.6	16.1	26.7

TABLE 10 (continued)

Region, country and period	Sex	Age-specific rural-urban net migration rates										
		5-9	10-14	15-19	20-24	25-29	30-34	35-39	40-44	45-49	50-54	55-59	60-64
1967-1977	M	26.8	42.1	62.9	20.7	26.0	29.7	23.6	27.3	18.8	15.2	12.7	4.2
	F	29.2	33.6	31.7	14.2	16.1	22.9	27.1	26.1	26.0	16.1	28.5	7.7
Israel													
1973-1983	M	46.4	36.4	39.5	46.8	29.4	31.6	27.5	30.4	29.6	31.0	26.8	17.0
	F	50.8	45.3	50.1	52.2	28.4	33.8	28.8	36.1	36.1	38.0	33.6	20.4
Syrian Arab Republic													
1960-1970	M	12.8	17.2	14.9	14.3	18.1	11.1	10.8	7.9	7.4	5.9	1.3	-0.9
	F	14.1	13.7	13.9	10.0	6.4	9.6	9.0	7.8	10.7	3.9	8.8	-3.0
1972-1982	M	10.9	9.5	6.7	8.4	13.4	1.3	1.2	4.4	-0.1	-0.2	11.6	-0.9
	F	9.9	8.8	6.4	6.7	5.5	3.2	6.3	6.3	7.2	-1.2	9.0	-2.0
Turkey													
1960-1970	M	19.6	31.3	48.7	22.8	-7.9	13.3	13.2	11.1	7.6	7.3	5.0	2.9
	F	16.4	19.5	22.6	15.1	15.0	17.4	15.2	9.6	11.4	7.4	13.0	4.0
1970-1980	M	19.7	28.2	42.6	27.8	3.9	12.2	9.6	9.9	6.0	3.7	1.6	-0.9
	F	18.9	20.9	26.6	30.1	21.2	15.7	13.1	9.9	11.0	6.6	7.4	3.8

C. *Latin America and the Caribbean*

Region, country and period	Sex	5-9	10-14	15-19	20-24	25-29	30-34	35-39	40-44	45-49	50-54	55-59	60-64
Caribbean and Central America													
Costa Rica													
1963-1973	M	11.6	14.6	15.8	14.9	14.3	12.9	9.8	8.3	14.9	12.1	10.4	9.1
	F	14.2	24.5	24.8	13.0	6.9	12.5	10.0	14.8	17.0	11.6	22.7	10.5
El Salvador													
1961-1971	M	4.2	9.5	10.6	4.0	0.7	-0.0	2.0	1.9	4.7	1.1	2.1	2.7
	F	6.7	17.9	15.3	0.5	0.7	0.9	3.8	3.4	8.1	2.7	8.0	5.7
Guatemala													
1963-1973	M	6.0	8.7	9.3	6.2	3.2	2.7	2.9	2.8	3.4	3.6	-2.2	1.0
	F	9.0	15.7	11.7	3.8	3.2	5.4	5.0	5.0	6.3	5.3	4.8	4.6
1971-1981	M	-2.9	-1.5	-3.5	-7.0	-11.4	-10.0	-7.5	-7.9	-5.9	-5.9	-11.4	-4.9
	F	-1.2	2.9	-1.4	-9.8	-11.1	-11.0	-7.3	-7.3	-5.8	-6.8	-11.0	-5.7
Honduras													
1964-1974	M	9.9	13.3	16.1	12.2	7.8	5.9	4.6	6.1	5.0	1.7	2.7	3.4
	F	12.9	21.8	19.6	10.1	6.5	7.8	6.7	6.7	8.1	4.9	8.7	5.9
Mexico													
1960-1970	M	16.6	21.3	25.7	23.5	19.2	21.3	16.4	20.5	13.1	14.6	7.7	8.5
	F	19.4	29.6	29.5	20.3	17.4	22.3	16.9	20.2	15.2	17.8	13.4	14.9
Nicaragua													
1961-1971	M	11.2	16.5	14.9	7.0	8.9	17.1	12.8	9.6	4.1	5.0	-2.0	2.1
	F	19.8	32.3	23.2	6.4	4.0	15.9	12.4	5.0	9.1	9.6	4.3	8.9
Panama													
1960-1970	M	12.1	20.7	24.1	19.0	15.0	11.9	8.8	9.1	5.0	5.8	1.2	2.9
	F	18.4	39.4	34.5	12.7	12.2	11.9	9.0	10.8	8.2	9.9	7.5	9.1
1970-1980	M	6.7	15.6	18.0	11.4	4.7	-0.7	1.7	1.9	0.7	-1.5	-3.8	-2.6
	F	11.0	29.0	25.8	-0.4	1.8	3.9	2.5	3.2	5.8	3.6	1.1	3.5
Cuba													
1960-1970	M	7.0	11.8	16.6	18.7	13.6	4.0	2.6	3.1	-2.0	-0.8	-9.0	-8.8
	F	9.8	16.1	20.1	19.4	8.0	-1.1	0.6	-1.1	-2.0	5.2	-1.1	2.6
1971-1981	M	28.4	27.9	26.7	29.1	32.3	28.8	24.8	18.8	16.3	15.7	14.1	11.3
	F	31.2	32.6	32.6	37.9	38.4	31.1	25.9	22.9	21.0	22.5	22.5	22.2

TABLE 10 (continued)

Region, country and period	Sex	Age-specific rural-urban net migration rates											
		5-9	10-14	15-19	20-24	25-29	30-34	35-39	40-44	45-49	50-54	55-59	60-64
Dominican Republic													
1960-1970	M	13.1	16.5	24.0	19.2	16.0	13.7	10.6	8.8	10.0	8.1	10.7	7.3
	F	19.5	29.2	29.2	15.9	12.6	11.1	10.9	11.0	11.8	8.1	23.7	9.1
1971-1981	M	16.8	25.9	32.8	30.3	23.0	14.7	9.8	12.0	15.5	9.4	13.2	7.7
	F	25.3	39.9	39.7	29.2	21.5	16.7	15.0	17.6	19.2	15.7	21.1	14.0
Haiti													
1961-1971	M	6.9	8.4	7.2	6.3	0.8	-0.1	-0.2	0.1	-1.6	-0.3	-1.1	-1.9
	F	14.6	18.9	13.8	5.5	-2.3	-0.1	2.5	1.5	1.4	0.6	-1.0	0.1
South America													
Argentina													
1970-1980	M	24.7	36.7	59.4	57.6	38.7	19.3	4.7	2.0	12.9	9.6	-1.0	-0.4
	F	38.0	49.4	72.3	52.5	43.0	20.4	6.3	8.3	19.5	14.6	8.8	14.0
Brazil													
1960-1970	M	21.2	24.7	28.0	28.4	27.1	23.7	22.8	14.3	13.6	20.8	17.6	9.2
	F	24.1	33.3	32.5	28.2	26.0	24.2	19.7	23.5	16.8	29.8	28.6	15.6
1970-1980	M	34.6	39.5	44.0	45.4	38.9	34.3	31.4	23.9	27.3	18.4	16.1	9.6
	F	38.9	48.5	47.5	44.1	39.9	37.8	30.0	31.3	29.1	26.0	24.5	14.7
Chile													
1960-1970	M	23.1	31.5	36.9	38.5	34.6	29.0	19.8	13.8	10.7	9.3	7.0	10.1
	F	30.5	51.3	60.8	37.2	26.0	24.2	17.3	15.5	15.8	17.8	16.1	17.7
1972-1982	M	28.8	32.6	36.1	33.7	32.5	27.0	20.9	11.5	18.6	12.7	12.5	13.9
	F	35.8	53.8	64.2	39.1	26.3	28.0	24.3	17.3	27.5	23.1	23.2	22.8
Colombia													
1963-1973	M	13.1	10.7	5.0	4.9	5.4	2.3	2.2	0.7	5.6	-1.8	7.6	-2.6
	F	19.4	35.8	25.5	2.1	-0.5	9.6	4.5	11.0	10.2	0.2	16.0	-4.9
1975-1985	M	33.0	24.2	27.4	33.0	41.9	35.1	23.8	24.1	19.1	25.4	13.4	24.7
	F	40.2	46.7	51.8	26.3	28.3	28.7	25.8	17.6	26.0	21.7	22.5	35.7
Ecuador													
1964-1974	M	8.0	14.7	15.2	9.1	8.9	6.7	4.8	6.4	4.9	3.8	1.3	0.3
	F	13.1	25.1	18.9	7.0	8.2	8.3	6.6	6.1	7.3	5.1	4.6	1.9
1972-1982	M	17.9	25.1	33.1	26.8	20.4	15.1	13.9	14.7	15.6	10.9	10.4	5.6
	F	20.9	34.2	38.5	20.2	15.2	13.5	13.0	14.0	14.6	13.4	10.3	7.9
Guyana													
1960-1970	M	18.8	22.5	23.6	17.8	18.0	19.0	20.1	21.7	18.7	19.5	16.1	17.7
	F	19.8	23.4	24.3	19.1	20.0	21.3	22.7	24.0	21.3	22.6	18.3	25.0
Paraguay													
1962-1972	M	7.7	15.8	5.1	-9.1	4.3	4.3	5.4	4.5	2.5	3.8	2.9	1.7
	F	12.6	19.4	9.5	0.8	1.7	4.1	6.0	5.1	5.8	5.5	6.0	5.2
1972-1982	M	11.1	22.4	16.7	4.9	12.8	13.0	12.5	9.3	9.9	6.2	8.4	6.5
	F	16.3	24.8	22.0	10.5	10.1	10.3	9.9	8.5	11.0	8.7	10.8	10.8
Peru													
1962-1972	M	26.9	42.1	44.4	29.0	18.8	19.6	18.5	17.1	16.0	15.4	9.8	8.2
	F	30.2	48.9	40.9	23.0	20.3	22.3	17.0	18.5	17.5	16.8	15.5	10.8
1971-1981	M	19.9	32.6	39.5	20.4	12.2	12.1	12.7	12.5	12.4	13.2	3.4	6.5
	F	22.9	38.6	39.0	17.4	15.1	13.0	12.2	13.7	12.9	14.5	6.6	10.1
Uruguay													
1965-1975	M	5.6	1.5	-1.7	-1.4	5.7	-0.2	-11.4	-8.6	-3.7	-6.7	-6.4	3.6
	F	15.6	19.8	17.2	7.0	5.1	3.8	2.1	3.5	4.2	5.5	19.5	12.8

TABLE 10 (continued)

Region, country and period	Sex	Age-specific rural-urban net migration rates											
		5-9	10-14	15-19	20-24	25-29	30-34	35-39	40-44	45-49	50-54	55-59	60-64
1975-1985	M	30.4	10.9	9.3	26.1	30.9	26.3	19.0	14.5	11.0	10.9	14.1	21.9
	F	40.4	43.6	44.8	31.6	30.9	34.5	30.1	27.0	26.8	32.1	33.9	37.9
Venezuela													
1961-1971	M	18.2	31.1	46.1	30.0	12.0	4.0	-2.3	1.4	-0.5	-2.2	-3.1	-0.4
	F	28.7	51.5	52.1	27.5	19.4	14.3	10.9	15.4	13.7	13.3	11.2	9.3
1971-1981	M	26.2	39.9	52.8	51.1	34.1	29.9	22.6	21.3	18.1	15.3	13.7	12.6
	F	34.4	53.9	61.4	42.0	35.2	28.5	25.8	26.6	26.6	24.0	26.7	19.2

as Bangladesh, India and Pakistan, female migration rates tended to be fairly low and those for men tended to be higher over several age groups. In contrast, in Western Asia, Israel and Turkey exhibited higher female than male migration rates over most of the age range.

Thus, the general pattern of variation of net rural-urban migration rates by sex and age was the following: at younger ages (under 14 or 19) female migration rates tended to exceed those of men; over the middle of the age range (20-29 or even, in a number of cases, 20-39 or 20-44), male migration rates were higher; from then on, however, the rates for women tended to exceed those for men. Although elements of this distinctive pattern could be found in all regions, in Latin America and in some countries of Western and South-eastern Asia, female migration rates tended to exceed male migration rates in almost every age group.

With respect to changes over time, in most countries with data available for two intercensal periods, the female net migration rates tended to increase, at least over age range 5-29, and the estimated increases tended to be considerable in most cases, often implying at least a doubling of migration rates at the peak ages.

Migration rates cannot indicate whether the relative participation of women in migration flows has increased. To assess that aspect, the percentage of women in net rural-urban migration by age group was calculated (see table 11). Such calculations are, however, not straightforward, because net migration may be negative for men and positive for women or vice-versa, or it can be negative for both. In cases where male and female net migration have opposite signs, only that of female migration is shown in table 11. In cases where both have the same sign, the percentage of women has been calculated and shown with the respective sign. Thus, a negative proportion of women indicates how large a relative loss they represent for urban areas.

The data shown in table 11 indicate that women tend to predominate among the net number of rural-urban migrants aged 5-14 in Africa, South-eastern Asia, and Latin America and the Caribbean. In other parts of Asia, women are not as likely to be overrepresented in the younger age groups. Over most of the age range 15-39, women tend to be underrepresented in the African countries considered. They also tend to be underrepresented over the age range 20-29 in most Latin American countries. In Asia, however, there is considerable variation in the relative representation of women as migrants over the middle age range. In countries of Southern Asia, in particular, women tend to account for relatively high proportions of net migrants aged 25-29 or, if net migration is negative, for low proportions of the migration losses registered in that age group. Both in Latin America and the Caribbean and in most countries of Asia, women tend to account for fairly high proportions of the net migrants aged 45-64. In Africa, there is considerably more variation in the estimates for older age groups, probably because the quality of the underlying data is worse; and although women tend to account for a majority of migrants in certain age groups, a firmer generalization does not seem possible. Similarly,

TABLE 11. PERCENTAGE OF WOMEN IN NET RURAL-URBAN MIGRATION, BY AGE, SELECTED COUNTRIES IN MAJOR AREAS BY REGION, 1960-1980

Region, country and period	Percentage of women in net rural-urban migration by age											
	5-9	10-14	15-19	20-24	25-29	30-34	35-39	40-44	45-49	50-54	55-59	60-64

A. *Africa*

Region, country and period	5-9	10-14	15-19	20-24	25-29	30-34	35-39	40-44	45-49	50-54	55-59	60-64
Eastern Africa												
Kenya												
1969-1979	59.5	54.1	38.8	31.8	22.2	32.4	54.1	64.4	+	+	+	+
Tanzania, United Republic of												
1968-1978	54.5	49.8	44.8	42.2	43.0	44.1	42.8	45.6	55.2	48.2	60.5	63.4
Zimbabwe												
1972-1982	66.7	56.8	42.9	38.3	39.8	81.1	+	+	-46.7	+	-65.8	-39.6
Northern Africa												
Egypt												
1966-1976	65.5	52.3	46.5	36.9	22.5	24.0	63.6	37.4	67.6	20.7	96.7	12.0
Libyan Arab Jamahiriya												
1963-1973	49.1	49.6	47.2	43.8	40.3	43.5	40.5	40.1	43.0	44.7	48.7	50.3
Morocco												
1961-1971	66.9	54.7	26.9	-	54.4	59.4	49.3	48.3	+	96.9	+	-51.4
1971-1981	57.6	48.9	35.9	29.3	35.1	49.4	50.4	47.7	56.3	52.7	45.0	-
Tunisia												
1965-1975	50.9	51.4	52.4	68.6	75.3	56.1	49.4	54.0	53.2	50.2	51.8	53.2
1974-1984	53.0	51.7	43.4	35.7	32.7	47.7	35.1	47.4	68.8	54.9	64.4	62.7
Southern Africa												
Botswana												
1961-1971	66.1	62.0	51.2	45.7	43.0	41.1	36.3	37.5	35.4	34.9	41.9	43.8
1971-1981	85.6	56.5	39.9	35.0	38.4	34.4	27.8	7.0	-	-	-31.3	-20.1
Western Africa												
Ghana												
1960-1970	68.5	46.5	30.7	31.2	53.8	+	100.0	69.0	+	71.2	+	+
Togo												
1960-1970	62.1	39.3	17.2	75.0	56.3	41.4	62.1	65.9	60.6	74.1	63.9	+

B. *Asia*

Region, country and period	5-9	10-14	15-19	20-24	25-29	30-34	35-39	40-44	45-49	50-54	55-59	60-64
Eastern and South-eastern Asia												
Republic of Korea												
1960-1970	49.0	50.7	54.7	48.4	41.9	40.3	44.6	49.9	60.6	73.4	86.0	86.3
1970-1980	45.7	50.9	58.0	48.8	37.3	43.7	49.5	51.8	61.1	71.8	82.7	84.3
Indonesia												
1961-1971	58.8	50.6	31.7	-	-22.6	+	45.2	67.3	54.0	49.2	+	+
1970-1980	54.0	52.1	42.2	41.0	77.7	60.5	54.8	50.9	55.3	46.9	60.5	65.3
Malaysia												
1970-1980	49.6	50.1	51.7	53.3	49.1	46.5	45.6	48.1	52.6	60.7	65.2	61.5
Philippines												
1970-1980	53.4	61.4	56.9	41.2	43.5	54.2	59.1	60.8	64.7	68.1	80.1	83.0
Thailand												
1970-1980	53.5	55.1	51.1	53.1	50.7	53.5	52.9	54.2	54.7	56.9	58.2	60.7

TABLE 11 (continued)

Region, country and period	Percentage of women in net rural-urban migration by age											
	5-9	10-14	15-19	20-24	25-29	30-34	35-39	40-44	45-49	50-54	55-59	60-64
Southern Asia												
Bangladesh												
1964-1974	50.7	41.3	23.0	35.5	61.5	47.4	40.0	44.5	38.6	48.1	51.3	63.8
1971-1981	49.1	43.4	34.9	33.3	41.0	41.8	40.9	40.9	47.6	42.0	47.0	43.9
India												
1961-1971	50.4	41.1	30.2	41.3	+	53.8	41.3	65.0	+	+	+	+
1971-1981	49.8	45.3	37.5	42.6	56.4	48.2	43.7	44.6	73.6	85.2	+	95.6
Iran (Islamic Republic of)												
1966-1976	43.1	38.0	35.2	44.2	68.0	49.6	44.9	44.5	50.6	52.5	38.8	58.8
Nepal												
1961-1971	52.6	34.8	22.8	2.4	-29.9	+	85.8	14.9	+	-34.8	-19.4	+
1971-1981	47.5	43.9	40.1	49.4	59.6	54.6	50.1	45.8	49.8	53.8	48.3	44.9
Pakistan												
1971-1981	61.4	46.8	14.7	-	-91.0	57.7	40.9	21.8	+	-9.4	+	+
Sri Lanka												
1961-1971	48.5	41.2	34.7	40.5	61.7	69.2	58.9	52.6	55.1	62.0	79.1	77.1
1971-1981	46.7	26.1	11.0	-	-22.1	-29.1	-35.3	-34.7	-21.7	-21.7	-21.2	-1.9
Western Asia												
Iraq												
1955-1965	48.9	46.4	48.6	53.9	51.7	60.3	56.6	54.6	42.9	50.7	53.3	79.0
1967-1977	49.6	40.7	37.5	40.8	41.7	47.4	53.9	50.2	55.4	51.3	67.7	64.2
Israel												
1973-1983	50.4	53.0	51.9	49.3	48.1	50.2	50.6	54.6	55.1	55.5	56.9	54.2
Syrian Arab Republic												
1960-1970	49.3	41.4	48.3	40.4	30.0	48.5	46.8	48.0	56.8	41.3	85.4	-78.2
1972-1982	45.9	45.7	48.5	44.2	31.3	72.6	85.1	59.0	+	-81.9	41.9	-68.7
Turkey												
1960-1970	44.1	36.5	31.6	45.6	+	59.9	53.7	48.2	56.6	53.2	68.9	62.0
1970-1980	47.9	41.3	39.3	56.3	85.8	60.2	59.7	52.6	63.4	66.1	80.9	+

C. *Latin America and the Caribbean*

	5-9	10-14	15-19	20-24	25-29	30-34	35-39	40-44	45-49	50-54	55-59	60-64
Caribbean and Central America												
Costa Rica												
1963-1973	54.0	61.2	58.6	44.1	31.4	47.0	49.5	60.9	49.3	45.4	64.6	47.4
El Salvador												
1961-1971	60.7	63.2	58.6	11.9	52.4	+	64.8	62.7	62.1	69.8	77.5	64.1
Guatemala												
1963-1973	58.9	62.1	54.4	37.2	49.5	65.0	62.8	61.3	61.5	57.5	+	79.7
1971-1981	-27.9	+	-27.9	-58.6	-49.9	-50.9	-49.0	-45.7	-47.3	-50.6	-45.1	-48.8
Honduras												
1964-1974	55.6	60.3	54.7	46.3	47.1	57.0	59.5	51.9	60.8	73.5	75.0	60.6
Mexico												
1960-1970	52.9	56.0	52.4	47.1	48.3	50.0	49.5	48.3	51.8	53.4	60.7	60.9
Nicaragua												
1961-1971	62.7	63.0	59.3	46.9	30.9	46.6	47.7	32.2	66.7	62.8	+	77.8
Panama												
1960-1970	59.4	63.3	55.2	37.3	42.6	46.8	47.3	49.5	56.7	56.4	83.1	70.4
1970-1980	61.7	62.5	55.2	-	26.4	+	57.1	59.1	87.5	+	+	+

TABLE 11 (continued)

Region, country and period	Percentage of women in net rural-urban migration by age											
	5-9	10-14	15-19	20-24	25-29	30-34	35-39	40-44	45-49	50-54	55-59	60-64
Cuba												
1960-1970	57.0	55.8	53.6	47.3	33.8	-	16.5	-	-41.8	+	-7.7	+
1971-1981	51.0	51.9	53.1	54.2	51.3	48.5	48.1	51.0	51.4	52.4	54.3	56.7
Dominican Republic												
1960-1970	59.0	61.7	54.9	45.5	43.6	43.4	48.1	50.1	48.5	44.4	59.7	48.6
1971-1981	59.2	58.8	53.4	47.7	47.2	51.6	59.3	55.5	50.9	56.8	53.3	57.6
Haiti												
1961-1971	67.9	67.1	64.1	48.6	-	-49.5	+	95.7	+	+	-45.2	+
South America												
Argentina												
1970-1980	59.6	55.2	50.3	44.7	48.7	47.1	53.2	77.3	53.8	53.6	+	+
Brazil												
1960-1970	52.1	56.3	52.9	49.2	48.3	48.6	46.2	59.1	51.9	55.0	56.8	58.3
1970-1980	52.1	53.9	50.9	48.6	49.1	50.0	47.1	54.2	48.8	55.9	55.9	56.7
Chile												
1960-1970	55.9	59.5	57.3	43.7	38.9	41.4	43.6	48.5	55.7	60.9	65.0	58.6
1972-1982	54.4	60.1	58.7	47.2	39.9	46.2	49.5	55.3	55.4	59.8	59.7	56.5
Colombia												
1963-1973	58.4	75.4	81.3	27.0	-	80.4	66.2	93.2	61.0	+	63.7	-60.9
1975-1985	52.9	55.9	51.1	41.6	42.5	46.1	48.1	46.8	47.4	52.7	46.8	57.0
Ecuador												
1964-1974	61.0	60.6	53.5	42.7	47.8	53.9	57.4	46.9	58.3	55.1	76.4	87.6
1972-1982	52.9	55.9	51.1	41.6	42.5	46.1	48.1	46.8	47.4	52.7	46.8	57.0
Guyana												
1960-1970	50.6	50.7	51.1	52.4	53.7	52.8	52.4	51.1	49.9	50.3	49.2	56.4
Paraguay												
1962-1972	60.7	52.3	65.1	+	28.1	47.6	53.4	52.3	71.4	58.5	68.1	75.6
1972-1982	58.2	50.0	56.2	66.4	42.5	41.8	43.9	45.3	52.8	56.3	55.2	61.9
Peru												
1962-1972	52.2	51.0	46.4	45.6	53.8	53.2	49.9	52.3	53.1	52.8	61.6	58.8
1971-1981	53.0	51.9	48.2	46.4	56.6	51.7	50.8	52.1	51.6	52.0	65.1	61.3
Uruguay												
1965-1975	71.1	91.9	+	+	40.1	+	+	+	+	+	+	68.6
1975-1985	55.6	77.4	77.0	45.7	42.2	48.7	53.0	55.5	61.8	64.9	59.2	51.4
Venezuela												
1961-1971	59.8	59.1	48.5	46.4	60.1	76.8	+	90.5	+	+	+	+
1971-1981	55.5	54.6	49.3	42.5	47.9	46.0	50.5	51.7	55.2	56.2	60.5	54.4

NOTE: A positive or negative sign without a number indicates the sign of female migration when male and female net rural-urban migration had opposite signs. A negative sign followed by the percentage female indicates that both male and female net rural-urban migration were negative.

consideration of countries with data for two intercensal periods reveals no consistent pattern of change.

D. CONCLUSIONS AND POLICY IMPLICATIONS

The data presented here indicate that net rural-urban migration in developing countries contributes substantially to urban population growth; and that during the 1970s, that contribution reached a median value of some 47 per cent. However, the set of countries with data available is still too limited and so variable that a stronger conclusion cannot be reached. In terms of the sex distribution of net rural-urban migration and of the relative values of net in-migration rates to urban areas, the partial evidence available suggests that, on average, during the 1960s women accounted for a larger proportion of net rural-urban migration than did men.

During the 1970s, however, women lost some ground and men accounted, on average, for slightly more than half of net rural-urban migration in the developing countries considered. Net in-migration rates to urban areas, though reflecting smaller differences by sex than the proportion of women in net rural-urban flows, nevertheless tended to be higher for women than for men, particularly in Asian countries and in Latin American and Caribbean countries, indicating that in relative terms women were contributing more to the growth of urban areas through migration than men.

Consideration of net rural-urban migration rates by age revealed that those rates tended to be higher for women than for men over age range 5-14 or 5-19, that the reverse was often true over a certain middle range that varied from region to region and that at older ages (45-64) the female net migration rates tended once more to exceed those of men. In terms of the relative participation of women in net rural-urban migration flows by age, they tended to outnumber men in most regions over age range 5-14, they were often outnumbered by men over a middle range that varied from region to region and they again tended to outnumber men at older ages (45-64). However, there was considerable variation between the age-specific net migration rates of different countries and even between those of the same country through time. Consideration of those countries having data for two intercensal periods did not indicate the existence of a consistent pattern of change in the relative participation of women in net migration by age.

The analysis presented here validates the importance of migration for the urbanization process. In contrast with earlier assessments of the contribution of net rural-urban migration to urban population growth, the data for the 1970s indicate that a substantial proportion of urban population growth is attributable to net migration and reclassification. Rural-urban migration deserves therefore special attention in devising urban development policies. Furthermore, as women account for a major proportion of rural-urban migration flows in most countries, special attention must be given to their special needs, particularly in developing countries where female migrants often constitute one of the most dynamic population subgroups.

NOTES

[1] It is impossible with this method to distinguish the effects of net urban migration from those of reclassification of rural areas into urban areas. However, as pointed out in United Nations (1985), the effect of reclassification is likely to be small, especially if the effect of migration on reclassification is taken into account. In other words, the reclassification of rural areas as urban often results from an increase in the population of those rural areas brought about by migration. In that sense, reclassification could be subsumed under migration. For these reasons, the text that follows usually makes no reference to reclassification, although it is understood that reclassification does play a role. A more serious problem of the estimation method used is that it assumes that the population under study is closed to international migration. To the extent that international migration contributes to increase the urban population of a country from one census to the next, rural-urban migration will be overestimated. Conversely, to the extent that urban areas experience net international emigration during the intercensal period, rural-urban migration will be underestimated and may even become negative. Given the sex selectivity of international migration, those effects are unlikely to be equal for both sexes.

[2] Information for either urban or rural areas would suffice, but it happens that whenever one is provided, the other is also usually available.

[3] Some countries or areas were excluded because they present special situations with respect to rural-urban migration (e.g., Hong Kong) or because their small populations make the estimation of migration unreliable (e.g., Macau and Maldives).

[4] Of the now Department for Economic and Social Information and Policy Analysis of the United Nations Secretariat.

[5] This paper is based on the age- and sex-specific urban-rural database prepared by the Population Division. The author thanks the Division for making the file available and would also like to acknowledge the assistance of Steven Strickland in processing the data for the present analysis.

REFERENCES

Preston, Samuel H. (1979). Urban population growth in developing countries: a demographic reappraisal. *Population and Development Review* (New York), vol. 5, No. 2 (June), pp. 195-215.

Singelmann, Joachim (1988). Age and sex profiles of internal migration in Ghana. Baton Rouge: Louisiana State University, Center for Life Course and Population Studies.

_____, and J. H. Li (1992). Place of birth and past place of residence in South Korea: methodological considerations for migration research. In *Migration and Economic Development*, Klaus F. Zimmermann, ed. Heidelberg, Germany: Springer Verlag.

United Nations (1980). *Patterns of Urban and Rural Population Growth*. Population Studies, No. 68. Sales No. E.79.XIII.9.

_____ (1985). *Migration, Population Growth, and Employment in Metropolitan Areas of Selected Developing Countries*. ST/ESA/SER.R/57.

_____ (1986). *Review and Appraisal of the World Population Plan of Action, 1984 Report*. Population Studies, No. 99. Sales No. E.86.XIII.2.

United Nations Secretariat (1983). Metropolitan migration and population growth in selected developing countries, 1960-1970. *Population Bulletin of the United Nations* (New York), No. 15, pp. 50-62. Sales No. E.83.XIII.4.

V. TYPES OF FEMALE MIGRATION

United Nations Secretariat*

As Petersen (1958) notes, migration, in contrast with fertility and mortality, lacks a physiological basis and is therefore unlikely to be explained or characterized in terms of general "laws". In addition, given the complexity of population mobility and the fact that its attributes vary over a broad continuum that is difficult to apprehend in its entirety, the use of "typologies" becomes mandatory if only to establish the subset of movements that is to be the object of discourse. It is therefore not surprising to find a plethora of typologies in the literature. The aim of this paper is not to delve into them nor to propose yet another set but rather to elucidate the concepts underlying most typologies and their relation to measurement issues, particularly with respect to female migration.

As is well known, the study of female migration, especially that occurring within countries, has generally been neglected. Perhaps for that reason, there have been few attempts to propose a migrant typology that is either specific to female migration or that, being more general, takes explicitly into account the attributes of migrating women. To the limited extent that the existing literature on female migration considers different types of migrants, it usually borrows typologies developed for the study of male migration or, even more often, those dictated by the idiosyncrasies of the data at hand. Consequently and especially with respect to female migration, typologies can rightly be criticized as being little more than taxonomic tools that leave little room for generalization and even less for the development of theory (Forbes, 1981).

Indeed, the advances made in understanding the migration process in general and female migration in particular are still hampered from yielding useful generalizations or testable hypotheses by the inadequacy of the data sources available. As long as data continue to be gathered using a variety of definitions and approaches that compromise their comparability either between countries or over time, knowledge of the migration process in general and especially of the role played by women will remain fractured and tentative.

The discussion here is structured around the main criteria that have been used to identify types of migrants. The first two, space and time, are inextricably linked to the conceptualization of migration. How they are operationalized in practice is important because different measurement approaches may lead to the selective elimination of women from the category of "migrants". A similar problem may arise in relation to the third criterion defining migrants, namely, the reasons or motivation for mobility. When only movements motivated by a narrow set of reasons are considered relevant for the study of migration, women are likely to be disregarded. Lastly, criteria related to the actual unfolding of the migration process and its relation to the mobility of women at different stages of the life cycle have generally been given scant attention; yet, their potential for yielding useful insights about the significance of migration in women's lives is high.

A. Spatial criteria

Distance

At the root of the concept of mobility is the movement from one place to another. A crucial issue is therefore to identify different "places". In general, existing administrative units are used as the geographical areas that allow the distinction between migrants and other movers. A weakness of this approach is that administrative units vary in size both within and between countries. To the extent that Ravenstein's (1885; 1889) well-known "law" on female migration holds true, namely, that women are more mobile over short than over long distances, the use of larger administrative units in one context and smaller ones in another will compromise the comparability or repre-

---

*Population Division of the Department of International Economic and Social Affairs (now the Department for Economic and Social Information and Policy Analysis).

sentativeness of the data, particularly with regard to its distribution by sex.

The question that arises then is: how universal is the validity of Ravenstein's law? Data that would allow its examination at the level of countries as a whole are scanty, but they suggest that in the modern world distance may not be a unidirectional correlate of the relative participation of women in migration. Consider, for instance, the cases summarized in table 12. For the four countries listed there, migration has been measured according to at least two distinct spatial criteria: the crossing of interdistrict borders; and that of interstate ones. Since states are constituted of districts of smaller size, intrastate migration between districts can be taken as an indicator of the extent of migration over short distances. Although this procedure is clearly not ideal to establish the distinction between short- and long-distance movements (the distance between non-contiguous districts within the same state may be greater than that between contiguous districts belonging to different states), it nevertheless reflects a distinction that is relevant for the measurement of migration because, as mentioned above, district or state equivalents are the geographical units most commonly used to distinguish migrants from other movers.

The original question can therefore be reformulated as: if interstate migration is the only type considered, will it misrepresent the extent of female participation in migration flows defined more generally? The data given in table 12 suggest that the answer to this question varies according to the country concerned. In Brazil in 1970, contrary to what was expected according to Ravenstein's law, women were more numerous than men among interstate migrants than among intrastate migrants, though the difference in the relative share of women in each type of flow was small (51 compared with 49 per cent). However, in the three other countries with census data available, women were, as expected, more numerous than men in intrastate than in interstate migration. Yet, even among those few countries, the differences between the proportions of women in intrastate and interstate flows varied considerably, being very small in Thailand (0.7 percentage point), moderate in the Libyan Arab Jamahiriya (2.7 percentage points) and very marked in India (over 10 percentage points for the country as a whole). For the last-named country, the availability of data on migration at the intradistrict level further underscores the differential participation of women in migration over short distances. Thus, women accounted for at least three quarters of all intradistrict migrants in India, compared with only slightly over half of those moving between states. Yet, India appears to be a very special case. The widespread custom of village exogamy associated with patrilocal residence in a country where early and virtually universal marriage is the rule is deemed responsible for the large number of women who migrate over short distances, especially within rural areas. Thus, the data for 1981 indicate that nearly 49 per cent of all rural women were lifetime migrants, whereas only 17 per cent of all rural men belonged to that category.

In Malaysia, data from the Labour Force and Migration Survey carried out annually also indicate that women account for greater shares of intrastate than of interstate migration: 49.1 versus 46.5 per cent in 1981 and 1982; 49.5 versus 45.7 per cent in 1983; and 49.5 versus 47.4 per cent in 1986 (Heng, 1989), but again the largest difference between the proportion of women in the two types of flows amounted to only 3.8 percentage points.

Although the few countries considered above are scarcely representative of the entire world, their data confirm both that the share of women in intrastate migration tends to be higher than that in migration between states and that there are important exceptions to that rule (e.g., Brazil). They also suggest that, at the country level, women's differential participation in intrastate and interstate migration is likely to be very marked only in special circumstances. Yet, this conclusion can only be validated if more countries gather and tabulate migration data according to geographical units at different levels of aggregation. The practice of recording migration only at the interstate level, aside from having the risk of misrepresenting the proportion of women participating in overall migration flows, is also likely to provide a biased picture in terms of other characteristics of migrants. Furthermore, when censuses or surveys code migration information only at the

TABLE 12. INTRASTATE AND INTERSTATE MIGRANTS BY SEX, SELECTED DEVELOPING COUNTRIES
(*Number of migrants in thousands*)

Country, census year and data type	Type of migrant	Male (percentage)	Female (percentage)	Percentage female
A. Africa				
Libyan Arab Jamahiriya, 1973 Place of birth	Intrastate	60.2	57.5	49.2
	Interstate	39.8	42.5	46.5
	Total number of migrants	326	352	48.1
B. Asia				
India, 1981 Place of birth				
Rural	Intradistrict	56.1	72.1	77.7
	Intrastate	27.4	21.2	67.6
	Interstate	16.4	6.7	52.5
	Total number of migrants	43 742	118 544	73.0
Urban	Intradistrict	28.5	35.5	63.7
	Intrastate	41.5	41.5	58.4
	Interstate	30.0	22.9	51.8
	Total number of migrants	13 947	19 598	58.4
Total	Intradistrict	49.4	66.9	76.4
	Intrastate	30.8	24.0	65.1
	Interstate	19.7	9.0	52.2
	Total number of migrants	57 876	138 427	70.5
India, 1981 Previous residence				
Rural	Intradistrict	59.9	73.6	77.2
	Intrastate	25.3	20.1	68.7
	Interstate	14.9	6.3	53.8
	Total number of migrants	43 911	120 977	73.4
Urban	Intradistrict	30.3	36.8	61.1
	Intrastate	41.1	41.0	56.4
	Interstate	28.6	22.1	50.1
	Total number of migrants	15 759	20 424	56.4
Total	Intradistrict	51.9	68.2	75.7
	Intrastate	29.4	23.2	65.1
	Interstate	18.6	8.6	52.3
	Total number of migrants	59 921	141 785	70.3
Thailand, 1980 Residence in 1975	Intrastate	31.5	30.9	52.2
	Interstate	68.5	69.1	51.5
	Total number of migrants	1 128	1 053	51.7

TABLE 12 (continued)

Country, census year and data type	Type of migrant	Male	Female	Percentage female
		(percentage)		
	C. *Latin America*			
Brazil, 1970				
Place of birth	Intrastate	51.1	53.6	48.7
	Interstate	48.9	46.4	51.2
	Total number of migrants	15 110	15 160	49.9

Sources: Brazil, *VIII Recenseamento Geral do Brasil, 1970*, National Series, No. 1 (Rio de Janeiro, Fundação Instituto Brasileiro de Geografia e Estatística, 1973); India, *Census of India, 1981: Report and Tables Based on 5 Per Cent Sample Data*, Series 1, part II, special (New Delhi, Ministry of Home Affairs, Registrar General; and Census Commissioner of India, 1985); Libyan Arab Jamahiriya, *1973 Population Census: Final All Country Results* (Tripoli, Census and Statistics Department, 1979); Thailand, *1980 Population and Housing Census; Subject Report No. 2: Migration* (Bangkok, Office of the Prime Minister, National Statistical Office, 1984).

state level, the possibility of exploiting such data for a more in-depth and textured analysis of migration by place of origin is precluded. Indeed, distance is often used as a proxy for other, more relevant characteristics of the place of origin which are more likely to be captured directly if data for a finer geographical mesh are available.

Rural and urban places

A second approach to the identification of different "places" suggests that, from both an analytical and a policy perspective, a more relevant way of conceptualizing "place" would be with respect to geographical characteristics of analytical interest (Standing, 1984a). The most evident use of this principle is the characterization of places as "urban" or "rural". Despite the broad variety of ways in which urban and rural areas are defined in practice,[1] the distinction between them remains relevant because it attempts to reflect basic differences in modes of production and human settlement. The overwhelming attention given to the study of rural-urban migration attests to the value of such an approach.

Perhaps not surprisingly, therefore, the analysis of female migration has also focused mainly on rural-urban migrant flows (e.g., Fawcett, Khoo and Smith, 1984). Indeed, since the move from a rural to an urban environment is often conceived as the passage from a traditional to a modern society, interest in ascertaining the consequences of that experience for women is high. Yet, it is worth asking if devoting so much attention to only one type of flow has not biased the assessment of the importance of female migration and its consequences for women.

To address this issue, one may consider the distribution of migrants by sex and type of migration stream in selected developing countries (see table 13). In most cases, the data presented in table 13 are derived from censuses where migrants were identified by considering whether their place of birth or that of residence at some point preceding the census differed from their place of residence at the time of enumeration[2]. For Brazil and India, a distinction was also made between intrastate and interstate flows. As in the case of migration by size of administrative unit, the data show that the relative participation of women in the different types of migration flows linking rural and urban areas varied considerably between countries. In India, for instance, women constituted an overwhelming majority of rural-rural migrants (77 and 79 per cent in 1971 and 1981, respectively) and that flow was dominant in terms of the proportion of migrants involved: 46 per cent of all male migrants in 1981; and 74 per cent of female migrants. In contrast, urban-urban migration was dominant in Brazil, involving 49 per cent of interdistrict male migrants and 52 per cent of their female counterparts, with the latter outnumbering males slightly (similar proportions were registered with respect to interstate migration).

Rural-urban migration was often not the dominant type for either men or women. In Brazil, only some 18 per cent of all interdistrict lifetime migrants had moved from a rural to an urban area by 1970. In Egypt the proportion of rural-urban migrants was only 28 per cent for males and 24 for females. In Malaysia, Pakistan and Thailand, where migrant status was ascertained on the basis of a change of residence during the five years preceding the census, rural-urban migrants constituted even lower proportions of all

TABLE 13. MIGRANTS BY SEX AND TYPE OF FLOW, ACCORDING TO URBAN OR RURAL ORIGIN AND DESTINATION
(*Number of migrants in thousands*)

Country, census year and data type	Migration stream	Male (percentage)	Female (percentage)	Percentage female
A. Africa				
Egypt, 1976 Previous residence Interstate	Rural-urban	27.8	24.1	46.3
	Urban-urban	56.9	53.5	48.3
	Rural-rural	8.9	15.1	62.9
	Urban-rural	6.4	7.2	52.7
	Total number of migrants	2 544	2 527	49.8
B. Asia				
India, 1971 Place of birth Intrastate	Rural-urban	21.6	9.3	52.1
	Urban-urban	13.1	5.6	52.3
	Rural-rural	57.8	80.2	77.8
	Urban-rural	7.5	4.9	62.5
	Total number of migrants	39 682	100 587	71.7
Interstate	Rural-urban	35.2	21.4	36.8
	Urban-urban	32.7	28.6	45.7
	Rural-rural	24.0	42.2	62.8
	Urban-rural	8.1	7.9	48.2
	Total number of migrants	9 384	9 009	49.0
Total	Rural-urban	24.2	10.3	48.6
	Urban-urban	16.8	7.5	50.0
	Rural-rural	51.4	77.1	77.0
	Urban-rural	7.6	5.2	60.2
	Total number of migrants	49 066	109 596	69.1
India, 1981 Place of birth Intrastate	Rural-urban	24.9	10.9	53.7
	Urban-urban	15.6	7.1	54.7
	Rural-rural	52.0	76.8	79.7
	Urban-rural	7.5	5.2	64.8
	Total number of migrants	48 627	129 260	72.7
Interstate	Rural-urban	39.2	24.5	40.7
	Urban-urban	33.4	29.2	48.9
	Rural-rural	20.0	38.2	67.8
	Urban-rural	7.4	8.1	54.7
	Total number of migrants	11 044	12 141	52.4
Total	Rural-urban	27.6	12.1	50.9
	Urban-urban	18.9	9.0	53.0
	Rural-rural	46.0	73.5	79.1
	Urban-rural	7.5	5.5	63.3
	Total number of migrants	59 671	141 401	70.3

TABLE 13 (continued)

Country, census year and data type	Migration stream	Male	Female	Percentage female
		(percentage)		
Malaysia, 1970				
Residence in 1965	Rural-urban	8.9	8.7	46
	Urban-urban	20.6	19.3	45
	Rural-rural	38.5	39.2	47
	Urban-rural	32.1	32.7	47
	Total number of migrants	484	421	46.5
Pakistan, 1973				
Residence in 1965	Rural-urban	18.0	16.3	42.3
	Urban-urban	39.0	38.4	44.2
	Rural-rural	30.2	35.5	48.7
	Urban-rural	12.7	9.7	38.1
	Total number of migrants	1 137	917	44.6
Philippines, 1973				
Residence in 1965	Rural-urban	35.0	42.6	60.6
	Urban-urban	25.5	25.1	55.5
	Rural-rural	22.4	17.5	49.8
	Urban-rural	17.0	14.8	52.5
	Total number of migrants	1 321	1 676	55.9
Birth to 1965	Rural-urban	42.5	44.4	52.2
	Urban-urban	11.4	14.0	56.2
	Rural-rural	35.0	30.3	47.5
	Urban-rural	11.1	11.3	51.6
	Total number of migrants	2 376	2 487	51.1
Republic of Korea, 1966				
Residence in 1961	Rural-urban	36.7	36.6	52.6
	Urban-urban	32.0	31.9	52.6
	Rural-rural	20.8	21.6	53.6
	Urban-rural	10.4	10.0	51.6
	Total number of migrants	1 179	1 314	52.7
Republic of Korea, 1970				
Residence in 1965	Rural-urban	47.8	49.4	51.5
	Urban-urban	24.5	23.2	49.3
	Rural-rural	17.0	17.5	51.3
	Urban-rural	10.7	9.9	48.7
	Total number of migrants	1 856	1 905	50.6
Republic of Korea, 1975				
Residence in 1970	Rural-urban	42.7	44.2	54.1
	Urban-urban	29.2	28.3	52.4
	Rural-rural	14.1	13.9	52.8
	Urban-rural	14.0	13.7	52.7
	Total number of migrants	1 886	2 147	53.2

TABLE 13 (continued)

Country, census year and data type	Migration stream	Male	Female	Percentage female
		(percentage)		
Thailand, 1980				
Residence in 1975	Rural-urban	13.6	17.3	53.7
	Urban-urban	17.1	20.0	51.6
	Rural-rural	58.6	53.1	45.3
	Urban-rural	10.6	9.7	45.5
	Total number of migrants	1 430	1 308	47.8
C. Latin America				
Brazil, 1970				
Place of birth				
Intrastate	Rural-urban	17.5	18.4	51.4
	Urban-urban	48.6	52.2	51.9
	Rural-rural	27.4	23.9	46.7
	Urban-rural	6.6	5.5	45.8
	Total number of migrants	15 105	15 155	50.1
Interstate	Rural-urban	17.1	17.8	49.9
	Urban-urban	48.6	52.4	50.7
	Rural-rural	28.2	24.6	45.4
	Urban-rural	6.2	5.1	43.9
	Total number of migrants	7 392	7 035	48.8
Honduras, 1983				
Residence in 1978	Rural-urban	20.9	29.8	65.3
	Urban-urban	29.3	34	60.5
	Rural-rural	33.5	24.1	48.7
	Urban-rural	16.3	12.1	49.5
	Total number of migrants	1	2	56.9

Sources: Brazil, *VIII Recenseamento Geral do Brasil, 1970*, National Series, No. 1 (Rio de Janeiro, Fundação Instituto Brasileiro de Geografia e Estatística, 1973); Egypt, *1976 Population and Housing Census: Fertility and Internal Migration and Movement of Workers and Students*, vol. 2, *Total Republic* (Cairo, Central Agency for Public Mobilisation and Statistics, n.d.); Elizabeth U. Eviota and Peter C. Smith, "The migration of women in the Philippines"; Siew-Ean Khoo and Peter Pirie, "Female rural-to-urban migration in Peninsular Malaysia"; Nasra M. Shah, "The female migrant in Pakistan"; and Sawon Hong, "Urban migrant women in the Republic of Korea", all in *Women in the Cities of Asia: Migration and Urban Adaptation*, James T. Fawcett, Siew-Ean Khoo and Peter C. Smith, eds. (Boulder, Colorado, Westview Press, 1984); Honduras, *Encuesta Demográfica Nacional de Honduras (EDENH II 1983)*, vol. 3; CELADE Series A, No. 1047/III (San José, Costa Rica, Centro Latinoamericano de Demografía, 1986); India, *Census of India, 1981: Report and Tables Based on 5 Per Cent Sample Data*, Series 1, part II, special (New Delhi, Ministry of Home Affairs, Registrar General; and Census Commissioner of India, 1985)); Thailand, *1980 Population and Housing Census; Subject Report No. 2: Migration* (Bangkok, Office of the Prime Minister, National Statistical Office, 1984).

migrants: some 9 per cent for each sex in Malaysia; 18 per cent among males and 16 per cent among females in Pakistan; and 14 and 17 per cent, respectively, in Thailand. In India, rural-urban migration was considerably more common for men than for women (involving 28 per cent of all male migrants and only 12 per cent of all female migrants in 1981), but women still outnumbered men slightly in the rural-urban flow. Only in the Philippines and in the Republic of Korea was rural-urban migration the dominant type for both sexes; and in both cases, women outnumbered men among rural-urban migrants.

The relative importance of urban-urban migration in certain countries must be noted. In Egypt, it involved some 57 per cent of all male migrants and 54 per cent of females. In Brazil, as stated above, it also accounted for nearly half of all migrants. In Pakistan, almost 40 per cent of those migrating between 1965 and 1973 moved from one urban area to another urban area, and in Honduras, urban-urban migration was dominant among migrant women (34 per cent of them engaged in that type of movement) and slightly less so among migrant men (29 per cent).

Rural-rural flows were dominant not only in India but also in Malaysia and Thailand. In addition, they constituted the second largest flow in several countries, including Brazil, Honduras, Pakistan and the Philippines (in terms of lifetime migrants). Urban-rural flows generally accounted for the lowest share of all migrants; in Malaysia, however, this type of flow was the second most important and involved about one third of all migrants.

In terms of the relative weight of women in the different types of flows, the situation is equally varied. In Brazil, Honduras, the Philippines and Thailand, women tended to be more numerous than men in flows converging to urban areas and to be less numerous in those converging to rural areas. In Egypt and India, women outnumbered men by considerable margins in rural-rural flows, but only in India did those flows constitute a relatively high proportion of all migrants. In Malaysia and Pakistan, women accounted for a larger proportion of rural-rural flows than for those of other types, but they were generally less numerous than men in all types of migration. Lastly, in the Republic of Korea, where changes over time in the relative participation of women in migration flows can be assessed, a decline occurred in the proportion of female migrants of each type between 1961-1966 and 1965-1970, followed by a rise from 1965-1970 to 1970-1975. It is noteworthy, however, that women consistently outnumbered men among all migrants during the three periods considered.

The implications of this analysis for the question posed earlier are clear: since rural-urban migration often accounts for a relatively small proportion of all migration in a country and since its distribution by sex may not be representative of migration flows in general, it is not appropriate to assume that findings pertaining to rural-urban migration are applicable to all migration flows. Given the relative importance of rural-rural or urban-urban migration in many countries and the differential participation of women in those flows, more attention should be devoted to them so as to obtain a more balanced assessment of the role of women in internal migration in developing countries.

B. Temporal criteria

Traditionally, migration has been conceptualized as involving a "permanent" change of residence. The limitations of such a conceptualization are well known (Bedford, 1981; Standing, 1984a; Zlotnik, 1987), and there have accordingly been many calls for a relaxation of the temporal criteria used to distinguish migration from other types of movements. In particular, increasing attention is being paid to temporary movements, such as those which Zelinsky (1971) grouped under the label "circulation", namely, movements having in common the lack of any declared intention of permanent or long-lasting change of residence.

No matter what time-limits are used to distinguish the movements of interest from other forms of mobility, there are intrinsic difficulties in making the transition from the conceptual to the operational because existing data-collection techniques are hard-pressed to yield information that conforms strictly with the elusive concepts being pursued. Thus, lacking a continuous observation system that records all movements as they occur and allows the analyst to select those spanning any duration of interest, information must usually be gathered on a retrospective basis, with all the recall problems that such a procedure entails.

In particular, the criteria most commonly used by censuses to identify migrants effectively eliminate certain categories of movers from the statistical record. That is the case when migrants are considered to be persons whose place of residence at the time of the census is different from their residence at a certain point in the past. Such an approach disregards all migrants who moved from A to B and back to A during the intervening period, as well as those who moved from A to B and died before enumeration. Similarly, when censuses use a *de jure* approach to enumerate the population, persons are allocated to their "usual place of residence" irrespective of their place of enumeration, and thus most of the persons that could be said to engage in circulation are not reflected in the statistics. With regard to female migration, the relevant question is whether the distribution by sex and other characteristics of the unrecorded migrants are different from those of the migrants accounted for by the data. Unfortunately, it is not possible to provide a general answer to this question.

A related issue, however, is the claim that women tend to participate less than men in short-term migration and, particularly, in circulation (Hugo, 1993; Standing, 1984b). When short-term migration is interpreted to encompass changes of residence of a shorter than usual duration, possibly no longer than a year, some evidence can be brought to bear on the issue. As concerns circulation, however, the problem of ascertaining the relative participation of women in it is compounded by the fact that there is as yet no consensus about how to define circulation and much less about how to measure it. Bedford (1981) documents the use of a bewildering array of definitions to distinguish circulation from other types of mobility. Thus, circulation has been considered to be: *(a)* an absence from the village for up to 12 months; *(b)* an absence involving sleeping at destination for continuous periods of up to six months; *(c)* a movement across the *duhuk* boundary for at least one day but less than one year; *(d)* a move involving an absence of more than a month, where the intention of the mover is to return to live in the village at some stage; or even *(e)* a movement whereby a migrant returns to his village of origin after a period in residence elsewhere and has no plans for subsequent movement (a definition that matches closely that of "return" migration).

Note that some of these definitions incorporate elements that attach more than temporal connotations to the term "circulation". Thus, mention of "the village" indicates that only rural origins are considered. Similarly, although these definitions do not illustrate the point, "circulation" is often used to mean implicitly "labour circulation", that is, the temporary migration of workers. Indeed, *Labour Circulation and the Labour Process* is the title of a book edited by Standing (1984b) which contains scarcely any discussion of female migration. One could even argue that, without those types of connotations, tourists could be considered the archetypal "circulators" and that is plainly not the intention of migration researchers. Yet, the exclusion of movements by persons that have no ostensible economic reason for moving is likely to lead to the selective exclusion of women. These observations suggest that conceptual fuzziness and measurement biases need to be investigated further as possible causes of the apparent low participation of women in circulation. There is some evidence that when only strictly temporal criteria are used to define circulation, the participation of women in it is not much lower than that of men. Thus, in a study of migration from a village in Central Java, short-term circular migration is defined as "the process of migrating regularly to urban places for a period of one to three months or longer, and then returning to the village" (Hetler, 1989, p. 73); and it was found that among the approximately 550 circular migrants recorded, 49 per cent were women.

With regard to short-term movements of a less transitory nature, census data provide some indication of their extent and their composition by sex. Table 14 presents data on migrants by duration of stay at their usual place of residence. In most of the censuses considered, migrants were identified as persons whose place of birth was different from their place of residence at the time of enumeration and their duration of stay at the latter was recorded. Migrants were then classified by duration of residence in comparable groups, namely, less than one year, from one to four years, from five to nine and 10 or more. Because most censuses were carried out on a *de jure* basis, movements of a transitory nature are not reflected in the data presented. Moreover, since many "recent" migrants (those whose duration of stay was less than a year at the time of enumeration) would likely become long-term migrants as time elapsed, they cannot be considered representative of short-term migrants. Despite these deficiencies in coverage, however, it is still useful to consider the differential composition of migrants by sex in the different duration categories.

The data presented in table 14 show that, excluding the Congo in 1974, Panama in 1980 and Venezuela in 1981, the proportion of women among recent migrants is indeed lower than that among migrants reporting longer durations of stay in eight countries. In the four Latin American countries considered, however, the difference between the highest proportion of women in other duration categories and that among recent migrants is fairly small (amounting to at most 2.4 percentage points in Panama). A similar pattern is noticeable in Cameroon, the Congo (1984) and the Libyan Arab

TABLE 14. MIGRANTS BY SEX AND DURATION OF STAY AT PLACE OF CURRENT RESIDENCE RECORDED BY CENSUSES OF SELECTED DEVELOPING COUNTRIES
(*Number of migrants in thousands*)

Country, census year and current residence	Duration of residence (years)	Male	Female	Both sexes	Percentage female
		(percentage)			

A. Africa

Country, census year and current residence	Duration of residence (years)	Male	Female	Both sexes	Percentage female
Cameroon, 1976 All country	Less than 1	13.4	12.6	13.0	45.7
	1-4	36.6	36.2	36.4	47.0
	5-9	19.7	20.2	19.9	47.8
	10 or more	30.2	31.0	30.6	47.9
	Number of migrants	1 010	906	1 916	47.3
	Migrants as percentage of total	28.9	24.9	26.9	-
Congo, 1974 All country	Less than 1	25.0	26.4	25.7	50.1
	1-4	8.1	8.8	8.4	50.9
	5-9	18.8	19.1	19.0	49.1
	10 or more	38.9	34.9	36.9	46.0
	Number of migrants	133	126	259	48.7
	Migrants as percentage of total	21.0	18.4	19.7	-
Congo, 1984 All country	Less than 1	11.9	11.6	11.8	49.1
	1-4	33.3	32.6	33.0	49.3
	5-9	17.1	17.6	17.3	50.6
	10 or more	32.4	32.7	32.5	50.2
	Number of migrants	331	329	660	49.9
	Migrants as percentage of total	37.7	35.5	36.5	-
Egypt, 1976 All country	Less than 1	5.5	4.7	5.1	46.1
	1-4	28.1	28.0	28.0	49.6
	5-9	16.7	17.6	17.2	51.1
	10 or more	49.7	49.7	49.7	49.8
	Number of migrants	2 571	2 548	5 119	49.8
	Migrants as percentage of total	13.8	14.2	14.0	-
Egypt, 1976 Urban	Less than 1	5.6	5.0	5.3	44.9
	1-4	27.8	28.7	28.2	48.5
	5-9	15.9	17.3	16.5	49.7
	10 or more	50.7	49.0	49.9	46.7
	Number of migrants	2 178	1 980	4 158	47.6
	Migrants as percentage of total	26.7	25.5	26.1	-
Egypt, 1976 Rural	Less than 1	4.9	3.8	4.3	52.5
	1-4	29.9	25.2	27.1	54.9
	5-9	21.3	18.8	19.8	56.1
	10 or more	43.8	52.2	48.8	63.2
	Number of migrants	393	568	962	59.1
	Migrants as percentage of total	3.8	5.6	4.7	-

TABLE 14 (continued)

Country, census year and current residence	Duration of residence (years)	Male	Female	Both sexes	Percentage female
		(percentage)			
Libyan Arab Jamahiriya, 1973					
All country	Less than 1	6.7	6.7	6.7	47.8
	1-4	30.9	32.0	31.4	48.9
	5-9	24.4	24.9	24.6	48.6
	10 or more	38.0	36.4	37.2	47.0
	Number of migrants	387	358	745	48.0
	Migrants as percentage of total	36.6	36.0	36.3	-

B. *Asia*

Bangladesh, 1974					
All country	Less than 1	13.5	12.0	12.8	42.9
	1-4	28.2	24.5	26.5	42.4
	5-9	17.5	17.3	17.4	45.5
	10 or more	40.9	46.2	43.3	48.8
	Number of migrants	2 828	2 389	5 218	45.8
	Migrants as percentage of total	7.6	6.9	7.3	-
Urban	Less than 1	11.9	11.0	11.5	38.3
	1-4	34.0	32.6	33.4	39.2
	5-9	17.9	18.7	18.2	41.3
	10 or more	36.2	37.7	36.8	41.2
	Number of migrants	1 794	1 207	3 001	40.2
	Migrants as percentage of total	50.7	44.1	47.8	-
Rural	Less than 1	16.2	13.0	14.5	47.9
	1-4	18.1	16.3	17.1	50.7
	5-9	16.8	15.9	16.3	51.9
	10 or more	48.9	54.8	52.0	56.2
	Number of migrants	1 034	1 182	2 217	53.3
	Migrants as percentage of total	3.1	3.7	3.4	-
India, 1981					
All country	Less than 1	8.5	3.7	5.1	50.7
	1-4	26.0	17.0	19.7	60.8
	5-9	16.7	14.8	15.4	67.8
	10 or more	42.0	61.1	55.4	77.5
	Number of migrants	59 671	141 401	201 072	70.3
	Migrants as percentage of total	17.3	44.0	30.2	-
Urban	Less than 1	6.1	4.8	5.4	45.8
	1-4	26.9	23.9	25.4	48.8
	5-9	17.8	18.0	17.9	52.0
	10 or more	44.5	13.9	20.3	54.2
	Number of migrants	27 722	29 738	57 459	51.8
	Migrants as percentage of total	33.1	40.3	36.4	-

TABLE 14 (continued)

Country, census year and current residence	Duration of residence (years)	Male	Female	Both sexes	Percentage female
		(percentage)			
Rural	Less than 1	10.6	3.4	5.0	52.8
	1-4	25.1	15.2	17.4	67.8
	5-9	15.7	14.0	14.4	75.7
	10 or more	46.7	69.3	64.6	84.9
	Number of migrants	31 949	111 664	143 613	77.8
	Migrants as percentage of total	12.3	45.1	28.3	-
Nepal, 1981 All country	Less than 1	2.5	2.1	2.3	46.9
	1-5	33.1	30.1	31.5	49.6
	6-11	22.8	21.6	22.2	50.7
	10 or more	41.5	46.2	44.0	54.7
	Number of migrants	611	662	1 272	52.0
	Migrants as percentage of total	8.0	9.2	8.6	-

C. *Latin America and the Caribbean*

Country, census year and current residence	Duration of residence (years)	Male	Female	Both sexes	Percentage female
Brazil, 1970 Interdistrict All country	Less than 1	11.9	11.5	11.7	49.2
	1-4	23.9	23.6	23.8	49.7
	5-10	23.3	23.3	23.3	50.1
	11 or more	40.8	41.6	41.2	50.6
	Number of migrants	15 110	15 160	30 270	50.1
	Migrants as percentage of total	32.6	32.4	32.5	-
Urban	Less than 1	11.1	10.9	11.0	51.3
	1-4	22.6	22.3	22.5	51.4
	5-10	22.7	22.6	22.6	51.6
	11 or more	43.6	44.2	43.9	52.1
	Number of migrants	9 976	10 697	20 673	51.7
	Migrants as percentage of total	39.5	39.8	39.7	-
Rural	Less than 1	13.4	12.9	13.2	45.4
	1-4	26.5	26.6	26.5	46.6
	5-10	24.6	25.0	24.8	47.0
	11 or more	35.5	35.5	35.5	46.5
	Number of migrants	5 135	4 463	9 598	46.5
	Migrants as percentage of total	24.3	22.4	23.4	-
Interstate All country	Less than 1	7.8	7.7	7.7	48.2
	1-4	17.7	17.9	17.8	49.0
	5-10	21.9	22.3	22.1	49.2
	11 or more	52.5	52.1	52.3	48.6
	Number of migrants	7 395	7 039	14 434	48.8
	Migrants as percentage of total	16.0	15.0	15.5	-
Urban	Less than 1	8.0	7.9	8.0	50.2
	1-4	17.5	17.7	17.6	50.7
	5-10	20.6	21.1	20.8	51.0
	11 or more	53.8	53.3	53.5	50.2
	Number of migrants	4 853	4 946	9 799	50.5
	Migrants as percentage of total	19.2	18.4	18.8	-

TABLE 14 (continued)

Country, census year and current residence	Duration of residence (years)	Male	Female	Both sexes	Percentage female
		(percentage)			
Rural	Less than 1	7.4	7.0	7.2	43.6
	1-4	18.2	18.5	18.3	45.6
	5-10	24.4	25.2	24.8	46.0
	11 or more	50.0	49.2	49.7	44.8
	Number of migrants	2 543	2 093	4 635	45.1
	Migrants as percentage of total	12.0	10.5	11.3	-
Panama, 1980					
All country	Less than 1	9.6	9.7	9.7	52.0
	1-4	13.9	13.5	13.7	51.0
	5-9	11.7	11.3	11.5	50.8
	10 or more	16.9	15.5	16.2	49.6
	Number of migrants	158	170	328	51.7
	Migrants as percentage of total	19.7	21.5	20.6	-
Trinidad and Tobago, 1980					
All country	Less than 1	—	—	—	—
	0-4	38.9	38.5	38.7	53.5
	5-9	23.3	22.1	22.6	52.3
	10 or more	36.3	38.0	37.2	54.9
	Number of migrants	123	143	266	53.7
	Migrants as percentage of total	24.9	28.8	26.8	-
Venezuela, 1981					
All country	Less than 1	10.4	10.6	10.5	51.0
	1-4	25.4	24.8	25.1	49.9
	5-9	18.7	19.1	18.9	50.9
	10 or more	31.6	32.8	32.2	51.4
	Number of migrants	3 887	3 957	7 844	50.4
	Migrants as percentage of total	53.5	54.5	54.0	-

Sources: Bangladesh, *Population Census of Bangladesh, 1974: National Volume, Report and Tables*, (Dacca, Bangladesh Bureau of Statistics, 1977); Brazil, *VIII Recenseamento Geral do Brasil, 1970,* National Series, No. 1 (Rio de Janeiro, Fundação Instituto Brasileiro de Geografia e Estatística, 1973); Cameroon, *Recensement général de la population et de l'habitat d'avril 1976*, vol. II, *Analyse*; tome 5, *Migrations internes* (Yaoundé, Bureau central du recensement, n.d.); Congo, *Recensement général de la population du Congo, 1974*, vol. IV, *Tableaux statistiques détaillés* (Brazzaville, Direction des statistiques démographiques et sociales, 1978); Congo, *Recensement général de la population et de l'habitat de 1984*, vol. 3, *Résultats définitifs;* tome I, *Ensemble du pays* (Brazzaville, Bureau central du recensement, 1987); Egypt, *1976 Population and Housing Census: Fertility and Internal Migration and Movement of Workers and Students*, vol. 2, *Total Republic* (Cairo, Central Agency for Public Mobilisation and Statistics, n.d.); India, *Census of India, 1981: Report and Tables Based on 5 Per Cent Sample Data,* Series 1, part II, special (New Delhi, Ministry of Home Affairs, Registrar General; and Census Commissioner of India, 1985); Libyan Arab Jamahiriya, *1973 Population Census: Final All Country Results* (Tripoli, Census and Statistics Department, 1979); Nepal, *Population Monograph of Nepal* (Kathmandu, National Planning Commission Secretariat, Central Bureau of Statistics, 1987); Panama, *Censos Nacionales de 1980: Octavo Censo de Población y Cuarto Censo de Vivienda,* vol. V, *Compendio general de población* (Panama, Dirección de Estadística y Censo, n.d.); Trinidad and Tobago, *Population and Housing Census, 1980*, vol. 4, *Internal Migration* (Port-of-Spain, Central Statistical Office, 1984); Venezuela, *XI Censo General de Población y Vivienda (20 de octubre de 1981): Total nacional* (Caracas, Oficina Central de Estadística e Informática, 1985).

Jamahiriya, implying that the selectivity of recent migration with respect to sex is relatively weak. In contrast, in Bangladesh, Egypt and Nepal, such selectivity is considerably more pronounced, so that the proportion of women among recent migrants is at least 5.0 percentage points lower than that in the duration group with the highest proportion of women. India, once more, displays the most extreme differences, with 51 per cent of recent migrants being women, compared with 78 per cent among migrants reporting durations of 10 years or more. In India, as in Bangladesh and Egypt, the sex selectivity of migration by duration of residence is more marked in rural than in urban areas.

Among the exceptions cited above, the unusual pattern of sex selectivity by duration observed in Panama is likely to result from poor reporting, as nearly 49 per cent of all migrants failed to state a duration of stay. The same may be true for the Congo in 1974 where, although the level of non-response was only a modest 10 per cent, there are doubts about the accuracy of the published data. Given these data problems, the tendency for women to be less well represented among recent migrants than among those having greater durations of stay may be more general than the data presented in table 14 suggest. If that is the case and one can assume that the propensity for migrants to remain at destination has remained constant over time, it would mean that women tend indeed to constitute a smaller proportion of short-term migrants than of those staying longer periods at destination.

The data given in table 14 suggest that, by characterizing migrants in terms of two criteria simultaneously, important effects on sex selectivity may be observed. Thus, in Brazil, women constitute a larger proportion of recent migrants among those crossing interdistrict boundaries (49 per cent) than among those moving between states (48 per cent). In addition, migrants with lower durations of stay tend to have greater weight among interdistrict than among interstate migrants. That is, among migrants moving over shorter distances, those with shorter durations of stay in the areas of destination are more common, and women tend to be better represented among the latter.

Similar interactions are observed between duration of stay and the rural versus urban character of the place of destination. Thus, in Bangladesh, Egypt and India, women accounted for higher proportions of recent migrants resident in rural areas than among those resident in urban areas. In Brazil, however, the reverse was true. Thus, the sex selectivity of short-term migration appears to be linked both to the geographical setting and to the temporal characteristics of migration.

This section concludes with the consideration of a set of data that has the potential to reflect better the variety of human mobility in terms of temporal characteristics. The data were obtained through a dual-record system operating in the rural areas of Burundi during the period 1970-1971 (Burundi, 1974). In such a system of data collection, the registration subsystem involves the continuous recording of demographic events: births; deaths; changes in marital status; and population movements. The survey in Burundi produced information on both out-migrants and in-migrants (persons intending to change their place of residence) and on absent residents and temporary visitors (*personnes de passage*). Among out-migrants and in-migrants, women outnumbered men almost two to one (66 per cent of all emigrants and 68 per cent of immigrants were women). Among absent residents and temporary visitors, however, men predominated (accounting for 79 per cent of the former and 67 per cent of the latter). Although, at first sight, the criteria used to determine migration status appeared to be gender-neutral, being based on residence status and on the actual presence or absence of a person from the survey area, careful analysis of the survey methodology showed that not all moves were treated equally. Thus, whereas women moving to get married were automatically considered out-migrants or in-migrants irrespective of their intended or even actual length of stay away from their village of origin, men moving to engage in seasonal work were not. Such measurement biases are probably more common than is recognized (the description of survey methodologies is often vague or confusing about those and other issues) and they derive from the general, if tacit, assumption that the reasons for a move are important in distinguishing migration from other types of mobility. The relevance of such criteria for the measurement of female migration is explored next.

C. REASONS FOR MOVING

The reasons for moving have generally figured prominently among the criteria used to distinguish types of geographical mobility. In developing typologies of mobility, researchers have proposed reasons ranging from the general and the abstract to those that can be ascertained on the basis of fairly tangible evidence. Thus, Petersen (1958) discusses "ecological push", "higher aspirations" and "social momentum" as reasons impelling different types of movements. Today, one is more likely to find such terms as "labour migration", "marriage migration" or "associational migration" to indicate that the reasons for moving are related to engaging in an economic activity, getting married or accompanying someone else. Because the latter are more amenable to measurement, they are the main topic of the following discussion. However, the relevance for the study of female migration of some elements of the more abstract typologies proposed is also worth noting.

A crucial distinction with regard to the reasons for migration is between the forced and the voluntary nature of the movement. Forced migration has been common throughout history and, at least in the international arena, currently remains an important component of population mobility (witness the high and growing number of refugees worldwide). Within countries, forced movements of people have occurred as a result of civil war, political strife, environmental deterioration or natural disasters. The term "displaced persons" is generally used to refer to persons that have been forced to leave their usual place of residence but have remained within the borders of their own country. There are no data sources providing a comprehensive assessment of the number of displaced persons worldwide. Definitional problems coupled with the massive, sudden and often short-term nature of the movements involved make their adequate quantification difficult. Yet, the number of displaced persons is probably at least as high as the number of refugees (some 17 million persons in early 1989, according to United Nations, 1992), and women are likely to account for a higher proportion of those displaced than men, particularly in situations of civil conflict where adult men are involved in the fighting.

Another notion colouring certain typologies is that the social forces leading to migration may be just as important as the economic factors. Indeed, "marriage migration" and "family migration" are two broad categories identifiable in terms of social linkages between people. At a more general level, it has been observed that in some societies migration has become an established pattern of behaviour, so much so that individuals are expected to migrate at certain stages of their life. Petersen (1958) called "social momentum" the forces giving rise to migration in those circumstances. More recently, social networks have been identified as the mechanism that, by facilitating migration, helps maintain the momentum of migration streams (Gurak and Caces, 1992). It is likely that men and women play different roles in using and maintaining the social networks that facilitate migration. This topic, however, remains largely to be explored.

With regard to the "proximate" reasons for movement most commonly used to identify migrants, those based on economic activity are usually underscored. Indeed, as mentioned earlier in discussing circulation, movements of short duration are often ignored unless related to economic activity. Thus, in gathering statistics about commuters to selected cities, the Republic of Korea focused only on persons aged 12 or over moving daily to and from a city to work or study there (Republic of Korea, 1982). Consequently, women constituted only 33 per cent of the 4.8 million persons classified as commuters to Seoul in 1980. Given the low labour force participation rates among women recorded by most data sources in the developing world, the use of such criteria to identify migrants is likely to lead to a gross underrepresentation of the mobility of women.

When focusing on female mobility *per se*, the reasons explored or imputed as giving rise to female migration are often presumed to be only those related to family ties. Mention has already been made of such migrant categories as marriage migration, family migration and associational migration. As with other commonly used terms, the meaning of each is vague. Thus, marriage migration can be interpreted to mean anything from moving in order to contract a planned marriage to moving in search of a potential husband or even moving away from a husband after a marriage has been dissolved. Family migration may encompass all persons moving simultaneously as a family group, only the "dependent" family members moving simultaneously with the family head, only the "dependent" family members moving to join the family head who migrated earlier or only women and children moving to join relatives. Associational migration is a catch-all term that has only one constant attribute: it is usually applied only to women. Men are often presumed automatically not to move in "association", even if they do so in the company of family members. Also in the case of women, the opposite of associational migration is usually described as "individual" migration, a term that is increasingly acquiring economic connotations. Thus, in certain contexts, the growing importance of female migration is predicated on the basis of an increasing number of women moving "individually" to work at the places of destination.

Despite evidence to the contrary, marriage has seldom been considered an "economic" strategy. Thadani and Todaro, in an effort to model the migration of women in terms of rational (i.e., economic) choices, consider explicitly the existence of "mobility marriage", noting that "the importance of marriage as a means of upward social mobility for women, in both developed and developing societies, has been generally acknowledged" (1984, p. 47). They go on to identify four variants of female migration that are relevant for understanding its dynamics, namely: *(a)* married women moving in search of urban employment and induced to migrate by perceived urban/rural differentials; *(b)* unmarried women in search of urban employment and induced to migrate for economic or marital reasons; *(c)* unmarried women induced to migrate solely for marriage reasons; and *(d)* married women engaged in associational migration with no thought of employment. Note that Thadani and Todaro focus only on rural-urban migration and that they posit a clear-cut dichotomy between women having economic motivations for migration and those having only social reasons to move. Although it is helpful to recognize explicitly that women may have the two types of motivations and often have them simultaneously, the real world is unlikely to arrange itself into the clear-cut categories that those authors suggest.

Next to be considered is some evidence on the reasons reported for the migration of men and women. Once more, the data have been obtained from censuses investigating in relatively rough ways the main reasons for migration (see table 15). At least four different types of reasons have been distinguished in each case—those related to employment, to education, to movement of the family and to marriage. In cases where a census gathered information on a more detailed set of reasons, they were combined to produce, as far as possible, categories comparable to those of other countries. The term "marriage-related" was used to indicate that the census concerned had recorded separately whether migration had taken place at the time of marriage or because of its dissolution.

Although the number of countries considered is small, it is clear that in all of them a majority of women are reported to migrate because their family moved or because of marriage-related reasons. It is also evident that only a relatively small proportion of women are reported to have moved because of employment-related reasons. Yet, there is considerable variation between countries. Thus, whereas in India, 73 per cent of women moved because of marriage and fewer than 2 per cent did so for employment considerations, in Thailand, only 9 per cent of women migrated because of marriage and 24 per cent because of employment. In Egypt, where the proportion of women moving for employment reasons was also reported to be low (fewer than 5 per cent), women were more likely to migrate with their families than because of marriage. That is the case also in Malaysia and Thailand. In Burundi, 46 per cent of the out-migrant women recorded by a dual-record system in 1970-1971 reported moving for marriage-related reasons (29 per cent to get married, 17 per cent because of separation), whereas 39 per cent did so to accompany the head of the family (Burundi, 1974).

These observations confirm the general view that the migration of women is more likely to be reported as deriving from social rather than economic reasons. It is less well recognized, however, that the migration of a very significant proportion of men is also attributed to social reasons, mainly to accompany family members. Thus, in Egypt, among the population aged 10 or over, over 34 per cent of males moved as part of the family or for marriage-related reasons. In India, one in every three male migrants moved for those reasons, and in Malaysia and among the population aged 5 or over in Thailand, the equivalent proportion reached 38 per cent. In the survey in Burundi cited above, nearly half of all male out-migrants (48 per cent) moved to accompany the head of the family or because of marital separation (Burundi, 1974). In fact, in most of the

TABLE 15. MIGRANTS BY SEX AND REASON FOR MIGRATION, SELECTED DEVELOPING COUNTRIES
(*Number of migrants in thousands*)

Country, census year and data type	Reason for migrating	Male (percentage)	Female (percentage)	Percentage female
	A. Africa			
Egypt, 1976				
Aged 10 or over	Employment	49.8	4.5	8.2
	Education	5.9	2.1	26.4
	Family moved	32.1	63.6	66.3
	Marriage-related	2.3	23.9	91.3
	Other	9.8	5.8	37.1
	Total number of migrants	2 359	2 345	49.9
	B. Asia			
India, 1981				
Rural-rural	Employment	19.5	1.1	18.0
	Education	4.2	0.4	28.0
	Family moved	33.7	8.6	49.2
	Marriage	5.5	81.7	98.3
	Other	37.1	8.1	45.1
	Total number of migrants	27 468	103 936	79.1
Urban-rural	Employment	27.0	3.3	17.6
	Education	3.2	1.0	35.2
	Family moved	31.9	21.2	53.4
	Marriage	2.2	59.3	97.9
	Other	35.7	15.1	42.2
	Total number of migrants	4 481	7 728	63.3
Urban-urban	Employment	41.1	4.5	10.9
	Education	5.2	2.2	32.4
	Family moved	31.5	35.9	56.2
	Marriage	1.0	43.6	98.0
	Other	21.2	13.9	42.5
	Total number of migrants	11 278	12 696	53.0
Rural-urban	Employment	47.5	4.2	8.4
	Education	8.1	2.6	24.9
	Family moved	23.5	29.3	56.3
	Marriage	1.2	51.5	97.9
	Other	19.7	12.4	39.5
	Total number of migrants	16 443	17 042	50.9
Total	Employment	31.9	1.9	12.5
	Education	5.4	0.9	28.0
	Family moved	30.3	14.3	52.7
	Marriage	3.2	73.4	98.2
	Other	29.3	9.6	43.6
	Total number of migrants	59 921	141 785	70.3
Malaysia, 1980	Employment	42.2	13.3	24.2
	Education	5.0	3.8	43.5
	Family moved	32.6	46.5	59.1
	Marriage	4.9	23.4	82.7
	Other	15.3	13.0	46.2
	Total number of migrants	21	21	50.3

TABLE 15 (continued)

Country, census year and data type	Reason for migrating	Male	Female	Percentage female
		(percentage)		
Nepal, 1981	Employment	59.1	31.5	36.7
	Education	4.0	1.6	30.4
	Marriage-related	1.0	30.3	97.0
	Other	36.0	36.6	52.4
	Total number of migrants	611	662	52.0
Thailand, 1980 Aged 5 or over	Employment	40.1	23.8	35.1
	Education	5.1	5.8	50.9
	Family moved	26.9	50.7	63.3
	Marriage-related	11.5	8.8	41.2
	Return home	2.9	2.5	44.8
	Other	13.5	8.4	36.1
	Total number of migrants	1 540	1 408	47.7

Sources: Egypt, *1976 Population and Housing Census: Fertility and Internal Migration and Movement of Workers and Students*, vol. 2, *Total Republic* (Cairo, Central Agency for Public Mobilisation and Statistics, n.d.); India, *Census of India, 1981: Report and Tables Based on 5 Per Cent Sample Data*, Series 1, part II, special (New Delhi, Ministry of Home Affairs, Registrar General; and Census Commissioner of India, 1985); Malaysia, *General Report of the Population Census, 1980*, vol. 1 (Kuala Lumpur, Commissioner of Census, 1983); Nepal, *Population Monograph of Nepal* (Kathmandu, National Planning Commission Secretariat, Central Bureau of Statistics, 1987); Thailand, *1980 Population and Housing Census; Subject Report 2: Migration* (Bangkok, Office the Prime Minister, National Statistical Office, 1984).

countries considered, there were almost as many men engaging in "associational" migration as those reporting economic reasons for moving.

The distribution of the migration categories by sex indicates that among migrants moving as part of a family, women consistently outnumbered men, often by considerable margins. The marriage-related category was generally constituted almost exclusively of women, except in Thailand, where men outnumbered women. Among migrants reported as moving for employment reasons, women accounted for a relatively small proportion in Egypt and India (slightly over 8 per cent), for a quarter of those recorded in Malaysia and for over a third of those recorded in Nepal and Thailand. That is, the relative participation of women in economically motivated migration is substantial in a number of countries.

The case of India, where the majority of female migrants reportedly move in order to contract marriage and only a tiny minority for employment-related reasons, again merits special consideration. The data classified separately by type of move (rural-rural, rural-urban etc.) show striking differences by type of flow. Among rural-rural migrants, which constituted nearly 80 per cent of all female migrants in 1981, women moving for marriage reasons accounted for 82 per cent. The equivalent proportions in urban-rural and rural-urban flows were 59 and 51 per cent, respectively. Only in urban-urban flows did marriage-related migration among women involve fewer than half of the female migrants recorded. Marriage is therefore a powerful institution for the redistribution of women over the territory of India, particularly within rural areas. Through the dowry system, it also involves the spatial redistribution of wealth. Given that newly-wed wives have to move into the husband's home, often to perform household duties under the supervision of the mother-in-law, marriage can also be thought in this case as a means of redistributing both the productive and the reproductive capacities of women. By ensuring that women shall change environments at a fairly early age, in a context of maximum subordination, village exogamy and patrilocal residence are mechanisms that effectively perpetuate the dependent status of women in India. Migration is a key element of this system; yet, its consequences for women have not received the attention they deserve.

Data on the reasons for migration have also been gathered by a number of migration surveys which are rarely representative of entire countries. Some surveys have found that for particular regions within a country, economic reasons for female migration tend to be cited more often than the data presented above suggest. Thus, the Survey of Migration to Bangkok Metropolis carried out in 1981 indicates that 59 per cent of female migrants moved in order to change jobs or to look for work during the agricultural slack season. The equivalent proportion among male migrants was only slightly higher: 64 per cent (Soonthorndhada, 1983). Yet, a comparison of these data with the Thai census results presented in table 14 indicates that migration to Bangkok Metropolis represents a special case within Thailand.

Another example of high levels of female migration motivated for job-related reasons is provided by the results of a survey carried out in areas of origin located in the Sierra region of Ecuador. Respondents were requested to provide information about household members who had out-migrated during the five years preceding the interview. They were also requested to provide reasons for the migration of those who had left. They reported that 72 per cent of male out-migrants and 52 per cent of female out-migrants had left because there were not enough jobs or because incomes were insufficient in the area of origin (Bilsborrow and Fuller, 1988). The survey methodology, however, led to an underrepresentation of entire migrant families among out-migrants and was therefore likely to underestimate true levels of associational migration.

Although surveys are better able than censuses to elicit reliable answers to questions on the reasons for migration, they do not necessarily improve on census results. Thus, in a survey carried out in the town of Salem in Tamil Nadu, India, where 17 per cent of the workforce consisted of women, many of whom were migrants, 93.2 per cent of female migrants reported that they had moved for marriage-related or associational reasons (Nangia and Samuel, 1983). A high proportion of migrant men also cited associational or marriage-related reasons for migration (37 per cent). These results suggest that, especially in societies where there are still normative barriers to women's work outside the home, it is unlikely that respondents of either sex may declare economic or job-related reasons for the migration of women.

D. MIGRATION AND THE LIFE CYCLE

As previously mentioned, in some societies migration is a pattern of behaviour expected of persons at a certain stage of the life cycle. That is generally so for female migration and first marriage in India, for the movement of teenagers to pursue higher education away from home in the United States of America, and for migration after retirement in many parts of the world. Although the relation between certain migrant types and specific stages of the life cycle has sometimes been considered, it has not received the systematic attention it deserves. In the case of female migration in particular, a useful way of systematizing the variety of possible conceptualizations that underlie a term like "family migration" or "associational migration" is to focus on the stages of the life cycle of migrants in relation to that of their immediate families (which may or may not migrate). Thus, women may move as children either simultaneously with close family members, to join close family members or to be fostered (by relatives or strangers); young single women may migrate simultaneously with family members, to join them or other relatives at the place of destination, to carry out a prearranged marriage or to be on their own studying or working; married women may move soon after marriage together with their husbands or after they have children as part of a family group, following their migrant husband or on their own leaving the family behind. Information on the age and marital status of every migrant at the time of migration, whether the person was accompanied or not by close family members (parents, siblings, spouses or children) and whether the person joined family members or other relatives (or friends) at the place of destination would permit the systematization suggested. The availability of such information would allow a better assessment of the degree to which woman are "tied" movers and the extent to which they follow others rather than initiate a move. Such information is particularly important in the case of ever-married women, who usually constitute the largest proportion of female migrants, even if they tend to be underrepresented with respect to the non-migrant population.

A systematic consideration of the different stages of the life cycle would have the advantage of incorporating what are now rather awkward but nevertheless relevant types of migration. Migration of the aged, for instance, could be related to retirement or widowhood (since women predominate among the aged, that type of migration would be particularly relevant for them). Return migration, meaning a move to a place of previous residence with the intention of remaining there indefinitely, would also fit naturally as the conclusion of the migration process in the life cycle. Although data on return migration are scanty, they tend to indicate that the participation of women in that type of flow is generally lower than their participation in overall migration. Thus, women accounted for only 38 per cent of the return migrants enumerated in the Libyan Arab Jamahiriya (as compared with a 49 per cent share among all migrants) and for 48 per cent of those enumerated in Thailand (compared to 52 per cent overall). In addition, men predominated markedly among returnees in selected areas of southern Nigeria (Peil, Ekpenyong and Oyeneye, 1988). It appears that rather than returning to their places of origin, older women, especially if alone because of widowhood or separation, are more likely to join their adult children in new settings.

E. Conclusion

This analysis of the participation of women in various types of migration has shown that such participation is more extensive than is generally believed. For the major types of internal migration flows, be they within states or between states of a country, from rural to urban, rural to rural, urban to urban or urban to rural areas, in the majority of cases women accounted for over 45 per cent of the migrants involved and in many cases they outnumbered men for particular types of flows. There was, however, considerable variation in the extent of female migration from one country to another, and although certain patterns seemed dominant, there were generally important exceptions. Thus, whereas the share of women in intrastate migration was generally greater than their share in interstate migration, in Brazil, the reverse was true in 1970. In addition, although in several countries women were less likely to be involved in rural-urban migration than in either rural-rural or urban-urban flows, in others the highest proportion of women was recorded among rural-urban migrants. Similarly, although in a number of countries women tended to be better represented among long-term migrants than among those moving over the short term, one or two exceptions did arise.

The existence of such variability underscores the need to gather, tabulate and disseminate in a more consistent fashion data on internal migration by sex, particularly those obtained through censuses. The small number of cases considered here indicates that most countries fail to publish the data required for even the most basic analysis of female migration. Lack of adequate and accessible information often contributes to perpetuate many misconceptions about the relative importance and impact of the migration of women. The continued emphasis on the study of rural-urban migration when greater numbers of women are involved in rural-rural or urban-urban flows in a number of countries is a case in point. Another is the view that only women move in associational or marriage-related migration. As the data on the reasons for migrating indicate, about a third or more of the male migrants in certain countries were reported to move for associational or sometimes marriage-related reasons. That fact suggests, perhaps better than others, that even men can be both social and economic actors, and that being categorized as one and not the other at any particular time does not preclude them from operating in both arenas at other times. The same is true of women. Even if the majority report or are reported to migrate mostly because of social reasons, the reasons for a move do not preclude them from adopting a variety of roles once they have reached their destination. Given that women's economic roles are considered to be particularly important, especially by the research community if not by the women themselves, the question that should be posed is not whether women have economic motives to migrate but whether, once they have moved, they have the possibility of becoming economically active—regardless of whether they actually do—for how long and under what conditions.

Migration is an intrinsic part of the development process. Women and men are both active participants in that process and as migrants they represent one of the most dynamic groups in society. A better understanding of how they use migration to improve their lot and that of their families requires that a broad viewpoint be adopted and that care be taken to avoid eliminating from the universe of discourse either migrants that do not fit well into preconceived types or even whole categories of migrants that are often arbitrarily assumed to have little relevance. Even within the study of female migration, the tendency to validate it in terms of the economic roles of migrant women may be biasing the view of the migration process and preventing researchers from making an objective assessment of the other relevant roles that migrant women play within their families and in society at large.

NOTES

[1] For definitions, see United Nations (1985, pp. 183-186).

[2] In interpreting the data at hand, it is important to bear in mind their possible deficiencies, especially those deriving from varying definitions of urban and rural over time. Thus, the accuracy of information on the rural or urban nature of the place of origin may be questionable in countries where reclassification has taken place or in cases where the respondent knows little about the person involved (as when heads of household have to provide information about domestic servants living in the household). For a more extensive discussion of data deficiencies, see Bilsborrow (1993).

REFERENCES

Bangladesh (1977). *Population Census of Bangladesh, 1974: National Volume, Report and Tables*. Dacca: Bangladesh Bureau of Statistics.

Bedford, R. D. (1981). The variety of forms of population mobility in Southeast Asia and Melanesia: the case of circulation. In *Population Mobility and Development: Southeast Asia and the Pacific*, G. W. Jones and H. V. Richter, eds. Development Studies Centre, Monograph No. 27. Canberra: The Australian National University.

Bilsborrow, Richard E. (1993). Issues in the measurement of female migration in developing countries. Chapter VI in the present volume.

_____, and Richard Fuller (1988). La selectividad de los emigrantes rurales en la sierra ecuatoriana. *Estudios Demográficos y Urbanos* (Mexico City), vol. 3, No. 2 (Mayo-Agosto), pp. 265-290.

Brazil (1973). *VIII Recenseamento Geral, 1970: Censo demográfico*. National Series, vol. 1. Rio de Janeiro: Fundação Instituto Brasileiro de Geografia e Estatística.

Burundi (1974). *Enquête démographique Burundi, 1970-1971*; vol. I, *Résultats définitifs*. Bujumbura: Département de statistiques; and Paris: Institut national de la statistique et des études économiques.

Cameroon (n.d.). *Recensement général de la population et de l'habitat d'avril 1976*, vol. II, *Analyse*; tome 5, *Migrations internes*. Yaoundé: Bureau central du recensement.

Congo (1978). *Recensement général de la population du Congo, 1974*, vol. IV, *Tableaux statistiques détaillés*. Brazzaville: Direction des statistiques démographiques et sociales.

_____ (1987). *Recensement général de la population et de l'habitat de 1984*, vol. 3, *Résultats définitifs*, tome I, *Ensemble du pays*. Brazzaville: Bureau central du recensement.

Egypt (n.d.). *1976 Population and Housing Census: Fertility and Internal Migration and Movement of Workers and Students*, vol. 2, *Total Republic*. Cairo: Central Agency for Public Mobilisation and Statistics.

Eviota, Elizabeth U., and Peter C. Smith (1984). The migration of women in the Philippines. In *Women in the Cities of Asia: Migration and Urban Adaptation*, James T. Fawcett, Siew-Ean Khoo and Peter C. Smith, eds. Boulder, Colorado: Westview Press.

Fawcett, James T., Siew-Ean Khoo and Peter C. Smith, eds. (1984). *Women in the Cities of Asia: Migration and Urban Adaptation*. Boulder, Colorado: Westview Press.

Forbes, Dean (1981). Mobility and uneven development in Indonesia: a critique of explanations of migration and circular migration. In *Population Mobility and Development: Southeast Asia and the Pacific*, G. W. Jones and H. V. Richter, eds. Development Studies Centre, Monograph No. 27. Canberra: The Australian National University.

Gurak, Douglas T., and Fe Caces (1992). Migration networks and the shaping of migration systems. In *International Migration Systems: A Global Approach*, Mary M. Kritz, Lin Lean Lim and Hania Zlotnik, eds. Oxford: Clarendon Press.

Heng, T. S. (1989). Female migration in the context of national migration trends and patterns in Peninsular Malaysia, 1981-1986. Paper presented at the Population Studies Unit Colloquium on Women and Development: Implications for Planning and Population Dynamics, held at Kuala Lumpur, Malaysia, 10-12 January.

Hetler, Carol B. (1989). The impact of circular migration on a village economy. *Bulletin of Indonesian Economic Studies* (Jakarta), vol. 25, No. 1 (April), pp. 53-75.

Honduras (1986). *Encuesta Demográfica Nacional de Honduras (EDENH II 1983)*, vol. 3. CELADE Series A, No. 1047/III. San José, Costa Rica: Centro Latinoamericano de Demografía.

Hong, Savon (1984). Urban migrant women in the Republic of Korea. In *Women in the Cities of Asia: Migration and Urban Adaptation*, James T. Fawcett, Siew-Ean Khoo and Peter C. Smith, eds. Boulder, Colorado: Westview Press.

Hugo, Graeme J. (1993). Migrant women in developing countries. Chapter III in the present volume.

India (1985). *Census of India, 1981: Report and Tables Based on 5 per cent Sample Data*. Series 1, part II, Special. New Delhi: Ministry of Home Affairs, Registrar General; and Census Commissioner of India.

Khoo, Siew-Ean, and Peter Pirie (1984). Female rural-to-urban migration in Peninsular Malaysia. In *Women in the Cities of Asia: Migration and Urban Adaptation*, James T. Fawcett, Siew-Ean Khoo and Peter C. Smith, eds. Boulder, Colorado: Westview Press.

Libyan Arab Jamahiriya (1979). *1973 Population Census: Final All Country Results*. Tripoli: Census and Statistics Department.

Malaysia (1983). *General Report of the Population Census, 1980*, vol. 1. Kuala Lumpur: Commissioner of Census.

Nangia, S., and M. J. Samuel (1983). Determinants and characteristics of female migration: A case study of Salem City in Tamil Nadu, India. *Population Geography* (Chandigarh, India), vol. 5, Nos. 1-2 (June-December), pp. 34-43.

Nepal (1987). *Population Monograph of Nepal*. Kathmandu: National Planning Commission Secretariat, Central Bureau of Statistics.

Panama (n.d.). *Censos Nacionales de 1980. Octavo Censo de Población y Cuarto Censo de Vivienda*, vol. V, *Compendio general de población*. Panama: Dirección de Estadística y Censo.

Peil, Margaret, Stephen K. Ekpenyong and Olotunji Y. Oyeneye (1988). Going home: migration careers of Southern Nigerians. *International Migration Review* (Staten Island, New York), vol. 22, No. 4 (Winter), pp. 563-585.

Petersen, William (1958). A general typology of migration. *American Sociological Review* (Washington, D.C.), vol. 23, No. 2 (June), pp. 256-265.

Ravenstein, E. G. (1885). The laws of migration. *Journal of the Royal Statistical Society* (London), vol. 48, No. 2 (June), pp. 167-235.

_____ (1889). The laws of migration. *Journal of the Royal Statistical Society* (London), vol. 52, No. 2 (June), pp. 241-302.

Republic of Korea (1982). *1980 Population and Housing Census Report*, vol. 2, *Internal Migration*. Seoul: National Bureau of Statistics.

Shah, Nasra M. (1984). The female migrant in Pakistan. In *Women in the Cities of Asia: Migration and Urban Adaptation*, James T. Fawcett, Siew-Ean Khoo and Peter C. Smith, eds. Boulder, Colorado: Westview Press.

Soonthorndhada, A. (1983). The determinants and consequences of female migration in Thailand. *Population Geography* (Chandigarh, India), vol. 5, Nos. 1/2 (June-December), pp. 5-11.

Standing, Guy (1984a). Conceptualising territorial mobility. In *Migration Surveys in Low-Income Countries: Guidelines for Survey and Questionnaire Design*, Richard E. Bilsborrow, A. S. Oberai and Guy Standing, eds. Beckenham, United Kingdom; and Sydney, Australia: Croom Helm.

_____, ed. (1984b). *Labour Circulation and the Labour Process*. London: Croom Helm.

Thadani, Veena N., and Michael P. Todaro (1984). Female migration: a conceptual framework. In *Women in the Cities of Asia: Migration and Urban Adaptation*, James T. Fawcett, Siew-Ean Khoo and Peter C. Smith, eds. Boulder, Colorado: Westview Press.

Thailand (1984). *1980 Population and Housing Census; Subject Report No. 2: Migration*. Bangkok: Office of the Prime Minister, National Statistical Office.

Trinidad and Tobago (1984). *Population and Housing Census, 1980*, vol. 4, *Internal Migration*. Port-of-Spain: Central Statistical Office.

United Nations (1985). *Demographic Yearbook, 1983*. Sales No. E/F.84.XIII.I.

_____ (1992). *World Population Monitoring, 1991: With Special Emphasis on Age Structure*. Population Studies, No. 126. Sales No. E.92.XIII.2.

Venezuela (1985). *XI Censo General de Población y Vivienda (20 de Octubre de 1981): Total Nacional*. Caracas: Oficina Central de Estadística e Informática.

Zelinsky, Wilbur (1971). The hypothesis of the mobility transition. *Geographical Review* (New York), vol. 61, No. 2 (April), pp. 219-249.

Zlotnik, Hania (1987). The concept of international migration as reflected in data collection systems. *International Migration Review* (Staten Island, New York), vol. 21, No. 4 (Winter), pp. 925-946.

VI. ISSUES IN THE MEASUREMENT OF FEMALE MIGRATION IN DEVELOPING COUNTRIES

*Richard E. Bilsborrow**

Women's roles as economic actors are gaining importance in developing countries, a change that is closely linked to socio-economic development. Since access to better economic opportunities often involves migration, the participation of women in internal migration would be expected to increase, particularly because the growing educational levels of women in developing countries, not only in absolute but in relative terms with respect to those of men, are leading to a rise in women's aspirations which, in many cases, can only be realized through migration. The evidence available, however, although partial and less than current, does not indicate that women's propensity to migrate has increased at the global level. Rather, trends continue to be mixed, varying considerably across regions and across countries within each less developed region (see Singelmann, 1993; and United Nations Secretariat, 1993).

In order to understand the selectivity, determinants and consequences of female migration, accurate data on the extent and characteristics of the phenomenon are needed. It is important, therefore, to consider to what extent existing information is compromised by biases leading to the selective misrepresentation of female migrants. Such biases may be inherent in the data sources available or may derive from the way in which the data are collected. Whether such biases exist and why is the issue considered here.

The difficulty of the task at hand should be mentioned at the outset: research on female migration in developing countries is scarce, but even more so is that on methodological issues relating to the study of female migration. Thus, an examination of the index of articles published in *International Migration Review* during 1990 showed that no articles referred to both "methodology" and "female migration". Similarly, a recent review of citations on migration studies on Africa indicated that from over 1,500 references, about 135 referred to data collection and methodology, and only 37 to female migration; none considered both subjects simultaneously (UAPS, 1990).

A. DEFINING MIGRATION

Because of its inherent complexity, migration is difficult to conceptualize and define,[1] and it therefore poses special challenges with regard to measurement. Not only does the determination of whether migration occurs depend upon considerations involving space and time but it also involves the consideration of how human mobility takes place. Since the migration of an individual and particularly that of many women is often dependent upon that of someone else, it is important to differentiate individual from family migration. Furthermore, whereas people are born and die only once, migration may be a recurrent event in a lifetime and data sources generally fail to reflect the various migrations in which a person has been involved. The factors influencing migration are probably more numerous than those determining fertility or mortality and must be defined in terms of at least two distinct geographical locations, if not multiple locations: the place of origin; and all those of potential destination.

The spatial criteria determining when migration occurs usually involve two considerations, both to some extent subjective and arbitrary: that movement takes place across a political or administrative boundary (so that spatially trivial moves, such as to the house next door, can be ignored); and that movement involves a change of "usual residence". Political boundaries, being politically instituted, can be changed. Their variation over time often compromises the comparability of migration statistics even for a single country. Furthermore, political or administrative boundaries within a country often determine units that, in terms of geographical size or population, may be very

---

*Carolina Population Center, University of North Carolina at Chapel Hill, North Carolina, United States of America.

different, especially from one country to another. Thus, some provinces of China or India are geographically larger or contain more people than most countries of the world. Such differences should be borne in mind in comparing measures of internal migration across countries.

In most countries, there are several levels of geographical subdivisions that can be used to determine when migration occurs. Countries usually consist of states or provinces, which are then subdivided into districts or counties, which may further consist of subdistricts. The task of ascertaining whether migration occurs at the subdistrict level is often cumbersome because the number of subdistricts involved is generally large. Consequently, many data sources on migration fail to reflect migration between subdistricts. When they do, only rarely are the data published in sufficient detail at the subdistrict level, in part to save printing and dissemination costs and in part because in many developing countries centralized planning and decision-making has been dominant. Data for small administrative units, such as villages, localities or urban neighbourhoods—which are very useful in local planning—are rarely produced and even less often made available to local authorities. Thus, migration data are more commonly available for moves between major rather than minor civil divisions and, consequently, tend to reflect more fully moves over longer distances than those over shorter distances. To the extent that the participation of women in migration varies according to the distance involved, that practice may tend to misrepresent female participation in migration.

A further complication in ascertaining when migration occurs is related to establishing when a change of "usual residence" has occurred. For some population groups, determination of usual residence may not be possible without a series of specialized questions (e.g., street-dwellers, transients, circulators, pastoralists and nomads). In the case of female migrants, problems are likely to arise with respect to those working as live-in domestic servants, who may declare as their usual place of residence that of their family of origin instead of their employer's house, especially if they have only been present in the latter residence for a short time. In censuses or surveys enumerating the population on a de facto basis, live-in domestic servants should be considered usual residents of the employer's house. But heads of household may not always declare them as such. It is therefore likely that domestic servants are underreported, especially in censuses. To the extent that those workers include high proportions of female migrants, they would also be selectively omitted.

Place of residence is often determined on the basis of the actual or expected length of stay in a given location. Therefore, migrants are identified as persons whose actual or expected duration of stay surpasses a certain lower limit. Alternatively, all people that move are considered migrants, but a differentiation is made between those surpassing that lower limit—that is, "permanent" or long-term migrants—and those that do not, short-term or temporary migrants. Among the latter group, migration is often a recurrent event whose exact timing and other characteristics may lead to the further differentiation of other types of migrants, including, for example, nomads, seasonal migrants and those engaging in circulation (Standing, 1984). Existing data sources and data-collection practices tend to define migration only in terms of long-term changes of residence, so that, to the extent that women's participation in migration varies according to whether long-term or temporary changes of residence are involved, their overall participation in spatial mobility may be misrepresented.

Similarly, most data sources tend to reflect better migration that is separated by longer time intervals than that occurring over relatively short intervals. Indeed, most censuses and surveys, even labour force and migration surveys, fail to include the questions necessary to identify short-term migrants (such as those proposed by Oberai, 1984). Thus, even the intensive migration surveys carried out in the Ecuadorian Sierra or in the Punjab (India) in the late 1970s failed to collect information on temporary out-migration (Bilsborrow, Oberai and Standing, 1984; Oberai and Singh, 1983). The failure to collect such information may lead to a misrepresentation of women's participation in migration.

Although the reasons for migration should not be the factor determining whether someone is considered a migrant, the emphasis that migration research has usually put on labour migration—or, more generally, on economically motivated migration—has often led those in charge of data collection to disregard other types of migrants. Thus, migration surveys have often obtained information only on the migration of men (e.g., Oberai and Singh, 1983). When motives or reported motives are taken into account in determining the universe of interest, women are very likely to be eliminated on the grounds that they are considerably less likely than men to migrate for economic reasons. An associated issue is that respondents to census or survey questions on out-migration from the household may omit persons that have left for non-economic reasons, most of whom are women.

The issue of respondent bias is also relevant with respect to other aspects of migration. When only heads of household, who are usually men,[2] are questioned about the motives leading to the migration of other household members, their responses may not be accurate, particularly where women are concerned. Underlying such practices is the generalized assumption that women are passive followers of men, particularly when they migrate in the company of family members. In Southern Asian societies, for instance, male household heads are routinely asked to report the reasons for their wives' or daughters' migration under the presumption that men made the decision to migrate. Such practices can severely bias the information obtained.

Lastly, despite the fact that Gary Becker, a recent Nobel prize winner in economics, developed an economic theory of marriage, it has scarcely been considered an economic process worthy of study in relation to migration. Yet, marriage migration is important not only in Southern Asia but in a number of countries in other regions, including China (Ji, Zhang and Liu, 1986), Cameroon (Simmons, Diaz-Briquets and Laquian, 1977) and Nigeria (Watts, 1983). It is therefore unwarranted to disregard such migration, whether from the data-collection perspective or as a subject of study.

B. Sources of data on internal migration

The standard sources of demographic data are population censuses, vital registration systems, sample surveys and population registers. In developing countries, censuses and sample surveys are the most important sources of information on migration, and they are the focus of attention here. Vital registration systems produce data on births and deaths that are usually not linked to the migration status of parents and are therefore of marginal importance for the study of migration. Population registers are important sources of migration data in developed countries, but although a few developing countries have such registers, their operation is not sufficiently reliable to become the basis of demographic information in general and of that on migration in particular. The first such register can be traced back over two thousand years to China; and as of 1967, population registration systems existed in about one third of the countries of the world (65), including 36 developing countries (Shryock and Siegel, 1976), most of which were in Asia or had centralized national planning systems.

Another data-collection system that can provide information on migration is that known as a "dual-record system", which combines a continuous population registration system with sample surveys. Assuming that both systems record the events of interest (births, deaths, migration) independently from each other, the number of events recorded by both or either of them can be used to estimate those events missed by both systems and thus correct for underregistration (Chandrasekar and Deming, 1949). Most countries making use of dual-record systems have gathered data only on births and deaths. One exception is the Sample Vital Registration Project of the Central Bureau of Statistics of Indonesia, carried out during the period 1977-1979, which consisted of a vital registration subsystem covering a sample population of 230,000 in 112 urban and rural villages of 10 provinces and a retrospective sample survey of the same population conducted every 12 months. The two systems gathered data not only on births and deaths but on migration into and out of the sampled areas. However, although the dual-record system yielded fairly accurate estimates of birth and death rates once they were adjusted for underregistration, the data on migration were too defective for the adjustment to be applied.

Population censuses

Since 1960, most countries of the world have periodically undertaken population censuses (usually every 10 years). Censuses have the advantage of covering the entire population of a country as of a reference date (usually the census "day"). By allowing the identification of migrants and non-migrants according to a combination of simple criteria, census data make possible the comparison of the demographic and socio-economic characteristics of the two groups. However, because they cover a large population, censuses can only incorporate a limited number of questions and therefore cannot provide data of sufficient breadth and depth to study the determinants and consequences of migration (see Goldstein and Goldstein, 1979; Bilsborrow, Oberai and Standing, 1984). In particular, census information refers to the characteristics of migrants at the time of the census and not at the time of migration, so that even their adequacy for the study of migration selectivity may be questionable when the characteristics considered are likely to have changed after migration.

Migration data obtained from censuses are also limited by the criteria that can be used to identify migrants. The standard census questions on place of birth, place of previous residence or place of residence at some fixed date prior to the census are typically used to identify migrants. Place of birth, used to identify lifetime migrants, is probably reported fairly well in terms of large geographical areas, but it becomes less accurate the greater the geographical disaggregation used. In addition, it is not known when lifetime migrants moved. The older the migrant, the longer the span over which migration may have taken place and the more likely that multiple moves are involved, only one of which is reflected by the data. Therefore, a better strategy for the identification of migrants is to use information on their place of residence at some fixed date prior to the census, such as exactly five years earlier. The number of persons whose place of residence five years prior to the census was different from that at the time of the census represents the net number of migrants over the five-year period preceding the census. Although these data also fail to reflect intermediate moves within that five-year period and return migration, they are better indicators of migration over a given period than those derived from information on place of birth. Another variant used to identify migrants is to ask place of previous residence and the length of residence in the place of enumeration, so as to ascertain the exact timing of the most recent change of residence. Such information may provide some indication of short-term migration if the respondent considers that residence is established after only a few months or weeks. However, true short-term migration can only be measured by using a battery of questions that most censuses cannot accommodate.

By coding place of birth, place of previous residence and place of current residence with sufficient detail, censuses are the best potential sources of information on migration over a range of political or administrative subdivisions, from provinces or states to districts, counties, municipios or even subdistricts. Unfortunately, in many cases, the necessary information is either not gathered or fails to be coded with sufficient detail. Consequently, many censuses only produce information on migration at the interstate or interprovincial level. Even when the necessary information is available, only interstate migration data are published. In such cases, special tabulations on migration at the interdistrict or intradistrict levels may be obtained from census tapes or other machine-readable versions of the census (often available only for census samples), but access to them is generally limited. A similar problem arises when the tabulations published fail to reflect the distribution of migrants by sex (a very common practice). Although such information is potentially available from census tapes or special tabulations, their restricted access severely limits the study of female migration.

In principle, there should be equal coverage of men and women in population censuses regardless of the questions used and the problems respondents may have with census concepts. Biases in measuring the relative volume of female migration or its characteristics may arise, however, because of the procedures used in collecting, processing and analysing the information. Such biases are discussed below.

Household surveys

Household surveys are flexible data-collection instruments that can be designed to cover specific populations or areas using detailed or probing questionnaires. Unlike censuses, household surveys can be specifically designed to investigate internal migration. A single-round retrospective survey on migration can record a migrant's situation in the previous place of residence and his or her activities and status there. As concerns economic activities, for instance, the survey may record primary and secondary employment, type of occupation, its sector or industry, the duration and regularity of employment during the year preceding migration, wage levels and earnings, job satisfaction and job search activity. If the respondent is engaged in agricultural activities, one can inquire about land-ownership and land use, receipts from products sold in the market, regularity and seasonality of work, agricultural input and access to technology, credit or agricultural extension services. The characteristics of the dwelling in the previous place of residence may also be recorded, as well as the reasons for leaving and for selecting the current place of residence. Similar information can be obtained with regard to economic activities or dwelling characteristics in the current place of residence, so that the situations before and after migration can be compared.

It is important to compare the situation of migrants with that of the appropriate comparison group. If the determinants of migration are to be explored, the comparison group should consist of non-migrants in the place of origin. Alternatively, if the consequences of migration are at issue, the appropriate comparison group should encompass non-migrants in the place of destination (Bilsborrow, Oberai and Standing, 1984). Lack of suitable data often prevents researchers from carrying out the appropriate comparisons and severely limits the understanding of the processes leading to migration and of its consequences. Surveys carried out in the areas of origin that obtain information about out-migrants from proxy respondents are meant to shed light on the determinants of migration, especially if they allow that factors at the individual, household and community or area levels be taken into account (Bilsborrow, Oberai and Standing, 1984; Massey, 1990; Guest, 1993). Such surveys should collect retrospective information about both out-migrants and non-migrants concerning their situation at the mean time of out-migration of the migrants in the study, so that the situations of both at the time of migration can be compared. It is therefore advisable to focus on recent migrants to minimize recall problems.

Surveys in the area of destination that gather information about in-migrants and non-migrants should try to ascertain their situation at the mean time of in-migration, as well as at the time of the survey, to determine how much migrants have benefited from migration in comparison with non-migrants. The vast majority of migration surveys have been carried out only in places of destination (usually equated with urban areas) and thus have limited the types of inferences that can appropriately be drawn. However, a perusal of the conclusions in the migration literature indicates that modesty has been all too rare (Bilsborrow, Oberai and Standing, 1984).

To obtain a more comprehensive picture of migration and its relation with other events in the life cycle, migration surveys can gather information on the migration history of each person. Migration histories typically record all changes of residence over a person's life (or since some initial age, say 12 or 15, when active participation in decision-making may begin). A migration history can be expanded into a life history by obtaining information about other key events in a person's life, such as changes of employment, changes in marital status and dates of children's births. Obtaining information through a questionnaire that links the timing of one event to another contributes to reduce recall errors (Freedman and others, 1988). If additional information is collected on wage levels, occupation, number of hours worked, housing conditions etc., one can carry out a longitudinal analysis of the determinants and, in particular, of the consequences of migration over time. Life-history data are likely to be especially useful for the study of how different events in a woman's life, such as marriage, child-bearing, entry into the labour force, employment or divorce, relate to migration (Peters, 1987; Gurak and Gilbertson, 1991). However, because the collection of life-history data is very demanding and costly, it is more likely that surveys will continue to focus on the most recent migration.

Because of concerns about the quality of the data gathered by single-round surveys where information about out-migrants from the areas of origin must be obtained from proxy respondents, tracing surveys that seek out and interview the actual out-migrants in the place of destination have been proposed and occasionally carried out (see Byerlee and Tommy, 1976, on Sierra Leone). Although the appeal of such surveys is considerable, their cost is higher than that of single-round surveys and can be cost-effective only in relatively small countries or regions with adequate maps, address lists and good transport systems.

Despite the considerable advantages of household surveys for the study of migration, they have some inherent limitations, in addition to those resulting from the inadequate use of the data they yield. Thus, surveys are usually unable to produce adequate measures of either levels or rates of migration because they tend not to be nationally representative and are, as a rule, usually not designed to produce estimates of the population at risk of migrating. Since surveys are carried out on samples, their statistical reliability depends upon the adequacy and type of the sample used and their results are always subject to sampling error. When surveys are designed to obtain information about household out-migrants from household members left behind, they will omit all those migrants whose entire households left the area. To the extent that those migrants have different characteristics from those who left some relatives behind to report on them, biases will arise.

The flexibility of surveys also increases the potential for the adoption of arbitrary or incorrect survey designs and analyses. The adoption of unnecessarily restrictive definitions of key concepts, particularly of migration itself, is a case in point. Thus, in a well-planned survey of rural-urban migration in the Indian Punjab, the universe under investigation was limited to male heads of household and then only to those stating that they had migrated for economic reasons (Oberai and Singh, 1983). Those types of restrictions are common in migration surveys and especially in migration analyses and are largely responsible for the invisibility of female migrants. Similarly, the studies of Bilsborrow and colleaques (1987) on the determinants of out-migration from rural communities in the Sierra region of Ecuador and of Saefullah (1992) on the impact of out-migration on two villages in West Java, Indonesia focus only on "economic" and "working" migrants, therefore eliminating most women from the universe of interest.

C. REASONS TO EXPECT BIASES IN THE MEASUREMENT OF FEMALE MIGRATION

The possible causes of bias in the measurement of female migration in developing countries can be classified into several categories: (*a*) those resulting from the types of migration in which women engage as compared with those of men; (*b*) those inherent in the activities in which women are reported to engage in; (*c*) those inherent in established social and cultural norms concerning, in particular, the appropriate roles and behaviour of women; (*d*) those related to errors of omission or commission made by the respondent providing information about migrant women. These causes of bias often operate not in isolation but in conjunction with one another. Some result in biases at the data-collection stage and others in biases relating to how the data are processed and disseminated, and some lead to a biased analysis of female migration.

One of Ravenstein's laws of migration (1885) states that women are more mobile than men over shorter than over longer distances. Therefore, the proportion of women among migrants moving over shorter distances is likely to be higher than that among migrants moving over longer distances. To the extent that migration between major civil divisions (such as states or provinces) involves longer distances than migration across smaller civil divisions (such as districts), women are likely to be better represented among intrastate than among interstate migrants. Given the widespread practice of publishing migration data only at the interstate level, female migration is likely to be generally underrepresented. Unfortunately, evidence on the relative participation of men and women in interstate and intrastate migration is scanty. Table 12 in this volume presents data for only four countries and indicates that in India, the proportion of women among intrastate migrants was considerably higher than that among interstate migrants, but in the Libyan Arab Jamahiriya and Thailand, the differences, though in the expected direction, were small. In Brazil, the proportion of women was higher among interstate than among intrastate migrants.

The results of other empirical studies also provide support for Ravenstein's law. Thus Radloff (1982) reports that, according to the 1970 census of Malaysia, the proportion of women among lifetime migrants moving within states was higher than that among lifetime migrants moving between states. Similarly, according to a migration survey carried out in Ecuador in 1977/78, women accounted for 49 per cent of the out-migrants from rural areas moving short distances whereas they accounted for only 39 per cent of those moving over longer distances (to non-contiguous provinces) (Bilsborrow and Fuller, 1988). Data for Neuquén City in Argentina and for the Senegal River Valley of Mali reported in this volume are also consistent with that general tendency (cf., Recchini de Lattes and Mychaszula, 1993; and Findley and Diallo, 1993, respectively). Consequently, the practice of Governments to process and publish only data on migration between states or provinces will tend to underrepresent differentially female migrants.

Such underrepresentation has implications not only for the measurement of female migration but also for the analysis of both the determinants and consequences of migration. According to Radloff: "Migration measures which identify only long-distance movers systematically select more successful and higher status migrants" (1982, p. 323). Such selectivity applies to both men and women and leads to biased conclusions about the nature and consequences of migration. In addition, rural-rural migrants are more likely than rural-urban migrants to be underrepresented, because their migration tends to occur within provinces. Such underrepresentation would tend to be more severe among women in countries characterized by high levels of marriage migration, such as India. It is clear that nothing can be said about migrants—their selectivity, determinants or consequences—when their very existence is not reflected in available statistics.

The second potential cause of bias in the measurement of female migration is that arising from the types of activities in which women are reported to engage. Because of their child-rearing responsibilities, married women are more likely to be unable or unwilling to respond to lengthy survey questionnaires. Women engaged in illegal or socially disapproved activities, such as prostitution, are also unlikely to volunteer information. Women working in domestic service—most of whom are migrants—are also rarely interviewed directly and, as "non-family members", may not even be reported to interviewers.

A far more pervasive and insidious bias exists because of the generalized tendency to underreport the economic activities of women and therefore to misrepresent their labour force status. Given the tendency of migration research to focus on the economic aspects of migration, women that appear not to be economically active are summarily disregarded. Thus, migrant women are relevant subjects of study only to the degree that they are economically active. Consequently, the need to ensure that women's economic activity shall be adequately measured is essential to help promote the study of female migration.

With regard to the work of women, it is surprising to find that cross-national statistics indicate that female labour force participation rates in developing countries have declined slightly despite the positive effects that would be expected from increasing levels of female education, growing urbanization and changing sex roles. Female labour force participation rates in developed countries have risen steadily, from 53 per cent in 1960 to 57 in 1980 and 58 in 1990; in developing countries, however, they have reportedly fallen from 46 per cent in 1960 to 42 in 1980 and then to 37 in 1990 (United Nations, 1990). Although there is evidence that women's labour force participation is significantly understated, the fact that it has always been understated suggests that correcting for such understatement may not alter the trend implied by the statistics reported above.

Many sources of bias affect the labour force participation rates of women. Boserup (1970), for example, points out the tendency to disregard the subsistence production activities of women in rural areas in both labour force statistics and national accounts. Benería (1991) and others stress the tendency to disregard women's economic activities in the urban informal sector. Wainerman and Recchini de Lattes (1981) report that censuses in Latin America are more likely to omit women's work in rural than in urban areas. Furthermore, the tendency of women to occupy lower status jobs and to receive lower wages than men in low-income countries is well documented[3] and contributes to the undervaluation of women's economic activities and of their roles in migration. The extent to which women's labour force activity is underreported and undervalued leads to an underestimation of the importance of economic or labour force motivations as determinants of the migration decisions of women and, correspondingly, to the arbitrary imputation of motives consistent with traditional views about women's roles. Better measurement of the economic contributions of women would reduce that important source of bias in migration studies.

Population censuses have generally underestimated women's labour force participation (Standing, 1983; Dixon-Mueller and Anker, 1988; Waring, 1988). Thus, a comparison of female labour force participation rates derived from Latin American census data with those estimated from household surveys (presumed to be more accurate because of the use of better trained interviewers and more detailed questions) revealed that the former were subject to a systematic downward bias (Wainerman and Recchini de Lattes, 1981). Anker and colleagues have developed questionnaires and interviewing procedures to improve the measurement of the economic activities of women (Anker, 1983; Anker, Khan and Gupta, 1988; Anker and Anker, 1988). Those procedures include the use of time-budget studies and activity lists, of more detailed and probing questions, of female interviewers trained to provide more careful explanations of what constitutes work and of the practice of interviewing women directly rather than by proxy. When detailed questions based on a list of 19 activities and a broader definition of what constitutes work were used in a survey carried out in Egypt, the labour force participation rates of women in rural areas doubled, from 29 to 58 per cent. A survey conducted in Bangladesh in 1990, using the procedures outlined above, produced an even greater increase in female labour force participation rates: from 8 to over 60 per cent. Efforts to improve the measurement of women's economic activities are to be commended not only because they show the important economic roles that women play in developing societies but because the data obtained are likely to shed light on heretofore hidden links between migration and women's labour force participation.

Women's invisibility as economic actors is closely linked to their limited rights to own property or to have control over financial and other productive assets. Until women have and are able to exercise equal rights as men to own, inherit, buy and sell land or other productive assets, their economic roles will continue to be undervalued. Even in much of Latin America, where the status of women is considered to be relatively high, women only recently have acquired rights equal to those of men with regard to property ownership and in some countries those rights are still far from being enforced. In Ecuador, for instance, only in 1978 did women earn the right to own property on more or less the same grounds as men and to obtain a divorce (further changes in the same direction were made to the *Código civil* in 1992). Despite those legal changes, however, landownership is still largely in the hands of men, partially because women are not fully aware of their rights. In many other parts of the world the situation is worse. Thus, Palmer (1988) reports that in most of sub-Saharan Africa, land is patrilineally inherited and notes that in Cameroon most of the land cultivated by women is compound land under the control of men. In those cases where women have either ownership or usufruct rights over land, they are generally allotted land of inferior quality, land that is fragmented or land that is more distant from their homes. Such a situation is likely to lead some women, especially those belonging to younger generations, to rebel and leave the farms to seek employment in urban areas. Married women, whose permanent relocation to urban areas is less likely, may engage in circulation to secure an income rather than work on the family plot for their husbands (Palmer, 1988).

Women's capacity to own or control resources, as well as society's perception about the value of their economic activities, is largely dependent upon the norms and values that determine which roles and behaviour are appropriate for women in any given society. Researchers must be aware of the pervasive nature of social perceptions of the acceptability of certain roles and conduct among women. Respondents to any census or survey questionnaire, being members of society, tend to shape their responses in accordance with social norms and expectations, thereby introducing specific biases. The next section explores the nature of those biases and their effects on the measurement of female migration.

D. Respondent bias and its effect on the measurement of female migration

The literature on non-sampling errors in survey research distinguishes between errors deriving from non-response (persons that decline to be interviewed or are not available for interview) and "response effects", which include biases resulting from the interaction of the data-collection instrument, characteristics of the interviewer and characteristics of the respondent.[4] The latter type of error was first discussed by Rice (1929), who observed significant interview bias in a survey on the causes of destitution in the United States.

This section focuses mainly on the issue of respondent bias, especially because of the widespread practice of obtaining information on migrants from only one household member: the one judged to have the greatest authority within the household, namely, the head of household, who is usually identified as a male. The issue is therefore to explore whether heads of household tend to underreport the migration of women or to distort its characteristics. The limited research available indicates that although biases may result from defects in the survey instrument (the questionnaire used) or from the interviewer's application of the questionnaire, or from the mode and environment in which data collection takes place (in the presence of others, for instance), a more common source of bias is the respondent. Biases arising from the survey instrument and from the respondent have, in general, been found to be larger than those resulting from the interviewer (Bradburn, 1983; Singleton and others, 1988; Hox, de Leeuw and Kreft, 1990).

Survey error due to the respondent's characteristics may be introduced as a consequence of the respondent's cognitive processes (Forsyth and Lessler, 1990), which are said to comprise: (*a*) previous ability to encode and store information or knowledge; (*b*) comprehension and interpretation of the question (influenced by the interviewer, his or her characteristics and dress, and the purpose of the data-collection effort as explained by the interviewer); (*c*) memory recall or the ability to retrieve the information at the time of interview; (*d*) judgements about what response is appropriate; and (*e*) communication or articulation of the answer selected (adapted from Groves, 1989).

An issue related to the ability of the respondent to encode and store information is the selection or identification of the person who is most likely to have the knowledge to respond accurately, that is, the so-called "respondent rule effects" (Groves, 1989). People know more about their own activities than about those of others, but to save interviewing time and costs, the use of proxy respondents is common in surveys. In most societies, knowledge of activities across generations is greater among persons of the same sex than among those of opposite sexes; that is, mothers are more likely to know about their daughters' activities than are fathers. Consequently, women are usually better proxy respondents for other women.

With regard to the comprehension and interpretation of the questions posed, in many cultures the sex of the interviewer in relation to the sex of the respondent is of paramount importance for the investigation of certain topics (Ballou, 1991). However, that concern should not be overstated. Thus, Anker and Anker (1988), and Anker, Khan and Gupta (1988) found that the sex of the interviewer did not bias the data on women's economic activities either in rural Egypt or in India. It seems reasonable to assume that a similar finding would apply with regard to the investigation of female migration.

The extent to which memory recall ability may be a problem leading to erroneous responses depends upon the length of the recall period (whether a person migrated a few months before the interview or several years before), the saliency of the event and the effort made in recalling it, although probing usually improves reporting (Cannell, Miller and Oksenberg, 1981; Singleton and others, 1988). The exponential decline in recall ability over time provides a strong argument for obtaining detailed information only for recent events (Som, 1973; Groves, 1989). That approach is especially relevant in migration surveys, which need to gather retrospective information from migrants about their situation prior to migration.

Yet, perhaps the most relevant source of survey measurement error is the respondent's bias deriving from his or her judgement about the answer that is most appropriate or socially acceptable. That is, respondents tend to provide answers that paint a good picture of themselves and of the out-migrant, a picture consistent with societal norms.[5] The interview situation involves a social interaction between the interviewer and the respondent in which the latter, in addition to providing information, wishes to make a good impression. The respondent thus evaluates the psychological meaning of the response in relation to personal goals extraneous to the survey and may alter the response when the correct response is deemed embarrassing or uncomfortable. This process has come to be called the "social desirability bias" (Cannell, Miller and Oksenberg, 1981, p. 395). Responses are therefore altered or biased to provide a more socially desirable response.[6] Respondents may thus tend to exaggerate or overreport characteristics and activities that they consider socially desirable and underreport or omit those thought to be undesirable or sensitive (Cannell, Miller and Oksenberg, 1981; Singleton and others, 1988; Groves, 1989). From another perspective, sensitive questions are those in which the motives to be uncooperative (to maintain one's social identity) have higher priority and are in conflict with those leading to cooperation (Hubbard, Lessler and Caspar, 1990).

Of course, what is considered "desirable" or "sensitive" is culture-specific. In many developing countries, especially in rural areas, views concerning appropriate activities for women are highly restrictive. It is often considered not only undesirable but inappropriate for women to work outside the home, even if they are still living at home, and therefore even more inappropriate for them to migrate from the natal community in order to work. The typical male head of household, when acting as a proxy respondent, is thus likely to underreport the migration of female household members or to misreport their characteristics, motives, current activities etc. Such biases are compounded if the male respondent has, in addition, incomplete knowledge of the activities, motivations and attitudes of the women concerned.

Consequently, self-reporting is likely to be more accurate and complete than proxy reporting because of the person's greater knowledge of his or her own activities, attributes and motives. However, when the characteristic or activity being investigated is itself considered socially undesirable, a proxy respondent may provide more accurate information than the person concerned. For example, in a Survey of Income and Program Participation carried out in the United States, proxy respondents tended to underreport less the participation of others in government transfer programmes than the recipients of those transfers themselves (Moore, 1990).

More germane are the experiments by Anker and others to compare female labour force participation and economic activities as reported by the women themselves versus those reported by the head of household (usually a man) in two field experiments conducted in Egypt and India. The study in Egypt (Anker and Anker, 1988) is based on a survey of 1,000 rural households carried out in 1984. Experiments were conducted using three different approaches or sets of questions: (*a*) standard census-type questions; (*b*) "key words" to probe and draw out responses as well as examples of common kinds of women's non-market economic activities; and (*c*) a full list of 19 activities. Although the 1980 census showed that only 5 per cent of rural women worked for pay and only 12 per cent were in the labour force, according to standard ILO definitions, the survey found 11 per cent in paid work, 54 per cent in "ILO work" and 58 per cent in the labour force according to a broader labour force definition recommended by Anker (1983) and by Dixon-Mueller and Anker (1988). The estimates obtained, however, differed greatly according to whether the respondent was the woman herself or a proxy (72 per cent of whom were men): whereas 19 per cent of women reported having worked for pay during the year preceding the interview and 15 per cent reported having worked for pay for at least 10 hours during the week preceding the interview, the proxy respondents reported only 11 and 8 per cent, respectively. Differences in specific activities suggest further statistically significant differences in paid work involving work away from home, in contrast to work at home.[7] Anker and Anker (1988) conclude that those results provide support for the widely held belief that men from developing countries are reluctant to mention to a stranger, that is, to the interviewer, that a female household member worked as a wage-earner, although such effects vary according to the culture and country involved.

The evidence of a proxy respondent bias (generally of male respondents) in reports concerning women's economic activities is only indirectly suggestive of a bias with regard to the measurement of female migration. There is, in fact, very little direct evidence of the latter bias, in part because of the small number of surveys on internal migration in developing countries and in part because of the lack of attention paid to methodological issues in migration surveys in general (Bilsborrow, Oberai and Standing, 1984). There is, however, some evidence that considerations about social desirability are likely to lead to an underreporting of women's migration and to distortions of their characteristics. Normative prescriptions against women's migration exist in many societies (Fawcett, Khoo and Smith, 1984; Guest, 1993; Lim, 1993; Rodenburg, 1993). Thus, Hetler (1989, cited in Saefullah, 1992) describes the social disapproval that higher class village women express towards women migrating away from their home village in Java. Societal norms can also lead the respondents to distort the reasons for out-migration: in the Senegal River Valley of Mali, male heads of household rarely mentioned economic reasons for women's out-migration in order to "save face" (Findley and Diallo, 1993). Even female respondents appeared to tailor their responses to satisfy the need for social desirability and thus tended not to mention economic reasons as leading to female migration.

Stronger evidence about respondent bias can be obtained from the Survey of Internal Migration in the Ecuadorian Sierra carried out in 1977-1978. Representative probability samples of households were selected in rural and urban areas of the Sierra region, which contained about half the population of Ecuador. In the rural sample, households with at least one out-migrant to urban areas in the Sierra region were oversampled and so were households in the urban sample with at least one in-migrant from rural areas in the Sierra region. The final sample encompassed 3,429 households in rural areas and 1,701 in urban areas. The survey instructions stipulated that the interviewer should "interview only the head of the family or his [sic] representative". While the sex of the actual respondent was not recorded in the survey, 81 per cent of the heads of household in rural areas and over 90 per cent of those in urban areas were men. Since the purpose of the survey was to investigate rural-urban migration, the rural survey was essentially a survey of areas of origin that gathered information on out-migrants and had therefore to rely upon proxy respondents because the migrants themselves were not present.[8] The respondent was thus asked to report all household members aged 12 or over that had migrated during the five years preceding the interview. Questions were asked about the characteristics of the out-migrant at the time of departure, including name, sex, age, educational attainment and marital status. Data were also obtained on place of destination, main activity and earnings prior to departure and reasons for migration, as well as the person's current situation and economic activity. The results, summarized in Bilsborrow and Fuller (1988), showed a surprisingly low proportion of women among rural-urban out-migrants, compared with either the proportion of women among the in-migrants from rural areas reported in the urban part of the survey or that among the rural-urban migrants recorded by the population census. Thus, the rural survey recorded 1,729 male and 1,229 female recent out-migrants and 5,545 male and 5,612 female non-migrants. The proportion of women among out-migrants in the rural survey was 42 per cent, far below the 48 and 49 per cent female in the population of urban areas according to the 1974 and 1982 population censuses, respectively. Given that the vast majority of the out-migrants reported in rural areas were children of the head of the household, this evidence suggested that fathers were less inclined to report that their daughters had out-migrated to the city than to report the out-migration of their sons, presumably because rural men considered migration to be socially undesirable (Bilsborrow and Fuller, 1988).

A more detailed comparison of the results of the rural and the urban parts of the survey of the Ecuadorian Sierra indicated that even when respondents in rural areas reported female out-migrants, they often provided erroneous information about their reasons for migration and their activities prior to and subsequent to migration (work status, occupation or income). Thus, comparisons between the characteristics of female and male out-migrants reported by the rural survey and those of female and male in-migrants interviewed in urban areas that reported migrating on their own, that is, not in the company of their entire family, disclosed important differences. Among female out-migrants, for instance, only 29 per cent were reported to be working prior to the move, whereas 39 per cent of the in-migrant women that moved on their own to urban areas reported themselves as having worked during the year prior to their migration. Similarly, respondents in rural areas reported that 53 per cent of female out-migrants were currently working at the place of destination, in contrast to a figure of 73 per cent reported by the female migrants themselves in urban areas (Yang and Bilsborrow, 1992). Interestingly, proxy respondents in rural areas provided responses for male out-migrants that were biased in the opposite direction, perhaps also for reasons of perceived social desirability. Thus, the percentage of male out-migrants reported as working prior to migration by respondents in rural areas was 75 per cent, whereas only 59 per cent of the male in-migrants in urban areas reported themselves as having worked in the year prior to their migration.

A second, very different type of data, also relating to Ecuador, provides further evidence of respondent bias in the same direction. In 1987, a community-level survey was carried out in 27 rural communities by the Consejo Nacional de Desarrollo (CONADE) of Ecuador to evaluate the demographic impact of integrated rural development projects (Bilsborrow and Ruiz, 1989). Almost all of the community leaders interviewed were male. The same year, Hubacher conducted a household survey whose respondents were evenly distributed by sex and resided in three of the same 27 communities located in the rural Sierra. The results yielded by the community-level survey and the household survey with regard to levels of recent out-migration from the three villages concerned indicated that male community leaders tended to underreport female migration in comparison with the results yielded by the household survey (Hubacher and Bilsborrow, 1990).

These examples indicate that the use of male proxy respondents can lead to an understatement of female migration and introduce serious biases in the characteristics of female migrants in a direction that reduces its perceived importance. Since Ecuador is probably an average developing country in terms of women's overall roles and status, this discussion is relevant for other contexts as well. Male respondent bias is likely a common source of error with regard to information on women obtained through surveys or censuses in other developing countries. Consequently, analyses of the selectivity or characteristics of female migrants or of the determinants and consequences of female migration based on existing data sets may yield distorted and unreliable results. Correction of such biases is not always straightforward; but, as the cases of the urban and rural surveys of Ecuador suggest, gathering information on migration at both ends of the migration process—origin and destination—can allow checks of data quality and even suggest ways of minimizing errors. It would also be very useful to record systematically the sex of the respondent and his or her relation to the migrant concerned so that further tests of respondent bias can be carried out.

E. Conclusion

Migration research has been seriously constrained by the limitations of the main sources of migration data, namely, population censuses and household surveys. Such limitations, rather than being intrinsic, are closely related to the lack of funding for migration surveys and their subsequent analyses, a situation that contrasts starkly with the support available for fertility surveys and analyses in recent decades.

The approach chosen to measure migration affects the level and patterns of migration. Such effects can be differential by sex. This paper has documented how the questions used, the manner in which the data are processed and published and the choice of respondent can each on its own or in combinations with others lead to the differential omission of female migrants. The questions used and respondent bias can also distort the characteristics of female migrants in ways that reduce the perceived importance of women's migration. Such distortions may significantly compromise the validity of studies on migrant selectivity and on the determinants and consequences of female migration.

Several measures to reduce the biases affecting the measurement of female migration can be proposed. First, in carrying out either population censuses or surveys it should not be assumed that the best respondent is the male head of household. Women in positions of authority within the household should be given equal chances as those of men to respond to census or survey questionnaires. Secondly, an effort should be made to measure female economic activity more accurately, particularly in censuses. Wainerman (1991) documents how the addition of only one or two questions can significantly improve the measurement of women's economic activity in censuses of developing countries. Thirdly, censuses should code, process and publish or disseminate in machine-readable form migration data by sex between units at two or three different levels of geographical disaggregation (the number of levels would depend upon the size of the country and the average population of the units at each level). Lastly, countries that are particularly interested in short-term migration and its trade-offs with long-term changes of residence should consider gathering data on short-term movements as part of a census sample.

In household surveys, even in multi-purpose surveys not specifically focusing on internal migration, a few additional questions could be added to the customary ones on the timing of the most recent change of residence and place of previous residence to identify short-term, temporary or seasonal migrants. The contributions of those migrants to household income and the relations between their economic and other activities with those of household members left behind could then be investigated. Although women seem to be less well represented in short-term migration flows, biased measurement schemes may be at least partially responsible for that outcome and efforts to adopt more even-handed approaches should be encouraged.

Surveys should incorporate more detailed and probing questions on economic activity which will yield a more realistic view of the economic contributions of women (Anker, Khan and Gupta, 1988; United Nations, 1989) and thus contribute to a better understanding of the interrelations of economic activity and female migration. Whenever feasible, information on economic activity should be obtained directly from the women concerned. If proxy respondents are used, women that are closely related to the women concerned should be sought to provide information on female migrants. In any case, surveys should record and process the sex of the respondent and his or her relationship to the migrant or non-migrant concerned so that respondent biases can be assessed. This practice would make possible the methodological research that is sorely needed to document how serious respondent biases are, in what contexts they arise and what measures can be taken to reduce them.

Improvements in the measurement and understanding of the internal migration of women in developing countries also require more detailed questions to identify female migrants better and to obtain more accurate information about them. With respect to the former, Grove (1989) reports that biases associated with the social desirability of a response can be reduced by using more detailed questions, probing or prefacing the question with a statement implying that the undesirable trait is common. With regard to female migration such a statement might be: "We know that women often leave this community to live elsewhere. We are interested in the women who have left the community in the past five years. Has any female member of your household gone to live somewhere else within the past five years?"

With respect to information about other aspects of female migration, efforts should be made not only to improve data on women's economic activities but to gather information allowing a better identification of various types of migrants (Oberai, 1984), including information on the role that women play in the decision-making process and on their motives to migrate. In obtaining such information, probing questions should be used with regard to both economic and non-economic motives for migration and to identify linkages between the two types of motives.

In conclusion, there is an urgent need for more and better information on internal migration in general and on female migration in particular. Well-designed household surveys are likely to be the best means to obtain that information, but as long as only a handful are carried out each year, migration research will continue to advance at a snail's pace. At the same time, migration will continue to change the face of this planet at an ever-increasing pace and female migrants will continue to play an important part in those changes.

Notes

[1] Some of these definitional issues are touched upon—rarely more than that—in standard demographic textbooks, such as Shryock and Siegel (1971). A more imaginative discussion, which nevertheless leaves major issues unresolved, is found in Standing (1984). The field of migration is in need of a definitive text that establishes widely accepted criteria on which to base definitions.

[2] Almost all censuses and surveys in developing countries continue this practice, which has been abandoned in the United States and other developed countries.

[3] See Benería (1982), Standing (1983), Anker and Hein (1986, 1987), Dixon-Mueller and Anker (1988), Palmer (1988) and Benería (1991).

[4] See Neter and Waksberg (1965), Phillips (1971), Sudman and Bradburn (1974, 1982), Bradburn (1983), Singleton and others (1988); and Cannell, Miller and Oksenberg (1981).

[5] Unfortunately, there has been little research on which characteristics of respondents are uniformly associated with poor data quality and few studies have obtained measures from respondents concerning their own perceptions of what is socially desirable (Groves, 1989). If these perceptions were known, the information could be used to adjust the biased responses resulting from the respondent's judgement about what is appropriate.

[6] In a 1963 household survey on hospitalizations in the United States, respondents were asked about the duration of and reasons for hospital stays. Responses were compared with actual hospital records. Reasons were classified into three groups, ranging from "not embarrassing or threatening at all" to "highly threatening or embarrassing". It was

found that hospitalizations associated with clearly embarrassing conditions were underreported at over twice the rate as those considered not embarrassing (21 per cent versus 10 per cent). See Cannell, Miller and Oksenberg (1981).

[7]Thus, for example, the percentages of women working for pay in non-agricultural activities or for the Government were 4.0 and 1.2 per cent, respectively, according to the women themselves and to proxy respondents, and those of women farming for others for pay were 12.8 and 8.8 per cent, respectively. In contrast, the percentage of women working in farm activities for the family were 16.7 and 16.4 per cent, according to themselves and to proxy respondents, respectively. There were also relatively minor differences in the reports of women themselves and of proxy respondents about the participation of women in virtually all other non-paid activities, including fetching water, grinding grain or caring for chickens.

[8]The issue here is not whether the proxy respondent knows about the out-migrant's activities—a general concern in household surveys—but rather whether there are systemmatic biases in the responses obtained. In many situations, proxy respondents (for example, heads of household) cannot provide accurate information about out-migrants. In a household survey conducted in 1989-1990 in two villages of Indonesia, 15 per cent of the heads of household interviewed did not know the place of destination to which the out-migrant had gone (Saefullah, 1992).

REFERENCES

Anker, Richard (1983). *Effect on Reported Levels of Female Labour Force Participation in Developing Countries of Questionnaire Design, Sex of Interviewer, and Sex/proxy Status of Respondent.* Population and Policies Programme, Working Paper, No. 137. Geneva: International Labour Organisation.

_____, and M. Anker (1988). *Improving the Measurement of Women's Participation in the Egyptian Labour Force: Results of a Methodological Study.* Population and Labour Policies Programme, Working Paper No. 163. Geneva: International Labour Office.

Anker, Richard, and Catherine Hein, eds. (1986). *Vers la mesure des activités économiques des femmes.* Geneva: International Labour Office.

_____ (1987). *Desigualdades entre hombres y mujeres en los mercados de trabajo urbano del Tercer Mundo.* Geneva: International Labour Office.

Anker, Richard, M. E. Khan and R. B. Gupta (1988). *Women's Participation in the Labour Force: A Methods Test in India for Improving Its Measurement.* Women, Work and Development Series, No. 16. Geneva: International Labour Office.

Ballou, Janice (1990). Respondent/interviewer gender interaction effects in telephone interviews. Paper prepared for the International Conference on Measurement Errors in Surveys, Tucson, Arizona, 11-14 November.

Benería, Lourdes (1982). Accounting for women's work. In *Women and Development: The Sexual Division of Labour in Rural Societies*, Lourdes Benería, ed. New York: Praeger.

_____ (1991). The measurement of women's economic activities: assessing the theoretical and practical work of two decades. Paper prepared for Meeting of Experts on Social Development Indicators, Rabat, Morocco, 8-11 April. Geneva: United Nations Research Institute for Social Development.

Bilsborrow, Richard, and Richard Fuller (1988). La selectividad de los emigrantes rurales en la sierra ecuatoriana. *Estudios Demográficos y Urbanos* (Mexico City), vol. 3, No. 2 (Mayo-Agosto), pp. 265-290.

Bilsborrow, Richard E., and L. Ruiz Pozo (1990). Impactos demográficos de proyectos de desarrollo: una metodología aplicada al Ecuador. *Forum Valutazione* (Rome), vol. 0, pp. 33-61.

Bilsborrow, Richard E., A. S. Oberai and Guy Standing (1984). *Migration Surveys in Low-Income Countries: Guidelines for Survey and Questionnaire Design.* Beckenham, United Kingdom; and Sydney, Australia: Croom Helm.

Bilsborrow, Richard E., and others (1987). The impact of origin community characteristics on rural-urban out-migration in a developing country. *Demography* (Washington, D.C.), vol. 24, No. 2 (May), pp. 191-210.

Boserup, Ester (1970). *Woman's Role in Economic Development.* London: George Allen and Unwin; and New York: St. Martin's Press.

Bradburn, Norman M. (1983). Response effects. In *Handbook of Survey Research*, Peter Rossi, James D. Wright and Andy B. Anderson, eds. New York: Academic Press.

Byerlee, Derek, and Joseph L. Tommy (1976). *An Integrated Methodology for Migration Research: The Sierra Leone Rural-Urban Migration Survey.* East Lansing: Michigan State University; and Njala University College, Sierra Leone.

Cannell, Charles F., Peter V. Miller and Lois Oksenberg (1981). Research on interviewing techniques. In *Sociological Methodology*, vol. 11, Samuel Leinhardt, ed. San Francisco, California: Jossey-Bass.

Chandra Sekar, C., and W. Edwards Deming (1949). On a method of estimating birth and death rates and the extent of registration. *Journal of the American Statistical Association* (Alexandria, Virginia), vol. 44, No. 245 (March), pp. 101-115.

Dixon-Mueller, Ruth, and Richard Anker (1988). *Assessing Women's Economic Contribution to Development.* Population, Human Resources and Development Planning, Paper No. 6. Geneva: International Labour Office.

Fawcett, James T., Siew-Ean Khoo and Peter C. Smith (1984). Urbanization, migration and the status of women. In *Women in the Cities of Asia: Migration and Urban Adaptation*, James T. Fawcett, Siew-Ean Khoo and Peter C. Smith, eds. Boulder, Colorado: Westview Press.

Findley, Sally E., and Assitan Diallo (1993). Social appearances and economic realities of female migration in rural Mali. Chapter XIII in the present volume.

Forsyth, Barbara H., and J. T. Lessler (1990). Cognitive laboratory methods: a taxonomy. Paper prepared for the International Conference on Measurement Errors in Surveys, Tucson, Arizona, 11-14 November.

Freedman, Deborah, and others (1988). The life history calendar: a technique for collecting retrospective data. In *Sociological Methodology Nineteen Eighty-Eight*, vol. 18, Clifford C. Clogg, ed. Washington, D.C.: American Sociological Association.

Goldstein, Sidney, and Alice Goldstein (1979). Surveys of internal migration in developing countries: a methodological view. Background paper prepared for the International Statistical Institute/World Fertility Survey Expert Group Meeting on Methodology of Migration Measurement. London, 25-27 September.

Groves, Robert M. (1989). *Survey Errors and Survey Costs.* New York: John Wiley and Sons.

Guest, Philip (1993). The determinants of female migration from a multilevel perspective. Chapter XII in the present volume.

Gurak, Douglas T., and G. A. Gilbertson (1991). Female headship and the migration process: an event-history analysis of marital disruption among Dominican and Colombian immigrants. Paper presented at the Annual Meeting of the Population Association of America, Washington, D. C., 21-23 March.

Hetler, Carol B. (1989). The impact of circular migration on a village economy. *Bulletin of Indonesian Economic Studies* (Jakarta), vol. 25, No. 1 (April), pp. 53-75.

Hox, Joop J., E. D. de Leeuw and I. G. G. Kreft (1990). The effect of interviewer and respondent characteristics: a multilevel analysis. Paper prepared for the International Conference on Measurement Errors in Surveys, Tucson, Arizona, 11-14 November.

Hubacher, David, and Richard Bilsborrow (1990). *Efectos demográficos de grandes proyectos de desarrollo*. Conference of UNFPA/CELADE/CEDEM. Havana, Cuba, July. San José, Costa Rica: Imprenta Nacional for Centro Latinoamericano de Demografía.

Hubbard, Michael L., Judith T. Lessler and Rachel A. Caspar (1990). Sensitive questions in surveys. Paper prepared for the International Conference on Measurement Errors in Surveys, Tucson, Arizona, 11-14 November.

Ji, Ping, Kaiti Zhang and Dowei Liu (1986). Marriage-motivated population movement in the outskirts of Beijing. *Social Sciences in China* (Beijing), vol. 7, No. 1 (March), pp. 161-180.

Lim, Lin Lean (1993). The structural determinants of female migration. Chapter XI in the present volume.

Massey, Douglas S. (1990). Social structure, household strategies, and the cumulative causation of migration. *Population Index* (Princeton, New Jersey) vol. 56, No. 1 (Spring), pp. 3-26.

Moore, Jeffrey C. (1990). Proxy reports: results from a record check study. Paper prepared for the International Conference on Measurement Errors in Surveys, Tucson, Arizona, 11-14 November 1990.

Neter, J., and J. Waksberg (1965). *Response Errors in Collection of Expenditures Data by Household Interviews: An Experimental Study*. Technical Paper No. 11. Washington, D. C.: United States Bureau of the Census.

Oberai, A. S. (1984). Identification of migrants and collection of demographic and social information in migration surveys. In *Migration Surveys in Low-Income Countries: Guidelines for Survey and Questionnaire Design*, Richard E. Bilsborrow, A. S. Oberai and Guy Standing, eds. Beckenham, United Kingdom; and Sydney, Australia: Croom Helm.

_____, and H. K. Manmohan Singh (1983). *Causes and Consequences of Internal Migration in a Developing Country: A Study in the Indian Punjab*. Delhi and New York: Oxford University Press.

Palmer, Ingrid (1988). *Gender Issues in Structural Adjustment of sub-Saharan African Agriculture and Some Demographic Implications*. Population and Labour Policies Programme, Working Paper No. 166. Geneva: International Labour Office.

Peters, H. Elizabeth (1987). *Retrospective Versus Panel Data In Analyzing Life-Cycle Events*. Chicago, Illinois: Economics Research Center, NORC.

Phillips, Derek L. ((1971). *Knowledge from What? Theories and Methods in Social Research*. Chicago, Illinois: Rand McNally and Co.

Radloff, Scott Ray (1982). Measuring migration: a sensitivity analysis of traditional measurement approaches based on the Malaysian family life survey. Doctoral dissertation. Providence, Rhode Island: Brown University, Department of Sociology (available from University Microfilms).

Ravenstein, E. G. (1885). The laws of migration. *Journal of the Royal Statistical Society* (London), vol. 48, No. 2 (June), pp. 162-277.

Recchini de Lattes, Zulma, and Sonia María Mychaszula (1993). Female migration and labour force participation in a medium-sized city of a highly urbanized country. Chapter VIII in the present volume.

Rice, Stuart A. (1929). Contagious bias in the interview: A methodological note. *American Journal of Sociology* (Chicago, Illinois), vol. 35, No. 3 (November), pp. 420-423.

Rodenburg, Janet (1993). Emancipation or subordination? Consequences of female migration for migrants and their families. Chapter XV in the present volume.

Saefullah, Asep Djadja (1992). The impact of population mobility on two village communities of West Java, Indonesia. Doctoral dissertation. Adelaide: The Flinders University of South Australia.

Shryock, Henry S., and Jacob S. Siegel and associates (1976). *The Methods and Materials of Demography*, vols. 1 and 2. Washington, D.C.: United States Bureau of the Census.

Simmons, Alan, Sergio Diaz-Briquets and Aprodicio A. Laquian (1977). *Social Change and Internal Migration: A Review of Research Findings from Africa, Asia, and Latin America*. Ottawa, Canada: International Development Research Centre.

Singelmann, Joachim (1993). Global assessment of levels and trends of female internal migration. Chapter IV in the present volume.

Singleton, Royce, Jr., and others (1988). *Approaches to Social Research*. New York and Oxford: Oxford University Press.

Som, Ranjan Kumar (1973). *Recall Lapse in Demographic Enquiries*. New York: Asia Publishing House.

Standing, Guy (1983). *A Labour Status Approach to Labour Statistics*. Population and Labour Policies Programme, Working Paper No. 139. Geneva: International Labour Office.

_____ (1984). Conceptualising territorial mobility. In *Migration Surveys in Low-Income Countries: Guidelines for Survey and Questionnaire Design*, Richard E. Bilsborrow, A. S. Oberai and Guy Standing, eds. Beckenham, United Kingdom; and Sydney, Australia: Croom Helm.

Sudman, Seymour, and Norman M. Bradburn (1974). *Response Effects in Surveys: A Review and Synthesis*. Chicago, Illinois: Aldine Publishing Company.

_____ (1982). *Asking Questions: A Practical Guide to Questionnaire Design*. San Francisco, California: Jossey-Bass.

Union for African Population Studies (1990). *Literature Review on Migration Studies in Africa*. Dakar.

United Nations (1989). *Improving Statistics and Indicators on Women Using Household Surveys*. Studies in Methods, Series F, No. 48. Sales No. E.88.XVII.11.

_____ (1990). *Global Outlook, 2000*. Sales No. E.90.II.3.

United Nations Secretariat (1993). Types of female migration. Chapter V in the present volume.

Wainerman, Catalina H. (1991). *Improving the Accounting of Women Workers in Population Censuses: Lessons from Latin America*. World Employment Programme, Research Working Paper No. 178. Geneva: International Labour Office.

_____, and Zulma Recchini de Lattes (1981). *El Trabajo femenino en el banquillo de los acusados: la medición censal en América Latina*. Colección Economía y Sociedad. Mexico, D.F.: The Population Council/Editorial Terra Nova.

Waring, Marilyn (1988). *If Women Counted: A New Feminist Economics*. San Francisco, California: Harper Collins.

Watts, Susan J. (1983). Marriage migration, a neglected form of long-term mobility: a case study from Ilorin, Nigeria. *International Migration Review* (Staten Island, New York), vol. 17, No. 4 (Winter), pp. 682-698.

Yang, Xiushi, and Richard Bilsborrow (1992). Survey locales and biases in migration data collection and analysis. Chapel Hill, North Carolina: Carolina Population Center. Unpublished.

Part Four

CHARACTERISTICS OF FEMALE MIGRANTS AND SELECTIVITY

VII. CHARACTERISTICS OF FEMALE MIGRANTS ACCORDING TO THE 1990 CENSUS OF MEXICO

María de la Paz López*, Haydea Izazola**
and José Gómez de León***

The impact of migration on areas of origin and destination depends upon not only the magnitude of the flows involved but also the socio-economic and demographic characteristics of migrants. The selectivity of migration in terms of age, sex, education, work experience and qualifications, to name only a few, is likely to affect the marriage market, the labour-market, the demand for housing and services and the household composition of both the communities of origin and those of destination. Just as migrants in general, female migrants tend to be selected on the basis of specific characteristics. Understanding the dimensions of migration selectivity in the case of women is a necessary step towards a better understanding of the forces that give rise to their migration.

Recent studies on female migration in developing countries have underscored its relevance (Hugo, 1993). However, despite efforts to achieve a more thorough characterization of female migration, much remains to be done. The inadequacy of data sources and the continued prevalence of narrow conceptual frameworks still hinder the analysis of the processes leading to the migration of women.

In Mexico, most of the studies focusing on migration at the macrolevel either disregard its female component altogether or focus only on the age and sex differentials of migration.[1] Studies focusing on the local level or the microlevel, which are mostly of a sociological or anthropological nature, tend to address more thoroughly certain issues of relevance to female migration.[2] These studies indicate that migrant women differ in many respects from non-migrant women in both the areas of origin and destination. Unfortunately, their conclusions can only rarely be generalized to the regional or national level.

This paper uses the information gathered by the 1990 population census of Mexico to explore the distinctive characteristics of female internal migrants. The characteristics of all migrants at the national level are compared with those enumerated in four different states, each representing a specific socio-economic context. The four federal states chosen are Baja California, the state of Mexico, Quintana Roo and Zacatecas.

Baja California is the easternmost state of Mexico bordering the United States. It is one of the most rapidly growing states in the country, particularly because of migration. The expansion of the *maquiladora* industry along the border during the 1970s and 1980s has been credited with attracting a large number of migrants to the region. Around 1990, there were a total of 1,880 *maquiladoras* in Mexico, 85 per cent of which were located in the states bordering the United States and 37 per cent of which (703) were in Baja California. The *maquiladoras* employed approximately 87,000 workers; nearly 60 per cent of them were women (Carrillo and Hernández, 1985; Margulis and Tuirán, 1986; Zenteno, n.d.). The state of Baja California also contains the border city of Tijuana, one of the major points of entry of undocumented migrants to the United States, and thus attracts many would-be emigrants from throughout Mexico and Central America.

The state of Mexico, which is adjacent to the Federal District and therefore to the capital of the country, is one of the major migrant-receiving states in Mexico. Some of its *municipios* are part of the Mexico City metropolitan area and belong therefore to one of the

---

*Asesora del Subsecretario de Coordinación y Desarrollo de la Secretaría de Salud.
**Consultora, Centro de Estudios de Población y Salud, Secretaría de Salud.
***Director General, Centro de Estudios de Población y Salud, Secretaría de Salud.

largest urban concentrations in the world. Through the expansion of the Mexico City conurbation, the state of Mexico is an important attraction pole for migrants from throughout the country. However, some of its rural *municipios* are relatively poor and have traditionally been the source of emigrants to the United States and of out-migrants to other parts of Mexico (Szasz, 1990).

With an estimated growth rate of 8 per cent per annum, Quintana Roo is the fastest growing state in Mexico and much of its growth is due to migration. The main pull factor in the state has been the growth of the tourist industry associated with the development of Cancún. The state has therefore attracted a large number of workers in the service sector (CONAPO, 1984a). Quintana Roo is located in the south-eastern part of Mexico, bordering Belize and Guatemala.

Zacatecas is one of the poorer states of the country. Located in the central plateau of Mexico, its economy depends mainly upon two currently depressed activities: traditional agriculture; and mining. People from Zacatecas have a long tradition of engaging in circular migration to the United States (CONAPO, 1984b).

The data used were obtained from a sample of the preliminary results of the XI Population and Housing Census of Mexico, conducted in March 1990. The sample was drawn with the double aim of checking the quality and validity of the census results during the different processing stages and of producing preliminary results with some degree of detail. Each of the 32 federal states of Mexico (including the Federal District) is fully represented in the sample. Although the sampling units are dwellings, the data used here refer to the characteristics of individuals.

Information on internal migration derived from censuses has both advantages and limitations. In Mexico, the census is the only statistical source yielding migration information for all the population of the country and it allows the consideration of a number of variables that are thought to be relevant for the migration process. By its very nature, however, the census can only include a limited set of questions and cannot probe to improve the quality of the information obtained. The 1990 census of Mexico allows the identification of interstate migrants on the basis of a question on place of residence exactly five years prior to the census. Only the federal states and "abroad" were accepted as responses to that question. Therefore, the state is the smallest unit that can be used to identify migrants. As Bilsborrow (1993) notes, this approach is likely to understate female migration because migration over shorter distances is not reflected properly in the data at hand. In addition, because states include both urban and rural areas and no attempt was made to record the urban or rural origin of migrants, the different types of flows (rural-urban, rural-rural, urban-urban and urban-rural) cannot be measured.

Throughout this paper, therefore, migrants are defined as persons who reported at the time of the 1990 census that their state of residence in 1985 was different from that of their current residence. At the national level, the total number of migrants thus defined can be interpreted as either the in-migrants to all the federal states or the out-migrants from them. At the state level, however, distinct measures of in-migration and out-migration are possible.

The 1990 census of Mexico also permits the identification of migrants on the basis of place of birth, but the measures of lifetime migration obtained on that basis are less than ideal because the time of migration cannot be controlled for, nor is there any certainty that only one move has occurred. It is generally accepted that the identification of migrants on the basis of a question on place of residence at a fixed point in the past yields better estimates than those obtained from information on place of birth. Neither measure, however, properly reflects multiple moves and both exclude as migrants those migrating and returning to their place of origin within the interval considered (the preceding five years or since birth, as the case might be).

With respect to the topics selected for analysis, two sets of census variables representing factors commonly cited in the literature as relevant for the understanding of female migration are considered. The first includes sociodemographic variables, such as age, marital status and relationship to the head of household. The second consists of several socio-economic variables, such as education, labour force participation, occupation or income, which are closely related to the economic aspects of migration.

A. SOCIODEMOGRAPHIC CHARACTERISTICS OF
FEMALE MIGRANTS

The 1990 census of Mexico enumerated approximately 3.6 million recent migrants, that is, persons who in 1985 had lived in a state different from that in which they were enumerated. Among those migrants, women outnumbered men by nearly 100,000, accounting for 51.4 per cent of the total (table 16). This pattern of relative female dominance in total migration is consistent with that observed in most of the other Latin American countries. Overall, recent migrants constituted about 5 per cent of the population aged five years or over. The total number of lifetime migrants (persons whose state of birth was different from that of enumeration) was higher, amounting to 14 million persons and constituting about 17.4 per cent of the total population. Among lifetime migrants, women were somewhat more dominant, accounting for 52.2 per cent of the total.

There were considerable differences between the four states considered with regard to the relative weight of women among recent migrants. As table 16 indicates, women accounted for 47.2 per cent of all in-migrants to Quintana Roo, 48.9 per cent of those to Baja California, 51.3 per cent of those to Zacatecas and 52 per cent of those enumerated in the state of Mexico. Interestingly, women failed to constitute a majority among the recent migrants enumerated in the two border states, Baja California and Quintana Roo, which have been experiencing the most dynamic economic transformation. It is especially noteworthy that despite its thriving *maquiladora* industry, the northern state of Baja California did not appear to attract women selectively. It was rather among migrants to the long-established attraction pole, represented here by the state of Mexico, that women dominated.

In considering the sex selectivity of migration at the state level it is important to bear in mind the relative

TABLE 16. DISTRIBUTION OF THE POPULATION AGED FIVE YEARS OR OVER BY MIGRATION STATUS, SEX AND STATE OF ORIGIN OR DESTINATION, MEXICO, 1990
(*Percentage*)

State	Total	Non-migrant	In-migrant	Out-migrant	Net migration (thousands)
A. *Male*					
Mexico (thousands)	34 600	32 470	1 725	1 725	-
Baja California	2.1	1.8	6.1	1.4	81
State of Mexico	12.1	11.5	23.0	7.6	266
Quintana Roo	0.6	0.5	2.9	0.6	40
Zacatecas	1.5	1.6	1.1	1.9	-13
B. *Female*					
Mexico (thousands)	36 354	34 105	1 826	1 826	-
Baja California	2.0	1.8	5.5	1.2	80
State of Mexico	12.1	11.5	23.5	7.7	288
Quintana Roo	0.6	0.5	2.4	0.6	34
Zacatecas	1.6	1.6	1.1	1.9	-15
C. *Percentage female*					
Mexico	51.2	51.2	51.4	-	-
Baja California	50.1	50.5	48.9	46.6	49.6
State of Mexico	51.2	51.1	52.0	51.9	52.0
Quintana Roo	47.9	48.1	47.2	50.9	46.1
Zacatecas	51.6	51.7	51.3	51.9	-52.6[a]

[a] The minus sign indicates that both male and female net migration are negative.

importance of migration within each context. In Quintana Roo, for instance, recent migrants constituted 22 per cent of the total population aged five years or over. The equivalent proportion was 14 per cent in Baja California, 10 per cent in the state of Mexico and just 3.5 per cent in Zacatecas. In terms of total numbers of migrants, however, the state of Mexico was dominant, having attracted about 23 per cent of all recent migrants enumerated in the country. Baja California occupied second place, accounting for approximately 6 per cent of all recent migrants. Quintana Roo with slightly under 3 per cent and Zacatecas with slightly over 1 per cent followed suit. That is, although migration was clearly very important in relative terms for the border states of Baja California and Quintana Roo, they were considerably less attractive for migrants than the state of Mexico and, with respect to female migration in particular, the latter attracted about three times as many women than the two border states put together (see table 16).

There are also important differences in the relative participation of women in out-migration from the different states. Thus, whereas women constitute a majority of the out-migrants from Zacatecas (52 per cent), the state of Mexico (52 per cent) and Quintana Roo (51 per cent), they are considerably underrepresented among out-migrants from Baja California (47 per cent). Such differences become accentuated when net migration is considered. In terms of net migration, the state of Mexico is the only one gaining more women than men. Baja California gains slightly more men than women and Quintana Roo gains considerably more men than women. Zacatecas, being a state of net emigration, loses more women than men (see table 16).

Age selectivity

It is well known that migrants constitute a selected group in terms of age. With respect to the non-migrant population, migrants tend to be overrepresented in age range 15-39 or 15-44 and to be underrepresented at younger and older ages. The age distribution of migrants generally reaches a peak somewhere within age range 15-29. Female migrants tend to be slightly more concentrated in the younger ages of age range 15-39 than are their male counterparts. Census data confirm that recent migrants in Mexico conform to such patterns of age selectivity (table 17). It is important to bear in mind, however, that the data on age produced by the census refer to the age of migrants at the time of enumeration and not to their age at the time of migration. However, by focusing only on recent migrants (those changing residence within the five years preceding the census), it can be assumed that, on average, migrants were about 2.5 years younger at the time of migration than at the time of the census. The present discussion, however, is in terms of the age reported at the time of the census.

Table 17 shows that for the country as a whole, female migrants tend to be even more concentrated in age groups 15-19 and 20-24 than male migrants and that their overrepresentation in age group 30-44 is less marked than that among male migrants. Among the different states, in-migrants to the state of Mexico display age distribution differentials by sex similar to those of the country as a whole, with a clear concentration of migrant women over age range 15-24. Zacatecas also displays a more marked concentration of female migrants than males in that age range. In Quintana Roo, in contrast, migrant women are more concentrated in age group 5-14 than migrant men; and in Baja California, the age distributions of male and female in-migrants are remarkably similar.

When the age distribution of female in-migrants is compared with that of female out-migrants two patterns emerge. In Baja California and Quintana Roo, female out-migrants tend to be more concentrated in age group 30-44 and in older age groups than in the younger age groups where female in-migrants are concentrated. In Zacatecas and to a lesser extent in the state of Mexico, female out-migrants show a tendency towards being concentrated in the younger age groups of age range 15-44, just as in-migrants are. Although one can only speculate about the causes of such differences, it is worth noting that the pattern of age selectivity in out-migration displayed by Baja California and Quintana Roo suggests that out-migrants tend to be slightly older and that perhaps return migration is an important component of out-migration. In Zacatecas, in contrast, out-migration is likely to be dominated by first-time migrants and therefore its age distribution resembles more closely that of in-migrants in other states.

TABLE 17. DISTRIBUTION OF THE POPULATION AGED FIVE YEARS OR OVER BY MIGRATION STATUS, SEX AND AGE GROUP, SELECTED STATES OF ORIGIN AND DESTINATION, MEXICO, 1990
(Percentage)

Age group	Male			Female		
	Non-migrant	In-migrant	Out-migrant	Non-migrant	In-migrant	Out-migrant
A. Mexico						
5-14	29.4	24.9	-	27.4	23.9	-
15-19	13.2	13.5	-	13.1	15.7	-
20-24	10.9	14.7	-	11.4	16.4	-
25-29	9.1	12.7	-	9.3	13.0	-
30-44	18.8	22.8	-	19.3	20.2	-
45-59	10.6	7.4	-	10.9	6.2	-
60+	7.6	3.8	-	8.1	4.2	-
TOTAL	99.7	99.7	-	99.5	99.6	-
B. Baja California						
5-14	24.5	21.4	24.2	23.1	23.6	25.0
15-19	12.6	16.5	11.9	13.0	15.1	15.6
20-24	11.8	21.6	16.2	11.7	21.1	13.1
25-29	10.8	13.9	13.9	11.0	13.4	10.8
30-44	20.6	18.2	20.0	21.1	17.7	23.5
45-59	11.6	6.0	8.4	12.0	5.7	8.5
60+	7.7	2.3	5.2	7.6	3.0	2.9
TOTAL	99.6	99.9	99.7	99.5	99.5	99.5
C. State of Mexico						
5-14	29.5	26.7	28.4	27.7	24.0	25.7
15-19	13.4	11.3	13.1	13.0	13.1	16.2
20-24	11.5	12.6	11.5	12.1	14.8	14.5
25-29	9.8	13.0	12.0	9.9	14.3	11.5
30-44	20.1	25.9	23.9	20.4	22.8	21.1
45-59	9.9	6.8	7.0	10.1	6.1	6.3
60+	5.6	3.3	3.9	6.4	4.3	4.1
TOTAL	99.7	99.7	99.6	99.6	99.5	99.5
D. Quintana Roo						
5-14	32.4	19.6	25.9	32.3	25.0	26.0
15-19	12.1	18.0	12.5	13.5	17.2	13.7
20-24	10.9	19.6	11.6	12.2	18.7	12.0
25-29	9.7	15.0	9.2	9.6	13.8	10.6
30-44	20.7	18.9	31.9	19.9	18.1	26.3
45-59	9.4	6.5	5.6	8.9	5.3	4.4
60+	4.5	2.2	2.8	3.3	1.7	5.8
TOTAL	99.6	99.8	99.4	99.8	99.9	98.9
E. Zacatecas						
5-14	33.9	35.0	25.1	31.4	32.5	26.0
15-19	14.2	9.7	17.2	14.9	15.2	17.4
20-24	10.6	11.4	17.3	11.0	13.8	16.7
25-29	6.6	10.9	9.0	7.3	8.8	11.0
30-44	15.0	22.6	16.3	16.0	18.1	15.5
45-59	10.5	5.9	7.8	10.8	7.2	8.3
60+	8.9	4.2	7.0	8.3	4.1	5.2
TOTAL	99.7	99.7	99.7	99.6	99.7	100.0

These comparisons cannot but be illustrative. Various mixes of contextual factors that selectively impinge upon migration by age underlie the differences detected. Indeed, age selectivity itself results from the processes leading to migration, which are in turn strongly related to the individual life cycle of the migrant, whether male or female.

Status within the household

The relation between migration and the status of the migrant within the household is complex, particularly because causality can run both ways, since a certain status within the household may be more or less conducive to migration and that migration will often modify the household composition itself (Oliveira, 1984). Census data are insufficient to explore the interrelations between household composition and migration. Nevertheless, they indicate that certain patterns exist.

The census defines a household as a domestic unit and household members are identified in terms of their kinship ties with the head of the household, making allowance for the existence of unrelated co-dwellers. The types of household members considered in the analysis are: the head of household; his or her spouse (or cohabitant); children of the head of household; other kin; domestic servants and other unrelated persons. Persons living alone are identified separately as one-person households.

As in most countries, most households in Mexico are headed by men (81.5 per cent of all heads of household and persons living alone are men). Among migrants, the proportion of men among household heads and persons living on their own is slightly higher, amounting to 84.2 per cent. Men account for 83.2 per cent of non-migrants declared as heads of household and for 85.5 per cent of their migrant counterparts. The difference between migrants and non-migrants is considerably more marked among persons living on their own: 54 per cent of non-migrants in that category are men whereas among migrants the equivalent proportion is 70 per cent.

The preponderance of men among heads of household is not as high in Mexico as in other Latin American countries (De Vos, 1987). According to the 1990 census, nearly one in every five households is headed by a woman (18.5 per cent). However, migrant women are less well represented as heads of household than their non-migrant counterparts. They are also considerably less well represented than non-migrants among persons living alone (only 30 per cent of the migrant one-person households consist of a woman living alone, compared with 46 per cent among the corresponding non-migrant category).

A comparison of the distribution of migrants with non-migrants in terms of their status within the household indicates that, at the level of the country as a whole, male migrants are somewhat more likely that their non-migrant counterparts to be the head of household and female migrants are more likely that non-migrant women to be the spouse of the head of household (see table 18). Although female migrants are slightly less likely than non-migrant women to be a head of household, if the two categories, head of household and spouse, are taken together, migrants of both sexes are somewhat better represented in them than non-migrants. In contrast, both male and female migrants are strongly underrepresented as children of the head of the household. The difference between the proportion of non-migrants and migrants in that category is largely counterbalanced by the relative excess of migrants over non-migrants in the categories of other relatives, unrelated co-dwellers and persons living alone in the case of men or domestic servants in the case of women. Thus, whereas only 7.6 per cent of male non-migrants are found in those four categories, the equivalent proportion among migrants is 19 per cent. Among women, the comparison is between 9.7 and 19.6 per cent for non-migrants and migrants, respectively. These differences corroborate that migrants are more likely than non-migrants to live away from their immediate relatives (i.e., spouses and children), especially as other relatives or unrelated co-dwellers within a household.

The patterns discussed above at the national level are largely repeated at the state level. Thus, in-migrants of both sexes are considerably less likely than non-migrants to be the children of the head of household and they tend to be more likely to be the head of household or the spouse (see table 18). However, male and female in-migrants to Baja California and, to a lesser extent,

TABLE 18. DISTRIBUTION OF THE POPULATION AGED FIVE YEARS OR OVER BY RELATIONSHIP TO HEAD OF HOUSEHOLD, MIGRATION STATUS AND SEX, SELECTED STATES OF ORIGIN AND DESTINATION, MEXICO, 1990
(Percentage)

Relationship to head of household	Male			Female		
	Non-migrant	In-migrant	Out-migrant	Non-migrant	In-migrant	Out-migrant

A. Mexico

Head of household	39.2	41.8	-	7.5	6.7	-
Spouse of head	0.6	0.7	-	34.6	37.3	-
Children of head	49.1	34.1	-	43.8	31.4	-
"Independent" members	7.7	18.9	-	9.7	19.7	-
Other relative	5.1	11.3	-	7.0	11.8	-
Unrelated co-dweller	0.7	4.2	-	0.8	2.9	-
Domestic servant	0.1	0.4	-	0.5	3.7	-
One-person household	1.7	3.1	-	1.4	1.2	-
Unknown	3.4	4.5	-	4.3	4.9	-

B. Baja California

Head of household	43.4	37.9	36.7	9.7	8.6	6.6
Spouse of head	0.8	1.0	0.5	38.7	37.0	36.0
Child of head	44.1	29.7	48.1	39.7	30.0	40.5
"Independent" members	9.0	26.6	13.0	8.8	19.3	12.4
Other relative	5.3	14.6	8.7	5.8	12.1	8.7
Unrelated co-dweller	1.1	8.1	1.9	0.9	5.0	2.3
Domestic servant	0.1	0.1	0.0	0.2	1.1	0.3
One-person household	2.6	3.7	2.5	1.9	1.0	1.0
Unknown	2.7	4.8	1.6	3.2	5.2	4.4

C. State of Mexico

Head of household	40.1	46.1	40.8	7.0	6.7	6.0
Spouse of head	0.5	0.5	0.7	35.6	41.8	33.3
Child of head	50.0	37.2	38.8	44.8	32.1	34.2
"Independent" members	6.0	12.9	16.1	8.3	15.3	21.2
Other relative	4.3	9.5	10.4	6.1	10.7	10.5
Unrelated co-dweller	0.5	1.5	2.5	0.6	1.3	2.7
Domestic servant	0.1	0.2	0.6	0.5	2.3	6.9
One-person household	1.1	1.7	2.6	1.1	1.1	1.1
Unknown	3.5	3.3	3.6	4.2	4.1	5.2

D. Quintana Roo

Head of household	38.9	39.5	43.5	5.8	5.6	10.9
Spouse of head	1.0	0.8	0.6	36.9	39.9	37.7
Child of head	47.2	29.7	33.9	43.5	31.1	30.8
"Independent" members	8.6	22.8	17.7	7.8	17.1	15.1
Other relative	4.8	12.9	10.9	6.0	10.3	10.2
Unrelated co-dweller	1.2	6.4	3.5	0.7	3.3	1.7
Domestic servant	0.4	0.6	0.0	0.5	2.1	1.6
One-person household	2.3	2.8	3.4	0.6	1.4	1.6
Unknown	4.3	7.3	4.3	5.9	6.4	5.5

TABLE 18 (continued)

Relationship to head of household	Male			Female		
	Non-migrant	In-migrant	Out-migrant	Non-migrant	In-migrant	Out-migrant

E. *Zacatecas*

Relationship	Non-migrant	In-migrant	Out-migrant	Non-migrant	In-migrant	Out-migrant
Head of household	36.2	37.0	33.8	5.7	6.5	5.9
Spouse of head	0.5	0.6	0.6	32.2	32.2	34.3
Child of head	55.0	47.0	34.0	51.1	43.4	32.3
"Independent" members	4.8	12.7	25.6	6.8	14.9	22.1
Other relative	3.3	7.2	19.7	4.9	10.0	16.0
Unrelated co-dweller	0.5	3.2	4.1	0.6	3.5	2.7
Domestic servant	0.0	0.0	0.0	0.1	0.0	2.7
One-person household	0.9	2.3	1.8	1.2	1.3	0.7
Unknown	3.5	2.7	6.0	4.2	3.0	5.3

male in-migrants to Quintana Roo are not as well represented among heads of household and their spouses as are non-migrants. Consequently, especially in those two states, there is a marked concentration of migrants in the four "independent" categories of household members: other relatives; unrelated co-dwellers; domestic servants; and persons living on their own. In Baja California, for instance, nearly 27 per cent of all male in-migrants are in those categories, compared with only 9 per cent of male non-migrants. The equivalent figures for women are 19 per cent for in-migrants and 9 per cent for non-migrants. Quintana Roo displays equally sharp differentials: 23 per cent of male and 17 per cent of female in-migrants belong to the four "independent" categories, compared with 9 and 8 per cent of male and female non-migrants, respectively. In the state of Mexico and Zacatecas, the percentage of persons in those categories tends to be lower, but the differences between migrants and non-migrants are equally marked. Furthermore, in both of those states a higher percentage of female in-migrants belongs to the four "independent" categories than that of males: 15 versus 13 per cent in both cases. That is, in both Baja California and Quintana Roo, female in-migrants are more likely to live with their immediate relatives than are their male counterparts, whereas the reverse is true for those in the state of Mexico and Zacatecas. However, both male and female in-migrants are considerably more likely to live away from their immediate relatives if they find themselves in Baja California and Quintana Roo than if they live in the state of Mexico or Zacatecas.

With respect to out-migrants, few generalizations can be made. Indeed, among out-migrants from Baja California, persons who are either the head of household or the spouse of the head are underrepresented in relation to non-migrants, and children of heads of household are overrepresented. In most of the other states the reverse is true, thus repeating in the case of out-migrants the pattern common with respect to in-migrants. The relative concentration in the four "independent" categories observed among in-migrants is also apparent in the case of out-migrants, but in this case women leaving the state of Mexico and Zacatecas are far more likely to be in those categories than are those leaving Baja California and Quintana Roo. In addition, only in the case of the state of Mexico are female out-migrants more likely than males to be in the "independent" categories.

Although these data are far from ideal to establish the type of migration involved, they nevertheless suggest that states like Baja California or Quintana Roo have been more likely to attract male and female migrants moving on their own, that is, without their immediate family members, than the other two states considered. Similarly, the state of Mexico and Zacatecas have been more likely to be the source of such migrants. Once at destination, however, the majority of those migrants live in multi-person households, mostly as other relatives of the head of household or as unrelated co-dwellers. Male migrants also tend to live on their own, whereas female migrants are almost as likely to be in domestic service.

Marital status

Another characteristic closely associated with the propensity to migrate, particularly in the case of women, is marital status. The 1990 census gathered information on whether the population aged 12 or over was single, married (by a religious ceremony, by law or both), living in a consensual union, or separated, divorced or widowed. Table 19 shows the distribution of migrants and non-migrants by marital status. As in the case of all the variables considered here, marital status reflects the situation of the enumerated population at the time of the census and not at the time of migration. There is no way to adjust for changes of marital status that may have taken place after migration.

At the level of the country as a whole, the data in table 19 indicate that migrants, whether male or female, are slightly less likely to be single than non-migrants. They are also more likely to be married or in a consensual union than non-migrants; and although the percentage of separated and divorced persons is slightly higher among migrants than non-migrants, migrants are less likely to be in the combined category of separated, divorced or widowed than are non-migrants. Even within the category of migrant, a higher proportion is married or in consensual union than single: 56 versus 40 per cent among men; and 57 versus 36 per cent among women. According to these data, therefore, migrants, whether male or female, cannot be characterized as being mostly young and single.

There are important differences in the distribution by marital status of the migrants in the different states considered. Male in-migrants to Baja California and Quintana Roo are considerably more likely to be single than non-migrants and are also less likely to be married than non-migrants. The reverse is true for male in-migrants to the state of Mexico and Zacatecas. Female in-migrants to Quintana Roo are also more likely to be single than non-migrants but in all other states they are less likely than non-migrants to be single. The difference in the proportion single of female in-migrants and non-migrants is smallest in Baja California which, together with Quintana Roo, is a state where female in-migrants are less likely to be married than non-migrants. However, in Baja California, the percentage of female in-migrants that are either married or in consensual union surpasses that of non-migrants. That is, the data on marital status confirm to a certain extent the suggestions made on the basis of data on status within the household. Baja California and Quintana Roo attract a higher proportion of unattached migrants (single in this case), although their attractiveness is stronger with respect to men.

With respect to out-migration, the patterns by state are less clear. Female out-migrants originating in the state of Mexico and Quintana Roo are more likely to be single or divorced and less likely to be married than non-migrants. Male out-migrants from Baja California display similar differences in relation to non-migrants. Otherwise, out-migrants tend to be less likely than non-migrants to be single and more likely to be married or in a consensual union.

B. SOCIO-ECONOMIC CHARACTERISTICS OF FEMALE MIGRANTS

As with all migration, women that move are known to constitute a selected group in terms of certain socio-economic characteristics, including their level of education, their labour force participation and their occupation. The analysis of migration selectivity in terms of those variables is again limited by the scope and quality of the census information available. In particular, the census information on economic activity is likely to understate female labour force participation (Wainerman and Recchini de Lattes, 1981) and it fails to characterize adequately the formal or informal nature of the economic activity in which women engage. In addition, although the census gathered information on income, the quality of such information is known to be poor, representing at best a crude approximation to the actual income earned by those reported as being employed. With those caveats in mind, the characterization of migrants in terms of those variables is examined below.

Educational attainment

Educational attainment is one of the characteristics more commonly considered in migration studies, since migrants usually constitute a selected group in terms of education. For the purposes of this analysis, four levels

TABLE 19. DISTRIBUTION OF THE POPULATION AGED 12 YEARS OR OVER BY MARITAL STATUS, MIGRATION STATUS AND SEX, SELECTED STATES OF ORIGIN AND DESTINATION, MEXICO, 1990
(Percentage)

Marital status	Male			Female		
	Non-migrant	In-migrant	Out-migrant	Non-migrant	In-migrant	Out-migrant
A. Mexico						
Single	41.7	40.2	-	37.0	35.5	-
Married	46.8	47.0	-	45.1	45.7	-
Consensual union	7.6	9.2	-	7.9	10.8	-
Separated or divorced	1.1	1.4	-	3.0	3.1	-
Widowed	1.7	1.0	-	6.1	4.0	-
Unknown	1.1	1.3	-	0.9	0.9	-
B. Baja California						
Single	40.2	47.9	43.9	34.7	33.2	32.8
Married	45.4	36.2	41.8	45.1	41.8	49.8
Consensual union	9.5	12.2	10.5	9.6	16.8	11.1
Separated or divorced	1.6	1.1	2.0	3.6	3.7	3.0
Widowed	1.4	0.7	0.8	5.6	3.2	2.1
Unknown	1.8	2.0	0.9	1.4	1.3	1.2
C. State of Mexico						
Single	41.2	35.1	38.7	36.7	31.0	37.9
Married	48.5	50.6	48.7	46.8	48.0	44.3
Consensual union	6.9	10.6	9.5	7.2	11.8	10.1
Separated or divorced	0.9	1.4	1.9	3.0	3.4	3.6
Widowed	1.3	1.0	0.8	5.4	4.8	3.3
Unknown	1.2	1.3	0.4	1.0	0.9	0.8
D. Quintana Roo						
Single	39.9	45.4	35.0	32.0	34.3	34.8
Married	48.7	42.5	53.5	52.6	48.1	48.4
Consensual union	7.8	8.8	7.1	8.5	12.3	8.3
Separated or divorced	1.5	1.5	1.5	3.0	2.6	3.9
Widowed	1.3	0.3	0.7	3.4	1.5	2.6
Unknown	0.7	1.5	2.1	0.6	1.2	1.9
E. Zacatecas						
Single	44.2	43.7	42.6	42.6	38.2	36.5
Married	49.9	50.4	47.2	48.0	49.2	47.4
Consensual union	2.5	3.1	4.5	2.4	5.9	7.3
Separated or divorced	0.6	0.0	2.0	1.4	1.4	2.6
Widowed	1.5	0.4	1.3	4.8	4.4	4.8
Unknown	1.2	2.4	2.4	0.8	0.9	1.5

of educational attainment are considered: zero schooling; from one to three years of primary school; from three to six years of primary school; and post-primary education. The last category lumps together a wide range of educational levels but its use has the advantage of avoiding small numbers.

As table 20 indicates, at the national level men display a more favourable distribution of educational attainment than do women, with lower proportions in the zero schooling category and higher ones in the category with more than six years of schooling. Furthermore, as expected, the distribution by educational attainment of migrants is considerably more favourable than that of non-migrants. Thus, whereas only 33 per cent of non-migrant men had more than six years of schooling, the equivalent proportion was 47 per cent among migrants. Among women, the difference, though smaller, was still considerable: 31 versus 42 per cent. Indeed, the distribution by educational attainment of migrant women as a whole is more favourable than that of all non-migrant men.

TABLE 20. DISTRIBUTION OF THE POPULATION AGED 12 YEARS OR OVER BY EDUCATIONAL ATTAINMENT, MIGRATION STATUS AND SEX, SELECTED STATES OF ORIGIN AND DESTINATION, MEXICO, 1990
(Percentage)

Years of schooling	Male			Female		
	Non-migrant	In-migrant	Out-migrant	Non-migrant	In-migrant	Out-migrant
A. Mexico						
Zero	15.8	11.4	-	18.1	12.5	-
One to three	21.3	15.7	-	20.3	15.9	-
Four to six	27.3	23.8	-	28.2	27.4	-
Over six	33.1	47.0	-	30.5	41.8	-
Unknown	2.6	2.1	-	2.9	2.5	-
B. Baja California						
Zero	10.4	9.8	9.7	10.3	11.1	12.8
One to three	15.9	15.1	14.9	16.0	17.0	18.5
Four to six	25.4	25.4	23.3	27.1	27.7	25.3
Over six	45.2	46.2	50.9	43.4	40.3	41.4
Unknown	3.0	3.5	1.1	3.2	4.0	2.0
C. State of Mexico						
Zero	12.2	10.1	10.0	15.6	11.5	12.9
One to three	18.5	14.5	16.3	18.8	15.0	16.2
Four to six	27.5	25.4	27.0	28.2	28.2	29.5
Over six	39.8	48.3	45.0	34.7	43.0	39.0
Unknown	2.0	1.7	1.7	2.6	2.2	2.3
D. Quintana Roo						
Zero	16.1	11.0	14.9	18.3	15.7	13.6
One to three	24.1	18.2	14.3	25.9	19.5	13.5
Four to six	27.9	24.4	19.0	26.9	24.1	20.7
Over six	29.4	43.2	51.3	25.6	36.3	49.2
Unknown	2.6	3.2	0.6	3.2	4.3	3.1
E. Zacatecas						
Zero	15.9	13.1	18.0	15.5	14.6	14.8
One to three	29.3	21.5	20.5	26.6	22.9	19.5
Four to six	32.3	27.1	30.4	35.4	27.8	40.0
Over six	20.5	36.5	28.1	20.1	33.8	22.9
Unknown	2.1	1.8	3.0	2.4	0.9	2.9

At the state level, there are considerable differences in the educational attainment of the non-migrant population. Zacatecas displays the most unfavourable distribution by educational attainment, with only about 20 per cent of its population having more than six years of schooling and nearly 16 per cent having no schooling at all. At the other end of the spectrum, Baja California displays the most favourable distribution, with 44 per cent of the population having at least six years of schooling and only 10 per cent having zero schooling. Consequently, the fact that only in Baja California do in-migrants fail to display a better distribution by educational attainment than the non-migrant population is less an indication of migration selectivity than a result of the high standards set by the state. With that exception, in-migrants of both sexes in all the other states considered consistently display a more favourable distribution by educational attainment than the non-migrant population. However, favourable differentials tend to be higher for males than for females. In particular, the proportion of female in-migrants with more than six years of schooling is consistently lower than that of their male counterparts. On the whole, the state of Mexico attracts the best qualified in-migrant population in terms of education. Baja California is not far behind, followed by Quintana Roo and then by Zacatecas.

With respect to out-migration, a positive selection in terms of education is clearly in operation in most cases. The main exception is that of women leaving Baja California; they tend to be somewhat less well educated than their non-migrant counterparts. The high selectivity of out-migration from Quintana Roo is worth underscoring. On the whole, that state seems to export more highly qualified people than those it imports. Baja California is in a similar position, particularly with respect to male out-migrants. However, given the relatively low educational attainment of the non-migrant population of Quintana Roo, the impact of the educational selectivity of migration is likely to be stronger there. Lastly, it is worth noting that in both the state of Mexico and Zacatecas the distribution by educational attainment of in-migrants is more favourable than that of out-migrants and that the differentials in favour of the receiving state are stronger in the case of women.

Labour force participation

The labour force participation of women in Mexico is generally low. Two factors contributing to that state of affairs are the prevalence of a male-oriented labour-market and of norms and values that confine women to the home. Nevertheless, Mexico has been experiencing a gradual increase in the labour force participation of women, particularly of those living in cities (Pedrero, 1990). According to the 1990 census, 19.5 per cent of the women aged 12 years or over were effectively employed during the week preceding the census. The corresponding figure for men in the same age group was 67 per cent. Among male migrants that proportion reached 72 per cent, whereas among migrant women it rose to 26 per cent (see table 21). That is, migrants are more likely to be employed than non-migrants, regardless of their sex.

The data in table 21 indicate that women are highly concentrated in the category of "homemakers". Thus, the 1990 census recorded over 60 per cent of all non-migrant women and 55 per cent of all female migrants in that category. Interestingly, the proportion of persons aged 12 or over that were classified as students was similar for men and women, though it was slightly higher for the former. For both sexes, migrants were less likely to be students than were non-migrants. Migrants were also less likely than non-migrants to be in the "other" category, which included the retired and the disabled.

At the state level, there was considerable variation in the labour force participation of both men and women. Zacatecas, the poorest state among those considered, displayed relatively low levels of both male and female labour force participation, with the economically active population among non-migrants amounting to only 63 and 12 per cent, respectively, among men and women. The state of Mexico displayed labour force participation rates among non-migrants similar to those of the country as a whole, whereas in both Baja California and Quintana Roo the labour force participation of men was relatively high. With respect to women, only in Baja California did the labour force participation of non-migrants surpass by a considerable margin that of the country as a whole. In all cases,

TABLE 21. DISTRIBUTION OF THE POPULATION AGED 12 YEARS OR OVER BY LABOUR FORCE PARTICIPATION STATUS, MIGRATION STATUS AND SEX, SELECTED STATES OF ORIGIN AND DESTINATION, MEXICO, 1990
(Percentage)

Labour force participation status	Male			Female		
	Non-migrant	In-migrant	Out-migrant	Non-migrant	In-migrant	Out-migrant
A. Mexico						
Economically active	68.7	74.3	-	19.6	26.8	-
Employed	66.8	72.3	-	19.1	26.2	-
Unemployed	1.9	2.0	-	0.4	0.6	-
Not economically active	29.2	23.7	-	78.4	71.2	-
Students	16.5	14.4	-	14.8	13.4	-
Homemakers	1.3	0.8	-	60.3	54.9	-
Other	11.4	8.5	-	3.3	3.0	-
Unknown	2.1	2.1	-	2.0	2.0	-
B. Baja California						
Economically active	71.4	79.5	67.7	27.1	34.4	19.1
Employed	69.8	76.9	65.9	26.7	33.6	19.1
Unemployed	1.6	2.6	1.8	0.4	0.7	0.0
Not economically active	25.0	17.9	30.2	69.3	62.9	78.6
Students	14.0	9.0	17.1	14.9	8.5	15.2
Homemakers	0.8	0.8	1.5	50.2	50.4	61.5
Other	10.2	8.1	11.7	4.1	4.0	1.9
Unknown	3.5	2.5	2.0	3.6	2.7	2.4
C. State of Mexico						
Economically active	67.5	75.8	71.8	20.8	26.1	26.0
Employed	65.4	73.7	69.8	20.3	25.6	25.4
Unemployed	2.1	2.1	2.0	0.5	0.4	0.6
Not economically active	30.3	22.2	26.2	77.1	72.0	72.4
Students	19.4	15.1	16.6	17.5	13.5	14.8
Homemakers	1.6	0.8	0.8	56.9	56.0	54.3
Other	9.2	6.4	8.8	2.7	2.5	3.3
Unknown	2.3	1.9	2.0	2.1	1.9	1.6
D. Quintana Roo						
Economically active	75.9	83.8	76.6	18.9	29.8	18.2
Employed	74.6	81.5	71.1	18.7	29.2	18.2
Unemployed	1.3	2.3	5.4	0.2	0.6	0.0
Not economically active	22.3	13.6	21.8	79.1	68.0	80.5
Students	15.7	7.5	11.8	15.3	11.1	20.5
Homemakers	0.6	1.0	1.4	61.7	55.1	56.6
Other	6.0	5.1	8.6	2.2	1.9	3.5
Unknown	1.8	2.6	1.6	2.0	2.1	1.3
E. Zacatecas						
Economically active	63.1	66.6	78.3	11.6	21.1	25.0
Employed	60.6	64.1	76.1	11.4	20.4	23.9
Unemployed	2.5	2.5	2.2	0.2	0.7	1.1
Not economically active	34.2	31.0	17.6	86.6	77.4	72.3
Students	13.9	16.3	7.3	12.8	14.4	7.0
Homemakers	3.4	1.3	0.4	71.1	60.7	62.8
Other	16.9	13.3	10.0	2.8	2.3	2.5
Unknown	2.7	2.5	4.1	1.8	1.5	2.7

the economically active population as a percentage of the total was higher among in-migrants than among non-migrants. The differences between the two groups were especially marked among women. It is clear that female migrants were considerably more likely to be in the labour force than their non-migrant counterparts. Unfortunately, it was not possible to standardize the data by age to ascertain to what extent such differences are the result of the different age distributions of migrants and non-migrants.

As with other variables, there was considerably more variation with regard to the economic activity of out-migrants. Both male and female out-migrants from the state of Mexico and Zacatecas were more likely to be economically active than non-migrants. In fact, the economic activity rate of male out-migrants from Zacatecas was among the highest recorded. In contrast, out-migrants from Baja California and Quintana Roo tended to be less economically active than non-migrants (the only exception was male out-migrants from Quintana Roo). Among female migrants, some of the lowest activity rates were recorded among out-migrants from those states. Out-migrants from the two border states were also more likely to be students that the non-migrant population. That tendency was specially marked among male out-migrants from Baja California and female out-migrants from Quintana Roo. Male out-migrants from Quintana Roo again constituted an exception, having a lower proportion of students than non-migrants. That is, migrants leaving the less economically dynamic states were more likely to be in the labour force than the non-migrant counterparts that they left behind, whereas migrants from the more prosperous states, especially if they were women, were less likely to be as economically active as their non-migrant counterparts remaining in their states of origin. Lastly, the need to secure a better education appeared to be an important motivating factor for out-migration from the more prosperous states.

Occupation

Two aspects of the type of occupation of those employed at the time of the census are considered here. Attention is first focused on the manual or non-manual character of the economic activity exercised by those employed, and their sector of economic activity is then discussed. In Mexico as a whole, approximately 61 and 37 out of every 100 employed persons work in manual and non-manual occupations, respectively. Most of those employed in a manual occupation are men (85 per cent). As table 22 shows, non-migrant men tend to be more concentrated in manual occupations than their migrant counterparts, but the reverse is true for women. That is, at the level of the country as a whole, employed female migrants tend to be disproportionately selected from the group of manual workers. An issue that remains to be explored is the relation of type of occupation with educational attainment. Among migrant women, for instance, 78 per cent of those employed in non-manual jobs had more than six years of schooling whereas among those employed in manual jobs, only 35 per cent had attained that level.

There are interesting differences at the state level. Whereas male in-migrants to most states are less likely to be in manual occupations than their non-migrant counterparts, in Baja California the reverse is true. Baja California is also the state where the percentage of in-migrant women in manual occupations exceeds that of non-migrant women by over 10 percentage points. In all other states considered, those two values are at most within three percentage points of each other. These differences suggest that the growth of the *maquiladora* industry in the border state of Baja California has indeed had an impact on the type of employment that both male and female migrants are likely to get. Its impact on migrant women appears to be especially strong in relative terms, but more detailed information would be needed to ascertain to what extent the migration of women and their likely employment in a manual occupation are linked.

With respect to out-migrants, all flows conform to the general pattern so that men who leave are less likely to be in manual occupations than those who stay and female out-migrants are more likely to be in manual occupations than those who stay. It is worth noting that, among out-migrants, the percentage in manual occupations is particularly high for both men and women originating in Zacatecas. Among female out-migrants, those originating in Quintana Roo are the least likely to be in a manual occupation.

TABLE 22. DISTRIBUTION OF THE EMPLOYED POPULATION BY MANUAL OR NON-MANUAL OCCUPATION, MIGRATION STATUS AND SEX, SELECTED STATES OF ORIGIN AND DESTINATION, MEXICO, 1990
(PERCENTAGE)

Type of occupation	Male			Female		
	Non-migrant	In-migrant	Out-migrant	Non-migrant	In-migrant	Out-migrant
A. Mexico						
Manual	68.3	53.5	-	38.1	45.9	-
Non-manual	29.7	44.5	-	59.0	52.1	-
Unknown	2.0	2.0	-	2.9	2.0	-
B. Baja California						
Manual	58.4	60.0	50.2	38.4	50.1	46.9
Non-manual	39.4	37.3	46.8	58.5	47.5	50.6
Unknown	2.2	2.7	3.0	3.1	2.4	2.5
C. State of Mexico						
Manual	62.4	50.0	53.0	39.6	40.2	50.8
Non-manual	35.6	48.7	45.1	57.9	58.2	47.3
Unknown	2.0	1.4	1.9	2.5	1.6	1.9
D. Quintana Roo						
Manual	64.4	50.9	54.4	26.8	28.0	32.7
Non-manual	33.1	45.5	43.5	70.1	71.0	67.3
Unknown	2.6	3.6	2.1	3.1	1.0	0.0
E. Zacatecas						
Manual	77.8	63.3	70.2	37.4	40.1	67.7
Non-manual	19.8	34.7	27.8	58.5	56.3	31.4
Unknown	2.5	2.0	2.0	4.1	3.6	0.9

Sector of economic activity

Information on the sector of economic activity of those employed permits a better assessment of the occupational selectivity of migrants. Three major sectors of economic activity are distinguished: agriculture; industry; and services. The last-named sector is further subdivided into the following categories: commerce; transport and communications; communal services; personal services; and other services (table 23). The categories of communal and personal services include several occupations that are common among women, such as teaching and nursing (communal) or domestic service (personal).

At the level of the country as a whole, the distribution by sector of economic activity for men according to migration status indicates that migrants are positively selected from both the industrial and the service sectors. Among women, however, the occupational distribution of migrants and non-migrants by major sector is very similar, indicating that female migrants are not especially selected in terms of their occupational sector. Both migrant and non-migrant women tend to be highly concentrated in the service sector (over 70 per cent of the employed women work in that sector) and it is within that sector that some differentials between migrants and non-migrants can be discerned. The main difference between the two groups is that migrant women are more likely to work in personal services than are their non-migrant counterparts. When female workers in personal services are classified by their level of skills, those in an unskilled occupation account for the majority and are largely responsible for the

TABLE 23. DISTRIBUTION OF THE EMPLOYED POPULATION BY SECTOR OF ECONOMIC ACTIVITY, MIGRATION STATUS AND SEX, SELECTED STATES OF ORIGIN AND DESTINATION, MEXICO, 1990
(Percentage)

Sector of economic activity	Male			Female		
	Non-migrant	In-migrant	Out-migrant	Non-migrant	In-migrant	Out-migrant
A. Mexico						
Agriculture	30.6	12.2	-	3.6	2.9	-
Industry	29.0	34.0	-	20.2	21.0	-
Services	37.6	50.7	-	70.6	71.8	-
Commerce	11.6	15.1	-	18.4	14.8	-
Transport and communications	5.2	5.5	-	1.9	1.8	-
Communal services	4.7	6.4	-	21.8	18.7	-
Personal services	7.5	8.6	-	13.1	21.6	-
Other services	8.6	15.0	-	15.5	14.9	-
Unknown	2.8	3.1	-	5.6	4.3	-
B. Baja California						
Agriculture	13.7	8.4	15.7	4.5	3.2	4.1
Industry	29.7	42.4	25.6	27.1	41.6	22.9
Services	53.5	46.2	53.5	63.7	51.4	70.5
Commerce	16.3	13.5	17.0	17.2	14.1	11.7
Transport and communications	6.0	4.0	4.2	2.0	1.5	0.0
Communal services	5.3	3.2	6.0	19.3	11.5	10.9
Personal services	12.5	9.1	7.9	8.6	11.1	9.4
Other services	13.4	16.2	18.3	16.6	13.0	38.4
Unknown	3.2	3.0	5.2	4.7	3.7	2.4
C. State of Mexico						
Agriculture	12.5	1.3	8.3	1.4	0.2	0.6
Industry	40.4	39.5	35.2	25.8	23.0	16.3
Services	44.2	56.6	53.6	67.0	71.7	78.6
Commerce	14.5	17.9	18.2	19.2	16.3	14.5
Transport and communications	7.1	7.7	6.2	1.8	2.5	1.7
Communal services	4.2	6.5	6.0	19.3	19.5	15.7
Personal services	8.8	10.5	9.8	12.5	17.0	32.8
Other services	9.5	13.9	13.4	14.2	16.4	13.8
Unknown	3.0	2.7	2.9	5.8	5.1	4.6
D. Quintana Roo						
Agriculture	32.9	12.0	18.5	0.9	0.0	0.0
Industry	14.4	17.0	22.2	5.2	6.8	11.2
Services	50.0	67.4	52.2	88.5	87.5	82.4
Commerce	11.4	14.5	8.0	23.4	20.2	37.7
Transport and communications	8.7	9.4	7.5	3.9	4.7	0.0
Communal services	3.7	2.8	10.4	20.7	8.9	15.0
Personal services	7.4	7.9	6.1	14.2	19.3	7.1
Other services	18.8	32.7	20.1	26.2	34.4	22.7
Unknown	2.7	3.6	7.0	5.4	5.7	6.4

TABLE 23 (continued)

Sector of economic activity	Male			Female		
	Non-migrant	In-migrant	Out-migrant	Non-migrant	In-migrant	Out-migrant

E. *Zacatecas*

Sector of economic activity	Non-migrant	In-migrant	Out-migrant	Non-migrant	In-migrant	Out-migrant
Agriculture	48.9	25.2	19.2	6.5	1.5	6.6
Industry	21.9	29.2	53.1	9.5	11.7	39.5
Services	26.4	43.1	25.5	77.9	80.2	52.2
Commerce	7.9	14.2	6.4	19.7	21.7	11.1
Transport and communications	2.5	2.2	2.7	1.3	1.5	1.7
Communal services	4.3	6.9	4.0	25.7	24.4	9.0
Personal services	6.0	8.4	6.0	14.9	16.5	24.9
Other services	5.7	11.5	6.3	16.2	16.0	5.4
Unknown	2.8	2.4	2.3	6.1	6.6	1.7

differentials between migrants and non-migrants. Thus, whereas only 10 per cent of female non-migrants are unskilled workers providing personal services, the equivalent proportion among female migrants is 19 per cent. Because of their relative concentration in personal services, female migrants are less likely than non-migrants to work in other types of services.

At the state level, striking differences arise, reflecting in large part the structure of employment that characterizes each area of destination. Thus, both male and female in-migrants to Baja California are considerably more likely than non-migrants to be working in the industrial sector. In Quintana Roo, in contrast, the tendency for both in-migrants and non-migrants is to be concentrated in the service sector, but whereas male in-migrants are more likely than their non-migrant counterparts to work in that sector, female in-migrants are only as equally likely as non-migrants to be employed in the service sector. Within that sector, the category of "other services", which includes many of those related to tourism, tends to attract a high proportion of in-migrants and both male and female in-migrants are more likely to be in that category than their non-migrant counterparts.

In the state of Mexico, both male and female in-migrants tend to be more highly concentrated in the service sector than non-migrants, to the detriment of both the industrial sector and especially the agricultural sector. Among women, the relative preponderance of in-migrants in the categories of personal and other services largely accounts for their stronger concentration in services than non-migrants. In Zacatecas, the only state among those considered where 49 per cent of the non-migrant male population are engaged in agriculture, male in-migrants also tend to be relatively well represented in that sector, their positive selectivity towards the industrial and service sectors notwithstanding. Female in-migrants are also better represented than non-migrants in industry and services, but the differences are small. As in other states, the somewhat greater concentration of female in-migrants in personal services and commerce accounts for most of the overall difference in their participation in the service sector in relation to non-migrants. It is also noteworthy that relatively high proportions of migrant and non-migrant women in Zacatecas are engaged in communal services.

With respect to out-migration, the situation varies considerably from state to state. Out-migrants from Baja California are fairly representative of the non-migrant population, though male out-migrants tend to be slighly more concentrated in agriculture and female out-migrants in services than their non-migrant counterparts. Both male and female out-migrants from the state of Mexico tend to be more concentrated in services than non-migrants, to the detriment of the other two sectors. Among women, it is particularly noteworthy that nearly one third of all out-migrants from the state work in personal services, whereas only 12 per cent of female non-migrants are in that category. Lack of skills may be prompting women to migrate in order to work in domestic service instead of trying to find a job locally in other and presumably better occupations.

Out-migrants from Quintana Roo tend to be more concentrated in the industrial sector than non-migrants, an outcome that is more the result of the lack of industrial activity in Quintana Roo than of the high selectivity of out-migrants. Interestingly, among female out-migrants, a smaller proportion is engaged in personal services than that among non-migrants. In Zacatecas, the opposite holds true: a higher proportion of out-migrant women than of non-migrants works in personal services. Yet, overall, female out-migrants from Zacatecas are more concentrated in the industrial sector than their non-migrant counterparts, to the detriment of the service sector. Male out-migrants show similar traits, though in their case, concentration in the industrial sector is associated with relatively low proportions in agriculture.

This analysis suggests that although there are certain general patterns regarding the occupational distribution of men and women that usually underlie those of male and female migrants, the eventual occupational experience of the latter is highly dependent upon the opportunities available in the place of destination. How such opportunities interact with the human capital of migrants to produce a certain occupational distribution is a matter that deserves to be explored. Unfortunately, the data available do not permit a more in-depth consideration of the issue.

Income

Since migration is deemed as a strategy to improve the economic well-being of migrants and their families, it is worth exploring whether migrants do indeed earn better incomes than their non-migrant counterparts. In addition, it is important to consider whether income is yet another source of gender asymmetries. Data on income, however, are probably the least reliable of those considered so far. Two sources of misreporting bias are common: the tendency for the highest income groups to underreport their income; and the tendency for persons engaged in the informal sector of the economy to omit reporting any income. To minimize the first problem, only two broad income categories are considered—persons earning up to twice the minimum wage and those earning more than that. Only employed persons were asked about their income.

In Mexico as a whole, about 55 per cent of the employed population earns up to twice the minimum wage and only 33 per cent earn more than that, with a further 7 per cent reporting no income. According to table 24, women are considerably more likely to be in the low-income category than men, irrespective of their migration status. In fact, whereas male migrants have a more favourable distribution by income than male non-migrants, the distributions by income level of migrant and non-migrant women are very similar and both are worse than that of non-migrant men.

Marked differences in the distribution by income level of employed persons are apparent in the four states considered. Baja California has the least skewed distribution by income and the highest level of average income, whereas Zacatecas displays a distribution heavily concentrated in the low end of the scale. However, in Baja California, both male and particularly female in-migrants have a less favourable distribution by income than their non-migrant counterparts. That outcome evokes a similar finding made earlier with respect to educational attainment: because of the relatively well-off position of Baja California, the characteristics of the non-migrant population of the state are difficult to match. In Zacatecas, in contrast, the distribution of in-migrants by income level, though not particularly favourable, is considerably better than that of non-migrants, because the latter is so unfavourable. A noteworthy aspect of the income distribution of Zacatecas is that the percentages with unknown income are high, especially among female in-migrants, making a comparison with other states far from straightforward.

In the state of Mexico, male in-migrants have a more favourable distribution by income level than non-migrants but female migrants are not much better off than their non-migrant counterparts. In fact, women in the state of Mexico, whether migrant or not, have one of the worst distributions by income level among the groups of women considered here, though it is close to the mean for the country as a whole. In contrast, in-

TABLE 24. DISTRIBUTION OF THE EMPLOYED POPULATION BY LEVEL OF INCOME, MIGRATION STATUS AND SEX, SELECTED STATES OF ORIGIN AND DESTINATION, MEXICO, 1990
(Percentage)

Income as multiple of minimum wage	Male			Female		
	Non-migrant	In-migrant	Out-migrant	Non-migrant	In-migrant	Out-migrant
A. Mexico						
No income	8.3	2.2	-	2.5	2.0	-
Up to twice	52.7	46.9	-	63.9	64.3	-
More than twice	33.0	46.5	-	27.9	29.3	-
Unknown	5.9	4.4	-	5.7	4.3	-
B. Baja California						
No income	1.2	0.4	4.2	0.9	0.7	4.7
Up to twice	32.2	37.7	39.8	45.5	57.4	56.0
More than twice	59.6	58.3	51.3	46.6	36.9	31.8
Unknown	7.0	3.5	4.8	7.0	5.0	7.6
C. State of Mexico						
No income	3.9	0.7	3.3	1.6	0.8	2.7
Up to twice	55.0	51.6	49.1	66.2	66.2	67.3
More than twice	36.3	43.8	43.2	27.0	29.4	23.8
Unknown	4.8	3.9	4.4	5.2	3.7	6.2
D. Quintana Roo						
No income	12.5	4.7	2.3	3.4	0.5	9.8
Up to twice	43.0	36.7	36.6	50.0	40.1	52.2
More than twice	38.0	54.5	56.0	41.1	54.2	35.1
Unknown	6.5	4.1	5.2	5.5	5.3	2.9
E. Zacatecas						
No income	19.4	7.3	2.3	5.4	1.6	2.5
Up to twice	51.2	46.3	62.8	67.4	59.7	84.1
More than twice	20.6	38.6	30.6	20.2	26.2	11.7
Unknown	8.8	7.7	4.2	7.0	12.5	1.8

migrants to Quintana Roo, whether they be men or women, display one of the most favourable distributions by income level. In that state, migrants of both sexes appear to be significantly better off than their non-migrant counterparts. In addition, female in-migrants are equally if not slightly better off than their male counterparts, an important development indeed.

With regard to the distribution of out-migrants by income level, men tend to display a more favourable distribution than their non-migrant counterparts except when they originate in Baja California. In sharp contrast, female out-migrants display in all cases a less favourable distribution by income level than the women who have remained in the states of origin. That is, in terms of income, women scarcely seem to benefit from migration.

C. CONCLUSION

This exploration of the main characteristics of male and female migrants in Mexico on the basis of recent census information indicates that, just as men, women that migrate represent a selected group in terms of specific characteristics. There are, however, significant differences according to the type of migration flow considered. Migrants at the national level tend to reflect the traditional selectivity traits. Thus, female migrants tend to be somewhat younger than their male counterparts and to be highly concentrated in age range 15-29, in relation to non-migrants. Like male migrants, female migrants tend to be underrepresented as children of the head of household and overrepresented in the group of persons that are not immediate relatives of the head of household (other relatives, unrelated co-dwellers, one-person households and domestic servants). In addition, female migrants, just as their male counterparts, are more likely to be married or in a consensual union than are non-migrants and less likely to be single or in the combined category of separated, divorced or widowed. Their distribution by educational attainment is generally more favourable than that of non-migrants and they are more likely to be economically active. However, in terms of both education and economic activity, they lag behind male migrants. They are therefore more likely than migrant men to work in a manual occupation, and if they appear to be selected at all in terms of occupation, it is because a higher proportion of them works in domestic service than that found among non-migrants. In terms of income, female migrants generally earn much lower salaries than those earned by men. Indeed, the evidence available suggests that whereas men improve their income-earning capacity by migrating, women hardly do so.

This analysis shows, however, that important differences arise in relation to the contexts in which migration takes place. Thus, prosperous regions with a developing and growing economy offer considerably better opportunities for migrants than poorer ones, and in such favourable circumstances women can sometimes benefit. That is the case, for instance, in Quintana Roo, where the promotion of tourism has attracted a considerable number of both male and female in-migrants, many of whom work and whose income distributions are both similar and favourable. The other prosperous state considered did not, however, register such a positive outcome. Indeed, in Baja California, the data on income suggested that female migrants were not better off than either male migrants or their non-migrant counterparts. A more detailed analysis is clearly needed to ascertain which factors contribute to a positive outcome of migration for women.

Notes

[1] See Tabah and Cosío (1970), Cabrera (1976), Ordorica and others (1976), Nolasco (1979), Corona (1984), del Castillo Negrete (1986) and Partida (1989).

[2] See Balán, Browning and Jelin (1973); Muñoz, Oliveira and Stern (1977); Allub and Michel (1982), Verduzco (1982, 1984), Arizpe (1985), Lezama (1985); Arroyo, Winnie and Velásquez (1986); and Arizpe (1989).

References

Allub, Leopoldo, and Marco Antonio Michel (1982). Migración y estructura ocupacional en una ciudad petrolera: Villahermosa, Tabasco. In *Impactos regionales de la política petrolera en México*. Mexico: Centro de Investigación para la Integración Social.

Arizpe, Lourdes (1985). *Campesinado y migración*. Mexico: Secretaría de Educación Pública. Foro 2000.

_____ (1989). *La mujer en el desarrollo de América Latina*. Mexico: Universidad Nacional Autónoma de México-Centro Regional de Investigaciones Multidisciplinarias.

Arroyo, Jesús, William Winnie and Luis Arturo Velázquez (1986). *Migración a grandes centros urbanos en una región de fuerte emigración: El caso del occidente de México*. Jalisco: Universidad de Guadalajara, Centro de Investigaciones Sociales de la Facultad de Economía.

Balán, Jorge, Harley Browning and Elizabeth Jelin (1973). *Men in a Developing Society: Geographical and Social Mobility in Monterrey, Mexico*. Austin, Texas: Institute for Latin American Studies.

Bilsborrow, Richard E. (1993). Issues in the measurement of female migration in developing countries. Chapter VI in the present volume.

Cabrera, Gustavo (1976). La migración interna en México, 1950-1960: aspectos metodológicos y cuantitativos. *Demografía y Economía* (Mexico), vol. 1-3.

Carrillo, Jorge, and Alberto Hernández (1985). *Mujeres fronterizas en la industria maquiladora*. Mexico: Secretaría de Educación Pública, Centro de Estudios Fronterizos del Norte de México.

Consejo Nacional de Población (1984a). *Quintana Roo demográfico: Breviario 1983*. Mexico.

_____ (1984b). *Zacatecas demográfico: breviario 1983*. Mexico.

Corona, Rodolfo (1984). La medición indirecta de la migración interna en México. In *Los factores del cambio demográfico en México*. Mexico: Siglo XXI Editores, Instituto de Investigaciones Sociales de la Universidad Nacional Autónoma de México.

De Vos, Susan (1987). Latin American households in comparative perspective. *Population Studies* (London), vol. 41, No. 4 (November), pp. 501-517.

Del Castillo Negrete, Miguel (1986). La migración interna en México, 1970-1980. Bachelor's thesis. Universidad Nacional Autónoma de México.

Hugo, Graeme J. (1993). Migrant women in developing countries. Chapter III in the present volume.

Lezama, José Luis (1985). Características generales de la migración en el período petrolero en Tabasco. Master's thesis in demography. El Colegio de México.

Margulis, Mario, and Rodolfo Tuirán (1986). *Desarrollo y población en la frontera norte: el caso de Reynosa*. Mexico: El Colegio de México.

Muñoz, Humerto, Orlandina de Oliveira and Claudio Stern (1977). *Migración y desigualdad social en la Ciudad de México*. Mexico: El Colegio de México, Instituto de Investigaciones Sociales de la Universidad Nacional Autónoma de México.

Nolasco, Margarita (1979). *Migración municipal en México, 1960-1970*, vols. I and II. Mexico: Secretaría de Educación Pública, Instituto Nacional de Antropología e Historia.

Oliveira, Orlandina de (1984). Migración femenina, organización familiar y mercados laborales. *Comercio Exterior* (Mexico), vol. 34, No. 7, pp. 676-687.

Ordorica, Manuel, and others (1976). *Migración interna en México, 1960-1970*. Mexico: Secretaría de Industria y Comercio.

Partida, Virgilio (1989). Niveles y tendencias de la migración entre ocho regiones de México, 1950-1980. In *Memorias de la Tercera Reunión Nacional sobre Investigación Demográfica en México*. Mexico: Universidad Nacional Autónoma de México.

Pedrero, Mercedes (1990). Evolución de la participación económica femenina en los ochenta. *Revista Mexicana de Sociología* (Mexico), año LII, No. 1 (enero-marzo).

Szasz, Ivonne (1990). Migración temporal y permanencia de población rural: el caso de Malinalco en el estado de México. Doctoral dissertation. El Colegio de México, Centro de Estudios Demográficos y de Desarrollo Urbano.

Tabah, León, and Ma. Eugenia Cosío (1970). Medición de la migración interna a través de la información censal: el caso de México. *Demografía y Economía* (Mexico), vol. 4, No. 1, pp. 43-85.

Verduzco, Gustavo (1982). *Campesinos itinerantes: colonización, ganadería y urbanización en el trópico petrolero de México*. Mexico: El Colegio de Michoacán.

_____ (1984). Nuevas perspectivas en el estudio de la migración interna en México. In *Los factores del cambio demográfico en México*. Mexico: Siglo XXI Editores-Instituto de Investigaciones Sociales de la Universidad Nacional Autónoma de México.

Wainerman, Catalina H., and Zulma Recchini de Lattes (1981). *El trabajo femenino en el banquillo de los acusados: la medición censal en América Latina*. Colección Economía y Sociedad. Mexico, D.F.: The Population Council/Editorial Terra Nova.

Zenteno, René (n.d.). Migración hacia la frontera norte de México: Tijuana, B.C. Master's Thesis. El Colegio de México: Centro de Estudios Demográficos y de Desarrollo Urbano.

VIII. FEMALE MIGRATION AND LABOUR FORCE PARTICIPATION IN A MEDIUM-SIZED CITY OF A HIGHLY URBANIZED COUNTRY

Zulma Recchini de Lattes and Sonia María Mychaszula***

Although migration research in Latin America has been more abundant than in other regions, relatively little has been devoted to the study of female migration, even though it is well known that women have outnumbered men in rural-urban migration in most countries of the region from 1950 to 1970 (ECLAC, 1990). Studies on the labour force participation of female migrants in urban areas of Latin American countries consistently indicate that domestic service is more frequently performed by recent migrants than by long-term migrants or non-migrants.[1] The literature on the subject is highly dominated by the view that single young women migrate from rural areas to join the urban labour-market as domestic servants—or sometimes as pedlars in countries where the indigenous population is an important component of the total—though some authors have noted the heterogeneity characterizing female migration (Orlansky and Dubrovsky, 1978; Herold, 1979; Raczynski, 1983).

Most of the studies available consider migration during the 1950s and 1960s, but important changes occurred in both the patterns of mobility and the status of women in the region during the 1970s and 1980s. The proportion urban reached very high levels in most countries of the region and rural-urban migration, which had tended to predominate during the 1950s and 1960s, became less important in several countries during more recent decades (Lattes, 1984 and 1990). That is, migration in general became a more complex phenomenon, as different types of movements of relatively equal importance coexisted. There are also indications that the migration flows directed to the largest cities in the region may have become less important in relative terms, whereas several medium-sized cities have become more attractive for migrants (Lattes, 1990). Indeed, an increasing proportion of the younger residents of the largest cities, many of whom are the children of migrants, are moving to smaller urban centres where job opportunities are growing and the quality of life is better.

During the period 1960-1990, Latin American women benefited from changes associated with the urbanization and modernization processes, such as the general improvement of their educational levels and changes in the roles and status of women associated with the growing feminist movement and the action of international and other organizations during the United Nations Decade for Women. In addition, in Latin America as a whole, the share of women in the labour force increased as a result of both a decrease of male labour force participation and an increase of that of women (ECLAC: 1990, and Pedrero: 1992). However, one must interpret such trends with some caution, because they may be the result of better statistical accounting of the labour force participation of women. Yet, the evidence indicates that female participation increased even in the modern economic activities where their selective underregistration is less likely (Wainerman and Recchini de Lattes, 1981). Despite those positive trends, the employment of women continues to be highly concentrated in occupations that have been traditionally considered "female", most of which are generally less prestigious and worse paid than those where men dominate (PREALC, 1978).

In a study of female migration in Chile, Herold (1979) underscores the heterogeneity characterizing it. In particular, she notes the distinct nature of migration to the largest urban agglomeration, Santiago, as compared with that of migration directed to other urban areas of Chile. Female migrants enumerated in small and medium-sized cities were usually older, better educated and, if economically active, engaged in higher status occupations than those at Santiago. The findings from another analysis of 28 Chilean cities (Raczynski, 1983) agreed with Herold's study. Raczynski concludes that the characteristics of in-migrants to Santiago,

---
*Centro Nacional de Estudios de Población-Consejo Nacional de Investigación Científica y Técnica, Buenos Aires, Argentina.
**Centro Nacional de Estudios de Población, Buenos Aires, Argentina.

Argentina: location of Neuquén City and of the main regions of origin of internal migrants

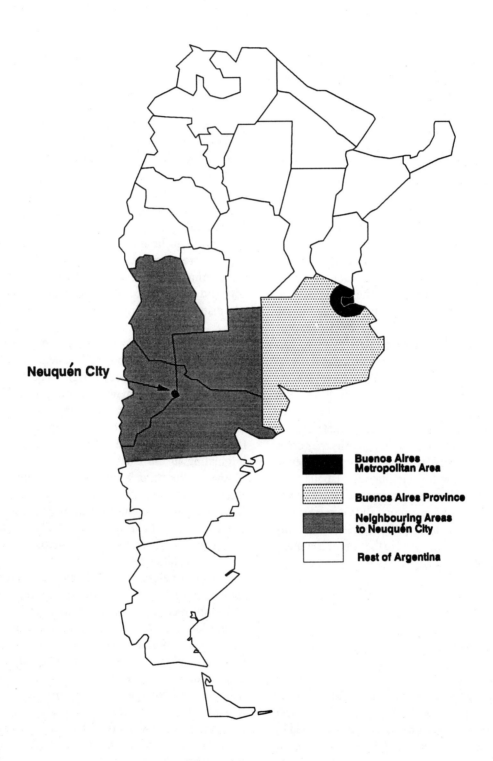

whether male or female, are quite different from those of in-migrants to other Chilean cities. Furthermore, women migrating to the three largest cities in the country are doubly affected by being migrants and by the typical sex segregation of the labour market. The characteristics of the cities of destination are important determinants of the occupational situation of the women in them, whether migrants or non-migrants. Those studies and the increasing complexity of both migration and the labour force participation of women imply that in order to understand the labour-market experience of migrant women, different groups of migrants must be considered in conjunction with the characteristics of their places of destination.

The present study tries to shed light on the interrelations between migration and the labour force participation of women by considering different types of migrant women. Those types are differentiated according to the women's demographic and socio-economic characteristics, their area of origin and the timing of their migration. Such factors, in conjunction with the job opportunities available in the place of destination, determine whether migrant women are likely to participate in the labour force and their particular mode of insertion into the labour-market. To the extent that the basic characteristics of migrant women differ from those of non-migrant women, both their labour force participation and the modes of labour-market insertion will differ. In some cases, complementarity may arise, as when women engaged in domestic service, whether migrants or non-migrants, facilitate the labour force participation of middle-class women in more prestigious occupations (García, Muñoz and Oliveira, 1982, cited by Oliveira and García: 1984). The heterogeneity of female migration is analysed in the case of Neuquén, a medium-sized city of Argentina.

A. Data used

The data used here were gathered by the 1980 population census and refer to the population aged 14 or over resident and present at Neuquén City at the time of the census, unless otherwise stated. Three types of information were used to identify migrants: (*a*) place of usual residence at the time of the census, coded by province, locality and small area; (*b*) place of birth; and (*c*) place of residence five years prior to the census date. The last two pieces of information were coded by province; and it was indicated whether they referred to provincial capital cities and one or more categories for each province, encompassing in most cases only the rest of the province and in a few cases a city or group of cities as well. Neuquén City was identified according to its official boundaries, so that it did not include the broader metropolitan area associated with it.

Two types of migrants were identified—recent and settled migrants. The former were defined as persons who in 1975 lived in a place other than Neuquén City. Settled migrants were persons that had been born outside Neuquén City but were already resident there in 1975 and were enumerated there in 1980. Barring the possibility of migration and return either before 1975 or during the period 1975-1980, settled migrants can, in general, be assumed to have arrived at Neuquén City before recent migrants. Lastly, non-migrants were defined as persons who had been born at Neuquén City and whose place of residence in 1975 and 1980 was also Neuquén City.

In addition, with respect both to recent and to settled migrants, five different migration categories were identified on the basis of place of origin. The first category is that of migrants from neighbouring areas who originated in the rest of the Province of Neuquén and in the three bordering provinces (Rio Negro, Mendoza and La Pampa); the second includes all those migrants originating in the Buenos Aires Metropolitan Area (BAMA); the third is constituted of migrants from Buenos Aires Province but excluding BAMA; the fourth includes migrants from the rest of Argentina (18 provinces); and the fifth comprises all migrants originating in foreign countries (see map). Among migrants in the latter category, recent migrants originate mainly in the neighbouring provinces of Chile whereas settled migrants comprise both European immigrants and more recently arrived Chileans. The first four categories encompass all internal migrants to Neuquén City and were defined on the basis of both empirical (a sizeable number of cases) and theoretical criteria (level of development of the region of origin). The areas neighbouring Neuquén City are the least urbanized and their inhabitants have the lowest educational levels. In contrast, BAMA is the most urbanized area and its inhabitants have the highest educational levels in the country. The other parts of Buenos Aires Province, as well as the rest of the country, are characterized by medium levels of urbanization and education (see table 25).

Women were considered to be in the labour force if they worked during the week preceding the census or if, being unemployed, they were looking for work during that period and had worked before. Those who had never worked were excluded from the labour force estimates because there was no information on their occupation. The latter category constituted a very small proportion of the total female labour force.

TABLE 25. LEVEL OF URBANIZATION AND DISTRIBUTION OF WOMEN BY EDUCATIONAL ATTAINMENT, REGIONS OF ARGENTINA, 1980

Region	Percentage of population in urban areas	Percentage of women aged 14 or over by educational attainment[a]		
		Low	Medium	High
Neighbouring areas	68.5	37.7	46.3	16.0
Buenos Aires Metropolitan Area	99.4	20.3	54.9	24.8
Buenos Aires Province	82.9	26.4	53.9	19.8
Rest of Argentina	69.9	38.0	44.0	18.0

Sources: Argentina, Instituto Nacional de Estadística y Censos, Censo Nacional de Población y Vivienda, 1980:
   Series B, Características generales: total del país (Buenos Aires, n.d.);
   Series D, Población: total del país, por provincia, departamento y localidad, República Argentina (Buenos Aires, n.d.);
   Series B, Características generales: Capital Federal (Buenos Aires, 1981);
   Series B, Características generales: partidos del gran Buenos Aires (Buenos Aires, 1981); Series B, Características generales: La Pampa (Buenos Aires, 1981);
   Series B, Características generales: Neuquén (Buenos Aires, 1981);
   Series B, Características generales: Río Negro (Buenos Aires, 1981);
   Series B, Características generales: Provincia de Buenos Aires (Buenos Aires, 1982);
   Series B, Características generales: Mendoza (Buenos Aires, 1982).
   [a]Low indicates incomplete primary school; medium indicates completed primary school but incomplete secondary school; high indicates completed secondary school or higher levels of education.

B. URBANIZATION AND FEMALE LABOUR FORCE PARTICIPATION IN ARGENTINA

Argentina is one of the most urbanized countries in the world (Lattes, 1990) because, even in comparison with developed countries, its process of urbanization began early (Recchini de Lattes, 1975). Its relatively small rural population began to decrease in the 1950s and its urban population has traditionally been highly concentrated in the Buenos Aires Metropolitan Area, whose population size has always been more than 10 times that of the second largest city in the country. However, the process of population concentration in the largest urban agglomeration stopped in the 1950s (see table 26). Thus, both the BAMA share of the total urban population of the country and its rate of growth have been decreasing, especially since 1970 (Lattes, 1990). Such trends are the result of the increasing out-migration experienced by BAMA coupled with a reduction of its attractiveness for in-migrants, both those originating in other regions of Argentina and those from abroad (Lattes and Mychaszula, 1985). In contrast, migration to medium-sized cities in Argentina (those having between 50,000 and 999,999 inhabitants) has been increasing and their share of both the total and overall urban population of the country has been growing (see table 26). Furthermore, the total number of medium-sized cities in Argentina rose from 15 to 41 during 1950-1980 (Vapnarsky and Gorojovsky, 1990). Because of the high level of urbanization in Argentina and the dynamism of its cities, urban-urban migration has predominated in recent decades.

In Argentina, female labour force participation is high by Latin American standards but low when compared with that in developed countries, and most economically active women are concentrated in a narrow set of occupations. The proportion of economically active women grew rapidly from 1947 to 1970 and then more slowly until 1980, reaching 26.9 per cent among women aged 14 or over. The share of women in the total labour force reached 27.5 per cent in 1980, the highest in several decades, as female labour force participation rose concomitantly with a decline in male participation.

TABLE 26. INDICATORS OF URBANIZATION AND URBAN STRUCTURE, ARGENTINA, 1950-1980

Year	Percentage urban in Argentina	Buenos Aires Metropolitan Area as a percentage of		Medium-sized cities[a] as a percentage of	
		Total Argentina	Urban Argentina	Total Argentina	Urban Argentina
1950	65.8	30.6	46.4	16.2	24.3
1960	73.3	33.5	45.8	20.5	26.9
1970	79.3	36.1	45.5	24.8	31.3
1980	83.0	35.6	42.9	28.4	34.2

Sources: Alfredo E. Lattes and Sonia María Mychaszula, "Urbanization, migration and urban deconcentration in Argentina", Buenos Aires, 1985 (mimeographed); and César A. Vapnarsky and Néstor Gorojovsky, *El crecimiento urbano en la Argentina*, Colección Estudios Políticos y Sociales (Buenos Aires, Grupo Editor Latinoamericano, 1990).

[a]Those with between 50,000 and 999,999 inhabitants.

The levels of female labour force participation displayed a fair degree of variation among the provinces and the federal capital, ranging from 22.2 to 33.7 per cent among women aged 14 or over in 1970. In 1980 that range had widened, with a low of 21.3 and a high of 40.2 per cent among women aged 14 or over. In 1980, the provinces with the highest female labour force participation levels were those located in the Patagonian region, where in-migration was also the highest (Mychaszula, Geldstein and Grushka, 1989; and CELADE, 1990). As in other Latin American countries, the incorporation of women into the Argentine labour market has been dual, with many of them working in manual occupations, particularly as domestic servants, and significant numbers working in non-manual occupations that include professionals and clerical or sales workers (ECLAC, 1989).

C. ECONOMIC AND DEMOGRAPHIC EXPANSION OF NEUQUEN CITY

Neuquén City is the capital of the Province of Neuquén, located in the northern Patagonian region, in an area of fluvial valleys known as the Alto Valle. A river separates Neuquén City from a neighbourhood of Cipolletti City, in the Province of Río Negro. In fact, Neuquén City is part of a larger metropolitan area—the Alto Valle de Río Negro y Neuquén or, in short, the Alto Valle Metropolitan Area—which encompasses both Neuquén City and Cipolletti City, as well as 14 smaller municipalities located mainly in the Province of Río Negro (Vapnarsky and Pantelides, 1987). Although it would have been desirable to analyse the migration and labour force participation of women in terms of that metropolitan area, given the important economic and social interactions within it, the data did not permit such analysis because neither place of birth nor place of residence in 1975 was coded in such a way as to allow identification of the Alto Valle Metropolitan Area. Focusing on Neuquén City was the best possible compromise and it has some advantages in terms of policy implications because the city is administratively independent of that part of the metropolitan area that belongs to the Province of Río Negro.

During the 1930s and 1940s, when Neuquén was still a national territory rather than a province, Neuquén City had few administrative functions, sharing with other cities of the region the commercial and financial services required by the agricultural colonies located in Alto Valle. During those decades, its demographic growth was moderate. In 1955, when Neuquén was granted provincial status, the official functions of the city were multiplied and it began to grow faster. Other economic changes and the political stability that characterized the province for almost 30 years favourably affected the socio-economic structure of both the province and the city, leading to remarkable economic and demographic growth which greatly contrasted with the national process, especially in the 1970s. Thus, during the period 1970-1980, gross domestic product grew at an average annual rate of 10.7 per cent in the Province of Neuquén, as compared with 1.0 per cent for the country as a whole (Kloster, 1992).

When the north-western part of the Province of Neuquén, historically the most populated area, was affected by adverse policies against the economic activities predominating in that area, the population began moving to areas closer to Neuquén City, located in the eastern part of the province. In the early 1960s, the exploitation of oil and natural gas increased considerably in the province, attracting a number of entreprises and related services to the city. In 1968, the construction of a hydroelectric complex in the province also triggered the growth of businesses, as well as of financial, personal and social services in the City. During the 1970s, the growth of the energy sector was accompanied by an increase in the manufacturing sector. The provincial government created an industrial park at Neuquén city and adopted tax incentives to attract investment. The movement of both capital and people to Neuquén City necessarily entailed the development of basic infrastructure. The construction sector grew continuously, together with wholesale and retail trade, hotels, restaurants, transportation, communications, entertainment and recreation, and professional and social services. All these activities generated increasing employment opportunities that attracted migrants from other parts of Argentina and from the neighbouring Chilean provinces.

Migration played an important role in the growth of Neuquén City from the time of its inception at the beginning of this century. The city has been populated by several waves of migrants, most of whom originated in the city of Buenos Aires and Buenos Aires Province as well as in Europe. Table 27 presents indicators of the population growth of Neuquén City and of the role played by migration. The population almost doubled during the 1960s and more than doubled again during the 1970s. From a population of 12,900 in 1950,[2] the City reached 90,000 in 1980[3], with net migration contributing more than 55 per cent of total population growth in every period since 1950. Since most migrants were in their prime reproductive ages upon arrival, they also contributed positively to the natural increase of Neuquén City. As is further illustrated below, the important contribution of migration to the demographic growth of Neuquén City has had profound consequences for its population structure, which is largely shaped by the different cohorts of migrants. In addition, at the provincial level, sharp decreases in both infant mortality and total fertility were recorded for the period 1970-1980. Those trends were probably parallelled by the city and are indicative of the very dynamic process of demographic and socio-economic change that it has been undergoing, which includes a substantial increase in the labour force participation of women as indicated by the gross number of years of working life.

D. THE CHARACTERISTICS OF FEMALE IN-MIGRANTS TO NEUQUÉN CITY

In 1980, migrants constituted over 77 per cent of all women aged 14 or over in Neuquén City. A majority (51 per cent) were settled migrants, that is, persons that in 1975 were already residents (see table 28). Recent migrants (those who had moved to Neuquén City after 1975) constituted 26 per cent of the women aged 14 or over, thus surpassing the proportion of non-migrants

TABLE 27. DEMOGRAPHIC INDICATORS OF NEUQUÉN CITY, 1950-1980

	Neuquén City				Neuquén Province		Neuquén City
Year	Population	Growth rate per 1,000	Growth due to net migration (percentage)	Population as percentage of province population	Infant mortality	Total fertility	Gross years of working life for women
1950	12 850	-	-	14.8	..	..	..
1960	22 500	56.0	56.0	20.5	..	..	..
1970	43 001	64.8	67.3	27.8	108.4	5.2	16.5
1975	60 097	66.9	57.0	..	..	4.8	..
1980	90 089	81.0	64.3	36.9	32.3	4.3	18.9

Sources: César A. Vapnarsky and Edith A. Pantelides, eds., *La formación de un área metropolitana en la Patagonia: población y asentamiento en el Alto Valle*, Informes de Investigación del CEUR, No. 7 (Buenos Aires, Centro de Estudios Urbanos y Regionales, 1987); and Sonia María Mychaszula and E. E. Kloster, "Crecimiento migratorio de la ciudad de Neuquén, cambio de la participación económica y del tamaño medio de la familia", solicited paper for the Conference on The Peopling of the Americas, Veracruz, Mexico, 1991.

TABLE 28. DISTRIBUTION OF WOMEN AGED 14 OR OVER BY AGE GROUP, MARITAL STATUS AND EDUCATIONAL ATTAINMENT, ACCORDING TO MIGRATION STATUS AND REGION OF ORIGIN, NEUQUÉN CITY, 1980

(Percentage)

Migration status and region of origin	Number of women	Per-centage	Age group			Marital status			Educational attainment		
			14-24	25-44	45-69	Single	Married	Widowed, divorced, separated	Low	Medium	High
Non-migrants	6 482	22.7	35.6	18.3	13.6	33.5	18.7	15.9	20.5	26.8	16.8
Total number of migrants	22 040	77.3	64.4	81.7	86.4	66.5	81.3	84.1	79.5	73.2	83.2
TOTAL	28 522	100.0	100.0	100.0	100.0	100.0	100.0	100.0	100.0	100.0	100.0
Recent migrants Argentina	7 432	26.1	30.2	27.7	17.0	27.7	26.4	19.6	20.3	24.9	39.1
Neighbouring areas	3 945	13.8	18.6	13.3	8.2	16.4	13.2	10.4	13.9	13.5	14.6
Buenos Aires Metropolitan Area	898	3.1	2.3	3.8	3.1	2.3	3.4	3.6	1.3	2.7	7.5
Buenos Aires Province	718	2.5	2.0	3.1	2.1	2.2	2.7	2.3	1.1	2.3	5.6
Rest of Argentina	1 205	4.2	4.3	5.0	2.5	4.2	4.6	2.4	2.0	4.0	8.9
Other countries	666	2.3	3.0	2.5	1.0	2.6	2.5	0.9	2.1	2.4	2.5
Settled migrants Argentina	14 608	51.2	34.2	54.0	69.4	38.9	54.8	64.5	59.1	48.3	44.1
Neighbouring areas	7 558	26.5	20.3	27.7	32.7	23.1	27.3	31.5	36.3	24.0	15.1
Buenos Aires Metropolitan Area	834	2.9	2.3	3.0	3.7	2.5	3.0	3.6	0.8	3.2	6.1
Buenos Aires Province	1 314	4.6	2.5	4.1	8.5	2.9	5.1	6.7	2.5	5.2	6.9
Rest of Argentina	1 708	6.0	3.5	7.1	7.3	4.4	6.8	5.8	3.5	5.8	10.9
Other countries	3 194	11.2	5.7	12.1	17.1	6.0	12.7	16.9	16.0	10.2	5.1

^aLow indicates incomplete primary school; medium indicates completed primary school but incomplete secondary school; high indicates completed secondary school or higher levels of education.

(22.7 per cent). Among both settled and recent female migrants, more than half in each category originated in neighbouring areas; and among settled female migrants, approximately one fifth originated outside Argentina, mainly in neighbouring provinces of Chile.

The contribution of migrants varied considerably according to age group. Among the youngest women (those aged 14-24), migrants accounted for only 64 per cent of the total mainly because that group includes many of the locally born daughters of migrants who arrived during the 1950s and 1960s. In contrast, migrants accounted for 82 per cent of women aged 25-44 and for 86 per cent of those aged 45 or over. As in the case of the total female population aged 14 or over, settled migrants accounted for greater proportions of the female population in each age group than recent migrants and the proportions of settled migrants increased with age. Thus, among women aged 25-44, 54 per cent were settled migrants and the equivalent proportion was 69 per cent among women aged 45 or over. Recent migrants, in contrast, accounted for declining proportions of women as age increased, reflecting the fact the migrants are generally concentrated at younger ages at the time of migration. Interestingly, the proportion of female migrants originating in foreign countries was especially high among women aged 45 or over (18 per cent) and most belonged to the settled category, indicating the effect that past levels of international migration, mostly from Europe, had had on Neuquén City.

Similar distribution patterns were observed with respect to marital status, as it is highly correlated with age. Thus, migrants accounted for a relatively low proportion of single women (67 per cent) and for considerably higher proportions of married (81 per cent) and of widowed, divorced or separated women (84 per cent). Settled female migrants were more numerous among all marital status groups, particularly among the widowed, divorced or separated, whereas recent migrants accounted for slightly over one quarter of both single and married women.

With regard to educational attainment, migrants were somewhat overrepresented among women with incomplete primary education and among those with at least a completed secondary-school education. They were slightly underrepresented among women who had completed primary education but had not completed secondary school. In relation to their proportion in the entire population, recent migrants tended to be overrepresented among the most educated group of women. Such overrepresentation was especially marked among recent migrants from BAMA, Buenos Aires Province and the rest of Argentina. In contrast, settled female migrants, especially those originating in neighbouring areas and in foreign countries, tended to be underrepresented in the group of women with high educational attainment. Settled migrants from the other three regions were all overrepresented in that group.

Although in 1980 the number of female migrants in Neuquén City was almost the same as the number of male migrants (the sex ratio was 99.9 men per 100 women), there were important differences between the two populations (see table 29). Among recent migrants, men constituted 52 per cent, thus outnumbering women, whereas among settled migrants, they constituted 49 per cent, being therefore outnumbered by women. The differences were even more marked for the different migration streams (see sex ratios in table 29). Women tended to outnumber men among migrants from neighbouring areas, both with respect to recent and to settled migrants, and there was also a preponderance of women among recent migrants from foreign countries (most of whom originated in Chile). In contrast, men outnumbered women in every other stream. Therefore, these data appear to corroborate the hypothesis made by Ravenstein (1885) with regard to the fact that women tend to predominate in migration flows over shorter distances.

Table 29 also permits a comparison of the age distribution of different groups of migrant women with that of non-migrants. The non-migrant female population is highly concentrated in age group 14-24, which accounts for about half of all non-migrant women aged 14 or over. This remarkable concentration is the result of the earlier migration of women of reproductive ages whose children constitute a large proportion of the non-migrant population. Recent migrants tend to be more concentrated in age group 25-44 and even in that aged 45 or over. Settled migrants display an even older age distribution, with a very high proportion in age group 45 or over, reflecting indirectly the time elapsed since migration. Among recent female migrants, those originating in neighbouring areas and in foreign countries tend to be significantly younger than the rest. In contrast, among settled female migrants, those originating in Buenos Aires Province and in foreign countries tend to be older.

There is a high correlation between the age distribution and that by marital status. Thus, the proportion single is higher among those groups having the highest proportions of young women (non-migrants and recent migrants, especially those coming from neighbouring areas and from foreign countries). To control for the effect of age, the distributions by marital status have been standardized. Such standardization reduces the differences between the different groups considered, indicating that age is the major factor behind the differences observed at first. It is worth noting, however, that according to the standardized distributions, migrant women are slightly more likely to be married than non-migrants and that they are also considerably less likely to be widowed, divorced or separated.

With respect to the distribution by educational attainment, table 29 shows that there are important differences between migrant and non-migrant women. In particular, a higher proportion of migrant women

TABLE 29. SEX RATIO BY MIGRATION STATUS AND DISTRIBUTION OF WOMEN AGED 14 OR OVER BY MIGRATION STATUS AND REGION OF ORIGIN, ACCORDING TO AGE GROUP, MARITAL STATUS[a] AND EDUCATIONAL ATTAINMENT[a], NEUQUÉN CITY, 1980
(Percentage)

Migration status and region of origin	Number	Sex ratio	Age structure			Marital status			Age-standardized marital status			Educational attainment[b]			Age-standardized educational attainment[b]		
			14-24	25-44	45-69	Single	Married	Widowed, divorced, separated	Single	Married	Widowed, divorced, separated	Low	Medium	High	Low	Medium	High
Non-migrants	6 482	90.7	49.7	36.8	13.5	42.9	49.7	7.4	30.5	58.2	11.3	31.0	54.6	14.3	34.8	49.8	15.4
Total number of migrants TOTAL	22 040	99.9	26.4	48.4	25.2	25.1	63.4	11.5	28.6	61.0	10.4	35.3	43.9	20.8	34.6	45.0	20.4
	28 522	97.8	31.7	45.7	22.6	29.1	60.3	10.6	29.1	60.3	10.6	34.4	46.3	19.3	34.4	46.3	19.3
Recent migrants	7 432	107.8	36.7	48.6	14.7	30.9	61.1	8.0	28.9	60.4	10.7	26.8	44.2	29.0	29.3	44.1	26.6
Argentina	3 945	94.4	42.6	44.0	13.5	34.6	57.5	8.0	28.8	59.8	11.4	34.5	45.1	20.4	36.7	43.5	19.8
Neighbouring areas Buenos Aires Metropolitan Area	898	123.9	23.2	54.8	22.0	21.7	66.0	12.2	27.7	60.8	11.6	14.0	39.9	46.1	14.4	44.4	41.2
Buenos Aires Province	718	173.0	25.5	55.7	18.8	24.9	65.6	9.5	27.3	62.4	10.4	14.9	42.2	42.9	17.3	46.7	35.9
Rest of Argentina	1 205	119.5	32.2	54.3	13.5	28.6	65.4	6.0	29.4	61.9	8.7	15.9	43.4	40.7	20.0	46.2	33.8
Other countries	666	74.2	40.4	49.7	9.9	32.3	63.5	4.2	29.2	61.5	9.3	31.1	47.9	21.0	36.6	45.7	17.6
Settled migrants	14 608	95.9	21.2	48.2	30.6	22.1	64.6	13.3	28.6	61.0	10.4	39.7	43.7	16.6	36.8	46.5	16.7
Argentina	7 558	83.0	24.3	47.8	27.9	25.3	62.1	12.6	30.0	59.1	11.0	47.0	41.9	11.0	44.7	44.2	11.1
Neighbouring areas Buenos Aires Metropolitan Area	834	118.8	25.1	46.3	28.7	25.3	61.5	13.2	29.4	59.4	11.2	9.4	50.0	40.6	8.6	50.1	41.3
Buenos Aires Province	1 314	110.6	17.2	40.9	41.9	18.3	66.4	15.3	28.1	63.0	8.9	18.7	52.5	28.8	13.5	53.9	32.6
Rest of Argentina	1 708	107.1	18.3	54.1	27.6	21.4	68.4	10.2	30.1	61.3	8.6	20.2	44.5	35.2	18.5	47.6	33.9
Other countries	3 194	108.6	16.0	49.5	34.4	15.5	68.5	16.0	24.3	65.6	10.1	49.1	42.1	8.8	45.6	45.7	8.6

[a] Observed and standardized by age. The age distribution used as standard is that of all women aged 14-69 resident in Neuquén City.
[b] Low indicates incomplete primary school; medium indicates completed primary school but incomplete secondary school; high indicates completed secondary school or higher levels of education.

have completed secondary school or higher levels of education than non-migrants and that difference is maintained after standardization by age. Recent female migrants are better educated than both settled migrants and non-migrants, especially when they originate in BAMA, in Buenos Aires Province or in other non-neighbouring provinces of Argentina. Settled migrants with the same origins also display relatively high levels of educational attainment, especially those coming from BAMA, who may have arrived in Neuquén in relatively recent periods. That is, migrant women from within Argentina originating in other than neighbouring areas constitute an educated élite among the female residents of Neuquén City. In contrast, among migrants from neighbouring areas and those from foreign countries, the proportion of women who have not completed elementary education is relatively high, even higher than among non-migrants.

All these comparisons indicate the heterogeneity characterizing migrant women. Recent female migrants from neighbouring areas, whether from Argentina or from neighbouring countries, tend to be younger and have lower levels of educational attainment than other recent female migrants. Those originating in other regions of Argentina, including Buenos Aires Province and BAMA, tend to be older and to have higher levels of educational attainment. Among settled migrants, the patterns are not so distinct because the group itself is more heterogeneous, incorporating as it does the net migration gain over a period of several years of various in-migration waves. Yet, settled migrants from neighbouring areas and those from foreign countries display also considerably lower levels of educational attainment that those originating in other areas.

E. Labour force participation of female in-migrants to Neuquén City

In Latin America, migrant women tend to have higher labour force participation than non-migrant women at the place of destination (Raczynski, 1983; Elton, 1978; and Orlansky and Dubrovsky, 1978). With very few exceptions (see Raczynski, 1983; Herold, 1979; and Martine and Peliano, 1978), most studies on the labour force participation of migrant women refer either to capital cities or very large metropolitan areas and do not control for characteristics that are expected to influence labour force participation among women, such as marital status, education or number of children. Raczynski (1983) notes that the proportion of women in the labour force, whether migrant or non-migrant, is higher in those cities having an employment structure in which manufacturing and service activities predominate.

The literature comparing the economic activity of migrants with that of non-migrants in the place of origin is even scarcer; and the few studies available refer to periods when migration originated mainly in rural areas, where female labour force participation has been traditionally low in most Latin American countries, at least as far as available statistics indicate. Economic activity tends to increase when migrants arrive in urban areas, especially large metropolitan areas (Elton, 1978). However, such experience is becoming less relevant for countries like Argentina, where most internal migrants are now moving from one urban area to another and sometimes from large urban agglomerations to smaller ones.

To compare the labour force experience of female migrants at Neuquén City and non-migrants according to the 1980 census, the gross number of years of working life was calculated in the usual way, that is, by multiplying the age-specific activity rates by the length in years of each age interval and adding them up over the full age range being considered. The resulting indicators for each group of women considered are shown in table 30. Two groups of non-migrants were used. Those listed as "total" correspond to the population of non-migrants at Neuquén City in 1980. Those identified by region of origin include all persons resident in the respective regions in 1980. Ideally, recent migrants at the place of destination should be compared with the population at the place of origin as it was before migration (in this case, as of 1975), but the information needed to perform that comparison is not available. The closest approximation possible is to consider the characteristics of the resident female population, irrespective of migration status, as of 1980. Because at the provincial level in 1980, recent in-migrants constituted a small proportion of the total resident population (CELADE, 1990), the inclusion of recent in-migrants in the calculation of labour force indicators for the areas of origin is not likely to bias those indicators significantly.

TABLE 30. GROSS NUMBER OF YEARS OF WORKING LIFE FOR WOMEN AGED 14-69, BY AGE GROUP, MIGRATION STATUS AND REGION OF ORIGIN, NEUQUÉN CITY, 1980

Region of origin	Non-migrants	Recent migrants	Settled migrants
A. *Age group 14-24*			
Neighbouring areas	3.4	4.9	4.0
Buenos Aires Metropolitan Area	4.4	3.8	3.8
Buenos Aires Province	3.7	4.4	4.1
Rest of Argentina	3.0	4.1	4.0
TOTAL	4.0a	4.7	4.0
B. *Age group 25-44*			
Neighbouring areas	6.2	8.9	8.8
Buenos Aires Metropolitan Area	7.8	9.7	11.1
Buenos Aires Province	7.1	10.1	9.9
Rest of Argentina	6.4	8.9	10.6
TOTAL	9.4a	9.2	9.4
C. *Age group 45-69*			
Neighbouring areas	3.6	6.0	6.1
Buenos Aires Metropolitan Area	4.9	5.5	6.1
Buenos Aires Province	4.3	4.6	5.6
Rest of Argentina	3.9	2.9	6.8
TOTAL	6.4a	5.2	6.1
D. *Total*			
Neighbouring areas	13.2	19.8	18.9
Buenos Aires Metropolitan Area	17.1	19.0	21.0
Buenos Aires Province	15.1	19.1	19.6
Rest of Argentina	13.3	15.9	21.4
TOTAL	19.8a	19.1	19.5

Source: For resident female population in regions of origin, Argentina, Instituto Nacional de Estadística y Censos: *Censo Nacional de Población y Vivienda, 1980*; Series D, *Población: total del país, por provincia, departamento y localidad* (Buenos Aires, n.d.).

a Refers to non-migrant women in Neuquén City. It is therefore not the weighted average of the rest of the figures in this column which refer to the resident female population in the different regions of origin in 1980.

As table 30 indicates, there is relatively little difference between the estimated gross number of years of working life of non-migrant women in Neuquén City and those of migrant women, whether recent or settled migrants. Indeed, non-migrant women have a slightly higher gross number of years of working life than recent migrants. The differentials, however, vary considerably by age group. Thus, among those aged 14-24, recent migrants have 0.7 year of working life more than non-migrants, a difference of 18 per cent. At ages 25-44, the difference between the two groups is minimal, 0.2 year in favour of non-migrant women, but it increases again for age group 45-69, with non-migrants surpassing once more recent migrants by 1.2 years. That is, although young recent migrants tend to work more than non-migrants and settled migrants, over age 25 the latter work for longer periods than the former. There are also differences between the various migration streams. Among recent female migrants, the number of gross years of working life is markedly lower for those originating in the rest of Argentina, whereas among settled migrants the lowest value occurs among those from neighbouring areas, although the differences between streams are less marked.

When the years of working life are calculated for populations in the area of origin, they indicate that both recent and settled migrant women in Neuquén City would work considerably longer during their lives than women in the areas of origin were the labour force participation rates observed in 1980 to remain constant. This finding supports the hypothesis that most women migrate for economic reasons and female labour force participation is strongly determined by existing economic opportunities. The largest differences are between recent female migrants from areas neighbouring Neuquén City and the female residents of those regions (6.6 years) and between settled female migrants from the rest of Argentina and female residents of that region (8.1 years). The consideration of specific age groups further indicates that for both of those areas of origin, the number of years of working life is higher among female migrants, whether recent or settled, in each age group than among the female population resident in the areas of origin. For BAMA, however, younger female residents (ages 15-24) have more years of working life than their migrant counterparts in Neuquén City, whereas for other Argentine provinces, recent female migrants aged 45-69 have less years of working life than either residents of those provinces or migrants from those provinces that settled in Neuquén City.

TABLE 31. GROSS NUMBER OF YEARS OF WORKING LIFE FOR WOMEN AGED 14-69, BY MIGRATION STATUS, AGE GROUP AND MARITAL STATUS, NEUQUÉN CITY, 1980

Age group	Single			Married			Widowed, divorced, separated		
	Non-migrants	Recent migrants	Settled migrants	Non-migrants	Recent migrants	Settled migrants	Non-migrants	Recent migrants	Settled migrants
14-24	5.3	6.4	5.5	2.1	1.9	1.7	a	a	a
25-44	15.9	17.1	17.0	7.5	7.1	6.8	16.2	16.7	16.5
45-69	10.3	12.7	11.9	5.2	4.2	4.3	8.7	6.6	8.3
TOTAL	31.5	36.2	34.4	14.8	13.2	12.8	24.9	23.3	24.8

^aNot available because of the small number of cases observed.

Given that age is highly correlated with marital status and that the latter factor is also highly correlated with female labour force participation, it is important to consider the gross number of years of working life according to type of migrant, marital status and age (see table 31). The non-migrants considered in this case are only those enumerated in Neuquén City in 1980. Interestingly, only among single women do migrants, whether recent or settled, consistently have more years of working life than non-migrants in every age group. Among married women, in contrast, the number of years of working life is consistently higher among non-migrants than among migrants, whether recent or settled; and the same relationship tends to hold among widowed, divorced or separated women except for age group 25-44. That is, the distribution by marital status is crucial in determining the types of differentials between migrant and non-migrant women. In terms of the differences between recent and settled female migrants, there is a tendency for the former group to have more years of working life than the latter if they are single or married and for almost every age group. However, the differences between the two groups of migrant women are generally smaller than those between them and non-migrants.

To take into account variations arising from the place of origin, the number of years of working life were calculated for two groups of women, single women aged 14-24 and married women aged 25-44, by migration status and place of origin (see table 32). For all the regions of origin considered, recent young single migrants have more years of working life than their settled counterparts. Among married women, however, settled migrants originating in Buenos Aires Province, BAMA and the rest of Argentina have more years of working life than both their recent migrant counterparts and married non-migrants. Those groups of settled migrant women, in addition to being highly educated, also have in their favour a longer stay in the city and a better knowledge of it that is likely to facilitate their making arrangements to take care of their domestic duties even when they themselves work outside the home.

TABLE 32. GROSS NUMBER OF YEARS OF WORKING LIFE FOR SINGLE MIGRANT WOMEN AGED 14-24 AND MARRIED MIGRANT WOMEN AGED 25-44, BY REGION OF ORIGIN, NEUQUÉN CITY, 1980

Region of origin	Single aged 14-24		Married aged 25-44	
	Recent migrants	Settled migrants	Recent migrants	Settled migrants
All migrants	6.4	5.5	7.1	6.8
Argentina Neighbouring areas	6.7	5.8	6.9	6.5
Buenos Aires Metropolitan Area	5.5	4.7	8.3	10.0
Buenos Aires Province	6.5	5.2	8.4	8.7
Rest of Argentina	5.8	4.6	6.4	9.1
Other countries	6.1	5.7	5.3	4.9

A direct comparison of the labour force participation of recent female migrants to Neuquén City with that of the population in the areas of origin by age and marital status was only possible through the indirect standardization of the labour force participation rates sepa-

TABLE 33. COMPARISON OF OBSERVED AND AGE-STANDARDIZED[a] PROPORTIONS OF SINGLE AND MARRIED WOMEN IN THE LABOUR FORCE, BY SELECTED REGIONS OF RESIDENCE OR ORIGIN

Region of residence or origin	Single		Married	
	Observed	Standardized	Observed	Standardized
Neighbouring areas	43.2	61.2	17.3	28.6
Buenos Aires Metropolitan Area	50.9	51.7	22.7	30.2
Buenos Aires Province	43.9	60.9	21.3	30.8
Rest of Argentina	37.1	54.5	18.4	23.4

Source: Argentina, Instituto Nacional de Estadística y Censos, *Censo Nacional de Población y Vivienda, 1980;* Series D, *Población: total del país, por provincia, departamento y localidad* (Buenos Aires, n.d.).

[a] The proportions were standardized by multiplying the resident population by age and marital status by the proportion of migrant women in the labour force of Neuquén City according to region of origin.

rately for single and married women. Standardized indicators were calculated by multiplying the resident population of each area of origin classified by age and marital status by the proportions of women in the labour force observed among recent migrants to Neuquén City classified by age, marital status and area of origin (see table 33). Standardization was not applied to the group of widowed, divorced and separated women that were recent migrants because their labour force participation rates were based on a very small number of cases.

As table 33 indicates, the standardized proportions of women in the labour force which represent the experience of recent female migrants in Neuquén City are consistently higher than those observed among the resident population of the areas of origin. That is, even after controlling for age and marital status, recent female migrants to Neuquén City have higher labour force participation rates than the resident population of their places of origin. It is noteworthy that only among single women originating in BAMA are the observed and standardized labour force participation rates relatively similar, indicating that both female residents in BAMA and female migrants originating there have equal propensities to participate in the labour force.

F. THE LABOUR FORCE PARTICIPATION OF MIGRANT WOMEN AND THEIR EDUCATIONAL ATTAINMENT

The evidence concerning the relation between education and female labour force participation is mixed: although most case-studies show that a positive relation exists between the two factors, some studies document that the relation follows a U-shaped curve (Standing, 1978). The data for the female population of Argentina as a whole show a positive relation, with women having higher levels of educational attainment being more likely to participate in the labour force, a relation that holds true even when controlling for age and family status (Wainerman, 1979; Sautu, 1991). The data on non-migrant and migrant women at Neuquén City corroborate the existence of a positive relation between educational attainment and female labour force participation among both female non-migrants and settled migrants (see table 34), but for recent migrants the relation is better described as J-shaped, with women that did not complete elementary school and those that completed secondary school or attained a higher level having more years of working life than recent female migrants with intermediate levels of educational attainment.

Table 34 also shows the number of years of working life by age group, educational attainment and migration status. There are, however, few generalizations that can be made from those data. The number of years of working life tend to be highest among women who have completed secondary school or attained a higher level, irrespective of migration status. Among those women, the differentials between migrants and non-migrants vary by age group. Under age 45, the highest number of years of working life are exhibited by non-migrant women, followed by settled migrants and lastly by recent migrants. For age group 45-69, the 9.7 years of working life among settled migrants is considerably higher than the 8.3 or the 8.1 years of recent migrants or non-migrants, respectively.

TABLE 34. GROSS NUMBER OF YEARS OF WORKING LIFE, BY AGE GROUP, EDUCATIONAL ATTAINMENT AND MIGRATION STATUS OF WOMEN AGED 14-69, NEUQUÉN CITY, 1980

Age group	Non-migrants	Recent migrants	Settled migrants
A. Low educational attainment			
14-24	3.2	4.7	3.4
25-44	6.3	6.8	6.5
45-69	5.5	5.2	5.3
TOTAL	15.0	16.7	15.2
B. Medium educational attainment			
14-24	3.7	4.1	3.5
25-44	9.2	6.8	7.9
45-69	6.5	3.9	5.3
TOTAL	19.4	14.8	16.7
C. High educational attainment			
14-24	6.4	4.7	5.8
25-44	15.2	13.1	14.1
45-69	8.1	8.3	9.7
TOTAL	29.7	26.1	29.6
D. Total			
14-24	4.0	4.6	3.9
25-44	9.4	9.1	8.8
45-69	6.4	5.2	5.8
TOTAL	19.8	18.9	18.5

ᵃLow indicates incomplete primary school; medium indicates completed primary school but incomplete secondary school; high indicates completed secondary school or higher levels of education.

Similarly, among women with intermediate levels of educational attainment (completed elementary school but incomplete secondary), non-migrants have higher years of working life if they are over age 25. Settled migrants exhibit the next higher levels, followed by those of recent migrants. Only among the youngest women, those aged 14-24, do recent migrants with intermediate educational levels have more years of working life than their non-migrant and settled migrant counterparts. It would seem, therefore, that education as a promoter of labour force participation has a greater impact on non-migrant women or on settled migrants than on women who have migrated more recently, probably because women belonging to the first two groups have had time to develop better strategies to combine their reproductive and their productive roles.

Among the women with the lowest educational attainment (incomplete primary), recent migrants have a higher number of years of working life than non-migrants and settled migrants when under age 45. For those aged 45-69, non-migrants and settled migrants again exhibit higher number of years of working life, although the differences between the groups are relatively small.

Differentials by region of origin are considered only for age group 25-44; and they indicate that among women with intermediate and higher levels of educational attainment, settled migrants tend to have longer years of working life than recent migrants. The few exceptions include women originating in Buenos Aires Province (excluding BAMA), though for them the differences between settled and recent migrants are small; and women from foreign countries with an intermediate educational level. Also noteworthy is that among those with low educational attainment, recent migrants have a slightly higher number of years of working life than settled migrants, especially among migrants originating in other countries. With regard to differentials by region of origin and educational attainment, no clear pattern emerges among either recent or settled migrants (see table 35).

These comparisons have shown that the labour force participation of both migrant and non-migrant women varies considerably according to level of educational attainment and age group. In general, the number of years of working life among women aged 25-44 are higher in both absolute and relative terms than among younger or older women; and for that age group, the years of working life tend to increase with educational attainment for each group of women considered—non-migrants, recent and settled migrants—thus corroborating the traditional relation between educational attainment and labour force participation typical of the Argentine population. The only possible exception to this pattern is that of recent migrants, for whom the number of years of working life among women with low and intermediate educational levels remains the same. That lack of increase, coupled with the low number of years of working life observed among recent migrants aged 14-24 and 45-69, with medium levels of education, is responsible for the J-shaped relationship observed between the educational attain-

TABLE 35. GROSS NUMBER OF YEARS OF WORKING LIFE FOR MIGRANT WOMEN AGED 25-44, BY EDUCATIONAL ATTAINMENT,[a] NEUQUÉN CITY, 1980

Age group	Low		Medium		High	
	Recent migrants	Settled migrants	Recent migrants	Settled migrants	Recent migrants	Settled migrants
All migrants	6.8	6.5	6.8	7.9	13.1	14.1
Argentina						
Neighbouring areas	7.1	7.0	7.2	8.9	13.7	14.2
Buenos Aires Metropolitan Area	[b]	[b]	6.6	8.5	12.2	14.1
Buenos Aires Province	[b]	[b]	7.3	7.2	14.5	14.1
Rest of Argentina	[b]	[b]	5.5	7.2	13.0	15.3
Other countries	6.3	5.8	7.5	6.5	9.0	10.8

[a]Low indicates incomplete primary school; medium indicates completed primary school but incomplete secondary school; high indicates completed secondary school or higher levels of education.
[b]Not available because of the small number of cases observed.

ment and the labour force participation of recent migrants in general. These comparisons therefore suggest that recent migrants have a significantly different experience from either their settled or their non-migrant conterparts in terms of how their educational attainment relates to their labour force participation. As was suggested above, it may be that recent migrants face added constraints or, in some cases, added pressures to participate in the labour force in comparison with those experienced by women that had been living at Neuquén City for longer periods. In particular, their marital status and other family characteristics are likely to play a significant role in mediating the relation between education and labour force participation.

G. THE POSITION OF MIGRANT WOMEN IN THE LABOUR-MARKET

As is well known, economically active women are usually confined to a narrow set of occupations that are labelled "women's work" and include some of the less prestigious and more poorly paid jobs with few prospects for promotion. Given that in Argentina economically active women tend to be either manual workers, especially domestic servants, or professional, clerical and sales workers (ECLAC, 1989), the question is whether the different types of migrants in Neuquén City find themselves segregated into the same set of occupations and to what extent that segregation varies between migrant and non-migrant women.

To address that issue, the occupational distributions of non-migrant women, recent and settled female migrants by region of origin are compared. According to the distributions by occupation presented in table 36, women in Neuquén City appear to conform to the dual incorporation into the labour-market already described for Argentina as a whole. Thus, irrespective of migration status, high proportions of economically active women work as clerical and administrative workers or as sales workers, on the one hand, and as domestic service workers, on the other. Among non-migrant women, nearly 51 per cent work as clerical or sales workers, compared with 36 per cent among recent migrants and 38 per cent among settled migrants. Those in domestic service account for 19 per cent of non-migrant women, 28 per cent of recent migrants and 22 per cent of settled migrants. In contrast, the group of occupations requiring higher qualifications—namely, professionals, administrative and managerial workers, teachers, clerical supervisors, managers and foremen, and technical workers—accounts for 13 per cent of non-migrant women, 25 per cent of recent migrants and 20 per cent of settled migrants. That is, higher proportions of migrant women than of non-migrants tend to work in occupations requiring higher skills, but migrants are also more likely than non-migrants to work in domestic service, thus corroborating their greater tendency to experience a dual incorporation into the labour-market.

It is worth noting that, given the rapid economic and demographic growth of Neuquén City, active campaigns for the recruitment of highly skilled workers, particularly professionals, were carried out in the rest of the country, especially by disseminating vacancy announcements in the national universities for the

TABLE 36. DISTRIBUTION OF WOMEN AGED 14-69 IN THE LABOUR FORCE, BY OCCUPATIONAL GROUP, MIGRATION STATUS AND REGION OF ORIGIN, NEUQUÉN CITY, 1980
(Percentage)

Occupational group	Non-migrants	Recent migrants	Settled migrants
A. Distribution by migration status			
Total distribution	22.6	28.5	48.9
Professional	6.7	56.8	36.5
Administrative and managerial workers	22.0	24.4	53.7
Teachers	13.6	36.5	49.9
Clerical supervisors, managers and foremen	18.8	25.9	55.4
Technical workers	21.2	25.3	53.5
Clerical and related workers	29.1	27.1	43.8
Sales workers	27.4	22.3	50.3
Specialized workers	21.5	20.3	58.2
Labourers and other unqualified workers	25.3	11.6	63.2
Domestic service workers	18.8	35.1	46.1
Occupations inadequately described	21.5	30.7	47.9
B. Distribution by occupational group			
Professional	0.8	5.3	2.0
Administrative and managerial workers	0.4	0.3	0.4
Teachers	6.7	14.3	11.4
Clerical supervisors, managers and foremen	0.9	0.9	1.2
Technical workers	4.4	4.2	5.1
Clerical and related workers	32.7	24.2	22.8
Sales workers	17.9	11.6	15.3
Specialized workers	6.5	4.9	8.1
Labourers and other unqualified workers	8.0	2.9	9.2
Domestic service workers	19.2	28.4	21.7
Occupations inadequately described	2.7	3.0	2.8
TOTAL	100.0	100.0	100.0
Highly skilled workers	13.2	25.0	20.1
Medium-level workers	57.1	40.7	46.2
Unskilled workers	27.2	31.3	30.9

recruitment of civil servants. One can indirectly ascertain the success of such campaigns by noting that when each occupational category is distributed according to migrant status, recent female migrants are heavily overrepresented among professionals (see the lower panel of table 36). They are also overrepresented among teachers and slightly less so among domestic workers and occupations inadequately described (probably encompassing mostly unqualified occupations). Settled female migrants, in contrast, are either underrepresented or adequately represented in all those occupational categories, but they are overrepresented among administrative and managerial workers, clerical supervisors, managers and foremen, technical workers, sales workers, specialized workers, and labourers and other unqualified workers. Despite such differences, however, both groups of migrant women tend to be highly overrepresented both in occupations requiring higher skills and in those requiring minimum skills. Non-migrant women, in contrast, are overrepresented in the middle-level occupations.

With respect to region of origin, there are marked differences in the occupational distribution of migrant women originating in neighbouring areas and foreign countries, on the one hand, and those originating in

BAMA and the rest of Buenos Aires Province and in other Argentine provinces on the other (see table 37). Among both recent and settled female migrants, those originating in areas neighbouring Neuquén City tend to be concentrated in unskilled work, especially in domestic service, or in middle-level occupations (clerical and related workers, sales workers and specialized workers). Thus, the former category accounts for 42 and 39 per cent, respectively, of recent and settled female migrants from neighbouring areas, whereas the

TABLE 37. DISTRIBUTION OF WOMEN AGED 14-69 IN THE LABOUR FORCE BY OCCUPATIONAL GROUP AND MIGRATION STATUS, NEUQUÉN CITY, 1980
(*Percentage*)

Occupational group	Neighbouring areas	Buenos Aires Metropolitan Area	Buenos Aires Province	Rest of Argentina	Other countries
A. *Recent migrants*					
Professional	1.7	13.9	13.2	8.3	0.4
Administrative and managerial workers	0.1	0.3	1.3	0.6	0.0
Teachers	10.7	18.0	20.3	26.2	1.3
Clerical supervisors, managers and foremen	1.0	1.6	0.6	0.6	0.9
Technical workers	3.1	6.3	6.8	4.7	4.4
Clerical and related workers	22.6	28.3	26.0	31.8	10.1
Sales workers	11.0	13.9	14.8	10.1	11.0
Specialized workers	4.6	5.4	6.4	3.4	7.0
Labourers and other unqualified workers	4.0	1.1	2.9	1.0	2.2
Domestic service workers	37.9	8.2	6.4	10.8	59.6
Occupations inadequately described	3.5	3.0	1.3	2.4	3.1
TOTAL	100.0	100.0	100.0	100.0	100.0
Highly skilled workers	16.6	40.1	42.2	40.4	7.0
Medium-level workers	38.2	47.6	47.2	45.3	28.1
Unskilled workers	41.9	9.3	9.3	11.8	61.8
B. *Settled migrants*					
Professional	0.6	10.1	3.6	4.1	0.7
Administrative and managerial workers	0.4	0.3	0.8	0.7	0.0
Teachers	6.5	24.5	24.8	26.8	2.0
Clerical supervisors, managers and foremen	0.8	3.2	1.1	2.0	0.8
Technical workers	5.6	4.0	4.0	4.7	5.0
Clerical and related workers	22.9	29.7	27.2	29.5	11.4
Sales workers	13.6	17.9	18.9	12.6	19.8
Specialized workers	8.0	3.7	9.5	5.7	11.8
Labourers and other unqualified workers	12.3	2.6	2.9	3.5	10.1
Domestic service workers	26.6	1.2	4.0	8.2	35.4
Occupations inadequately described	2.7	2.9	3.2	2.3	3.0
TOTAL	100.0	100.0	100.0	100.0	100.0
Highly skilled workers	13.9	42.1	34.3	38.3	8.5
Medium-level workers	44.5	51.3	55.6	47.8	43.0
Unskilled workers	38.9	3.8	6.9	11.7	45.4

latter accounts for 38 and 45 per cent, respectively, of the same groups. Among migrants originating in other countries, those that arrived recently are even more concentrated in unskilled occupations (62 per cent), particularly in domestic service (60 per cent), with middle-level occupations accounting for considerably lower proportions than in other groups (28 per cent). Settled migrants from other countries also have high percentages in unskilled occupations (45 per cent) and in middle-level occupations (43 per cent), but the distribution between the two is more balanced.

In contrast, migrant women originating in the rest of Argentina tend to be fairly evenly distributed between the highly skilled occupations and middle-level work. Recent female migrants, in general, comprise higher proportions in the highly skilled occupations than settled migrants, though some exceptions arise by region of origin. Thus, among recent migrants originating in BAMA, 40 per cent were in highly skilled occupations, compared with 42 per cent among settled female migrants from the same region. For Buenos Aires Province and the other provinces of Argentina, the equivalent proportions of highly skilled workers were 42 and 40 per cent among recent migrant women and 34 and 38 per cent among settled migrants. In all cases, the proportion of female migrants originating in those three regions and working in middle-level occupations surpassed 45 per cent and even reached 56 per cent among settled migrants originating in Buenos Aires Province.

Another interesting comparison is that of the occupational distribution of women in the regions of origin with that of recent migrant women in Neuquén City by region of origin. Such a comparison, however, must be interpreted with some caution, because the occupational distribution in both the area of origin and that of destination is dependent upon the economic structure of each location. Table 38 presents the occupational

TABLE 38. OBSERVED AND STANDARDIZED[a] DISTRIBUTIONS OF WOMEN AGED 14-69 IN THE LABOUR FORCE BY OCCUPATIONAL GROUP AND REGION OF ORIGIN
(*Percentage*)

Occupational group	Resident population of							
	Neighbouring areas		Buenos Aires Metropolitan Area		Buenos Aires Province		Rest of Argentina	
	Observed	Standardized	Observed	Standardized	Observed	Standardized	Observed	Standardized
Professional	2.2	1.8	3.4	12.1	2.6	11.0	2.3	7.4
Administrative and managerial workers	0.2	0.1	0.3	0.2	0.2	1.0	0.1	0.5
Teachers	13.1	11.7	7.9	14.9	12.0	16.8	14.1	25.5
Clerical supervisors, managers and foremen	0.8	1.0	0.9	2.2	0.6	1.8	0.6	0.5
Technical workers	4.9	3.9	4.8	7.2	4.7	9.2	4.9	4.6
Clerical and related workers	19.1	21.4	25.2	27.6	18.2	23.9	17.9	30.2
Sales workers	13.7	11.1	13.4	15.1	13.6	15.3	12.8	12.1
Specialized workers	14.7	5.8	18.9	6.4	18.1	7.8	13.5	4.1
Labourers and other unqualified workers	7.0	4.0	3.7	2.2	5.0	4.2	5.6	0.9
Domestic service workers	21.2	35.2	18.5	9.6	19.8	7.9	23.5	11.5
Occupations inadequately described	3.2	4.1	3.0	2.6	5.2	1.2	4.7	2.7
TOTAL	100.0	100.0	100.0	100.0	100.0	100.0	100.0	100.0
Highly skilled workers	21.2	18.5	17.3	36.6	20.1	39.8	22.0	38.5
Medium-level workers	47.5	38.3	57.5	49.1	49.9	47.0	44.2	46.4
Unskilled workers	28.2	39.2	22.2	11.8	24.8	12.1	29.1	12.4

Source: Argentina, Instituto Nacional de Estadística y Censos, *Censo Nacional de Población y Vivienda, 1980*; Series D, *Población: total del país, por provincia, departamento y localidad* (Buenos Aires, n.d.).

[a] Standardized distributions were calculated by multiplying the resident population by age group by the proportion of recent migrant women classified by occupational group according to region of origin.

distribution of the female labour force resident in the different regions of origin and the standardized distribution obtained by multiplying the resident population by age group by the proportions of recent migrants originating in the relevant region in each occupational category.

The comparison between the observed and the standardized occupational distributions indicates that whereas migrants from areas neighbouring Neuquén City are selected downward in the occupational scale with respect to the population in the areas of origin, those from other regions are selected upward. Thus, for BAMA, the proportion of highly skilled workers among the female labour force resident in the area amounted to 17 per cent, whereas that implied by the occupational distribution of recent female migrants to Neuquén City was more than double, reaching almost 37 per cent. The equivalent comparison for the unskilled categories amounted to 22 per cent among residents versus 12 per cent according to the migrant distribution. As table 38 indicates, the comparisons for both Buenos Aires Province and other Argentine provinces indicate similar differentials. In contrast, the economically active female population resident in areas neighbouring Neuquén City comprised 21 per cent of highly skilled workers, 48 per cent in the middle-level occupations and 28 in the unskilled jobs, which compare favourably with the percentage distribution implied by the occupations of recent migrants—19 in highly skilled occupations, 38 in middle-level and 39 in unskilled. That is, recent migrants from areas near Neuquén City are highly selected from the lower end of the occupational scale and adequately selected from the high end to the detriment of those in middle-level occupations. Those from farther away are, on the contrary, adequately selected from the middle range of the occupational scale and highly selected from the upper end, implying that they can exercise greater selectivity in entering the local labour-market than can migrants from areas in the vicinity.

Further insight into the segmentation of the labour-market can be gained by considering the labour force participation of women in the formal and informal sectors of the economy. The literature on the topic is abundant (see, for example, PREALC, 1990a and 1990b; Portes, 1990); and it generally emphasizes the relative vulnerability of workers in the informal sector, given that they often join the labour-market because of survival needs and must accept working conditions that are far below those of workers in the formal sector. Thus, informal sector workers normally lack all types of social benefits, earn lower incomes and are more likely to be subject to environmental hazards. Undocumented migrants, ethnic minorities, the young and women are more likely to work in that sector (Castells and Portes, 1990).

The identification of workers in the informal sector was carried out using the PREALC definition, which includes all non-remunerated family workers, all own-account workers except professionals and all domestic servants. Table 39 presents the proportion of men and women in the formal and informal sectors by migration status, age group and two broad regions of origin. In this case, only internal migrants have been considered, since many migrants from other countries have an illegal status that may influence their relative propensity to join the informal sector. The data indicate that among women, those in age groups 14-24 and particularly those over age 45 have the highest propensity to work in the informal sector, irrespective of their migration status. Overall, however, recent female migrants are considerably more likely to work in the informal sector than either settled female migrants or non-migrant women. That is, the younger and older recent female migrants appear to be the most vulnerable in terms of their likely employment, a finding that corroborates the widespread view that young female migrants have a high tendency to work in domestic service and that older women who work do so by necessity, often because they lack male support. According to the data given in table 39, domestic service is the predominant form of work among women participating in the informal sector, especially among those aged 14-24 and, to a lesser extent, among older women, whatever their migration status. Commerce is also important, but far fewer women engage in it. Yet, again irrespective of migration status, commerce is a more likely activity among women over age 45.

When the data by area of origin are considered, they confirm the important differences existing between female migrants originating in areas neighbouring Neuquén City and those originating in the rest of Argentina: the former are two or three times more likely to work in the informal sector than the latter,

TABLE 39. DISTRIBUTION OF THE MALE AND FEMALE LABOUR FORCE BY SECTOR, MIGRATION STATUS, AGE GROUP AND REGION OF ORIGIN, NEUQUÉN CITY, 1980
(*Percentage*)

Sector and industry	Total				Neigbouring areas				All other Argentina			
	14-24	25-44	45-69	Total	14-24	25-44	45-69	Total	14-24	25-44	45-69	Total
A. Recent migrants												
Female												
Formal	52.3	78.3	57.0	66.9	40.7	68.8	52.5	54.7	80.8	87.9	64.0	84.2
Informal	47.7	21.7	43.0	33.1	59.3	31.2	47.5	45.3	19.2	12.1	36.0	15.8
Of which:												
Commerce	2.3	4.7	9.2	4.2	2.4	5.7	6.5	4.3	1.9	3.7	13.5	4.0
Domestic service	42.9	13.9	27.2	25.8	53.9	22.5	34.5	37.7	15.9	5.4	15.7	9.0
Male												
Formal	86.8	84.5	78.3	84.2	86.6	82.6	79.7	83.2	86.9	86.6	76.4	85.4
Informal	13.2	15.5	21.7	15.8	13.4	17.4	20.3	16.8	13.1	13.4	23.6	14.6
Of which:												
Commerce	4.5	4.9	7.9	5.2	3.6	3.8	6.1	4.1	5.7	6.0	10.2	6.5
Domestic service	0.2	0.0	0.2	0.1	0.4	0.1	0.2	0.2	0.0	0.0	0.3	0.0
B. Settled migrants												
Female												
Formal	67.9	75.6	62.0	71.2	62.1	69.1	53.0	64.2	83.1	86.4	77.2	83.9
Informal	32.1	24.4	38.0	28.8	37.9	30.9	47.0	35.8	16.9	13.6	22.8	16.1
Of which:												
Commerce	3.3	5.4	9.1	5.7	2.5	5.0	9.0	5.2	5.4	5.9	9.3	6.5
Domestic service	26.9	15.3	21.4	19.0	33.8	22.1	30.5	26.6	8.8	4.1	6.0	5.3
Male												
Formal	87.5	83.3	77.9	82.6	88.1	82.7	77.5	82.7	85.9	84.1	78.3	82.5
Informal	12.5	16.7	22.1	17.4	11.9	17.3	22.5	17.3	14.1	15.9	21.7	17.5
Of which:												
Commerce	3.1	4.6	7.7	5.2	1.9	3.6	5.9	3.7	6.5	6.1	9.6	7.3
Domestic service	0.1	0.0	0.0	0.0	0.1	0.1	0.1	0.1	0.0	0.0	0.0	0.0
C. Non-migrants												
Female												
Formal	70.7	80.2	62.6	74.2	-	-	-	-	-	-	-	-
Informal	29.3	19.8	37.4	25.8	-	-	-	-	-	-	-	-
Of which:												
Commerce	2.5	4.7	10.9	4.4	-	-	-	-	-	-	-	-
Domestic service	25.4	12.1	21.8	18.9	-	-	-	-	-	-	-	-
Male												
Formal	86.9	83.0	78.6	84.0	-	-	-	-	-	-	-	-
Informal	13.1	17.0	21.4	16.0	-	-	-	-	-	-	-	-
Of which:												
Commerce	3.0	4.4	6.4	4.1	-	-	-	-	-	-	-	-
Domestic service	0.2	0.1	0.0	0.1	-	-	-	-	-	-	-	-

whether they be recent or settled migrants. There are, however, important differences between recent and settled female migrants originating in neighbouring areas. Whereas among female migrants from other areas of Argentina about 16 per cent in either migrant category, recent or settled, work in the informal sector, among female migrants originating near Neuquén City, the proportion of settled migrants in the informal sector, 36 per cent, is considerably lower than that among recent female migrants, 45 per cent. Consideration of differentials by age indicates that whereas settled and recent female migrants from areas near Neuquén City have similar tendencies to work in the informal sector if they are over age 25, younger women (those aged 14-24) are considerably more likely to work in the informal sector if they are recent migrants (59 per cent) than if they are settled migrants (38 per cent).

To conclude, it is worth comparing the experience of women in terms of their insertion into a segmented labour-market with that of men. As table 39 indicates, the proportion of female migrants in informal activities is considerably higher than that among male migrants, whether recent or settled. Thus, whereas among male migrants, 16 and 17 per cent, respectively, of recent and settled migrants work in the informal sector, the equivalent proportions among female migrants are 33 and 29 per cent. Differences are more marked between male and female migrants originating in areas neighbouring Neuquén City, whose proportions in the informal sector are 17 and 45 per cent, respectively, for recent migrants; and 17 and 36, respectively, for settled migrants. In contrast, among migrants from other parts of Argentina, the differences by sex are small; and among settled migrants, males have a slightly higher proportion in the informal sector (17.5 per cent) than females (16.1 per cent).

In general, the different groups of men considered show similar tendencies to participate in the informal sector, irrespective of migration status or origin, so that the overall proportions in that sector vary over a relatively narrow range, from 14.6 to 17.5 per cent. In contrast, the equivalent range for women is from 15.8 to 45.3 per cent. In addition, there is a clear tendency among men for the proportion in informal sector activities to increase with age, a tendency that is not so clear-cut among women, for whom informal sector activity is relatively high at younger ages (14-24), particularly because of those engaging in domestic service. Lack of similar employment possibilities for young man and the fact that they probably spend more time in school are a couple of the factors keeping their informal sector participation low.

H. Conclusion

The labour force participation of migrant women has not received sufficient attention and thus the general view that most female migrants in Latin America are young single women moving to work as domestic servants in the cities has not been based on sufficient empirical evidence. This study, by focusing on a medium-sized city of Argentina which has largely been populated through migration, indicates that the migration of women is a considerably more complex phenomenon which cannot be properly characterized by such simplistic stereotypes.

The evidence with regard to Neuquén City, where 77 per cent of the female population can be classified as in-migrant, amply exemplifies the heterogeneity characterizing female migration. The most interesting differences detected have been those associated with region of origin. Thus, female migrants originating in areas neighbouring Neuquén City, which are less developed than the rest of the country, tend to be downwardly selected in terms of both education and occupation. Among recent female migrants from those areas, 35 per cent had not even completed elementary education. In addition, among the economically active women, 38 per cent worked as domestic servants and 45 per cent were classified as working in the informal sector. It is this group, without doubt, that best conforms to the stereotype mentioned above. However, it constitutes a relatively small proportion of recent female migrants (fewer than one fourth). Furthermore, recent female migrants from areas neighbouring Neuquén City that are economically active also include nearly 17 per cent working in highly skilled occupations (mostly as teachers) and a majority (55 per cent) working in the formal sector.

At the other end of the spectrum, recent female migrants from BAMA and from the rest of Buenos Aires Province are upwardly selected in terms of educational attainment and occupation. They exhibit relatively high labour force participation rates; and among the economically active women, at least 40 per cent work in highly skilled occupations. Very few engage in domestic service (only 8 per cent of those originating in BAMA do) and their levels of participation in the informal sector are likely to be low and similar to those of migrant men originating in the same areas.

Settled female migrants originating in BAMA have similar characteristics to those of recent female migrants from the same area, tending to have relatively high levels of educational attainment and a tendency to work in highly skilled occupations. By virtue of the longer time that they have spent in Neuquén City, settled female migrants from Buenos Aires are probably better off than those arriving more recently, because the former are more likely to have developed better strategies to combine their reproductive and their productive roles. An indication of their "privileged" position is that the proportion in domestic service is the lowest in any migrant group (1.2 per cent). Given their modes of insertion into the labour force, female migrants from Buenos Aires, whether recent or settled, may be taken to represent the most "independent" component of the migration stream, since their migration is likely to have been prompted by economic considerations related to labour-market opportunities. Nevertheless, it is important to note that, as with any other migrant group, most women originating in BAMA, whether recent or settled, have been married.

Although the case of Neuquén City is very special, both within Argentina and even more within Latin America, this study sheds light on the important role that female migrants have played in a city characterized by rapid economic growth. Among all migrants enumerated at Neuquén City, women are almost as numerous as men, though they are slightly underrepresented among recent migrants. Their participation in the labour force is high in comparison with that of women in the areas of origin. There are many indications that female migrants are able to take advantage of the labour-market opportunities open to them in Neuquén City. Highly qualified female migrants are attracted from relatively distant areas, whereas nearby areas are the sources of generally less skilled female migrants. The costs of migration associated with distance probably contribute to that dichotomy. Although distance may not be the determining factor behind that dichotomy in other situations, the dichotomy itself is likely to arise more generally. Indeed, the coexistence in female migration streams of highly skilled women and the unskilled is likely to characterize many other situations in Latin America, especially as internal migration becomes increasingly dominated by urban-urban flows. Thus, at Neuquén City, most economically active women among recent migrants worked either in highly skilled occupations (25 per cent) or in middle-level occupations (41 per cent). Consequently, the slightly over 28 per cent that worked in domestic service can scarcely be called representative. Although the vulnerability of the latter group cannot be denied, it is important not to stress it at the expense of ignoring the experience of their better educated sisters. A more balanced approach to the study of female migration is clearly necessary.

Notes

[1] See Simmons, Diaz-Briquets and Laquian (1977); Elton (1978), Martine and Peliano (1978); and bibliographical reviews by Jelin (1978), Crummett (1987), and Tienda and Booth (1988).

[2] This figure and that for 1960 were estimated by Vapnarsky and Pantelides (1987) by adjusting the 1947 and 1960 census figures and interpolating them. The adjustments made were based on a detailed analysis of settlement maps of the period. The census figures themselves indicated that smaller numbers of persons were present in 1947 and 1960, namely, 9,165 and 16,738, thus implying still higher rates of population growth.

[3] According to Vapnarsky and Gorojovsky (1990), Neuquén City and Cipolletti City constituted an integrated urban agglomeration of 131,000 inhabitants in 1980. The Alto Valle Metropolitan Area (including Neuquén City, Cipolletti City and another 14 smaller urban centres), had increased from 81,000 persons in 1950 to 305,000 in 1980. That is, Neuquén City has grown faster than the rest of the Alto Valle Metropolitan Area (Vapnarsky and Pantelides, 1987).

References

Argentina, Instituto Nacional de Estadística y Censos (n.d.). *Censo Nacional de Población y Vivienda, 1980*. Series B, *Características generales: total del país*. Buenos Aires.

────── (n.d.). *Censo Nacional de Población y Vivenda, 1980*. Series D, *Características generales: total del país, por provincia, departamento y localidad, República Argentina*. Buenos Aires.

────── (1981a). *Censo Nacional de Población y Vivienda, 1980*. Series B, *Características generales: Capital Federal*. Buenos Aires.

_____ (1981b). *Censo Nacional de Población y Vivienda, 1980*. Series B, *Características generales: partidos del gran Buenos Aires*. Buenos Aires.

_____ (1981c). *Censo Nacional de Población y Vivienda, 1980*. Series B, *Características generales: La Pampa*. Buenos Aires.

_____ (1981d). *Censo Nacional de Población y Vivienda, 1980*. Series B, *Características generales: Neuquén*. Buenos Aires.

_____ (1981e). *Censo Nacional de Población y Vivienda, 1980*. Series B, *Características generales: Río Negro*. Buenos Aires.

_____ (1982a). *Censo Nacional de Población y Vivienda, 1980*. Series B, *Características generales: Provincia de Buenos Aires*. Buenos Aires.

_____ (1982b). *Censo Nacional de Población y Vivienda, 1980*. Series B, *Características generales: Mendoza*. Buenos Aires.

Castells, Manuel, and Alejandro Portes (1990). El Mundo sumergido: los orígenes, la dinámica y los efectos de la economía informal. In *La economía informal: en los países desarrollados y en los menos avanzados*, Alejandro Portes, ed. Buenos Aires: Planeta, Política y Sociedad.

Centro Latinoamericano de Demografía (1990). *La migración interna en la Argentina, período 1975-1980*. CELADE Series A, No. 209. Santiago, Chile.

Crummett, María de los Angeles (1987). Migración rural femenina en América Latina y el Caribe y su efecto en las pequeñas unidades campesinas. In *Mujeres campesinas en América Latina: desarrollo rural, migración, tierra y legislación*. Santiago, Chile: Food and Agriculture Organization.

Elton, Charlotte (1978). *Migración femenina en América Latina: factores determinantes*. CELADE Series E, No.26. Santiago, Chile: Centro Latinoamericano de Demografía.

Garcia, Brígida, Humberto Muñoz and Orlandina de Oliveira (1982). *Hogares y trabajadores en la Ciudad de México*. Mexico: El Colegio de México/Universidad Autónoma de México.

Herold, Joan M. (1979). Female migration in Chile: types of moves and socioeconomic characteristics. *Demography* (Washington, D.C.), vol. 16, No. 2 (May), pp. 257-278.

Jelin, Elizabeth (1976). *Migración a las ciudades y participación en la fuerza de trabajo de las mujeres latinoamericanas: el caso del servicio doméstico*. Estudios sociales, No. 4. Buenos Aires: Centro de Estudios de Estado y Sociedad.

Kloster, Elba Eleonora (1992). Características generales, económicas y sociodemográficas de la provincia y de la ciudad. Draft.

Lattes, Alfredo E. (1984). Territorial mobility and redistribution of the population: recent developments. In *Population Distribution, Migration and Development*. Proceedings of the International Conference on Population, Migration and Development, Hammamet, Tunisia, 21-25 March 1983. Population Studies, No. 89. Sales No.E.83.XIII.3. New York: United Nations.

_____ (1990). La urbanización y el crecimiento urbano en América Latina, desde una perspectiva demográfica. In *La investigación urbana en América Latina: caminos recorridos y por recorrer: Las ideas y su contexto*, vol. 3, José Luis Coraggio, ed. Quito: CIUDAD.

_____, and Sonia María Mychaszula (1985). Urbanization, migration and urban deconcentration in Argentina. Mimeographed.

Martine, George, and José Carlos P. Peliano (1978). *Migrantes no mercado do trabalho metropolitano*. Estudos para o Planejamento, No. 19. Brasilia: Instituto de Planejamento Economico e Social/IPLAN.

Mychaszula, Sonia María, and Elba E. Kloster (1992). Crecimiento migratorio de la ciudad de Neuquén, cambio de la participación económica y del tamaño medio de la familia. In *Proceedings of the Conference on The Peopling of the Americas, Veracruz, 1992*. Veracruz, Mexico: International Union for the Scientific Study of Population.

Mychaszula, Sonia María, R. N. Geldstein and C. Grushka (1989). *Datos para el estudio de la participación en la actividad económica*. Información Documental y Estadística, No. 4. Buenos Aires: Centro Nacional de Estudios de Población.

Oliveira, Orlandina de, and Brígida García (1984). Urbanization, migration and the growth of large cities: trends and implications in some developing countries. In *Population Distribution, Migration and Development*. Proceedings of the Expert Group on Population Distribution, Migration and Development, Hammamet, Tunisia, 21-25 March 1983. Population Studies, No. 89. Sales No. E.83.XIII.3. New York: United Nations.

Orlansky, Dora, and Silvia L. Dubrovsky (1978). *Efectos de la migración rural-urbana sobre la función y la condición de la mujer en América Latina*. Informes y Documentos de Ciencias Sociales, No. 41. Paris: United Nations Educational, Scientific and Cultural Organization.

Pedrero Nieto, Mercedes (1992). División sexual del trabajo y cambio demográfico en América Latina, 1950-1990. In *Proceedings of the Conference on The Peopling of the Americas, Veracruz, 1992*. Veracruz, Mexico: International Union for the Scientific Study of Population.

Portes, Alejandro, ed. (1990). *La economía informal en los países desarrollados y en los menos avanzados*. Buenos Aires: Planeta, Política y Sociedad.

Programa Regional del Empleo para América Latina y el Caribe (1978). *Participación laboral femenina y diferencias de remuneraciones según sexo en América Latina*. Investigaciones sobre Empleo, No. 13. Santiago, Chile: International Labour Organisation.

_____ (1990a). *Urbanización y sector informal en América Latina, 1960-1980*. Santiago, Chile: International Labour Organisation.

_____ (1990b). *Empleo en América Latina y la heterogeneidad del sector informal*. PREALC Documentos de Trabajo, No. 346. Santiago, Chile: International Labour Organisation.

Raczynski, Dagmar (1983). *La población migrante en los mercados de trabajo urbanos: el caso de Chile*. CIEPLAN Notas técnicas, No. 55. Santiago, Chile: Corporación de Investigaciones Económicas para América Latina.

Ravenstein, E. G. (1885). The laws of migration. *Journal of the Royal Statistical Society* (London), vol. 48, No. 2 (June), pp. 167-235.

Recchini de Lattes, Zulma (1975). Urbanización. In *La población de Argentina*, Zulma Recchini de Lattes and Alfredo E. Lattes, eds. CICRED Series. Buenos Aires.

Sautu, Ruth (1991). Oportunidades ocupacionales diferenciales por sexo en Argentina, 1970-1980. *Estudios del Trabajo* (Buenos Aires), No. 1 (Primer semestre), pp. 47-69.

Simmons, Alan, Sergio Diaz-Briquets, and Aprodicio A. Laquian (1977). *Social Change and Internal Migration: A Review of Research Findings from Africa, Asia, and Latin America*. Ottawa, Canada: International Development Research Centre.

Standing, Guy (1978). *Labour Force Participation and Development*. Geneva: International Labour Office.

Tienda, Marta, and Karen Booth (1988). Migration, gender and social change: a review and reformulation. In *Conference on Women's Position and Demographic Change in the Course of Development, Oslo, 15-18 June: Solicited Papers*. Liège: International Union for the Scientific Study of Population.

United Nations, Economic Commission for Latin America and the Caribbean (1989). *Transformación ocupacional y crisis social en América Latina*. Sales No. S.90.II.G.3. Santiago, Chile.

_____ (1990). *Los grandes cambios y la crisis: impacto sobre la mujer en América Latina y el Caribe*. Sales No. S.90.II.G.13. Santiago, Chile.

Vapnarsky, César A., and Néstor Gorojovsky (1990). *El crecimiento urbano en la Argentina*. Colección Estudios Políticos y Sociales. Buenos Aires: Grupo Editor Latinoamericano.

Vapnarsky, César A., and Edith A. Pantelides, eds. (1987). *La formación de un area metropolitana en la Patagonia: población y asentamiento en el Alto Valle*. Informes de Investigación del CEUR, No. 7. Buenos Aires: Centro de Estudios Urbanos y Regionales.

Wainerman, Catalina H. (1979). Educación, familia y participación económica femenina en la Argentina. *Desarrollo Económico* (Buenos Aires), vol. 18, No. 72 (enero-marzo), pp. 511-537.

_____, and Zulma Recchini de Lattes (1981). *El trabajo femenino en el banquillo de los acusados: la medición censal en América Latina*. Colección Economía y Sociedad. México: The Population Council/Editorial Terra Nova.

IX. THE LABOUR-MARKET ASPECTS OF FEMALE MIGRATION TO BANGKOK

Pasuk Phongpaichit*

During the past 30 years, development shifted into high gear in Thailand. Per capita income increased more than 17 times, from $102 in 1960 (Ingram, 1971) to $1,797 in 1992 (Thailand, 1992). There was a significant shift in the structure of the economy away from agriculture and towards industry and services. The National Economic and Social Development Board reports that the share of agriculture in gross domestic product (GDP) dropped from 35 to 14 per cent between 1960 and 1989 and that of services rose from 55 to 62 per cent during the same period. Since the early 1980s, the economy has been reoriented towards manufactured exports so that by 1990 the percentage of manufactured exports in total exports reached 75 per cent, up from a mere 2 per cent in 1960 (Bank of Thailand, 1976 and 1991).

Concomitantly, the level of urbanization also increased. The percentage of people living in urban areas rose from 13 per cent in 1965 to 22 per cent in 1989. The change was not as dramatic as that experienced by some other countries in the region. In the Republic of Korea, for instance, over the same period the level of urbanization increased from 32 to 71 per cent. In Malaysia the level of urbanization was already 26 per cent by 1965 and it rose to 42 per cent in 1989 (World Bank, 1991). The level of urbanization in Thailand has tended to lag behind that of many comparable countries, mainly because the continued expansion of agriculture has helped to retain people in the countryside. During the past 10 years, however, growth in agriculture has slowed considerably, with the growth of agricultural output declining from an annual rate of 4.2 per cent in the 1970s to 3.7 per cent in 1980-1986 and to 1.9 per cent during 1986-1988.

In terms of urbanization, Bangkok Metropolis, which includes the cities of Bangkok proper and adjacent Thonburi, and the five provinces surrounding Bangkok, which together with Bangkok Metropolis constitute the Bangkok Metropolitan Area, have developed into a major industrial centre: the majority of the factories are located there. They constitute a powerful centre of attraction for people from all parts of the country. Although several provincial towns have also experienced significant spurts of growth, they have not matched that of Bangkok. One striking feature of recent urbanization has been the increasing role of women in labour migration to urban areas and especially to Bangkok Metropolis.

This paper examines the extent and characteristics of female migration to Bangkok Metropolis, taking into account the developmental context in which migration has evolved. It discusses the conditions that give rise to that flow and the impact of migration on the women involved and on the labour market at destination. Attention is also given to the policy implications of increasing female labour migration and to the need to improve the labour-market situation of migrant women in Bangkok Metropolis.

A. THE CONTEXT OF THE ECONOMIC DEVELOPMENT STRATEGY: SERVICE AND EXPORT-LED GROWTH IN THAILAND

Economic development in Thailand has been based both on the expansion of labour-intensive and export-oriented manufacturing and on the proliferation of the service sector, both as a source of foreign-exchange earnings and as a source of employment. During the past 30 years, the service sector in Thailand has always been more important than the industrial sector in terms of its contribution to GDP and as an employment generator. Rather than experiencing the traditional form of industrialization, Thailand has undergone a transformation driven mostly by export and service-led growth. This development strategy has been a deliberate policy on the part of the Government (Phongpaichit, 1991a).

During the 1960s, economic growth was based largely on the expansion of agricultural exports and, to a lesser extent, on import substitution. Beginning in the mid-

---

*Faculty of Economics, Chulalongkorn University, Bangkok, Thailand.

1970s, however, the earnings from agricultural exports declined; and although there were attempts to compensate for such a decline by shifting to manufactured exports, the results were not significant before the mid-1980s. Faced with a deteriorating balance of trade and a mounting foreign debt, the Government actively promoted the service sector, especially tourism and international labour migration, to earn foreign exchange. Its efforts were largely successful and tourism grew rapidly through the 1980s to become the major source of foreign exchange in Thailand by the end of the decade. The international migration of labour, directed mostly to Western Asia, also expanded and made a significant contribution to foreign earnings.

In the mid-1980s, several new factors reoriented the international position of Thailand. First, the decline in the price of oil, the major import, significantly altered the terms of trade of Thailand. Secondly, the major adjustment of the currencies of Eastern and South-eastern Asian countries, set off by the rise of the value of the yen that began in 1985, triggered a relocation of industrial investment. With capital inflows from Japan and other sources, Thailand emerged as a major centre of manufacturing exports. Thirdly, the Government facilitated that trend by adopting policies designed to encourage foreign investment and export-led growth. However, those developments did not dampen the expansion of the service sector, they merely supplemented it. From 1986 onward, Thailand enjoyed four years of double-digit growth in GDP, driven largely by the expansion of services and the exportation of manufactured goods.

The continued importance of agricultural exports and the active promotion of the service sector shaped the nature of economic development of Thailand in a way that differed significantly from that of other newly industrializing countries in Asia. This difference can be seen from a comparison with the Republic of Korea, another country that has undergone a radical transformation of its economic structure.

In 1965, the share of the agricultural sector in GDP was roughly the same in the Republic of Korea and Thailand: about 38 and 32 per cent, respectively. By 1980, that share had fallen to 16 per cent in the Republic of Korea, but it took another five years to achieve a similar level, 17 per cent in 1985, in Thailand (table 40). In the Republic of Korea, between 1965 and 1989 the shift in production from agriculture to the industrial and service sectors was shared almost equally by those sectors (44 and 46 per cent of GDP, respectively). In Thailand, the shift to services was larger than that to industry. Therefore, in 1989, the industrial sector accounted for only 38 per cent of GDP, while the service sector accounted for 47 per cent.

These changes in output structure had different implications for the structure of employment in the Republic of Korea and in Thailand. First, Thailand retained most of its labour force in agriculture so that even by 1987 almost two thirds of the Thai labour force was still in that sector. In the Republic of Korea, however, only 19 per cent of the labour force remained in agriculture by 1989. Secondly, the Republic of Korea experienced a somewhat less marked shift towards the service sector than did Thailand. By 1987, Thailand had twice as many workers in the service

TABLE 40. STRUCTURE OF PRODUCTION AND THE LABOUR FORCE, REPUBLIC OF KOREA AND THAILAND, 1965-1985

Sector	Republic of Korea			Thailand		
	1965	1980	1989	1965	1985	1989

A. *Percentage distribution of gross domestic product*

Agriculture	38	16	10	32	17	15
Industry	25	42	44	23	30	38
Services	37	42	46	45	53	47

B. *Percentage distribution of labour*

	1965	1980	1989	1970	1987	1989
Agriculture	59	34	19	78	64	..
Industry	13	29	29	6	12	..
Services	28	37	52	15	24	..
Urban population	32	..	71	13	22	..

Source: For gross domestic product and percentage of the population in urban areas in both the Republic of Korea and Thailand, World Bank, *World Development Report*, various years (New York, Oxford University Press); for the Republic of Korea, distribution of the labour force derived from the Republic of Korea, *Korean Economic Indicators*, various years (Seoul, Economic Planning Board, National Bureau of Statistics); and for Thailand equivalent figures taken from Thailand, *Population and Housing Census, 1970* (Bangkok, National Statistical Office, 1970); and *Report of the Labour Force Survey, Whole Kingdom, Round 3* (Bangkok, National Statistical Office, 1987).

sector as in industry (24 per cent of labour force versus 12 per cent), whereas in the Republic of Korea, the ratio of service sector workers to industrial workers in 1989 was 1.8 (52 versus 29 per cent).

In terms of urbanization, the pace in Thailand was considerably slower than that of the Republic of Korea. In Thailand, the urban population as a proportion of the total rose from some 13 per cent in 1965 to 22 per cent in 1989. In the Republic of Korea, the equivalent proportion rose from 32 to 71 per cent between 1965 and 1988 (see table 40). Rural-urban migration has played an important part in both urbanization and industrialization. In Thailand, the urban population grew much faster than that of the entire country. Between 1970 and 1980, the urban population grew at an annual rate of 5.3 per cent, whereas the rural and total population growth rates were 2.2 and 2.7 per cent per annum, respectively. In more recent years, (1980-1990), the growth rate of the urban population declined to 2.9 per cent.[1] This slow-down, however, is somewhat artificial because it does not take into account the geographical expansion of urban areas, especially that of Bangkok Metropolis. The statistics suggest that the urban sector draws a substantial portion of its increased population from in-migration from rural areas.

Rising levels of rural-urban migration in Thailand have been closely associated with the expansion of industry and service activities in urban areas. A study based on the 1980 population census estimated that in 1980, recent migrants from rural areas (that is, those that had migrated between 1975 and 1980) accounted for 50-60 per cent of the growth in urban employment in all of Thailand (ESCAP, 1988).

A special characteristic of Thai urbanization has been the role of Bangkok as a primate city. In 1980, Bangkok Metropolis alone housed 61.5 per cent of the total urban population and had 46 times the population of the next largest city, Chiang Mai. The primacy of Bangkok has been strengthened further because the majority of the new industrial development has been concentrated there and in the Bangkok Metropolitan Area. In addition, a major proportion of tourist-related services has been concentrated in Bangkok. The capital city has therefore become a major attraction pole for rural-urban migrants.

The new urban economy, with its emphasis on service activities and export-oriented manufactures, has created a wide range of new job and entrepreneurial opportunities for which women have been acceptable and willing applicants. Within the service sector, such opportunities have opened up in retailing, construction (in 1988, women constituted 18 per cent of all construction workers in Thailand), food preparation and a wide range of activities related to tourism (Thailand, 1988). Within manufacturing, those opportunities included factory work in the textile and garment industry, the food industry, the electronics industry and a broad variety of light industries. Thus, in 1987/88, women accounted for between 70 and 95 per cent of the workforce in the export-oriented industries located in the provinces of Ayuthaya, Chachoengsao, Nonthaburi, Patumthani, Samutprakarn and Samutsakorn, which include four within the vicinity of Bangkok and constitute the hub of export-oriented industry in Thailand (Kanjana-uksorn, 1991).

The importance of female workers derives from the lack of alternative sources of labour for the new productive activities in urban areas. Urban areas lacked an adequate supply of unemployed or underemployed persons of the right age with the necessary disposition to work in factories for relatively low wages. During the 1970s, the open unemployment rate in Thailand was fairly low, oscillating between 2 and 3 per cent. In urban areas, relatively higher unemployment rates were found among the educated (those with secondary education or more), who were not willing to work for low wages in labour-intensive manufacturing. Thus, in 1987 the unemployment rate among urban-dwellers with at least a secondary education was at least 7 per cent, whereas that for those with an elementary education or less was at most 2.5 per cent (Thailand, 1987).

Despite several decades of economic development and urbanization, Thailand has not experienced the drain of labour from the countryside that has characterized many developing States. The major reason for that difference lies in the good performance of the agricultural sector, at least until the mid-1980s. The relatively high land-man ratio that persisted until the late 1970s allowed the agricultural sector to retain the underemployed rural workers and forestalled the flood of pauperized men migrating to join the unemployed or underemployed in urban areas. Consequently, the growing demand for unskilled workers in urban areas exerted a powerful pull mostly on the peripheral labour resources of the agricultural sector, namely, women.

B. THE CHANGING RURAL ECONOMY AND ITS IMPACT ON RURAL-URBAN MIGRATION

An important feature of Thai development during the second half of the twentieth century has been the continued growth of the rural sector even during the industrial expansion of the 1970s and 1980s. In other newly industrializing countries or areas of Asia, agriculture was either unimportant (Hong Kong and Singapore) or was rapidly restructured during industrialization (the Republic of Korea and Taiwan Province of China). In both the Republic of Korea and Taiwan Province of China, the land/man ratio was already low when the industrialization drive began and the incidence of tenancy and landlessness was relatively high. Consequently, the agricultural sector quickly declined in importance as a source of employment when farms were mechanized and rural labour was transferred to industry.

In contrast, when Thailand embarked on a path of modern economic development during the post-war period, the country still had a high land/man ratio. In the 1970s, small and medium-sized farms still constituted over 80 per cent of all farms. Tenancy was high in selected areas but overall tenancy rates were lower than in other Asian countries. Landlessness was also low by Asian standards (about 8 per cent in 1975). Between the periods 1958-1960 and 1983-1985, the area under cultivation increased 2.6 times, from 7.5 million to 19.2 million hectares. Thus, even during the period of rapid industrialization, the agricultural sector in Thailand continued to experience growth in cultivated land area at a rate possibly unequalled in Asia during the twentieth century.

While the expansion of cultivation continued to generate employment in rural areas, the nature of agriculture in Thailand meant that underemployment also rose. Because Thailand is located in a monsoonal agricultural setting, farming is largely rain-fed, with irrigated areas accounting for less than 20 per cent of the total area under cultivation. Agriculture under monsoon conditions is highly seasonal, and, consequently, seasonal unemployment and underemployment reach relatively high levels in rural areas. Much of the expansion of cultivation since the 1950s has taken place in upland and marginal areas characterized by low rainfall and limited irrigation. By the early 1980s, the number of persons in rural areas that were working less than 20 hours per week in the dry season and would have liked to work more (those underemployed in terms of hours worked) reached about 500,000 (Thailand, 1983). In its final stages, much of the expansion of land under cultivation involved the clearing and colonization of marginal lands which provided inadequate income. If underemployment is defined in terms of income (those receiving less than a certain standard[2]), total underemployment could be as high as 3 million (Thailand, 1982). Among the unemployed and the underemployed, women constituted a majority.

As the urban economy grew while agriculture remained largely extensive and low in technology, rural/urban income differentials increased (see table 41). Then, as the Thai economy was rocked by the chaos in commodity markets brought about by the second oil crisis of the late 1970s, the rural sector bore the brunt of the slow-down. Average rural income declined in absolute terms (table 41). Moreover, by the 1980s, the mode of extensive agricultural growth had nearly reached its natural limits and new agricultural land was growing scarce (most forests had already been cut). Thus, as of the late 1970s, the Thai rural sector faced a growing problem characterized by stagnant or declining real incomes, widening urban/rural differentials (see table 41) and a high incidence of poverty in rural areas, where the proportion landless increased from 8 to 13 per cent between 1975 and 1988 (Siamwalla, 1991). Government attempts to structure the economy to deal with the worldwide recession of the mid-1980s did not benefit the rural sector. If anything, since the mid-1980s, government outlays have favoured urban areas more than before. Although the agricultural problem was not so severe as to prompt a mass exodus from the countryside, the end of the period of extensive expansion of the cultivated area meant that there was a need to restructure the rural economy.

TABLE 41. PER CAPITA INCOME BY REGION AND SECTOR, AT CURRENT PRICES, THAILAND, 1975/76-1985/86

Region and sector	1975/76	1980/81	1985/86
A. *Percentage of national average*			
By region			
North	86.5	92.8	89.1
North-east	71.3	65.6	58.5
Central	122.2	112.1	111.4
South	95.6	98.2	93.9
Bangkok	194.8	223.4	253.5
National average in United States dollars	209.3	277.9	255.2
B. *National average in United States dollars*			
By sector			
Agriculture	148.2	301.6	288.4
Non-agricultural	307.9	692.4	787.2
Non-agricultural/ agricultural	2.1	2.3	2.7

Source: J. Ashkul, "Development of urban areas: problems and policies", in *The Directions of Thai Economy in the Next Decade*, Proceedings of a Symposium organized by the Faculty of Economics (Bangkok, Chulalongkorn University, 1990), in Thai; cited in Suthy Prasartset, *Democratic Alternatives to Maldevelopment: The Case of Thailand*, Occasional Papers Series, No. 10 (Yokohama, Japan, PRIME, International Peace Research Institute Meigaku, 1991).

NOTE: Original figures in baht (B) were converted using a rate of B 20 per United States dollar.

Some rural households responded to increasing adversity by reducing their reliance upon markets and switching to more self-sufficient farming (Lertvicha, 1991). Others invested in new production technology to reduce costs and raise productivity. But that strategy requires a large capital outlay, which small and marginal farmers did not have. Selecting family members to migrate in search of work and wages appeared to be the easiest way out. Most commonly, rural households responded to the crisis by retaining their assets (land) but increasing their income from off-farm work, usually outside the rural sector. If necessary, they invested in labour-saving machinery on the farm so that they could release family members to earn supplementary income from off-farm sources.

Since the mid-1970s, migrant labour from the rural sector has played an increasing role in the Thai economy. Because of the seasonality of rural activities, a significant proportion of rural-urban migration is still short-term and seasonal. In addition, women constitute a sizeable proportion of the flow because they are more likely to be unemployed and underemployed in rural areas and because young women can be released from the rural household without greatly affecting the household's agricultural productive capacity. In the past seven or eight years, the urban labour demand, which expanded considerably because of the growth of tourism and labour-intensive industries, has attracted many young women from rural areas.

C. PATTERNS OF MIGRATION IN THAILAND

In Thailand, data on migration come from three main sources: the Population Census; the Labour Force Survey; and the Survey on Migration to Bangkok Metropolis and other major urban centres. The decennial population census gathers data on place of birth, which permits the identification of lifetime migrants, and on the number of persons that changed their place of residence during the five years preceding the census (recent migrants).

The Labour Force Survey provides the basic labour statistics for the entire country. Although it does not focus specifically on migration, it records the place of residence of all persons aged 11 or over that changed residence at any time during the five-year period preceding the survey (up to the survey week). The Labour Force Survey was carried out annually from 1963 to 1970 and twice a year between 1971 and 1983; it has been conducted three times a year since 1984. The February-March round of the survey is probably the best to measure the extent of labour migration, because that is the beginning of the dry season when rural-urban migration increases. In fact, rural-urban migration peaks in April, one month after the survey is completed. Since the survey misses the migration peak, its data may underestimate the true extent of rural-urban migration, particularly that involving short-term movements. Furthermore, the survey does not gather detailed information specifically on migrants; and because urban areas have not been reclassified to take account of the spatial expansion of cities, it is likely to understate the extent of migration directed to urban areas and overstate that directed to rural areas.

The annual Survey on Migration to Bangkok Metropolis and other major urban centres gathers information on persons that moved to those places during the two years preceding the survey. It gathers more detailed information about migrants, including their age, sex, occupation, earnings, place of birth and remittances, but it does not collect detailed demographic information about them, such as family size or number of children ever born. Data collection for Bangkok Metropolis began in 1974, with a lapse in 1986 and 1987. The most recent data available are for 1988. The next survey is expected to take place in 1993. In 1983, the survey covered for the first time not only Bangkok Metropolis but three additional provinces on an experimental basis. The 1984 survey was extended to cover Bangkok Metropolis and its five surrounding provinces. After 1984, the survey was enlarged to cover other urban centres, namely, Khon Kaen in 1985, Chiang Mai in 1986; and Nakorn Ratchasima, Chonburi and Songkla in 1987. In 1989, the surveys of Chiang Mai and Khon Kaen were repeated and an additional survey was carried out for a new urban centre, Surat Thani. However, migration surveys of cities other than Bangkok have had several shortcomings arising from incompatible questions and incomplete returns.

Migrants constitute a significant proportion of the urban population of Thailand. Based on the 1990 population census, 1,450,000 people aged 5 or over (that is, 14 per cent of the total urban population) were classified as recent migrants (table 42). About half were rural-urban migrants. According to the different censuses, the number of recent rural-urban migrants has increased steadily over time, from 348,000 in 1970 to 420,600 in 1980 and 738,400 in 1990. Because the area classified as urban has not been expanded to keep up with the real growth of Bangkok Metropolis and other cities, these figures almost certainly underestimate the absolute number of migrants into urban places and especially their rate of increase over the past decade.

Data on recent migrants drawn from the Labour Force Surveys for 1982-1989 are broadly consistent with those from the censuses (table 43). Rural-rural migration accounts for the largest proportion of all migrants, followed by urban-rural, rural-urban and urban-urban migration. The number of recent rural-urban migrants has fluctuated according to economic conditions. From a high of 466,000 in 1982, the number declined to 418,000 in 1985 because of the

TABLE 42. NUMBER OF MIGRANTS DURING THE FIVE YEARS PRECEDING EACH CENSUS, THAILAND, 1970-1990

Classification	1970	1980	1990
Population aged 5 or over	28 736 400	38 940 500	50 065 700
Total urban population	4 553 102	7 928 000	10 206 900
Total recent migrants	3 331 100	2 947 700	4 026 100
Urban destination			
Urban-urban	297 000	506 000	545 100
Rural-urban	348 000	420 600	738 400
Unknown-urban	118 400	98 300	165 200
TOTAL	763 400	1 024 900	1 448 700
Rural destination			
Rural-rural	2 086 700	1 532 900	1 645 100
Urban-rural	180 400	278 300	508 900
Unknown-rural	300 600	111 600	423 400
TOTAL	2 567 700	1 922 800	2 677 400

Source: Thailand, *1990 Population and Housing Census: Migration*, Subject Report No. 1 (Bangkok, National Statistical Office, forthcoming).

TABLE 43. PERCENTAGE DISTRIBUTION OF MIGRANTS, BY TYPE OF MIGRATION, THAILAND, 1982-1989

Year	Urban-urban	Rural-urban	Urban-rural	Rural-rural	Total number of migrants (thousands)
1982	6.7	16.6	12.1	64.6	2 810
1983	5.0	12.9	17.5	64.6	4 213
1984	5.3	11.6	18.8	64.3	3 861
1985	6.2	11.6	21.8	60.3	3 606
1986	7.1	14.3	19.8	58.8	3 573
1987	5.4	12.5	22.0	60.0	4 439
1988	6.5	14.4	22.6	56.5	3 963
1989	6.3	16.7	23.3	53.8	4 245

Sources: Thailand, *Report of the Labour Force Survey: Whole Kingdom, Round 1, February* (Bangkok, National Statistical Office, various years).

mid-decade recession and then rose to reach 709,000 in 1989 as the urban economy expanded during the second half of the decade.

Because of its nature, the Labour Force Survey is likely to miss an important proportion of short-term labour migration, particularly that involving circulation. A number of studies at the village level have documented higher levels of short-term and circular migration,[3] indicating that many rural-dwellers tend to migrate only temporarily. Some engage only in seasonal migration, others leave for longer periods but tend, nevertheless, to return. Thus, in the late 1970s, in a village in Ayudhaya, north of Bangkok, 18 per cent of the people participating in the harvest had worked in Bangkok for periods of from one to two years, and another 13 per cent had migrated regularly to work there for shorter periods (Lauro, 1979).

In the north-east, the poorest and most arid area of the country, circular migration has been customary. In earlier periods, when the population was less dense and settlements more sparse, drought compelled entire villages to move to areas with better water-supplies, from which they would usually return once the drought had passed. More recently, with the growth of urban employment opportunities, rural-dwellers are more likely to go to cities in search of work. Thus, short-term and circular migration has become part of the survival strategy of rural families; and because the agricultural economy has come under greater pressure since 1985, such migration from rural to urban areas is more likely to be for a longer period.

D. THE ROLE OF WOMEN IN MIGRATION FLOWS

One major change in migration over the past decade has been the increasing proportion of young women with low levels of educational attainment originating in the poorer areas of the country. Before 1984, men outnumbered women in rural-urban migration flows, but during 1985-1987, the percentage of women increased rapidly. According to the 1988 Survey on Migration to Bangkok Metropolis, among the 110,000 migrants who arrived in Bangkok Metropolis between September 1986 and August 1988, 60 per cent were women. Among both male and female migrants, the reason for migrating most often reported was "work": 72 per cent of the men and 65 per cent of the women cited that reason (table 44). A majority of the migrants to Bangkok Metropolis originated in rural areas—63 and 67 per cent among men and women, respectively—and about two of every five male migrants and nearly half of all female migrants had been born in the north-east, the poorest region in the country. Female migrants were slightly less likely to be employed than male migrants (69 versus 75 per cent). Among employed migrants, the vast majority had relatively low levels of educational attainment. Thus, 80 per cent of the employed female migrants had at most completed elementary school and 70 per cent of their male counterparts were in the same category. Employed migrants of both sexes tended to be young, but women were considerably younger than men: over

TABLE 44. CHARACTERISTICS OF MIGRANTS TO BANGKOK METROPOLIS, 1986-1988
(*Percentage*)

Characteristics	Male	Female	Total
Reason for migration			
Education	9	11	10
Work	72	65	68
Other reasons	19	24	22
Number of respondents	41 380	68 324	109 704
Previous place of residence			
Urban area	37	33	35
Rural area	63	67	65
Number of respondents	41 390	68 335	109 725
Place of birth			
North	18	17	17
Central	34	29	30
North-east	42	47	45
South	6	8	7
Foreign countries and unknown	0.4	0.3	0.2
Number of respondents	41 394	68 334	109 728
Age group of employed migrants			
10-19	30	52	43
20-29	48	38	43
30 or over	22	10	24
Number of respondents	29 782	44 462	74 244
Education of employed migrants			
No education	1	2	2
Elementary or less	70	80	76
Secondary	22	14	18
Higher than secondary	7	4	4
Number of respondents	30 918	47 183	78 101

Source: Thailand, *Survey of Migration to Bangkok Metropolis, 1988* (Bangkok, National Statistical Office, 1988).

TABLE 45. NUMBER OF MIGRANTS TO BANGKOK METROPOLIS
PERCENTAGE FEMALE, BY PERIOD OF ARRIVAL
AND PLACE OF PREVIOUS RESIDENCE

Period of arrival	Region of previous residence				
	Total	Central	North	North-east	South
A. Total number of migrants					
Nov. 1973-Oct. 1975	67 213	28 210	7 372	24 891	6 740
Sept. 1986-Aug. 1988	100 482	24 320	19 686	48 669	7 807
B. Percentage female					
Nov. 1973-Oct. 1975	53	54	52	54	49
Sept. 1986-Aug. 1988	62	59	61	65	68

Source: Thailand, *The Survey of Migration to Bangkok Metropolis, 1973, 1975, 1988* (Bangkok, National Statistical Office, various years).

half of all employed female migrants were aged 10-19, compared with only 30 per cent of their male counterparts.

The number of female migrants arriving annually in Bangkok Metropolis appears to have increased substantially over time. Thus, data from the 1975 Survey on Migration to Bangkok Metropolis and those from the 1988 Survey suggest that during 1973-1975, the annual flow of female migrants amounted to about 18,000, whereas during 1986-1988, that flow had risen to about 31,000. The share of women among all migrants to Bangkok had also increased from 53 to 62 per cent (table 45). Furthermore, the proportion of women aged 10-19 among all migrants also rose, from 21 per cent in 1974-1976 to 28 per cent in 1986-1988.

E. LABOUR FORCE EXPERIENCE OF FEMALE MIGRANTS

Using data from the Survey on Migration to Bangkok Metropolis, this and the following sections document the labour force experience of female migrants in that city. Table 46 shows that the labour force participation rates of female migrants aged 11 or over is below that of males, although it is still high. Over three quarters of female migrants are in the labour force. The highest participation rate for female migrants is found among those aged 11-19, the only age group where female migrants display higher participation rates than male migrants. It is likely that migrant men aged 11-19 have a low labour force participation rate because many are still in school.

For comparison purposes, table 46 also displays the labour force participation rates for the total population of Bangkok Metropolis as of 1987, obtained by the Labour Force Survey. Unfortunately, data exclusively for non-migrants in Bangkok as of 1988 are not available. The data available, however, indicate that migrants of both sexes have considerably higher labour force participation rates than the total population of Bangkok Metropolis and that the differences are more marked for women, especially for those under age 25.

TABLE 46. LABOUR FORCE PARTICIPATION RATES,
BY MIGRATION STATUS, AGE GROUP AND SEX,
BANGKOK METROPOLIS
(*Percentage*)

Age group	Male	Female
A. Recent migrants as of 1988		
11-19	74.3	78.7
20-29	91.2	78.0
30-39	98.5	74.3
40-49	100.0	75.8
50-59	82.4	54.1
60 or over	26.2	13.8
TOTAL	85.6	76.7
B. Total population as of 1987		
11-14	4.2	7.8
15-19	32.7	42.4
20-24	71.4	65.0
25-29	95.5	76.1
30-34	97.3	76.2
35-39	98.5	74.2
40-49	97.4	70.8
50-59	87.8	50.0
60 or over	34.7	17.4
TOTAL	70.0	55.8

Sources: For data on migrants in 1988, Thailand, *Survey of Migration to Bangkok Metropolis, 1988* (Bangkok, National Statistical Office, 1988); for data on total population of Bangkok Metropolis in 1987, Thailand, *Report of the Labour Force Survey, Round 3* (Bangkok, National Statistical Office, 1987).

TABLE 47. UNEMPLOYMENT RATES, BY MIGRATION STATUS, AGE GROUP AND SEX, BANGKOK METROPOLIS
(Percentage)

Age group	Male	Female
A. Recent migrants as of 1988		
11-19	3.7	2.9
20-29	3.8	4.6
30-39	3.1	7.4
40-49	1.8	a
50-59	3.5	9.9
TOTAL	3.5	3.9
B. Total population as of 1987		
11-14	a	1.6
15-19	15.5	11.6
20-24	16.3	13.5
25-29	7.1	7.2
30-34	3.8	3.8
35-39	3.4	2.4
40-49	0.7	0.3
50-59	2.0	0.8
TOTAL	2.8	5.9

Sources: For data on migrants in 1988, Thailand, *Survey of Migration to Bangkok Metropolis, 1988* (Bangkok, National Statistical Office, 1988); for data on total population of Bangkok Metropolis in 1987, Thailand, *Report of the Labour Force Survey, Round 3* (Bangkok, National Statistical Office, 1987).

a Sample too small.

As table 47 shows, overall unemployment rates among both male and female migrants to Bangkok Metropolis are less than 4 per cent, although among women aged 20 or over they rise steadily with age and reach relatively high levels among older female migrants. Indeed, the low unemployment rates observed among all migrant women are largely due to the very low unemployment registered among teenaged female migrants. A comparison with the unemployment rates of the total population of Bangkok Metropolis in 1987 indicates that both male and female migrants have a very different experience with regard to unemployment from that of the total population of the city. Thus, among the latter, overall unemployment is higher among women than among men, and except for both men and women under age 20 and men aged 50-59, unemployment rates tend to decline with age for both men and women. In addition, in contrast to the experience of female migrants, for all female residents of the city unemployment rates tend to be highest when they are aged 15-24.

Table 48 shows that most migrants to Bangkok Metropolis that were aged 11 or over and were employed at the time of interview had worked previously in agriculture, though, as with low educational attainment, the proportion working in agriculture was slightly higher among female migrants (79 per cent) than among male migrants (70 per cent). Since among the same group of migrants, similar proportions had a low educational attainment, it is not surprising that they mainly found work either in unskilled factory work or in the informal sector, which is usually covered under the service, sales and production occupations of the urban economy. Thus, as table 48 indicates, about 83 per cent of the employed male migrants in Bangkok Metropolis and 94 per cent of their female counterparts reported that they worked as a production worker, a service worker or in sales. The distribution within those occupations, however, varied considerably between male and female migrants. Male migrants tended to be far more concentrated in production jobs than female migrants, for whom those jobs were, nevertheless, the second most important source of employment. As in many other societies, the service sector was the main employer of female migrants.

Among the growing number of young women migrating to Bangkok Metropolis and finding jobs in the service sector, a significant number are involved in the sex industry. It is not possible, however, to quantify

TABLE 48. PREVIOUS AND CURRENT OCCUPATION OF EMPLOYED MIGRANTS BY SEX, BANGKOK METROPOLIS, 1988
(Percentage)

Occupation	Male	Female
Previous occupation		
Agriculture	70	79
Production worker	12	6
Other	18	15
Current occupation		
Professional	1.9	2.3
Managerial	1.2	0.4
Clerical	3.4	2.0
Sales	11.2	9.2
Agriculture, mining	1.9	0.6
Transport	7.1	0.1
Production worker	60.7	35.0
Service worker	10.8	50.0
Other	1.8	0.4

Source: Thailand, *Survey of Migration to Bangkok Metropolis, 1988* (Bangkok, National Statistical Office, 1988).

with accuracy either the number of female migrants involved in sexual services or changes over time. Government surveys largely fail to capture that segment of the female population. The Labour Force Survey, for instance, only accounts for a few thousand women involved in the massage business. Casual estimates of the total number of women involved in sexual services in urban areas (masseuses, bar girls, prostitutes etc.) range from 200,000 to over 1,000,000. However, figures based on casual observations may grossly misrepresent the true situation. According to the Centre for the Prevention of the Abduction of Females for Prostitution, 200,000 is the most plausible number of women involved in the sex industry in Thailand as a whole. There are about 700 sex-related establishments in Bangkok Metropolis. Assuming that each engages on average 30-40 women, the estimated number of women involved in sexual services would be between 21,000 and 28,000. Because many female migrants working in those services go back to their region of origin to help with the harvest from May to August, the number in Bangkok would vary according to the season.

According to the Labour Force Survey, in 1988 recent migrants from rural areas accounted for 30 per cent of the non-professional labour force in Bangkok Metropolis and for nearly 38 per cent of that in all urban areas (see table 49). In both Bangkok Metropolis and all urban areas, female migrants from rural areas accounted for considerably higher proportions of all female non-professional workers than their male counterparts did of all non-professional male workers. Thus, female migrants from rural areas accounted for 35 per cent of non-professional female workers in Bangkok Metropolis and for 46 per cent of those in all urban areas. The equivalent proportions for men were 25 and 32 per cent, respectively.

F. Searching for a Job

Employed female migrants in Bangkok Metropolis reported that they relied mainly upon friends (37 per cent) and relatives (35 per cent) to help them secure a job and only 19 per cent reported that they relied upon their own initiative (table 50). Employed male migrants showed a somewhat lower tendency to depend upon relatives (23 per cent) and a greater tendency to

TABLE 49. EMPLOYED RURAL MIGRANTS AS A PERCENTAGE OF NON-PROFESSIONAL WORKERS, BY REGION AND SEX, THAILAND, 1988
(*Thousands*)

	Male	Female	Total
A. *Bangkok Metropolis, 1988*			
(1) Non-professional workers	577.4	490.4	1 067.8
(2) Employed five-year rural migrants	143.8	172.8	316.6
(3) (2) as percentage of (1)	24.9	35.2	29.6
B. *All urban areas of Thailand, 1988*			
(1) Non professional workers, all urban areas, Thailand	873.8	678.9	1 552.7
(2) Employed recent rural migrants	281.3	312.4	593.7
(3) (2) as percentage of (1)	32.2	46.0	38.2

Sources: For data on Bangkok Metropolis, Thailand, *Survey of Migration to Bangkok Metropolis, 1988* (Bangkok, National Statistical Office, 1988); for data on all urban areas, Thailand, *Report of the Labour Force Survey, Round 1* (Bangkok, National Statistical Office, 1988).

rely upon their own initiative (32 per cent). Both male and female migrants reported making little use of employment agencies (only 2 per cent of men and 5 per cent of women used them); and if they did use such agencies, they tended to use private agencies rather than those run by the Government.

It is known that networks of friends and relatives are particularly important for female migrants looking for work in the informal sector. Villagers with friends or relatives who had migrated earlier to the city often secured information about available jobs from them. During the 1980s, networks also proved important for the recruitment of workers for small garment shops in Bangkok. A 1990 study of small garment workshops in a low-rent district of Bangkok showed that virtually all workers were women under age 20, mostly recruited among friends and relatives of the owner or from the owner's village. The families of those young women probably felt more secure if their daughters were working for someone they knew. Ironically, however, many young rural women who engage in prostitution are also recruited into the trade by relatives and friends. Agents and "mamasans" are known to contact the parents directly to purchase the under-age girls. Even village élites and teachers have been reported to play a part in that recruitment.

TABLE 50. METHODS USED BY MIGRANTS TO SEEK WORK, BY SEX, BANGKOK METROPOLIS, 1986-1988

Method	Number of males	Percentage	Number of females	Percentage
All methods	30 921	100	47 168	100
Labour department	377	1	781	2
Private employment agencies	252	1	1 284	3
Relatives	7 177	23	16 341	35
Friends, acquaintances	10 474	34	17 298	37
Self	10 299	33	9 291	19
Transfer from previous jobs	1 713	6	1 561	3
Others, unknown	629	2	630	1

Source: Thailand, *Survey of Migration to Bangkok Metropolis, 1988* (Bangkok, National Statistical Office, 1988).

The constraints female migrants face in securing good jobs are no different from those faced by unskilled male and female workers in general. Thus, the most important constraint is their low educational attainment. In addition, to secure work in the informal sector, lack of sufficient capital and inability to learn the necessary skills quickly are also important obstacles (Phongpaichit, 1991b).

G. VULNERABILITY OF FEMALE MIGRANT WORKERS

Migrant female workers often face poor working conditions in small factories and workshops operating in the informal sector of the economy. Such working conditions are not only offences under the law, they also contribute to low worker productivity and to the persistence of relatively low wages among female migrants. In addition, migrant women working in textile, frozen food, electronics or chemical factories are often subject to health hazards in the workplace and women providing sexual services are commonly exposed to sexually transmitted diseases[4] and to the risk of pregnancy. Lastly, up to 1992, children under age 15 could be legally employed doing light work, such as child care or helping with household chores, but there were, nevertheless, problems associated with the mistreatment of young migrants being employed as child labour, particularly young female migrants.

The extent of these problems is not properly reported in any of the official surveys but their existence is well known (Thongudai, 1991). Government bodies handling such problems (the Department of Labour, the Social Welfare Department, the Public Health Department and the Police Department) are well aware of them, but either there is not enough commitment to enforce existing laws that would combat them or little attention has been given to finding effective ways of addressing the problems. In the name of market liberalization, the Government has tended to disregard labour abuses, particularly those involving migrant women.

H. EARNINGS AND REMITTANCES OF MIGRANT WORKERS

Data for the urban areas of the central region of Thailand, which is dominated by Bangkok, show that recent migrants (those migrating within the five years preceding the interview) earn less than the average wage of workers in the region (table 51). Unfortunately, there is no information on migrants' wages by sex. Data on how wages vary according to educational attainment suggest that the low wages of migrants are mostly the result of their low skill and educational levels. Yet, migrants earn considerably more than they would have earned in rural areas. In 1980, Thongudai (1982) found that a sample of female migrants had earned an average nominal wage of 753 baht (B) per month in rural areas before migration, compared with B1,306 per month after migration, an increase of 73 per cent. For those that had not worked before, migration provided the opportunity to secure an urban job and to earn a wage for the first time. A study by Fuller and others (1983) shows that female migrants earned less than their male counterparts and received a higher proportion of their income in kind, in the form of food and accommodation. It has been estimated that among all urban workers, being a woman is itself a factor that reduces earnings by 20 per cent in relation to those of men (Patamasiriwat, 1991).

Migrant women providing sexual services can earn significantly higher amounts. Earnings of women working in massage parlours, nightclubs, barber shops,

TABLE 51. AVERAGE WAGES, BY SEX, YEARS OF EDUCATION AND MIGRATION STATUS, CENTRAL REGION OF THAILAND, 1988

	Baht per month	Percentage of labour force
Both sexes	3 440	100.0
Male	3 887	54.9
Female	2 894	45.1
Education (years)		
5-10	2 937	24.0
11-14	4 279	25.6
15 or more	7 143	11.2
Wages of recent migrants	1 888	2.8

Source: Direk Patamasiriwat, "Work experience and income: a case study of workers in the Central Region", Bangkok, Thailand Development Research Institute, 1991; mimeographed.

NOTE: The central region of Thailand is where most industries are concentrated. Migrants are persons that migrated to the central region during the period 1983-1988.

bars and other entertainment places have been reported to be quite high. A study in 1980 reported the income of masseuses to be about B5,000 per month (Phongpaichit, 1982).

Excluding those in the sex trade, female migrants generally have lower earnings than non-migrants. However, they are still able to send remittances to their families in the village of origin. In a study of north-eastern migrants, conducted in 1978-1979, it was found that 61 per cent sent remittances back home. On average, the remittances from both male and female migrants amounted to B614 per month or 48 per cent of the mean income of rural households in north-eastern Thailand in 1978 (Fuller and others, 1983).

Among in-migrants to Bangkok Metropolis in 1988, 38 per cent of men and 56 per cent of women reported sending remittances back to their village (table 52). Employed women were both more likely to send remittances and to send them more frequently than employed men, probably because most of the employed migrant women were still single (72 per cent, compared with 65 per cent among men) and tended to have stronger ties with their families of origin than men did. When asked what was positive about being in Bangkok, about two thirds of migrants of both sexes cited the income they could earn.

Various studies have shown that migrant remittances have become a significant proportion of the incomes of rural households (Thongudai, 1982; Phongpaichit, 1982). In effect, migrant remittances have contributed to the survival of rural society despite the deteriorating agrarian economy and may have delayed the need to restructure the agrarian economy.

I. CONCLUSIONS AND POLICY IMPLICATIONS

During the 1970s, the Thai Government began to promote the service sector to bolster the faltering economy. The policy was successful and the service sector grew rapidly, mainly by tapping the unemployed and underemployed labour force in rural areas, in which women, particularly young women, accounted for a significant proportion.

Today, migrant women constitute a large proportion of the workers in the export-oriented industries located around Bangkok and of those in services, including tourism, an important source of foreign exchange for the country. Female migrants from rural areas consti-

TABLE 52. EMPLOYED MIGRANTS, BY SEX, AMOUNT OF REMITTANCES SENT HOME PER ANNUM AND FREQUENCY OF REMITTANCES, BANGKOK METROPOLIS, 1988

Method	Number of males	Percentage	Number of females	Percentage
Remittances sent				
<700 baht	5 790	18.7	14 326	30.4
>700 baht	5 842	18.9	11 533	24.4
Unknown	126	0.4	327	0.7
Not sending	19 163	62.0	20 999	44.5
TOTAL	30 921	100.0	47 185	100 0
Frequency of sending remittances				
One to three times	6 622	21.4	15 587	33.0
Four to six times	2 668	8.6	6 093	12.9
Seven or more times	2 290	7.4	4 155	8.8
Unknown	175	0.6	354	0.7
Not sending	19 161	62.0	20 999	44.5
TOTAL	30 916	100.0	47 188	100.0

Source: Thailand, *Survey on Migration to Bangkok Metropolis, 1988* (Bangkok, National Statistical Office, 1988).

tute 46 per cent of all non-professional workers in urban areas in Thailand and 35 per cent of those in Bangkok Metropolis. They have been crucial for the growth of labour-intensive export-oriented manufacturing and for that of tourism, the two economic activities sustaining the economic growth of Thailand during the past decade.

In 1988, about two thirds of the recent migrant women in Bangkok originated in rural areas; and among the 69 per cent that were employed, four out of every five had a very low level of educational attainment. Employed migrant women tended to be concentrated in service occupations, many of which are in the informal sector, and in production activities that generally involve working in factories in both the formal and the informal sectors. The earnings of female migrants were low, compared with those of both migrant men and non-migrant women, probably because of their lack of education and work experience. However, rural female migrants earned more than they would have earned in their villages of origin and over half of them were able to send remittances to the family left behind.

As a consequence of the economic strategy advocated by the Thai Government, migration has significantly increased the supply of labour in Bangkok Metropolis and has tended to keep wages low. Low wages have also been possible because of the fact that, for many rural migrants, urban wages are only a supplementary income. In times of economic slowdown, migrants—particularly female migrants—can return to their village and thus effectively subsidize the urban economy. It is thus that low-wage industries have expanded so quickly in Thailand and have been able to compete in the world market.

However, the nature of the labour-market and the short-term profitability of the use of cheap and unskilled labour perpetuate short-term thinking on the part of entrepreneurs and policy makers. The relatively easy availability of migrant workers has reduced the incentives for manufacturers to invest in training and skill acquisition to raise productivity. Similarly, the constant flow of young women to work in the sex industry contributes to its growth and continued profitability. The Government has been reluctant to disturb this state of affairs. It has done little to induce industries to invest in worker training and it has adopted a lax attitude towards the issue of prostitution even as the levels of HIV infection rise.

Although the Thai economy has been able to grow rapidly because of the policies adopted to promote tourism and export-oriented manufacturing, in the middle to longer term such policies may lose effectiveness, especially as Thailand faces growing competition from new low-wage countries, such as China and Viet Nam. Therefore, Thailand needs to work towards raising the skills and productivity of the labour force. The country cannot continue to rely upon cheap female migrant workers to earn the foreign exchange it needs. A new approach to human resource development is called for. Although in recent years the lack of high-level manpower, especially of engineers, has led to an overhaul of policies on higher education, such changes are not sufficient. Human resources must be upgraded on a wider scale so that the population in rural areas can benefit from better job prospects and possibilities for occupational mobility. The main policy thrust therefore must be to expand the provision of secondary education in rural areas, particularly to young women. Subsidies that facilitate the secondary education of low-income groups in both urban and rural areas are needed. Efforts to upgrade the skills of school-leavers, whether male or female, also need to be pursued, especially in rural areas.

To increase labour productivity, training must be provided not just to workers but also to the owners of small and medium workshops, many of whom employ female migrant workers. Better management practices and better labour relations would greatly contribute to gains in productivity. Special measures need to be taken to protect women engaged in sexual services, particularly when they are young migrants from rural areas. Provision of efficient job placement services also seems necessary, whether by the Government or through private agencies. The latter, however, must be regulated so that abuses are prevented.

NOTES

[1] Calculated from Thailand (1970, 1980); and from preliminary results of the Population and Housing Census, 1990, as reported in Suvi (1991).

[2] The minimum level of income used was $90 per month for Bangkok Metropolis and its five surrounding provinces; $78 per month for all urban areas of other provinces; and less than $25 per month for all rural areas. The minimum level of income was based on the minimum wage paid by the government sector. See Thailand, 1982.

[3] See Texter (1961), De Young (1963), Kirsch (1966), Moerman (1968), van Roy (1971), Klausner (1972), Goldstein (1974), Lefferts (1974), Singhanetra-Renard (1980), and Fuller and others (1983).

[4] Figures from the Ministry of Public Health show that 14 per cent of the prostitutes in Bangkok are HIV-positive. See "AIDS figures not plausible", *Bangkok Post*, 23 August 1991.

REFERENCES

Ashkul, J. (1990). Development of urban areas: problems and policies. In *The Directions of the Thai Economy in the Next Decade*. Proceedings of a Symposium organized by the Faculty of Economics. Bangkok: Chulalongkorn University. In Thai.

Bank of Thailand (1976). *Bank of Thailand Monthly Bulletin* (Bangkok), June.

_____ (1991). *Bank of Thailand Monthly Bulletin* (Bangkok), May.

De Young, John E. (1963). *Village Life in Modern Thailand*. Berkeley: University of California Press.

Fuller, Theodore D., and others (1983). *Migration and Development in Modern Thailand*. Bangkok: The Social Science Association of Thailand; Chulalongkorn University.

Goldstein, Sidney, and Pichit Patektepsombati (1974). *Migration and Urban Growth in Thailand: An Exploration of Interrelations Among Origin, Recency and Frequency of Moves*. Institute of Population Studies, No. 14. Bangkok: Chulalongkorn University.

Kanjana-uksorn, Teeranart (1991). The political economy of prostitution: the case of Thailand. Paper presented at the Seminar on Political Economy, Bangkok, The Political Economy Centre of the Faculty of Economics of Chulalongkorn University, 7 August 1991. In Thai.

Kirsch, A. Thomas (1966). Development and mobility among the Phu Thai of northeast Thailand. *Asian Survey* (Berkeley, California), vol. 6, No. 7 (July), pp. 370-378.

Klausner, W. J. (1972). The northeast migration problem. In *Reflections in a Log Pond*, W. J. Klausner, ed. Bangkok: Suksit Siam.

Lauro, D. J. (1979). The demography of a Thai Village. Unpublished doctoral dissertation. Canberra: The Australian National University, Research School of Social Science.

Lefferts, H. L. (1974). *Baan Dong Phong: Land Tenure and Social Organisation in a Northeastern Thai Village*. Ann Arbor, Michigan: University Microfilms.

Lertvicha, Pornpilai (1991). The potential of the Thai rural economy. In *Thai Dynamics*, Pasuk Phongpaichit and Sungsidh Piriyarangsan, eds. Bangkok: Chulalongkorn University, The Political Economy Centre, Faculty of Economics.

Moerman, H. (1968). *Agricultural Change and Peasant Choice in a Thai Village*. Berkeley: University of California Press.

Patamasiriwat, Direk (1991). A study on work experiences and earnings: the case of the Central Region in Thailand. Bangkok: Thailand Development Research Institute. Mimeographed.

Phongpaichit, Pasuk (1982). *From Peasant Girls to Bangkok Masseuses*. Women, Work and Development Series, No. 2. Geneva: International Labour Office.

_____ (1991a). The service sector of Thailand. In *The Thai Economy*, Peter G. Warr, ed. Cambridge, United Kingdom: Cambridge University Press.

_____ (1991b). Nu Nit, Noi and Thailand's informal sector in rapid growth. In *Human Resources Development Strategy in Thailand: Past, Present and Future*, Chira Hongladarom and Shieru Itoga, eds. Tokyo: Institute of Developing Economies.

Prasartset, Suthy (1991). *Democratic Alternatives to Maldevelopment: The Case of Thailand*. Occasional Papers Series, No. 10. Yokohama, Japan: PRIME, International Peace Research Institute Meigaku.

Republic of Korea (various years). *Korean Economic Indicators*. Seoul: Economic Planning Board.

Singhanetra-Renard, A. (1980). Mobility in North Thailand: a view from within. Paper presented at the Development Studies Centre Conference on Population Mobility and Development, Canberra, Australia.

Suvi, Vilas (1991). Trends and observations on the migration into Bangkok Metropolis between 1982 and 1988. Paper presented at the Seminar on National Demographic Studies, Royal River Hotel, Bangkok, 21-22 November.

Texter, R. B. (1961). *From Peasant to Pedicab Driver*. Southeast Asian Studies Cultural Report Series, No. 9. New Haven, Connecticut: Yale University Press.

Thailand, Joint Public-Private Consultative Committee (1992). *Thailand Update*. No. 2 (August).

_____, National Statistical Office (1970). *Population and Housing Census, 1970*. Bangkok.

_____ (1980). *Population and Housing Census, 1980*. Bangkok.

_____ (1982). *Report of the Labour Force Survey, Whole Kingdom, Round 1*. Bangkok.

_____ (1983). *Report of the Labour Force Survey*. Bangkok.

_____ (1987). *Report of the Labour Force Survey, Whole Kingdom, Round 3*. Bangkok.

_____ (1988). *Report of the Labour Force Survey, Whole Kingdom, Round 1*. Bangkok.

_____ (various years). *The Survey of Migration to Bangkok Metropolis*. Bangkok.

_____ (forthcoming). *1990 Population and Housing Census: Migration*. Subject Report No. 1. Bangkok.

Thongudai, Pawadee (1982). Women, migration and employment: a study of migrant workers in Bangkok. Unpublished doctoral dissertation. New York: New York University, Department of Economics.

_____ (1991). The labour markets of factory workers. Paper presented at the Annual Seminar of the Faculty of Economics, Thammasat University, on The Labour Markets in Thailand: Man is Not a Factor of Production, 12-13 February. In Thai.

United Nations, Economic and Social Commission for Asia and the Pacific (1988). *Internal Migration and Structural Change in the Labour Force*. Asian Population Studies Series, No. 90. Bangkok.

van Roy, Edward (1971). *Economic System of Northern Thailand: Structure and Change*. Ithaca, New York: Cornell University Press.

World Bank (1991). *World Development Report, 1991*. New York: Oxford University Press.

Part Five

DETERMINANTS OF FEMALE MIGRATION

X. MIGRATION DECISIONS: THE ROLE OF GENDER

Nancy E. Riley* and Robert W. Gardner*

This paper examines the role of women in the decision-making process leading to migration. In doing so, the close links between decision-making and other aspects of the migration process are recognized, since many of the factors that influence the role of women in the decision-making process are the same as those which affect their role in migration more generally. Models of migration decision-making usually include a consideration of two aspects: content (determinants) and process. In general, the focus here is on the process except in cases where the determinants of female migration interact directly with it. Although the main purpose is to discuss decisions relating to internal migration, examples are also drawn from the literature on international migration, because the decision-making process has common elements in both.

Generalizing to all women is, of course, fraught with difficulties. Although distinctions between women in different contexts are made as appropriate, it is not possible to undertake here the kind of textured analyses of differences among women deriving from such factors as the class, caste, ethnic and racial stratification systems characterizing different societies. Such analyses are clearly necessary to achieve a more thorough understanding of the role of women in decision-making. At the very least, however, consideration must be given to how a woman's stage in the life cycle, in relation to that of her family, affects her ability to participate actively in decision-making. Thus, young women, who are usually at the bottom of the two power hierarchies determined by age and gender, are especially likely to be dominated by the decisions of others.

In all societies, gender is a basic factor determining the range of options open to individuals, both with regard to migration and to other behaviour. Studies have shown that gender and gender stratification systems are involved in all aspects of the migration process, including the relations between societies of origin and of destination (Fernández-Kelly, 1983a, 1983b; Kearney, 1986), migrant recruitment strategies and influences (León de Leal and Deere, 1979), the sex ratio of migration streams (Ravenstein, 1885) and the way in which people participate in making decisions about migration.

In this paper, migration decisions are defined broadly to include decisions to migrate, decisions not to migrate and decisions about where to migrate. Three ways in which women may be involved in the migration decision-making process are distinguished. First, those moves—either a woman's own or that of family members—which occur without the woman's participation in the decision to migrate are considered. Then, decisions jointly made by a woman and at least another member of her family or household[1] are discussed. Lastly, attention is turned to decisions made by women themselves, independently from other family members.

It is important to consider both the decisions that result in a woman's migration and those which do not. The role that women play in making a decision about the migration of another family member are also considered in the light of the way in which gender stratification influences the women who may not even consider migration as an option for themselves.

When necessary, the different types of migration in which women may be involved are distinguished. Women may migrate as part of a family or household group, they may participate in making a decision about the migration of other family members although they themselves may not move or they may migrate alone. When migrating alone, a woman may do so with her family's support or even its pressure, she may follow a family member who migrated earlier or she may migrate by herself. Women may also migrate specifically to join their future husband and get married, thus engaging in marriage migration, a type that is consid-

---

*East-West Population Institute, Honolulu, Hawaii, United States of America.

ered both as an individual strategy of the woman concerned or as one deriving from a joint decision between her (or her family) and her future husband.

Aside from discussing the role that women play in migration decisions, factors that influence that role are also considered. Gender, of course, is a key factor, but other factors discussed include a woman's individual characteristics, such as age, stage in the life cycle and education; family characteristics, such as size, structure and the relationships between family members; and social and economic factors external to the family in the societies of origin and destination (see Lim, 1989; Murray, 1987; Radcliffe, 1990a, 1990b; Thadani and Todaro, 1984). Economic position or class, in particular, is an important factor determining migration behaviour.

A. THE ROLE OF GENDER

Individuals are subject to constraints and opportunities which shape and are shaped by their decisions and behaviour. Those constraints and opportunities derive from the many facets of the environment in which the person lives. Some influence all members of society, some have strong effects on a particular group within a society and some affect only the individual. However, even a universal feature shaping the environment in which a society lives is likely to be perceived and handled differently by different members of that society. A person's response will depend upon his or her capacity to perceive and manipulate the environment according to his or her position and values within society.

Knowledge of one's own or of another's capacity to manipulate the environment also shapes responses to it. In the case of migration, gender often determines whether a person would even perceive migration as an option. Gender is also a crucial element differentiating what types of migration are available, whether the person has access to the resources required for migration, and whether or to what extent the person may participate in making the decision to migrate.

People's perceptions and behaviour with regard to migration are mediated by their position in the social world, of which gender is a major determinant. Those positions are also influenced by the place a particular society occupies in the world, by the organizing features of that society and the position of particular persons within it. Individual characteristics in turn mediate societal organizations and structures. Consequently, the decision-making process relating to migration cannot be abstracted from other background or contextual factors because, like any other decision, it does not result from discrete actions but rather from the cumulative experience and socialization of a lifetime.

In discussing the role of women in decision-making, it is important to recognize the pervasive effect of gender outside the decision-making process. The effect of gender is so powerful that it requires a more extensive treatment than simply estimating differences between males and females within existing decision-making models. Because gender ideology affects all aspects of life, including what constitutes a decision and how one acts on a decision, using models based on male migration may miss important aspects of the migration process and of decisions with regard to the migration of women (Boyd, 1989).

In most societies, men may engage in actions or strategies that differ considerably from those condoned for women. It is therefore important to consider not only whether and under what conditions women migrate but whether and to what extent they are able to manipulate their environment. If a society selectively bars women from even considering the possibility of migrating, an analysis of whether women actually migrate will miss the point. It must be recognized that "although decisions can be classed according to the amount of choice implicit in a decision, and the participants involved, cultural values help people discard or fail to consider certain alternatives" (Bentley, 1989, p. 75). In particular, one must not assume that women who do not migrate have consciously decided not to do so.

Although some studies take into account gender issues in studying migration (e.g., Young, 1986; and Shields and Shields, 1989), the general lack of attention to gender in most migration studies is still noticeable even after more than a decade of calls to correct such neglect (Morokvasic, 1983). For example, a study of Mexican migration to the United States scarcely acknowledges the role of gender, although the authors view migration as a social process determined by underlying structural institutions and changes in the societies of origin and destination (Massey and others, 1987). Not only does that study ignore the role of gender in the economic relations between the two countries (for a discussion of such relations, see Sassen-Koob, 1983; Brown, 1987; and Benería and Roldán, 1987), but the authors reduce the role of women in the decision that men should migrate to one of passive acquiescence. In that study, as in others, there is an implicit assumption that because women do not migrate as often as men, they are not active in the migration process. Although it is true that women may not be well represented in some migration flows between Mexico and the United States, other studies indicate that women are indeed active participants in the migration process between those countries not only as migrants (Woodrow and Passel, 1990) but through their influence within the family (Wiest, 1983)—by deliberately marrying migrants (Ahern, Bryan and Baca, 1985), by influencing the priorities set by their families and selecting the strategies to reach their goals (Findley and Williams, 1988), by participating in decisions about the migration of men (Baca and Bryan, 1985) and by accepting or even welcoming new roles as the household head while their husbands are in the United States (Ahern, Bryan and Baca, 1985; Baca and Bryan, 1985). By focusing only on the migration of men, the authors cited, as well as many others, miss an opportunity to understand the many facets of the migration process, including the crucial roles that women play in it.

B. Role of the individual versus that of others

In her critique of "reductionist" literature, Morokvasic (1983) warns:

"While emigration may be an individualized act, it cannot be explained as a matter of individual motivation, though many studies have tried to explain migration in those terms. Whether the individual women appear as free choosers and decision-makers...or as passive followers of men, the social constraints on the individual decision-maker must not be ignored. The subjective elements of migration, whether they concern males or females, must be assessed within the framework of social forces and structural conditions...." (1983, p. 29).

Since any discussion of migration decision-making must consider the social context in which it takes place, the pervasive influence of gender again comes into play. The migration process is structured by the social and economic make-up of the societies involved and the role that women play is shaped by the interaction of the respective gender systems with those structural and cultural aspects of society that impinge upon migration (Fernández-Kelly, 1983a; Boyd, 1989).

However, without underestimating the importance of the general social context, the need to examine individual behaviour remains. Women have agency, even given the constraints they face. Thus, it is important to understand the tension between women as individual actors and women as part of the socio-economic structures in which they live. For example, in discussing the role of women in decisions about the migration of entire households, the tension between women as individual actors and women as members of social groups (i.e., households) must be confronted. Because of differences in socialization, women in many societies may be more likely than men to subordinate their own needs to those of others. Studying the role of women in the decision-making process leading to migration involves understanding how women, who generally have fewer options and less authority than their male peers, are nevertheless not totally devoid of power and how they exercise that power in relation to migration.

Although information on an individual's participation in decision-making is often unreliable, it is illustrative to consider the results of a survey carried out in the Philippines among prospective migrants. The sample consisted of 1,744 residents of Ilocos Norte Province, of whom 269 were intending to migrate, 84 within the Philippines, 93 to an international destination and the balance to an as yet undefined destination. The Philippine Migration Study included the following question: "Would you say your decision to move was based 1) entirely on your own desire, 2) mostly on your own desire, 3) mostly on the desires of others, 4) entirely on the desires of others, or 5) equal desires of both?" Table 53 shows the distribution of the

TABLE 53. DISTRIBUTION OF PROSPECTIVE MIGRANTS ACCORDING TO HOW THEY TOOK THE DECISION TO MIGRATE, BY SEX AND TYPE OF DESTINATION, PHILIPPINE MIGRATION STUDY
(*Percentage*)

Basis for decision	Women	Men	Both sexes
A. All those intending to migrate			
Entirely on own desire	42.3	55.7	49.4
Mostly on own desire	23.1	23.2	23.2
Equal desire of both	25.5	14.5	19.7
Mostly on desire of others	6.7	3.4	4.9
Entirely on desire of others	2.4	3.2	2.8
TOTAL	100.0	100.0	100.0
Total number of cases	127	142	269
B. Those intending to migrate internally			
Entirely on own desire	41.7	64.6	54.8
Mostly on own desire	19.4	16.7	17.9
Equal desire of both	25.0	10.4	16.7
Mostly on desire of others	11.1	4.2	7.1
Entirely on desire of others	2.8	4.2	3.6
TOTAL	100.0	100.0	100.0
Total number of cases	36	48	84
C. Those intending to migrate internationally			
Entirely on own desire	41.9	44.0	43.0
Mostly on own desire	34.9	28.0	31.2
Equal desires of both	18.6	20.0	19.4
Mostly on desires of others	2.3	4.0	3.2
Entirely on desires of others	2.3	4.0	3.2
TOTAL	100.0	100.0	100.0
Total number of cases	43	50	93

responses obtained by sex of prospective migrant and by whether the intended destination was within or outside the Philippines.

In considering the results obtained, it is important to underscore that, among all prospective migrants, although women were somewhat more likely than men to be influenced by the desires of others, over 40 per cent of all women indicated that their decision was based entirely on their own desires. When only those intending to migrate to international destinations were included, there was relatively little difference between the proportion of men and women, indicating that their decision to migrate was entirely based on their own desires; and although the percentages were small, men were almost twice as likely as women to migrate internationally mostly or entirely because of the desires of others. In contrast, with regard to internal migration, there was a considerable difference in the proportions of men and women reporting that their migration was based entirely on their own desires (65 and 42 per cent, respectively), and women were considerably more likely than men to report that they were planning to migrate mostly because of the desires of others. These data confirm that in the population studied, women were more likely than men to base their migration decisions on the desires of others, but they also indicate that in the vast majority of cases, women exert considerable influence on the decision to migrate by basing it entirely or mostly on their own desires or by giving equal weight to the desires of others.

C. DECISIONS MADE BY OTHERS

Before discussing those moves which involve women but do not involve them in the decision to migrate, it is important to establish the circumstances in which such an event would occur. A move may be decided by fiat by someone outside the family, as when families are forcefully resettled by Governments. In those circumstances, women are unlikely to be excluded from making the decision to move solely because of their gender. There are also situations in which women may be forced to migrate or prevented from doing so by decisions taken solely by other family members. In the case of adult women, it is assumed that those cases arise only rarely because although some women may totally lack power or influence within their family, most adult women have some agency and therefore some means of influencing the course of events in which they are involved. That is not to say that women control the decision to migrate nor to deny that, in most societies, women do not have as much influence or power as the men with whom they live or work.

Women have various means of influencing decisions and outcomes in subtle or covert ways (Hollos and Leis, 1985). In addition, logistics dictate that if migration is to be successful, the women involved must acquiesce to it, even if they migrate under the auspices of the family. Especially when a woman migrates alone, leaving her immediate family behind, her acquiescence will facilitate migration and the maintenance of close ties with the family of origin, a necessary condition for the family to maintain some control over the migrant woman. A study of female migration in Latin America showed that it is possible for women to migrate alone while still remaining in a tightly controlled social environment (Jelin, 1977). In the society studied, young women from rural areas migrated to a city to take a job as a domestic servant. Before the move, they were under the careful watch of family elders. Their migration took place only after their families had found them positions in the city where they would be watched equally carefully. Often, the young women stayed in the homes of family members in the area of destination. Thus, although young single women were sent to the city to take advantage of the job opportunities available there, their parents took several measures to maintain close control over them.

One of the most important factors influencing a woman's involvement in the decision to migrate is her age. At younger ages (that is, when females are minors), age may be a more important factor than gender. Most children, whether female or male, have little say in the migration decisions of the families in which they live. However, decision makers within the family may differentiate between sons and daughters when the migration envisioned is not that of the entire household. For instance, boys may be more likely than girls to be sent away at relatively young ages for schooling or training, whereas female children may be sent to the homes of relatives to help with domestic chores. In cases where selected adults within the household migrate, certain children may be chosen to accompany them while others are left behind. Generalizations are difficult, but whether any children migrate and which do so are likely to depend upon whether the primary migrant is the mother, the father or a sibling and upon the social conditions and the economic opportunities (especially those specific to males and females) at both origin and destination.

When women reach adult ages, age would probably be less important in determining their role in the decision-making process than their stage in the life cycle, which would interact strongly with gender. For example, a widowed woman may be compelled to migrate in order to join her offspring and be supported by them. Her situation, although related in part to age and marital status, would also be greatly influenced by attitudes related to gender ideology about whether and how older women can live by themselves. In such a situation, a woman's decision, though not entirely dictated by others or by societal attitudes, would nevertheless be conditioned in important respects by them.

Another stage in the life cycle that often involves relocation is the passage from single to married life. The term "marriage migration" has been coined to indicate migration deriving from customs establishing the place of residence of newlywed couples away from the bride's family of origin. In societies where arranged marriages are common and the custom of village exogamy is combined with patrilocal residence for the newlyweds, brides may be compelled to migrate without being involved in either the marriage or the migration decision. In India, the migration of women over short distances has generally been attributed to those practices. Despite the large numbers of women involved, hardly any attention has been given to understanding the role that women play in the decisions made and the consequences that such decisions have for them.

It is important to recognize, however, that even in circumstances where women are supposed to have no influence with regard to the decisions made on their behalf, there is considerable variation within societies. Thus, not all "arranged" marriages are alike: there is a wide continuum of parent/child involvement in marriage decisions that can be considered "arranged". Prospective brides sometimes have a fair amount of involvement in the decision made and may have veto power as to the chosen spouse. Because marriage determines the place to which the bride will migrate, her involvement in the decision about whom to marry clearly has implications for migration. In many instances, marriage is a strategy used by parents to improve the family's status through advantageous alliances. The place of residence of prospective sons-in-law is likely to be an important consideration, both because of its implications for the ease of maintaining family ties and because it may give the family of origin access to resources in other areas through remittances or other forms of family transfers.

D. JOINT DECISIONS

Among adult women, particularly those still in unions, joint decisions with regard to migration may well be the most common occurrence. Although most women do not have power equal to that of their male peers, they are unlikely to be totally excluded from the decision to migrate. Women's involvement in the decision-making process will depend upon a variety of factors, both within and outside the family.

In examining joint decisions on whatever issue, one must first define which decisions will be considered "joint". For this discussion, joint decisions include only decisions made by more than one person, of which at least one is a woman. The decisions made may involve the migration of a single person, whether male or female, of selected family members, of the whole household or even the decision not to migrate. Considering a wide array of possible decisions is crucial in studying the role of women in decision-making, because in societies where female migration is restricted, women may have few alternatives but to influence the migration of their male relatives.

In considering joint decisions, account must be taken of whether they are part of a household strategy directed to improving the average well-being of the household or family unit. The concept of household strategy presumes that there is some kind of consensus among household members. In reality, "household strategies" are more likely to derive from the decisions made by the most powerful household members, decisions that, by affecting all household members irrespective of their involvement in the decision-making process, may give rise to dissent or resistance. The extent to which such dissension or resistance tends to manifest itself differentially by sex should be considered. Because of socialization, women are probably more likely to acquiesce with little resistance to the decisions made by others.

The fact that joint decisions are common makes it imperative to examine them, although they pose difficulties in determining the extent of women's participation in taking them. Problems arise for several reasons, including misreporting or misperception of what actually occurs during the decision-making process (Spiro, 1983) and difficulty in measuring the relative influence exerted by different individuals (McDonald, 1980). Research has shown that in any decision that might be considered jointly made—either by the people making the decision or by outsiders—some persons inevitably have more input than others. However, self-reports of persons' roles in the process are often inaccurate (Wilk, 1989; Park, 1982). Reporting inaccuracies may be related to recall errors or to a conscious or unconscious need to change actual events (Ramu, 1988). In decisions made jointly by two or more household members, the degree of involvement of a person in the decision-making process reflects his or her relative power within the household. Age, generation, relationship to the head of household and gender would all influence the relative participation of different household members. Although in most societies women have less decision-making power than men within the household (Rosaldo, 1974), there is a continuum of the degree of influence that women have in making major decisions, such as those involving migration.

Studies that focus on the decision-making itself and ignore the context in which decisions take place are especially problematic for the study of women's involvement in the process because gender stratification and ideology influence not only the actual decision but also the way in which men and women define, organize and select goals and the strategies they use to attain them (Matthews, 1987). To perceive such differences, decisions must be studied within the social context in which they are made so that the power relations between those making joint decisions can be taken into account. In most societies, men's power within the household is just the reflection of the authority that men have in society at large, authority that can be thought of as the legitimacy to act in a particular manner. In this regard, Curtis states:

"As a right, it exists not in the one who exercises it, but in those who accept it. The right of ownership, then, is a social phenomenon consisting of the fact that vast numbers of people accept a given owner's use of a given property as he/she sees fit, given certain socially defined limitations. An individual woman confronts patriarchy in the fact that other men and women accept a man's right to make some decision for her. She may or may not do as she is told, but in order not to, she must overcome a social environment that accepts that man's right to make that decision." (1986, pp. 172-173)

Authority and expectations about the roles of men and women shape their responses to their social environment and their interactions with each other. In a study of power differentials between wives and husbands in the Netherlands, Komter (1989) found that although gender biases had been reduced in formal institutions, in legal provisions and even in prevailing sex roles, men remained dominant within their families because the gender ideology that legitimated inequality had not yet been totally eradicated. However, husbands manifested power in subtle and veiled ways. Women and men employed different strategies to initiate a change. Women tended to be cautious in suggesting change and were more likely to anticipate possible negative reactions by their husbands and to resign themselves to the current situation in order to prevent disruption or outright conflict (Komter, 1989). Men, in contrast, were more likely to ignore their wives' anger or desire for change.

In some households, men and women may have responsibility for different types of decisions (Wilk, 1989). Such specialization may be egalitarian or unequal. If women and men have specific roles in the family and community, their decision-making power is likely to be tied to those roles. In most societies, women are responsible for the domestic sphere while men exercise responsibility mainly outside the home. In such cases, it would be expected for men to have a greater say in migration decisions.

Although gender roles and ideologies influence the participation of all women in migration decisions, within households some women may have more say than others in decisions about moving. The age and position of a woman within the household are important determinants of her influence in decision-making. As stated above, minors, whether male or female, are likely to have little involvement in decision-making. Young unmarried women, particularly those who are still outside the labour force, would also have reduced influence in most migration decisions, unless the migration envisaged involved them in particular. The wife of the head of household would probably have the most influence among female household members, particularly if the family is nuclear. In extended families, intergenerational power structures would play an important role in determining the influence of different adult women and it should not be assumed that the interests of all female household members would coincide. In patrilocal societies, for instance, where younger married couples live with the parents of the husband, conflicts of interest between the wife and the mother-in-law may play themselves out in migration decisions (Wolf, M., 1972; Johnson, 1983).

Studies have shown that the effect of age dominance, whether by men or women, in family decisions lessens as societies change and as economies become increasingly oriented towards the market and away from the family (Caldwell, 1982). In such transitional economies, the family comes to rely increasingly upon the education, training and labour of young people, thus eroding the influence that family elders have traditionally exerted in decision-making within the family.

The benefits of migration may be perceived differently by different family members. For example, migration from Mexico to the United States has been shown to have a greater impact on women's social roles than on those of men, because once they are in the United States, Mexican women are more likely to work in the paid labour force than they were in Mexico (Briody, 1987; Guendelman, 1987). Similar changes have been documented in the Philippines and Thailand when women migrate from rural to urban areas (Tonguthai, 1987). Women and their husbands may evaluate such an anticipated change differently. If a woman welcomes it, she may seek a positive decision with regard to migration. If her husband wants her to contribute more to family income, he might also be in favour of migration. However, if he perceives her wife's work outside the home as threatening, he may delay or stop her migration altogether.

A change in a woman's economic contribution to household income does not, however, necessarily result in a commensurate increase in her power within the family. She may work outside the home to benefit the family and be unwilling or unable to increase her influence in decision-making within the domestic unit. Thus, a study of Greek-Cypriot women in London (Anthias, 1983) and that of Turkish women in the Netherlands (Brouwer and Priester, 1983) found that the economic activity of migrant women in their new environments had only partial or negligible influence on their power in relation to that of their husband. Foner (1986), however, found that changes in women's influence within the household were more complex among Jamaican immigrant women in New York and London. In some cases, women may lose power within the household because of migration. Guendelman (1987), for instance, reports that Mexican women in the United States sometimes have less autonomy than they have in Mexico because they lack the language and labour skills needed in their new environment and are therefore more dependent upon their husbands.

In making joint decisions when there is no consensus a priori, a woman is likely to make her decision prevail only if she has enough influence in relation to that of the other decision makers involved. A woman's influence is higher if she has access to resources. Research has shown that the size of a woman's contribution to household income is related to the role that she plays in making major decisions (Blood and Wolfe, 1960; Burgoyne, 1990). Education is also a determinant of influence. Thus, in Nigeria, young women that had attended school, even if for relatively short periods, saw their influence in family decision-making rise (Caldwell, 1979). The influence gained, however, is not always commensurate with the economic or social contributions that a woman makes to family well-being. In Hong Kong, for instance, Salaff (1981) describes the changes in young women's lives as they begin to make substantial contributions to their family's income. Although the young women gain some power in certain areas, they do not, in general, acquire influence proportional to their contribution (Standing, 1985). Furthermore, in some contexts, even the complete economic dependence of a woman upon her husband does not necessarily translate into her exclusion from the decision-making process (O'Connor, 1991). The relation between economic contribution and power in the family is thus not always direct, but appears to be related also to the expected roles of women within the family (Olsen, 1989). Even when women play an important economic role, societal norms and expectations may dictate that their involvement in making major family decisions be small (Qualls, 1987; Burgoyne, 1990).

Access to resources can influence the decision-making process in other ways. A woman's access to education is likely to facilitate her acquisition and evaluation of information about migration. Access to employment and financial resources, by making migration possible, would also allow a woman to be more assertive in the decision-making process leading to migration. Furthermore, women may have access to resources that men do not have or do not exploit as well. Among the most important is access to networks of kin and friends that are crucial in fostering migration by transmitting information, helping in effecting the move and providing assistance at the place of destination (Lomnitz, 1977; Tienda, 1980; Boyd, 1989). Women are often involved in the development and maintenance of such networks (di Leonardo, 1984; Benería and Roldán, 1987) and through their involvement they are in a position to influence decisions about migration.

In some contexts, women are constrained by gender stratification and ideology to the point that they are only able to participate in migration by influencing decisions concerning the migration of other family members, particularly males. Under such restrictions, women achieve their goals through the men around them (Safilios-Rothschild, 1985), participating in what have been called "bargains with patriarchy" (Kandiyoti, 1988). In places where only men migrate, women can be as actively involved in the migration decision as when they themselves or the whole household migrates. Women understand that the migration of a husband or a son may be the best or only way for her family or herself to achieve economic or other goals. In rural villages of Mexico, for instance, women who are not able to migrate to the United States strongly encourage their husbands to do so, because having at least one family member abroad is important to the well-being and sometimes the survival of the household (Wiest, 1983).

E. INDEPENDENT DECISIONS BY WOMEN

Independent decisions involving migration can result in the migration of the woman concerned, of one or more family members or of the entire family or household. In most societies, women usually lack the power and authority needed to make on their own decisions about the migration of others. Yet, at certain stages of the life cycle, the advantages of age or generation may overcome the pervasive influence of gender and lead to situations where women can or must decide for others. Widowed or divorced women may be in that position, as well as women left behind by the previous migration of close male relatives. It is likely, however, that most independent decisions on migration will result in the movement of the women taking the decision and those are the cases discussed below.

Women that are not in a union (the never-married, divorced or widowed) are more likely than married women to make independent decisions about migration. Although never-married women are generally subject to a number of restrictions, both within their families and in society at large, married women or women in unions usually confront more restrictions and have even fewer opportunities to operate independently. Divorced or widowed women are more likely to act independently, particularly if they need to migrate in order to find work and support their dependants.

Women that move on their own, with minimal family support, usually have greater access to the resources needed for migration than other women, so that they can secure information about possible areas of destination and pay the transport and other costs involved in migration. Such women must therefore have considerable free agency to operate outside of their immediate family. If social norms prevent women from such activities, migration by unattached women is unlikely to occur or even to be considered as an option.

In many contexts, never-married women migrate without the support or even against the wishes of their immediate families. In Indonesia, for instance, young women often leave rural areas to work in urban factories even though their parents oppose their move (Wolf, D., 1990). In Ireland, single women often emigrated on their own in the hopes of finding better marriage prospects and working opportunities abroad (Jackson, 1984). In Zaire, women migrate on their own to the towns to take advantage of the opportunities available in the informal sector and to gain independence from men (MacGaffey, 1988). Indeed, some women that migrate independently do so in order to rebel against social norms. Given the social obstacles to female migration prevailing in many societies, the importance of personality in making a decision to move independently cannot be overlooked. A woman moving away from her family on her own needs to overcome not only great economic barriers but a series of social prejudices. She must also have the emotional and psychological resilience to face the social opposition produced by behaviour that does not conform to existing social norms. Dandekar aptly describes the situation in discussing the experience of an Indian village with a high male out-migration:

"If the social atmosphere in the village becomes oppressive, a young man can move to the city. The question of a woman's honour, her chastity, and her credibility to the community at large as a potential marriage partner prevent her from making similar moves. In the past only destitute women moved to the city where they survived by serving meals. Most were forced to establish a liaison with a man. Women who survive in this fashion were and are maligned by villagers who look upon them with critical and jaundiced eyes. Gossip abounds. Thus, rural society discounts and devalues women who show initiative." (1986, pp. 116 and 118)

Because of such social constraints, women may use marriage as a means for migration. To the extent that women are free to choose their spouse, their decision to marry someone living in another location or someone intending to migrate may be part of their conscious or unconscious strategy to relocate. Women thus achieve their goals through men. Boulahbel-Villac (1990) describes such marriage strategies among Algerian women intending to go to France. Because marriage is involved, however, the decision leading to actual relocation will in all probability be a joint decision involving husband and wife.

F. CONCLUSION

In discussing the process leading to decisions on migration and the influence exerted by women, only scant attention has been paid to the determinants of female migration and therefore to the content of the migration decision. The focus has been on how women are involved in decisions about migration either involving themselves or other family members and on the importance of relative power within the household and its determinants, including household structure and factors beyond the household. Although individual characteristics have proved to be important, the role of women in making decisions on migration appears to depend greatly upon the prevailing gender ideology.

The relevance of women's involvement in the decision-making process with regard to migration can be judged from several perspectives. One relates to the relative participation of women in migration. Although there is no evidence indicating that greater involvement by women in decision-making would increase the propensity of women to migrate, the conditions that would foster such involvement are associated with a higher overall status of women. To the extent that society selectively bars women from considering migration as an option while it condones the migration of men, elimination of such barriers can only be beneficial for the women involved. Yet, migration should be an option for women to select or to reject freely. Norms that force women to migrate and deprive them of the option of staying in their usual place of residence are also unacceptable. Free agency, even if limited by a variety of practical constraints, needs to be assured to all adult women.

That a number of changes associated with modernization are likely to increase the participation of women in decision-making with regard to migration is a sign that such participation is a desirable outcome. Indeed, increasing female educational levels, providing better labour-market opportunities for women, equalizing male and female wages and assuring equal rights for women in terms of ownership of assets and access to credit are all measures that, by improving the status of women in society at large, are likely to improve their status within the home as well and to strengthen their position and influence with regard to major decisions, including those involving migration.

To the best of the authors' knowledge, there has been no study focusing on the way in which migration decisions are made, although many studies have looked at why migration decisions are made and a number have considered how decisions are made within families. Although the last-named studies yield some insights about the likely dynamics of decisions about migration, they are not an adequate basis for policy formulation. More information is needed on several aspects of decision-making in relation to migration. Data on who within the family or household participates or intervenes in making migration decisions are needed. A number of studies, such as the Philippine Migration Study cited above, have included one or two questions on who influences migration decisions. Information of that type relating to different societies would at least indicate who intervenes in decision-making on behalf of whom. It is important that in investigating the issue, relevant questions are posed both to migrants and to non-migrants, to men and to women, so that those factors which prevent certain persons from intervening in the decision-making process can be understood better and modified if possible.

As already noted, there are often problems in the quality or the possible interpretation of self-reports on any decision-making process. It is necessary to go beyond conventional sample survey methodologies to investigate that process. In-depth interview techniques, such as those used by anthropologists and psychologists, are needed to understand better not only who decides but also how and why a decision is made or the reasons for excluding certain persons from the decision-making process. To unearth the influence of gender ideology, the latter aspect has to be carefully delineated for each society and its impact on decision-making must be probed, taking into account the various facets of migration and its determinants at various levels.

NOTE

[1] For the purposes of this paper, a household includes all those persons living together, whether related or not, whereas a family includes both relatives living together and those living apart but playing an active and regular part in household matters (Yanagisako, 1979).

REFERENCES

Ahern, Susan, Dexter Bryan and Reynaldo Baca (1985). Migration and la mujer fuerte. *Migration Today* (Staten Island, New York), vol. 13, No. 1, pp. 14-20.

Anthias, Floya (1983). Sexual divisions and ethnic adaptation: the case of Greek-Cypriot women. In *One Way Ticket: Migration and Female Labour*, Annie Phizacklea, ed. London: Routledge and Kegan Paul.

Baca, Reynaldo, and Dexter Bryan (1985). Mexican women, migration and sex roles. *Migration Today* (Staten Island, New York), vol. 13, No. 3, pp. 14-18.

Benería, Lourdes, and Martha Roldán (1987). *The Crossroads of Class and Gender: Industrial Homework, Subcontracting, and Household Dynamics in Mexico City*. Chicago, Illinois: The University of Chicago Press.

Bentley, Jeffrey (1989). Eating the dead chicken: intra-household decision making and emigration in rural Portugal. In *The Household Economy: Reconsidering the Domestic Mode of Production*, Richard R. Wilk, ed. Boulder, Colorado: Westview Press.

Blood, Robert O., Jr., and Donald M. Wolfe (1960). *Husbands and Wives: The Dynamics of Married Living*. Glencoe, Illinois: Free Press.

Boulahbel-Villac, Yeza (1990). Algerian women in France: a negotiated status as a paradoxical form of integration. Paper presented at the United Nations Expert Group Meeting on International Migration Policies and the Status of Female Migrants, San Miniato, Italy, 27-30 March.

Boyd, Monica (1989). Family and personal networks in international migration: recent developments and new agendas. *International Migration Review* (Staten Island, New York), vol. 23, No. 3 (Fall), pp. 638-670.

Briody, Elizabeth (1987). Patterns of household immigration into south Texas. *International Migration Review* (Staten Island, New York), vol. 21, No. 1 (Spring), pp. 27-47.

Brouwer, Lenie, and Marijke Priester (1983). Living in between: Turkish women in their homeland and in the Netherlands. In *One Way Ticket: Migration and Female Labour*, Annie Phizacklea, ed. London: Routledge and Kegan Paul.

Brown, Richard (1987). The migrating self: persons and politics in the process of modernization. *Studies in Third World Societies* (Williamsburg, Virginia), vol. 39.

Burgoyne, Carole B. (1990). Money in marriage: how patterns of allocation both reflect and conceal power. *Sociological Review* (Keele, United Kingdom), vol. 38, No. 4 (November), pp. 634-665.

Caldwell, John C. (1979). Education as a factor of mortality decline: an examination of Nigerian data. *Population Studies* (London), vol. 33, No. 3 (November), pp. 395-413.

_____ (1982). *Theory of Fertility Decline*. London: Academic Press.

Curtis, Richard F. (1986). Household and family in theory on inequality. *American Sociological Review* (Washington, D.C.), vol. 51, No. 2 (April), pp. 168-183.

Dandekar, Hemalata (1986). *Men to Bombay, Women at Home*. Ann Arbor: University of Michigan, Center for South and Southeast Asian Studies.

di Leonardo, Micaela (1984). *The Varieties of Ethnic Experience: Kinship, Class and Gender among California Italian-Americans*. Ithaca, New York: Cornell University Press.

Fernández-Kelly, María Patricia (1983a). Mexican border industrialization, female labor force participation, and migration. In *Women, Men, and the International Division of Labor*, June Nash and María Patricia Fernández-Kelly, eds. Albany, New York: State University of New York Press.

_____ (1983b). *For We Are Sold, I and My People: Women and Industry in Mexico's Frontier*. Albany, New York: State University of New York Press.

Findley, Sally E., and Linda Williams (1991). *Women Who Go and Women Who Stay: Reflections of Family Migration Processes in a Changing World*. Population and Labour Policies Programme, Working Paper No. 176. Geneva: International Labour Office.

Foner, Nancy (1986). Sex roles and sensibilities: Jamaican women in New York and London. In *International Migration: The Female Experience*, Rita James Simon and Caroline B. Brettell, eds. Totowa, New Jersey: Rowman and Allanheld.

Guendelman, Sylvia (1987). The incorporation of Mexican women in seasonal migration: a study of gender differences. *Hispanic Journal of Behavioral Sciences* (Los Angeles, California), vol. 9, No. 3 (September), pp. 245-264.

Hollos, Marida, and Philip E. Leis (1985). "The hand that rocks the cradle rules the world": family interaction and decision making in a Portuguese rural community. *Ethos* (Washington, D.C.), vol. 13, No. 4 (Winter), pp. 340-357.

Jackson, Pauline (1984). Women in 19th century Irish immigration. *International Migration Review* (Staten Island, New York), vol. 18, No. 4 (Winter), pp. 1004-1020.

Jelin, Elizabeth (1977). Migration and labor force participation of Latin American women: the domestic servants in the cities. *Signs* (Chicago, Illinois), vol. 3, No. 1 (Autumn), pp. 129-141.

Johnson, Kay Ann (1983). *Women. The Family and Peasant Revolution in China*. Chicago, Illinois: University of Chicago Press.

Kandiyoti, Deniz (1988). Bargaining with patriarchy. *Gender and Society* (Newbury Park, California), vol. 2, No. 3 (September), pp. 274-290.

Kearney, Michael (1986). From the invisible hand to visible feet: anthropological studies of migration and development. In *Annual Review of Anthropology*, vol. 15, Bernard S. Siegel, ed. Palo Alto, California: Annual Reviews Inc.

Komter, Aafke (1989). Hidden power in marriage. *Gender and Society* (Newbury Park, California), vol. 3, No. 2 (June), pp. 187-216.

León de Leal, Magdalena, and Carmen Diana Deere (1979). Rural women and the development of capitalism in Colombian agriculture. *Signs* (Chicago, Illinois), vol. 5, No. 1 (Autumn), pp. 60-77.

Lim, Lin Lean (1989). The status of women in international migration. Background paper for the United Nations Expert Group Meeting on International Migration and the Status of Female Migrants, San Miniato, Italy, 27-30 March.

Lomnitz, Larissa Adler (1977). *Networks and Marginality: Life in a Mexican Shantytown*. Cinna Lomnitz, trans. New York: Academic Press.

MacGaffey, Janet (1988). Evading male control: women in the second economy in Zaire. In *Patriarchy and Class: African Women in the Home and Workforce*, Sharon Stichter and Jane Parpart, eds. Boulder, Colorado: Westview Press.

McDonald, Gerald W. (1980). Family power: the assessment of a decade of theory and research, 1970-1979. *Journal of Marriage and the Family* (Minneapolis, Minnesota), vol. 42, No. 4 (November), pp. 841-854.

Massey, Douglas S., and others (1987). *Return to Aztlan: The Social Process of International Migration from Western Mexico*. Berkeley: University of California Press.

Matthews, Holly E. (1987). Predicting decision outcomes: have we put the cart before the horse in anthropological studies of decision making? *Human Organization* (Oklahoma City, Oklahoma), vol. 46, No. 1 (Spring), pp. 54-61.

Morokvasic, Mirjana (1983). Women in migration: beyond the reductionist outlook. In *One Way Ticket: Migration and Female Labour*, Annie Phizacklea, ed. London: Routledge and Kegan Paul.

Murray, Colin (1987). Class, gender and the household: the developmental cycle in Southern Africa. *Development and Change* (London), vol. 18, No. 2 (April), pp. 235-249.

O'Connor, Pat (1991). Women's experience of power within marriage: an inexplicable phenomenon? *Sociological Review* (London), vol. 39, No. 4 (November), pp. 823-842.

Olsen, M. K. G. (1989). Authority and conflict in Slavonian households: the effect of social environment on intra-household processes. In *The Household Economy: Reconsidering the Domestic Mode of Production*, Richard R. Wilk, ed. Boulder, Colorado: Westview Press.

Park, C. Whan (1982). Joint decisions in home purchasing: a muddling through process. *Journal of Consumer Research* (Los Angeles, California), vol. 9, No. 2 (September), pp. 151-162.

Qualls, William J. (1987). Household decision behavior: the impact of husbands' and wives' sex role orientation. *Journal of Consumer Research* (Los Angeles, California), vol. 14, No. 2 (September), pp. 264-279.

Radcliffe, Sarah A. (1990a). Between hearth and labor market: the recruitment of peasant women in the Andes. *International Migration Review* (Staten Island, New York), vol. 24, No. 2 (Summer), pp. 229-249.

_____ (1990b). Ethnicity, patriarchy, and incorporation into the nation: female migrants as domestic servants in Peru. *Environment and Planning D: Society and Space* (London), vol. 8, pp. 379-393.

Ramu, G. N. (1988). Marital roles and power: perceptions and reality in the urban setting. *Journal of Comparative Family Studies* (Calgary, Alberta, Canada), vol. 19, No. 2 (Summer), pp. 207-227.

Ravenstein, E. G. (1885). The laws of migration. *Journal of the Royal Statistical Society* (London), vol. 48, No. 2 (June), pp. 167-235.

Rosaldo, Michelle Zimbalist (1974). Woman, culture and society: a theoretical overview. In *Women, Culture and Society*, Michelle Zimbalist Rosaldo and Louise Lamphere, eds. Palo Alto, California: Stanford University Press.

Safilios-Rothschild, Constantina (1982). Female power, autonomy and demographic change in the third world. In *Women's Roles and Population Trends in the Third World*, Richard Anker, Mayra Buvinic and Nadia Youssef, eds. London: Croom Helm.

Salaff, Janet (1981). *Working Daughters of Hong Kong: Filial Piety or Power in the Family?* Cambridge, United Kingdom; and New York: Cambridge University Press.

Sassen-Koob, Saskia (1983). Labor migration and the new international division of labor. In *Women, Men, and the International Division of Labor*, June Nash and María Patricia Fernández-Kelly, eds. Albany, New York: State University of New York Press.

Shields, Gail M., and Michael P. Shields (1989). Family migration and nonmarket activities in Costa Rica. *Economic Development and Cultural Change* (Chicago, Illinois), vol. 38, No. 1 (October), pp. 73-88.

Spiro, Rosann (1983). Persuasion in family decision-making. *Journal of Consumer Research* (Los Angeles, California), vol. 9, No. 4 (March), pp. 393-402.

Standing, Hilary (1985). Resources, wages and power: the impact of women's employment on the urban Bengali household. In *Women, Work, and Ideology in the Third World*, Haleh I. Afshar, ed. London: Tavistock.

Thadani, Veena N., and Michael P. Todaro (1984). Female migration: a conceptual framework. In *Women in the Cities of Asia: Migration and Urban Adaptation*, James T. Fawcett, Siew-Ean Khoo and Peter C. Smith, eds. Boulder, Colorado: Westview Press.

Tienda, Marta (1980). Familism and structural assimilation of Mexican immigrants in the United States. *International Migration Review* (Staten Island, New York), vol. 14, No. 3 (Fall), pp. 383-408.

Tonguthai, Pawadee (1987). Women and work in Thailand and the Philippines. In *Women's Economic Participation in Asia and the Pacific*. Bangkok: United Nations Economic and Social Commission for Asia and the Pacific.

Wiest, Raymond E. (1983). Male migration machismo, and conjugal roles: implications for fertility control in a Mexican municipio. *Journal of Comparative Family Studies* (Calgary, Alberta, Canada), vol. 14, No. 2 (Summer), pp. 167-181.

Wilk, Richard R. (1989). Decision making and resource flows within the household: beyond the black box. In *The Household Economy: Reconsidering the Domestic Mode of Production*, Richard R. Wilk, ed. Boulder, Colorado: Westview Press.

Wolf, Diane (1990). Daughters, decisions and domination: an empirical and conceptual critique of household strategies. *Development and Change* (London), vol. 21, No. 1, pp. 43-74.

Wolf, Margery (1972). *Women and the Family in Rural Taiwan*. Stanford, California: Stanford University Press. This volume refers to Taiwan Province of China.

Woodrow, Karen A., and Jeffrey S. Passel (1990). Post-IRCA undocumented immigration to the United States: an assessment based on the June 1988 CPS. In *Undocumented Migration to the United States: IRCA and the Experience of the 1980s*, Frank D. Bean, B. Edmonston and J. S. Passel, eds. Washington, D.C.: The Urban Institute Press.

Yanagisako, Sylvia Junko (1979). Family and household: the analysis of domestic groups. *Annual Review of Anthropology*, vol. 8, Bernard J. Siegel, ed. Palo Alto, California: Annual Reviews, Inc.

Young, Grace E. (1986). Incorporating an analysis of gender into the study of migration: the case of Peruvian migration patterns. *Migration News* (Geneva), vol. 35, No. 2 (April-June), pp. 26-31.

XI. THE STRUCTURAL DETERMINANTS OF FEMALE MIGRATION

Lin Lean Lim*

To explain the causes of migration, whether of men or women, both the underlying determinants of migration and the particular motives that result in the decision to migrate need to be taken into account. Although economic motives for migration are important for both men and women, the macro-forces underlying the economic reasons for migration are often gender-biased; moreover, economic variables are not the only factors that determine migration and cannot be considered in isolation from social and cultural factors (Hugo, 1981). Consideration of the basic structural factors determining migration is particularly important in explaining its sex selectivity because they tend to be closely linked to gender asymmetries in economic, sociocultural or political spheres in areas of origin and destination, thus reflecting different opportunity and constraint structures for male and female decision makers.

This paper focuses on the basic structural determinants of female migration, in particular, on the ways in which economic and social transformations and technological changes in Asia, particularly in South-eastern Asia, have influenced the increasing internal migration of women over the past three decades. One of the main aims of the paper is to show that the underlying macro-forces that affect female migration are the same as those which determine women's status and the integration of women into development. It is expected that a macrolevel approach will help throw light on the complex interrelations between economic development, social change, women's status and female selective migration. The macrolevel approach is also useful from a policy and planning perspective, because policies and programmes to influence female migration or female status must, by their very nature, be formulated at the macrolevel.

A review of the literature on the structural determinants of migration confirms not only that most macrolevel approaches are not gender-specific but also that it is useful to distinguish between the "intermediate" and the basic structural factors affecting migration. The former group includes those factors which persons can perceive, feel, articulate, relate to and evaluate as pertinent to themselves and their migration goals. The latter factors are beyond the consideration and often even the awareness of individuals; their influence is felt only through the intermediate factors (Gardner, 1981). It is thus important to show first the linkages between the different categories of intermediate factors and the reasons for migrating. The analysis turns then to the basic structural factors that have been important in influencing the internal migration of women and to the consideration of policy implications.

A. A REVIEW OF THE STRUCTURAL DETERMINANTS OF MIGRATION

The determinants of migration at the macrolevel have been variously described as place-related characteristics, economic and sociocultural factors, demographic factors and institutional and policy-related factors. Broadly, these factors can be considered: *(a)* to create opportunities or set constraints that influence individual migration behaviour; *(b)* to operate through the socialization of individuals so that they conform to given roles or through the enforcement of social norms or values at the individual level; or *(c)* to affect the access to and evaluation of information about alternative places of destination. These factors can impinge directly upon individual reasons for moving as either intermediate or proximate determinants; or they could be less proximate, more basic structural factors which operate or are filtered through the intermediate factors.

To understand how these factors influence migration decisions, Germani (1965) suggests the consideration of three levels:

(a) *The objective macrolevel.* This level has two main categories of variables. The first category is the

---
*International Labour Organisation, Regional Office for Asia and the Pacific, Bangkok, Thailand.

"push-and-pull" factors associated with places of origin and destination, including such factors as relative availability of job opportunities, producer assets (e.g., land), wage rates, educational opportunities and the attraction of the "bright lights". The second group includes variables related to the nature and conditions of communications, accessibility and contacts between places. Germani emphasizes, however, that objective influences do not operate in a vacuum so that, to understand them, it is necessary to consider the normative and psychosocial contexts in which they operate;

(b) *The normative level*. This level includes norms that need to be considered because people evaluate and perceive objective place-related factors against the framework of institutionalized roles, expectations and behavioural patterns that regulate migration; and

(c) *The psychosocial level*. The third level involves the attitudes and expectations of persons that may result in deviations from normative patterns.

The most commonly cited determinants at the macrolevel are those related to the objective characteristics of geographical areas, which are often considered "contextual" variables derived from aggregations of individual characteristics, such as the average level of education of all the people in a community. They can also be "setting" or "global" variables (Bilsborrow, Oberai and Standing, 1984; Freedman, 1974, 1979; Casterline, 1985), which are not based on aggregates of individual characteristics but are distinctive features of the geographical area or of the entire population in it. Setting or global variables cover locational, historical, institutional, physical or policy-related factors affecting the entire population in a particular location. Even among such variables, however, it is important to distinguish between those factors which directly influence the individual's or the family's decision on migration (the proximate determinants) and those which are the basic structural factors affecting migration decisions in a less proximate way.

The basic structural factors refer to the dominant forms of the economy, polity and social system characterized by particular organizational and institutional structures (e.g., Simmons, Diaz-Briquets and Laquian, 1977; Wood, 1982). They include such factors as land tenure systems, investment patterns, the emergence and expansion of capitalist modes of production, the overall style of development policy, a country's role in the international division of labour, the unequal levels of development between and within countries, the modernization of production techniques and the extent of social change and political conflict.

Although the relative economic advantages of places of destination provide the most cited reason for migration, researchers rarely consider gender differences in economic opportunities between places of origin and destination. For example, it is important to understand to what extent and how labour-market opportunities for men and women, and discrimination against women in employment or wages, have been changing as a consequence of industrialization or structural adjustments in different countries.

Many researchers, however, are aware that economic variables alone do not provide an adequate explanation of migration differentials and emphasize the significance of the social and cultural context in which migration takes place (see Mabongunje, 1970; Pryor, 1975; Hugo, 1981). Yet, no one has considered specifically how cultural or religious factors or societal norms, through their influence on the sexual division of labour and the status of women, influence decisions with regard to the migration of women. At the place of origin, cultural restrictions on the roles of women and their freedom to act or choose have been identified as important factors influencing female migration (Thadani and Todaro, 1979). The influence of cultural norms relating to marriage and women's participation in associational migration have also been underscored (Thadani and Todaro, 1979; Behrman and Wolfe, 1984). Nevertheless, attempts to explain sex differentials in migration have not systematically recognized the influence that historical and social processes have had in moulding the different roles and responsibilities of men and women (e.g., Benería and Roldán, 1987; UNFPA, 1990).

At the macrolevel, the demographic factors mentioned as affecting decisions on the migration of individuals include the relative population size and density of communities of origin and destination, their sex ratios, dependency ratios, imbalances in the male and female populations of marriageable age, kinship networks and chain migration.

Government policies can modify, either directly or indirectly, many place-related factors. However, the evidence suggests that explicit policies and programmes meant to influence internal migration tend to have smaller effects than those which are not explicitly meant to influence migration, such as policies on education, agricultural or industrial development, housing, ethnic relations, social welfare (see, e.g., Chan, 1981). Little attention has been given to the effects that those policies have on differences in territorial mobility by sex, by virtue of their differential effects on men and women.

The important role that the family or the group of household members has in influencing or even making the decision on the migration of individual women has been stressed. Empirical studies have shown that female migration is often better understood from a family rather than a strictly individual perspective (Findley and Williams, 1991). It has been suggested that considering the family as the structural context in which migration decisions take place is a useful approach that allows explicit consideration of the position and role of women within the family as determinants of female migration (Lim, 1988a). Although the family also exerts some influence on male migration, its consideration with regard to female migration is essential, because it is in the family that women's subordination to male authority is generally most obvious and immediate; it is the family that assigns or defines roles for women, which in turn determine their relative motivations and incentives to migrate; and it is the family that provides the resources and information that can support or discourage migration (Lim, 1988a).

Female migration, as part of a family or household survival strategy, is attracting increasing attention (see Findley and Williams, 1991; Arizpe, 1981; Jelin, 1977; Trager, 1984), in part because of the growing theoretical interest in household processes and the household economy (e.g., Redclift and Mingione, 1985; Netting, Wilk and Arnould, 1984). It still remains to be clarified, however, how the broader structural transformations taking place in developing countries affect the structure and functions of the household as well as other household processes and thereby the migration of female members.

B. A FRAMEWORK FOR THE EXAMINATION OF THE STRUCTURAL DETERMINANTS OF FEMALE MIGRATION

To place the discussion of the underlying structural determinants of female migration in perspective, it is useful to have a framework that links them to the decision-making process with regard to the migration of individual women. In this section, the framework proposed by Hugo (1981) is used to distinguish between the reasons for moving as perceived and as stated by individuals (that is, the "intermediate" or "proximate" determinants at the macrolevel) and the basic structural factors influencing decisions on migration. In doing so, special attention is given to gender dimensions and the familial context.

Hugo developed a framework based on the theory that migration results from a rational evaluation by a person that the perceived total benefits minus the costs of migration outweigh the anticipated difference between the benefits and costs of staying in the current place of residence. The latter place and potential destinations are assumed to have particular but diverse sets of attractive, unattractive and neutral factors.

The opportunity and constraint structures of different places reflect the effects of basic structural factors that Hugo denominates the "environment of social and spatial inequalities". Spatial inequalities derive from unbalanced development strategies, such as those favouring industry over agriculture, urban over rural areas or capital-intensive over labour-intensive production. Often, such development strategies also lead to gender biases in the characteristics of localities and therefore alter the differential attractiveness of potential destinations for men and women. In addition, opportunity and constraint structures are affected by the broader environment as determined by sociocultural and legal institutions, including laws of inheritance, marriage patterns, kinship systems and religion, which also affect the nature of gender relations in different places.

According to Hugo's framework, migration is a reaction to stress or pressures exerted by an individual's own physical, economic, social, political and cultural context. The current location induces stress in a potential female migrant when she secures information indicating that she would be better off in other locations in terms of "social freedom", employment, marriage prospects, housing, access to schooling etc. Various aspects of a woman's roles and position within the family and society, as determined by broad sociocultural and economic forces, affect her evaluation of the feasibility and attractiveness of migration. The higher her relative position within the family and society in the place of origin, the lower may be the incentive to migrate, although her ability to do so may be greater. The greater her subordination to male authority, the stronger her motivation to migrate, although her ability to move may be restricted. Thus, for women, the possibility of migrating can be seen as a function of various constraining and facilitating factors related to their position *vis-à-vis* men within the family and society.

In addition to the structural inequalities described above, Hugo (1981) distinguishes three interrelated sets of intervening variables: *(a)* those determining a person's perception of opportunities elsewhere; *(b)* those affecting the evaluation a person makes of available opportunities; and *(c)* those influencing a person's response to the evaluation made.

The first set refers to the nature, amount and source of information that affect the form the stress takes and the person's evaluation of it. In developing countries, much of this information arises from interpersonal communication. Women, especially in rural areas, are more dependent upon information obtained through social networks than men, who are more likely to have access to formal information channels. Migration is a more likely option for women with kin in the place of destination. Women make more use than men of the opportunities for transport, accommodation and employment arranged by relatives and friends (Lim, 1988a).

The second set of intervening variables includes people's individual demographic, educational and socio-economic characteristics, their ethnic and other background factors and their psychosocial make-up, which will affect the way in which those persons evaluate information and determine their predisposition to migrate.

The third set encompasses the social structure of the person's community of origin—its particular set of standards, values, beliefs and customs (Hugo, 1981)—which influences whether the evaluation made will result in migration. The institutionalized roles, expectations and behavioural patterns (which also determine gender relations and the status of women in a community) provide the normative context in which people evaluate and perceive the relative attractions or repulsions of particular locations. Borrowing a term from McNicoll (1985, p. 181), the "cognitive environment" is important because men and women have been socialized to assess options differently.

In addition to individual characteristics and community norms, the family plays an important role in influencing female migration, to the extent that, in some cases, the family rather than the woman herself decides whether she should migrate. Because development leads to changes in the functions and structure of the family, it also influences the status of women, their well-being, and their rights and obligations within the family, and it therefore affects their motivations and propensity to move. Consequently, the family or household group is "a primary arena for the expression of age and sex roles, kinship, socialization and economic cooperation where the very stuff of culture is mediated and transformed into action" (Netting, Wilk and Arnould, 1984, p. xxii). As Harbison (1981) suggests, there is a need for more systematic treatment of the family as the immediate context in which the decision to migrate is made.

The family, however, is far from static. Thus, as a woman passes through different stages of the life cycle, her family's configuration is likely to change and have a varying influence on her motivation to migrate and the likelihood of her migrating. Among unmarried daughters, for instance, birth order may affect their propensity to migrate, with younger daughters being more likely to do so than older ones who have been selected by the family or the parents to assume responsibility for necessary household chores (e.g., Salaff, 1981). Birth-order effects have also been noticed among male offspring, but they are usually linked to inheritance rights, with those expecting no inheritance being more likely to migrate.

Individual characteristics, the structure and functions of the family and social norms can be considered the filters through which information about the current place of residence and potential destinations passes and is judged, affecting both the nature and the level of stress experienced by the potential migrant. These filters thus influence the eventual decision taken about migration.

C. BASIC STRUCTURAL DETERMINANTS OF FEMALE MIGRATION

One can distinguish three types of structural forces impinging upon the objective characteristics of places and underlying the motives and potential for female migration: *(a)* those related to government policies, especially general development policies that are not explicitly intended to affect migration but that nevertheless determine the opportunities and constraints in different locations; *(b)* those related to the political system, legal provisions or institutional structures; and *(c)* those arising from the sociocultural system and related to community norms and values. This classification is useful because it provides an indication of the degree to which the factors involved are likely to respond to policy action. Thus, it is easier to alter or redirect government policies than to change institutional structures or legislative provisions, while changes in sociocultural norms and traditions may take even longer to occur.

The economic development context

The fundamental determinants of the sex selectivity of internal migration flows emanate from government policies that have implicitly or explicitly perpetuated or, in some cases, created various forms of inequalities that have not only spatial but gender-related dimensions. Of particular relevance are such policies as those establishing the economic growth strategies of the 1960s and 1970s and the structural adjustments of the 1980s in Asia and the Pacific. Although those policies have facilitated a notable increase in autonomous female migration by creating new economic opportunities for women, they have often been based on the exploitation of supposedly "feminine" qualities and the low status of women in many societies.

Women's participation in migration to urban areas has been significant in several countries or areas of Eastern and South-eastern Asia, including Hong Kong, Malaysia, the Philippines, the Republic of Korea, Singapore and Thailand (Lim, 1990), mainly because the economic growth strategies pursued by those economies—promoting labour-intensive, export-oriented industrialization, attracting foreign investment and encouraging tourism—have created unprecedented employment opportunities favouring female workers. Consequently, many young, single women have migrated on their own to become wage-earners in urban areas, whereas before they would have remained at home or on the farm, waiting to get married and have children.

In the type of industrialization pursued by the countries or areas mentioned above, female labour, an important proportion of which consists of migrants, has been necessary because male participation rates were already high, as is typical of the early stages of development. The successful industrialization of most of those economies has been possible because of women's willingness to migrate in order to fill the supply gap. In Eastern and South-eastern Asia, women have been able to respond to the growth of employment opportunities through autonomous migration because there are virtually no institutional nor sociocultural barriers to female labour force participation, and demographic trends together with educational gains have ensured that there shall be an ample supply of qualified female labour (Eisold, 1984; Jones, 1984; Khoo, 1987; Lim, 1988b).

Furthermore, women have provided a labour supply at relatively low and stable wages. Young women in the newly industrializing economies of Eastern and South-eastern Asia have been socially and economically oppressed for so long that they have both low "aspiration" wages and low "efficiency" wages (Standing, 1989). Consequently, employment opportunities have opened up for them largely because their wages are lower than those of equivalent male workers and their productivity is equally high (Lele, 1986). Because labour is the single largest cost of production in the types of industries being fostered, low wages are essential to maintain global competitiveness.

Lastly, female labour is particularly attractive to foreign investors: the vulnerability of women is one of their main attractions on the labour-market (United Nations, 1986). Supposedly "feminine" qualities, such as docility, manual dexterity, deference to command, willingness to withstand rigid discipline and the tedious monotony of the assembly line, and the lower likelihood of women joining or forming unions, have made of women ideal workers. Thus, multinational companies tend to hire recent female migrants from rural areas because they are more naïve and are not knowledgeable about working conditions; therefore, they are likely to be more passive and less demanding (Salih and others, 1985).

In so far as the increase in autonomous female migration can be attributed to the growth of employment opportunities in manufacturing, particularly that carried out in export-processing zones and industrial estates, it is worth noting that women's employment in the manufacturing sector grew substantially faster than that of men in almost all the Eastern and South-eastern Asian countries during the 1970s (excluding the Philippines) and that, except in the planned economies of Eastern Europe, female participation in manufacturing in those Asian countries was the highest in the world (Jones, 1984; Khoo, 1987; United Nations, 1989). Furthermore, the sectors that have been the engines of economic growth in the newly industrializing economies of Asia have also been those where female employment has been growing faster than that of males (Lim, 1990).

In Southern Asia, only Sri Lanka has recorded substantial female economic migration, particularly to export-processing zones. In other countries of the region, not only has economic growth been low during the past three decades and job creation modest, but the sociocultural context has not facilitated autonomous female migration. In Bangladesh, India and Pakistan, the migration of women, especially that from rural to urban areas, continues to be predominantly associational or marriage-related (Youssef, Buvinic and Kudat, 1979; Findley and Williams, 1991).

Another fundamental factor leading to expanded employment opportunities for migrant women has been the aggressive promotion by many South-eastern Asian countries of tourism as a source of needed foreign exchange. The tourist industry has employed more female workers than male not only because women accept lower wages but because Asian women have been an attractive selling-point by virtue of being portrayed as submissive, sentimental and sexually desirable. Considerable numbers of young women have migrated to the main tourist spots to work not only in hotels and restaurants but in various "hospitality" services as barbershop or massage girls, hostesses in "Japanese lounges" or *karaoke* bars, for escort services or as prostitutes. Young women are more likely to be drawn into prostitution or other socially banned occupations when they are away from their home towns. Although the migration of women to engage in prostitution has long been observed (Phongpaichit, 1982; Lerman, 1983), the link between the growth of prostitution as a highly organized trade and the expansion of the tourist industry in many Eastern and South-eastern Asian countries is increasing the likelihood that migrant women, particularly if young, will find themselves involved in prostitution (Lim and Wihtol, 1991).

During the 1970s, the rapid expansion of the public sector in many of the Eastern and South-eastern Asian countries also stimulated female migration indirectly by creating new employment opportunities for women in the civil service. Given the goals of providing equal educational opportunities for women and integrating them into development, the Governments of those countries set an example by expanding the female share of public sector employment (Standing, 1989). In Malaysia, for instance, the public sector ranked second after manufacturing in terms of the growth of female employment (Lim, 1989). Since public sector jobs tend to be concentrated in capital cities, their expansion probably stimulated internal migration. It is important to note, however, that even within the public sector, women tended to occupy lower status jobs, as nurses or paramedics rather than physicians, as clerical workers rather than managers, as telephone operators rather than engineers.

Although the basic structural factors discussed so far relate to the "pull" of increasing employment opportunities for women in urban areas, those pushing women from rural areas are also important. Female out-migration appears to be more likely from areas where men control agricultural resources and production or from those where women have been displaced by agricultural mechanization and the decline of cottage industries (Sassen-Koob, 1984; Young, 1982). Even where poverty is not widespread, the increasing differentials between rural and urban areas serve to fuel rural out-migration. There are, however, exceptions. In parts of India, for instance, technological advances and the commercialization of agriculture appear to have created new job opportunities for lower caste women involved in rural-rural migration (Findley and Williams, 1991).

In Thailand, the increasing difficulties of making a living from agriculture, given the growing population densities in some rural areas, environmental degradation, droughts and other problems related to climate coupled with the relative neglect of agriculture by the Government and the lack of employment alternatives for women, have led many young women from large rural families to migrate to the cities in search of a job. Some rural families have even been known to sell their daughters into prostitution. In Java, Indonesia, Collier (1981) documented how the introduction of mechanization in the milling of rice resulted in the displacement of large numbers of female workers, thus increasing the pressures for out-migration. Other innovations in the planting, growing and harvesting of rice have also had major labour displacement effects impinging disproportionately upon rural Javanese women (Hugo, 1993). In Malaysia too, machines have been substituted for female labour and rural out-migration has been a solution for those displaced from their traditional activities (Corner, 1981).

Yet, in Malaysia, the Government's educational policies have been a more significant factor leading to female out-migration from rural areas. To ensure that female rural children shall have an education, the Malaysian Government has set up urban residential hostels for children, both male and female, from the large rural land development schemes. The younger female populations in rural areas have typically attained at least a lower secondary level of education and have thus been motivated to find work beyond the farm or the home. However, the educational levels attained are still too low to ensure women satisfying jobs with enough scope for occupational mobility. Although better education has been an asset to facilitate industrialization, women still find themselves restricted largely to low-status, low-paying jobs (Lim, 1989).

Not all the forces behind the "push" from rural areas have been negative from a developmental perspective. In fact, the very emphasis given by Governments to rural development in terms of expanding educational opportunities for rural youth, improving transport systems and access to the mass media, can positively encourage overall development *in situ*, although such measures may also lead to the increased out-migration of both men and women. Economic growth may tend to retain population in general, but for women in particular the spread of modernization has helped to erode traditional value structures and prompted them to migrate in order to avoid restrictive village lifestyles (Ariffin, 1980).

The implications for female migration of the structural adjustment policies that the developing countries adopted in the 1980s in the wake of the world recession and the international debt crisis are important because "women, or the amount of labour that they do, today represent an *adjustment variable* in the context of the national efforts being made to bring the economy under control" (Vickers, 1991, p. 20). Although evidence is still limited, migration implications can be examined from two related perspectives: the relative availability and changing nature of jobs open to men and women; and the changing roles of women in families as they confront economic hardship.

Although differing in combination and strength from one country to another, the main components of structural adjustment policies have been: *(a)* supply-side policies relying upon economic liberalism, mainly through labour-market deregulation, flexible job structures and outward-looking strategies with a bias against non-tradables, such as agricultural food production; *(b)* demand-reducing policies, involving mainly cutbacks in government expenditure and the privatization of public enterprises; and *(c)* policies to improve international competitiveness, especially by keeping down production costs.

In so far as these policies have been responsible for creating new job opportunities for women in some Eastern and South-eastern Asian countries or areas during the 1980s, they can be assumed to have had a positive effect on female migration (Standing, 1989; Lim, 1990). Though at levels below those attained during the 1960s and 1970s, new job creation in the structural adjustment milieu has been proportionately higher among women than among men. For instance, the average annual growth rate of non-agricultural employment between 1980 and 1986-1987 was 6.7 per cent for women and 4.2 per cent for men in the Republic of Korea; 6.0 and 3.3 per cent, respectively, in Malaysia; 3.4 and 2.2 per cent in Hong Kong, 2.6 and 0.7 per cent in Singapore, and 6.3 and 5.2 per cent in Thailand (Lim, 1990). Although these differences in growth rates do not imply that more jobs were created for women than for men during the period considered (the base numbers of jobs for each sex were far from equal in most cases), other evidence indicates that the participation of women in export-oriented manufacturing, in services (especially community and personal services) and in trade or tourism increased in relation to that of men. In Malaysia and Singapore, for instance, women accounted for most of the increase in employment in the manufacturing sector during the 1980s.

As agents of "invisible adjustment", women in some South-eastern Asian countries have been increasingly involved in migration to take up non-agricultural employment. As Vickers reports:

"IMF adjustment practices have increased women's participation in cash crop production and other foreign exchange activities, but at the same time have devalued the traditional areas of women's work, such as subsistence agriculture, and reinforced their marginalization." (1991, p. 20)

Although in Western-bloc countries one response to the economic crisis of the 1980s has been for women to withdraw from the labour force (United Nations, 1989), in the ASEAN countries, hard economic circumstances have been more likely to force women to enter the labour force. To do so, many have had to resort to migration. Yet, the types of employment women have found—personal service jobs, such as catering, cleaning or domestic service (instead of civil service jobs, which were cut by austerity drives during the 1980s); informal sector hawking, street vending and food catering; tourism and entertainment; and casual, temporary or part-time work in manufacturing, which often involves subcontracting or outputting arrangements—suggest that women rarely achieve upward social or economic mobility through territorial mobility.

Women have been more likely than men to be affected by the job retrenchment that has accompanied structural adjustment. Although some migrant women that lost their jobs in urban areas have returned to their village of origin (ILO, various years; Ariffin, 1985; Young and Salih, 1986), the bulk of the evidence suggests that pressures for women to leave rural areas as part of household survival strategies have been increasing. Government policy biases against food production and unfavourable terms of trade for agricultural products, reduction of subsidies and inflation have all contributed to increase the relative unattractiveness of rural areas and strengthened push factors.

Perhaps more importantly, the forces linked to economic hardship have accelerated the process of proletarianizing of rural families and have indirectly contributed to changes in the roles of women within their family, thus influencing their motivation and propensity to migrate. The effects of structural adjustment policies have prompted rural families to assign new economic roles to women and to rely increasingly upon female migration for wage employment as a household survival strategy. Economic pressures help explain why social taboos on female mobility are being ignored or why the "niceties of proper female existence" are not applied to certain groups of migrant women.

Younger daughters from larger than average families tend to be those "selected" for migration because they are not needed to perform agricultural work or household chores and do not have viable job alternatives in rural areas. Daughters are considered particularly reliable sources of remittances because they tend to be more willing and faithful than sons in fulfilling family obligations (Trager, 1984) and remit a larger share of their income than do sons (Findley and Williams, 1991). Thus, in places where daughters used to be considered liabilities, they have become assets and families are more willing to invest in their education and delay their marriage. Role reversals have also occurred where job opportunities have been scarce for men but available for women. Wives have migrated on their own to take wage-earning jobs while husbands have stayed behind to take care of the family. In some cases, the tasks of absent female migrants have been undertaken by other female family members, such as grandmothers or older daughters (Lim, 1990).

There is also evidence of an increase in single-parent households, most of which are headed by women. The increase is related, at least in part, to the increasing out-migration of men in search of work and to higher levels of divorce and separation, perhaps triggered by the stresses associated with the economic crisis (United Nations, 1989). Migration rates tend to be high among divorced, separated or widowed women with children to support and limited wage-earning opportunities in rural areas.

The economic crisis has also contributed to the increase in international migration of women from Southern and South-eastern Asia to seek employment, particularly in domestic service and entertainment (often an euphemism for prostitution) but also in nursing, teaching and clerical work. With the demand for male workers slackening in the oil-producing countries of Western Asia and employment opportunities with attractive remuneration opening up for women in overseas labour-markets, women have been the ones giving up hearth and family to work overseas. Large numbers of Sri Lankan women, for instance, have migrated to Western Asia to work as domestic servants, despite strong cultural norms establishing that men should protect and provide for women and that married women should not leave the home for prolonged periods. Other countries sending considerable numbers of women to work abroad include Indonesia, the Philippines and Thailand. It has been suggested that the internal and international migration of women may be interrelated, so that one type leads to another, usually because rural women move first to urban areas, if only to secure the necessary travel documents, and also because those who are not successful in going abroad may tend to look for alternative employment in the urban areas of their own countries.

The institutional factors

In spite of moves spurred by the United Nations Women's Decade to promote the equality of women and to do away with discrimination against women in legislation or access to resources, there are still institutionalized gender inequalities that may either facilitate or hinder female migration. Laws restricting female internal migration, such as those which during the colonial period prohibited women from living in newly developed towns, mining camps and plantations, are largely a thing of the past. Where there are legal restrictions on female mobility, they apply generally to international migration and are intended to protect female workers. But there are other, subtler, institutional barriers to movement. Although it is not possible to provide a comprehensive list of all relevant institutional factors impinging upon female migration, the most relevant include the rights of women to individual ownership of land, other producer assets and housing; the laws and practices determining women's access to credit; inheritance practices, in terms both of laws and of actual customs, which may discriminate against women even when the law does not; labour and equal-wage legislation; the "typing" of certain jobs as "female" and others as "male", particularly on the basis of safety requirements or working conditions that restrict employers from hiring women for certain jobs; and education systems that discriminate against women or that discourage them from scientific or manual studies. The relevance of these factors in particular cases is discussed below.

Rules and regulations concerning women's rights or access to assets, such as education, housing, credit or land, influence their motivation and ability to migrate. Thus, when women have access to credit on their own, their capacity or incentives to migrate are likely to be significantly different from those of women who need male approval to secure a loan. The extent to which the needs of women, especially female heads of household, are taken into account in devising programmes for agricultural extension, training, credit or marketing is also likely to influence their decisions to move or stay in rural areas. In Thailand, for example, the increasing out-migration of women from rural areas and their reliance upon non-farm activities can be linked to the exclusion of female farmers from agricultural development programmes. This practice "retards agricultural productivity and prevents rural incomes from rising as fast as they would if both men and women were taught improved farming methods.... [and] creates a growing gap in the earning power of men and women" (Thomson, 1990, p. 14).

In many developing countries, the move to provide women with educational opportunities equal to those of men could also have an important impact, not only in terms of migration for educational reasons or to secure better jobs but also by encouraging individualism and innovative behaviour in dealing with sociocultural norms and traditions.

In Malaysia, where rural-rural migration is still the dominant type in internal flows, most rural-rural female migrants move in association with other migrants because only families qualify for Government-sponsored land settlement schemes. The criteria for selection of families participating in those schemes also determine the types of women likely to be involved in such migration—they must come from poor Malay families with an agricultural background, little or no land and a large family size. In addition, because the land cannot be subdivided and only one child can inherit, there is an in-built impetus for the out-migration of offspring, particularly daughters, who are unlikely to inherit and have limited employment opportunities within the settlements (Chan and Lim, 1980). In Malaysia, the Government's New Economic Policy for ethnic restructuring, which is directed to eliminating the identification of race with occupation and location, has favoured Malays over other groups and has provided various incentives for them to migrate from rural to urban areas. Although the implications of the New Economic Policy for migration may not be obviously sex-selective, they help explain the relatively more rapid increase of female rural-urban migration among Malays than among other ethnic groups (Lim, 1989).

Not only discriminatory institutional factors shape female migration; more gender-neutral institutional provisions can also have an impact. The availability of family planning services in rural areas, for instance, may eventually reduce migration pressures since female migrants tend to come from larger than average families (various studies in Malaysia show that the large majority of young female migrants come from families with more than six members, Lim, 1989). On the other hand, the mobility of women with high fertility is likely to be constrained by the presence of several children (Findley and Williams, 1991). Thus, the success of family planning programmes in Thailand may have had a substantial effect in freeing married women in rural areas to move to urban centres.

Institutional arrangements in places of destination may be particularly important for young, single female migrants. Provision, whether by Governments or employers, of subsidized and supervised accommodation and public transport facilities not only increases the attraction of those places but makes parents more willing to permit the autonomous migration of their young daughters (Lim, 1984). The extent to which neighbourhood institutions (such as social clubs, mothers' clubs and day-care centres), whether formal or informal, exist to facilitate the adjustment and adaptation of female migrants would also determine the evolution of migration as information is filtered back to the places of origin.

Social or kinship networks and informal arrangements, especially in ethnic enclaves, are institutional structures providing crucial assistance to migrants, whether in terms of accommodation or of job placement. The role of social networks is particularly important in fostering female migration, since the presence of kin at destination provides a guarantee for the well-being of women moving on their own. Furthermore, to the extent that networks facilitate the chain migration of family groups, they also promote the associational migration of women. In places of origin too, the presence of extended kinship groups may facilitate female migration by allowing women to leave their children behind while they migrate on their own.

Religion is another institutional factor affecting a woman's propensity to migrate through the internalization of values or norms concerning the roles and status of women *vis-à-vis* men through a system of beliefs. Furthermore, in some contexts, religion also has an impact as the basis of law or other social institutions that define or govern the rights, duties or obligations of women. The more encompassing the religious laws are in everyday life, the more closely religious precepts coincide with customary cultural socialization or the more religion bolsters traditional structures of patriarchy, the greater the underlying influence of religion is likely to be on female migration.

The Muslim religion, for instance, institutionalizes the inferior position of women. Thus, the Muslim law of inheritance entitles a daughter to only half of what is due a son and a widow to a quarter of her deceased husband's estate if there are no children and one eighth if there are. Because of their limited rights to resources, Muslim women may be prompted to migrate. Muslim law allows men to take up to four wives at a time and grants men unilateral power to divorce their wives. Divorced women, whose position may be insecure or unstable in the place of origin, may be induced to migrate. *Khalwat* laws (those prohibiting close physical proximity in a secluded place between a Muslim man and women who are not his wives) explain why Muslim parents are reluctant to allow young women to leave the protection of their homes. The custom of purdah, that is, of secluding or segregating women from public life and confining them to the protection of their homes, clearly restricts female mobility. Subtler influences may exist. A religion that sanctifies marriage and imposes censure on the single state institutionalizes the position of women as economic dependants, thus leaving little scope for women to engage in independent migration-related behaviour.

The socio-cultural influences

The basic structural determinants discussed so far relate to the economic motives for female migration. Although the economic motives tend to be stronger in South-eastern Asia than in many other parts of the developing world, they are closely intertwined with social motivations. In Southern Asia, women are more likely to move for family reasons (Findley and Williams, 1991), with mobility patterns shaped by social norms and traditions which define women's roles and responsibilities both within their families and in the broader society.

Especially because gender is a social construct, its underlying sociocultural determinants cannot be ignored. These determinants can be identified broadly in terms of social systems of gender roles and relations; sociocultural norms, values and expectations that either directly or indirectly sanction or interdict the migration of men or that of women. These normative factors tend to be particularly strong in traditional or religious societies. The more traditional the society, the stronger the pressure of expectations concerning the roles of women and the greater the social influence on the resources and satisfactions that women derive or the stresses that they experience in what they do or are able to do with their lives.

In highly traditional and patriarchal societies, where the position of women is subordinate, women are likely to take part mostly in associational migration decided by the patriarch or other male family members. Thus, as Japan became industrialized, migration decisions tended to be familial rather than individual because "the codified household law prohibited a change of residence without the consent of the head of household" (Taeuber, 1970, p. 378). In India, the dominance of women in rural-rural flows has been attributed to village exogamy and patrilocal residence, both deriving from a strong patrilineal tradition (Singh, 1984). In Pakistan, where women's movements are constrained and they are supposed to remain under the constant protection of their menfolk, they either remain in the care of their extended families if their husbands migrate or move in association with other family members (Shah, 1984).

In some matrilineal societies, it is expected, prescribed or approved behaviour for male but not female family members to leave their habitual place of residence. In the Minangkabau areas of Indonesia and Malaysia, for instance, the norm is for young men to *merantau* (move around geographically) in search of wealth and experience, a custom that has its roots in the matrilineal social system of inheritance (Hugo, 1981; Lim, Ogawa and Hodge, 1988). Women in those societies, by virtue of their control over property rights, their guardianship of customary laws and their responsibility to care for ancestral spirits, may see their ability to migrate constrained. In northern Thailand, for instance, daughters that have migrated to urban areas have been reluctant to return to inherit the land that traditionally would have been theirs (Findley and Williams, 1991).

In patriarchal systems where there is a clear sexual division of labour, with men assuming all economic roles and women assuming only domestic and child-care roles, the autonomous migration of women tends to be constrained. On the other hand, the desire to escape such role constraints and the limitations imposed by their subordinate position *vis-à-vis* men may induce women to migrate. Thus, young and single Malay women that had migrated to urban areas reported that the second most important reason for migrating was to achieve personal freedom and break away from the traditional roles, norms and values which dictate that Malay women in rural areas be obedient to their parents and elders, docile and gentle in their manners and efficient in carrying out their domestic chores and that their freedom be restricted until they are married (Ariffin, 1980).

A wide array of values or norms, although not directly defining migration behaviour, can impinge upon the individual's evaluation of migration as an option or his or her ability to migrate. In Papua New Guinea, for example, the range of social attitudes that constrain the migration of women includes:

"...a preference for girls to retain their traditional roles as gardeners and homemakers, limited finance for education, the belief that it is a waste of time and money to educate girls, the view that boys are more dispensable in the village than their hardworking sisters, the fear that girls may 'play around' and become pregnant or marry outside their communities with a consequent loss of control over marriage exchanges and brideprice payments or, finally, concern that girls will enter the westernized urban world and adopt unacceptable attitudes of behavior." (Connell, 1984, p. 966)

Sociocultural norms and prescriptions with regard to the role of women as daughters also influence their migration motivations and behaviour. In Thailand, gratitude and obedience are stressed as a daughter's virtues; to repay parents, especially by looking after them in their old age, is still very much part of a Thai woman's psyche. For a majority of young Thai women, migration is motivated by the desire to repay their parents.

For women more than men, sociocultural customs and traditions surrounding marriage are important. Where tradition decrees that a woman must marry into her husband's group as an outsider, marriage usually entails migration for the woman. In some societies, however, the man moves in with his wife's family. Where it is customary for the elders to arrange marriages, as in the South Pacific, women may choose to migrate in order to escape such marriages (Connell, 1984). Migration may also be used to evade family or church pressures that customarily proscribe separation or divorce. In some countries, divorced women are, in fact, expected to migrate (Hugo, 1981).

Once married, whether the woman moves with her husband in associational migration, stays behind in the place of origin when her husband migrates alone or engages in autonomous migration depends upon the cultural acceptability of the separation of husband and wife. Prolonged separation of spouses appears more acceptable in developing than developed countries, in part because the harsh realities of poverty may demand such separation. Thus, although middle-class Sri Lankan men claimed that they would never consider sending their wives to work as maids in another man's home, poor Sri Lankan families could not afford the luxury of conforming to social norms and had allowed their women to work even in homes overseas (Brochmann, 1987). Whether women accompany their husbands may also depend upon whether women have access to their own resources and upon the relative importance of a woman's economic role in the place of origin and her expected role in the place of destination.

D. POLICY IMPLICATIONS AND RECOMMENDATIONS

The advantage of focusing on the structural determinants of female migration at the macrolevel is that they are potentially amenable to policy manipulation. Policy implications, however, are complex because of the inevitable linkages between female migration, women's status and the role of women in the development process. In addition, the analysis of policy implications is complicated because the implementation of development strategies is itself affected by legal or institutional factors that are, in turn, products of the sociocultural context. In so far as gender inequalities in both places of origin and destination shape patterns of female migration, policy should be directed to eliminating those inequalities rather than to controlling migration. Even though the number of female migrants has increased in most countries, the gender biases of development policies and the pervasiveness of sociocultural norms that foster gender inequalities have meant that migration has in many cases led women to exchange a subordinate place within the family in the area of origin for an equally subordinate place in the workplace in the area of destination.

No general recommendations can be made a priori as to whether it is desirable to develop policies to stimulate or curb female migration without a clear assessment at the country level of the implications of territorial mobility on women's position *vis-à-vis* that of men, their occupational mobility, social freedom, access to and control over resources etc. Territorial mobility that results in increased female vulnerability to exploitation or that taps women's contribution to development but denies them its full benefits should be subject to government intervention. On the other hand, policies for the integration of women into mainstream development should not be formulated without taking into account their implications for female migration.

Given such complex interlinkages, the most effective strategy is for policy to focus on the structural factors underlying gender inequalities, so as to eliminate or attenuate them while at the same time enhancing women's human resource potential and their effective participation in development. In doing so, it is necessary to go beyond migration-directed policies and to consider those to empower women, modify gender relations and improve the conditions of women's labour force participation. Assuming that migration involves rational decision-making, if greater gender equality were achieved, the consequences of female migration would be more likely to be beneficial for the persons involved.

Because various forms of discrimination against women are a function of gender rather than migrant status, the policy implications discussed below apply to both migrant and non-migrant women. Even among female migrants, some groups, such as the young, recent migrants or those engaged in prostitution, are more vulnerable than others and would require special programmes.

Where Governments have formulated policies directed specifically to influencing migration, their goal has generally been to achieve a redistribution of the population that would facilitate the national or regional development objectives of the country, but there has been no consideration of their differential impact on men and women. To be effective, such policies need to be sensitive to women's motivations and ability to respond to migration incentives. Migration-directed policies have tended to deal with areal characteristics, but their intended impacts have often not been achieved or have been distorted by the underlying structural factors. Thus, the creation of job opportunities in a region may have failed to attract female migrants because insufficient attention was given to the sociocultural norms shaping the perception of such opportunities and the ability of women to respond to them. In addition, the aims of migration-directed policies are often subverted by other government policies and programmes. It is clear that greater awareness of the underlying structural factors and sensitivity to gender issues would improve the efficacy of migration-directed policies.

Of greater importance is to consider the range of Government policies that, without being specifically intended to affect migration, influence it nevertheless, usually by affecting women's status and migration behaviour. Thus, economic growth strategies emphasizing export-oriented industrialization, modern technologies, foreign direct investment and tourism, though undoubtedly having stimulated female migration, have been advocated on the basis of the availability of cheap and controllable female workers, many of whom are migrants. Such a rationale, by exploiting women's disadvantaged position, helps perpetuate it. In implementing such economic growth strategies it is essential that the focus be shifted from reliance upon the alleged "feminine" qualities and assumed elasticity of female labour supply to the need to enhance the human resource potentials of women, especially those who are migrants, and to ensure that the conditions of their mobility and subsequent participation in the labour force shall not be retrogressive in terms of their position *vis-à-vis* men.

A related requirement is that structural adjustment policies take gender into account by considering explicitly their impact on women. As mentioned above, women have been contributing disproportionately to the process of "invisible adjustment" by increasing their territorial mobility and their labour force participation. However, their vulnerability has also increased as the trend towards the casualization of the labour force and the adoption of flexible work arrangements has involved disproportionate numbers of women. Such trends require that there be constant reviews of formal provisions directed to reducing the inequalities between the sexes and that protective measures be taken to prevent the exploitation of women as their economic roles change.

The need for broader measures to assist female migrants derives also from their changing roles within the family, especially because women, particularly the young, are assuming crucial income-earning responsibilities. In some cases, the remittances sent back by migrant women represent the only monetary income of families in rural areas. Consequently, efforts to improve the labour-market opportunities for women would also have significant effects in improving rural well-being and alleviating poverty in rural areas.

It is also essential to ensure that women shall have equal access to education, employment, ownership of assets (both tangible and intangible), inheritance, credit, training programmes, agricultural extension schemes and subsidies, low-cost housing, sites to ply a trade etc. Changes in that direction would not only increase women's contribution to development but would help obviate the need to migrate in many instances. A more equal access to agricultural credit and training, for example, would make it easier for female heads of household to stay on the farm instead of migrating in search of non-agricultural jobs.

Access to adequate family planning services would also contribute to the well-being of women in general and to the reduction of migration pressures in the medium term, especially where migrants are more likely to belong to large families. Given that in some countries increasing numbers of female migrants are young and entering the family formation stage of their life, facilitating their access to family planning services would also be important, particularly because migrant women are more likely to be open to new possibilities and may help diffuse information in their places of origin.

Although government policies are less likely to influence directly the sociocultural forces shaping female migration and in most cases changes may occur only in the long run, efforts must nevertheless be made to modify them because they exert a crucial influence in determining the roles and status of women and thereby have a pervasive effect on the eventual outcomes of purely socio-economic policies intended to benefit women. To influence such sociocultural factors, use of education and the mass media is recommended, not just by providing women with more equal access to educational opportunities and realistic information concerning opportunity and constraint structures in different places but by using all acceptable means to alter gender relations and especially by raising awareness about the economic roles of women.

REFERENCES

Ariffin, Jamilah (1980). Industrial development in Peninsular Malaysia and rural-urban migration of women workers: impact and implications. *Journal Ekonomi Malaysia* (Kuala Lampur), vol. 1, No. 1.

Ariffin, R. (1985). Retrenchment: an exploratory study of the retrenchment experience of the textile and electronics workers in Penang. Penang: Universiti Sains Malaysia, School of Social Sciences. Mimeographed.

Arizpe, Lourdes (1981). Relay migration and the survival of the peasant household. In *Why People Move: Comparative Perspectives on the Dynamics of Internal Migration*, Jorge Balán, ed. Paris: United Nations Educational, Scientific and Cultural Organization.

Behrman, Jere R., and Barbara L. Wolfe (1984). Micro determinants of female migration in a developing country: labour market, demographic marriage market and economic marriage market incentives. In *Research in Population Economics*, T. Paul Schultz and Kenneth Wolpin, eds., vol. 5. Greenwich, Connecticut: JAI Press.

Benería, Lourdes, and Martha Roldán (1987). *The Crossroads of Class and Gender: Industrial Homework, Subcontracting and Household Dynamics in Mexico City*. Chicago, Illinois: The University of Chicago Press.

Bilsborrow, Richard E., A. S. Oberai and Guy Standing (1984). *Migration Surveys in Low-Income Countries: Guidelines for Survey and Questionnaire Design*. Beckenham, Kent, United Kingdom; and Sidney, Australia: Croom Helm.

Brochmann, Grete (1987). *Escape Route to Dependency? Female Migration from Sri Lanka to the Middle East*. PRIO Working Paper, No. 5. Oslo: International Peace Research Institute.

Casterline, John B., ed. (1985). *The Collection and Analysis of Community Data*. Voorburg, Netherlands: International Statistical Institute.

Chan, Paul (1981). Migration-related policies in Peninsular Malaysia: an evaluation. In *Population Mobility and Development: Southeast Asia and the Pacific*, G. W. Jones and H. V. Richter, eds. Development Studies Centre, Monograph No. 27. Canberra: The Australian National University.

_____, and Lin Lean Lim (1980). Report on ASEAN migration in relation to rural development: case study of migrant settlers in three land schemes in Peninsular Malaysia. Kuala Lumpur: University of Malaya, Faculty of Economics and Administration.

Collier, William L. (1981). Agricultural evolution in Java. In *Agricultural and Rural Development in Indonesia*, Gary E. Hansen, ed. Boulder, Colorado: Westview Press.

Connell, John (1984). Status or subjugation? Women, migration and development in the South Pacific. *International Migration Review* (Staten Island, New York), vol. 18, No. 4 (Winter), pp. 964-983.

Corner, Lorraine (1981). Linkages, reciprocity and remittances: the impact of rural outmigration on Malaysian rice villages. In *Population Mobility and Development: Southeast Asia and the Pacific*, G. W. Jones and H. V. Richter, eds. Development Studies Centre, Monograph No. 27. Canberra: The Australian National University.

Eelens, F., and Toon Schampers (1989). Survival migration: the Sri Lankan case. In *Women, Migrants and Tribals: Survival Strategies in Asia*, G. K. Lieten, O. Nieuwenhuys and L. Schenk-Sandbergen, eds. New Delhi: Manohar India.

Eisold, E. (1984). *Young Women Workers in Export Industries: The Case of the Semiconductor Industry in Southeast Asia*. World Employment Programme, Research Working Paper. Geneva: International Labour Office.

Findley, Sally E., and Linda Williams (1991). *Women Who Go and Women Who Stay: Reflections of Family Migration Processes in a Changing World*. Population and Labour Policies Programme, Working Paper No. 176. Geneva: International Labour Office.

Freedman, Ronald (1974). *Community-level Data in Fertility Surveys*. World Fertility Survey Occasional Papers, No. 8. Voorburg, Netherlands: International Statistical Institute.

_____ (1979). *Issues in the Comparative Analysis of World Fertility Survey Data*. East-West Population Institute Paper, No. 62. Honolulu, Hawaii: East-West Center.

Gardner, Robert W. (1981). Macrolevel influences on the migration decision process. In *Migration Decision Making: Multidisciplinary Approaches to Microlevel Studies in Developed and Developing Countries*, Gordon F. De Jong and Robert W. Gardner, eds. New York: Pergamon Press.

Germani, Gino (1965). Migration and acculturation. In *Handbook for Social Research in Urban Areas*, Philip M. Hauser, ed. Technology and Society Series, No. 13. Paris: United Nations Educational, Scientific and Cultural Organization.

Harbison, Sarah F. (1981). Family structure and family strategy in migration decision making. In *Migration Decision Making Multidisciplinary Approaches to Microlevel Studies in Developed and Developing Countries*, Gordon F. De Jong and Robert W. Gardner, eds. New York: Pergamon Press.

Hugo, Graeme J. (1981). Village-community ties, village norms, and ethnic and social networks: a review of evidence from the third world. In *Migration Decision Making: Multidisciplinary Approaches to Microlevel Studies in Developed and Developing Countries*, Gordon F. De Jong and Robert W. Gardner, eds. New York: Pergamon Press.

_____ (1993). Migrant women in developing countries. Chapter III in the present volume.

International Labour Organisation (various years). *Yearbook of Labour Statistics*. Geneva: International Labour Office.

Jelin, Elizabeth (1977). Migration and labour force participation of Latin American women: the domestic servants in the cities. In *Women and National Development*, The Wellesley Editorial Committee, ed. Chicago, Illinois: The University of Chicago Press.

Jones, Gavin W., ed. (1984). *Women in the Urban and Industrial Workforce: Southeast and East Asia*. Development Studies Centre, Monograph No. 33. Canberra: The Australian National University Press.

Khoo, Siew-Ean (1987). Development and women's participation in the modern economy: Asia and the Pacific. In *Women's Economic Participation in Asia and the Pacific*. Bangkok: United Nations Economic and Social Commission for Asia and the Pacific.

Lele, Una (1986). Women and structural transformation. *Economic Development and Cultural Change* (Chicago, Illinois), vol. 34, No. 2 (January), pp. 195-221.

Lerman, Charles (1983). Sex-differential pattern of circular migration: a case study of Semarang, Indonesia. *Peasant Studies* (Salt Lake City, Utah), vol. 10, No. 4 (Summer), pp. 251-269.

Lim, Lin Lean (1984). Towards meeting the needs of urban female factory workers in Peninsular Malaysia. In *Women in the Urban and Industrial Workforce: Southeast and East Asia*, Gavin W. Jones, ed. Development Studies Centre, Monograph No. 33. Canberra: The Australian National University.

_____ (1988a). Effects of women's position on migration. In *Conference on Women's Position and Demographic Change in the Course of Development, Oslo, 1988: Solicited Papers*. Liège: International Union for the Scientific Study of Population.

_____ (1988b). *Economic Dynamism and Structural Transformation in the Asian Pacific Rim Countries: Contributions of the Second Sex*. NUPRI Research Paper Series, No. 45. Tokyo, Japan: Nihon University, Population Research Institute.

_____ (1989). *Female Migration*. Report submitted to the Economic Planning Unit, Prime Minister's Department Malaysia for the Human Resources Development Plan. Kuala Lumpur: University of Malaya, Faculty of Economics and Administration.

_____ (1990). The feminization of labour in the Asian Pacific Rim Countries: from contributing to economic dynamism to bearing the brunt of structural adjustments. Paper presented at the Nihon University International Symposium on Sources of Economic Dynamism in the Asian and Pacific Region: A Human Resources Approach, Tokyo, November 1989.

_____ (1991). International labour migration in Asia: patterns, implications and policies. Paper prepared for the ECE/UNFPA Informal Expert Group Meeting on International Migration, Geneva, 16-19 July.

_____, and R. Wihtol (1991). The sex sector: prostitution, development and gender relations in South-east Asia. Bangkok: International Labour Office. Mimeographed.

Lim, Lin Lean, N. Ogawa and R. W. Hodge (1988c). The demographic impacts of an integrated agricultural development project in Peninsular Malaysia. Tokyo: Nihon University, Population Research Institute.

Mabogunje, Akin L. (1970). Systems approach to a theory of rural-urban migration. *Geographical Analysis* (Columbus, Ohio), vol. 2, No. 1 (January), pp. 1-18.

McNicoll, Geoffrey (1985). The nature of institutional and community effects on demographic behaviour: a discussion. In *The Collection and Analysis of Community Data*, John B. Casterline, ed. Voorburg, Netherlands: International Statistical Institute.

Netting, Robert M., Richard R. Wilk and Eric J. Arnould, eds. (1984). *Households: Comparative and Historical Studies of the Domestic Group*. Berkeley and London: University of California Press.

Phongpaichit, Pasuk (1982). *From Peasant Girls to Bangkok Masseuses*. Women, Work and Development Series, No. 2. Geneva: International Labour Office.

Pryor, Robin J. (1975). *The Motivation of Migration*. Studies in Migration and Urbanization, No. 1. Canberra: The Australian National University.

Redclift, Nanneke, and Enzo Mingione, eds. (1985). *Beyond Employment: Household, Gender and Subsistence*. New York and Oxford: Basil Blackwell.

Salaff, Janet (1981). *Working Daughters of Hong Kong: Filial Piety or Power in the Family?* Cambridge, United Kingdom; and New York: Cambridge University Press.

Salih, K., and others (1985). Young workers and urban services: a case study of Penang, Malaysia. Final report, Participatory Urban Services Project. Penang: Universiti Sains Malaysia.

Sassen-Koob, Saskia (1984). Notes on the incorporation of third world women into wage labor through immigration and off-shore production. *International Migration Review* (Staten Island, New York), vol. 18, No. 4 (Winter), pp. 1144-1167.

Shah, Nasra M. (1984). The female migrant in Pakistan. In *Women in the Cities of Asia: Migration and Urban Adaptation*, James T. Fawcett, Siew-Ean Khoo and Peter C. Smith, eds. Boulder, Colorado: Westview Press.

Simmons, Alan B., Sergio Diaz-Briquets and Aprodicio A. Laquian (1977). *Social Change and Internal Migration: A Review of Findings from Africa, Asia and Latin America.* Ottawa, Canada: International Development Research Centre.

Singh, Andrea Menefee (1984). Rural-to-urban migration of women in India: patterns and implications. In *Women in the Cities of Asia: Migration and Urban Adaptation*, James T. Fawcett, Siew-Ean Khoo and Peter C. Smith, eds. Boulder, Colorado: Westview Press.

Standing, Guy (1989). *Global Feminisation through Flexible Labour*. Labour Market Analysis and Employment Planning Working Paper, No. 31. Geneva: International Labour Office.

Taeuber, Irene B. (1970). Family, migration and industrialization in Japan. In *Readings in the Sociology of Migration*, Clifford J. Jansen, ed. Oxford and New York: Pergamon Press.

Thadani, Veena N., and Michael P. Todaro (1979). *Female Migration in Developing Countries: A Framework for Analysis.* Center for Policy Studies, Working Paper No. 47. New York: The Population Council.

Thomson, S. (1990). Gender issues in Thailand's development. Paper prepared for the United Nations Development Programme. Bangkok: Gender and Development Research Institute.

Trager, Lillian (1984). Family strategies and the migration of women: migrants to Dagupan City, Philippines. *International Migration Review* (Staten Island, New York), vol. 18, No. 4 (Winter), pp. 1264-1278.

Vickers, Jeanne (1991). *Women and the World Economic Crisis*. London; and Atlantic Highlands, New Jersey: Zed Books.

Ware, Helen (1981). *Women, Demography and Development*. Canberra, Australia: The Australian National University.

Wood, Charles H. (1982). Equilibrium and historical-structural perspectives on migration. *International Migration Review* (Staten Island, New York), vol. 16, No. 2 (Summer), pp. 298-319.

United Nations (1986). *World Survey on the Role of Women in Development*. Sales No. E.89.IV.2.

_____ (1989). *World Survey on the Role of Women in Development*. Sales No. E.86.IV.3.

United Nations Population Fund (1990). *Incorporating Women into Population and Development: Knowing Why and Knowing How*. New York.

Young, Kate (1982). The creation of a relative surplus population: a case study from Mexico. In *Women and Development: The Sexual Division of Labour in Rural Societies*, Lourdes Benería, ed. New York: Praeger.

Young, M. L., and K. Salih (1986). Industrialization, retrenchment and household processes: implications of the recession. Paper presented at the Himpunan Sains Sosial IV, Persatuan Sains Sosial Malaysia, Universiti Malaya, Kuala Lumpur.

Youssef, Nadia, Mayra Buvinic and Ayse Kudat (1979). *Women in Migration: A Third World Focus*. A study by the International Center for Research on Women. Washington, D.C.: United States Agency for International Development.

XII. THE DETERMINANTS OF FEMALE MIGRATION FROM A MULTILEVEL PERSPECTIVE

Philip Guest*

Migration research has traditionally ignored gender issues. Female migration has either been excluded completely from consideration or has been labelled "associational migration", with the implicit assumption that through such a labelling exercise female migration has been adequately explained. Although the migration of women has begun to be treated as an independent area of study (Fawcett, Khoo and Smith, 1984; Recchini de Lattes, 1989), analysis has remained grounded within the dominant perspectives that have structured the study of migration in general. At the microlevel, this view has entailed an emphasis on the human capital attributes of women, while at the macrolevel, the emphasis has been on changes in the spatial distribution of economic opportunities for women.

In both the macro- and the micro-perspective, the processes of economic and social development are important, although often implicit, factors in increasing the incidence of female migration (Skeldon, 1990). At the microlevel, development increases the probabilities of migration by improving the levels of human capital or by encouraging migration in order to improve those levels. At the macrolevel, structural changes that occur unevenly across regions generate spatial inequalities in the location of economic opportunities for women and consequently result in flows of female migrants (Morokvasic, 1984).

The segmentation of migration research between the macrolevel and the microlevel disregards the role that linkages between those levels play in determining migration. Yet, those linkages are particularly important for the study of migration differentials by gender because of the normative constraints on female migration that exist in many societies (Fawcett, Khoo and Smith, 1984; Paralikar, 1991). Norms concerning the economic and familial roles appropriate for women structure access to economic opportunities and hence have a major influence on female migration patterns.

A "multilevel" framework provides a basis for incorporating effects at different levels, because its aim is to specify not only how structural factors constrain or channel behaviour or how individual attributes motivate behaviour but also how linkages between macrolevel and microlevel factors determine behaviour (Bilsborrow, Oberai and Standing, 1984; Massey, 1990). A multilevel approach involves frameworks for analysis that include concepts or variables at more than one level of aggregation. It does not, however, entail the development of yet another theoretical orientation since migration has often been, implicitly or explicitly, investigated within a multilevel framework. Thus, macrolevel analyses of the determinants of migration based on an economic framework have used regional or areal variables (such as unemployment rates) while couching explanations in terms of individual or household responses to spatially structured inequalities (Todaro, 1976). Historical-structuralist approaches have also focused on the effects of political and economic structures on individual motivations (Wood, 1981; Portes and Walton, 1981). Microeconomic theories of migration have acknowledged the importance of spatial inequalities in opportunities while focusing on the way in which people respond to those inequalities (DaVanzo, 1981).

However, the transition from theory to empirical research has been slow and fitful, with only a few studies yielding results that help specify further the interrelations between different levels of analysis. Microlevel studies of mobility have helped by stressing the roles of community characteristics in determining levels and patterns of migration (Hugo, 1978; Roberts, 1982; Chapman, 1988; Guest, 1989), but most statistical analyses have concentrated on a single level. Thus, research has proceeded under the implicit assumption that processes operating at other levels (other than that at which variables are actually being

---

*Institute for Population and Social Research, Mahidol University, Bangkok, Thailand.

investigated) are given or can somehow be abstracted from. In the case of macrolevel analyses, that implies assuming away differences in individual motivations, skill levels or other sources of variation in the way in which people respond to spatial inequalities in opportunities. On the other hand, microlevel analyses fail to recognize attributes of the social setting structure, values and access to opportunities which directly influence migration.

The list of multilevel studies of migration, although still small, has been expanding over the past five years (Brown and Goetz, 1987; Bilsborrow and others, 1987; Findley, 1987; Guest and Praditwong, 1989; Baydar and others, 1990; Brown, 1991). Most have used the individual as the micro-unit and the region as the macro-unit, although Findley (1987) uses families and villages as the micro- and macro-units, respectively. All those studies have in common an explicit focus on how development processes have created differences in the context in which individuals or families reside and the way in which those differences influence migration behaviour.

Few of the multilevel studies mentioned above have considered gender differences in migration decisions. There are, however, theoretical reasons to argue that a multilevel perspective would be particularly useful in understanding gender differences in levels and patterns of mobility (Smith, Khoo and Go, 1984). Those differences cannot be adequately explained by recourse solely to the different attributes of the persons involved or by focusing exclusively on gender-related spatial differences in opportunities.

To understand the determinants of gender differences in migration flows it is necessary to recognize that, within a society, sex roles, although not immutable, are historically determined. Sex roles are expressed within familial and institutional settings that constitute the contexts in which individuals negotiate decisions about behaviour. There are thus two possible sources of variation in individual behaviour: differences in individual and family characteristics that determine decision-making power; and differences in the institutional setting. Institutional sources of variation may be historically determined or may result from differences in the pace and type of change occurring in different areas of a country.

The institutions that involve primary social contact are the family and community. These institutions can be expected to exert direct influences on mobility processes. Political and economic structures of societies, or even the position of a society within the international division of labour, can also influence migration (Young, 1982). Because much of the impact of societal processes can be analysed through their effects at the community and family levels, the latter two proximate institutional levels are the focus of this paper.

Migration is only one of several responses to conditions of structural change (Bilsborrow, 1987; Guest, 1989). The conditions leading to migration may also differ considerably among women. Migration for marriage or in association with other family members is likely to respond to different forces from individual migration undertaken primarily for the economic gain of the migrant and his/her family. However, central to all decisions concerning whether migration is the most appropriate response are societal norms relating to the conditions under which moves can be made. Since these norms are maintained and reinforced at the community level and internalized within the family, multilevel models are appropriate for the study of migration in general and of female migration in particular.

A. The normative basis for migration

The concepts of norms, values, roles and status are useful in providing a framework for understanding how female migration is socially structured. A norm may be defined as a socially shared expectation of how a person should behave in a given situation. Norms are often paired with values, which refer to general societal goals. Norms and values relate to specific social roles carried out by individuals, and status is obtained from the satisfactory performance of those roles. All people participate in a number of roles during their life; however, the value placed on each role may differ by sex. In most societies, the economic role is seen as paramount for men. The result is that men are generally responsive to the changing spatial distribution of economic opportunities and there are limited normative barriers to their movement. Because research to date has mainly focused on male migration, scant attention has been given to the normative context of migration decision-making.

For women, however, normative influences on migration are of particular importance. The roles undertaken by women are usually more complex than those of men because of the combination of reproductive and productive functions. Oppong (1983) identifies seven roles of women: parental; occupational; conjugal; domestic; kin; community; and individual. The norms related to the performance of each of those roles have implications for mobility. Furthermore, there may be variations in the strength of social norms related to mobility for the different roles of women.

Societal concerns about the appropriateness of allowing unattached women to live away from the immediate control of the family or the community are at the root of many norms constraining female mobility (Boserup, 1970). In extreme cases, this concern can lead to the seclusion of women (Pittin, 1984; Singh, 1984). However, in many societies where control over the functions of women is strong, marriage norms of village exogamy and patrilocal residence, such as those found in many parts of Southern Asia, ensure that every female shall migrate at least once. In this situation, female migration is synonymous with the transfer of roles centred on the family of origin to roles under the control of the family of procreation.

The degree to which norms vary over a woman's life cycle is a factor determining the age selectivity of female migration. For example, Khoo and Pirie (1984) note that, traditionally, young Malay rural women were kept at home to ensure their virginity and to make use of their labour. However, older Malay women, whose main reproductive roles were completed, were expected to engage in trade; and their mobility, although mainly short term, was therefore socially sanctioned. A weakening of the constraints on the mobility of young Malay rural women has taken place in recent years through a reduction in the domestic demand for their labour and through increases in female factory employment in urban areas.

Strong normative influences on the mobility of women are a reflection of the low status and lack of decision-making power of women. In many societies, women's interests are subordinated to those of their families of origin or their families of procreation. Such subordination often restricts the mobility of women, especially where emphasis is on their reproductive roles. Those roles, which revolve around maintaining the domestic unit, may tie women to the area of origin. Skeldon (1990), commenting on the very low levels of female migration in Papua New Guinea, argues that the important female role of maintaining the family agricultural holdings constrains their mobility while at the same time it frees men to circulate.

A lack of decision-making power among women can sometimes lead to high levels of female mobility. The most obvious case is marriage migration, in which a patrilocal marriage system operating in conjunction with village exogamy forces all women to move at least once in their lives. Movement with family members may also be a result of strong normative pressures which reflect the dependent role of women. There is almost no research examining the degree of influence women have in decisions about their migration when it occurs with other family members (cf. Riley and Gardner, 1993). McDevitt and Gadalla (1985), in a study of migration plans of rural Egyptian couples, found that a wife's intentions to move were strongly associated with her husband's prior migration experience and his financial gain from his previous move. Conversely, a husband's intention to move was not affected by his wife's characteristics. These results suggest that in that context the interests of the husband were dominant in migration plans.

Even where a woman migrates by herself and states that she moved for economic reasons, her movement does not denote autonomy in the migration decision-making process. As Huang (1983) notes in a study of single female migrants to Taipei, in almost 90 per cent of the moves the parents of the women were involved in the daughter's decision to move. Families may foster the migration of women precisely because their dependent status makes daughters more likely to acquiesce to the authority of the head of the family.

In relating women's status as a contextual variable to migration, the links between aspects of status and the roles of individuals are paramount. For example, in societies in which the prestige of women is high, where women have relative autonomy in decision-making and control over resources, a balance in production and reproduction roles is more likely. In societies where women's production roles are considered most important but are not tied to the place of origin, normative restrictions on their movement are likely to be fewer and migration is more likely to be an option than where these roles are tied to the place of origin.

Safilios-Rothschild (1982) notes that women's status interacts with household characteristics to determine the position of individual women. For example, women from households in higher economic strata are more likely to have high prestige and autonomy. If such a position leads to greater access to education or changes in the types of roles valued, it may result in important class-selectivity patterns of female migration. For example, many studies have found that the migration of women is positively associated with their level of education (Shah, 1984; Khoo and others, 1984; see also Findley and Williams, 1991).

This finding of a positive relation is not universal, however, as Bilsborrow and others (1987) found that the least educated women were most likely to migrate from rural to urban areas of Ecuador. They interpret this finding in terms of the nature of the employment opportunities available for women in the Ecuadorian labour-market. Such findings draw attention to the interplay between the roles of women, the distribution of employment opportunities and women's migration. In situations where employment opportunities for women are spatially concentrated, economic necessity may force women to migrate in contravention to prevailing community norms regarding the mobility of women (Findley and Diallo, 1993). Women from higher socio-economic classes, however, can afford the luxury of immobility (Hetler, 1990; Lessinger, 1990).

It has also been argued that low levels of female status might motivate women to migrate in order to gain autonomy (Boserup, 1970; Ware, 1981; Williams, 1987). However, Collins (1983) interprets low female mobility among the Aymara Indians of Peru as a result of a desire to avoid a situation in which their labour would be valued less than that of men, thus suggesting that fear of a decline in status may also sometimes inhibit the migration of women.

B. Economic development and female migration

Female migration will occur in response to employment opportunities if: (*a*) there is a significant demand for female labour; (*b*) there are inequalities in the spatial distribution of employment opportunities for women; (*c*) potential migrants are aware of opportunities; and (*d*) migration is acceptable in terms of prevailing norms concerning the roles of women.

It is generally agreed that economic development, although at first reducing employment opportunities for women in agriculture and cottage industries, ultimately increases their employment by creating new opportunities in the service and manufacturing sectors (Boserup, 1970; Acevedo, 1990; Presser and Kishor, 1991). Both in Asia, particularly South-eastern and Eastern Asia, and in Latin America, the concentration of opportunities for female employment in urban areas has fuelled large-scale rural-urban migration of women (Smith, Khoo and Go, 1984).

The opportunities for female wage employment have been increasing rapidly over the past two decades. Standing (1989) refers to the 1980s as a period of feminization of the global labour force, brought about by the deregulation of labour-markets that has prompted employers to hire unskilled female workers. Cross-national research by Schultz (1990) indicates that the absorption of women into wage labour has been slow in regulated labour-markets, such as those prevailing in Southern and Western Asia. Although levels of female labour migration are relatively low in Southern and Western Asia, high levels of female migration in many Latin America countries have been stimulated by employment opportunities in the service sector, particularly in domestic service (Recchini de Lattes, 1989). In Puerto Rico, there has been some increase in female employment in the industrial sector, but most of the growth in the female labour force has also come in the services and government sectors (Falcón, 1991). In Eastern and South-eastern Asia, however, a substantial component of female migration is associated with employment in manufacturing (Khoo and others, 1984). Women are preferred because they can be paid lower wages than men, are assumed to be more docile and are considered better suited to perform repetitive tasks (Ong, 1987; Porpora, Lim and Prommas, 1989; Skeldon, 1990; Lim, 1993). The expansion of the service sector in urban areas has also increased the demand for female migrant labour (Standing, 1989).

In many developing countries, a ready supply of female labour has resulted from structural changes in agriculture and its interrelations with the sexual division of labour in the agricultural sector (Lele, 1986). In general, increasing productivity in that sector is associated with decreasing opportunities of wage employment in agriculture for women and increasing ones for men (Schultz, 1990).

Changes in the location of employment opportunities have sometimes greatly influenced norms affecting female migration. Normative constraints on female migration are easier to maintain when the productive roles available to women can be carried out in the same location as can their domestic roles. As Khoo and Pirie (1984) state with respect to the weakening of norms constraining the mobility of unmarried rural Malay women, change occurred only after the mechanization of agriculture had reduced the economic roles of women in rural areas. At the same time, urban employment opportunities for women expanded, perhaps in part to take advantage of the pool of unemployed rural female labour. Ong (1987) describes how some rural parents, in anticipation of remittances, now actually encourage their daughters to migrate in search of factory employment.

However, the normative context of female migration is not determined solely by the distribution of economic opportunities resulting from economic development. Blanc-Szanton (1990) argues that in Thailand agricultural transformations and changes in inheritance laws have changed the norms of post-marital residence, thereby stimulating the rural-urban migration of women. She describes how in traditional Thai rural society men would migrate into the households of their parents-in-law. Upon the death of the parents, one daughter, usually the youngest, would inherit the house and agricultural holdings. Recent legal changes requiring equal inheritance among all children thus reduced the control of resources by women and also reduced their agrarian roles, forcing them to seek employment in other areas.

Norms that structure the role of women in relation to their families of origin and procreation may undergo fundamental changes in the process of development. Strauch (1984) describes how in traditional Chinese society, wives were expected to reside with their husband's parents and contribute to the maintenance of the parents-in-law's household. In analysing the situation in two ethnic Chinese communities, in Hong Kong and Malaysia, Strauch notes that the increasing availability of urban jobs has led to the separation of sons from rural-based parents, which in many cases has resulted in the associated migration of wives. This process has had another effect on migration by maintaining linkages between married women and their families of origin. When a woman lived with her parents-in-law, she was economically and, in many cases, socially lost to her own parents. Linkages are stronger between parents and daughters when the daughter resides apart from her parents-in-law. According to Strauch, parents are likely to encourage their daughter to migrate from the home of her parents-in-law to join her husband in urban areas because such a move increases the likelihood that they will receive remittances. Also, an urban-based married daughter can provide her siblings with help if they should later migrate to urban areas.

The role of social networks in providing means to modify traditional norms affecting female mobility so as to respond to locational changes in employment opportunities cannot be underestimated. Social networks play a special role in facilitating female migration since in most societies the migration of women is constrained because of fears with regard both to the presumed vulnerability of women and to the reduced control over their behaviour. Parents are more likely to allow the migration of single daughters if relatives or friends will house or aid them at destination (Fuller and others, 1983; Huang, 1983; Findley and Diallo, 1993). In India, where there are strong normative pressures against the migration of women for employment purposes, the presence of fellow villagers in the place of destination makes female labour migration possible (Lessinger, 1990), while the movement of women for marriage purposes is related to the presence of networks which allow the identification of suitable spouses. Even in the Philippines, where restrictions on female migration are weaker than in India, social networks play an important role in determining whether migration takes places and to what destination (Trager, 1988).

Social networks facilitating the mobility of individuals typically have both a kin and a community basis. Networks are integrated through the contacts that a family has with friends and kin in potential destinations. Social networks also have an effect at the community level by influencing norms concerning mobility. Once migration has occurred and networks have been established, it is likely that migration may be viewed as an acceptable, even a desirable, mode of behaviour. Such normative changes can give rise to distinctive patterns of migration by sex, as the case of Indonesia illustrates. Whereas both Hugo (1978) and Guest (1989) found very low participation of women in temporary migration in Western and Central Java, respectively, in the district of Nguter, located within five kilometres of the site studied by Guest, there were very high levels of female circulation to Jakarta. Hetler (1990) describes similar patterns within the same general area. In Nguter, the circulation of women to Jakarta to sell *jamu* (traditional Javanese herbal medicines) has been established over generations and knowledge from family and friends about accommodations and suitable areas for trading has reduced the risk of migration. It had become expected that women would migrate while men would remain behind.

The stage of development of social networks is an important factor in determining the sex selectivity of migrants. Men are likely to move first and as networks become established, more women tend to move (Zoomers, 1986; Breman, 1990). This pattern is associated with the level of risk that is deemed appropriate for the respective sexes in the migration process. Where social networks are rudimentary, migrants may find it difficult to obtain accommodation and suitable employment. But when networks have developed sufficiently to reduce uncertainty about what to expect upon migration, women are more likely to move.

The role of social networks in generating and sustaining migration flows has not been lost on employers of female labour. In many circumstances, recruiters have been used by companies to secure the needed female migrant workers (Standing, 1986). Once flows have been established, social and family ties can normally ensure that migration shall continue (Breman, 1990). For the smooth continuation of flows, it is important that employers guarantee the moral well-being of the women recruited. Thus, in a sense, employers take on a quasi-parental role by establishing dormitories for young women and instituting strict rules about what they can do during their free time (Ong, 1987). Such a role serves the interests of employers by ensuring that the migrant labour force shall remain relatively isolated from the receiving community and thus less likely to engage in industrial disputes or organize in labour unions.

The importance of the information and help that social networks provide migrants, particularly women, can have important policy implications. Studying the effects of the control of information on migration patterns in selected Thai villages, Fuller and others (1985) found that supplying information about employment opportunities available in regional urban centres helped direct migration flows to those centres and away from the traditional destination—Bangkok. To the extent that female migrants rely upon social networks to determine where they will move, they may not migrate to those areas where their employment opportunities would be maximized. In a study of Thai women, Leenothai (1991) found that female migration was not responsive to the potential income and occupational characteristics of potential destinations. For example, the income elasticities of the probability of being chosen as a destination were close to zero for most of the destinations considered. Net of the characteristics of potential destinations and individual attributes of women, however, the capital city of Bangkok was the most attractive destination. Leenothai argues that even though the development of regional growth centres and the movement of industry into provinces surrounding Bangkok had increased female wages in those areas, female migration continued to be directed towards Bangkok because of well-established social networks which reduced the uncertainty of migration.

C. COMMUNITY AS CONTEXT

The limited amount of multilevel research that has been conducted on migration has developed from a concern with the effects of location (Brown, 1991) and economic structure. This intellectual history is reflected in the selection of spatial units to define context, the choice of macroeconomic variables to measure aspects of the context and reliance upon distance as a measure of integration between contexts. These developments are theoretically sound when evaluated within the framework of human capital migration theory. As noted earlier, however, in the case of female migration, the normative context is important and may not support the expectations based on human capital theory. Although most multilevel studies have not examined gender issues in migration, it is instructive to take note that those which have conducted separate analyses for males and females report much lower explanatory power for female models than for male models (Bilsborrow and others, 1987; Guest and Praditwong, 1989).

Some of the lower levels of explanation of female multilevel migration models may result from the definition of community used. In almost all multilevel studies, community is defined in terms of geographical location. This conceptualization only partially captures the complexity of the normative context in which decisions about female migration are made. In many contexts, community cannot be restricted to a specific geographical location. The existence of cross-cutting bases of community membership may mean that people living within the same area have very different norms relating to mobility and other life-course events that relate to mobility. In Malaysia, for instance, the intersecting ethnic and sexual division of labour results in different migration patterns among women belonging to different ethnic groups (Guest, 1983; Ariffin, 1991). The status of women and the existence of normative constraints against their movement also vary between groups, as in India, where women belonging to certain castes do not migrate, apart from moving upon marriage to the village of their husband (Singh, 1984). In contrast, women of other castes have relatively high levels of migration after marriage. In Thailand, Blanc-Szanton (1990) describes how the role of women differs considerably between Thais of Chinese descent and other Thai women and results in different levels of mobility, even among women in the same geographical community.

The solution to a situation in which mobility norms within a geographical community may be affected by exposure to the values of several different social groups is to bring explicitly into the analysis the dimensions of community and group membership. This extension of migration research has also been advocated by other authors; for example, Goldscheider (1987) stresses the need to identify homogeneous groups within society in analysing migration, although it would not be advisable to conduct the analysis separately for each group identified. An issue that would need to be addressed is the extent to which the norms and values of one group affect the migration behaviour of members of other groups that interact with the first group. For example, is the mobility behaviour of Chinese living in predominantly Chinese communities in Malaysia the same as the behaviour of Chinese living in predominantly Malay communities? Multilevel analysis has the capability of addressing those issues by incorporating several levels of analysis and specifying interactions between the different levels.

Community linkages

Households exist within geographically based communities which are linked, in varying degrees and by various types of linkages, to other communities. By affecting the type and number of opportunities available, those linkages influence the way in which families allocate labour through migration. For example, rural communities located near urban areas display a greater diversification in production and employment opportunities compared with those farther away from urban centres.

In attempting to explain differences in migration levels and patterns among villages of Western Java, Hugo (1981) stresses the role of migration networks. Other researchers similarly underscore the role of information flows (Fuller, Lightfoot and Kamnuansilpa, 1985). One research tradition has focused on the differential levels of economic integration among communities and the process of transformation from non-capitalist to capitalist modes of production (Amin, 1974; Portes, 1985). The growing interlinkages between different communities can be observed at many levels in the developing world. Those linkages raise aspirations for consumer goods and help promote migration in order that those aspirations may be fulfilled.

Ideally, independent, albeit interrelated, community characteristics, such as the degree of economic integration, the existence and strength of information flows or migration networks and the ease of access to other communities, should be considered separately in analysing their effects on migration. Unfortunately, in many studies influenced by the gravity-model theory of migration, distance between communities is often taken as a proxy for all those characteristics (Brown, 1991). Multilevel models, with their greater emphasis on a range of contextual factors, can overcome that shortcoming.

Although the direct effect of distance on the probability of migrating is generally negative (Connell and others, 1976), the introduction of indicators of economic and social integration may cause the effects of distance to lose significance (Guest and Praditwong, 1989); that is, physical distance would be a deterrent to migration only when reinforced by other processes fostering economic and social isolation. Findley (1987) found that community accessibility, measured as a combination of transport availability and distance to a local regional centre, was related to out-migration only in those communities with higher levels of living. The relationship was positive and was interpreted as an indication that heightened aspirations occurred with higher levels of living and that migration would be more likely to occur to pursue those aspirations where communities were accessible from a large urban centre. Bilsborrow and colleagues (1987) also found a non-linear relationship between distance and the probability of sons migrating out of rural areas in Ecuador. Although distance from the capital city, Quito, had a generally negative effect on the probability of out-migration, the effects were smaller for households owning more than five hectares of land, a finding that was interpreted as indicating that households in a more advantageous economic position had the means to cover the extra costs of migration related to longer distances.

Moreover, Bilsborrow and colleagues (1987) found that in the Ecuadorian Sierra, distance was not significantly associated with the probability of out-migration of daughters, suggesting that locational factors other than the ability to cover the costs of migration were important. The authors conclude that since Quito offered far more employment opportunities for women than other destinations, migration to it was not deterred by distance. Similarly, weak effects of distance on the propensity of women to migrate have been observed in other contexts. Considering the case of Thailand, Arnold and Piampiti (1984) argue that improved transport systems have reduced the importance of distance as a determinant of migration propensities. Indeed, because most employment opportunities for women are concentrated in Bangkok, better transportation has affected their migration more than that of men. Leenothai's (1991) findings corroborate that conclusion, indicating that distance was a significantly greater deterrent to female migration directed to places other than Bangkok than to the capital city itself. Such differences were attributed to the existence of well-established social networks linking Bangkok to sending areas.

Economic opportunities at the community level

The economic structure of communities provides the framework in which migration decisions are made. Most effects of economic opportunities at the community level can be analysed in terms of the access of families to employment. In general, a lack of local employment opportunities can be expected to stimulate out-migration. Where access to opportunities differs by sex, gender differences in out-migration can be expected.

In research by Brown and Goetz (1987), Findley (1987), Bilsborrow and others (1987) and Brown (1991), it has consistently been found that in rural communities the local availability of off-farm employment results in lower probabilities of out-migration. In many areas of the developing world, modes of agricultural development that encourage consolidation of land holdings, mechanization in the production and processing of crops and higher capital input into production can also affect the availability of agricultural employment. In many situations, labour displacement from agricultural development has been gender-specific (Lele, 1986). Furthermore, agricultural development has often been associated with the substitution of family labour, usually female, by hired labour, usually male (Singh, Squire and Strauss, 1986), further decreasing the availability of agricultural employment for women.

On the other hand, a few multilevel studies show that there is no significant relationship between agricultural development and out-migration (Findley, 1987; Guest and Praditwong, 1989). In the study by Guest and Praditwong (1989), based on Thai data, the analysis was conducted separately for males and females. However, since the effects of mechanization and commercialization of agriculture on the availability of female labour vary according to the type of agriculture practised (Heyzer, 1989), the impact of agricultural development on female migration needs to be assessed under different agricultural systems.

Changes in land tenure systems, the types of agriculture practised and the availability of land are also associated with out-migration. In explaining out-migration from rural areas of Costa Rica, Brown (1991) identifies three major push factors: (*a*) land consolidation; (*b*) curtailment of commercial agriculture; and (*c*) expansion of commercial cattle production. Rhoda (1983) states that land reform programmes are one of the few development interventions that tend to reduce the probability of out-migration from rural areas. In a multilevel analysis of rural development programmes in Malaysia, Baydar and others (1990) report that an agricultural settlement scheme in which land was provided for the production of commercial crops (such as oil-palm) had a negative effect on male out-migration. To the extent that women are also involved in agricultural production, increased access by women or their families to agricultural land would also tend to decrease female out-migration, as is suggested in a number of studies, most based on African data, which indicate that women are likely to stay behind when men migrate if they have a major role in agriculture (Colfer, 1985; Skeldon, 1990; Findley and Williams, 1991).

Although local access to farm and non-farm employment is important in determining the probability of migration, it is unlikely that the effects of the availability of each type of employment are simply additive. The existence of a more differentiated local labour-market allows families to use broader risk-diversification strategies in the allocation of labour in lieu of out-migration. Since families appear to combine the sexual division of labour with sectoral diversification (Guest, 1989), the presence of opportunities in different sectors for both sexes tends to reduce out-migration.

Inequalities between families in a community can affect migration levels by structuring access to employment opportunities (Peek, 1981; Roberts, 1982). Connell and others (1976) suggest that in villages where strong inequality prevails, poorer households deprived of access to local employment and richer households investing in education are both likely to foster the out-migration of some of their members. Arguing that migration can also be partially explained in terms of "relative deprivation", Stark (1984b) suggests that families evaluate their level of living in terms of their relative position within the community. If their position is below that of the reference group, they are more likely to engage in migration.

The demographic structure of communities is another factor affecting migration. For example, in communities where young men tend to leave, young women may also do so to improve their marriage prospects. On the other hand, in communities characterized by heavy male out-migration, the probability of female migration may be reduced because the absence of male labour may increase both women's productive responsibilities and their local employment opportunities (Lele, 1986; Kandiyoti, 1990). Although formerly less common, the situation observed in one Indonesian village, where female migration was a more attractive option than male migration and resulted in men taking over the domestic responsibilities of female migrants (Hetler, 1990), may now occur with more frequency because of the high demand for female labour in the urban areas of some societies. Situations like these underscore the importance of analysing male and female mobility within the same framework.

Services and infrastructure

The effects of the provision of community infrastructure and services on female migration have generally not been explored. As migration is the outcome of a decision-making process that involves the relative evaluation of the desirability or utility of different places, changes in the facilities available either in the place of origin or in potential destinations alter the probability of migration. Robinson goes so far as to state that "the most important cause of migration is the urban bias in health, education, and human-capital related public services" (1987, p. 126). Services most likely to affect the decision-making process with regard to migration include schools, health facilities, extension services, transportation systems and credit facilities.

Introducing services into a community, however, does not always reduce out-migration. In so far as the services provided help integrate the community into the economic system or increase the aspirations of its population, their effect on migration may be positive

(Rhoda, 1983). A multilevel study that included a measure of the availability of a range of community services, such as schools, clinics and extension services, found no direct effect of services on migration. However, high levels of community services were associated with high levels of out-migration in areas where the productivity of agriculture was high, whereas out-migration was low where access to community services was high but agricultural productivity was low (Findley, 1987). The interaction of these two community-level variables was interpreted in terms of the ability of households in communities with adequate resources derived from high agricultural productivity to sponsor the out-migration of household members. It is argued that it was in those communities which had high levels of access to services that heightened aspirations provided a motivation for migration.

It is the issue of raised aspirations that is often linked to increased out-migration. In so far as the provision of community services affects aspirations, an impact on migration might be expected. Where these effects conflict with normative expectations which limit women's productive roles to the household and farm or family business, the effects on female migration are likely to be significant. The expansion of access to educational facilities would appear likely to have the largest effect in this regard through its effects on employment aspirations. For example, in some rural secondary schools in Thailand, vocational courses intended to prepare female students for positions in the urban-based tourist industry essentially are preparing students for out-migration. In a study of migration in Venezuela, Brown (1991) notes how the expansion of education into rural areas created an educated rural workforce but that the employment opportunities that the educated aspired to were mainly in urban areas. This development led to an increase in migration, especially for women because of the higher concentration of working opportunities for them in urban areas. Khoo and Pirie (1984) argue that increased access to education for rural Malay girls increased the probability of migration because many girls migrated to urban areas to continue their secondary and college education. Migration to pursue one's education is a major factor in female and often in male migration as well as in many societies, with Findley and Williams (1991) finding that studies across a wide variety of contexts consistently show that about 10 per cent of female migrants cited education as their reason for moving.

The demonstration effect from the introduction of educational facilities into a community is as likely to have as pervasive effects on future migration as on increasing levels of education. Exposure to education, and educators, can instil in rural children the desire to experience a different way of life. For example, Keyes (1987) reports that the expansion of primary schools in Thailand, combined with the employment of female teachers, provided role models for village girls in occupations far removed from the rice fields of the village. Employment in health facilities, also often staffed by women, provides another model for rural women. It is the contact with the wider world that occurs through the provision of education, health and communication services, among others, that helps orient people to opportunities in other areas (Skeldon, 1990).

The provision of services, such as electricity, also brings urban and rural places into closer contact. The expansion of electricity networks is a process well under way in most developing countries. Porpora and Lim (1987) argue that one of the main factors leading to an increase in migration from north-eastern Thailand to Bangkok has been the spread of electrification and the consequent rise in demand for consumer goods, combined with the lack of local employment opportunities that might permit the eventual satisfaction of that demand. Two multilevel studies that have included electrification as a contextual variable have reported contradictory results. In a study of migration in Ecuador, Bilsborrow and others (1987) observe that lack of electricity is a significant determinant of male out-migration but not of female out-migration. In Thailand, however, Guest and Praditwong (1989) found that the higher the level of electrification, the higher is male out-migration and, to a somewhat lesser extent, female migration. Such different findings underscore the need to examine how electrification has influenced other aspects of community and family life, particularly by affecting employment structures.

The link between community characteristics and family labour-allocation strategies is an area that has not been fully explored. The modelling of migration as a risk-diversification strategy of families focuses attention on aspects of the community that might reduce risk. Massey (1990) hypothesizes that access to local capital markets, through which affordable credit could be made available to help ensure against long-term risk, might reduce the probability of out-migration. The stimulating effects that credit availability could have on other areas of the local economy, such as providing capital for the creation of new businesses, might also affect migration probabilities. Although no study has been undertaken at the village level on the effects of access to capital markets on migration, Guest and Praditwong (1989), using provincial data for Thailand, found that the availability of commercial banking had a significant effect on reducing out-migration probabilities at the provincial level. Furthermore, the inhibiting effect was stronger for women than for men. Given the normative constraints on the migration of women in most societies, one possible interpretation of such results that is consistent with the risk-diversification framework is that families located in communities where there are alternative options to ensure against risk are likely to give priority to reducing the out-migration of women rather than that of men.

D. THE FAMILY INFLUENCE ON MIGRATION

Some efforts directed to integrating the structural and individual bases of mobility behaviour have focused on the role of the household or family unit in allocating labour among geographically dispersed labour markets (Wood, 1981; Harbison, 1981; McGee, 1988; Guest, 1989; Massey, 1990; Root and De Jong, 1991). In developing societies, families are linked to labour-markets in two important ways. First, access to employment is often tied to family or community affiliation (Jellinek, 1978; Stretton, 1981; Hugo, 1981). Kin networks provide information and contacts which are essential for a family member to find employment, and identification with the family of origin remains important for continued access to employment opportunities. Secondly, the family ensures against long-term risk by diversifying its sources of income over space and time (Stark, 1984a; Grindle, 1988; Lauby and Stark, 1988; Massey, 1990).

The treatment of migration as a family strategy does not require, as seems to be assumed by some researchers (Porpora, Lim and Prommas, 1989; Wolf, 1990), that all family members play an active role in decision-making, although such involvement often occurs (Huang, 1983; Trager, 1988). Socialization carried out within the family and community ensures that family members shall be aware of their obligations to the survival of the household and of their roles within it (McGee, 1988). It is the role of the family in transmitting and interpreting societal and community norms that provides the greatest family influence on the migration of females.

A major obligation of migrants in many societies is the remittance of cash or goods to the family of origin (Lucas and Stark, 1984). The migration of a daughter may be preferred to that of a son if daughters are viewed as more likely to provide support to the family of origin after migration. That is the case in the Philippines (Trager, 1988) and among female migrant workers in Thailand (Porpora, Lim and Prommas, 1989). The strong normative expectation of material support from daughters is reinforced in a number of societies by structural factors. Perhaps the most important is the relationship between gender roles and the prevailing kinship system. In Thailand, the cultural norm is for a man to marry and spend a certain period in the home of the wife's parents. The youngest daughter is expected to care for her ageing parents and to inherit their house (Porpora, Lim and Prommas, 1989). Such an arrangement ensures that daughters shall have an ongoing stake in their family of origin.

Occupational structures may also provide support to norms relating to the provision of parental support. The occupational opportunities open to women in developing societies are generally not conducive to the attainment of long-term economic independence and this may encourage remittances from female migrants to their families of origin. Lauby and Stark (1988), and others, observe that many urban occupations for women are secure only in the short term and that women's wages are lower than those of men. In those circumstances, women are more likely than men to remain dependent upon their family of origin and, consequently, to have a greater incentive to remit.

In the absence of economic ties between migrants and their families of origin, affective ties can still play an important role in promoting movement. Migrants can help other family members to move by providing them with accommodation and assisting them in their search for employment. In fieldwork undertaken in Chinese communities in Hong Kong and Malaysia, Strauch (1984) notes that even though economic relationships between daughters and their family of origin are traditionally severed upon marriage, the links remain important for promoting the migration of other family members to whom married daughters can provide assistance in the place of destination. Such assistance is often of special importance to unmarried female siblings whose migration without the existence of kin in the place destination would probably not be allowed.

Family socio-economic conditions

Gender differences in the returns expected from the migration of family members are linked to the relation between the socio-economic position of households and their survival strategies. The risk-diversification model of migration developed by Stark (1984a) treats the labour of family members as the principal factor of production available to families in developing countries. In that model, the main goal of families is to sustain long-term viability through the allocation of labour in different labour-markets under the assumption that such a strategy will diversify production risks. Families using such a strategy are likely to encourage female rather than male migration if they expect to retain greater control over the earnings of female migrants. A number of factors, including family needs and the possibility of exercising more effective control over the earnings of daughters who have limited skills, suggest that families selecting women as out-migrants in risk-diversification strategies are more likely to belong to lower socio-economic strata (Lauby and Stark, 1988).

The socio-economic resource base of a family also has indirect effects on the probability of out-migration, although the direction of those effects will vary according to the normative environment. In societies where there are strong normative pressures against the independent migration of women, it is likely that only poorer families will experience sufficient economic need to violate those norms (Findley and Diallo, 1993). Thus, a study of female migration from a Javanese village showed that female migrants were concentrated in poorer families and documented the social disapproval that élite village women expressed with regard to female mobility (Hetler, 1990). Such disapproval centred mostly on the detrimental effects that migration was assumed to have on the performance of traditional female roles within the family. In other contexts, disapproval has focused on the risk of sexual misbehaviour to which migrant women are believed to be exposed (Ong, 1987; Lessinger, 1990).

Family control over non-labour factors of production, including capital and land, also determines whether migration is used as a risk-diversification strategy. Several studies have shown that the probability of migrating is related to the class position of the families to which potential migrants belong (Connell and others, 1976; Roberts, 1982; Findley, 1987; Guest, 1989), although the class most likely to use migration may vary according to the socio-economic context. A common finding is that middle-strata families are less likely to include migrants, compared with families in both the upper and lower strata (e.g., Bilsborrow and others, 1987). Findley (1987) takes note, however, that where social networks have reduced the risks of out-migration, middle-class families are more likely to include female out-migrants.

Such findings suggest the existence of different types of family strategies involving migration. McGee (1988) makes a distinction between strategies where migration is primarily a means of risk diversification and those where it is a means of accumulation. In the latter case, the rational course of action would be to select for migration the family member who is able to maximize earnings by migrating. In those situations where male labour is not required for family production or where female labour cannot substitute for the labour of the male family member, the customary sex discrimination in occupational and educational markets of developing countries would dictate that a young male be the person to migrate. Families adopting a risk-diversification strategy, on the other hand, might take advantage of the typical occupational segregation by sex by selecting for out-migration women who remain dependent upon the family of origin. Trager (1984) makes a distinction similar to that of McGee when she contrasts families using migration as a survival strategy and those using it to achieve upward mobility. In the Philippines, the first strategy is likely to lead to the migration of young women with low levels of education, while the second is more likely to involve the out-migration of both sexes to urban areas for the purpose of furthering their education.

Family structure

Both the amount of labour and the way it is allocated by a family are a function of the availability of labour. Demographic factors determining such availability include the size, composition and life-cycle stage of the family. If a minimum level of family labour is required to meet family production and reproduction requirements, the migration of family members will take place only if some combination of the following occur: (*a*) the minimum level of labour required for production can be met using family resources remaining net of out-migration; (*b*) affordable hired labour is available to substitute for family labour (Roberts, 1982); or (*c*) the labour of remaining family members is used more intensively (Deere, 1982; Palmer, 1985).

According to a review of available literature by Connell and others (1976), the evidence indicates that migrants come primarily from large households. Four major reasons are suggested: (*a*) a household requires a few productive members before it can use risk-diversification strategies which include migration; (*b*) large households increase pressures on resources, especially if resources are fixed; (*c*) the larger the household, the greater the probability that it may have links to a migration network; and (*d*) parents with only a few children are loathe to have them live outside the household. The last point would seem to depend to a large extent upon societal norms concerning appropriate patterns of parental-child residence. Furthermore, those norms are likely to change over the life cycle and may differ by sex.

The life-cycle stage of families is closely related to its size and hence to the existence of relative labour surpluses. When surpluses exist, migration can be used to utilize fully the labour available and alleviate economic stress. Arizpe (1981), for instance, found that the relationship of a migrant worker to the head of the family depended upon the life-cycle stage of the household. When children were young, it was usually the head of the family who engaged in temporary migration, with the offspring of the head more likely to migrate when they had reached working ages.

Both family size and structure are likely to be related to the sex selectivity of migration. In the rural areas of most developing countries, women are expected not only to provide the labour necessary for family maintenance (reproduction) but to work in production activities. Although the latter are not necessarily tied to one location, reproduction activities are. Therefore, the relation between reproduction and production activities will determine the extent to which female labour for production purposes can be allocated across space through migration.

Mangkuprawira (1981) notes that larger households involve conflicting demands on women because, on the one hand, more of their labour is needed for production activities while, on the other, reproduction and child-care demands are also greater. Depending upon the life-cycle stage of the family, such conflicts may be reduced by allocating some of the reproduction activities to female offspring. However, whereas hired labour can undertake the production activities assigned to women, it cannot be relied upon to carry out all the reproduction activities of women. Hence, female migration is more likely when there are other women in the family who can undertake the necessary reproduction activities. Thus, in the Philippines, the number of offspring in a family is positively related to the out-migration of daughters (Lauby and Stark, 1988). The case-studies of female migrants reported by Trager (1988) also show either that there are female siblings at home who can help parents or that migrant women tend to return frequently to perform needed tasks at the parental home.

In societies where the sexual division of labour is pronounced, families may take advantage of it by diversifying the allocation of family labour among different occupations. A study of household patterns of labour allocation in central Java found that, holding the size of the household labour force constant, the difference in the within-household sexual division of labour was greatest for larger households and for those in stages of the life cycle where young children were present in the household (Guest, 1989).

Associational migration

The discussion so far has focused mostly on women migrating out of the parental home, usually as part of a family migration strategy. Yet, a large proportion of women migrate either in conjunction with other family members or to join family members who migrated previously. This form of migration, often identified as "associational", has traditionally been analysed in terms of the characteristics of the head of the family, typically a male (Thadani and Todaro, 1984). Even here, however, the roles of women within the family may have significant impacts on family migration. For example, using data from a longitudinal survey, Root and De Jong (1991) found that family migration was related to a different set of family characteristics than the migration of individual family members. They define family migration as the movement of all family members as a group, while individual migration is defined as the movement of only some of the family members. Ties to kin in the community of origin were found to be important in constraining family migration, whereas family structure and level of resources were important in determining the migration of individuals out of the family. The existence of social ties in the community of origin often had economic implications that affected the decision to migrate, as, for instance, in terms of reducing the costs of child care.

The economic activities of women in the area of origin and their potential earnings in the area of destination may also be important determinants of family migration. Female employment as a factor determining family migration has been examined mainly in the context of developed economies, where studies have consistently shown that the wife's market earnings in the area of origin are negatively associated with the out-migration of the family (e.g., Sandell, 1977; Mincer, 1978). In developing countries, the productive activities of women in areas of origin (especially in rural areas) have generally been ignored in the analysis of family migration. The few studies that have considered them found their effects on the probability of family out-migration to be significant. Thus, a study in Costa Rica shows that the education of wives, used as a proxy for potential earnings, is significant and positively associated with the probability of family migration over long distances, particularly to the capital, San José (Shields and Shields, 1989). This finding is considered a reflection of the concentration of economic opportunities for women in the capital city.

Roles in the family

The structural changes that have transformed the occupational opportunities open to women have not left the family untouched. In many societies, the changes taking place in the family can be broadly characterized as involving a reduction of intergenerational control (Thornton and Fricke, 1987). There are several interdependent areas where a loss of control might be expected to increase the propensity of women to migrate. A reduction of the familial role in socialization, the increased education of girls, the weakened position of parents in controlling their children's access to resources, a greater participation of offspring in the selection of their marriage partners and other aspects of sexual relations, all result in the increased autonomy of the second generation and of women in particular.

The role of families in socialization has been weakened through the separation of the place of work from that of residence and through the increased importance of formal schooling. The implications of such changes are often more profound for women than for men. The change from work within the family to formal employment outside the family is evident in most societies (Schultz, 1990). Women's access to formal education has also increased vastly in most societies (McDonald, 1985). Higher levels of education of women are related to increased access to employment opportunities in the formal labour-market, which increases the probabilities of migration, especially to urban areas. For example, Huang (1983), in an analysis of increases in female migration in Taiwan Province of China, considers the higher levels of education obtained by women in rural areas to be instrumental in providing female rural-urban migrants with better opportunities to participate in an expanding urban service sector.

The changes in women's production and reproduction roles, increased decision-making power through independent access to resources, the emergence of an educational gap between generations which decreases the amount of parental authority over female children (Boserup, 1990) and exposure to new ideas are all related to higher levels of investment in female children and the growing independence of women (Thornton and Fricke, 1987).

The same factors are instrumental in increasing the freedom of adolescents to choose their marriage partners and engage in freer interaction with the opposite sex (Xenos, 1988). These processes are in turn associated with delayed marriage. It is this combination of greater freedom for adolescent women and an extended period before marriage when they contribute to the family economy that can make female migration for employment more likely. In a review of the existing literature on female migration, Findley and Williams (1991) conclude that later ages at marriage among women in parts of Asia may account for the higher proportion of "economic" reasons given by migrants for their moves.

E. METHODOLOGICAL ISSUES

Several methodological issues are important in the formulation and application of multilevel models (Bilsborrow and Guilkey, 1987). Some of these issues, including the levels of analysis and selection of variables, have been mentioned earlier. Others, including the appropriate methods of analysis, estimation techniques and the incorporation of temporal change, are briefly discussed below.

Microlevel research has allowed the formulation and testing of multilevel hypotheses about migration. With respect to female migration, for instance, microlevel analysis has furthered the understanding of the interrelations between family structure and patterns of female migration (Strauch, 1984; Wolf, 1984; Trager, 1988; Hetler, 1990). An area in which microlevel studies of female migration are badly needed is that involving the effects of community structure on out-migration decisions. The selection of a small number of villages for intensive analysis can be most illuminating for the study of migration (Hugo, 1988). If villages are selected on the basis of pre-specified structural characteristics, hypotheses concerning the interrelations between community structure and individual or family migration can be formulated (Roberts, 1982; Guest, 1989; Wimberley, Berry and Flinn, 1989). Formal statistical testing, however, requires larger and representative samples of both communities and families within communities (Bilsborrow, 1984). Thus, in order to obtain results that can be generalized and to incorporate a range of variables at different levels of analysis, the use of survey data covering a large number of contexts and communities is desirable.

The statistical challenges posed by multilevel analysis have received increasing attention in recent years. The main thrust has been to expand techniques that integrate, within one equation or a system of equations, the effects of variables measured at different levels (Bilsborrow and Guilkey, 1987). At the most basic level, overall macro-effects can be estimated by including variables that index the higher level of aggregation employed in the analysis. For example, a series of dummy variables indicating spatial units can be used in ordinary least-squares regression (Firebaugh, 1979). An analogous single-equation approach which tests for the presence of "grouping" effects of data collected at more than one level of analysis involves the application of random-effect logistic regression models (Curtis, McDonald and Diamond, 1991). Both of these types of models, however, which can also include interactions between the random effect (the macro-effect) and variables at lower levels of aggregation, can only test for the presence or absence of macro-effects but not for their source.

Analyses directed to specifying the components of macro-effects have generally followed two paths. First, there have been attempts to apply decision-making models that integrate characteristics of potential destinations into the analysis of decision-making with regard to migration. Two related methods of analysis are important, although both involve the assumption that behavioural decisions are based on characteristics of higher level units. Using mixed conditional logistic regression models, the choice of destination of migration is modelled as a function of the characteristics both of the decision maker and of alternative destinations (Leenothai, 1991). As economic opportunities for women are often more spatially concentrated than those for men, this model could help provide useful insights into patterns of female migration (Leenothai, 1991).

Nested-logistic models are another type used in multilevel migration research. They allow the modelling of migration as a two-stage process, with the first stage being the decision to move and the second the selection of a place of destination (Odland and Ellis, 1987; Liaw, 1990). Factors measured at different levels of analysis can enter into each stage of the decision-making process. Introducing both origin and destination characteristics simultaneously into the model provides a strong basis for investigating structural effects on the probability of migration by sex. For example, Odland and Ellis (1987) found that the concentration of service-sector occupations in places of destination was an important determinant of female migration in Ecuador, while Liaw (1990) reports that migrant women in Canada respond less than men to employment growth in the place of destination.

The mixed conditional logit and nested-logit models which have been applied to migration have emphasized the choice of destination of migration. The macro-variables employed typically relate to characteristics of available destinations. Another type of analysis, however, focuses on specifying or measuring macrolevel variables in terms of the substantive characteristics of the contexts in which individuals or families reside. Multilevel migration research based on this framework has used fixed-effect multilevel models, expressed either in additive or interactive form (Findley, 1987; Guest and Praditwong, 1989; Brown, 1991). The development of random coefficient models which incorporate stochastic variation in the coefficients of microlevel variables across contexts allows for a wider range of conceptual models to be tested (Mason, Wong and Entwisle, 1983; Entwisle and Mason, 1985; Wong and Mason, 1985). Simultaneous equations models where some of the microlevel variables are seen as not independent of each other but rather as endogenous can also be estimated (Bilsborrow and Guilkey, 1987). Random-coefficient and simultaneous-equation models have not yet been applied in multilevel studies of migration decisions.

Another important methodological issue in multilevel models is the temporal aspects of the effects of interest. Massey (1990) considers analyses of migration based on synchronic versus diachronic terms as one of the four major areas of debate in the field of migration. The changing selectivity of migration can be analysed on the basis of historical-structural changes that have taken place in society (Amin, 1974; Balán, 1983) or by incorporating measures of structural change at the family or community levels into statistical models (Wimberley, Berry and Flinn, 1989).

More generally, attention must be paid to the recursive nature of multilevel models in analysing behaviour by assuming the existence of effects at different levels. Wood (1981), Bilsborrow (1984) and Massey (1990) discuss the need to combine the neoclassical economic approach, according to which migration results from an individual human-capital maximization decision, with the historical-structuralist approach, which incorporates factors at the broader "community" level, such as market expansion, labour recruitment and capital accumulation. In studies of female migration, the interrelations across levels are important, but the analysis of the processes linking them demands high quality longitudinal data at both the microlevel and the macrolevel.

F. Conclusion

Literature on the determinants of female migration is sparse and fragmented. Research has been carried out mostly either within a micro- or a macro-perspective. Yet, the determinants of female migration are not confined to either of those somewhat arbitrary divisions. Since migration is selective in terms of both gender and the characteristics of women, the determinants of selectivity operate at different levels. Consequently, a multilevel framework is most appropriate for studying the effects of individual characteristics and family and community factors on female migration. That framework permits to take into account the effects of norms concerning female mobility and economic roles, social networks and income-earning opportunities both within and outside the community of residence, as well as community services and infrastructure.

A multilevel perspective on migration suggests that policy formulation must simultaneously take into account the microlevel and macrolevel factors affecting migration decisions. As Shrestha (1987) points out, to understand the effects of policies explicitly directed to modifying migration patterns, it is necessary to examine the complementarity of institutional policies and individual needs and motivations. Although most

Governments express dissatisfaction with the distribution of their populations, explicit policies designed to change migration patterns have seldom been successful. More often it is policies in other areas that have the greatest (though often unintended) effects on migration (cf. Simmons, 1993).

Female mobility is further complicated in that the individual interests of women are often subordinated to those of other kin and community members. The migration of women, or its restriction, is in many cases a reflection of that subordination. Hence, policies designed to promote the interests of women through migration should, at a minimum, take into account the normative context in which female migration decisions are made. For example, a policy directed to providing urban employment for young women displaced from agricultural employment is unlikely to have immediate effects in a context in which there are strong normative proscriptions against the movement of women away from the oversight of other family members.

Since the promotion of women's position in society is now clearly recognized by most Governments as a valued social goal, policies designed to affect the norms and values that define and underpin women's subordinate role in the migration process should be formulated. One strategy would be to encourage greater participation of women in the migration decision-making process. Because migration is just one area in which women's lack of status is manifested, policies need to be directed to the institutional structures that reinforce unequal gender relations. Providing women with equal access to education, for example, will help them acquire the knowledge and skills to participate in decision-making. Efforts to employ women in government services, especially in rural areas, should be encouraged to demonstrate to women the possible range of employment opportunities that they or their daughters could pursue. Also recommended are policies that provide women with the information needed to make a decision on migration on the basis of their interests. To date, informational activities for migrants have not been effectively employed by most Governments (Gardner, 1981).

In many societies, it is the structure of intergenerational relations, embodied in rules of inheritance, post-nuptial residence and control over property, that determines the extent to which women enjoy some level of autonomy in decision-making. In some cases, Governments have little overt power or desire to legislate changes in kinship relations that have evolved over many generations. In other instances, however, economic development has changed the bases upon which intergenerational and family relationships develop and policy interventions to ensure that women's rights shall be protected may be in order. For example, policies to ensure that daughters, wives, divorcees and widows shall receive fair access to family resources will allow more women to make migration decisions free from constraints. Measures undertaken to require the formal agreement of women in marriage and divorce decisions may also have some influence on the status of women and hence on their movement.

References

Acevedo, Luz del Alba (1990). Industrialization and employment: changes in the patterns of women's work in Puerto Rico. *World Development* (Oxford), vol. 18, No. 2 (February), pp. 231-255.

Amin, Samir (1974). *Modern Migrations in Western Africa*. London: Oxford University Press.

Ariffin, Jamilah (1991). Internal migration in Peninsular Malaysia-trends and patterns in the 1980's. Paper presented at the International Conference on Migration, Singapore, 7-9 February.

Arizpe, Lourdes (1981). Relay migration and the survival of the peasant household. In *Why People Move: Comparative Perspectives on the Dynamics of Internal Migration*, Jorge Balán, ed. Paris: United Nations Educational, Scientific and Cultural Organization.

Arnold, Fred, and Suwanlee Piampiti (1984). Female migration in Thailand. In *Women in the Cities of Asia: Migration and Urban Adaptation*, James T. Fawcett, Siew-Ean Khoo and Peter C. Smith, eds. Boulder, Colorado: Westview Press.

Balán, Jorge (1983). Agrarian structures and internal migration in a historical perspective: Latin American case studies. In *Population Movements: Their Forms and Functions in Urbanization and Development*, Peter A. Morrison, ed. Liège: Ordina Editions.

Baydar, Nazli, and others (1990). Effects of agricultural development policies on migration in Peninsular Malaysia. *Demography* (Washington, D.C.), vol. 27, No. 1 (February), pp. 97-109.

Bilsborrow, Richard E. (1984). The need for and design of community-level questionnaires. In *Migration Surveys in Low Income Countries: Guidelines for Survey and Questionnaire Design*, Richard E. Bilsborrow, A. S. Oberai and Guy Standing, eds. Beckenham, United Kingdom; and Sydney, Australia: Croom Helm.

_____ (1987). Population pressures and agricultural development in developing countries: a conceptual framework and recent evidence. *World Development* (Oxford), vol. 15, No. 2 (February), pp. 183-203.

_____, and David K. Guilkey (1987). *Community and Institutional Influence on Fertility: Analytical Issues*. Population and Labour Policies Programme, Working Paper No. 157. Geneva: International Labour Office.

Bilsborrow, Richard E., A. S. Oberai and Guy Standing (1984). *Migration Surveys in Low-Income Countries: Guidelines for Survey and Questionnaire Design*. Beckenham, United Kingdom; and Sydney, Australia: Croom Helm.

Bilsborrow, Richard E., and others (1987). The impact of origin community characteristics on rural-urban out-migration in a developing country. *Demography* (Washington, D.C.), vol. 24, No. 2 (May), pp. 191-210.

Blanc-Szanton, M. Cristina (1990). Gender and inter-generational resource allocation among Thai and Sino-Thai households. In *Structures and Strategies: Women, Work and Family*, Leela Dube and Rojni Palriwala, eds. New Delhi: Sage.

Boserup, Ester (1970). *Women's Role in Economic Development*. London: Allen and Unwin; and New York: St. Martin's Press.

_____ (1990). Population, the status of women, and rural development. In *Rural Development and Population: Institution and Policy*, Geoffrey McNicoll and Mead Cain, eds. New York: The Population Council; Oxford and New York: Oxford University Press.

Breman, Jan (1990). *Labour Migration and Rural Transformation in Colonial Asia*. Amsterdam: Free University Press.

Brown, Lawrence A. (1991). *Place, Migration and Development in the Third World: An Alternative View*. London and New York: Routledge.

_____, and Andrew Goetz (1987). Development-related contextual effects and individual attributes in Third World migration processes: a Venezuelan example. *Demography* (Washington, D.C.), vol. 24, No. 4 (November), pp. 497-516.

Chapman, Murray (1988). Population movement studied at microscale: experience and extrapolation. In *Micro-Approaches to Demographic Research*, John Caldwell, Allan Hill and Valerie Hull, eds. London: Kegan Paul International.

Colfer, Carol (1985). On circular migration: from the distaff side. In *Labour Circulation and the Labour Process*, Guy Standing, ed. Beckenham, United Kingdom; and Sydney, Australia: Croom Helm.

Collins, Jane L. (1983). Fertility determinants in a high Andes community. *Population and Development Review* (New York), vol. 9, No. 1 (March), pp. 61-75.

Connell, John, and others (1976). *Migration from Rural Areas: The Evidence from Village Studies*. New Delhi: Oxford University Press.

Curtis, Sian, John McDonald and Ian Diamond (1991). *Random-effects Models for Birth Interval Effects on Infant Mortality in Brazil*. Population Studies Working Paper, No. 91.2. Southampton, United Kingdom: University of Southampton, Department of Social Statistics.

DaVanzo, Julie (1981). Microeconomic approaches to studying migration decisions. In *Migration Decision Making: Multidisciplinary Approaches to Microlevel Studies in Developed and Developing Countries*, Gordon F. De Jong and Robert W. Gardner, eds. New York: Pergamon Press.

Deere, Carmen Diana (1982). The division of labour by sex in agriculture: a Peruvian case study. *Economic Development and Cultural Change* (Chicago, Illinois), vol. 30, No. 4 (July), pp. 795-811.

Entwisle, Barbara, and William M. Mason (1985). Multilevel effects of socioeconomic development and family planning programs on children ever born. *American Journal of Sociology* (Chicago, Illinois), vol. 91, No. 3 (November), pp. 616-649.

Falcón, Luis (1991). Migration and development: the case of Puerto Rico. In *Determinants of Emigration from Mexico, Central America, and the Caribbean*, Sergio Diaz-Briquets and Sidney Weintraub, eds. Boulder, Colorado; and Oxford, United Kingdom: Westview Press.

Fawcett, James T., Siew-Ean Khoo and Peter C. Smith (1984). Urbanization, migration, and the status of women. In *Women in the Cities of Asia: Migration and Urban Adaptation*, James T. Fawcett, Siew-Ean Khoo and Peter C. Smith, eds. Boulder, Colorado: Westview Press.

Findley, Sally E. (1987). *Rural Development and Migration: A Study of Family Choices in the Philippines*. Boulder, Colorado: Westview Press.

_____, and Assitan Diallo (1993). Social appearances and economic realities of female migration in rural Mali. Chapter XIII in the present volume.

Findley, Sally E., and Linda Williams (1991). *Women Who Go and Women Who Stay: Reflections of Family Migration Processes in a Changing World*. Population and Labour Policies Programme, Working Paper No. 176. Geneva: International Labour Office.

Firebaugh, Glenn (1979). Assessing group effects: a comparison of two methods. *Sociological Methods and Research* (Newbury Park, California), vol. 7, No. 4 (May), pp. 384-395.

Fuller, Theodore, and others (1983). *Migration and Development in Modern Thailand*. Bangkok: The Social Science Association of Thailand; Chulalongkorn University.

Fuller, Theodore D., Paul Lightfoot and Peerasit Kamnuansilpa (1985). Towards migration management: a field experiment in Thailand. *Economic Development and Cultural Change* (Chicago, Illinois), vol. 33, No. 3 (April), pp. 601-621.

Gardner, Robert W. (1981). Macrolevel influences on the migration decision process. In *Migration Decision Making: Multidisciplinary Approaches to Microlevel Studies in Developed and Developing Countries*, Gordon F. De Jong and Robert W. Gardner, eds. New York: Pergamon Press.

Goldscheider, Calvin (1987). Migration and social structure: analytic issues and comparative perspectives in developing nations. *Sociological Forum* (Ithaca, New York), vol. 2, No. 4 (Fall), pp. 674-696.

Grindle, Merilee S. (1988). *Searching for Rural Development*. Ithaca, New York: Cornell University Press.

Guest, Philip G. (1983). Internal migration and the change of the ethnic and sexual divisions of labor in Peninsular Malaysia. Unpublished Master's thesis. Providence, Rhode Island: Brown University.

_____ (1989). *Labor Allocation and Rural Development: Migration in Four Javanese Villages*. Boulder, Colorado: Westview Press.

_____, and Tanaporn Praditwong (1989). A contextual model of Thai migration. Paper presented at the Annual Meeting of the Population Association of America, Baltimore, Maryland, 30 March-1 April.

Harbison, Sarah (1981). Family structure and family strategy in migration decision making. In *Migration Decision Making: Multidisciplinary Approaches to Microlevel Studies in Developed and Developing Countries*, Gordon F. De Jong and Robert W. Gardner, eds. New York: Pergamon Press.

Hetler, Carol B. (1990). Survival strategies, migration and household headship. In *Structures and Strategies: Women, Work and Family*, Leela Dube and Rajni Palriwala, eds. New Delhi: Sage.

Heyzer, Noeleen (1989). Asian women wage earners: their situation and possibilities for donor intervention. *World Development* (Oxford), vol. 17, No. 7 (July), pp. 1109-1123.

Huang, Nora L. H. Chiang (1983). Female migration to Taipei—process and adaptation. *Population Geography* (Chandigarh, India), vol. 5, No. 1/2 (June-December), pp. 12-33.

Hugo, Graeme J. (1978). *Population Mobility in West Java*. Yogyakarta, Indonesia: Gadjah Mada University Press.

_____ (1981). Village-community ties, village norms, and ethnic and social networks: a review of evidence from the third world. In *Migration Decision Making: Multidisciplinary Approaches to Microlevel Studies in Developed and Developing Coun-*

tries, Gordon F. De Jong and Robert W. Gardner, eds. New York: Pergamon Press.

_____ (1988). Micro-approaches to the study of population movement: an Indonesian case study. In *Micro-Approaches to Demographic Research*, John Caldwell, Allan Hill and Valerie Hull, eds. London: Kegan Paul International.

Jellinek, Lea (1978). Circular migration and the *pondok* dwelling system. In *Food, Shelter and Transport in Southeast Asia and the Pacific*, P. J. Rimmer, D. W. Drakakis-Smith and T. G. McGee, eds. Canberra: The Australian National University, Research School of Pacific Studies.

Kandiyoti, Deniz (1990). Women and rural development policies: the changing agenda. *Development and Change* (London), vol. 21, No. 1, pp. 5-22.

Keyes, Charles F. (1987). *Thailand: Buddhist Kingdom as Modern Nation-State*. Boulder, Colorado: Westview Press.

Khoo, Siew-Ean, and Peter Pirie (1984). Female rural-to-urban migration in Peninsular Malaysia. In *Women in the Cities of Asia: Migration and Urban Adaptation*, James T. Fawcett, Siew-Ean Khoo and Peter C. Smith, eds. Boulder, Colorado: Westview Press.

Khoo, Siew-Ean, and others (1984). Women in Asian cities: policies, public services, and research. In *Women in the Cities of Asia: Migration and Urban Adaptation*, James T. Fawcett, Siew-Ean Khoo and Peter C. Smith, eds. Boulder, Colorado: Westview Press.

Lauby, Jennifer, and Oded Stark (1988). Individual migration as a family strategy: young women in the Philippines. *Population Studies* (London), vol. 42, No. 3 (November), pp. 473-486.

Leenothai, Sunee (1991). *The Role of Growth Centers in Migration of Women: Destination Choices of Female Migrants in Thailand*. Working Paper in Demography, No. 26. Canberra: The Australian National University, Research School of Social Sciences.

Lele, Uma (1986). Women and structural transformation. *Economic Development and Cultural Change* (Chicago, Illinois), vol. 34, No. 2 (January), pp. 195-221.

Lessinger, Johanna (1990). Work and modesty: the dilemma of women market traders in Madras. In *Structures and Strategies: Women, Work and Family*, Leela Dube and Rajni Palriwala, eds. New Delhi: Sage.

Liaw, Kao-lee (1990). Joint effects of personal factors and ecological variables on the interprovincial migration patterns of young adults in Canada: a nested logit analysis. *Geographical Analysis* (Columbus, Ohio), vol. 22, No. 3 (July), pp. 189-208.

Lim, Lin Lean (1993). The structural determinants of female migration. Chapter XI in the present volume.

Lucas, Robert E. B., and Oded Stark (1984). *Motivations to Remit: Evidence from Botswanna [sic]*. Migration and Development Program, Discussion Paper No. 10. Boston, Massachusetts: Harvard University.

Mangkuprawira, S. (1981). Married women's work pattern in rural Java. In *The Endless Day*, T. Scarlett Epstein and R. Watts, eds. Oxford: Pergamon.

Mason, William M., George Y. Wong and Barbara Entwisle (1983). Contextual analysis through the multilevel linear model. In *Sociological Methodology, 1983-84*, S. Leinhardt, ed. San Francisco, California: Jossey-Bass.

Massey, Douglas S. (1990). Social structure, household strategies, and the cumulative causation of migration. *Population Index* (Princeton, New Jersey), vol. 56, No. 1 (Spring), pp. 3-25.

McDevitt, Thomas M., and Saad M. Gadalla (1985). Incorporating husband-wife differences in place utility differentials into migration decision models. *Population and Environment* (New York), vol. 8, No. 1-2 (Spring-Summer), pp. 98-119.

McDonald, Peter (1985). Social organization and nuptiality in developing societies. In *Reproductive Change in Developing Countries: Insights from the World Fertility Survey*, John Cleland and John Hobcraft, eds. London: Oxford University Press.

McGee, Terrence (1988). Shadows on the household: some preliminary thoughts on changing economic characteristics of households in Southeast Asia. Paper presented at the Working Group Meeting on Socioeconomic Transformation, Demographic Change and the Family in Southeast Asia, Honolulu, East-West Center, 27-29 May.

Mincer, Jacob (1978). Family migration decisions. *Journal of Political Economy* (Chicago, Illinois), vol. 86, No. 5 (October), pp. 749-773.

Morokvasic, Mirjana (1984). Birds of passage are also women ... *International Migration Review* (New York), vol. 18, No. 4 (Winter), pp. 886-907.

Odland, John, and Mark Ellis (1987). Disaggregate migration behavior and the volume of interregional migration. *Geographical Analysis* (Columbus, Ohio), vol. 19, No. 2 (April), pp. 111-124.

Ong, Aihwa (1987). *Spirits of Resistance and Capitalist Discipline: Factory Women in Malaysia*. Albany: State University of New York Press.

Oppong, Christine (1983). Women's roles, opportunity costs, and fertility. In *Determinants of Fertility in Developing Countries*, vol. 1, *Supply and Demand for Children*, Rodolfo A. Bulatao and Ronald D. Lee, eds., with Paula E. Hollerbach and John Bongaarts. New York: Academic Press.

Palmer, Ingrid (1985). *The Impact of Male Out-migration on Women in Farming*. West Hartford, Connecticut: Kumarian Press.

Paralikar, Kalpana (1991). Women in migration: theoretical, moral, practical and legal issues concerning plans and policies for their development. Paper presented at the International Conference on Migration, Singapore, 7-9 February.

Peek, Peter (1981). Agrarian change and rural emigration. In *Why People Move: Comparative Perspectives on the Dynamics of Internal Migration*, Jorge Balán, ed. Paris: United Nations Educational, Scientific and Cultural Organization.

Pittin, Renée (1984). Migration of women in Nigeria: the Hausa case. *International Migration Review* (Staten Island, New York), vol. 18, No. 4 (Winter), pp. 1293-1314.

Porpora, Douglas V., and Mah Hui Lim (1987). The political economic factors of migration to Bangkok. *Journal of Contemporary Asia* (Manila), vol. 17, No. 1, pp. 76-89.

Porpora, Douglas V., Mah Hui Lim and Usanee Prommas (1989). The role of women in the international division of labour: the case of Thailand. *Development and Change* (London), vol. 20, No. 2 (April), pp. 269-294.

Portes, Alejandro (1985). The informal sector and the world-economy: notes on the structure of subsidized labor. In *Urbanization in the World Economy*, Michael Timberlake, ed. Orlando, Florida: Academic Press.

_____, and John Walton (1981). *Labor, Class, and the International System*. New York: Academic Press.

Presser, Harriet B., and Sunita Kishor (1991). Economic development and occupational sex segregation in Puerto Rico: 1950-80. *Population and Development Review* (New York), vol. 17, No. 1 (March), pp. 53-85.

Recchini de Lattes, Zulma (1989). Women in internal and international migration with special reference to Latin America. *Population Bulletin of the United Nations, 1989* (New York), No. 27, pp. 95-107. Sales No. F.89.XIII.7.

Rhoda, Richard (1983). Rural development and urban migration: can we keep them down on the farm? *International Migration Review* (Staten Island, New York), vol. 17, No. 1 (Spring), pp. 34-64.

Riley, Nancy E., and Robert W. Gardner (1993). Migration decisions: the role of gender. Chapter X in the present volume.

Roberts, Kenneth D. (1982). Agrarian structure and labor mobility in rural Mexico. *Population and Development Review* (New York), vol. 8, No. 2 (June), pp. 299-322.

Robinson, Warren C. (1987). Implicit policies and the urban bias as factors affecting urbanization. In *Urbanization and Urban Policies in Pacific Asia*, Roland J. Fuchs, Gavin W. Jones and Ernesto M. Pernia, eds. Boulder, Colorado: Westview Press.

Root, Brenda Davis, and Gordon F. De Jong (1991). Family migration in a developing country. *Population Studies* (London), vol. 45, No. 2 (July), pp. 221-233.

Safilios-Rothschild, Constantina (1982). Female power, autonomy and demographic change in the third world. In *Women's Roles and Population Trends in the Third World*, Richard Anker, Mayra Buvinic and Nadia Youssef, eds. London: Croom Helm.

Sandell, Steven H. (1977). Women and the economics of family migration. *Review of Economics and Statistics* (Amsterdam), vol. 59, No. 4 (November), pp. 406-414.

Schultz, T. Paul (1990). Women's changing participation in the labor force: a world perspective. *Economic Development and Cultural Change* (Chicago, Illinois), vol. 38, No. 3 (April), pp. 457-488.

Shah, Nasra M. (1984). The female migrant in Pakistan. In *Women in the Cities of Asia: Migration and Urban Adaptation*, James T. Fawcett, Siew-Ean Khoo and Peter C. Smith, eds. Boulder, Colorado: Westview Press.

Shields, Gail M., and Michael P. Shields (1989). Family migration and nonmarket activities in Costa Rica. *Economic Development and Cultural Change* (Chicago, Illinois), vol. 38, No. 1 (October), pp. 73-88.

Shrestha, Nanda R. (1987). Institutional policies and migration behavior: a selective review. *World Development* (Oxford), vol. 15, No. 3 (March), pp. 329-345.

Simmons, Alan B. (1993). Government policies, women and migration: a review of research findings and policy options in developing countries. Chapter XIX in the present volume.

Singh, Andrea Menefee (1984). Rural-to-urban migration of women in India: patterns and implications. In *Women in the Cities of Asia: Migration and Urban Adaptation*, James T. Fawcett, Siew-Ean Khoo and Peter C. Smith, eds. Boulder, Colorado: Westview Press.

Singh, Inderjit, Lyn Squire and John Strauss (1986). The basic model: theory, empirical results, and policy conclusions. In *Agricultural Household Models: Extensions, Applications and Policies*, Inderjit Singh, Lyn Squire and John Strauss, eds. Washington, D.C.: The World Bank.

Skeldon, Ronald (1990). *Population Mobility in Developing Countries*. London and New York: Belhaven Press.

Smith, Peter, Siew-Ean Khoo and Stella P. Go (1984). The migration of women to cities: a comparative perspective. In *Women in the Cities of Asia: Migration and Urban Adaptation*, James T. Fawcett, Siew-Ean Khoo and Peter C. Smith, eds. Boulder, Colorado: Westview Press.

Standing, Guy (1986). Labour circulation and the urban labour process. *Journal of Economic and Social Geography* (Amsterdam), vol. 77, No. 5, pp. 389-398.

_____ (1989). Global feminization through flexible labor. *World Development* (Oxford), vol. 17, No. 7, pp. 1077-1095.

Stark, Oded (1984a). Migration decision making: a review article. *Journal of Development Economics* (Amsterdam), vol. 14, No. 1-2 (January-February), pp. 251-259.

_____ (1984b). Rural-to-urban migration in LDCs: a relative deprivation approach. *Economic Development and Cultural Change* (Chicago, Illinois), vol. 32, No. 3 (April), pp. 475-486.

Strauch, Judith (1984). Women in rural-urban circulation networks: implications for social structural change. In *Women in the Cities of Asia: Migration and Urban Adaptation*, James T. Fawcett, Siew-Ean Khoo and Peter C. Smith, eds. Boulder, Colorado: Westview Press.

Stretton, A. W. (1981). The building industry and urbanization in Third World countries: a Philippine case study. *Economic Development and Cultural Change* (Chicago, Illinois), vol. 29, No. 2 (January), pp. 325-339.

Thadani, Veena N., and Michael P. Todaro (1984). Female migration: a conceptual framework. In *Women in the Cities of Asia: Migration and Urban Adaptation*, James T. Fawcett, Siew-Ean Khoo and Peter C. Smith, eds. Boulder, Colorado: Westview Press.

Thornton, Arland, and Thomas E. Fricke (1987). Social change and the family: comparative perspectives from the West, China, and South Asia. *Sociological Forum* (New York), vol. 2, No. 4 (Fall), pp. 746-779.

Todaro, Michael (1976). *Internal Migration in Developing Countries*. Geneva: International Labour Office.

Trager, Lillian (1984). Family strategies and the migration of women: migrants to Dagupan City, Philippines. *International Migration Review* (Staten Island, New York), vol. 18, No. 4 (Winter), pp. 1264-1278.

_____ (1988). *The City Connection: Migration and Family Interdependence in the Philippines*. Ann Arbor: University of Michigan Press.

Ware, Helen (1981). *Women, Demography and Development*. Canberra: The Australian National University.

Williams, Linda (1987). Migration, women's intra-familial decision-making power, and fertility: the case of rural central Java. Unpublished doctoral dissertation. Providence, Rhode Island: Brown University.

Wimberley, Dale W., E. Helen Berry and William L. Flinn (1989). Structural influences on outmigrant selectivity: a panel study of three rural Colombian communities. *Rural Sociology* (College Station, Texas), vol. 54, No. 3 (Fall), pp. 339-364.

Wolf, Diane (1984). Making the bread and bringing it home: female factory workers and the family economy in rural Java. In *Women in the Urban and Industrial Workforce: Southeast and East Asia*, Gavin W. Jones, ed. Development Studies Centre, Monograph No. 33. Canberra: The Australia National University.

_____ (1990). Daughters, decisions and domination: an empirical and conceptual critique of household strategies. *Development and Change* (London), vol. 21, No. 1, pp. 43-74.

Wong, George Y., and William M. Mason (1985). The hierarchial logistic regression model for multilevel analysis. *Journal of the American Statistical Association* (Alexandria, Virginia), vol. 80, No. 391 (September), pp. 513-524.

Wood, Charles H. (1981). Structural change and household strategies: a conceptual framework for the study of rural migration. *Human Organization* (Oklahoma City, Oklahoma), vol. 40, No. 4 (Winter), pp. 338-344.

Xenos, Peter (1988). Issues in Southeast Asian family change: historical context and contemporary evidence. Paper presented at the Conference of the Northwest Center for Southeast Asian Studies, Eugene, Oregon, 30 September-2 October.

Young, Mei Ling (1982). Circular mobility and its policy implications. In *Third Asian and Pacific Population Conference, Colombo, 20-26 September*. Asian Population Studies, No. 58. Bangkok: United Nations Economic and Social Commission for Asia and the Pacific.

Zoomers, E. B. (1986). From structural push to chain migration: notes on the persistence of migration to Ciudad Juarez, Mexico. *Tijschrift voor Economiseke en Sociole Geographie/Journal of Economic and Social Geography* (Amsterdam), vol. 77, No. 1, pp. 59-67.

XIII. SOCIAL APPEARANCES AND ECONOMIC REALITIES OF FEMALE MIGRATION IN RURAL MALI

Sally E. Findley* and Assitan Diallo**

Until recently, studies on migration rarely focused on women as migrants because they were seen as moving primarily for marriage or associational reasons. In recent years, however, the characterization of female migrants as "passive" or dependent has been called into question. Among a number of studies about female migration in Africa, Asia, and Latin America and the Caribbean, over 40 per cent cite economic factors as crucial in motivating the migration of women (Findley and Williams, 1991). Yet, the view that women do not migrate on their own for economic reasons continues to be dominant in sub-Saharan Africa (Findley, 1987). Part of the problem is that the motives reported by respondents are often mixed, as in the Sahel, where women interviewed in the cities cite economic reasons for their migration (Dupont, 1989; Findley, 1988; ISH, 1984), while both household heads and women living in rural areas say that women migrate only to get married or because of other family reasons.

In this paper, the reasons for those mixed reports are discussed, the characteristics of female migrants are presented and an exploration of the factors leading to their migration is carried out using data from a longitudinal survey conducted in 1982 and 1989 in the Senegal River Valley of rural Mali. Because the survey was designed to examine detailed family-level responses to drought conditions prevailing around the middle of the observation period, it included detailed questions on both male and female migration. Those data were supplemented by qualitative information from an intensive survey conducted in 1987 in seven villages that had either very high or very low levels of out-migration, according to the 1982 survey.

A. FEMALE MIGRATION: A RESPONSE TO ECONOMIC STRESS

Standard economic models view migration as the mechanism enabling labour to move to areas of greater or more favourable demand. Under the assumption that stable and well-paid employment is preferred, persons with the most favourable labour qualifications are expected to migrate, namely, men with relatively high educational attainment, skills or prior employment experience (Findley, 1982). Persons lacking such qualifications, including many women in developing countries, are not expected to migrate or to do it only to accompany or follow the economically active male migrant.

In the Senegal River Valley, labour migration to France and to other countries of Africa generally conforms to that model. The migrant, usually a young single man, stays abroad for several years to earn the money he needs to marry and establish a family. Remittances are used to support the family of origin during his absence but may also be invested in farm implements, irrigation or non-agricultural activities. Migrants may also establish a fund for village improvements. Upon return or on periodic home visits, migrants may use their savings to get married (Adams, 1977; Barou, 1976; Condé and Diagne, 1986; Finnegan, 1980; Coulibaly, Gregory and Picke, 1980).

Regardless of whether the migrant is successful in sending back money to his family, his migration reinforces the image that men are the providers for the family. Interviews conducted in 1987 consistently showed that men saw migration as vital to fulfilling their ascribed role as heads of the family and main breadwinners. Although women did not like the long absences of men entailed by migration, they continued to support the migration of their male relatives because they saw no other reliable way for the family to achieve economic stability or progress.

---

*Center for Population and Family Health, Columbia University, New York, New York, United States of America.
**Population Studies and Training Center, Brown University, Providence, Rhode Island, United States of America.

Because men are considered the supporters of the family, women are not expected to earn money or supply basic foodstuffs. Since men control the family grain supply, women may not even know the extent of reserves or the lack thereof (Pollet and Winter, 1971). In principle, therefore, women are expected not to migrate and especially not to do so for economic reasons. Indeed, a sign of family status is that women do not have to work for pay and are therefore free to do no more than socialize during visits to other areas.

Despite this view, women do contribute to nurture the family. They assist their husbands with cultivation and are responsible for the preparation of all meals, implying that they must supply everything but the grain: cooking fuel; water; peanuts; vegetables; spices; meat (Rondeau, 1987). Women are responsible for actually feeding the family; and if husbands do not provide the necessary millet or rice, women ultimately have to obtain it as well.

In these circumstances, it is important to consider what happens in cases of sudden or severe economic stress. The distressed families no longer view migration only as a human capital investment; rather, it becomes part of the family's options to cope with the sudden and often unexpected shortfall in income. In several African countries affected by economic crisis, there is evidence of migration as a survival strategy (*PopSahel*, 1991; Touré, 1985; Barbière, 1985). Unlike refugee movements, migration for survival is generally short-term, with family members being away for at most a few months to earn whatever they can.

Typically, short-term migrants have been young men, especially those with little or no education who belong to impoverished families and go to nearby cities to work as petty traders, pulling carts, in construction or in other low-status and poorly paid jobs. Studies from Burkina Faso, the Niger, Senegal and Togo show that such migrant men usually stay away for less than a year and return to help with the farm work (Barou, 1976; Remy, 1977; Finnegan, 1980; Amselle, 1978; Minvielle, 1985).

During an economic crisis, role expectations may be loosened so that women can become more directly involved in strategies to provide basic staples. As in other societies faced with subsistence crises, some of these strategies involve reductions in food consumption or expenditures while others extend networks for the sharing of food or resources (Scott, 1976; ISH, 1984).

In Mali, families reduce their consumption by eating less, eating more wild (and therefore free) foods or purchasing less. They sometimes reduce also the number of persons that have to be fed by sending some family members elsewhere either temporarily or permanently through marriage. Although this practice is not common in all of Mali, migrants from the region of Kayes, for example, generally receive free room and board from kin in places of destination.

Even if children or women out-migrate to reduce immediate food demands, the family is unlikely to acknowledge explicitly the economic basis for the migration. Instead, children will be sent to live elsewhere according to social custom, such as for Koranic studies under a master living in another village or by fostering the child out to distant kin, even if in the same village (Findley and Diallo, 1988).

Women may also be encouraged to migrate in order to reduce consumption, but as with children, their migration is unlikely to be viewed in that light. In the 1987 survey, male heads of household were asked about the motives for female migration and in virtually no case was female migration attributed to economic factors. Similarly, village elders declared that women would not be sent to cities to work, even in times of dire need, though they did admit to sending women to Bamako or other cities in order to buy food. Therefore, even if the need to reduce consumption is a factor motivating out-migration, it is not likely to be reported, in order to save face.

Most female migration falls under the guise of visiting family or other social reasons. Even if women are desperate to find work as domestic servants or traders, they themselves tend to avoid reporting an economic reason as their primary motive for migration. Yet, once in the city and settled with kin, women may end up working with the other women in the household in income-generating activities.

As in many societies, a change in marital status often triggers migration. In the Senegal River Valley, women normally move to the husband's home shortly after marriage, and women that divorce or separate return to their natal home. In addition, changes in marital status may lead to other socially acceptable migrations. Normally, women getting married wish to accumulate some savings and are therefore more likely to engage in circular migration during the year prior to their marriage.

Even under the guise of social visiting, not all women migrate during times of economic stress. Since it is not socially acceptable for women to become wage-earners or major contributors to the household's income, women with higher economic status are the least likely to migrate. Within any given family, the women expected to move are those with the lowest status in relation to other women, such as single adolescents; divorced, widowed or separated women; higher order wives in a polygamous family and other female kin not directly related to the head of household. Childless married women, whose status is low in this society, are also more likely to migrate, as are women that already have migration or employment experience.

Women with heavy family responsibilities will be less likely to migrate, even in times of economic distress. Thus, female migration is less likely in families with large numbers of children in the household compound. However, if there are several women living in the compound who can take over child-care responsibilities, some women with children may be freed to migrate.

Although men are relatively free to migrate, even to places where they know no one, the head of a family will not favour a woman's migration unless he can be assured that the woman will stay with someone who can be responsible for her welfare. Women that have already migrated or those from families that have already sent other migrants are expected to find it easier to secure the necessary hosts.

Given that female migration other than that for marriage or family reasons is frowned upon, women are likely to migrate for economic reasons only under conditions of significant economic stress, when low incomes or the total lack of cash income or low levels of grain availability force them to do so. Although women are not themselves responsible for food production, families that are chronically short on cereals will be under severe economic stress and will be more likely to encourage female out-migration.

Similarly, villages with higher levels of socio-economic development are likely to have fewer female out-migrants, because women will find greater opportunities to secure food or money in the village itself. Employment opportunities for women, however, are different than those for men and the development activities typically promoted in villages (e.g., irrigated agriculture) are unlikely to change the economic opportunities open to women or their migration motivations. Changes that may make a difference with regard to female employment or access to cash include the promotion of alternative vegetable crops (melons, beans etc.) or the raising of small ruminants (sheep or goats).

Lastly, because women are not directly responsible for food supplies, the effect of periodic droughts on women's out-migration is a function not only of whether there are food shortfalls but of the difficulty in finding drinking-water. In villages with poor supplies of drinking-water or no irrigation, women play an important role in seeking water and are thus less likely to out-migrate, especially if the household has few women that can share in fetching water.

B. THE STUDY AREA

The upper Senegal River Valley, stretching from Matam, Senegal to Diamou, Mali, is one of the least developed river regions of the western Sahel. Subject to enormous changes in water-levels between the dry and wet seasons, it has never supported a year-round river transport network. In addition, most of the valley consists of rough terrain lacking railway or adequate road service, and is therefore largely inaccessible to the rest of the world. Although partially served by the Dakar-Niger rail line, the region has failed to generate significant exports and is characterized by a subsistence agro-pastoral economy (Mali, 1985; OMVS, 1980). Kayes, the regional capital of the Malian portion, is little more than a local administrative and trade centre.

The dominant ethnic group in the region, the Soninke or Sarakolle, is Islamic and rigidly patrilineal. Among the Soninke, families live as "grand families", which may include up to 100 persons. The oldest male heads the compound, which includes the families of each son and grandson. Historically, the Soninke were the region's traders, but with the collapse of the gum-arabic market upon which this trade was based, the Soninke have become better known for their labour exchanges, especially in the French labour market (Pollet and Winter, 1971; Minvielle, 1986).

The village economy is basically one of subsistence agriculture, based on millet, sorghum and corn. The average level of rainfall, around 600 millimetres per annum, is sufficient only for extensive unirrigated agriculture. Even maintaining subsistence levels of production is problematic, as rainfall is highly variable. Therefore, farmers traditionally build large granaries and store up to a three-year supply as a reserve against the inevitable dry years. Since the drought of 1968-1974, however, rainfall has tended to be below average, so few farmers have been able to produce enough to feed their families each year. Millet yields in 1982 were low, less than 245-600 kilograms per hectare (Mali, 1985); and in over half the villages, production was insufficient to meet local needs. According to the 1982 survey, families had to buy up to 40 per cent of their food needs.

In most of the villages, cereal cultivation is complemented by pastoral activities. In 1982, 75 per cent of the households kept some form of livestock. Cows dominated the pastoral activities, with an average of 23.7 heads per family. Herds are generally too small to survive a severe drought (Silitshena, 1990), so most families use livestock as a form of savings. During dry years, animals are sold or exchanged for grain, whenever possible before they lose value through weight loss.

C. DATA SOURCES

Observations of migration and related family and community characteristics are drawn from surveys conducted in 1982 and 1989. During the intervening period, there was a severe drought (1983-1985) and from 1986 onward a deepening economic crisis that affected much of Western Africa. The surveys were conducted by the Centre d'études et de recherche sur la population et pour le développement (CERPOD), part of the Sahel Institute at Bamako, Mali. The original survey was undertaken jointly with the Development Centre of the Organisation for Economic Co-operation and Development (OECD), and involved surveys in both France and the Senegal River Valley. A sample of 99 villages in the valley was selected to represent areas with high rates of emigration to France. In each village, questionnaires were addressed to village elders, heads of household, migrants and women (Condé and Diagne, 1986). The present analysis is restricted to the Malian subsample of 39 villages with its sample of 327 households.

Migration data for the period 1982-1989 were collected by the 1989 Follow-up Migration Survey of the Senegal River Valley. All of the original households were reinterviewed, even if the head of household or household membership had changed. The 1989 Survey encompassed 7,263 persons in 327 households. Interviews were conducted with each head of household, who supplied information on all household members, including out-migrants. If the head had died or migrated since 1982, the newly designated head of household was interviewed. Village elders were assembled and asked questions about the current village characteristics and those in 1982. Interviews were also conducted with all women aged 15 or over. They included a fertility history, though only the total number of children ever born is used in the present analysis.

Migration status was determined from the question on residential status, as well as from questions on up to three migrations in the intervening period 1982-1989. A migrant was any person who had been a member of the household in 1982, had moved away for a total of at least six months at any time prior to the 1989 interview or was listed as a temporarily absent resident in 1989. There were no screening questions for migration motives, so that the moves recorded included both economically and non-economically motivated migration. Out-migrants were identified on the basis of data obtained from a migration history of every person, including new members of the household, which recorded all migrations between the two interview rounds. Any absence of one month or more to work or study was recorded, as well as any circular move during the drought of 1983-1985. For new members of the household, a migration was counted only if it was a departure after taking up residence in the household.

The data from the 1982 and 1989 surveys were linked by means of individual identifiers. After cleaning and eliminating the 18 households where household-level information was missing, 7,079 persons and 309 households remained. The present analysis is restricted to the 1,552 women and 1,375 men over age 14 at the time of the baseline survey in 1982.

These quantitative data are supplemented by qualitative data collected in 1987 under CERPOD auspices. That survey was conducted to test the follow-up methodology, to verify that households could be reinterviewed and to check the extent of memory recall about the drought period 1983-1985. In addition, the interviews were designed to provide an in-depth profile of migration patterns already evident in the 1982 survey. In 1987, in-depth interviews were conducted with 71 families in 7 of the 39 Malian villages belonging to the original 1982 sample. In 1982, the villages selected had had levels of temporary or permanent out-migration that were significantly higher or lower than the average for the 39 villages. In the high-migration villages, an average of 13.5 per cent of village residents were absent at the time of the 1982 survey, while 20 per cent were out-migrants; in the low-migration villages, only 0.6 per cent of residents were absent and 3.6 per cent were out-migrants. In 1987 interviews were conducted with the heads of household and with 33 returned migrants, 46 randomly selected male non-migrants, 56 randomly selected females over age 14 and 34 wives of absent migrants. The questionnaire used probed for details about household economic conditions, the agricultural system, the role and effect of migration on the family economy, the history of migration within the household and in the village, attitudes towards migration and suggestions concerning migration and development policies.

D. Characteristics of migrants

Between 1982 and 1989, women were half as likely as men to migrate at least once. As is shown in table 54, 635 males, or 46 per cent of the men over age 14, had migrated, compared with 438 females or 28 per cent of the women. Female migration was thus far from insignificant. In fact, women constituted 41 per cent of the total migrant population, although that percentage was far below the 53 per cent of the total adult population accounted for by women.

TABLE 54. FEMALE AND MALE MIGRATION FROM THE SENEGAL RIVER VALLEY, MALI, 1982-1989

Sex	Migrant Number	Migrant Percentage	Non-migrant Number	Non-migrant Percentage	Total Number	Total Percentage
Male	635	59	740	40	1 375	47
Female	438	41	1 116	60	1 554	53
TOTAL	1 073	100	1 856	100	2 929	100

Source: Centre d'études et de recherche sur la population et pour le développement, *Enquête renouvellée de migration dans la Vallée du fleuve Sénégal* (Bamako, Sahel Institute, 1982 and 1989).

TABLE 55. FEMALE AND MALE MIGRANTS BY DURATION, SENEGAL RIVER VALLEY, MALI, 1982-1989

Duration	Female Number	Female Percentage	Male Number	Male Percentage
Less than six months or circulated	254	58	231	36
Permanent migration	184	42	404	64

Source: Centre d'études et de recherche sur la population et pour le développement, *Enquête renouvellée de migration dans la Vallée du fleuve Sénégal* (Bamako, Sahel Institute, 1982 and 1989).

Most female migrants moved for relatively short periods, returning to their home after absences of less than six months. As is shown in table 55, out of 438 women migrants, 254 (58 per cent) returned after short absences and only 184 (42 per cent) left for over six months. In contrast, 64 per cent of male migrants were gone for periods exceeding six months.

Table 56 shows that most of the female migrants moved over short distances. Many stayed in the same *cercle* or county, one tenth went to the cities of Bamako or Kayes and another 26 per cent went to unspecified destinations in Mali, yielding a total of 59 per cent going to Malian destinations. However, one fifth did migrate to other countries in Africa and another one tenth went to France. In contrast, among male migrants, the largest share (41 per cent) went to France and the second largest contingent (29 per cent) to other African countries. It should be noted that for nearly one fifth of the female out-migrants and just over one

TABLE 56. FEMALE AND MALE MIGRANTS BY DESTINATION, SENEGAL RIVER VALLEY, MALI, 1982-1989

Destination	Female Number	Female Percentage	Male Number	Male Percentage
Same circle	60	16	23	4
Rural Mali or Senegal River Valley	23	6	14	2
Bamako or Kayes	40	11	42	8
Mali, unspecified	95	26	79	14
Other African	74	20	166	29
France	41	11	232	41
Other	36	10	14	2
Total known destinations	369	100	570	100

Source: Centre d'études et de recherche sur la population et pour le développement, *Enquête renouvelée de migration dans la Vallée du fleuve Sénégal* (Bamako, Sahel Institute, 1982 and 1989).

TABLE 57. CHARACTERISTICS OF FEMALE MIGRANTS AND NON-MIGRANTS, SENEGAL RIVER VALLEY, MALI, 1982-1989

Characteristics	Migrant	Non-migrant
Mean age in 1982	24.8	30.1
Percentage never married or divorced	23	17
Percentage married in 1982	55	69
Percentage married before age 15	18	15
Percentage in polygamous unions	40	35
Percentage childless	30	19
Percentage with primary schooling	5	3
Percentage with cash income in 1982	5	4
Percentage with migration experience	35	3
Average number of children under age 5 in 1982 per compound	1.7	2.1

Source: Centre d'études et de recherche sur la population et pour le développement, *Enquête renouvelée de migration dans la Vallée du fleuve Sénégal* (Bamako, Sahel Institute, 1982 and 1989).

tenth of the male out-migrants, the place of destination was not recorded.

In most respects, female migrants conform to expectations in terms of being more likely than non-migrants to be young, single and to have lower social status (see table 57), as reflected by their age, and marital and motherhood situations. The average age of a migrant woman was 24.8 years, compared with 30.1 for non-migrants (making the difference significant at a probability level of 0.026).

Although 69 per cent of non-migrant women were married in 1982, only 55 per cent of migrant women were, the difference being significant at the 0.001 level. More migrant than non-migrant women were in polygamous unions (40 compared with 35 per cent). As expected, migrant women were also significantly more likely to be childless, compared with non-migrants—30 and 19 per cent, respectively—and far more likely to have had an earlier migration experience.

Another measure of social status is the woman's age at marriage. In general, the younger the woman at the time of marriage, the greater the age difference between herself and her husband, and the more subordinate she is in her husband's family. In this sample, the average age at marriage was 16.4 years. Among migrants, 18 per cent had married before age 15, compared with only 15 per cent of non-migrants. That difference was not significant, however, and this variable was not used subsequently as a measure of social status.

In many studies, status has also been measured in terms of a woman's level of education or her participation in the labour force. However, in the valley region, fewer than 4 per cent of the women had ever attended primary school and fewer than 5 per cent had some form of cash income in 1982. Consequently, although migrant women were slightly more likely to have had some cash earnings in 1982, the small numbers involved led the authors to exclude those variables from the subsequent analysis.

In considering the reasons stated for female migration, it is important to recall that they were reported retrospectively by the head of household and are therefore subject to errors related both to the motive that the migrant reported to the head of household and to the reinterpretation that the latter person made of it at the time of interview. It is likely that this reinterpretation would be influenced by the outcome of migration, in particular, by the migrant's success in sending food or money back home. Migrants that failed to send something back might well be deemed to have engaged in migration primarily for personal or social reasons.

In any case, economic and human capital reasons are rarely reported as the main motives for female out-migration in this Malian sample. As is shown in table 58, only 2.3 per cent of the women were reported to migrate to work or study. As expected, personal and social reasons dominated, with by far the largest numbers reported as having left in order to join (29 per cent) or visit (18 per cent) relatives or to get married, or after marital dissolution. It is clear that the male heads of household did not attribute economic motives to women who migrated from rural Mali.

E. EMPIRICAL RESULTS

According to the foregoing discussion, although economic motives are not cited explicitly, they are likely to influence female migration. Thus, female migrants are expected to be concentrated in families and communities having fewer economic resources or opportunities in relative terms, and the demographic composition of families is expected to influence female migration. These and other predictors of female migration are considered next. Table 59 lists the independent predictors used and indicates the ex-

TABLE 58. MOTIVES ATTRIBUTED TO FEMALE MIGRATION, SENEGAL RIVER VALLEY, MALI, 1982-1989

Reason for migrating	Number	Percentage
Marriage	75	17
Marital dissolution	54	12
To join family or spouse	124	29
To visit	79	18
To study or work	10	2
Health	35	8
To return home	14	3
To move the family	9	2
Other or unknown	37	9

Source: Centre d'études et de recherche sur la population et pour le développement, *Enquête renouvellée de migration dans la Vallée du fleuve Sénégal* (Bamako, Sahel Institute, 1982 and 1989).

TABLE 59. STATUS, FAMILY AND COMMUNITY VARIABLES EXPECTED TO AFFECT FEMALE MIGRATION, SENEGAL RIVER VALLEY, MALI, 1982-1989

Variable	Description	Expected direction	Actual direction
A. Marital status			
MARRIED	Married in 1982 (1 = Yes)	−	−
POLYMARR	In polygamous union (1 = Yes)	+	+
B. Family facilitators and constraints			
PRIORMIG	Women's previous migration experience (1 = Yes)	+	+
FABSENT	Number of household members absent in 1982	+	+
WOMENCMPD	Interactive effect of women in compound if woman has children	−	−
CHILDDEP	Number of children under age 5 in the household compound	−	−
C. Family economic situation			
FAMINCOME	Logarithm of family cash income in 1982	−	−
FOODDEFCT	Per capita kilograms of millet deficit in 1982	+	a
D. Village economic development			
VILLINC	Logarithm of average village income in 1989	−	a
DEVTACTIV	Any village development activities	−	a
VILLFOOD	Village generally food sufficient	−	a
E. Village economic opportunities for women			
SHEEP	Women raise sheep in village	−	−
OTHERCROP	Other fruits or vegetable crops	−	a
F. Environmental stress			
DROUGHTIRR	Affected by drought and lack of irrigation	−	a

NOTE: For definition of variables, see annex.
aNot significant.

pected signs for their coefficients. More detailed descriptions of the variables used as predictors are found in the annex. Most variables are measured as of 1982, using data from the baseline survey or data collected retrospectively in 1989. Exceptions are village income, which was not obtained reliably for 1982; and number of women working in the family fields, which was not asked in 1982. The independent variables used are indicators of the factors discussed above that are thought to be related to the social status of women. They can be grouped under marital status, family facilitators and constraints, family economic situation, village economic development, village economic opportunities for women and environmental stress. Because age at marriage and childlessness varied so little, they were excluded from the analysis; and instead of using a separate variable indicating that a woman belonged to a polygamous marriage, the model incorporated an interaction using the variable POLYMARR (equal to one if the woman belonged to a polygamous union and to zero otherwise). All correlations between independent variables were less than 0.50, so that multicollinearity did not appear to be an important problem.

The dependent variable used was an indicator of the woman's migration status during the period 1982-1989, that is, it took the values zero or one. Since the dependent variable was dichotomous, the model was fitted using logistic regression, where the dependent variable becomes the odds ratio of migrating versus not migrating. The equation takes the following form:

$$\text{logit(mig8289)} = a + b_1 STATUS + b_2 FAM + b_3 FAMECON + b_4 ECONDEVT + b_5 WOMENOPP + b_6 ENVIRON.$$

The logistic regression coefficients, denoted as b_1 in the equation, indicate the change in the logarithm of the odds of migrating given a unit change in the independent variable. The equation indicates the six categories of independent variables. The complete estimation equation, whose coefficients are shown in table 60, has 14 independent variables. Coefficients significantly different from zero imply that the associated variable has a statistically significant effect on the probability of migrating. Significance is measured by the t-statistic for each regression coefficient and is also displayed in table 60. Any t-statistic whose absolute value is greater than 1.645 is significant at the 10 per cent level or better.

Roughly 400 cases had to be dropped from the estimation procedure because of incomplete informa-

TABLE 60. LOGISTIC REGRESSION COEFFICIENTS FOR FACTORS AFFECTING FEMALE MIGRATION, FROM A COMPLETE MODEL, SENEGAL RIVER VALLEY, MALI, 1982-1989
(*Log likelihood* = -436.59)

Variable	Coefficient	Standard error	t	Probability > |t|	Mean
MARRIED	-0.876[a]	0.217	-4.044	0.000	0.735
POLYMARR	0.371[b]	0.222	1.673	0.095	0.319
PRIORMIG	2.849[a]	0.282	10.101	0.000	0.086
FABSENT	0.049[a]	0.020	2.419	0.016	6.071
WOMENCMPD	-0.100[a]	0.026	-3.794	0.000	2.810
CHILDDEP	-0.112[a]	0.046	-2.449	0.014	2.108
FAMINCOME	-0.035[b]	0.021	-1.700	0.089	11.476
FOODDEFCT	-0.000	0.001	-0.477	0.634	46.406
VILLINC	0.026	0.030	0.866	0.387	7.091
DEVTACTIV	-0.188	0.321	-0.585	0.558	0.139
VILLFOOD	-0.105	0.188	-0.561	0.575	0.560
SHEEP	-0.475[b]	0.245	-1.944	0.052	0.825
OTHERCROP	-0.270	0.227	-1.187	0.236	0.270
DROUGHTIRR	-0.163	0.191	-0.851	0.395	0.500
CONSTANT	-0.300	0.412	-0.728	0.467	1.000

Sources: Estimates prepared using STATA.
NOTES: Number of observations = 1,087; dependent variable is mig8289 with mean 0.198; chi square (14) = 208; probability > chi square = 0.0.
[a]Significant at the 0.05 level.
[b]Significant at the 0.10 level.

tion on family income and family food deficits. Since the means and standard deviations for the cases included and those excluded were similar, the excluded cases can be assumed to have the same basic characteristics as those included. The only significant differences noted pertained to marital status and family size, with the excluded cases being more likely to be single and to belong to slightly smaller households. To check further the effect of such exclusions, the estimation equation was also fitted to the total number of cases omitting the income and food deficit variables, with the result that the signs of the coefficients and their relative magnitudes were similar. Owing to the larger number of observations, however, the levels of significance were higher, but only one additional variable, DROUGHTIRR, became almost significantly different from zero. Its negative sign suggested that, as expected, women were deterred from migrating in the most drought-prone areas, probably because they were needed to fetch water.

The fitted model presented in table 60 supports the hypotheses for the two marital status variables, namely that married female migrants have a lower likelihood of out-migrating, except if they are in polygamous unions, an indicator of their lower social status. Family structure and the existence of persons that could facilitate migration, as indicated by the second group of variables listed in table 59, strongly affect women's migration in the predicted direction. Thus, women who have contacts in the place of destination, gained either through their own previous migration (PRIORMIG) or through that of other members of the household compound to which they belong (FABSENT), are more likely to migrate. Women living in households with high numbers of children under age 5 in 1982, as indicated by the CHILDDEP variable, are less likely to migrate. The presence of other adult women in the household compound, as indicated by the number of women active in cultivating family parcels in 1989 (WOMENCMPD), also reduces the probability of migration. Note, however, that WOMENCMPD is introduced as an interactive variable that is set to zero if the woman whose probability of migration is being modelled has no children of her own. Thus, WOMENCMPD only has a negative effect on the migration probability of women with children of their own. That is, contrary to expectations, the presence of other women in the compound does not necessarily make it easier for women with children to migrate.

The variable indicating the economic status of the family is also significant in influencing the probability that women migrate. The coefficient for the variable indicating the level of family cash income in 1982 (FAMINCOME) shows that women from families with low incomes are more likely to out-migrate. This outcome is consistent with the hypothesis that women, just as men, are compelled to migrate by poverty. However, the extent of the family's food deficit in 1982, as measured by the variable FOODDEFCT, did not have a significant effect on women's migration, perhaps because of problems in securing reliable reports on it from survey respondents or because the family's food deficit in 1982 was not strongly related to its food deficit during the period 1982-1989 when migration occurred.

None of the variables indicating the village's economic development had a significant effect on the probability of female out-migration. This outcome is not due to multicollinearity, because none of the pairwise correlations between variables in this group exceeded 0.20, but it may be caused by the fact that the effect of low family incomes in compelling women to migrate operates mainly at the family level and that the existence of development activities in a village, as indicated by the variable DEVTACTIV, does not necessarily imply that they have an effect on women. Indeed, if such activities benefit mostly men, they may have an impact on the migration of the latter but be irrelevant for the migration of women (development activities at the village level do have some effect on male migration to France, as reported in Findley and Ouedraogo, 1992). In the valley, most development projects involve small-scale irrigation schemes that direct water to river-bank plots farmed mostly by men.

The variable indicating village food sufficiency (VILLFOOD) lacked significance in determining female migration, an outcome consistent with the fact that chronic village food shortages may not directly influence female out-migration because women have little responsibility for the provision of grains. However, this outcome may also be the result of inadequate measurement, since VILLFOOD refers to the village status with regard to food sufficiency in 1982, which may not be a good indicator of the food status of the village during the entire period 1982-1989, when migration took place.

In contrast to the poor predictive performance of variables indicating general economic development at the village level, one of the two variables reflecting the economic opportunities open specifically for women in the village, namely the one indicating that sheep or goats are raised in the village (SHEEP), is significant and has the expected negative effect on the probability of female out-migration. Sheep and other small ruminants are viewed as women's responsibility and the women who raise them can dispose of them for their own benefit. The other variable in the group, OTHERCROP, indicating whether other fruit or vegetable crops are grown in the village, also has a negative effect on female out-migration but is not significant. The non-cereal crops viewed as belonging to women's domain include melons, beans and indigo. They are often grown in marshy areas or along riverbanks, so that even during dry years they can be a source of income or alternative food.

The variable indicating environmental stress, DROUGHTIRR, was not significant in affecting the probability of female out-migration, although it had the expected negative coefficient. It had been argued that women living in particularly vulnerable villages that were affected by severe drought and had no alternative source of water for agriculture would be less likely to out-migrate than women in villages with more stable water-supplies, because women were responsible for fetching water.

According to the results presented so far, a major factor determining the probability of migration of a woman is her own previous migration experience (PRIORMIG). To explore how much that variable influences the effects of the others, a second model was fitted eliminating PRIORMIG from the equation (see table 61). The results obtained confirm the high significance of marital status, the presence of children under age 5 and of other adult women in the household compound and the migration experience of other members of the compound in determining the probability of migration of individual women. In addition, the significance of family income increases, as does that of the variable indicating whether sheep and goats are raised in the village. But more importantly, the variable indicating average village income becomes highly significant and affects the probability of migration of individual women positively. That result is consistent with the expectation that women in better-off communities are likely to have higher aspirations and to use migration as a means of satisfying them.

TABLE 61. LOGISTIC REGRESSION COEFFICIENTS FOR FACTORS AFFECTING FEMALE MIGRATION, MODEL EXCLUDING PRIOR MIGRATION, SENEGAL RIVER VALLEY, MALI, 1982-1989
(Log likelihood = -497.25)

Variable	Coefficient	Standard error	t	Probability > $|t|$	Mean
MARRIED	-0.742[a]	0.194	-3.831	0.000	0.735
POLYMARR	0.084	0.201	0.420	0.675	0.319
FABSENT	0.083[a]	0.018	4.490	0.000	6.071
WOMENCMPD	-0.083[a]	0.024	-3.541	0.000	2.810
CHILDDEP	-0.128[a]	0.042	-3.066	0.002	2.108
FAMINCOME	-0.035[b]	0.019	-1.864	0.063	11.476
FOODDEFCT	-0.001	0.001	-0.559	0.576	46.406
VILLINC	0.061[a]	0.025	2.447	0.015	7.524
DEVTACTIV	-0.137	0.296	-0.462	0.644	0.139
VILLFOOD	0.010	0.173	0.057	0.955	0.560
SHEEP	-0.470[a]	0.223	-2.103	0.036	0.825
OTHERCROP	-0.248	0.206	-1.199	0.231	0.270
DROUGHTIRR	-0.149	0.175	-0.853	0.394	0.500
CONSTANT	-0.523	0.388	-1.349	0.178	1.000

Sources: Estimates prepared using STATA.

NOTES: Number of observations = 1,087; dependent variable is mig8289 with mean 0.198; chi square (13) = 86.89; probability > chi square = 0.0.

[a] Significant at the 0.05 level.
[b] Significant at the 0.10 level.

F. CONCLUSION

In the Senegal River Valley, the dominant image of migration is one of men leaving to work in France. Although the international migration of men continues to figure prominently in family mobility strategies, there is also a growing but less well acknowledged flow of female migrants. Data from a longitudinal survey conducted in the same households in 1982 and 1989 document the migration of household members during the period 1982-1989. The data show that women accounted for 41 per cent of the migrants from the Malian portion of the region, of whom 17 per cent attributed their migration to marriage, 12 per cent to the dissolution of marriage, 31 per cent to other family reasons and only 2 per cent to study or work. Thus, economic reasons were hardly mentioned in the reported motives, although they included a wide range of social reasons other than marriage.

At least in regions like the Senegal River Valley, where traditional ways of life coexist with powerful economic reasons compelling women to migrate, it is likely that female migration will continue to be attributed to socially acceptable reasons. Both women and men find it easier to view women's migration as conforming to social norms so that it cannot be attributed to the failure of male relatives to provide adequately for the women concerned. Indeed, by failing to acknowledge the economic benefits accruing from female migration, respondents may present it as proof of men's ability to provide the resources needed for migration.

Nevertheless, there is some evidence concerning the growing importance of economic considerations in prompting female migration. Studies in Sahelian cities have found significant numbers of women citing economic motives for their migration, even when the timing and destination of the move were dictated by social circumstances (Vaa, Findley and Diallo, 1989). The case of a young woman interviewed in a survey of low-income Bamako women is enlightening: although she declared moving to Bamako to visit her relatives, she was actually working full-time as a domestic servant to earn money for her trousseau. Another survey of migrant women in Bamako and Segou showed both strong economic motivations for migration and high labour force participation among them (ISH, 1984).

The analysis of factors affecting the out-migration of women from the Kayes region of north-western Mali indicates that certain groups of women tend to be overrepresented among migrants. Thus, migrant women include higher proportions of single women and of those from families with lower incomes than the overall population of the place of origin. Currently married women have lower probabilities of migrating than their single, widowed, divorced or separated counterparts, but they still make up the largest proportion of female migrants. The number of children under age 5 in a household compound has a negative impact on the probability of migration of the adult women in it, and that effect is not reduced by the presence of other adult women who are active in cultivating family parcels, probably because the latter group cannot devote much time to child care. Interestingly, the most highly significant variables in determining the probability of female migration are a woman's marital status, her prior migration experience and the number of women working in family parcels. Women that migrate once appear to be highly likely to migrate again, probably because they have already developed successful migration strategies in terms both of social acceptability and of practical feasibility. The existence of other temporary migrants belonging to a household compound also has a significant positive effect on the probability of migration of the adult women in it, a fact that suggests that having adequate contacts in the area of destination is very important in facilitating migration.

There is evidence, however, that women's migration does respond to economic forces. Thus, women from poorer families are more likely to migrate than those from households with higher cash incomes and the significance of that variable increases when a woman's prior migration is not included in the equation fitted. Similarly, when sheep or goats are raised in the village, women are less likely to migrate because that activity provides them with some income. These findings suggest that improving the income-earning opportunities of village families in general and of women in particular can reduce the out-migration of women. However, at the village level, an increase of mean village income can lead to further migration if the expectations of the population rise.

Recognizing that economic problems are likely to persist in Mali and that female migration will probably increase, a number of steps can be taken to improve the income-generating opportunities for women, both in the villages of origin and in the areas of destination. However, because the status of female migrants tends to be low compared with that of male migrants (Findley, Ouaidou and Ouedraogo, 1988), initiatives to enhance the positive aspects of female migration are needed, including programmes that would make it easier for poor women to migrate, work and return home better able to meet their obligations.

As discussed above, demographic factors are important determinants of female migration. Female migration would be facilitated, for instance, if age at marriage were increased and child-bearing were delayed. One strategy to achieve that end would be for the Malian Family Planning Association to strengthen outreach and service delivery in rural areas, especially those from which significant numbers of migrants to urban areas originate, such as the Kayes region.

Because parents in Mali are usually unwilling to let their daughters migrate away without entrusting them to kin living in town, young women living in families without previous migration experience or contacts in town may be unable to move. To facilitate their migration, the Ministry for Women's Affairs could work with local social clubs, especially migrants' associations, to help migrant women find secure housing.

Mothers that migrate often need help with child care. Married women, who constitute the largest number of migrants, often migrate on their own, leaving their children with relatives in the place of origin. Women in polygamous unions can entrust their children to other co-wives and are therefore more likely to migrate. But in times of economic stress, when women may be compelled to migrate to aid the family, such arrangements may prove difficult. It is clear that the availability of child-care services for migrant women in the major cities of destination, such as Bamako and Segou, would be very beneficial. Women's migrant and social clubs could also explore the possibility of organizing cooperative child care.

The powerful effect of prior migration experience—at both the family level and the individual level—in fostering further migration suggests that activities that increase the flow of information between areas of origin and those of destination would be useful. Since many female migrants work in domestic service (ISH, 1984), placement services for such workers would be desirable. In addition, migration clubs established in areas of origin can help potential female migrants meet families that already have migration experience and contacts in the areas of destination.

Because poverty is one of the factors triggering female migration, long-term efforts to raise family income levels in both places of destination and places of origin would give women more latitude in deciding whether to migrate. Programmes that enhance the income-earning capabilities of women, including training and job exchange programmes, the promotion of literacy in rural areas, lessons in accounting and commercial practices and the establishment of savings and loan clubs for women should be given priority. In particular, savings clubs operating in village and city could play pivotal roles in facilitating saving while in the city as well as after the return to the village. Tontines already operate in Bamako and in the larger villages, but their functions could be expanded to include assistance in settling migrants, expediting remittances and accumulating savings to facilitate return.

In the long term, the development of better income-earning opportunities for women in their places of origin is the most attractive strategy. Since the drought in 1965-1974, the shift away from cattle-raising has benefited women. More could be done to help them establish themselves commercially as goat and sheep breeders by providing them with loans and training in breeding schemes and animal husbandry. Similarly, it would be important to strengthen the ability of women to grow and market alternative cash crops.

Although existing rural development activities did not have a significant effect on women's out-migration, they must be reconsidered in the light of the economic dilemma facing men and women in the Senegal River Valley. Women must be provided with means to meet their own economic needs even when programmes address mostly the needs of men. For example, in one of the villages surveyed, the men began the irrigation perimeter but the women used part of it to cultivate tomatoes.

Although the suggestions made here seem appropriate for the region of Kayes, they are not necessarily appropriate for other regions of Mali or for other countries. Some characteristics of Kayes do not apply to the rest of Mali: for instance, male dominance in the production of cereals; or a strong reliance upon family migration. Yet, a comparison of the characteristics of female migrants from Kayes with those identified in a national study (ISH, 1984) shows a high degree of similarity.

This study has documented the high volume of women's out-migration from the Senegal River Valley and explored its determinants, but many aspects of this migration remain to be explored. For example, the information on women's work and family income was too inadequate to establish the extent to which migrant women contribute to family income. Future projects in Africa should recognize the important economic factors influencing women's migration and should take measures to reflect them adequately in both the data-gathering and the analysis phases.

ANNEX

Definition of variables used in the analysis and their means and standard deviations

Variable	Definition
MARRIED	A dichotomous variable. It is 0 if the respondent was not married at the time of the 1982 survey (i.e., she was single, separated, divorced or widowed) and 1 if she was married. Mean = 0.665; SD = 0.472.
POLYMARR	A dichotomous variable. It is 0 if the respondent was not married at the time of the 1982 survey or not in a polygamous union and 1 if she was married and in a polygamous union. Mean = 0.291; SD = 0.455.
PRIORMIG	A dichotomous variable. It was 1 if the respondent had migrated between 1978 and 1982 or was registered as temporarily absent in 1982 and 0 otherwise. Mean = 0.097; SD = 0.297.
FABSENT	The number of household members temporarily absent or who had migrated out of the village by the time of the 1982 survey. Mean = 5.97; SD = 4.84.
WOMENCMPD	The number of women active in cultivating family parcels in 1989. This variable was made to operate only when the woman considered had children of her own; otherwise, it was set equal to 0. Mean = 3.47; SD = 4.74.
CHILDDEP	The number of children under age 5 in the household compound at the time of the survey in 1982. Mean = 2.01; SD = 2.31.
FAMINCOME	The logarithm of the per capita household cash income in 1982. Due to incomplete reporting on economic variables, there are 402 cases with no information on this variable. Mean = 9.975; SD = 0.914.

Variable	Definition
FOODDEFCT	Per capita kilograms of millet that the family purchased in 1982 to cover its food needs after exhausting its own grain reserves. This variable was also not reported in 402 cases. Mean = 46.51; SD = 92.87.
VILLINC	Average of the logarithm of household cash income in a given village. The average was calculated on a per capita basis. This variable was calculated using data reported in the 1989 survey to obtain a better coverage of village households (in 1982, over 400 households did not report income). It does not include remittance income and does reflect the real decline in income for this region during the period 1982-1989. Mean = 6.14; SD = 3.61.
DEVTACTIV	A dichotomous variable. It is 1 if there was a development project or projects active in the village in 1982 (e.g., small-scale irrigation, farmer demonstration project or community-based health care project) and 0 otherwise. Projects could be run either by the Government or by non-governmental organizations. Mean = 0.153; SD = 0.361.
VILLFOOD	A dichotomous variable. It is 1 if the village elders considered in 1982 that the village was generally capable of producing enough cereal grains to meet its needs and 0 otherwise. Mean = 0.559; SD = 0.497.
SHEEP	A dichotomous variable. It was 1 if small ruminants (sheep or goats) were raised in the village in 1982 and 0 otherwise. Because raising these animals is part of women's responsibilities, it is an indicator of economic opportunities for women. Mean = 0.845; SD = 0.361.
OTHERCROP	A dichotomous variable. It is 1 if non-cereal cash crops were grown in the village in 1982 and 0 otherwise. These cash crops are also part of women's responsibilities so that this variable is also an indicator of economic opportunities for women. Mean = 0.267; SD = 0.443.
DROUGHTIRR	A dichotomous variable. It is 1 if a village was considered exceptionally susceptible to severe drought (compared to other villages in the region) in 1982 and if the village did not have any other source of water for agriculture, and 0 otherwise. Mean = 0.547; SD = 0.497.

All means and standard deviations are reported for the 1,489 cases in the file, except for the variables FINCOME and FOODDEFCT, as noted above.

REFERENCES

Adams, Adrian (1977). *Le long voyage des gens du fleuve.* Paris: Francois Maspero.

Amselle, Jean-Loup (1978). Migration et société néotraditionelle: le cas des Bambara du Jitumu (Mali). *Cahiers d'études africaines* (Paris), vol. 18, No. 72, part 4, pp. 487-502. English summary.

Barbière, Jean Claude, ed. (1985). *Femmes du Cameroun: mères pacifiques, femmes rebelles.* Paris: Karthala Press.

Barou, Jacques (1976). L'émigration dans un village du Niger. *Cahiers d'études africaines* (Paris), vol. 16, No. 3-4, pp. 627-632.

Centre d'études et de recherche sur la population et pour le développement (1982 and 1989). *Enquête renouvellée de migration dans la Vallée du fleuve Sénégal.* Bamako: Sahel Institute.

Condé, Julien, and others (1986). *Les migrations internationales sud-nord: une étude de cas; les migrants maliens, mauritaniens et sénégalais de la Vallée de fleuve Sénégal, en France.* Paris: Organisation for Economic Co-operation and Development, Development Centre.

Coulibaly, Sidiki, Joel Gregory and Victor Piché (1980). *Les migrations voltaïques: importance et ambivalence de la migration voltaïque,* tome I. Ottawa, Canada: International Development Research Centre; and Centre voltaïque de la recherche scientifique and Institut national de la démographie.

Dupont, Véronique (1989). Insertion différentielle des migrants dans les marchés du travail de trois villes moyennes de région de plantation (Togo). In *L'Insertion urbaine des migrants en Afrique,* Philippe Antoine and Sidiki Coulibaly, eds. Collection colloques et seminaires. Paris: Office de la recherche scientifique et technique outre-mer.

Findley, Sally E. (1982). Internal migration: determinants. In *International Encyclopedia of Population*, John A. Ross and others, eds. New York: Free Press.

_____ (1987). Les femmes aussi s'en vont. *PopSahel, Bulletin de Population de CERPOD* (Bamako), No. 4 (September), pp. 20-22.

_____ (1988). Les migrations féminines dans les villes africaines: leurs motivations et expériences. In *L'Insertion urbaine des migrants en Afrique*, Philippe Antoine and Sidiki Coulibaly, eds. Collection colloques et seminaires. Paris: Office de la recherche scientifique et technique outre-mer.

_____, and Assitan Diallo (1988). Foster children: links between urban and rural families. In *Proceedings of the Second African Population Conference, Dakar*, vol. 2. Liège: International Union for the Scientific Study of Population.

Findley, Sally E., and D. Ouedraogo (1992). Africa versus France: factors affecting the choices of Malian migrants. Presented at the Annual Meeting of the Population Association of America, Denver, Colorado, 30 April-1 May.

Findley, Sally E., and Linda Williams (1991). *Women Who Go and Women Who Stay: Reflections of Family Migration Processes in a Changing World*. Population and Labour Policies Programme, Working Paper No. 176. Geneva: International Labour Office.

Findley, Sally E., N. Ouaidou and D. Ouedraogo (1988). From seasonal migration to international migration: an analysis of factors affecting the choices of families in the Senegal River Valley. In *Proceedings of the Second African Population Conference, Dakar*, vol. 2. Liège: International Union for the Scientific Study of Population.

Finnegan, Gregory A. (1980). Employment opportunity and migration among the Mossi of Upper Volta. In *Research in Economic Anthropology*, George Dalton, ed., vol. 3. Greenwich, Connecticut: JAI Press.

Institut des sciences humaines (1984). *Exodes des femmes au Mali: main d'oeuvre domestique feminine à Bamako et Segou*. Bamako.

Mali (1985). *Diagnostic de la region de Kayes*. Bamako: Comité regional de développement, Kayes: Ministère du plan.

Minvielle, Jean-Paul (1985). *Paysans migrants du Fouta Toro: Vallée du Sénégal*. Travaux et documents de l'ORSTOM, No. 191. Paris: Editions de l'ORSTOM.

Organisation pour la mise en valeur du fleuve Sénégal (1980). *Etude socio-économique du bassin du fleuve Sénégal*. Dakar/Saint Louis.

Pollet, Eric, and Grace Winter (1971). *La société Soninké (Dyahunu, Mali)*. Editions de l'Institut de sociologie. Bruxelles: Université Libre de Bruxelles.

PopSahel (1991). La migration comme stratégie de survie. *PopSahel, Bulletin de Population de CERPOD* (Bamako, Mali), No. 16 (April).

Remy, Gérard (1977). Mobilité géographique et immobilisme social: un exemple voltaïque. *Revue du tiers-monde* (Paris), vol. 18, No. 71 (juillet-septembre), pp. 617-653.

Rondeau, Chantal (1987). Paysannes du Sahel et stratégies alimentaires. *Revue internationale d'action communautaire* (Montreal), No. 1767.

Scott, J. (1976). *The Moral Economy of the Peasant: Rebellion and Subsistence in Southeast Asia*. New Haven, Connecticut: Yale University Press.

Silitshena, R. M. K. (1990). Social science research on drought in Botswana, Lesotho and Swaziland: a state-of-the-art review. In *Drought in Africa: Proceedings of a Workshop Held in Timbuktu, Mali, 24-28 November 1986*. Ottawa, Canada: International Development Research Centre.

Touré, Abdou (1985). *Les petits metiers à Abidjan: l'imagination au secours de la conjoncture*. Paris: Karthala Press.

Vaa, Mariken, Sally E. Findley and Assitan Diallo (1989). The gift economy: a study of women migrants' survival strategies in a low-income Bamako neighborhood. *Labour, Capital and Society* (Montreal), vol. 22, No. 2 (November), pp. 234-260.

XIV. THE ROLE OF WAGE DIFFERENTIALS IN DETERMINING MIGRATION SELECTIVITY BY SEX: THE CASE OF BRAZIL

*Alicia Puente Cackley**

Despite the fact that women have outnumbered men in rural-urban migration in most countries of Latin America for a long time and that female migration is increasing in other parts of the developing world (Thadani and Todaro, 1984), in the economics literature, female labour migration has been assumed to be either negligible or comparable to that of men in its motivation and direction.

When looking at the labour migration of both men and women, the decision to migrate may be conceptualized in more than one way. A person may migrate as an individual, as one of the members of a married couple or as part of a larger family unit. When two or more persons migrate as a group, the possibility arises that what is optimal for the couple or family unit as a whole may be suboptimal for a particular individual, resulting in the existence of "tied movers" or "tied stayers" (Mincer, 1978).

Although this issue has been raised in the economics literature, there have been few attempts to incorporate it into an empirical study of women's migration, particularly in a developing country. This paper compares sex-specific migration models for individuals and married couples in two regions of Brazil in order to show how the traditional "male" model, which assumes that migration decisions are made by the individual alone, is often inappropriate when examining the factors influencing the migration of women.

A. LITERATURE REVIEW

Migration models

The early economics literature on migration makes almost no mention of the role of gender. Sjaastad (1962), for example, considers migration in a cost/benefit framework, treating the decision to migrate as an investment in human capital that can be evaluated in terms of current values in alternative locations. Although the current value of the costs and benefits associated with migration may well differ systematically between men and women in a society, depending on how motives or goals vary by sex and upon the sociocultural constraints that men and women face, such issues were not addressed.

Harris and Todaro (1970) propose a model of rural-urban migration in developing countries based on the maximization of the expected utility by a (sexless) single "worker", whose age, level of education and work experience determine such utility. Labour is assumed to be homogeneous, so that its propensity to move from the rural to the urban sector does not depend upon the sex of the workers concerned or their family ties. Later variations of the Harris-Todaro model (Fields, 1975, and Choi, 1989, among many others) also fail to incorporate indicators of differences between the sexes. Thus, early economic models of migration were constructed only with men in mind. Women were not considered to play important economic roles and were therefore ignored. More recent economic models of migration acknowledge that a migrant may be either male or female, but there is still little or no recognition of the different motives that lead men and women to migrate.

Thadani and Todaro (1984) were among the first to propose a conceptual framework for female migration in developing countries. They argue that although the migration of women, like that of men, may be driven by economic considerations, a "distinguishing feature" of female migration is the importance of marriage as a reason for migration. They thus identify four variants of female rural-urban migration: (*a*) currently married women in search of urban employment induced to migrate by perceived urban/rural wage differentials; (*b*) unmarried women in search of urban employment induced to migrate for economic or marital reasons;

---

*United States General Accounting Office, Washington, D.C., United States of America.

(c) unmarried women induced to migrate solely for marriage reasons; and (d) currently married women engaged in associational migration with no thought of employment (Thadani and Todaro, 1984). In discussing how marriage motives might impel women to move, Thadani and Todaro recognize that marriage could be a means of social and economic mobility for women and hence should not be disregarded. They suggest that the probability of migrating from a rural area i to an urban area j could be modelled as a function of the expected income differential between i and j, the income differential reflecting an unattached woman's chances of achieving a certain expected income through marriage with a resident of j, the relative probability of finding a husband in j rather than i, variables measuring sociocultural obstacles that constrain women's mobility and a residual term reflecting all other influences on female migration.

Apart from the relatively modest amount of literature on the estimation of migration models in developing countries, there is a large body of economics literature on the causes and consequences of migration in the developed world. Beginning with a seminal paper by Mincer (1978), a subset of this literature looks specifically at the migration decisions of family units or couples. The premise of these studies is that the optimal migration strategy for a person acting alone may differ from that of someone who is part of a family acting as a unit. Mincer assumes that a family consists of at least two married adults, with or without dependent children. He shows how the migration of a married couple can create "tied movers" and "tied stayers", and how the difference between the individual's and the couple's optimal strategy depends upon the degree of correlation in the gains from migration of the husband and the wife. Only when there is a perfect correlation do the optimal strategies of the individual and the married couple coincide (Mincer, 1978).

The work by Borjas (1987) is also relevant in the present context, even though it focuses on international migration. He considers individual migrants first and determines the circumstances in which they are positively or negatively selected in terms of ability from the population in the area of origin. He shows how the extent of income inequality between places of origin and destination influences the type of person that migrates: if income inequality is greater at the place of destination, then people with higher than average skills have an incentive to migrate because they can earn a higher relative wage in the area of destination; and conversely, if income inequality is greater in the place of origin, they lack an incentive. In a later paper, Borjas and Bronars (1989) show how a Mincer type of married-couple framework of migration decision-making changes the distribution of abilities of migrants and non-migrants, weakening the effects of selection by ability. Some low-skilled migrants that would not have migrated on their own to a place with a high level of income inequality may do so if they are married to highly skilled persons. These "tied" migrants with lower skills are not likely to fare as well in the labour-market of the area of destination and therefore may reduce the average wage for migrants as a whole. Borjas and Bronars test their model using data on foreign male immigrants to the United States of America and find that the decision to migrate taken at the level of the married couple has an important impact in lowering the average wages of immigrants (Borjas and Bronars, 1989).

Recent work by Cobb Clark (1990) also considers the characteristics of immigrants to the United States in the context of migration of married couples. She finds that both the magnitude and the direction of immigrant selectivity are affected by whether a woman migrates as part of a couple or alone, as well as by such factors as the prevailing United States immigration policy (including the types of visas granted) and the relative economic and social conditions in countries of origin and destination.

Empirical analyses of labour migration

In economics, empirical studies on labour migration can be based on either aggregate data or on data at the individual level. Most of the former studies automatically exclude women because they implicitly assume that women's labour force participation is too low for a labour supply model of migration to predict it accurately. Examples of that type of study are those by Sahota (1968) and Fields (1982), using data for Brazil and Colombia, respectively.

Even among studies based on individual data, often only the migration decisions of men are studied because of problems in measuring women's labour force participation[1], particularly in developing countries. Thus, the studies by Tunali (1982) and Falaris (1987) are among the many examples that consider only men.

Three studies that did consider female migrants explicitly are those of Yap (1976), Taylor (1984) and Bilsborrow and others (1987). All three assume that the appropriate model for investigating the migration decisions of women is the same as that for men. According to Yap and Taylor, the decision to migrate is based solely on individual maximization of income. Using 1960 census data for Brazil, Yap compares the incomes of migrants in places of destination following rural-urban migration with the current incomes of non-migrants in the rural places of origin. She finds that being female has a negative and significant effect on a migrant's income gain, but she does not control for marital status. Taylor looks at the out-migration decisions of men and women in Mexico as a function of individual and family characteristics. To test the effects of family ties on migration choices, Taylor uses a dummy variable equal to one if the migrant resides permanently away from the family. Taylor hypothesizes that families perform a risk-reducing role in the decision to migrate and finds a distinct tendency for men to predominate in migration from Mexico to the United States, but for both sexes to be equally likely to engage in internal migration.

Bilsborrow and colleagues (1987) study the determinants of the rural-urban out-migration of individuals (daughters or sons) from rural families in Ecuador, including factors at the individual, household and community levels. The fact that they include family variables in the estimation indicates that they view the decision to migrate as one made in a family context. Their findings show that being married has a statistically significant negative effect on the probability of out-migration of daughters but no significant effect on that of sons.

Behrman and Wolfe (1984) present a study of the interregional migration of women in Nicaragua that follows the Thadani-Todaro framework. The study compares estimates of expected outcomes in each of three regions with the actual migratory flows between those regions to see how important the incentives associated with the labour-market, the demographic marriage market and the economic marriage market are in explaining women's migration. While far from conclusive, their results appear to show that a woman's own expected wage is not the only factor influencing her decision to migrate. Economic marriage market incentives, measured by the estimated earnings of potential male companions in a particular region, appear to be more consistent with the migration flows of women in Nicaragua than are strictly demographic marriage market incentives, measured by the estimated probability that a woman will find a future male companion in each region.

There are also several relevant studies of female migrants in the United States. Among these, DaVanzo (1976) uses data from the Panel Survey of Income Dynamics to estimate the determinants of whether a couple (husband and wife) will migrate, as a function of their joint income. She finds that wives' characteristics have indeed an influence on the migration of couples. Nakosteen and Zimmer (1980) estimate a model of migration between states in the United States using data for both men and women from the Social Security Administration Continuous Work History Sample. Using standard income maximization theory, they hypothesize that women are less likely than men to migrate due to the effect of family ties on their mobility. Their results do indeed indicate that being female has a negative effect on the probability of migrating. However, although the expected wage equations are corrected for sample selection bias due to the migration decision itself, they are not corrected for a second potential source of bias deriving from the lower labour force participation rates of women.

B. MODELS AND DATA USED

The aim of modelling

For most of the past 25 years, migration has been conceptualized as resulting from an individual decision based on the optimization of income or utility. Although research on migration decisions in developed countries has increasingly incorporated a couple or a family perspective, it is evident from the review presented above that such an approach has been rare in the analysis of migration in developing countries, although it would seem even more appropriate in that context.

According to Mincer (1978) and Borjas (1987), a model that assumes that migration decisions are made by individuals based only on their own characteristics cannot adequately predict the migration propensities of married couples. Such prediction requires the maximization of a bidimensional utility function which is unlikely to produce the same results as the combination of each individual's utility function. Maximization of a couple's utility function results in the creation of tied movers or stayers, that is, persons that migrate or not according to what is best for the couple, even though the optimization of their own individual utility functions would dictate a different migration decision (Mincer, 1978). According to Mincer, the effects of modelling the migration of a married woman according to the maximization of her own individual utility are likely to be more misleading than those resulting from adopting the same strategy for married men, because married women are more likely to be tied movers or stayers.

In the following discussion and according to the conventional maximization approach based on individual utility functions, men and women are assumed to maximize separately the current discounted value of their lifetime income streams across areas of origin and destination, net of the costs of migration. It is further assumed that, other things being equal, an individual (or couple) will migrate if the net current discounted value of lifetime income is greater at the place of destination than at the place of origin and will remain at the place of origin if the reverse is true.

The decision rule for an individual woman or man may then be established in terms of the value of the function D defined as:

$$D_i^I = W_{ij} - W_{ik} - C^I, \quad (1)$$

where the index I indicates that this is a migration model based on the individual, i represents the particular individual, j and k indicate the place of destination and origin, respectively; W_{ij} and W_{ik} represent the current discounted value of lifetime income in the areas of destination and origin, respectively; and C^I is the cost of migration for the individual. Only if D_i^I is positive does the individual migrate.

In the version of this model for married couples, currently married women and men are assumed to be part of a unit that maximizes the sum of the current discounted values of lifetime income of both husband and wife across areas of origin and destination, net of their joint migration costs. The decision rule for the married couple therefore depends upon a different variant of D, defined as:

$$D_i^M = (W_{ij}^f - W_{ik}^f) + (W_{ij}^m - W_{ik}^m) - C^M, \quad (2)$$

where the index M indicates that this is a model for the migration of married couples, f identifies the wife's characteristics, m those of the husband and the costs C^M now refer to those of the couple and are assumed to increase with the size of the family. As in the case of an individual, a married couple migrates only if D_i^M is positive.

Correcting for selectivity bias

An accurate assessment of the impact of lifetime income differentials between places of origin and destination on a person's probability of migrating requires that those differentials be adequately measured. Since discounted lifetime income cannot be measured a priori, a common proxy used is some measure of individual earnings, such as the hourly wage rate. Because the actual wages of an individual cannot be observed at both the place of origin and the place of destination at the same time, a common practice is to use information about individual characteristics together with data on the relative earnings of migrants and non-migrants to estimate the potential wage of each person in both locations. If, as is common, migrants do not constitute a randomly selected subset of the population in the place of origin, the wages of non-migrants in the place of origin constitute a biased estimate of the wages that migrants would have earned if they had not moved. The same is true of the wage of migrants as an estimate of the wage that non-migrants would have earned if they had moved. That is, there are likely to be unobservable, systematic differences between migrants and non-migrants that affect the wage that each would have otherwise earned at the places of origin and destination. Use of these wage estimates leads therefore to biases in the estimation of wage differentials and consequently to biases in the estimation of the effects of wage differentials and any other variables considered to be determinants of migration (Heckman, 1979).

The problem of selection bias in estimates of wages or earnings has been raised in contexts other than the study of migration. Heckman (1979), for example, considers the general issue of selection bias, Lee (1978) the effect of selection bias (union membership) on estimates of the effects of labour union membership on wage levels, and Willis and Rosen (1979) the effect of selection bias on the estimation of the effects of college education on expected lifetime earnings. In each instance, correction for selection bias led to statistically unbiased and consistent, although somewhat inefficient, estimates of the coefficients of the structural equation proposed.

The method of estimation for migration models for individuals and couples

In keeping with the models presented above, the probability of migrating from one region to another is estimated as a function of the difference of the natural logarithms of the expected hourly wage rate that an individual earns in each region ($\ln(W_{ij}) - \ln(W_{ik})$) and of a set of individual characteristics, denoted by Z_i, that affect the migrant's utility function independently of wage differentials. In the version of the model for married couples, the equivalent differences of the natural logarithms of expected hourly wages for husband and wife are included.

The logarithm of the expected wage is assumed to be a linear function of a set of personal characteristics, denoted by the vector X_i, which includes age, education, occupation and urban or rural residence. In the case of Brazil that is analysed below, each of these variables refers to a person's status as of 1970, except that urban or rural residence refers to the person's place of residence in 1976. Thus, the logarithm of the expected wage at the places of destination and origin can be represented by the following equations:

$$\ln W_{ij} = \alpha_{0j} + \alpha_{1j} X_{ij} + e_{ij} ; \qquad (3)$$

$$\ln W_{ik} = \alpha_{0k} + \alpha_{1k} X_{ik} + e_{ik} , \qquad (4)$$

where the subindices j and k indicate areas of destination and origin, respectively; α_{0j}, α_{1j}, α_{0k} and α_{1k} represent coefficients that are to be estimated; W_{ij} and W_{ik} represent the hourly wages that a migrant would have earned at the place of destination and origin, respectively; X_{ij} and X_{ik} are vectors representing the personal characteristics of the workers involved; and e_{ij} and e_{ik} are the error terms in the estimation equation which are each assumed to have a normal distribution with mean 0 and standard deviation σ_j and σ_k, respectively.

On the basis of the expected wages, the decision rule for the migration of an individual depends upon the value of:

$$D_i^I = \delta_0 + \delta_1 (\ln W_{ij} - \ln W_{ik}) + \delta_2 Z_i^I - \varepsilon_i^I , \qquad (5)$$

where δ_0, δ_1 and δ_2 represent coefficients; Z_i^I is a vector of personal characteristics expected to affect the probability of migrating independently of the wage differential; and ε_i^I is an error term. The characteristics denoted by Z_i^I include the type of residence prior to migration (i.e., urban or rural residence in 1970) and the number of household members over age 6 in 1976. The error term ε_i^I is again assumed to have a normal distribution with mean 0 and standard deviation σ_ε^I. If D_i^I is positive, the person would migrate; no migration would take place otherwise.

The decision rule for a married couple depends similarly upon the value of the function D^M, which has the form:

$$\begin{aligned} D_i^M = \delta_0 &+ \delta_1 (\ln W_{ij}^f - \ln W_{ik}^f) \\ &+ \delta_2 (\ln W_{ij}^m - \ln W_{ik}^m) \\ &+ \delta_3 Z_i^M - \varepsilon_i^M , \end{aligned} \qquad (6)$$

where Z_i^M represents the characteristics of both husband and wife; and ε_i^M is again assumed to have a normal distribution with mean 0 and standard deviation σ_ε^M. As in the case of the individual model, migration would occur only if D_i^M is positive.

Ideally, the estimation of the coefficients of equations (3) and (4) should be carried out using the wages that migrants had before migration at the place of origin k and the wages that they earned after migration in the place of destination j. However, the data on Brazil that are used in the analysis only include information on wages for a fixed date, 1976, for all people that were residents of the place of origin in 1970 and were either still origin residents in 1976 or had migrated to the destination by 1976. Consequently, those data had to be used to infer the expected wages at the place of origin for migrants and non-migrants alike, taking into account the effects of migration selectivity. To do that, equation (3) had to be estimated only for migrants, whereas (4) was estimated only for non-migrants at the place of origin. That procedure, however, meant that the error terms in equations (3) and (4) would no longer have the zero means required to use ordinary least squares fitting procedures, since the selectivity involved implied that their means would be $E(e_{ij} | D = 1)$ and $E(e_{ik} | D = 0)$, that is, the expected value of e_{ij} conditional on the fact that only migrants were being considered ($D = 1$ implies that migration occurred) and the expected value of e_{ik} conditional on the fact that only non-migrants were considered ($D = 0$ implies no migration). Consequently, some correction had to be introduced in equations (3) and (4) before estimation was possible. Following Lee (1978), a procedure that estimates the means $E(e_{ij} | D = 1)$ and $E(e_{ik} | D = 0)$ in equations (3) and (4) and adjusts the error terms so that they have zero means was used. The result is a non-linear least squares equation that can be estimated in two steps.

To do that, the first step was to combine equations (3) and (4) with (5), so that equation (5) could be expressed exclusively in terms of the exogenous explanatory variables in the following reduced form:

$$D_i^I = \gamma_0 + \gamma_1 X_i + \gamma_2 Z_i - E_i^I, \quad (7)$$

where γ_0, γ_1 and γ_2 represent coefficients and the error term has been normalized so that its standard deviation, σ_E^I, equals 1. Similarly, in the case of the model for married couples, D_i^M was expressed as:

$$D_i^M = \gamma_0 + \gamma_1 X_i^f + \gamma_2 X_i^m + \gamma_3 Z_i^M - E_i^M. \quad (8)$$

It turns out that the expected values of the original error terms (e_{ij}, e_{ik}) can be expressed as $(-\sigma_{1\varepsilon} f(\psi_i)/F(\psi_i))$ and $(\sigma_{2\varepsilon} f(\psi_i)/(1-F(\psi_i)))$, respectively, where f is the probability density function, F is the cumulative distribution function of the normal distribution and

$$\psi_i = \gamma_0 + \gamma_1 X_i. \quad (9)$$

One can therefore modify equations (3) and (4) as follows:

$$\ln W_{ij} = \alpha_{0j} + \alpha_{1j} X_i - \sigma_{1\varepsilon}(f(\psi_i)/F(\psi_i)) + \eta_{ij}; \quad (10)$$

$$\ln W_{ik} = \alpha_{0k} + \alpha_{1k} X_i + \sigma_{2\varepsilon}(f(\psi_i)/(1-F(\psi_i))) + \eta_{ik}, \quad (11)$$

so that even when they refer to hourly wages conditional on migrant status their error terms η_{ij} and η_{ik} have conditional means equal to zero, that is,

$$E(\eta_{ij} | D = 1) = E(\eta_{ik} | D = 0) = 0. \quad (12)$$

Consequently, the first step of the estimation procedure is to fit equations (7) and (8) using an independent variable D that is equal to one if the person or couple in question is migrant and to zero otherwise and using maximum likelihood probit methods to obtain estimates of the coefficients γ. Those coefficients are then used in equation (9) to calculate ψ_i, whose values are substituted in the normal density and distribution functions, $f(\psi_i)$ and $F(\psi_i)$, to calculate the adjustment terms in equations (10) and (11). The next step is to estimate those equations using ordinary least squares. This method produces consistent estimates of the coefficients in equations (10) and (11) and of the standard deviations $\sigma_{1\varepsilon}$ and $\sigma_{2\varepsilon}$.

The estimates of the coefficients are then used to estimate the expected wages in each location for every individual in the survey sample. Thus, equation (10) is used to estimate the expected wages of non-migrants in the place of origin as if they had migrated, and of migrants in the place of destination, whereas equation (11) is used to estimate the wages of non-migrants in the place of origin and of migrants as if they had remained in the place of origin. Those calculations produce expected wages for all migrants and non-migrants in the sample, a necessary input for the estimation of equations (5) and (6) to determine the relative importance of the different factors affecting the probability of migrating.

To conclude this discussion of the methodology used, it should be mentioned that another source of selectivity bias must be taken into account when fitting models in relation to female wage-earners. Indeed, since female labour force participation in general is relatively low and not all working women receive a wage, focusing only on those that do is likely to introduce biases because of the selectivity involved. Hence, a procedure similar to that described above was used to correct for the selectivity bias associated with the wage-earning status of women. The procedure used was derived from the work of Tunali (1982) and of Fishe, Trost and Lurie (1981), and is described in detail in Cackley (1990). The resulting models of individual and married-couple migration therefore incorporate a correction for two types of selectivity and are consequently based on unbiased estimates of the expected wages of both migrants and non-migrants by sex.

The data used

The data used in this analysis are from the Pesquisa Nacional por Amostra de Domicilios (PNAD) in 1976, one of a series of national sample surveys carried out in Brazil. Due to limitations in the basic data and to the complexities of modelling the decision to migrate, the analysis is limited to estimating the probability of migration between only two of the major geographical regions, namely, from the north-east to the extended south-east, which was defined as comprising the states of Espirito Santo, Minas Gerais, Rio de Janeiro and São Paulo, plus the Federal District that borders Minas Gerais and includes the country's capital, Brasilia. Together, those two major regions accounted for 70 per cent of the Brazilian population in 1970 (Merrick and Graham, 1979).

Because the model refers only to labour migration, the universe of interest includes only women aged 20-40 and men aged 20-45 that were either currently married or never married in 1976 and that had been resident in the north-eastern region of Brazil in 1970. A person was considered to be in the labour force if he or she had a non-zero wage in 1976, thus excluding unpaid family workers. Analysis of the characteristics of paid and unpaid female workers indicated no systematic differences between the two subgroups that would significantly bias the estimation of wage functions. It was found that 8 per cent of married women and 9 per cent of unmarried women were unpaid family workers.

The information gathered by the 1976 PNAD permitted the calculation of the values of certain variables as of 1970. Thus, age was calculated by subtraction, educational attainment was estimated by assuming that each school cycle was completed in a certain number of years, marital status was derived from information on the time of marriage and information on occupation was obtained by assuming that non-migrants had in 1970 the same occupation that they reported for 1976 and that migrants had in 1970 the same occupation that they were reported to have had in their previous place of residence. The data on wages, however, were only available for 1976. Therefore, in using equations (10) and (11), wages in 1976 were associated with personal characteristics referring to 1970, that is, prior to migration. Although wage data for 1970 would have been preferable for this purpose, they were not available.

A migrant was identified by three questions in the survey: current state and *municipio* of residence; length of stay in the current *municipio* (less than two years, from two to six years or six years or more), and state of residence prior to the current one. A person who was living in the extended south-eastern region of Brazil at the time of interview, had lived there less than six years and was reported to have lived in the north-east prior to migration was considered a migrant for the purposes of this study.

The universe of interest was further restricted because of the nature of the data on marital status. Since the year of marriage was not recorded for men and women who were separated, divorced or widowed by 1976, those persons had to be dropped from the analysis. The number of women in that category was relatively small; and the number of men even smaller, so that the resulting bias is probably not important. Table 62 shows the number of persons residing in the north-east in 1970 by sex and marital status as of 1970 and by work and migration status as of 1976.

Two variables were used to indicate the costs associated with migration. One was a dummy variable set equal to one if a person was living in an urban *municipio* in 1970 and to zero otherwise. That variable can be interpreted as a crude proxy for the access that a prospective migrant in the north-east had to information about conditions in the main potential areas of

TABLE 62. RESIDENTS OF THE NORTH-EASTERN REGION OF BRAZIL IN 1970, BY SEX AND MARITAL STATUS IN 1970 AND MIGRANT AND WAGE-EARNING STATUS IN 1976

Sex and marital status in 1970	Number of residents in north-eastern Brazil in 1970	Number with non-zero wage data in 1976		Number with non-zero wage who migrated to the extended south-east by 1976	
		Percentage	Number	Percentage	Number
Never-married women	4 369	50	2 195	15	635
Never-married men	6 857	84	5 744	22	1 535
Married women	3 480	14	489	2	55
Married men	3 480	97	3 390	11	386

Source: Brazil, *Pesquisa Nacional por Amostra de Domicílios, 1976* (Rio de Janeiro, Fundação Instituto Brasileiro de Geografia e Estatística).

destination (the extended South-east, which is considerably more urbanized than the north-east). Since the more information a migrant has about the place of destination, the lower the costs of moving, the dummy variable used would be expected to have a positive effect on the probability of migrating. However, another interpretation possible is to view that variable as a measure of the relative economic conditions people face at their place of origin. Poorer conditions in rural areas, in relation to urban areas, may push people to out-migrate. This interpretation would imply a negative effect of urban residence on the probability of out-migrating. The second variable indicating costs is the number of household members over age 6 in 1976. As the number of household members increases, both types of costs rise, thus leading to a reduction in the probability of migration.

The data available are especially useful for the analysis intended because they facilitate the identification of migrants by age, sex and marital status at a time close to that of migration. In addition, the large sample size allows the estimation of separate migration functions for all four groups of currently married and never-married men and women in 1970.

Data limitations

For the purposes of this investigation, however, there are several significant limitations in the data available, especially because they do not permit the identification of all characteristics of household members nor the composition of the household prior to migration. Thus, in order to have some indicator of the number of household members at the time of migration, it was necessary to make the simplistic assumption that the household remained intact after migration (except for the person who out-migrated, in the case of individual migration), so that all persons in the household over age 6 in 1976 were assumed to have also been household members in 1970, prior to migration. Although this variable is clearly less than ideal as a measure of true household size at the time of migration, it is the best available.

A second limitation of the data at hand is that migrants could only be identified as such if they changed their state of residence. The information available did not permit the identification of those who had moved from one *municipio* to another within the same state. For that reason, the analysis could only be undertaken at the level of regions comprising several states. Furthermore, since the analysis only focused on migration from the north-east to the extended south-east, to the extent that different factors influence other migration flows in the country, the results obtained are not representative of those flows.

A further limitation of the analysis carried out is that wages are estimated only on the basis of individual characteristics, without regard to those of the areas of origin or destination. PNAD 1976 did not gather information on contextual variables at either the municipal or the state level and no attempt was made to obtain such information from other sources. Consequently, the resulting estimates of expected wages are not very precise, because they lump together persons from a large geographical region without making allowance for location-specific factors that affect wages.

Like other studies based on data from a single cross-sectional survey, the present study is limited by the fact that migrants are only observed in the place of destination. Therefore, their actual wages just before and just after migration are not observed and can only be estimated making allowance for the selection bias of migration as discussed above. Although it is preferable to have the actual pre-migration and post-migration wage for each migrant, the correction procedure for migration selectivity may adequately cope with that limitation.

Lastly, there is the problem of the exclusion of potentially important variables. For example, household assets, which may be location-specific, are excluded (see DaVanzo, 1976, on their effects). Other household composition variables, such as the age, sex composition or labour force activity of other adult household members (including those who can provide child care in place of the mother), are also not considered. Even education is included only indirectly, through its effects on estimated wages, although it may have other effects on migration by changing tastes or enhancing access to information.

D. THE ESTIMATED MODELS

The models to be compared include the individual model applied to currently married and never-married women and men, as well as the married-couple model applied only to married women and men. First, the models are estimated, correcting only for migration-related selection bias. The models are then re-estimated, correcting also for selection bias related to the earning of a non-zero wage by women. The purpose of estimating different models is to explore the changes in the effects of wage differentials on a woman's probability of migrating when correcting for different types of biases. Along the way, differences in the functions estimated for men and women are noted.

The individual model

The individual-level model has as its dependent variable the probability that a person migrated from the north-eastern region of Brazil to the extended southeast between 1970 and 1976. First, the effects associated with the expected wage differential between destination and origin are presented, correcting only for the selection bias associated with migration itself. The estimated effects (that is, coefficients) and their standard errors for the four groups considered, namely, never-married women, never-married men, currently married women and currently married men, are shown in table 63. They are positive and significant for three groups—namely, never-married women, currently

TABLE 63. RESULTS FROM A PROBIT MODEL OF THE INDIVIDUAL PROBABILITY OF MIGRATING FROM THE NORTH-EASTERN REGION OF BRAZIL TO THE EXTENDED SOUTH-EASTERN REGION

	Sex and marital status in 1970			
Variable	Never-married women	Never-married men	Married women	Married men
Constant	-1.79[a] (0.12)	-1.96[a] (0.10)	-1.71[a] (0.32)	-2.17[a] (0.14)
Expected migrant wage minus expected non-migrant wage	1.11[a] (0.12)	1.25[a] (0.13)	0.20 (0.14)	0.98[a] (0.15)
Lived in an urban *municipio* in 1970	-0.10 (0.06)	0.35[a] (0.04)	-0.04 (0.21)	0.33[a] (0.09)
Number of household members over age 6 in 1976	-0.02 (0.01)	-0.06[a] (0.01)	-0.01 (0.04)	-0.01 (0.02)

NOTE: Standard errors are shown in parentheses.
[a]Significant at the 0.05 level.

married men and never-married men—but the coefficient for the wage differential is not significant in the case of currently married women.

The coefficients of the two independent variables indicating migration costs are generally statistically significant at the 5 per cent level for men, whether they are currently or never married, the exception being the coefficient for the number of household members over age 6 in the case of currently married men. In the case of men, the sign of the coefficient of the dummy variable indicating urban residence in 1970 is positive, meaning that urban residence in the north-east increases the probability of migrating. For both groups of women, in contrast with men, neither of the two variables indicating migration costs was significant.

The coefficients of the expected wage differential for the different population groups support Mincer's hypothesis that the determinants of migration for married couples and especially those for married women should be investigated using a household or at least a married-couple perspective. Thus, for currently married women, the expected wage differential has a relatively small coefficient that is not significant, whereas the equivalent coefficient for never-married women is large and significant. Indeed, a differential in the same direction exists between the coefficient of the expected wage differential for currently married men and that for never-married men, though both are significant. Such differentials suggest that factors excluded from the estimation equations, such as the earning prospects and other characteristics of spouses, may influence the migration probability of both currently married men and women.

The married-couple model

The model for married couples has as its dependent variable the probability that a married couple will migrate jointly from the north-eastern region to the extended south-eastern region. Table 64 shows the results of fitting the model using as independent variables the expected wage differentials of both husband and wife, making allowance for the selection bias of migration.

In the model for married couples, the estimated coefficient of the husband's expected wage differential is positive, significant and greater in magnitude than the corresponding coefficients for currently married men, never-married men or never-married women, according to the individual model. On the other hand, the coefficient of the wife's expected wage differential, although positive, continues to lack significance. Another important change with respect to the coefficients yielded by the individual model is that the coefficient for the variable indicating urban residence in 1970 is now negative and significant.

Results from models incorporating corrections for the selectivity of women as wage-earners

Using another adjustment strategy, the coefficients for the individual and married-couple models were estimated again and are displayed in table 65. The new adjustment strategy permits the estimation of expected wage differentials for women while at the same time adjusting for the selectivity inherent not only in migration but in the fact that only a relatively small and selected number of women are wage-earners. According to the re-estimated individual model, a woman's expected wage differential is still a significant positive predictor of her probability of migrating if she has never been married, although the size of the coefficient is smaller than that presented in table 63. For currently married women, however, the coefficient of the expected wage differential continues to lack statistical significance and is now negative in both the individual and the married-couple models. The husband's expected wage differential in the married-couple model, on the other hand, continues to have a significant and positive effect on the couple's probability of migrating, although the magnitude of its coefficient is only about 60 per cent of that estimated without adjusting for the selectivity of wage-earning among women (see table 64).

By correcting for the bias associated with the status of women as wage-earners, the coefficient of the variable indicating urban residence in 1970 becomes positive and significant for all groups presented in table 65, thus bringing these results in line with the previous ones for currently married and never-married men (see table 63). The positive sign suggests that those with previous urban residence face lower physical and psychological costs associated with migration, probably by having greater access to information about possible destinations. In contrast, the sign of the

TABLE 64. RESULTS FROM A PROBIT MODEL OF A MARRIED COUPLE'S PROBABILITY OF MIGRATING FROM THE NORTH-EASTERN REGION OF BRAZIL TO THE EXTENDED SOUTH-EASTERN REGION

Variable	Model: married couple	Standard error
Constant	-2.40ᵃ	0.41
Wife's expected migrant wage minus wife's expected non-migrant wage	0.27	0.16
Husband's expected migrant wage minus husband's expected non-migrant wage	1.75ᵃ	0.46
Lived in an urban *municipio* in 1970	-0.64ᵃ	0.28
Number of household members over age 6 in 1976	-0.01	0.05

ᵃSignificant at the 0.05 level.

TABLE 65. RESULTS FROM PROBIT MODELS OF THE PROBABILITY OF INDIVIDUAL WOMEN AND MARRIED COUPLES MIGRATING FROM THE NORTH-EASTERN REGION OF BRAZIL TO THE EXTENDED SOUTH-EASTERN REGION

	Marital status in 1970		
	Never-married women	Married women	Married couples
Constant	-1.58[a] (0.10)	-1.78[a] (0.13)	-2.11[a] (0.15)
Own predicted wage differential	0.73[a] (0.11)	-0.07 (0.04)	-0.09 (0.04)
Husband's predicted wage differential	-	-	0.96[a] (0.15)
Lived in an urban *municipio*	0.12[a] (0.06)	0.55[a] (0.08)	0.35[a] (0.09)
Number of household members over age 6 in 1976	-0.05[a] (0.01)	-0.01 (0.02)	-0.01 (0.02)

NOTE: Standard errors are shown in parentheses.
[a] Significant at the 0.05 level.

coefficient for the number of household members over age 6 continues to be negative in all the cases presented in table 65, as was expected, but is statistically significant only for never-married women. The lack of significance of this variable may be due to the fact that it is not based on household structure before migration because, as explained above, that information was lacking.

The changes in the results obtained by modifying the estimation procedures corroborate that it is appropriate to model the migration of married and never-married women differently because they are operating in different contexts and responding to different incentive structures. Although the probability of migrating for never-married women increases as the difference between their expected wages at destination and at origin rises, the same is not true for currently married women. For the latter group, the probability of migrating is more strongly determined by the expected wage differential of their husbands. This conclusion is consistent with Mincer's hypothesis.

E. CONCLUSION

This paper analyses differences in the effects of several factors on the migration probabilities of never-married and currently married women and compares them with those for never-married and currently married men in Brazil. The analysis corroborates that for currently married women migration is often not an optimal strategy in terms of their own potential, but they may, nevertheless, choose or be compelled to migrate as part of a family or, as modelled here, in the company of their husbands, so that as a couple, the expected joint gains of both husband and wife are maximized. In contrast, never-married women appear to be better able to migrate when their own interests are being served, as is proved by the fact that their probability of migrating is determined by factors similar to those determining the migration of men, in particular, the expected wage differential between destination and origin.

The preceding analysis also makes clear that migration is often a viable economic strategy for women, both those migrating when still not married and those moving as part of a couple. Thus, in every instance, the differential of either women's own or their husband's expected wages between the areas of destination and those of origin had a positive and significant effect on the probability of migrating.

NOTE

[1] See Bilsborrow (1993) and references therein to studies by Anker and others.

REFERENCES

Behrman, Jere R., and Barbara L. Wolfe (1984). Micro determinants of female migration in a developing country: labor market, demographic marriage market and economic marriage market incentives. In *Research in Population Economics*, vol. 5, T. Paul Schultz and Kenneth I. Wolpin, eds. Greenwich, Connecticut: JAI Press Inc.

Bilsborrow, Richard E., and others (1987). The impact of origin community characteristics on rural-urban out-migration in a developing country. *Demography* (Washington, D.C.), vol. 24, No. 2 (May), pp. 191-210.

Borjas, George J. (1987). Self-selection and the earnings of immigrants. *American Economic Review* (Nashville, Tennessee), vol. 77, No. 4 (September), pp. 531-553.

_____, and Steven G. Bronars (1989). Immigration and the family. Unpublished paper.

Brazil (1978). *Pesquisa Nacional por Amostra de Domicílios, 1976*. Rio de Janeiro: Fundação Instituto Brasileiro de Geografia e Estatística.

Cackley, Alicia Puente (1990). Female migration in Brazil: the role of marital status in the migration decisions and wages of women. Unpublished doctoral dissertation. Ann Arbor, Michigan: University of Michigan.

Choi, Jung Whan (1989). Migration and economic development in less developed countries. Unpublished doctoral dissertation. Ann Arbor, Michigan: University of Michigan.

Cobb Clark, Deborah A. (1990). Immigrant selectivity: the role of immigration policy and household structure. Unpublished doctoral dissertation. Ann Arbor, Michigan: University of Michigan.

DaVanzo, Julie (1976). *Why Families Move: A Model of the Geographic Mobility of Married Couples*. Report R-1972-DOL. Santa Monica, California: The Rand Corporation.

Falaris, Evangelos M. (1987). A nested logit migration model with selectivity. *International Economic Review* (Osaka, Japan), vol. 28, No. 2 (June), pp. 429-443.

Fields, Gary S. (1975). Rural-urban migration, urban unemployment and underemployment, and job-search activity in LDCs. *Journal of Development Economics* (Amsterdam), vol. 2, No. 2 (June), pp. 165-187.

_____ (1982). Place-to-place migration in Colombia. *Economic Development and Cultural Change* (Chicago, Illinois), vol. 30, No. 3 (April), pp. 539-558.

Fishe, Raymond P. H., R. P. Trost and Philip M. Lurie (1981). Labor force earnings and college choice of young women: an examination of selectivity bias and comparative advantage. *Economics of Education Review* (Oxford, United Kingdom), vol. 1, No. 2 (Spring).

Harris, John R., and Michael P. Todaro (1970). Migration, unemployment and development: a two-sector analysis. *American Economic Review* (Nashville, Tennessee), vol. 60, No. 1 (March), pp. 126-142.

Heckman, James J. (1979). Sample selection bias as a specification error. *Econometrica* (Cambridge, Massachusetts; and London), vol. 47, No. 1 (January), pp. 153-161.

Lee, Lung-fei (1978). Unionism and wage rates: a simultaneous equations model with qualitative and limited dependent variables. *International Economic Review* (Osaka, Japan), vol. 19, No. 2 (June), pp. 415-433.

Merrick, Thomas W., and Douglas H. Graham (1979). *Population and Economic Development in Brazil: 1800 to the Present*. Baltimore, Maryland: The Johns Hopkins University Press.

Mincer, Jacob (1978). Family migration decisions. *Journal of Political Economy* (Chicago, Illinois), vol. 86, No. 5 (October), pp. 749-773.

Nakosteen, Robert A., and Michael Zimmer (1980). Migration and income: the question of self-selection. *Southern Economic Journal* (Chapel Hill, North Carolina), vol. 46, No. 3 (January), pp. 840-851.

Sahota, Gian S. (1968). An economic analysis of internal migration in Brazil. *Journal of Political Economy* (Chicago, Illinois), vol. 76, No. 2 (March/April), pp. 218-245.

Sjaastad, Larry A. (1962). The costs and returns of human migration. *Journal of Political Economy* (Chicago, Illinois), vol. 70, No. 5, part 2 (October), pp. 80-93.

Taylor, J. Edward (1984). *Differential Migration, Networks, Information and Risk*. Migration and Development Program, Discussion Paper No. 11. Cambridge, Massachusetts: Harvard University, Center for Population Studies.

Thadani, Veena N., and Michael P. Todaro (1984). Female migration: a conceptual framework. In *Women in the Cities of Asia: Migration and Urban Adaptation*, James T. Fawcett, Siew-Ean Khoo and Peter C. Smith, eds. Boulder, Colorado: Westview Press.

Tunali, F. Insan (1982). A common structure for models of double selection: with an application to migration selectivity on income. Unpublished paper.

Willis, Robert J., and Sherwin Rosen (1979). Education and self-selection. *Journal of Political Economy* (Chicago, Illinois), vol. 87, No. 5, part 2 (October), pp. 57-536.

Yap, Lorene Y. L. (1976). Rural-urban migration and urban underemployment in Brazil. *Journal of Development Economics* (Amsterdam), vol. 3, No. 3 (September), pp. 227-243.

Part Six

CONSEQUENCES OF MIGRATION FOR WOMEN

XV. EMANCIPATION OR SUBORDINATION? CONSEQUENCES OF FEMALE MIGRATION FOR MIGRANTS AND THEIR FAMILIES

Janet Rodenburg*

Throughout history, both a wide range of structural changes in society and personal reasons have led men and women to migrate. Particularly in modern times, the development process has triggered forces that have led to unprecedented migration levels. Despite the deficiencies of existing migration statistics, it is clear that at the global level, the numerical importance of female migration has been comparable to that of men. It is more than appropriate, therefore, to inquire what the consequences of migration have been for the role and status of female migrants and their families.

Despite growing research on female migration, relatively little has focused on the impact of migration on women and their families. Instead, existing research often provides only descriptive profiles of migrants and fails to address the more complex questions concerning the social and economic impact of migration. In order to address such issues, either longitudinal or retrospective data are needed, but such data are still extremely scarce. Consequently, the information presented here is sometimes impressionistic and patchy. It is hoped, however, that this review will provide a foundation for future detailed inquiries.

In order to understand how changes in women's roles interact with changing family structure and functioning, one must first know which women migrate, where to, for what reason and what their living and working conditions were prior to their move. Therefore, a brief account of the various backgrounds from which women migrate is presented and some of the existing links between income generation in urban areas and subsistence production in the rural sector are indicated. A problem with much of the literature is to explore "what causes what"—for example, whether it is the move from a rural to an urban area or the entry into the workforce that changes women's attitude and status. This is clearly not an "either-or" situation but one with many simultaneous changes interacting in complex ways.

When reviewing migration studies, a common methodological problem is the frequent absence of a comparative standard by which to judge conditions in which female migrants find themselves. Very few studies compare the circumstances of female workers in a certain occupation with control groups of non-migrant women, or even men, or with those working in other occupations. For example, to know that female factory workers in a developing country earn $2 an hour or $2 a day tells us nothing about how much such employment is worth to the workers themselves. The impact of employment on women's lives and their position in and relations within their family must also be assessed in comparison with what they would have been in the absence of employment. Thus, for a young woman, how does living in a city on her own, earning a wage and marrying when and whom she chooses compare with the alternative of staying at home with her parents, performing unpaid labour in the family farm and being married off while still a teenager to a man of her parents' choice?

This paper highlights various consequences of internal female migration. An overview of this type is necessarily selective and requires a simplified presentation of complex issues. A first selection is to focus on rural-urban migration, which is generally thought to entail more fundamental changes in women's position than rural-rural moves. Secondly, although most of the examples presented refer to South-eastern Asia, the situation in that region is sufficiently varied that some useful generalizations are possible. However, it is important to note that there are important biases in the research literature with regard to the regions covered, with the result that overall generalizations can only be tentative.

---

*Anthropological-Sociological Centre, Department of South and Southeast Asia Studies, University of Amsterdam, Amsterdam, The Netherlands.

A. Major approaches to migration theory

Migration studies are, in general, based on one of two paradigms deriving from opposing ideological views (for reviews, see Bach and Schraml, 1982; and Wood, 1982). The first view, based on the equilibrium model of migration, focuses on the individual migrant, who is seen as moving to improve his or her economic situation. In most of the studies based on this model, "change" is conceptualized as a passage (an evolution) from tradition to modernity, modernity being synonymous with promotion, betterment and freedom (Morokvasic, 1983). This perspective is usually ahistorical and ignores the underlying structural forces that also affect the migration decision-making process, including the social, cultural and political aspects of labour migration. The relevance of, for example, class background, household structure and political power structures at both the local and the national level is overlooked.

The historical-structural perspective, on the other hand, emphasizes class conflict and uneven regional development between rural and urban areas within countries. Such considerations are important, because even within a single society, migrants' perceptions of and responses to changing work opportunities are influenced by their race or class. Unfortunately, by emphasizing only the structural conditions leading to migration, this approach has barely given attention to the individuals and families involved, let alone to the problems characteristic of women.

Dissatisfaction with these two major approaches to the analysis of migration has resulted in efforts to interrelate them by proposing the family or household as a link between the microlevel and the macrolevel. By shifting the unit of analysis to the household, migration can be viewed as a group decision-making process in which individuals take part, as well as a process related to the overall conditions of households linked to one another through larger community and regional ties (Crummett, 1987; Harbison, 1981). As Radcliffe (1990) demonstrates in her study of migration in the Andes, the household is an important mediator between peasant women and the labour market. As a rule, parents and siblings initiate and organize the work of young female household members. The household further influences migration because of the association of different roles with birth order of siblings. Older children in the Andes often sacrifice their own education by working to pay for younger children's schooling and tend to migrate at an earlier age than other children (Radcliffe, 1990). As Trager (1988) notes for the Philippines, the migration of young women and their subsequent remittances are part of a strategy that, in the long run, helps maintain the family as a unit. This strategy involves the management and organization of different resources: income and wealth; job opportunities for family members; possibilities of domestic production of goods and services; and networks of social relations.

Several studies have stressed that it is important not to view households as harmonious units (Folbre, 1988; Wolf, 1990). Conflicts of interest exist within families, especially between women and men or between generations. Within households, young women are among the least powerful, being under the control of both men and their elders, and being constrained by kinship obligations (see, e.g., Salaff, 1981). Many female migrants do not sever their links with their parents' household because their migration is functional to the household. In other words, they are fulfilling the role that they have been assigned within the division of labour in the peasant household (Arizpe, 1982). Daughters tend to be seen as more likely than sons to be obedient and less likely to spend money on themselves (Trager, 1984). Gender and age differences within the family are of great importance in understanding the behaviour of migrants, especially the extent to which ties are maintained among family members living in different places (Crummett, 1985; Radcliffe, 1990; Riley and Gardner, 1993). This interdependence between migrants and non-migrants implies that, to understand the migration process fully, family ties and kinship networks need to be analysed.

B. Conditions determining the migration of women

According to the most widely accepted economic framework for migration (Todaro, 1976), one of the key determinants of migration is the probability of finding a job paying a better wage at destination than at origin. This framework has generally been used to study labour migration, particularly the migration of men, who are assumed to act as independent decision makers. The same framework has not been judged suited for the study of female migration, since it has been suggested that women are often motivated to migrate for other than purely economic reasons (Thadani and Todaro, 1984). It is often assumed that a woman who moves in association with others (husband, father or other relatives) is not an economic actor. So ingrained is the view that women's migration matters little, that even the women themselves tend to downplay their role in it. It is therefore not surprising to find that when asked, most respondents indicate that women migrate to accompany or join family members or to get married (United Nations Secretariat, 1993). The fact that in some countries a significant proportion of women are being recognized as economic migrants is an important step forward. For instance, in Malaysia, the 1980 census showed that some 13 per cent of all female migrants had moved for employment-related reasons. The equivalent proportion in Thailand was 24 per cent. In her study of southern Indian working-class migrants at Delhi, Kasturi (1981) shows that migrant women have higher labour force participation rates than migrant men, are primary or equal earners and thus contribute substantially to family income.

The consequences of migration for women are likely to differ according to the type of migration involved and the circumstances in which migration occurs. In assessing the impact of migration on female status, it has been noted that both positive and negative changes may be expected depending upon, among other things, the timing of migration with respect to a woman's life cycle, the type of migration involved, the set of cultural or social constraints to which women are subject and the resources that women have at their disposal. Such resources include not only material assets but a woman's own skills and capabilities (Zlotnik, 1993).

The overall socio-economic situation in many developing countries is one in which large numbers of people live at or below minimum standards of living. A major issue for many persons is survival—how to obtain enough income to feed and to satisfy the basic necessities of their families. Families classified as "middle income", although not living at the margins of existence, are nevertheless struggling to increase family incomes. In studying the consequences of migration, a distinction needs to be made between "survival" and "mobility" migrants. Although it is difficult to make that distinction in practice, women that command little human capital and few resources are likely to belong to the former rather than the latter category and thus probably benefit less from migration.

Survival migration

Women that migrate to escape rural poverty are usually called "survival migrants". In Africa, many women leave their villages because they are widowed, divorced or repudiated and have to find some way of surviving. Others migrate because their husbands or families do not provide for them. They migrate to escape an intolerable marriage, to avoid being beaten by a husband or being forced into another marriage, to escape the control of their families or to secure economic independence (Tabet, 1989). In Nigeria, the drought in 1973 led many women to migrate to urban areas (Pittin, 1984). In the Philippines, when the land reform programme established by the Marcos Government forced land tenants to buy the land they tilled at 6 per cent interest payable to the landlords and to pay a land-tax on top, peasant women had to migrate to seek employment in the expanding export industries, in the military bases, as domestic servants or, if necessary, even as prostitutes in the cities. In general, survival migrants have relatively little education and, consequently, tend to secure only informal sector occupations.

Research on Latin America shows that structural changes in production and the poverty that results from them often lead families to send their daughters to town to earn extra money for the support of the family or household unit (Arizpe, 1982; Young, 1982; Crummett, 1985). An example comes from Mexico, where peasant households are said to use migration as a strategy for survival and reproduction. In one of the villages studied by Arizpe (1982), a high level of unemployment has resulted from a combination of the fragmentation and erosion of land, the disappearance of traditional occupations, and the unequal terms of exchange through prices for agricultural products. Arizpe reports: "By sending the father and later the offspring in progressive order to work in salaried employment, the peasant household obtains resources which enable it to continue in agriculture and ensure its social reproduction" (1982, p. 22). In those households, the migration of selected family members, who subsequently find work and send remittances home, is essential to the support of the rest of the family. Migrant daughters generally contribute to the family income prior to their marriage.

The mere out-migration of women to become self-sufficient in the area of destination reduces the strain on severely depleted family resources; and, as in all the cases cited above, the remittances ensure family survival. Without such remittances, the rural family would almost certainly be worse off, but the meagre amounts received do not permit any upward mobility.

Mobility migration

Although some women migrate because they would otherwise be destitute, others do so in order to improve their own level of living and those of their families, even when families object to their working or have no pressing need for their income. In other words, rather than being "pushed" by structural poverty, mobility migrants are primarily "pulled" by better opportunities in the area of destination. In northern Sumatra, Indonesia, the main factors impelling women with middle-level education to leave their villages are their aversion to farming and their unwillingness to follow in their mothers' footsteps by remaining in the backward living conditions that prevail in the countryside. For them, the city, where opportunities are greater, provides an attractive and exciting alternative to rural life (Rodenburg, 1989).

This type of migration can also be seen as a household strategy, the aim of which is upward mobility. Parents educate their daughters so that they can perform occupations in the formal sector (Trager, 1988) or improve their chances of a favourable marriage. Regardless of whether those women obtain white-collar jobs in the city, they too are likely to send remittances home. However, their remittances tend to be used to further the education of their siblings rather than to satisfy basic necessities.

Middle- and upper-class professionals also migrate to improve their prospects of upward mobility. Because they are more likely to come from families with relatively high levels of education and income, their remittances are usually not essential for maintenance of the family. Women engaging in this type of migration are more likely to focus on individual goals as opposed to "family" goals, but there is too little information on them to make this point strongly.

C. EMPLOYMENT CONDITIONS AND JOB ORIENTATION

Participation in the labour force is one of the traditionally significant motives for male migration and is becoming increasingly significant for female migrants. Indeed, women that have migrated recently are more likely to be in the labour force than are non-migrant women. The majority of recent female migrants that work are young and single. Married migrant women appear to have a lesser need to work, probably because their husbands provide the necessary support for the family. It may also be that the lower activity rates found among recent female migrants that are married result from underreporting (Shah and Smith, 1984).

Whether the working experience of female migrants has a positive effect on their status depends in part upon the type of work they do. Women with medium levels of education can aspire to clerical and semi-professional jobs that carry some prestige, but those with little or no education are likely to be confined to low-wage occupations. Although rural-urban migrants may have, in general, more education than their rural counterparts, they tend to be less well educated than non-migrants in urban areas. This distinction seems to be stronger among female than male migrants. Furthermore, the proportion of female migrants in informal activities is considerably higher than that among male migrants (Recchini de Lattes and Mychaszula, 1993). In secondary cities in the Philippines, female migrants are especially prominent in informal sector occupations, including domestic service: 94 per cent of economically active recent female migrants to secondary cities worked in the informal sector, compared with 14 per cent of recent male migrants and 54 per cent of economically active native female residents of those cities (Trager, 1988).

Female migrants are often concentrated at the bottom of the wage pyramid. They usually have lower wage aspirations than non-migrants because they come from areas where incomes are low and the range of jobs limited. They are therefore more likely to accept menial or degrading jobs because anonymity is possible (Shah and Smith, 1984). Apart from socio-economic discrimination by employers, the low status of female migrants is also a result of gender-specific socialization patterns within the family. Consequently, the nature of women's work may assume very specific forms, at least in South-eastern Asia. According to Heyzer, there are:

> "...forms that allow the combination of work and child care, forms that are extensions of women's domestic responsibilities within the household, forms that require little capital outlay, forms that do not threaten the boundaries constructed by traditional ideology governing sex roles." (1986, pp. 49-50)

Rural-urban female migrants may not be able to secure clerical or professional jobs as soon as they migrate if they cannot secure the training that those jobs require in rural areas. Rather, young women frequently move to urban areas for secondary education, with the hope of later finding that type of employment. In Chile, one in five of the established female migrants in Santiago was a professional (Herold, 1979). A study in two villages of Northern Sumatra, Indonesia, indicates that 25 and 40 per cent, respectively, of economically active female migrants in urban areas worked in white-collar occupations or were students (Rodenburg, forthcoming). In a secondary city of the Philippines, there is evidence of high educational status and upward mobility among repeat female migrants (Trager, 1988). Unlike most women employed in the informal sector, white-collar workers are paid regular wages and receive a variety of Government-mandated benefits.

Although few studies systematically compare the occupational mobility of male and female migrants, the evidence suggests that mobility among female migrants is more limited than that among their male counterparts (Findley and Williams, 1991). The situation is even worse for migrant women that are married or have children. Married female migrants tend to play a different role in the urban labour market than single women, often supplementing their family's income by working part time in the informal sector (Young, 1982). Most of those women are in need of maternal and child health services and lack access to adequate child-care facilities in the city (Fawcett, Khoo and Smith, 1984).

Female migrants in domestic service

For many rural-urban migrant women in developing countries domestic service offers the main opportunity to gain some degree of economic independence. Very often, rural families allow their daughters to move to the city only because they can secure a job in domestic service, a job where their basic subsistence needs, food and shelter, are generally ensured. Parents feel that their daughters are safer, morally and psychologically, if they live with a family instead of having to make their own way in the impersonal urban environment (Jelin, 1977). Consequently, considerable proportions of recent female migrants work in domestic service. Surveys carried out during the 1970s in several Asian countries indicate that 45 per cent of economically active recent female migrants in Indonesia and approximately one quarter of those in Malaysia, the Republic of Korea and Thailand were employed in domestic service, compared with proportions of 8-15 per cent among long-term female migrants and 5-12 per cent among non-migrants (Shah and Smith, 1984). Such findings are consistent with those from studies in Latin America (Crummett, 1987; Jelin, 1977; Recchini de Lattes and Mychaszula, 1993).

Domestic servants are usually young. In Indonesia, for instance, three fourths of the migrant women working in domestic service were under age 25 (Crockett, 1985). Domestic service is an occupation in which the employer's authority is enhanced by the youth of the employee. Young migrant women often lack a place to live and are thus constrained to live in their employer's house and hence to work longer hours than what is normal in the formal sector (Young, 1982; Crockett, 1985). Because domestic service is usually not subject to government regulations or contractual arrangements, it provides the employee with few guarantees and no benefits. Furthermore, employers tend to dismiss women when they become older, get married or become pregnant. However, a study on southern Indian working-class migrants to Delhi showed that married migrant women preferred domestic service to other occupations because it could be carried out on a part-time basis, thus leaving them enough time to fulfil their household obligations (Kasturi, 1981). In the Caribbean, some married women, instead of becoming part-time domestic servants, undertake certain domestic chores, such as laundering or ironing, for pay (Despradel, 1984).

Like most workers in the informal sector, domestic servants are rarely unionized. Discussing the Latin American situation, Jelin (1977) argues that because domestic servants identify with their employers, they fail to develop the working-class identity that would prompt them to unionize. In addition, given their long working hours, their residential segregation and their relative youth and inexperience, domestic servants have few opportunities to establish relations with persons outside their jobs. In contrast, Kasturi (1981) documents how domestic servants in a neighbourhood of Delhi functioned as an informal labour union able to bargain for better working conditions in terms of higher wages, periodic leave and an annual bonus at the time of the major religious holiday.

Some studies contend that domestic service leads to a certain upward mobility (e.g., Smith, 1973), but it is difficult to test that hypothesis given the lack of adequate empirical evidence. Such a test would involve comparing the experience of migrant women entering the urban labour-market as domestic servants with that of women from similar socio-economic backgrounds that followed different paths, including those not migrating, those entering other types of occupations after migration and those that never worked. Since such comparisons are not possible, it is nevertheless useful to note cases in which domestic service may have positive effects in terms of upward mobility. In Bangkok, for instance, female migrants from rural areas may begin as low-level domestic servants and move up to become "head maids" with added responsibilities. In Argentina, Brazil or other highly urbanized countries, rural women may migrate first to medium-sized cities to work as domestic servants and then move to larger urban centres where domestic service is better paid (Jelin, 1977). The family environment in which domestic service takes place often facilitates the acculturation of domestic servants to urban life and may even promote the acquisition of skills that can be used to secure better paid occupations. In the Caribbean, women in domestic service often constitute a labour reserve that can be tapped for other, more productive, occupations, such as manufacturing (Despradel, 1984). The same is true in Peninsular Malaysia, where young single female migrants who work first in domestic service later move to factory work (Heyzer, 1986). That is only possible, however, if industrialization is growing. In Malaysia, for instance, already in 1970, 32 per cent of the economically active recent female migrants worked in production, compared with only 23 per cent in domestic service (Shah and Smith, 1984).

Despite such potentially positive impacts, most studies conclude that domestic service is generally a dead end. Since many female domestic workers lack a primary education, their prospects for other type of employment are limited (Young, 1982). Although domestic workers are assured of housing and food, their salaries are usually much lower than those of other workers, thus limiting their possibility to send remittances and to accumulate savings. Furthermore, the personal freedom of domestic servants is often restricted, both by the long hours of work involved and by the limited chances to socialize outside the job. Although some employers allow domestic servants to obtain formal training—permission to study being one of the most important "fringe benefits" of that occupation (Despradel, 1984; Jelin, 1977)—the skills most commonly acquired have little value in the labour-market. But perhaps more importantly, because of their youth, most women in domestic service have marriage as a goal, wishing to form their own families and devote themselves to housework (Jelin, 1977; Palabrica-Costello, 1984).

Export manufacturing

Women in both developed and developing countries tend to constitute a relatively low proportion of production workers (Anker and Hein, 1986). However, some developing countries registered relatively high rates of increase in the number of women in manufacturing activities during the 1970s and 1980s. Such increases were often associated with the establishment of export-processing zones, that is, industrial sites set up under special legislation allowing the duty-free import of raw materials for the assembly and manufacture of goods primarily destined for export. The number of export-processing zones has grown rapidly in recent years, passing from 79 in 25 developing countries in 1975 to 176 in 47 developing countries in 1986. In the mid-1980s, about 1.9 million persons were employed in export-processing zones, well over half of whom were women directly engaged in the production process (Zlotnik, 1993). In such countries as Barbados, India, Indonesia, Jamaica, Malaysia, Mauritius, Mexico, the Republic of Korea and Sri Lanka, over three quarters of all workers employed in export-processing zones were women (ILO, 1988). The zones have attracted labour-intensive industries producing electronics, clothing, footwear and toys, all of which require cheap labour to remain profitable and competitive. Women have been mobilized to work in those industries because "they are considered docile and insecure enough to be hired into the lowest ranks of the industrial hierarchy" (Heyzer, 1982, p. 183).

Not only is there a preference for female workers, but it appears that in several countries the workforce of export-processing zones includes high proportions of female migrants. In the northern border area of Mexico, for instance, 56 per cent of all employees in the *maquiladora* industry were migrants (Zlotnik, 1993), while in the Bataan Export Processing Zone of the Philippines, 62 per cent of all workers were recent migrants (Feranil, 1984). It is in the interest of the manufacturers to have a mobile workforce that is fully employed during business upswings but that can be laid off during contractions. Young rural women, whose income needs are assumed to be marginal, can be reabsorbed by rural families when laid off and are thus regarded as an ideal labour force. Analysing the migration of rural women to Taipei, Huang comments: "The village always provides a backstop for the migrant" (1984, p. 262).

Not in all industries are migrant women the preferred workforce. Especially in multinational electronics factories requiring higher levels of education, jobs tend to be filled by urban residents that have both the qualifications and the contacts to obtain that employment. In most countries, the poorest, least educated rural women cannot compete for those jobs. However, in some of the newly industrializing economies of Asia, especially in the Republic of Korea and Taiwan Province of China, qualified urban workers can afford to shun low-level production jobs in favour of better paid occupations, thus leaving open such employment opportunities for rural-urban migrants. In Malaysia, the Government's policy of using ethnic quotas to promote the employment of Malays has resulted in substantial rural-urban female migration to fill the quotas in export industries (Lim, 1990). Consequently, in the early 1980s, some 70 per cent of the workers in the export-processing zones of Malaysia were born in distant and mostly rural areas, though they were generally not recent migrants (Zlotnik, 1993).

What are the consequences of working in export-processing zones for female migrants? The situation of female workers in the export industries of developing countries is varied and complex, depending upon the type of industry involved, the economic climate and the provisions of labour law. Yet, the stereotypical view presented largely in feminist literature and the popular media is remarkably homogeneous and generally negative. According to it, multinational corporations representing the first world establish factories in third world export-processing zones and employ mostly young, single, female rural-urban migrants, "who are ruthlessly exploited in harsh factory environments where they suffer long hours, poor working conditions, insecure, unhealthy, and unsafe jobs, and wages so low that they are not even sufficient to cover individual subsistence" (Lim, 1990, p. 111). Although some situations may match that stereotype in some or all of its details, it does not represent the norm in all or even in most cases of female employment in export factories in the developing world. Although wages, working conditions and job security in such factories are inferior to those in developed countries, they are comparable if not superior to those prevailing in most of the other sectors employing women (or even men) in any given developing country.

Some sources take note that labour unions either do not exist or closely collaborate with management (Arizpe and Aranda, 1981). When compared with other sectors of the economy, however, it is apparent that women working in large modern factories are better able to organize in unions and, despite the obstacles they face, in many cases have become more unionized than sections of the male labour force in their own countries or female workers in similar industries in developed countries. Women have also undertaken militant labour actions, such as strikes and work slowdowns; and in countries like the Philippines and the Republic of Korea, they have been involved in even broader political action. Thus, female textile workers are considered to be among the most militant workers in the Republic of Korea (Lim, 1990).

The average length of employment for women in export-processing zones is only a few years. In Malaysia and Taiwan Province of China, only a minority of female migrants become long-term industrial workers with some prospect of upward occupational mobility (Salaff, 1981; Heyzer, 1986). It appears, however, that the length of time women work in factories varies by country and over time and is usually truncated by the increasing domestic responsibilities faced by women when they marry and have children, rather than by employer compulsion or market disruption (Huang, 1984; Lim, 1990). A similar conclusion was reached by Feranil (1984) when studying married female workers in the Bataan Export Processing Zone of the Philippines.

Long working hours, low wages and lack of occupational mobility are not conducive to improving the status of women. Indeed, given that managers in the export-processing zones are mostly male, researchers have concluded that female workers pass from the patriarchy of the home to that of the factory (Arizpe and Aranda, 1981; Mather, 1986). Yet, export-processing zones worldwide have offered women wage-earning opportunities that would have probably not existed in their absence. Thus, most workers in the Mexican strawberry industry considered their job to be a stage in their life that allowed them to get out of the daily routine of the village. When asked what type of work they liked best, 59 per cent answered that they preferred to work in a strawberry plant; only 4.5 per cent preferred to work on the land and 36.5 per cent would have preferred to be employed in an office (Arizpe and Aranda, 1981).

Sexual service

Pushed out of the countryside by poverty, women go to the cities in search of employment. In Thailand, the combined pressures of land shortage and proletarianization of the peasantry have led many women from the north, north-east and centre of the country to become prostitutes in Bangkok. It has even been reported that some young women have been sold into brothels by their own parents to relieve debt (Phongpaichit, 1982). Similarly, most of the prostitutes in Manila are from the central Philippine provinces of Leyte, Samar and Cebu, all economically depressed areas. A study of low-income migrants to Semarang, Indonesia, places the proportion of female migrants engaging in prostitution at 29 per cent (Lerman, 1983). Those women tend to be very poor, single and young, usually in age group 15-24. In Africa, in contrast, female migrants that enter prostitution are likely to have been married at least once (Sudarkasa, 1977; Obbo, 1980; Pittin, 1984; Tabet, 1989). Lacking the skills and education needed to secure other types of jobs, women have little choice but to engage in the occupations traditionally reserved for them. For many, prostitution is the only means to earn reasonable amounts of money quickly.

Despite their relatively good earnings, several studies indicate that prostitutes are exploited by intermediaries and end up earning relatively little themselves. In Manila, some "hospitality girls", especially those working in the tourist industry, earn less than 10 per cent of the total fees paid by clients (Neumann, 1979; Heyzer, 1986). Young prostitutes in Jakarta are reported to eat only one decent meal per day and some are even forced to sell their babies due to financial difficulties (Heyzer, 1986). The less urgent the economic need, the more choice women have as to the clients and working conditions that they are willing to accept and also about their use of money.

Although wage differentials vary, prostitutes can earn 5-10 times what the typical migrant woman might earn in a day. Seldom do women go into prostitution because they have no other choice: they do so because no other options provide such high returns (Phongpaichit, 1982; Pittin, 1984). Setting up a business is the ultimate goal many women have and sometimes they manage to realize it. At Yaoundé, Cameroon, for example, bars, restaurants, nightclubs, beauty parlors and European ready-to-wear boutiques are largely owned by prostitutes or former prostitutes (Tabet, 1989). Other women buy houses, plots of land or livestock for their family (Lerman, 1983). A study of Hausa prostitutes in Nigeria showed that many women had side occupations, ranging from petty trade to running a local restaurant (Pittin, 1984). As they became wealthier, their subsidiary occupation took precedence over prostitution, until they dropped that work to become full-time businesswomen and entrepreneurs.

The earnings of prostitutes enable them to support themselves and, especially in the Asian situation, to send cash or gifts to relatives in the countryside (Neumann, 1979; Lerman, 1983; Phongpaichit, 1982). Because so many African prostitutes are either divorced or escaping bad marriages, most do not remit to their family. However, showing how well one fares sometimes helps in getting acceptance from the family (Tabet, 1989). By sending money, women compensate for the possible loss of face resulting from their involvement in prostitution; and when demand for their services drops, women often go back to the village and are accepted both by family and community. In Nigeria, once the families of Hausa "courtesans" have resigned themselves to the women's new status, those women are allowed to visit the family in a normal fashion (Pittin, 1984).

Examples from South-eastern Asia also point to a general acceptance of prostitutes by their families. Parents of prostitutes in Central Java, Indonesia, are in such need of remitted income that even if they are aware of their daughter's occupation at Semarang, they will generally not oppose it. If a prostitute returns permanently to her village, her wealth will likely make her attractive to a potential husband (Lerman, 1983). Nor are prostitutes stigmatized in the rural communities of northern Thailand. Instead, there is generally an extensive network providing young rural women access to urban prostitution. In recent years, village élites and teachers have sometimes played a part in the recruitment of under-age women for prostitution (Phongpaichit, 1991). Evidence from north-eastern Thailand, on the other hand, indicates that prostitutes are often stigmatized; consequently, most of them keep their occupation secret. It seems that in north-eastern Thailand, masseuses seldom return to their rural village. Men in that area are said to be reluctant to marry former prostitutes, not because of moral concerns but out of fear that the migrants might have developed higher aspirations and expectations than local women (Phongpaichit, 1984). The sharp increase of HIV infection in Bangkok may also be a reason for preventing the eventual reintegration of ex-prostitutes into rural villages of Thailand, although there is still no evidence on that.

Petty trade

Female migrants are more likely than males to be found in petty trade, except in countries where cultural norms cause women to be secluded. Women traders outnumber men in such countries as Bolivia, El Salvador, Ghana, Indonesia, Peru and Thailand (Anker and Hein, 1986). A survey of migrants in three medium-sized cities of Togo revealed that 32 per cent of female migrants were merchants or traders, compared with 5 per cent of the male migrants (Dupont, 1987, cited in Findley and Williams, 1991).

Petty trade, whether through street hawking, market vending or store operation, absorbs large numbers of female migrants, typically belonging to older age groups than those in other informal activities. Moreover, the data, such as those gathered for Indonesia, indicate that sales occupations are more important to married and long-term female migrants than to recent migrants (Crockett, 1983). In Bangkok, the proportion of married female migrants that are self-employed (e.g., engaged in street-vending) is about eight times larger than those in salaried employment (Tongudai, 1984).

The trading opportunities for recent migrants are usually limited because credit is not easily available and success in trading requires experience and networks (Kasturi, 1981). A business like food-vending is not only highly competitive but usually has a low start. It takes several months or years before the regular clientele needed for a successful food-vending operation can be established. Longer term migrants or the native-born have a better chance of succeeding than short-term or circular migrants, who continue to move back and forth between the city and rural areas (Tongudai, 1984). Perhaps more important, petty trade assumes a capacity either to comply with or circumvent government regulations or licensing requirements for those engaged in street commerce (Jellinek, 1976; Hackenberg and Barth, 1984; Tongudai, 1984). Since such information is generally not readily available to recent migrants, the majority of pedlars are drawn from established urban residents.

Many female traders sell prepared food, as is the case for large numbers of Javanese women in Indonesia (Dewey, 1962; Jellinek, 1976). Female migrants can engage in such activities because of their low initial capitalization and the possibility of using unpaid family labour. Some women run a small shop at their own homes, an activity that allows them to perform household chores and take care of young children at the same time (Hackenberg and Barth, 1984). Other trading activities, however, may require women to be away from their homes. Several studies focus on female traders circulating between small towns and villages (Dewey, 1962; Lerman, 1983; Mantra, 1981; Sudarkasa, 1977). In Central Java, Indonesia, female traders migrate to urban areas for periods of from one to three months and then return home (Hetler, 1990). Since the village provides few income-earning opportunities for women, they leave husband and children to sell *jamu*, a herbal drink, in nearby towns. This strategy helps keep the children in school and husbands in agriculture.

For southern-Indian women, vending is a higher status occupation than domestic service. It is a less strenuous activity and does not involve the pollution that is implicit in "cleaning the dirt of others" (Kasturi, 1981, p. 21). Although working hours can be long and incomes small and uncertain, the flexible working hours may be an advantage for women who also run a household, and even a small income can make a critical difference to limited household earnings. In Indonesia, circulating female migrants engaging in petty trade sometimes contribute more than half the total income of their household (Hetler, 1990).

To summarize, recent female migrants fill very specific vacancies in the urban occupational structure—vacancies that are usually low-paid, demand long hours of work and are, in most cases, beyond the protection of labour unions or government regulation. In fact, it may be the very existence of such vacancies that encourages female migration. Migrant women are the most critically affected by the lack of economic alternatives and the majority either find work in domestic service or turn to self-employment in petty trade. Yet, despite the limited opportunities available, migrant women are unambiguously better off than they would have been without those jobs. In absolute terms, workers in export manufacturing may be the most privileged, but there are considerable differences between countries. Although urban areas offer a greater variety of jobs, only women with some education can take full advantage of them.

D. ECONOMIC CONSEQUENCES FOR FEMALE MIGRANTS

Irrespective of the reasons for migrating or the way in which migration takes place (with or without the company of close family members), migrant women often join the labour force at the place of destination and their wages are generally higher than what they would have been in rural areas. For those that did not work before, urban work provides the first opportunity to earn an income. Moreover, income and expenditure in the city are not subject to the seasonal variations typical of rural areas, where cash becomes scarce during the farming season and may be barely sufficient for subsistence.

Irrespective of occupation, women generally earn lower salaries than men. In most societies, being female is already a good reason to be paid less than a man, irrespective of the type of economic activity performed (ILO, 1988). Common justifications for those differences are that women have lower levels of education than men and less experience or even that they do not need as much money because they have fewer financial responsibilities than men. Whatever the rationalization, employers clearly benefit from women's lower wages and women are segregated to the lower strata of the occupational ladder.

Even when allowance is made for educational attainment and age, the incomes of female migrants are usually at the bottom. In the Republic of Korea, only 5 per cent of all working women are paid more than 70,000 won (W) per month, compared with about 45 per cent of working men. Moreover, about 43 per cent of all employed women, but only 11.6 per cent of employed men, earn less than W30,000 per month, which is the Government's minimum wage (Hong, 1984). Most migrant women working in Malaysian export manufacturing received a monthly income ranging from 70 to 200 ringgit (M$) which, by urban income standards, falls within the lowest category (Ariffin, 1984). Migrant women in sexual services can earn significantly higher amounts. In Jakarta, they earned roughly three times the average daily income of petty traders and five times the daily incomes of casual labourers (Papanek, 1975). A study in 1980 reported that the income of masseuses in Bangkok could be of about 5,000 baht (B) per month while a large majority of female migrants in other occupations were earning less than B 840 per month (Phongpaichit, 1982).

Despite their relatively low earnings, many female migrants are still able to generate a surplus for the rural family. In Asia, female migrants, especially the young and single, are more reliable sources of remittances than their brothers (Trager, 1984; Phongpachit, 1982; Ariffin, 1984). In the Philippines, migrants from poor backgrounds working in low-paying jobs were as likely to send remittances as those in higher paying occupations (Trager, 1988). Single women in cities in the Republic of Korea remitted about 55 per cent of their income home (Hong, 1984). Most Thai masseuses studied by Phongpachit (1982) claimed to send between one third and one half of their income to their family. In other studies, the numbers of those sending remittances are not presented, but it is reported that "most" women did so (LaGuerre, 1978; Connell, 1984; Huang, 1984).

Remittances have a substantial impact on the families receiving them. For those at the margins of survival, maintenance would be difficult without them and for others remittances can allow upward mobility. In the Philippines and Thailand, the money remitted by female migrants was used to supplement living expenses at home, to finance the education of siblings and to pay hired labour during the harvest season (Phongpaichit, 1982; Trager, 1988). Although few women thought their families would have suffered without their remittances, their contribution to village households was substantial.

A woman's financial contribution to her family and the help that she can provide for new arrivals from the village in the city enhance her status. Strauch (1984) shows that because of their improved access to resources, female migrants in Chinese communities in Hong Kong and Malaysia have greater power and status. That change may cause strains and conflicts within the family, but it also gives young women a greater sense of their own worth and a stronger basis for self-esteem. It is for those reasons that young female migrants, despite their limited options for employment in the cities, continue to move there (Khoo and others, 1984).

There is some evidence that married women who work after migration may see their status enhanced. In Mexico City, married female migrants doing industrial piecework found that their wages allowed them to avoid conflict with their spouses by reducing the frequency with which they had to ask for money or argue about expenditures: "Access to an independent income, even if it is small and is used to meet family rather than personal consumption needs, restores or strengthens these women's self-image and self-esteem" (Roldán, 1988, p. 245). Married female employees in the Bataan Export Processing Zone valued their work because it allowed them some social interaction outside the home (Feranil, 1984). To a certain extent, such changes may be part of the modernization process and of the fact that higher educational levels and the availability of industrial employment expand a woman's role outside the home.

Yet, most sources indicate that many female migrants, whether married or single, continue to engage in traditional female occupations in urban areas, especially in domestic service. Even in the realm of export manufacturing, traditional values that are thought to contribute to the productivity of female workers are encouraged, such as obedience to authority, hard work, honesty, discipline and self-denial. "Instead of urbanization presenting females with opportunities for social and economic advancement, the form it takes in South-east Asia maintains their static position in the labour force" (Crockett, 1984, p. 109).

In sum, despite the fact that most female migrants earn far less than their male counterparts, the economic benefits of their migration to the city are substantial when compared with their prospects in rural areas. Whether they work in the formal or the informal sector of the economy, a large proportion of female migrants is able to send home remittances or, in the case of married women, to supplement the income of their household. By becoming a wage-earner, women can enhance their self-esteem and their status within the family.

E. CONSEQUENCES OF FEMALE MIGRATION FOR THE POWER STRUCTURE WITHIN THE FAMILY

A host of social factors and values not only constrain female migration but prevent its consequences from being as beneficial as possible for women, whatever their origin, social class, education, destination or occupation. Norms concerning the family system and the roles of women within the family are especially important in determining the consequences of migration for women.

Several studies have shown that the extent to which Asian women benefit from migration depends upon the prevailing family system. For women in some Eastern and South-eastern Asian countries, becoming wage-earners may be a way of gaining autonomy (Trager, 1988; Karim, n.d.), but for women that adhere to Confucian ideology, as most of those in Hong Kong, the Republic of Korea and Taiwan Province of China, work is a sign of dependence (Huang, 1984; Salaff, 1981).

The economic obligations of migrants to their parents depend upon the strength of family ideology with regard to the "pooling of resources". Thus, many Malay female migrants consider their work in factories away from home as part of their obligation to their family and abide by the need to send money back home regularly. They may, however, experience some conflict between the norms and values of their home community and those prevalent in the city, especially since traditional values hold that young women should provide for the parental home even at the expense of their own interests, whereas in urban areas the pressures for modernization give greater weight to individual needs and aspirations (Ariffin, 1984; Mather, 1986).

A number of researchers analyse female migration in the context of the "filial daughter" ideology, according to which daughters establish strong ties binding women within the household and linking one generation to another. In the Republic of Korea, for instance, migrant daughters adhere more strictly than migrant sons to the ethics of "familism", maintaining close economic ties with their mother and sending her money regularly (Yoon, 1990). In addition, in both the Republic of Korea and Taiwan Province of China, the earnings of young migrant women enable their brothers to obtain the higher education needed to occupy high-status jobs (Greenhalgh, 1988; Cho, 1990).

Research conducted in Hong Kong provides the clearest example of filial piety. A majority of the migrant women studied remitted part of their earnings home: "Bringing home money is an expression of filial piety, and even married women bring money home on their visits" (Huang, 1984, p. 261). Salaff (1981) found that although the economic achievements of working daughters, especially their monetary earnings, enhanced the deference accorded to them at family gatherings where they might represent their family, they were not accorded privileges and power commensurate with their contributions and were excluded from major domestic decision-making. Moreover, because of their poorly paid jobs and the obligation to contribute to their family's budget, migrant women could not invest in productive assets and thus secure their own future.

In the Republic of Korea, some indications of change have been observed. Cho (1990) and Yoon (1990) write about young women that decided to find jobs in urban areas so as to escape their harsh rural life and village isolation. Their mothers, desiring a better fate for them, refuse to control their lives and no longer adhere to the hierarchy inherent to patriarchal societies. From the mothers' perspective, there is little future in agriculture for educated daughters: "Better to look elsewhere, to search for their own kind of womanhood" (Yoon, 1990, p. 270).

Despite all the drawbacks of migration, living away from home is generally viewed by the women themselves as "liberating", providing a degree of freedom and independence not possible in rural areas (Wilkinson, 1987). In Huang's study of Taiwan Province of China (1984), most female migrants who worked in urban areas found their experience rewarding because it gave them the opportunity to relate to others and obtain skills and education. Some adopted styles of dress, make-up and haircut considered "modern", thereby challenging the prevailing image of women as shy and modest. Moreover, migrant women tended to be more outspoken than non-migrant women. Thus, Indonesian female migrants working in export manufacturing who resented the treatment that they received from managers were dismayed by the unwillingness of local workers to participate in labour actions (Mather, 1986).

In Indonesia, female migrants belonging to the patrilineal Toba Batak of Northern Sumatra had become increasingly independent. They tended to keep their own income instead of adding it to the income pool of the family left behind: they did not consider that the need to help their families of origin was a reason for their employment in urban areas; instead, they mentioned their desire to buy clothes for themselves. The autonomy evinced by these young female migrants contrasted sharply with the generalized image of the docile Asian female migrant. Better educational attainment and a higher age at marriage probably encouraged the more assertive behaviour noticed among these adolescent women (Rodenburg, forthcoming).

For married women also, the chances to break out from a confined role appear to be greater in urban than in rural areas. By migrating, married women can evade the direct control of their rural family and their migration may weaken traditional family structures and encourage the development of new ones (Findley and Williams, 1991). Such outcomes are particularly important in patrilineal and patrilocal societies, where migration away from the woman's in-laws may encourage the development of more intimate and egalitarian relationships between husband and wife. Thus, a study of urban neighbourhoods in a city in northern India (Vatuk, 1972) found a weakening trend towards the incorporation of married women into their husbands' kin network and stronger ties between the women concerned and their family of origin than was typical in traditional rural India.

In the Islamic Republic of Iran, however, migration from rural areas was less positive for women who accompanied their husbands and fathers to Teheran (Bauer, 1984). Once in the city, wives were not allowed to work outside the house. Patriarchal structures conditioned by Islamic beliefs restrict women's behaviour in the public domain and confine women's roles to domestic activity. Bauer concludes:

"It is the reorganization of the household, with its emphasis on the nuclear family and the geographic distances separating the extended family, as well as the disparity between access to information and control over its use, that challenges the traditional ordering of family authority." (1984, p. 288)

Married women migrating from rural to urban areas of developing countries often experience not only a transition from an extended to a nuclear family but also an important change in the nature of their economic activity: from being unpaid family workers they become wage-earners. Such changes are likely to enhance the independence of women and to strengthen their role in decision-making within the family (Hugo, 1993), as is seen in the Caribbean, where women that migrate to accompany their husbands often find work before their male companions and where migrant women have higher labour force participation in productive activities than do migrant men or city-born women (Despradel, 1984). Consequently, Caribbean women often become the main economic actors of the household, thus attaining equality with men, something that they did not have in rural areas, where they were "second-class" producers.

In general, the higher a woman's income is as a proportion of total family income, the more power she holds in the family (Lu, 1984; Despradel, 1984). However, the wife's independent access to a cash income is not always related to her position of power in the household. Possible redefinitions of the roles of wives and husbands in household management also depend upon the characteristics of women's work. Thus, Roldán (1988) shows that domestic service, instead of enhancing women's self-esteem, reinforces the prevailing gender hierarchies in migrant households in Mexico City.

On the whole, few working wives receive help from men in housework. In the Philippines, fewer than 3 per cent of the women working in the Bataan Export Processing Zone had a husband who undertook some child-care duties while his wife was at work (Feranil, 1984). Another study on the Philippines (Miralao, 1984) showed that, compared with husbands of unemployed wives, more husbands of working wives undertook household tasks, such as buying groceries, washing the dishes, and cleaning and fixing the home. Although women's employment did not bring about dramatic redefinitions of the roles of wives and husbands in household management, it did result in greater sharing of household chores. Findings relating to

Indonesia also suggest that the employment of wives reduced the sex-typing of household decision-making areas (Hetler, 1990; Williams, 1990). Husbands in rural areas cooked, did the washing and cared for their children when their wives were away as circular migrants (Hetler, 1990).

Sex inequalities and the power of the husband within the family seem to be more persistent among migrant couples in Taiwan Province of China (Lu, 1984). Regardless of whether migrant wives participate in the workforce, whatever their employment status, type of occupation, location of work or level of income, there are no significant differences in their power within the family or in the roles that they play. The author notes that working women are not purposely using their economic contribution to modify family structure or relations. Changes may be brought about by necessity, but the traditional family ideal persists.

To summarize, in several societies, especially those where Confucian ideology predominates, single migrant women are expected to help support their family of origin. Yet, the economic support that they provide does not always lead to a better position of migrant women within the family. In some instances, the patriarchal structure is reinforced. When the economic obligations of children to parents are less strictly adhered to, migrant women are more likely to increase their independence. In addition, if migration to the city involves a shift from an extended to a nuclear family, the status of married women may improve, especially if they work for wages. In a number of Eastern and South-eastern Asian countries, the evidence suggests that the husbands of working women are sharing some household tasks.

F. Conclusion

Without immediately supporting Whiteford's optimistic view on the liberating and emancipating effects of rural-urban migration on women (Whiteford, 1978), the opportunities for female migrants in most urban areas of developing countries have unquestionably increased, especially in terms of their access to salaried employment and, in some cases, in terms of their enhanced status within the family. However, the social position of women in general and of female migrants in particular is shaped by structural forces and value systems that are not so easy to change.

Migration is a process that has important consequences for the women concerned, especially when it involves a change of residence from a rural to an urban environment. The change may be positive or negative, depending upon the conditions of female employment, the strength of the migrant's ties with her family of origin and on whether the norms prevalent in the area of destination reinforce traditional patterns of behaviour.

Most studies show that the status of female migrants is greatly influenced by their relative resources in terms of education, skills and income. Women that migrate as part of a survival strategy usually have little education or capital. Consequently, they are generally relegated to the worst-paid and largely unregulated jobs (such as those in domestic service, the informal sector or prostitution), where the potential for exploitation is high. Women that migrate to enhance their chances for upward mobility are usually better educated. As a result, they can secure better-paid jobs in the formal sector and enjoy better working conditions and higher salaries than those prevailing in the informal sector.

Female migrants are often at a disadvantage when compared with male migrants. Even when allowance is made for educational attainment and age, female migrants usually perceive lower wages than either male migrants or female non-migrants. Nevertheless, rural-urban migrant women are generally satisfied with the consequences of migration, because the wage-earning opportunities open to them in urban areas are considerably better than those in their region of origin.

In some cases, families prefer the migration of daughters to that of sons, since daughters who find employment tend to send remittances more regularly. In addition, migrant women working in the formal sector provide not only financial assistance to their family of origin but also the urban link needed to introduce younger siblings to the urban environment.

In some societies, however, the strength of traditional patriarchal ideology and the emphasis on women's familial roles prevent women from migrating or from reaping the full benefits of migration if they do. That is the case in some Muslim countries and in a number of those where Confucian ideology prevails. In those countries, migrant women are likely to experience a conflict between the norms and values prevailing in their community of origin and those prevalent in the city, and although female migrants will usually be accorded more respect because of their contribution to family income, their power within the family will not necessarily be enhanced.

There is scant information on the consequences of female migration for the status of women within their immediate family. Changes occurring in the domestic context are often the result of the adoption of urban lifestyles, the greater economic potential of women and their growing independence when they become wage-earners. However, even when migrant women have control over their own income, they do not necessarily gain power and status within the family. There is a need to understand better the social mechanisms, struggles and processes that perpetuate the domination of women within the household. To do so, the analysis of gender ideology and power relations, particularly of the processes by which power is exerted within the family or household, is necessary. It is also important to understand how intra-household asymmetrical processes are related to political and structural changes occurring in the society at large.

Although female migration has increased in many countries, the gender biases of development policies and the pervasiveness of sociocultural norms that determine the subordinate position of women have meant that by migrating, many women have merely exchanged their subordination within the household for their subordination in the workplace (Lim, 1991). Consequently, in many instances, migration and the associated employment of women have not been necessarily "liberating" for the women involved. However, because rural-urban migration is an integral part of the modernization process, female migrants, despite many drawbacks, are active participants in it. Whether they move to ensure the survival of their families or to improve their chances of upward mobility, women in developing countries go to the city largely on their own initiative and engage in urban employment that provides them with some measure of independence. Given the alternatives, such outcome has many positive facets that ought not to be dismissed.

REFERENCES

Anker, Richard, and Catherine Hein (1986). Sex inequalities in third world employment: statistical evidence. In *Sex Inequalities in Urban Employment in the Third World*, Richard Anker and Catherine Hein, eds. Essex, United Kingdom: Macmillan Press.

Ariffin, Jamilah (1984). Migration of women workers in Peninsular Malysia: impact and implications. In *Women in the Cities of Asia: Migration and Urban Adaptation*, James T. Fawcett, Siew-Ean Khoo and Peter C. Smith, eds. Boulder, Colorado: Westview Press.

Arizpe, Lourdes (1982). Relay migration and the survival of the peasant household. In *Towards a Political Economy of Urbanization in Third World Countries*, Helen I. Safa, ed. Delhi: Oxford University Press.

_____, and Josefina Aranda (1981). The "comparative advantages" of women's disadvantages: women workers in the strawberry export business in Mexico. *Signs* (Chicago, Illinois), vol. 7, No. 2 (Winter), pp. 453-473.

Bach, R. L., and L. A. Schraml (1982). Migration, crisis and theoretical conflict. *International Migration Review* (Staten Island, New York), vol. 16, No. 2 (Summer), pp. 320-341.

Bauer, Janet (1984). New models and traditional networks: migrant women in Tehran. In *Women in the Cities in Asia: Migration and Urban Adaptation*, James T. Fawcett, Siew-Ean Khoo and Peter C. Smith, eds. Boulder, Colorado: Westview Press.

Cho, Haejoang (1990). Transformation of gender structure in Cheju island. In *Structures and Strategies: Women, Work and Family*, Leela Dube and Rajni Palriwala, eds. New Delhi: Sage.

Connell, John (1984). Status or subjugation? Women, migration and development in the South Pacific. *International Migration Review* (Staten Island, New York), vol. 18, No. 4 (Winter), pp. 964-983.

Crockett, Virginia R. (1985). *Female Migrant Workers in Urban Indonesia*. Ann Arbor, Michigan: University Microfilms International.

Crummet, Maria de los Angeles (1985). Class, household structure, and migration: a case study from rural Mexico. Working Paper No. 92. Notre Dame, Indiana: University of Notre Dame.

_____ (1987). Rural women and migration. In *Rural Women and State Policy: Feminist Perspectives on Latin American Agricultural Development*, Carmen Diana Deere and Magdalena León, eds. Boulder, Colorado: Westview Press.

Despradel, Lil (1984). Internal migration of rural women in the Caribbean and its effects on their status. *Women on the Move: Contemporary Changes in Family and Society*. Paris: United Nations Educational, Scientific and Cultural Organization.

Dewey, Alice G. (1962). *Peasant Marketing in Java*. New York: Free Press of Glencoe.

Dupont, Véronique (1987). Insertion diferentielle des migrants dans les marchés du travail de trois villes moyennes de region de plantation (sud-ouest Togo). Paper presented at the Atélier du Travail sur l'insertion des migrants dans les villes de l'Afrique d'ouest et centrale, organized by CRDI, ORSTOM and URD-Benin, Lomé, Togo, 14-17 February.

Fawcett, James T., Siew-Ean Khoo and Peter C. Smith, eds. (1984). *Women in the Cities of Asia: Migration and Urban Adaptation*. Boulder, Colorado: Westview Press.

Feranil, Imelda Zosa (1984). Female employment and the family: a case study of the Bataan Export Processing Zone. In *Women in the Urban and Industrial Workforce: Southeast and East Asia*, Gavin W. Jones, ed. Development Studies Centre, Monograph No. 33. Canberra: The Australian National University.

Findley, Sally E., and Linda Williams (1991). *Women Who Go and Women Who Stay: Reflections of Family Migration Processes in a*

Changing World. Population and Labour Policies Programme, Working Paper No. 176. Geneva: International Labour Office.

Folbre, Nancy (1988). The black four of hearts: toward a new paradigm of household economics. In *A Home Divided: Women and Income in the Third World*, Daisy Dwyer and Judith Bruce, eds. Stanford, California: Stanford University Press.

Greenhalgh, Susan (1988). Intergenerational contracts: familial roots of sexual stratification in Taiwan. In *A Home Divided: Women and Income in the Third World*, Daisy Dwyer and Judith Bruce, eds. Stanford, California: Stanford University Press. This article refers to Taiwan Province of China.

Hackenberg, Beverly, and Gerald Barth (1984). Growth of the bazaar economy and its significance for women's employment: trends of the 1970s in Davao City, Philippines. In *Women in the Urban and Industrial Workforce: Southeast and East Asia*, Gavin W. Jones, ed. Development Studies Centre, Monograph No. 33. Canberra: The Australian National University.

Harbison, Sarah F. (1981). Family structure and family strategy in migration decision making. In *Migration Decision Making: Multidisciplinary Approaches to Microlevel Studies in Developed and Developing Countries*, Gordon F. de Jong and Robert W. Gardner, eds. New York: Pergamon Press.

Herold, Joan M. (1979). Female migration in Chile: types of moves and socioeconomic characteristics. *Demography* (Washington, D.C.), vol. 16, No. 2 (May), pp. 257-278.

Hetler, Carol B. (1990). Survival strategies, migration and household headship. In *Structures and Strategies: Women, Work and Family*, Leela Dube and Rajni Palriwala, eds. New Delhi: Sage.

Heyzer, Noeleen (1982). From rural subsistence to an industrial peripheral work force: an examination of female Malaysian migrants and capital accumulation in Singapore. In *Women and Development. The Sexual Division of Labour in Rural Societies*, Lourdes Benería, ed. New York: Praeger.

_____ (1986). *Working Women in South-East Asia: Development, Subordination and Emancipation.* Buckinghamshire, United Kingdom; and Milton Keynes, Philadelphia, Pennsylvania: Open University Press.

Hong, Sawon (1984). Urban migrant women in the Republic of Korea. In *Women in the Cities of Asia: Migration and Urban Adaptation*, James T. Fawcett, Siew-Ean Khoo and Peter C. Smith, eds. Boulder, Colorado: Westview Press.

Huang, Nora Chiang (1984). The migration of rural women to Taipei. In *Women in the Cities of Asia: Migration and Urban Adaptation*, James T. Fawcett, Siew-Ean Khoo and Peter C. Smith, eds. Boulder, Colorado: Westview Press.

Hugo, Graeme J. (1993). Migrant women in developing countries. Chapter III in the present volume.

International Labour Organisation (1988). *Economic and Social Effects of Multinational Enterprises in Export-processing Zones.* Geneva: International Labour Office.

Jelin, Elizabeth (1977). Migration and labor force participation of Latin American women: the domestic servants in the cities. *Signs* (Chicago, Illinois), vol. 3, No. 1 (Autumn), pp. 129-141.

Jellinek, Lea (1976). The life of a Jakarta street trader. Working papers. Melbourne, Australia: Monash University, Centre of Southeast Asian Studies.

Karim, W. J. (n.d.). Goods, classes and gender: the Malaysian example. Penang, Malaysia: Universiti Sains Penang.

Kasturi, L. (1981). Poverty, migration and women's status. *ICSSR Research Abstracts Quarterly* (New Delhi), vol. 10, Nos. 1 and 2, pp. 17-27.

Khoo, Siew-Ean, and others (1984). Women in Asian cities: policies, public services and research. In *Women in the Cities of Asia: Migration and Urban Adaptation*, James T. Fawcett, Siew-Ean Khoo and Peter C. Smith, eds. Boulder, Colorado: Westview Press.

LaGuerre, Michel S. (1978). The impact of migration on the Haitian family and household organization. In *Family and Kinship in Middle America and the Caribbean*, Arnaud F. Marks and Raymond A. Romer, eds. Curacao and Leiden: University of Netherlands Antilles.

Lerman, Charles (1983). Sex-differential patterns of circular migration: a case study of Semarang, Indonesia. *Peasant Studies* (Salt Lake City, Utah), vol. 10, No. 4 (Summer), pp. 251-269.

Lim, Linda Y. C. (1990). Women's work in export factories: the politics of a cause. In *Persistent Inequalities. Women and World Development*, Irene Tinker, ed. New York: Oxford University Press.

Lu, Yu-Hsia (1984). Women, work and the family in a developing society: Taiwan. In *Women in the Urban and Industrial Workforce: Southeast and East Asia*, Gavin W. Jones, ed. Development Studies Centre, Monograph No. 33. Canberra: The Australian National University. This article refers to Taiwan Province of China.

Mantra, Ida B. (1981). *Population Movement in Wet Rice Communities: A Case Study of Two Dukuh in Yogyakarta Special Region.* Yogyakarta, Indonesia: Gadjah Mada University Press.

Mather, Celia (1986). 'Rather than make trouble, it's better just to leave': behind the lack of industrial strife in the Tangerang region of West Java. In *Women, Work, and Ideology in the Third World*, Haleh I. Afshar, ed. London: Tavistock.

Miralao, Virginia A. (1984). The impact of female employment on household management. In *Women in the Urban and Industrial Workforce: Southeast and East Asia*, Gavin W. Jones, ed. Development Studies Centre, Monograph No. 33. Carberra: The Australian National University.

Morokvasic, Mirjana (1983). Women in migration: beyond the reductionist outlook. In *One Way Ticket: Migration and Female Labour*, Annie Phizacklea, ed. London: Routledge and Kegan Paul.

Neumann, L. A. (1979). Hospitality girls in the Philippines. *Southeast Asia Chronicle* (Berkeley), No. 66 / *Pacific Research* (Mountain View, California), vol. 9, Nos. 5-6.

Obbo, Christine (1980). *African Women: Their Struggle for Economic Independence.* London: Zed Press.

Palabrica-Costello, Marilou (1984). Female domestic servants in Cagayan de Oro, Philippines: social and economic implications of employment in a 'premodern' occupational role. In *Women in the Urban and Industrial Workforce: Southeast and East Asia*, Gavin W. Jones, ed. Development Studies Centre, Monograph No. 33. Canberra: The Australian National University.

Papanek, Gustav F. (1975). The poor of Jakarta. *Economic Development and Cultural Change* (Chicago), vol. 24, No. 1 (October), pp. 1-27.

Phongpaichit, Pasuk (1982). *From Peasant Girls to Bangkok Masseuses.* Women, Work and Development Series, No. 2. Geneva: International Labour Office.

_____ (1984). The Bangkok masseuses: origins, status and prospects. In *Women in the Urban and Industrial Workforce: Southeast and East Asia*, Gavin W. Jones, ed. Development Studies Centre, Monograph No. 33. Canberra: The Australian National University.

_____ (1993). The labour-market aspects of female migration in Thailand. Chapter IX in the present volume.

Pittin, Renée (1984). Migration of women in Nigeria: the Hausa case. *International Migration Review* (Staten Island, New York), vol. 18, No. 4 (Winter), pp. 1293-1314.

Radcliffe, Sarah A. (1990). Between hearth and labor market: the recruitment of peasant women in the Andes. *International Migration Review* (Staten Island, New York), vol. 24, No. 2 (Summer), pp. 229-249.

Recchini de Lattes, Zulma and Sonia María Mychaszula (1993). Female migration and labour force participation in a medium-sized city of a highly urbanized country. Chapter VIII in the present volume.

Riley, Nancy, and Robert Gardner (1993). Migration decisions: the role of gender. Chapter X in the present volume.

Rodenburg, Janet (1989). Migration and its socio-economic impact on women, their households and the village economy in North Tapanuli, Sumatra. Research report. Medan, Sumatra.

_____ (forthcoming). Staying behind: rural women and migration in North Tapanuli, Indonesia. Doctoral dissertation. Amsterdam: University of Amsterdam.

Roldán, Martha (1988). Renegotiating the marital contract: intrahousehold patterns of money allocation and women's subordination among domestic outworkers in Mexico City. In *A Home Divided: Women and Income in the Third World*, Daisy Dwyer and Judith Bruce, eds. Stanford, California: Stanford University Press.

Salaff, Janet (1981). *Working Daughters of Hong Kong: Filial Piety or Power in the Family?* Cambridge, United Kingdom; and New York: Cambridge University Press.

Shah, Nasra M., and Peter C. Smith (1984). Migrant women at work in Asia. In *Women in the Cities of Asia: Migration and Urban Adaptation*, James T. Fawcett, Siew-Ean Khoo and Peter C. Smith, eds. Boulder, Colorado: Westview Press.

Smith, M. L. (1973). Domestic service as a channel for upward mobility for the lower class woman: the Lima case. *Female and Male in Latin America*, A. Pescatello, ed. Pittsburgh, Pennsylvania: University of Pittsburgh Press.

Strauch, Judith (1984). Women in rural-urban circulation networks: Implications for social structural change. In *Women in the Cities of Asia: Migration and Urban Adaptation*, James T. Fawcett, Siew-Ean Khoo and Peter C. Smith, eds. Boulder, Colorado: Westview Press.

Sudarkasa, Niara (1977). Women and migration in contemporary West Africa. In *Women and National Development*, Wellesley Editorial Committee, ed. Chicago, Illinois: University of Chicago Press.

Tabet, Paola (1989). "I'm the meat, I'm the knife": sexual service, migration, and repression in some African societies. In *A Vindication of the Rights of Whores*, Gail Pheterson, ed. Seattle: The Seal Press.

Thadani, V. N., and Michael P. Todaro (1984). Female migration: a conceptual framework. In *Women in the Cities of Asia: Migration and Urban Adaptation*, James T. Fawcett, Siew-Ean Khoo and Peter C. Smith, eds. Boulder, Colorado: Westview Press.

Todaro, Michael P. (1976). *Internal Migration in Developing Countries*. Geneva: International Labour Office.

Tongudai, Pawadee (1984). Women migrants in Bangkok: an economic analysis of their employment and earnings. In *Women in the Urban and Industrial Workforce: Southeast and East Asia*, Gavin W. Jones, ed. Development Studies Centre, Monograph No. 33. Canberra: The Australian National University.

Trager, Lillian (1984). Family strategies and the migration of women: migrants to Dagupan City, Philippines. *International Migration Review* (Staten Island, New York), vol. 18, No. 4 (Winter), pp. 1264-1278.

_____ (1988). *The City Connection: Migration and Family Interdependence in the Philippines*. Ann Arbor: The University of Michigan Press.

United Nations Secretariat (1993). Types of female migration. Chapter V in the present volume.

Vatuk, Sylvia J. (1972). *Kinship and Urbanization: White Collar Migrants in North India*. Berkeley and London: University of California Press.

Whiteford, Michael B. (1978). Women, migration and social change: a Colombian case study. *International Migration Review* (Staten Island, New York), vol. 12, No. 2 (Summer), pp. 236-247.

Wilkinson, Clive (1987). Women, migration and work in Lesotho. In *Geography of Gender in the Third World*, Janet Henshall Momsen and Janet Townsend, eds. London: Century Hutchinson; and Albany, New York: State University of New York Press.

Williams, Linda B. (1990). *Development, Demography and Family Decision Making: The Status of Women in Rural Java*. Boulder, Colorado: Westview Press.

Wolf, Diane (1990). Daughters, decisions and domination: an empirical and conceptual critique of household strategies. *Development and Change* (London), vol. 21, No. 1, pp. 43-74.

Wood, Charles H. (1982). Equilibrium and historical-structural perspectives on migration. *International Migration Review* (Staten Island, New York), vol. 16, No. 2 (Summer), pp. 298-319.

Yoon, S. Y. (1990). Super motherhood: rural women in South Korea. In *Structures and Strategies: Women, Work and Family*, Leela Dube and Rajni Palriwala, eds. New Delhi: Sage.

Young, Kate (1982). The creation of a relative surplus population: a case study from Mexico. In *Women and Development. The Sexual Division of Labour in Rural Societies*, Lourdes Benería, ed. New York: Praeger.

Zlotnik, Hania (1993). Women as migrants and workers in developing countries. In "Sociology and social development in a time of economic adversity", James Midgley and Joachim Singelmann, eds. *International Journal of Contemporary Sociology* (Joensuu, Finland), vol. 30, No. 1, special issue, pp. 39-62.

XVI. INCOME ASPIRATIONS AND MIGRANT WOMEN'S LABOUR FORCE ACTIVITY IN MALAYSIA

Kanta Alvi* and Rebeca Wong**

Migration is a strategy often used by families or individuals to improve their socio-economic status. Until recently, migration research has been male biased and has ignored gender specificity. Although late in coming, the growing literature on female mobility suggests that not only are the numbers of female migrants on the rise but the types of movements are varied and complex. Most voluntary female migration movements are broadly categorized as either autonomous or associational (Findley and Williams, 1991; Hugo, 1993). In general, the term "autonomous" is used to describe women who are active participants in the decision to migrate and that move for economic reasons, whereas women are described as "associational migrants" when they move in the company of close family members and are not necessarily actively involved in making the decision to migrate. Associational migrants are frequently women that move in order to get married or to accompany or join their husbands. When women migrate in the company of family members, they are more likely to be "tied movers" (Mincer, 1978) and are often simplistically viewed as passive followers of men (Connell and others, 1976).

Research on female migration is relatively more advanced concerning the determinants than the consequences of such spatial mobility. With regard to the consequences of migration, relatively little attention has been paid to the economic behaviour of associational female migrants. This paper focuses on the experience of women migrating after marriage, either together with their family or to reconstitute their family unit in the urban area of destination. The migration flows considered are rural-urban and urban-urban. For the purpose of this analysis, a household is regarded as a migrant household if the wife of the head of household migrated after marriage.

It is assumed here that income aspirations not only provide the incentive to migrate but act as an important motivational factor that influences the labour force participation of different household members in the area of destination. The aim is to examine the economic activities of migrant wives and, in particular, to consider their allocation of time to market work as a strategy to help their households achieve specific economic goals. A conceptual framework relating the supply of labour by migrant wives to income aspirations is discussed first. Then, the particularities of the socio-economic setting of Peninsular Malaysia—the country whose data are used for the empirical analysis—are presented. A detailed description of the data used, the specification of the empirical model and the methodology used, and a description of the sample characteristics follow. Lastly, results of the empirical case-study are presented and discussed.

A. CONCEPTUAL FRAMEWORK

The relation between migration and labour force participation depends upon the strength of the factors that constrain or ease labour absorption in the area of destination. Factors that impede a migrant's access to desirable employment include lack of information, lack of appropriate skills and job experience, social or institutional barriers to entry and asymmetrical information about the skills of migrants on the part of employers (Standing, 1978a; Stark, 1988). Such barriers often cause migrants to have a lower acceptance wage rate than non-migrants (Shah and Smith, 1984; Findley and Williams, 1991). Moreover, recent migrants are less likely to have access to financial resources in the area of destination or sufficient accumulation of savings that would allow them to search for a job for a prolonged period. Migrants of modest rural

---

*Research Scientist, International Centre for Diarrhoeal Disease, Bangladesh; and Research Associate, The Johns Hopkins University School of Hygiene and Public Health, Baltimore, Maryland, United States of America.

**Assistant Professor, Department of Population Dynamics, The Johns Hopkins University School of Hygiene and Public Health, Baltimore, Maryland, United States of America.

background can also be assumed to have low income aspirations. In sum, the relatively low income aspirations of migrants increase the probability of their securing employment in the informal urban sector (Standing, 1978a and 1978b).

In the present analysis, a distinction is made between the current expected income (short-run wage income) of migrants and their aspired income, which may be considered an income goal in the long run. The former is what migrants expect to earn soon after migration when they are faced with various social and economic constraints preventing their assimilation into the area of destination. The wage rate they accept then does not necessarily reflect their income aspirations.

What is aspired income? Aspired income is that income which enables the migrant household to achieve the level of living of those with whom it compares itself. Aspired income may change as time elapses, depending upon the success or failure of migrants in the place of destination. Even though migration may lead to an improvement of the absolute income of the household that moved, the satisfaction of household members with this new income will depend upon the household's economic standing in relation to the levels of living of those with whom it compares itself. Such comparisons of relative positions with respect to economic gains occur because people are status-conscious. A person's income aspirations and behaviour are determined by the lifestyles and norms of the social class whose attitudes, values and interests are perceived as similar to his or her own (Duesenberry, 1949; Freedman, 1963; Hyman and Singer, 1968; Easterlin 1978; Oppenheimer, 1982; Elster and Kamlet, 1988a, 1988b). Aspired income comprises both wage and non-wage income and is a measure of the standard of living of the reference group. As migrants assimilate to the urban environment, it becomes more and more likely that the group used as reference is one from the area of destination.

Aspired income may be different from the wage income that a migrant may accept. This study does not assume a priori that the aspired income of migrants is lower than that of non-migrants with similar characteristics, but the initial supply price of a migrant's labour may well be lower than that of a non-migrant with similar characteristics. Migrant households, particularly soon after migration, are thus more likely to experience a gap between their actual and aspired incomes. This gap can create economic pressure that influences the work behaviour of the members of the migrant household. It is hypothesized that the perceived need for income created by such a gap will tend to increase the wife's allocation of time to income-generating and money-saving activities. By focusing on the labour force experience of women, this paper examines how migrant households function as a unit to fulfil their economic aspirations and how women respond to the family's economic circumstances.

B. The context of the study: Peninsular Malaysia

Malaysia has a multi-ethnic population consisting of 53 per cent Malays, 36 per cent Chinese and 11 per cent Indians. The ethnic groups display distinct characteristics in terms of culture, occupation, education, economic position and main place of residence. Malays are predominantly rural smallholders and urban public sector employees. Malay women have traditionally been active as traders, craftswomen and workers on family farms. The Chinese are concentrated in urban places and their two main sectors of employment are commerce and manufacturing. Traditionally, Chinese women have not been as economically active as Malay women, but their participation in market work has increased sharply, particularly in skilled jobs in the modern sector (ESCAP, 1986). The Indians are employed in the rubber plantations and oil-palm estates in rural areas and in the professions and services in urban areas. Ethnic differences have long been a major source of social tensions in Malaysia and many Government policies have been directed towards narrowing the socio-economic differences between ethnic groups.

In Malaysia, as elsewhere, the growth of urban areas has resulted from a combination of natural increase, migration and reclassification of rural places. During 1947-1957, there was a rapid growth of the urban population, in part as a result of Government policies that resettled rural Chinese in "new towns" (Goldstein and Goldstein, 1983) and in part because of the voluntary influx of rural-urban migrants, particularly Malays. After the independence of Malaysia in 1957, the proportion of the population living in urban areas grew slowly, rising from 27 to 29 per cent between 1957 and 1970 (ESCAP, 1986). Government policies that were intended to develop rural areas through the Federal Land Development Authority (FELDA), for instance, were partially responsible for the slow growth of urbanization. Ethnic differences in migration patterns resulted from the different opportunities open to the various ethnic groups. From 1970 to 1980, the pace of urbanization accelerated and the proportion urban reached 39 per cent by 1980 (ESCAP, 1986). Such rapid growth was mostly the result of concerted government efforts to increase the proportion of Malays in urban areas (Goldstein and Goldstein, 1984) and of the growth of employment opportunities in urban areas, particularly in the manufacturing, construction, utilities and service sectors. Regional development policies also led to the growth of small towns which attracted migrants from rural areas (Malaysia, 1986).

Analysis of the census data for 1957 and 1970 show that while female agricultural employment fell slightly (from 23 to 22 per cent), there was an overall increase in non-agricultural activities among women (Hirschman and Aghajanian, 1980). The changing structure of the Malaysian economy was largely responsible for such changes. Chinese women responded to the job opportunities in urban areas, while mechanization displaced Indian women from plantation agriculture. To reduce ethnic inequalities, government policies targeted job opportunities for Malays. During the period 1957-1970, the annual rate of increase of the number of Malay women working in the manufacturing sector was 16 per cent, compared to 17.3 per cent for Chinese female workers. By 1976, the rate of increase for Malay women had risen to 19.4 per cent, exceeding by about 8 per cent that of Chinese women (ESCAP, 1986).

C. Data and methods

Data sources

The data for the empirical analysis presented in this paper were drawn from the Malaysian Family Life Survey (MFLS) carried out in Peninsular Malaysia under the auspices of the Rand Corporation. The initial aim of the survey was to gather information on factors affecting fertility and thus the sample is not representative of the entire population of Peninsular Malaysia. The survey was carried out in three rounds, each four months apart, during the period 1976-1977. In the first round, it covered 1,262 households[1], each containing at least one ever-married woman under age 50. In the second and third rounds, there were 1,216 and 1,181 completed interviews, respectively. Only one ever-married woman was selected as the primary respondent in each household (Butz and others, 1978; Jones and Spoelstra, 1978). The analysis presented here considers a subsample of 412 urban households where the selected ever-married woman interviewed was the wife of the head of household and was still married at the time of interview (currently married).

The MFLS of 1976-1977 consisted of 11 questionnaires, out of which the analysis presented in this paper used information from: *(a)* the household roster (MF1); *(b)* the female retrospective questionnaire (MF2); *(c)* the female and male time budget (MF4, MF5); and *(d)* the income and wealth questionnaire (MF6).[2]

The empirical model and method

A standard model of female labour supply is used as a conceptual framework to model the labour force participation of married women (Mincer, 1962; Cain, 1966; Heckman, 1974; Schultz, 1978). This study assumes that the household is the decision-making unit and focuses on the allocation of time by individuals as members of a household unit.[3] It is assumed that a married woman's allocation of time to market work is affected by:

(a) *The relative value of the woman's time.* A person's human capital endowment is a major determinant of that individual's opportunity income. For a married woman, the time she devotes to market work can be interpreted as a response to her wage rate in relation to the value to her household of her domestic work and the ease with which that domestic work can be carried out by others. In this analysis, the value of a woman's market time is determined by factors affecting her wage, such as education and age; and that of a woman's non-market time is determined by such factors as her age, number of children in the household and the presence of domestic help. For the purpose of this analysis, the ethnicity of a woman is also considered in determining the value of a woman's market and non-market time;

(b) *The perceived need to work or the demand for income.* The household's economic condition determines the need to generate resources, thus affecting the labour supply responses of its members. Status consciousness also determines a taste or preference for certain levels of income, generating a pressure to achieve the aspired income level. The indicators of income demand used here include the household's income per adult (excluding the wife's income) and the gap between the household's actual and aspired income. That gap is measured as the income of the household relative to the income of its reference group;

(c) *The structure of the labour-market.* Measures used as indicators of the structure of the labour-market include the area of residence, whether the household head is an employer or is self-employed (a fact that is important to consider because his wife may have a greater likelihood of being employed if the head of household has a family business) and the type of employment that the woman has which determines the demands put on her time;

(d) *Migration status.* Migrants are a self-selected group in terms of their motivation to improve their economic status. They are likely to have a stronger awareness of their aspirations and economic goals than non-migrants, a factor that can affect the allocation of their time to work. Migrants may also have a greater need to work than non-migrants, particularly during the period immediately following their migration.

Multiple regression techniques and, in particular, ordinary least squares, are used to analyse a married woman's allocation of time to work. The employment status of the woman, that is, whether she is employed or not, is assumed to be exogenous in the model used. The main empirical goal is to identify factors that influence the time that a married woman spends in market work, given the woman's employment status.[4] Throughout the analysis, the term "wife" indicates that the wife of the household head is being considered. Definitions of the variables used in the regression models are provided in the annex. However, some of the definitions and measures of the variables require further explanation.[5]

A migrant wife's allocation of time to market work is measured as the total number of hours spent in different remunerated and non-remunerated market activities during a full year. Such activities exclude most housekeeping work, such as cooking, cleaning or child-care. The information on women's activities was gathered using the MFLS time-budget questionnaire that was administered three times, four months apart. Time spent in market work includes that spent in full-time or part-time wage employment; that spent working in one's own business, family business or farm; that devoted to working as an employer and that spent working in home production of goods and services for sale or for home consumption.[6] In each round and for each of the market activities, MFLS documented the number of hours spent in that activity during the most recent seven days in which the activity had been performed and the number of weeks in which the activity was performed during the previous four months.

A household is characterized as migrant if the wife of the head of the household migrated after marriage. The types of migration streams considered are rural-urban and urban-urban. However, if migration had taken place more than 15 years prior to the time of the survey, that is, if the time of residence in the place of interview exceeded 15 years, then neither the woman nor her household were considered to be migrant. The rationale for choosing a cut-off point of 15 years is that such a period is long enough for in-migrants to adjust to their new place of residence; and, consequently, beyond that point their motivations and behaviour are likely to be indistinguishable from those of natives.

The household's absolute income is measured as cash income flow from work and from the household's stock of assets during the year covered by the survey. Income is therefore measured in terms of two components. The first component consists of cash earnings from work in wage employment, self-employment, family business, as an employer or from home production of goods and services for sale. The income of all members of the household aged 15 years or over during the reference year from all the above-mentioned activities is added when measuring household income. The second component encompasses the return on non-business or non-farm assets owned by household members, which includes cash from renting land and buildings owned by household members, dividend income, net interest income, and insurance and employer's provident receipts (see Alvi, 1990; Fain, 1982). In the analysis of the wife's labour force participation, the relevant measure is household income without the wife's contribution. The effect of household composition on total household income is taken into account by considering household income per person aged 15 or over in the household as the measure of household income.

Relative income tries to capture a family's relative economic deprivation in relation to its aspired lifestyle. The family's aspired level of living is determined by the socio-economic position and status of its reference group. A household's minimum aspired income[7] is estimated as the mean income of the reference group. Reference groups are identified as households whose heads have a similar occupation and are in the same age group as the male head of the household in question. Two age groups (15-34 and 35 or over) and five occupational groups (professional and managerial, clerical and sales, production and services, agricultural and labourer, and non-working groups) were considered in identifying the reference group of each household. The measure of relative income for the ith household is then given by:

$$\frac{\frac{(y_i - w_i)}{A_i}}{\frac{\sum_{j=1}^{M_i} \overline{Z}_{ji}}{M_i}},$$

Where y_i = the absolute income of the ith household;

w_i = the wife's contribution to the income in the ith household;

A_i = the number of persons aged 15 or over in the ith household;

$\overline{Z}_{ji}$ = mean income per person aged 15 or over of the jth household; where j (= 1, ...M_i) is in the ith household's reference group;

M_i = the number of households in the ith household's reference group.

Profile of the sample

Among the 412 urban households in the sample used in the analysis, 100 (some 24 per cent of the total) were identified as migrant households. Non-migrant wives had a slightly younger age distribution than migrants, with a mean of 33.2 years for non-migrants, compared with 34.4 years for migrants. In the sample used in the analysis, 57 per cent of the households were Chinese, 28 per cent were Malay and 14.5 per cent were Indian, compared with the country's urban ethnic composition of 58.5 per cent Chinese, 27.6 per cent Malay and 12.8 per cent Indian in 1970 (ESCAP, 1986). Migration levels varied between ethnic groups (table 66). Chinese wives were the least likely to migrate after marriage, followed by Malay and Indian wives. Approximately 16 per cent of the Chinese wives had migrated after their most recent marriage, compared with 32 per cent of the Malay and 43 per cent of the Indian wives. There was only a small difference between the average number of years of schooling of migrant and non-migrant wives (5.4 years for migrants and 5.2 years for non-migrants). Household composition by migration status showed that non-migrant wives belonged to larger households than migrants (mean household size was 6.5 for non-migrants and 6.1 for non-migrants).

TABLE 66. DISTRIBUTION OF WIVES OF HEADS OF HOUSEHOLD BY MIGRATION STATUS AND ETHNICITY, MALAYSIA

Ethnicity	Total number	Migration status (percentage)	
		Migrants	Non-migrants
Malay	119	31.9	68.1
Chinese	235	15.7	84.3
Indian	58	43.1	56.9

The time-budget information shows that only 12.1 per cent of the wives spent no time in market work during the reference year. About 30 per cent of the wives worked more than 900 hours annually, that is, more than three hours a day on average. A high proportion of wives (44.7 per cent) stated that their primary employment was home production, meaning that definitions of labour force participation that fail to take into account work in home production are likely to underestimate women's participation in productive activities by wide margins. The participation of wives in wage employment did not vary by migration status. Most male heads of household were in wage employment (67 per cent), 98 per cent of whom were full-time workers. Overall, heads of migrant households were more likely to be in wage employment (82 per cent) than heads of non-migrant households (63 per cent), while a larger percentage of the heads of non-migrant households were in self-employment (either self-employed, working in a family business or as an employer) than the heads of migrant households (28 versus 10 per cent).

The hypotheses

Two hypotheses are examined in the empirical analysis: *(a)* migrant wives work longer hours than non-migrant wives in households where actual income falls short of the aspired level; and *(b)* the time allocated by migrant wives to market work is inversely related to the relative income of their households, where relative income is measured by the ratio of the household's actual income to its aspired income. These hypotheses can be illustrated using table 67, which relates migration status to relative income.

TABLE 67. MIGRATION STATUS IN RELATION TO RELATIVE INCOME, MALAYSIA

Migration status	Household's relative income without wife's contribution	
	Actual income ≤ minimum aspired income	Actual income > minimum inspired income
Non-migrant wives	A (227)	B (85)
Migrant wives	C (65)	D (35)

NOTE: Numbers in parentheses show the distribution of the 412 urban households in the sample used in the analysis.

The hypotheses suggest two relevant comparisons. First, to compare hours worked by women in cells A and C of table 67 in order to ascertain whether migrant wives work longer hours than non-migrant wives in households where aspired income is higher than the actual level. Secondly, to compare the work effort of migrant wives in the two relative income groups, that is, to compare C and D. It is also enlightening to investigate variations in hours worked within groups of migrant wives. That is, within cells C and D, how are women's working hours related to the household's relative income? Due to limitations imposed by the small sample size, the cases in cells C and D were combined to examine the relationship between wives' work behaviour and relative income in migrant households.

Table 67 can also be a useful tool in general migration research to set the context for more detailed empirical work. The literature on migration suggests that in the place of origin, the households or individuals most likely to migrate are concentrated in C while most non-migrants are in B (Stark, 1984). The conceptual framework for this study suggests that at the place of destination, particularly during the initial stages after migration, migrants would be expected to have higher percentages in C versus D than non-migrants would have in A versus B, especially because migrants would have a lower acceptance wage and probably higher general aspirations.

D. RESULTS

To examine the hypotheses stated in the previous section, two models are considered, the only difference between the two being the specification of the migration status and relative income variables. In both models, the dependent variable is the number of hours worked by the wife.

In model I, the relative income and migration status variables are treated as four dummy variables, distinguishing migrants in two relative income groups (≤ 0.9 and > 0.9) and having non-migrants also classified into two relative income groups (≤ 0.9 and > 0.9). The definition of these dummy variables implicitly divides the sample of households into two groups according to their relative income position, separating households whose actual income falls short of their minimum aspired income from those whose actual income exceeds it. By this criterion alone, a relative income ≤ 1.0 and > 1.0 would have been the most logical way of separating the sample. However, using 1.0 as the cut-off point divides the sample in a way that reduces the number of migrant households in the higher relative income group to a point where meaningful comparisons would be compromised. It was therefore considered that households with a relative income position above 0.9 would have a behaviour similar to that of those whose actual income exceeds their minimum aspired income.

TABLE 68. RESULTS OF FITTING MODEL I FOR WOMEN'S HOURS OF WORK, MALAYSIA
(Dependent variable: hours worked by wife of the household head)

Independent variable	B coefficient	t value
Age	15.8[a]	3.04
Education	-6.2	-0.69
Children under age 6	-21.2	-0.64
Children aged 6-14	5.8	0.26
Mother substitute	-58.8	-0.68
Chinese	46.7	0.59
Indian	-138.4	-1.31
Residence	39.7	0.60
Husband self-employed	89.0	1.03
Wage employment	1 211.0[a]	15.07
Self-employment	1 083.5[a]	11.85
Log of absolute income	-5.4	-0.25
Non-migrants in RIG ≤ 0.9	-	-
Non-migrants in RIG > 0.9	177.2[b]	1.95
Migrants in RIG ≤ 0.9	183.1[b]	1.95
Migrants in RIG > 0.9	-44.0	-0.34
Constant	-318.5	-1.23
R^2	0.46	-
Sample size	412	-

NOTE: RIG = relative income without the wife's contribution.
[a]Significant at 1 per cent level.
[b]Significant at 5 per cent level.

The results obtained by fitting model I (table 68) indicate that migrant wives work significantly longer hours than non-migrant wives in households facing a gap between their actual and aspired income. This result implies that migrant wives are more likely to respond to household aspirations than non-migrant wives. The findings also indicate that among non-migrant wives, those with higher relative income work significantly more hours than those with lower relative income. It is worth noting that the group of non-migrant wives whose relative income is greater than 0.9 includes a large proportion of Chinese. In the sample used, a relatively large proportion of Chinese women were either in wage employment or self-employed, that is, in types of employment where the number of working hours tends to be higher than in employment related to home production.

Model II (table 69) is used to test the second hypothesis, namely, that the working behaviour of migrant wives is inversely related to the household's relative economic position. In this model, relative income is specified as a continuous variable, migration status as a dummy variable set to one if the wife is a migrant and to zero if she is not, and an interaction term between migration status and relative income is included. According to this specification, the effect of migration status on the wife's allocation of time to market work will be determined by the coefficients of the migration status dummy variable plus that of the interaction term between migration status and relative income. The coefficient of the interaction term by itself is assumed to capture the responsiveness of a woman's work behaviour to relative income in migrant households.

TABLE 69. RESULTS OF FITTING MODEL II FOR WOMEN'S HOURS OF WORK, MALAYSIA
(Dependent variable: hours worked by wife of the household head)

Independent variable	B coefficient	t value
Age	15.9[a]	3.07
Education	-3.5	-0.40
Children under age 6	-29.2	-0.89
Children aged 6-14	8.3	0.37
Mother substitute	-69.9	-0.81
Chinese	46.9	0.59
Indian	-131.0	-1.25
Residence	63.2	0.96
Husband self-employed	116.0	1.35
Wage employment	1 211.0[a]	15.08
Self-employment	1 099.5[a]	12.04
Log of absolute income	5.9	0.25
Relative income	43.7	0.68
Migrants	263.3[b]	2.48
Migrants x relative income	-208.0[a]	-2.72
Constant	-414.0	-1.62
R^2	0.46	-
Sample size	412	-

[a]Significant at 1 per cent level.
[b]Significant at 5 per cent level.

The results of fitting model II indicate that migrant wives belonging to households with low relative income work significantly longer hours than non-migrant wives.[8] Our focus in model II is, however, on the coefficients of relative income and the interaction term (between migration status and relative income). The results suggest that for non-migrant wives, relative income does not affect the wife's hours of work. On the other hand, for migrant wives, the greater the need for income (measured by a low relative income position), the longer hours the wife works. To supplement these findings, the regression estimates of a separate model for migrant and non-migrant wives were examined. The results, presented in table 70, indicate that relative income has a significant influence only on the work behaviour of migrant wives, who work longer hours the larger the gap between their household's actual and minimum aspired income. These results support the notion that migrants are selected in terms of their higher level of motivation.

TABLE 70. RESULTS OF FITTING MODELS FOR MIGRANT AND NON-MIGRANT WOMEN'S HOURS OF WORK, MALAYSIA
(*Dependent variable: hours worked by wife of the household head*)

Independent variable	Migrants		Non-migrants	
	B coefficient	t value	B coefficient	t value
Age	21.7[a]	2.17	15.6[b]	2.56
Education	-23.5	-1.75	5.0	-0.45
Children under age 6	-42.6	-0.66	-26.4	-0.70
Children aged 6-14	-3.1	-0.07	10.0	0.39
Mother substitute	-252.6	-1.00	-31.6	-0.34
Chinese	353.0[a]	2.39	42.8	-0.46
Indian	-59.5	-0.39	-123.1	-0.90
Residence	-79.0	-0.62	78.0	1.02
Husband self-employed	93.3	0.40	135.0	1.44
Wage employment	1 465.0[b]	9.79	1 124.2[b]	12.00
Self-employment	853.3[b]	4.55	1 162.6[b]	11.18
Log of absolute income	50.9	1.21	-3.8	-0.14
Relative income	-161.0[b]	-2.65	41.4	0.60
Constant	-608.2	-1.27	-344.3	-1.13
R^2	0.58	-	0.44	-
Sample size	100	-	312	-

[a]Significant at 5 per cent level.
[b]Significant at 1 per cent level.

With respect to the other variables included in the different models, both models I and II yield similar results. There is a significant positive association between woman's age and time devoted to market work. Age is generally accepted as a proxy for experience and may thus partially capture the market value of woman's time. Women that work for wages or are self-employed work significantly longer hours than those working in other types of employment.[9]

Education, considered as a proxy for the market value of a woman's time, shows no significant effect on hours worked, in part because the definition of labour force participation used includes time spent in home production.[10] In addition, the results fail to support the hypothesis that the number of young children in the household limits the time a woman may devote to market work[11]. This result is partially attributable to the composition of the sample used in the analysis, where 64 per cent of the wives of household heads reported their main activity as that of being worker in a family business or farm or in home production. These activities are considered to be relatively compatible with child-care responsibilities. It is also possible that a woman's education and the number of young children in the household are important determinants of the type of employment chosen. If so, the coefficients of variables indicating a woman's employment status could be partially capturing the influence of her education and other constraints on the use of her time.

E. CONCLUSION

This study presents a conceptual framework that explains the relation between income aspirations and the work behaviour of migrant wives at the place of destination. In general, women that migrate in association with other family members are considered passive followers of men; and, consequently, their economic behaviour at the place of destination has received little attention. Even the literature on female migration is heavily tilted towards the analysis of the situation of women that migrate primarily and explicitly for economic reasons.

This paper is among the few that analyse the labour force participation of married women migrating with their family or to join family members in the place of destination, a group that constitutes a considerable proportion of female migrants in most countries. It is assumed that during the period immediately following migration, migrant households are likely to face a gap between their actual and aspired incomes. The question is whether migrant wives respond to their household's economic need by allocating more time to market work when that gap is large in relative terms. The empirical findings presented here and based on data for Peninsular Malaysia indicate that migrant wives work longer hours than non-migrant wives in households where actual income is below that aspired. The results also indicate that a migrant wife's allocation of time to market work is influenced by the household's perceived economic need. These findings show that migrant married women play an important economic role in their households and open up an important issue for further research: what do women gain out of their efforts? Presumably, the observed behaviour among migrant wives is motivated by the desire to increase the economic welfare of their household. The analysis presented, however, does not address the issue of how the life of a migrant woman is affected by her work and the relatively longer hours that she devotes to it.

NOTES

[1] A household is defined as a group of people who sleep under the same roof and eat from the same cooking pot. See Jones and Spoelstra (1978).

[2] For detailed information on the types of information collected and the survey instruments used, see Butz and others (1978) and Fain (1982).

[3] Mincer (1972), Becker (1965); Morgan, Sirageldin and Baerwaldt (1966); among others, have modified the model of individual utility maximization so as to account for utility maximization at the family level in explaining the allocation of time to productive activities by married women.

[4] As mentioned in the text, most women in the sample analysed participated in the labour market. Only 12.1 per cent of the wives spent no time in market work during the year preceding the survey.

[5] For extensive discussion on the measurement of the variables concerned and their limitations, see Alvi (1990).

[6] As, for instance, time spent growing and selling fruits, vegetables, animals or handicrafts or selling services; or time spent growing fruits and vegetables, raising animals or making clothes for home consumption.

[7] The mean income of the reference group population is referred to as the "minimum aspired income", because the income of some households will be below while that of others will be above the minimum threshold of aspired income.

[8] The comparison of the work behaviour of migrant and non-migrant wives using model II has a limitation. Differences should be interpreted with caution because the specification of the interaction term did not weigh non-migrants by their relative household income.

[9] The comparison group included women that were mainly engaged in home production or that spent no time in market work. When the models are tested including only working women, the sign and significance of all the coefficients remain the same.

[10] Other studies also indicate that the association between hours worked and educational level is not strong. See McCabe and Rosenzweig (1976), Peek (1976), and Angulo and Rodríguez (1978).

[11] Similar findings are reported in studies by Boulier (1976), Peek (1976), Angulo and Rodríguez (1978), Quizon and Evenson (1978).

ANNEX

List of variables

Variable	Definition
Hours worked	Hours worked in one year in formal and informal sectors by wife of the household head
Age	Years of age
Education	Completed years of schooling
Children under age 6	Number of children under age 6 in the household
Children aged 6-14	Number of children aged 6 to 14 in the household
Mother substitute	Presence of non-working women aged 15 or over in the household (1 = yes)

Variable	Definition
Chinese	Race is Chinese (1 = yes)
Indian	Race is Indian (1 = yes)
Residence	Place of residence is Ipoh, Penang or Kuala Lumpur (1 = yes)
Husband self-employed	Husband's main activity status is self-employed, employer or working in family business (1 = yes)
Wage employment	Main activity status of wife is full-time or part-time wage employment (1 = yes)
Self-employment	Main activity status of wife is self-employment, working in family business or employer (1 = yes)
Log of absolute income	Natural logarithm of household's actual income minus wife's contribution
Relative income	The ratio of household's income minus wife's contribution to household's aspired income. Aspired income is defined as the mean income of the household's reference group population
Migrant	The wife of the household head if she changed residence after last marriage and her duration of residence at the current place is 15 years or less (1 = yes)
Non-migrants in RIG[a] ≤ 0.9	Non-migrant wife (did not move after last marriage or if she moved her duration of stay at the current place is more than 15 years) in relative income group ≤ 0.9 (1 = yes)
Non-migrants in RIG > 0.9	Non-migrant wife in relative income group > 0.9 (1 = yes)
Migrants in RIG ≤ 0.9	Migrant wife in relative income group ≤ 0.9 (1 = yes)
Migrants in RIG > 0.9	Migrant wife in relative income group > 0.9 (1 = yes)

[a] Relative income without the wife's contribution.

REFERENCES

Alvi, Kanta (1990). Migrants' aspired income and women's motivation to work: the case of Peninsular Malaysia. Doctoral dissertation. Baltimore, Maryland: The Johns Hopkins University.

Angulo, Alejandro, and Cecilia L. de Rodriguez (1978). Female participation in economic activity in Colombia. In *Labour Force Participation in Low-income Countries*, Guy Standing and Gail Sheehan, eds. Geneva: International Labour Office.

Becker, Gary S. (1965). A theory of the allocation of time. *The Economic Journal* (London), vol. 75, No. 99, pp. 493-517.

Boulier, Bryan (1976). Children and household economic activity in Laguna, Philippines. Institute of Economic Development and Research, Discussion Paper. Quezon City, Philippines: University of the Philippines at Diliman.

Butz, William, and others (1978). *The Malaysian Family Life Survey, Appendix A: Questionnaires and Interviewer's Instructions*. R-2351/1-AID. Santa Monica, California: The Rand Corporation.

Cain, Glen G. (1966). *Married Women in the Labor Force: An Economic Analysis*. Chicago, Illinois: University of Chicago Press.

Connell, John, and others (1976). *Migration from Rural Areas: The Evidence from Village Studies*. New Delhi: Oxford University Press.

Duesenberry, James S. (1949). *Income, Saving and the Theory of Consumer Behavior*. Cambridge, Massachusetts: Harvard University Press.

Easterlin, Richard (1978). *Population, Labor Force, and Long Swings in Economic Growth: The American Experience*. New York: Columbia University Press.

Elster, Susan, and M. S. Kamlet (1988a). Income aspirations and married women's labor force participation. School of Urban and Public Affairs, Working Paper, Series 88-16. Pittsburgh, Pennsylvania: Carnegie Mellon University.

_____ (1988b). Reference groups, occupational class and married women's labor force participation. School of Urban and Public Affairs, Working Paper, Series 88-16. Pittsburgh, Pennsylvania: Carnegie Mellon University.

Fain, Terry (1982). *The Malaysia Family Life Survey: Codebook of the Individual Level Data Set*. N-1815-AID. Santa Monica, California: The Rand Corporation.

Findley, Sally E., and Linda Williams (1991). *Women Who Go and Women Who Stay: Reflections of Family Migration Processes in a Changing World*. Population and Labour Policies Programme, Working Paper No. 176. Geneva: International Labour Office.

Freedman, Deborah S. (1963). The relation of economic status to fertility. *American Economic Review* (Nashville, Tennessee), vol. 53, No. 3 (June), pp. 414-426.

Goldstein, Sydney, and Alice Goldstein (1983). *Migration and Fertility in Peninsular Malaysia: An Analysis Using Life History Data*. N-1860-AID. Santa Monica, California: The Rand Corporation.

_____ (1984). Inter-relations between migration and fertility: their significance for urbanization in Malaysia. *Habitat International* (Tarrytown, New York), vol. 8, No. 1, pp. 93-103.

Heckman, James J. (1974). Shadow prices, market wages and labor supply. *Econometrica* (Cambridge, Massachusetts; and London), vol. 42, No. 4 (July), pp. 679-694.

Hirschman, Charles, and Akbar Aghajanian (1980). Women's labor force participation and socio-economic development: the case of Peninsular Malaysia, 1957-1970. *Journal of South East Asian Studies* (Singapore), vol. 1, No. 1, pp. 30-49.

Hugo, Graeme J. (1993). Migrant women in developing countries. Chapter III in the present volume.

Hyman, Herbert H., and Eleanor Singer, eds. (1968). *Readings in Reference Group Theory and Research*. New York: Free Press.

Jones, Robert, and Nyle Spoelstra (1978). *The Malaysia Family Life Survey, Appendix C: Field and Technical Report*. R-2351/3-AID. Santa Monica, California: The Rand Corporation.

Lim, Lin Lean (1988). Effects of women's position on migration. In *Conference on Women's Position and Demographic Change in the Course of Development, Oslo, 1988: Solicited Papers*. Liège: International Union for the Scientific Study of Population.

Malaysia (1986). *Third Malaysia Plan, 1976-1980*. Kuala Lumpur: Government Printer.

McCabe, J. L., and M. R. Rosenzweig (1976). Female labor force participation, occupational choice, and fertility in developing countries. *Journal of Development Economics* (Amsterdam), vol. 3, No. 2, pp. 141-160.

Mincer, Jacob (1962). Labor force participation of married women: a study of labor supply. In *Aspects of Labor Economics*, H. G. Lewis, ed. Report of the Universities-National Bureau Committee for Economic Research. Princeton, New Jersey: Princeton University Press.

_____ (1978). Family migration decisions. *Journal of Political Economy* (Chicago, Illinois), vol. 86, No. 5 (October), pp. 749-773.

Morgan, James N., Ismail A. Sirageldin and Nancy Baerwaldt (1966). *Productive Americans: A Study of How Individuals Contribute to Economic Progress*. Ann Arbor, Michigan: The University of Michigan, Institute for Social Research.

Oppenheimer, Valerie Kincade (1982). *Work and the Family*. New York: Academic Press.

Peek, Peter (1976). A simultaneous equation model of household behaviour. World Employment Programme, Research Working Paper (restricted). Geneva: International Labour Office.

Quizon, E. I., and R. E. Evenson (1978). Time allocation and home production in Philippine rural households. New Haven, Connecticut: Yale University, Department of Economics. Mimeographed.

Schultz, T. Paul (1978). The influence of fertility on labor supply of married women: simultaneous equation estimates. In *Research in Labor Economics*, vol. 2. Greenwich, Connecticut: JAI Press.

Shah, Nasra M., and Peter C. Smith (1984). Migrant women at work in Asia. In *Women in the Cities of Asia: Migration and Urban Adaptation*, James T. Fawcett, Siew-Ean Khoo and Peter C. Smith, eds. Boulder, Colorado: Westview Press.

Standing, Guy (1978a). *Labour Force Participation and Development*. Geneva: International Labour Office.

_____ (1978b). Aspiration wages, migration and urban unemployment. *The Journal of Development Studies* (London), vol. 14, No. 2 (January), pp. 232-248.

Stark, Oded (1984). Rural-to-urban migration in LDCs: a relative deprivation approach. *Economic Development and Cultural Change* (Chicago, Illinois), vol. 32, No. 3 (April), pp. 475-486.

_____ (1988). *Migrants and Markets*. Discussion Paper No. 37. Cambridge, Massachusetts: Harvard University, Migration and Development Program.

United Nations, Economic and Social Commission for Asia and the Pacific (1986). *Population of Malaysia*. Country Monograph Series, No. 13. Bangkok.

XVII. THE CONSEQUENCES OF TEMPORARY OUT-MIGRATION FOR THE FAMILIES LEFT BEHIND: THE CASE OF JEQUITINHONHA VALLEY, BRAZIL

Franklin W. Goza*,
Eduardo Rios-Neto** and Paula Vieira**

Studies of internal migration from rural areas of developing countries have focused on peasant men who move to urban areas in search of better economic opportunities (Mascarenhas-Keyes, 1990). The relatively few studies examining the consequences of this movement for family members left behind have found that the women and children who remain either perform the tasks previously carried out by the out-migrant men or hire others to perform them if sufficient remittances are received. When the latter is not the case, the wife and other family members need to work harder to perform those tasks as well as their other duties (Cliffe, 1978; Deere and León de Leal, 1982; Hugo, 1985; Margolies and Suarez, 1978; Siegal, 1969). Even though women and children frequently assume those additional responsibilities, there is little certainty that this will result in any increase in their status (Safilios-Rothschild, 1985; Bisilliat and Fiéloux, 1987). Although women acting as the de facto head of household sometimes experience positive outcomes (e.g., increased economic power or prestige), that consequence is not uniform and may only be temporary when it occurs. Instead, it seems likely that women left behind will experience negative outcomes as a result of the absence of their male immediate relatives.

This paper contributes to the small but growing field of research on the consequences of migration for those left behind by examining the case of the Jequitinhonha Valley of Minas Gerais, Brazil. The emphasis is on economic aspects and the paper focuses almost exclusively on the consequences experienced by women married to temporary migrant workers. To a lesser extent, however, the consequences of temporary male migration on children are also discussed.

This project is unusual in two respects: it examines the consequences of short-term or circular out-migration; and it considers both the paid and unpaid activities of women married to migrants. The data analysed were collected with an instrument designed to measure women's economic activities in several ways, including a time-budget. Analyses of these data illustrate the limitations of standard measures of women's economic activity, a problem common to many censuses and surveys (Anker, 1983; Safilios-Rothschild, 1985; other papers in this volume) and underscore the value of careful data collection to avoid drastic undercounts of women's productive activities. In the present context, time-budget data are examined to determine changes in household activity patterns associated with temporary out-migration. In addition, two measures of women's economic activities are analysed as dependent variables in multivariate regressions to determine the effects of male out-migration on women's participation in the paid labour force, an activity that often represents a significant status change for women (positive, in most cases). The effects of the husband's previous migration status, as well as other important socio-economic variables, are also controlled for in the models used. The concluding analytical section reviews some of the social consequences of out-migration by examining its effects on the education of the children of migrants, women's attitudes and the overall social well-being of families left behind.

Prior to the examination of the outcomes of migration, the Jequitinhonha Valley and some of its important sociocultural and economic characteristics are described, including the prevalence of temporary male labour out-migration that has pervasive effects on the area. Next, the data and the methods used to collect them are discussed. After a brief review of relevant theoretical issues and hypotheses, the main body of the paper examines the consequences of out-migration for those left behind.

---

*Bowling Green State University, Bowling Green, Ohio, United States of America.
**Centro de Desenvolvimento e Planejamento Regional, Federal University of Minas Gerais, Belo Horizonte, Minas Gerais, Brazil.

A. THE JEQUITINHONHA VALLEY

The rural area examined in this study is the Jequitinhonha Valley of the state of Minas Gerais, located in south-central Brazil. The valley occupies 78,451 square kilometres in the north-eastern corner of the state and in 1991 had nearly 880,000 inhabitants, most small producers of beans, rice and corn. The valley occupies two distinct geographical regions, known as the Upper and the Lower Jequitinhonha. The Upper Jequitinhonha consists of a high plateau region characterized by *cerrado* (woodsy scrub-brush) vegetation and the Lower Jequitinhonha is a lowland region with savannah-type vegetation. The data discussed below refer only to the upper region because fieldwork was limited to municipalities in that area.

The valley is frequently portrayed as an economically stagnant area and one of the poorest regions of Brazil (Moura, 1988; Silva, 1988; Moura, Lacerda and Eigenheer, 1980). The agrarian structure is characterized by extreme inequality, consisting of a few large landholders and many small producers. Historically, the principal agricultural actors were linked through a latifundium/minifundium dualism. On the latifundium side, large *fazendas* (agricultural or cattle-raising estates) sheltered numerous familial production units. Those family units provided services to the *fazendeiro* (estate owner) in exchange for a residential dwelling, the right to farm for themselves on small subsistence plots within the *fazenda* and an occasional cash remuneration. Outside the *fazenda* were small producers or *minifundistas* who generally combined their agricultural production tasks with other activities, such as mining or craft production of ceramic, wood or cotton goods (Goza, 1992).

Recently, however, the valley has experienced numerous structural transformations. The mechanization of agriculture, government attempts to promote reforestation and coffee production and the expansion of local cattle ranches have led to drastic changes in the lives of the small producers (Goza, 1992; Silva, 1992). One result is that between 1960 and 1980 the valley lost nearly 500,000 residents, as many of those without a secure claim to land were displaced and left the region permanently (Silva and Silva, 1986). Those that remained, largely small landowners and their children, had to determine how to survive in a rural area that now required cash for most transactions but offered few employment opportunities.

One means of coping was for adult males to migrate to other parts of Brazil in search of temporary employment. Although numerous routes were explored, the preferred strategy came to be the seasonal migration of men to the sugar-cane fields in the Ribeirão Preto area of the state of São Paulo. Migrants in their late teens tend to stay away for several years during which they work and save enough money to buy a homestead and become eligible bachelors. After marriage, they tend to go only for several months a year or not at all. As their children get older, they usually stay away for from six to nine months at a time. By their late thirties to mid-forties, and sometimes sooner, most retire from the cane-cutting occupation (Goza and Rios-Neto, 1988). Thus, there is a clear connection between the stage of the migrants' family in the life cycle and the annual duration of their out-migration episodes.

In the Jequitinhonha Valley, many farmers produce two harvests each year. During the first season, which extends approximately from September to February, practically all rural heads of household, their spouses and children undertake agricultural activities associated with seeding, weeding and harvesting. During the remaining months, male heads of household have two options: to work locally or to migrate temporarily to cut sugar cane in São Paulo. Those migrating usually depart in February after planting their second crop. In addition to their normal tasks, the women and children remaining behind have to care for their small properties and subsistence crops. Most migrants return home between September and November, when the rains arrive and they have to plant their primary crop. Frequently, however, cane cutters must sign a labour contract prior to the initiation of their employment which requires that they remain until the end of the sugar harvest or forfeit from 10 to 25 per cent of their earnings (Goza and Rios-Neto, 1990). For that reason and as a consequence of the late return of the men, many women must assume all the duties associated with planting. Upon their return, most male migrants remain in the valley until the following February when the cycle begins again. Many men migrate every year for several decades (Goza and Rios-Neto, 1990). Thus, in keeping with Mitchell's definition (1985), this type of movement is denominated "circular migration", meaning the process whereby people regularly leave their permanent residence in search of employment in locations too far for them to commute on a daily, or in this case, even a monthly basis.

Data from the Upper Jequitinhonha Valley indicate that of the 2,252 persons over age 15 included in the survey sample, 35 per cent had left the area at least once for periods ranging from 3 to 12 months. This temporary or short-term movement was far more common among men than women, with 53 and 17 per cent, respectively, having migrated at least once. Over 93 per cent of the men leaving the area temporarily did so to work, while only 67 per cent of the women migrating reported work as their main objective. The data thus indicate that temporary labour migration in the area is very much gender-specific, as male out-migration continues to predominate.

Over 54 per cent of the 800 heads of household interviewed had migrated temporarily at least once. The average number of temporary moves made by heads of household migrating at least once was 4.2. These figures show the pervasiveness of that type of migration in the Jequitinhonha Valley. It is worth noting that in the traditional valley society, whenever a husband was part of the household, regardless of age or economic activity, he was always described as the head of household by the respondent (that is, either himself or his wife), even when a woman was the primary income-earner in the household. Thus, the present use of the term "head of household" reflects the way in which it was used by respondents of the Jequitinhonha Valley. Still, 127 households or 16 per cent of the total, were reported as having a female head (Goza and Rios-Neto, 1988).

Of the 1,816 temporary moves reported by all heads of household, over 80 per cent were directed to the Ribeirão Preto area of the state of São Paulo, where the principal migrant activity was sugar-cane harvesting (Goza and Rios-Neto, 1988). Consequently, the mean number of episodes for those male heads of household engaged in circular migration was 1,816/(0.54x800) or 4.5 times. The data also show that most short-term migrants departed alone (33.1 per cent) or with friends (28.2 per cent), and that only 1.4 per cent left with their spouse. Thus, wives remaining at home became the de facto heads of household during the absence of their husbands. The small number of women who did accompany their husbands to Ribeirão Preto generally found work either preparing food for the cane cutters or as cleaners of the large barracks where workers were housed or washing workers' clothes. Only a handful worked harvesting cane.

One of the four municipalities surveyed, Chapada do Norte had significantly higher rates of temporary labour out-migration than the others (Goza, 1992; Goza and Rios-Neto, 1988). Nearly 70 per cent of its adult men had worked temporarily elsewhere. In the municipalities of Minas Novas and Turmalina, this figure was approximately 50 per cent, while in São Gonçalo do Rio Preto, it was fewer than 30. Examination of temporary migration rates by age group for Chapada do Norte illustrates the degree to which an area of small agricultural producers can come to depend upon outside income to help meet its economic requirements. The percentages of men in age groups 15-24, 25-34, 35-44 and 45-54 that were migrants were 52, 86, 90 and 90 per cent, respectively. These figures are significantly higher than those for the other three municipalities studied.

Remittances received by family members that remained in the valley are an important consequence of circular migration (Goza, 1992). It is generally assumed that the primary way in which those left behind benefit from migration is through the remittances sent or savings brought back when the migrants return (Findley and Williams, 1991). When those funds are significant and received regularly, they will affect the entire family positively (Standing, 1984; Mascarenhas-Keyes, 1990), but if they are small, irregular or of unpredictable amounts, the entire household may suffer (Cliffe, 1978; Palmer, Subhadhira and Grisanaputi, 1985).

Over 17 per cent of the 800 households interviewed received funds of varying amounts during the 12 months preceding the interview. This figure is roughly equal to the number of male household heads that temporarily out-migrated in 1987. However, 14 per cent of households with a head who migrated received no remittances and 12 per cent of those whose head did not migrate received some remittances, often from sons, brothers, uncles and grandsons who were not household members. The wives left behind without any remittance assistance must have had to depend entirely upon their own initiative, the mercy of others or the *caderneta* system discussed below to make ends meet. The varying proportions of wives that reported receiving remittances in the four municipalities studied (i.e., ranging from 5 to 60 per cent) suggests that, in many cases, the de facto head of household must have experienced financial difficulties.

When asked about the uses made of the funds received, it became apparent that most households relied upon remittances for basic survival, with 67 per cent using them for household consumption purposes and to repay debt. Only 2 per cent used remittances to pay for the education of family members, 1 per cent to purchase land and another 1 per cent to finance the migration of others. No one reported using remittances to increase savings. Thus, the economic returns from temporary out-migration were largely used for the short-term enhancement of the migrant household's well-being, rather than to facilitate upward mobility.

B. Background

The data analysed in this study are from a two-phase project on labour migration originating in the Jequitinhonha Valley of Minas Gerais, Brazil that was conducted by the Centre for Development and Regional Planning (CEDEPLAR), Federal University of Minas Gerais, between January and August of 1988. During the first phase, multi-stage random sampling techniques were used to select 800 households in four municipalities of the Upper Jequitinhonha Valley (Chapada do Norte, Minas Novas, São Gonçalo do Rio Preto and Turmalina). The data gathered include brief migration histories of all household members and a life history for each head of household. The latter provides information on marriages, births and deaths in the respondent's household, as well as detailed information on migration, employment and agricultural production and holdings. Other questionnaire sections covered debt, remittances, agricultural innovations, household time-budgets and future migration plans. Despite its richness, the data gathered permit only an indirect assessment of some of the effects of temporary migration on those left behind.

During the second phase of data collection, 450 sugar-cane cutters were interviewed in the area of destination, in the Ribeirão Preto area of São Paulo. Those interviews were carried out at the 10 destinations most often cited by out-migrants from the Upper Jequitinhonha Valley during the first phase of data collection (Goza and Rios-Neto, 1988).

The questionnaire used in the area of origin measured the labour force participation of everyone over 15 years of age, using the same type of question utilized in Brazilian demographic censuses. According to this approach, all respondents were asked what their primary occupation was during the 30 days preceding the interview. This traditional way of investigating the topic, in Brazil and many other places (Anker, Khan and Gupta, 1988), is henceforth referred to as the "census question" approach.

The labour force activities of heads of household and their spouses were also measured in another manner, through a time-use schedule or time-budget. A variety of ways exist for constructing time-budgets (Anker, 1980). Although most, if not all, time-budgets have been attempts to ascertain better women's labour force participation, the number of activities evaluated and the ways in which they are measured is far from uniform. Another issue concerning the time-budget methodology is how to demarcate specific activities as either economic or home-oriented. Such distinctions are problematic because not all home activities occur completely outside of the market, nor do all economic activities take place completely within it.

In the formulation of the time-budget used, 17 types of activities were examined. Ten were classified as economic and the remainder as domestic. The 17 categories used were selected because of their importance to all households in the valley, especially those in rural areas. The groupings made were arbitrary in that they captured only a subset of all activities, although an attempt was made to select the most important. The economic activities included: wage labour; harvesting, weeding and seeding; cattle-raising; handicrafts; service sector production; hunting and fishing; domestic production; building construction; and mining. The domestic activities included: child care; fetching wood and water; home repairs; sale of home production; raising livestock; other domestic duties; and other domestic duties and child care combined. The fieldwork suggested that these activities and demarcations were those most appropriate for the Jequitinhonha Valley.

The time-budget recorded each activity from three different perspectives. The first two referred to the number of hours worked during a typical week and during the week prior to the interview. The third recorded the number of months during which an individual performed each activity during the year preceding the interview. In an attempt to measure correctly the activities of every household head and spouse, the goal was to collect data directly from the person in question. However, if after two return visits that person could not be located, proxy responses were solicited from the spouse. This situation arose less than 5 per cent of the time. Interviewers completed the time-budget on the basis of responses solicited from the respondents. Given the seasonal nature of many agricultural activities, as well as the authors' interest in monitoring the effects of a spouse's temporary absence, the focus was on the variables that measure activities performed over the past 12 months rather than during the past week, since most migrants had not yet departed for São Paulo. Although all questions concerning activities during the past week and year were collected in the same fashion, space limitations restrict the discussion to those most relevant to this paper.

Although the time-use method of ascertaining labour force activity is more demanding for both interviewer and respondent, some authors (Anker, 1980; Anker, Khan and Gupta, 1988) believe it is worth the extra time and cost because time-budget data enable one to obtain a better measure of the intensity and scope of economic activity. They may also permit a more detailed assessment of the division of labour by gender and should allow a better assessment of changes in the activity patterns of women, including those related to the migration of husbands. Lastly, the time-budget permits better identification of persons engaged in unpaid economic activities and thus reduces the underestimation of unpaid family workers (Anker, 1983).

Because the time-budget data were collected only from heads of household and their spouses and because the aim of this paper is to contrast the activities of the wives of migrants and non-migrants, all analyses of labour force participation reported below are limited to the 609 couples providing complete information. Because of space limitations, there is no discussion here of the activities of the 127 women who were head of household, most of whom were widows. Another 60 households were excluded because there was no wife present, since the male head of household was either a bachelor or a widower. Lastly, several cases had to be excluded because the respondents did not provide complete responses to the questions.

C. THEORETICAL CONSIDERATIONS

In the Jequitinhonha Valley, the entry of women into paid employment represents a break with tradition and is viewed by most women as a positive form of status adjustment, indicating the importance of the issue. Two theoretical frameworks are relevant to the examination of the effects of repeated, short-term, circular migration of husbands on the labour force participation of married women. The first is the basic theory of the sexual division of labour (Becker, 1991), which may be extended to rural areas of developing countries. Women that find themselves in traditional agricultural societies characterized by a rigid division of labour by gender are unlikely to experience positive changes as a result of their husbands' temporary absence, especially if women's contributions to agricultural activities are viewed as auxiliary and if the nature of temporary migration does not require that the pre-existing division of labour by gender be altered significantly.

In the Jequitinhonha Valley, as in many other areas of the world, the domestic production activities performed by wives are frequently undervalued by the normative, institutional and community level mechanisms that depreciate women's contributions to production, even though those activities may be crucial for household survival. In such contexts, even women themselves often underestimate their economic contributions by regarding them as a "wifely duty rather than as work" (Safilios-Rothschild, 1985, p. 300). Thus, in traditional societies women's work is often viewed as minor, superfluous or auxiliary. Economic activities such as seeding and weeding are essentially invisible to those gathering census data and are not captured by the traditional "census question".

Past research has shown that migrants from the Jequitinhonha Valley usually attempt to return home during the peak agricultural season to assist with plowing and planting (Goza and Rios-Neto, 1990). In the absence of a priori knowledge about the degree to which the activities of wives of out-migrants are altered by their husbands' absence, it is hypothesized that circular male migration will have a minor effect on the labour force activities of their wives and, therefore, the sexual division of labour will remain virtually unchanged.

The second relevant theoretical framework focuses on traditional agricultural societies characterized by a rigid division of labour by gender. However, it predicts that married women tend to enhance their status by assuming control over economic production in areas of origin, thereby enabling husbands to move to more lucrative salaried activities in other places (Gronau, 1977; Evenson, Popkin and King-Quizon, 1980). Although this income diversification strategy implies a double burden on married women as they undertake production for both the home and the market, an improvement of their status is expected from their more active role in agricultural production, commercialization and management of resources within the household. The pattern of agricultural specialization, income diversification and status enhancement suggested by this framework has been observed in Africa (Safilios-Rothschild, 1985; von Braun, 1989). Increased agricultural specialization by women may have occurred also in the Jequitinhonha Valley as migrant husbands often remain away for up to nine months per year.

D. Variables, hypotheses and models

Given the patriarchal nature of society in the Jequitinhonha Valley (Moura, 1988; Moura, Lacerda and Eigenheer, 1980), both the census question and time-budget data are expected to indicate a rigid division of labour by gender. However, because of their nature, the time-budget data are expected to show more clearly the differences in labour allocation by gender. In addition, since previous research suggests that women left behind generally take over many of the tasks normally carried out by men (Connell, 1984; Mitchell, 1961), significant differences are expected between the activities performed by the wives of migrants and those performed by the wives of non-migrants.

The variables used in the multivariate analyses presented below are defined in the annex. The variables AGE, age squared (AGE2), and number of children in the household that are under age 5 (KIDSLT5) are the household demographic variables to be examined. Although the importance of these variables in models of labour force participation is well documented, it is worth recalling that a wife's age, and by extension age squared, and the number of children she has that are under age 5 are all closely associated with the life cycle of the household. It is expected that age will be positively correlated with market participation, while age squared is expected to capture the negative, non-linear effects of increasing age. KIDSLT5 is hypothesized to indicate the negative effect of recent fertility on the labour force activities of women.

Among the socio-economic measures considered, education (measured as education squared, EDUCATION2) is of fundamental importance. It is expected to capture the usual positive impact of education on women's labour force participation. The other socio-economic indicators examined are electricity, debt, drought (whether the household experienced losses due to drought) and urban residence. Because it was not possible to obtain a reliable measure of household income, electricity and debt are used as proxies for household wealth, which is closely related to household income. Other proxy indicators of household income, including property ownership and materials used to construct the home, were examined but did not show statistical significance and therefore are not discussed further. Access to electricity is hypothesized to reflect the negative effect of relative wealth on the participation of women in paid activities. Household debt, interpreted as a proxy for household poverty, is expected to have a positive effect on female economic activity. The far from uniform weather patterns in the valley have left some areas remarkably verdant, while others are extremely parched. Such differences are probably the result of the extremely mountainous topography (Silva, 1992). The variable DROUGHT indicates the effect of drought conditions over the 12 months preceding the interview. Drought is expected to affect labour force participation positively, forcing households under stress to diversify their economic pursuits by, among other things, compelling wives to secure salaried employment. Urban residence is hypothesized to be positively correlated with female labour force participation since more employment opportunities are likely to be available in urban areas.

The effects of migration on female labour force participation are evaluated through three variables. The variable MIGRANT87 is used to capture the effect of husband's migration in 1987 on the wife's economic participation. Other things being equal, the temporary absence of husbands is expected to increase the labour force participation of the wives left behind because they have to generate income for consumption when their husbands are away. The other two migration variables are meant to capture the effects of husbands' past migration experience on women's labour force participation during the previous 12 months. The variable RETIRED indicates if the head of household migrated during the 10 years preceding the interview, while that denoted by MOVESTO87 indicates the number of moves a husband made prior to 1987.

Research has shown that an association exists between a family's stage in the life cycle, the migration of the head of household during the year preceding the interview and the activity rates of married women (Rios-Neto and Vieira, 1991 and 1992). More specifically, female activity rates increase with age, whereas male annual out-migration rates tend to decrease as men get older (Goza and Rios-Neto, 1988; Rios-Neto and Vieira, 1990). The impact of recent male out-migration on female labour force participation may thus be affected by countervailing life-cycle effects unless the age of wives is controlled for. In addition, there may be a separate effect of the husband's cumulative migration experience on the wife's labour force participation. That is, the more time a man spends away, the more likely it is that his wife will have to undertake additional economic responsibilities and acquire the skills needed to do so. Because cumulative male migration and married women's labour force participation are positively correlated with age, this hypothesis can be tested only by controlling for age and other indicators of the stage in the life cycle, such as KIDSLT5 and RETIRED.

E. CONSEQUENCES OF TEMPORARY OUT-MIGRATION

Economic consequences

Descriptive results

This section presents a comparison of the results obtained by the two different ways of gathering information on the economic activities of women and then discusses the sexual division of labour in the Jequitinhonha Valley on the basis of the data gathered. As expected, the time-budget measure for the number of months worked during the year preceding the interview and the census question on current labour force status produced very different estimates. According to the former measure, 52 per cent of all married women were economically active for at least a month, whereas according to the latter the proportion active amounted to only 36 per cent, a statistically significant difference. Part of the difference was due to the seasonal nature of many agricultural tasks, which cannot be captured by the census question because it relates only to the previous month. The time-budget question, in contrast, referred to activities performed for at least one month during the previous 12 months. Another cause of the differences observed is undoubtedly the "invisible" nature of many of the economic tasks performed by women. By explicitly eliciting the reporting of time spent on specific tasks, the time-budget approach leads to more complete and therefore more accurate measures of the economic activities of women.

An understanding of the sexual division of labour in the valley is helpful to determine the potential impact of the temporary migration of husbands on the status of women left behind, since it provides a baseline from which to monitor change. The time-budget documents that division well since it covers both economic (i.e., market and non-market) and domestic activities. Although the distinction between economic and domestic activities is somewhat arbitrary, the distinction is made on the basis of the time-budget classification suggested by Anker (1980). In the broadest sense, economic activities are those market and non-market activities directly associated with the formation of monetary income and the satisfaction of consumption needs through the production of non-market subsistence goods. Domestic activities are time-allocated tasks associated with the production of "commodities" or household services in the sense suggested by Becker (1965). The time-budget also illustrates the differences in the allocation of time by heads of household and their spouses.

In tables 71 and 72, panel A provides the time-budgets for economic and domestic activities of husbands and wives, respectively. In column (1), the tables indicate the number of persons engaged in each activity; in column (2), the average number of months during which each activity was performed over the 12 months preceding the interview; in column (3), the person-months during which the activity was performed; in column (4), the effective labour force allocation index; and in column (5), the potential labour force allocation index. The potential labour force allocation index is the ratio of the total number of person-months spent in economic or domestic activities divided by the maximum number of person-months available to individuals, assuming that only one activity can be performed per month (i.e., the potential labour supply is 12 times the number of males, that is, 7,440 person-months). This crude index provides an idea of the degree of labour force participation, labour seasonality and labour allocation slackness in the valley. However, it is affected by the fact that people can perform more than one task per month, as is indicated by the mean number of activities per person.

Husbands performed an average of 1.83 economic activities per person (see panel A of table 71) and used 87 per cent of their potential labour allocation index. Column (4) of table 71 indicates that husbands devoted over 70 per cent of their economic activities to wage labour, harvesting, and seeding and weeding. This figure was computed by summing the appropriate proportions found in column (4). Married women performed, on average, 0.76 economic activity per person (see table 72). They too concentrated more than 70 per cent of their economic activities on wage labour, harvesting, and seeding and weeding (see column (4) of table 72), but their potential labour allocation index was only 37 per cent, indicative of both a lower level of market work and a higher degree of seasonality in economic activities.

Panel B of tables 71 and 72 provides information on the domestic activities for which information is available. The average figure for domestic activity per husband was 0.41. The potential labour allocation index of husbands in this list of household activities (35 per cent) was low and suggestive of relative idleness in the domestic sphere. Husbands allocated more than 65 per cent of their domestic labour to tending livestock or hauling water and wood. In contrast, the potential domestic labour allocation index of wives was high (1.88), indicating that married women performed more than one household task simultaneously. More than 90 per cent of their time was devoted to cleaning, cooking and washing (33 per cent), child care (27 per cent), hauling water and wood (18 per cent) and raising livestock (14 per cent).

That wives performed, on average, 1.88 domestic tasks per month and husbands only 0.41 task indicates the traditional gender-based division of labour in the valley. If one compares the overall mean number of economic and domestic activities performed, married women performed an average of 2.64 activities while men performed 2.24. Without weighting the mean number of hours worked in each activity, this result cannot be interpreted as indicating a higher level of activity among wives with a consequent reduction of their leisure time—something found in other time-budget studies.

Comparing the total number of hours worked in the previous week between economically "active" and "inactive" women, Rios-Neto and Vieira (1992) found that economically active women in the valley work more hours per week and have less leisure than women that are not economically active. The latter group worked 72.1 hours per week in domestic activities, whereas active women worked 51.3 hours in domestic activities and 45.7 hours in economic activities, for a total of 97 hours per week. Therefore, active women had roughly 25 per cent less time to devote to leisure activities. "The participation of women in the labour market does not affect their responsibility for producing and reproducing the labour force; therefore, rural women generally work a 'double' day" (Deere, Humphries and de Leal, 1982, p. 106).

TABLE 71. ECONOMIC AND DOMESTIC ACTIVITIES PERFORMED BY MALE HEADS OF HOUSEHOLD, ACCORDING TO TIME-BUDGET DATA, JEQUITINHONHA VALLEY, BRAZIL

Activity	Persons engaged in activity Number (1)	Persons engaged in activity Percentage	Average months for those engaged in activity[a] (2)	Person-months per period (3) = (1)(2)	Effective labour allocation index (4) = (3)/6,465.4	Potential labour allocation index (5) = (3)/7,440
A. Average time in economic activity						
Wage labour	252	40.65	7.97	2 008.40	0.31	0.27
Harvesting	341	55.00	4.11	1 400.20	0.22	0.19
Weeding and seeding	330	53.23	4.10	1 354.30	0.21	0.18
Cattle-raising	45	7.26	9.56	430.00	0.07	0.06
Handicrafts	12	1.94	7.63	91.50	0.01	0.01
Services	81	13.06	9.74	789.00	0.12	0.11
Hunting and fishing	3	0.48	5.43	16.30	0.00	0.00
Home production	9	1.45	6.00	54.00	0.01	0.01
Building/construction	34	5.48	5.41	184.00	0.03	0.03
Mining	27	4.35	5.10	137.70	0.02	0.02
TOTAL	1 134	182.90	65.05	6 465.40	1.00	0.87
Number of persons	620	-	-	-	-	-
Potential labour supply	7 440	-	-	-	-	-
Average number of activities	1.83	-	-	-	-	-

Activity	Persons engaged in activity Number (1)	Persons engaged in activity Percentage	Average months for those engaged in activity[a] (2)	Person-months per period (3) = (1)(2)	Effective labour allocation index (4) = (3)/2,607.6	Potential labour allocation index (5) = (3)/7,440
B. Average time in domestic activity						
Child care	46	7.42	10.09	464.00	0.18	0.06
Fetching wood/water	95	15.32	11.00	1 045.00	0.40	0.14
Home repairs	15	2.42	5.97	89.60	0.03	0.01
Sale of domestic production	7	1.13	5.57	39.00	0.02	0.01
Raising livestock	64	10.32	10.55	675.00	0.26	0.09
Cleaning, cooking, washing	20	3.23	11.70	234.00	0.09	0.03
Other domestic duties and child care	6	0.97	10.17	61.00	0.02	0.01
TOTAL	253	40.81	65.05	2 607.60	1.00	0.35
Number of persons	620	-	-	-	-	-
Potential labour supply	7 440	-	-	-	-	-
Average number of activities	0.41	-	-	-	-	-

Source: Survey on Temporary Migration in the Jequitinhonha Valley: Causes and Consequences, 1988.

[a] In the 12 months preceding interview.

TABLE 72. ECONOMIC AND DOMESTIC ACTIVITIES PERFORMED BY WIVES OF HEADS OF HOUSEHOLD, ACCORDING TO TIME-BUDGET DATA, JEQUITINHONHA VALLEY, BRAZIL

Activity	Persons engaged in activity Number (1)	Persons engaged in activity Percentage	Average months for those engaged in activity[a] (2)	Person-months per period (3) = (1)(2)	Effective labour allocation index (4) = (3)/2,724.7	Potential labour allocation index (5) = (3)/7,440
A. Average time in economic activity						
Wage labour	94	15.16	9.47	890.00	0.33	0.12
Harvesting	149	24.03	3.84	572.35	0.21	0.08
Weeding and seeding	152	24.52	3.66	556.05	0.20	0.08
Cattle-raising	7	1.13	6.73	47.10	0.02	0.01
Handicrafts	24	3.87	11.17	268.00	0.10	0.04
Services	23	3.71	8.66	199.20	0.07	0.03
Hunting and fishing	0	0.00	0.00	0.00	0.00	0.00
Home production	20	3.23	7.70	154.00	0.06	0.02
Building/construction	0	0.00	0.00	0.00	0.00	0.00
Mining	5	0.81	7.60	38.00	0.01	0.01
TOTAL	474	6.45	58.82	2 724.70	1.00	0.37
Number of persons	620	-	-	-	-	-
Potential labour supply	7 440	-	-	-	-	-
Average number of activities	0.76	-	-	-	-	-

	Persons engaged in activity Number (1)	Persons engaged in activity Percentage	Average months for those engaged in activity[a] (2)	Person-months per period (3) = (1)(2)	Effective labour allocation index (4) = (3)/13,531.6	Potential labour allocation index (5) = (3)/7,440
B. Average time in domestic activity						
Child care	312	50.32	11.67	3 640.00	0.27	0.49
Fetching wood/water	207	33.39	11.58	2 396.60	0.18	0.32
Home repairs	11	1.77	10.18	112.00	0.01	0.02
Sale of domestic production	9	1.45	9.33	83.99	0.01	0.01
Raising livestock	167	26.94	11.39	1 902.00	0.14	0.26
Cleaning, cooking, washing	378	60.97	11.78	4 453.50	0.33	0.60
Other domestic duties and child care	80	12.90	11.79	943.50	0.07	0.13
TOTAL	1 164	187.74	77.72	13 531.60	1.00	1.82
Number of persons	620	-	-	-	-	-
Potential labour supply	7 440	-	-	-	-	-
Average number of activities	1.88	-	-	-	-	-

Source: Survey on Temporary Migration in the Jequitinhonha Valley: Causes and Consequences, 1988.
[a] In the 12 months preceding interview.

The means in tables 71 and 72 were compared using *t*-tests to examine gender differences in participation rates for all the economic and domestic activities recorded in the time budget. Except for the time devoted to home repair and the sale of home production, all gender differences were statistically significant: husbands engaged more in wage labour, harvesting, seeding and weeding, and cattle-raising; wives were more likely to care for children, fetch water or wood, tend livestock and perform other domestic activities.

Additional *t*-tests examined gender differences in the average number of months worked in each economic and domestic activity recorded with the time-budget. Among the 10 economic activities recorded, only wage labour and handicraft production resulted in statistically significant gender differences, since wives participating in those activities worked significantly more months than husbands.

A final series of comparisons involved the number of hours worked during the week prior to the interview (data not presented here) on economic and domestic activities. During that week, husbands, regardless of migration status during the year preceding the interview, averaged 50 hours of economic activity, whereas wives averaged only 13. Not surprisingly, the result was reversed for domestic activities, with wives averaging 57 hours of work compared with 6 for husbands. Together these figures indicate that, on average, husbands worked 56 hours a week, significantly less than the 70 hours averaged by their wives. In general, these statistics indicate that a clear-cut division of labour by gender exists in both economic and domestic activities, with men being most likely to work outside the home and women to work mostly in the household.

Turning to the question of whether the out-migration of husbands during 1987 affected the economic and domestic activities of their wives, panel A of table 73 presents time-budget data for women married to non-migrants and panel A of table 74 does the same for the wives of out-migrants. A comparison of these data indicates that in the Jequitinhonha Valley the temporary out-migration of husbands does not significantly affect the time married women allocate to economic activities, since the potential labour allocation index for wives of non-migrants is 37.2 per cent while that for wives of migrants is even lower at 34.4. The average number of paid activities per married woman is also virtually the same, regardless of the husband's migratory status. *T*-tests applied to differences in economic activity between the wives of migrants and non-migrants uncovered only two significant differences: more wives of non-migrant men engaged in wage labour (16.5 versus 9.3 per cent) and market-based service activities (4.9 versus 0.8 per cent) than the wives of migrants. It thus appears that the temporary migration of husbands affects women's economic activities in the opposite direction to that hypothesized, although the estimated differences are small.

Panel B of tables 73 and 74 indicates that differences in the domestic activities of the two groups of women are also small. The potential labour allocation index of wives of non-migrants was 1.78, compared with 2.00 for wives of migrants. Although the average number of home activities per person was higher for wives of migrants (2.1 versus 1.8), the difference was not significantly so. The *t*-tests on the differences in participation in domestic activities for the two groups again showed only two significant contrasts: wives of migrants were more likely to spend time fetching wood and water (43 versus 31 per cent) and tending to livestock (33 versus 26 per cent) than women married to non-migrants. Otherwise, both groups were similar in that they spent most of their time caring for children and performing other home-related chores. It is interesting, however, that the total workload of the wives of migrants as measured by the sum of the labour allocation indices, that is, 2.34, is greater than that for the wives of non-migrants, 2.15, implying that the former group had less leisure time and therefore experienced a real loss of welfare. Note also that the comparable figure for husbands is only 1.22, implying that they have far more leisure time than their wives, a finding that corroborates that of other time allocation surveys carried out throughout the world.

Consequently, the expectation that the migration status of husbands would affect the labour force participation of wives is not supported by the data yielded by the time-budget. Instead, wives left behind experience an increase in domestic activities, specifically in those where husbands tended to contribute the most, namely, the raising of livestock and the hauling of water and wood. The general lack of wage-earning

TABLE 73. ECONOMIC AND DOMESTIC ACTIVITIES PERFORMED BY WIVES OF NON-MIGRANT HEADS OF HOUSEHOLD, ACCORDING TO TIME-BUDGET DATA, JEQUITINHONHA VALLEY, BRAZIL

Activity	Persons engaged in activity Number (1)	Persons engaged in activity Percentage	Average months for those engaged in activity[a] (2)	Person-months per period (3) = (1)(2)	Effective labour allocation index (4) = (3)/2,238.2	Potential labour allocation index (5) = (3)/6,024
A. Average time in economic activity						
Wage labour	83	16.53	9.37	778.00	0.35	0.13
Harvesting	119	23.71	3.84	457.35	0.20	0.08
Weeding and seeding	119	23.71	3.59	427.55	0.19	0.07
Cattle-raising	5	1.00	5.82	29.10	0.01	0.01
Handicrafts	18	3.59	10.89	196.00	0.09	0.03
Services	22	4.38	8.51	187.20	0.08	0.03
Hunting and fishing	0	0.00	0.00	0.00	0.00	0.00
Home production	17	3.39	7.88	134.00	0.06	0.02
Building/construction	0	0.00	0.00	0.00	0.00	0.00
Mining	3	0.60	9.67	29.00	0.01	0.01
TOTAL	386	76.89	59.58	2 238.20	1.00	0.37
Number of persons	502	-	-	-	-	-
Potential labour supply	6 024	-	-	-	-	-
Average number of activities	0.77	-	-	-	-	-

Activity	Persons engaged in activity Number (1)	Persons engaged in activity Percentage	Average months for those engaged in activity[a] (2)	Person-months per period (3) = (1)(2)	Effective labour allocation index (4) = (3)/10,697.6	Potential labour allocation index (5) = (3)/6,024
B. Average time in domestic activity						
Child care	248	49.40	11.69	2 899.00	0.27	0.48
Fetching wood/water	156	31.08	11.56	1 803.60	0.17	0.30
Home repairs	8	1.59	10.38	83.00	0.01	0.01
Sale of domestic production	7	1.39	10.00	70.00	0.01	0.01
Raising livestock	128	25.50	11.35	1 453.00	0.14	0.24
Cleaning, cooking, washing	312	62.15	11.74	3 661.50	0.34	0.61
Other domestic duties and child care	62	12.35	11.73	727.50	0.07	0.12
TOTAL	921	183.47	78.45	10 697.60	1.00	1.78
Number of persons	502	-	-	-	-	-
Potential labour supply	6 024	-	-	-	-	-
Average number of activities	1.83	-	-	-	-	-

Source: Survey on Temporary Migration in the Jequitinhonha Valley: Causes and Consequences, 1988.

[a] In the 12 months preceding interview.

TABLE 74. ECONOMIC AND DOMESTIC ACTIVITIES PERFORMED BY WIVES OF MIGRANT HEADS OF HOUSEHOLD, ACCORDING TO THE TIME-BUDGET DATA, JEQUITINHONHA VALLEY, BRAZIL

Activity	Persons engaged in activity Number (1)	Persons engaged in activity Per-centage	Average months for those engaged in activity[a] (2)	Person-months per period (3) = (1)(2)	Effective labour allocation index (4) = (3)/486.5	Potential labour allocation index (5) = (3)/1,416
		A. Average time in economic activity				
Wage labour	11	9.32	10.18	112.00	0.23	0.08
Harvesting	30	25.42	3.83	115.00	0.24	0.08
Weeding and seeding	33	27.97	3.89	128.50	0.26	0.09
Cattle-raising	2	1.69	9.00	18.00	0.04	0.01
Handicrafts	6	5.08	12.00	72.00	0.15	0.05
Services	1	0.85	12.00	12.00	0.03	0.01
Hunting and fishing	0	0.00	0.00	0.00	0.00	0.00
Home production	3	2.54	6.67	20.00	0.04	0.01
Building/construction	0	0.00	0.00	0.00	0.00	0.00
Mining	2	1.69	4.50	9.00	0.02	0.01
TOTAL	88	74.58	62.08	486.50	1.00	0.34
Number of persons	118	-	-	-	-	-
Potential labour supply	1 416	-	-	-	-	-
Average number of activities	0.75	-	-	-	-	-

	Persons engaged in activity Number (1)	Persons engaged in activity Per-centage	Average months for those engaged in activity[a] (2)	Person-months per period (3) = (1)(2)	Effective labour allocation index (4) = (3)/2,834.0	Potential labour allocation index (5) = (3)/1,416
		B. Average time in domestic activity				
Child care	64	54.24	11.58	741.00	0.26	0.52
Fetching wood/water	51	43.22	11.63	593.00	0.21	0.42
Home repairs	3	2.54	9.67	29.00	0.01	0.02
Sale of domestic production	2	1.69	7.00	14.00	0.01	0.01
Raising livestock	39	33.05	11.51	449.00	0.16	0.32
Cleaning, cooking, washing	66	55.93	12.00	792.00	0.28	0.56
Other domestic duties and child care	18	15.25	12.00	216.00	0.08	0.15
TOTAL	243	205.93	75.39	2 834.00	1.00	2.00
Number of persons	118	-	-	-	-	-
Potential labour supply	1 416	-	-	-	-	-
Average number of activities	2.06	-	-	-	-	-

Source: Survey on Temporary Migration in the Jequitinhonha Valley: Causes and Consequences, 1988.

[a]In the 12 months preceding interview.

opportunities for women in the region under study is probably responsible for this outcome. Since women have few options for economic activity, they concentrate instead on domestic and subsistence activities. Besides, the earnings of their migrant husbands may reduce pressures for them to seek paid employment. The multivariate analysis presented below provides further insights on these issues.

Multivariate analysis

The neoclassical framework which has been widely used in the examination of labour force participation rates embodies two approaches: the labour-leisure choice model; and the household production model. The labour-leisure choice model deals with the impacts of substitution (price) and income effects on female labour force participation: an increase in the wage rate has two effects. First, it raises the price of leisure, thereby reducing the demand for leisure and increasing labour force participation (a substitution effect). Secondly, it increases earned income, thereby inducing an increase in the demand for leisure, which is assumed to be a normal good (the income effect). The net result is economically determined by the relative strength of these two effects through the Slutsky equation (Mincer, 1962).

The household production model proposed by Becker (1965) deals with time allocation not in terms of the demand for leisure but in terms of the time allocated between market and domestic activities. Substitution and income effects are still relevant, but new concepts of shadow prices and full income are added. Thus, the value of time in domestic activities is determined by the shadow price of that time. Women participate in the labour force when the value of market time (the wage rate) is larger than the value (shadow price) of domestic or non-market time.

The literature emphasizes a large number of variables affecting the value of market time, including female education, the demand for labour in a given area and labour-market tightness. Variables affecting the value of non-market time include the availability of market substitutes for time-intensive domestic activities (such as child care), fertility (high fertility induces an increase in the demand for time devoted to domestic activities), husband's income, wealth and non-earned income. Those variables which affect positively the value of non-market time contribute to a decrease in female labour force participation. While the regression equations estimated below are empirical representations of this theoretical framework, the variables used are also determined by data availability, the agricultural nature of the region studied and the hypothesized role of circular migration and remittances on women's economic activities.

Multivariate probit regression analysis is used to examine the effects of socio-economic and life-cycle variables on the economic participation of married women. Two sets of models are examined, each with a different measure of women's labour force participation in economic activity as the dependent variable. The first analyses the determinants of female labour force participation using a census measure as the dependent variable, while the second uses the time-budget measure. Because the latter is a more sensitive indicator of the economic activities of women, it is expected to yield both different and superior results compared with those obtained using the census measure.

Results for the model using the census measure are presented in table 75. Recall that the census measure reflects activities of relatively higher status and greater visibility than the larger set of activities reflected in the time-budget measure. To analyse the determinants of female labour force participation as indicated by the census measure, models 1 and 2 contain socio-economic and life-cycle variables whose importance was discussed earlier. Various other variables hypothesized to have significant effects on women's labour force participation according to the theoretical discussion above (viz., education, age of youngest child in household, number of adults in the household, number of women aged 10-19 in the household, ownership of property, receipt of remittances and amount received) were also examined but were not found to be significant in a variety of models. Educational level probably failed to reach significance because of the generally low level of educational attainment of women in the valley. Because of space limitations, the remaining discussion focuses only on the variables presented in tables 75 and 76.

TABLE 75. RESULTS OF PROBIT REGRESSION OF THE EFFECTS OF SOCIO-ECONOMIC AND LIFE-CYCLE CHARACTERISTICS ON THE LABOUR FORCE PARTICIPATION OF WIVES, AS MEASURED BY THE CENSUS-TYPE QUESTION

Independent variable	Model 1		Model 2	
	Regression coefficient	t-ratio	Regression coefficient	t-ratio
Constant	-1.624[a]	-4.037	-1.780[a]	-4.263
AGE	5.504[a]	2.958	5.380[a]	2.816
AGE2	-5.823[a]	-2.683	-5.638[a]	-2.539
EDUCATION2	1.299[a]	5.051	1.355[a]	5.255
KIDSLT5	-0.080	-1.380	-0.092	-1.552
LIGHTS	-0.148	-1.290	-0.213[b]	-1.736
URBAN	..	..	0.250	1.610
MIGRANT87	..	..	0.187	1.126
MOVESTO87	..	..	0.034[b]	1.899
RETIRED	..	..	0.455[b]	2.478
Chi-squared	37.563	-	53.939	-
Number of cases	609	-	609	-

Source: Survey on Temporary Migration in the Jequitinhonha Valley: Causes and Consequences, 1988.
[a]Significant at the 0.01 level.
[b]Significant at the 0.10 level.

TABLE 76. RESULTS OF PROBIT REGRESSION OF THE EFFECTS OF SOCIO-ECONOMIC AND LIFE-CYCLE VARIABLES ON THE ECONOMIC ACTIVITY OF WIVES, AS MEASURED BY THE TIME-BUDGET METHOD

Independent variable	Model 1		Model 2	
	Regression coefficient	t-ratio	Regression coefficient	t-ratio
Constant	-1.045[a]	-2.742	-0.971[b]	-2.515
AGE	5.614[a]	3.091	5.261[a]	2.882
AGE2	-7.374[a]	-3.383	-7.115[a]	-3.247
EDUCATION2	1.117[a]	4.159	1.119[a]	4.147
KIDSLT5	-0.060	-1.099	-0.061	-1.113
DEBT	-0.178	-1.627	-0.194[b]	-1.756
DROUGHT	0.403[a]	3.572	0.407[a]	3.592
LIGHTS	-0.323[a]	-2.853	-0.337[a]	-2.961
MIGRANT87	..	..	-0.205	-1.274
MOVESTO87	..	..	0.184	0.988
RETIRED	..	..	0.023	1.328
Chi-squared	55.881	-	59.828	-
Number of cases	609	-	609	-

Source: Survey on Temporary Migration in the Jequitinhonha Valley: Causes and Consequences, 1988.
[a]Significant at the 0.01 level.
[b]Significant at the 0.10 level.

Model 1 includes various socio-economic and life-cycle measures for wives and their households but excludes measures of husband's migration status. As expected, age (AGE) and education squared (EDUCATION2) have statistically significant, positive coefficients. Age squared (AGE2) is highly significant and negative, capturing the tendency of older women to work less than younger women. The number of children under age 5 in the household (KIDSLT5) is not significant, nor is electricity (LIGHTS), a proxy for income. To examine the impact of husbands' migration experience on the labour force participation of wives, model 2 includes three additional variables, MIGRANT87, MOVESTO87 and RETIRED, as well as an indicator of urbanization (URBAN), a measure at the community level. The inclusion of these variables improves considerably the overall fit of model 2. Electricity (LIGHTS) becomes a weakly significant negative predictor of the labour force participation of wives and the variable KIDSLT5, though not quite statistically significant, has the expected negative sign. Age and education continue to have statistically significant effects in the expected direction. Among the new variables introduced in model 2, URBAN almost attains statistical significance ($p < 0.11$) and its sign is in the expected direction. The variable MIGRANT87, indicating whether the head of household was a migrant during the year preceding the interview, does not have a significant effect on female economic activity, although its coefficient is positive. However, the two variables MOVESTO87 and RETIRED, reflecting the husband's past migration experience, are both significant and have positive coefficients, suggesting that women's off-farm employment tends to increase in the long run as a result of their husbands' migration and of the experience that they themselves gain as the de facto head of household.

Table 76 presents the results for models using the time-budget measure of labour force participation as the dependent variable. Not surprisingly, there are similarities and differences with the results presented in table 75. Age (AGE) and education squared (EDUCATION2) continue to be highly significant, the number of children under age 5 in the household continues to lack significance but the effect of electricity (LIGHTS) becomes stronger and significant. The observed significance of these socio-economic variables is consistent with neoclassical theory. Thus, electricity reflects the expected negative effect of relative wealth on the participation of women in paid economic activities. Education squared captures the traditional positive impact of female education on labour force participation. The effect is non-linear because it is only after a certain level of education that women in rural Brazil are prompted to enter the labour force. The positive and significant coefficient of the new variable added, DROUGHT, indicating household stress due to drought in the 12 months preceding the interview, supports the hypothesis that drought has a positive effect on female labour force participation. While the variable DEBT was not significant and was therefore excluded from the models presented in table 75, it is included in those presented in table 76 and borders on statistical significance, although in an unexpected negative direction. It is worth noting that the higher chi-squared statistic for model 1 in table 76 compared with that for model 1 in table 75 indicates the superior overall fit of the former and consequently suggests that using the time-budget measure of women's labour force participation is advantageous.

Model 2 in table 76, as does that in table 75, includes the three additional indicators of husbands' migration status. Those indicators have relatively small effects on the other variables of the model, except that DEBT becomes marginally significant. Although the negative coefficient of DEBT was not expected, it may be regarded as reflecting the ability to borrow and thus to find means other than female labour force participation to secure needed cash. Of greater interest is that the results for the three migration variables differ from those presented in table 75. First, although still lacking statistical significance, the husband's 1987 out-migration status (MIGRANT87) now has a negative sign, contrary to what was expected. In addition, the other two migration variables, MOVESTO87 and RETIRED, indicating the effects of the cumulative migration experience of husbands lose the weak significance levels that they had in table 75. These findings were found to be robust to various alternative combinations of these three migration variables. The authors thus conclude that the circular out-migration of men did not significantly affect their wives' economic activity and that the models based on census types of measures of such activity yielded misleading results in that respect.

Economic consequences of male out-migration

This study has examined the time married women allocate to economic and domestic activities. It was assumed at the onset that a traditional division of labour by gender prevailed in Jequitinhonha Valley. In that context, the possibility that the current and past migration experience of husbands increased their wives' economic activity was explored. It was hypothesized that, because male out-migration from the valley was temporary and seasonal, the effect of their migration would be less than that observed in some African regions where husbands were absent for long periods at a time (Safilios-Rothschild, 1985; von Braun, 1989). Empirical findings, particularly those based on the time-budget data, confirmed that hypothesis to the extent that male out-migration during 1987 did not affect wives' labour force participation during that period. Time-budget data also permitted the authors to corroborate that a traditional division of labour by gender prevailed in the region studied.

Nevertheless, household strategies and the stage in the life cycle appeared to be important determinants of both husbands' migration and married women's labour force participation. The labour force participation of married women increased as their own age increased and also responded positively to increases in the age of their children, as suggested by the negative impact of the number of children under age 5 in the household.

With respect to the negative impact of household debt on the economic activity of married women, it derives from specific institutional mechanisms operating in the valley. Thus, whereas agricultural seasonality and low labour demand during the lean season institutionally constrain female labour force participation, women have the option of using the consumption-loan mechanism instead of engaging in economic activity. The availability of credit can help households and especially wives acting as the head of household to satisfy the pressing cash needs that they face periodically. The consumption-loan mechanism, referred to locally as the *caderneta*, has been established by large and small traders in all villages. Whenever a purchase is made but not paid on the spot, both buyer and seller sign a notebook which remains with the seller until all debts are paid. Debts are erased by paying the current market value of goods purchased earlier. Prices are arbitrarily set by shop owners and generally include an implicit interest rate. In this way it is possible for a household to accrue a large amount of debt with several small shops in the area. Debt is therefore a means of facilitating consumption over time and thus spurring households to generate cash for debt repayment. Circular migration is one of the strategies used to raise cash. Yet, debt was not found to be positively related to circular migration in the valley (Rios-Neto and Vieira, 1991), implying that households have alternative strategies to generate funds. Moreover, since debt was found to be significant in reducing the economic activity of wives even after controlling for their husbands' recent and past migration, it would seem that the *caderneta* system alleviates some household economic pressure that would otherwise induce greater female labour force participation. Fifty-two per cent of the households surveyed in the valley had some kind of debt, 70.5 per cent of which had been accrued through the *caderneta* system.

Social consequences of male out-migration for the families left behind

Given the importance of education to social and economic mobility, the effects of temporary male out-migration on the education of the children left behind were explored. Specifically, it was asked whether the income earned through repeated, short-term migration helped facilitate the education of children. In the case of long-term migration that was also accompanied by significant remittances, a noticeable increase in the education of children left behind would be expected. This hypothesis has received empirical support in a recent study of families left behind in Goa, India (Mascarenhas-Keyes, 1990), but there are few studies on the subject.

Before discussing the results obtained in the case of the Jequitinhona Valley, note that the average number of years of schooling completed by those aged 10 or over in the valley were 2.3 and 2.7 for males and females, respectively. Few children in the valley attended school beyond age 10.

To examine the effect of parental migratory status on children's education, the educational levels of children of migrants and non-migrants were compared first. Given the very different duties of boys and girls in the region and the difference in access to schools in the four municipalities included in the survey, both the sex of the child and the place of residence were controlled for. The population was further divided into various age groups. Several interesting results emerged. First, even though the educational attainment of both migrant heads of household and their spouses was not significantly different from that of non-migrants, children in households with non-migrant heads of household had, at every age, completed more years of formal schooling than their counterparts with migrant heads. In many instances, the differences were statistically significant.

Persons aged 15-24 at the time of the interview are those most likely to have completed their formal education during the years when temporary migration was already a pervasive phenomenon in the valley (Goza, 1992). The high rates of temporary out-migration in Chapada do Norte and Turmalina over the period 1977-1987 suggest that children living there would have been the most fully exposed to the effects of temporary migration. For that reason, this discussion centres on those two municipalities. The *t*-tests controlling for the migration status of the head of the household, municipality of residence and gender of child indicate that the children of non-migrants always attained higher educational levels than children of migrants. Three of the four comparisons made (i.e., two gender comparisons per municipality) were statistically significant.

The prevalence of temporary out-migration in the municipality of Chapada do Norte over the period 1967-1987 provides an opportunity to examine shifts in educational levels between 1970 and 1980. Given the lack of any significant government investment in the region during the 1970s, any changes observed can be related to the influence of funds brought back to Jequitinhonha Valley by migrants. Table 77 indicates the literacy rates in 1970 and 1980 in the four municipalities considered. Chapada do Norte had the lowest overall literacy rates, not only among the four municipalities but in the entire valley, which contains 51 such units. Note, however, that the total gains recorded in the mostly rural Chapada do Norte during 1970-1980 were among the highest for the four municipalities,

TABLE 77. LITERACY RATES BY MUNICIPALITY AND URBAN
OR RURAL LOCATION, 1970 AND 1980

	Percentage of population age 5 or older								
	Urban		Percentage change	Rural		Percentage change	Total		Percentage change
Municipality	1970	1980		1970	1980		1970	1980	
Chapada do Norte............................	64.8	68.4	5	9.0	19.3	114	12.0	23.5	96
Sao Gonçalo do Rio Preto	63.9	66.6	4	38.6	40.5	5	45.8	49.6	8
Minas Novas	62.8	67.9	8	11.4	25.3	122	16.6	32.4	95
Turmalina	68.9	68.4	-1	23.8	32.0	34	35.4	45.9	30

Source: Brazil, Instituto Brasileiro de Geografia e Estatística, *Censo Demografico, 1970* (Rio de Janeiro, 1970), vol. III, table 53; and *Censo Demografico, 1980* (Rio de Janeiro, 1982), vol. III, table 3.

even though the other three had less temporary out-migration.

These results are consistent with the fact that only 2 per cent of remittances were spent in the education of family members. They also suggest a more disturbing trend. With the husbands' departure, wives must assume, at least temporarily, the role of the head of household, as well as responsibility for the domestic chores formerly carried out by the husband. Although data on the domestic activities of children were not gathered by the survey, they too are likely to have undertaken extra chores. The demanding nature of agricultural duties often requires considerable time, even for such tasks as tending livestock. Given the lack of educational differences between migrant and non-migrant heads of household or their spouses (differences that one would expect to affect the educational attainment of their children), the results obtained suggest that many children of migrants drop out of school to assist their families, particularly when their father is away.

To conclude, the possible effects of the out-migration of husbands on the fertility behaviour and attitudes of their wives are considered. Because migrant husbands become more aware of the "outside world", they—and their wives—would be expected to be more open to modern ideas about desired family size and the use of birth control. Statistical *t*-tests comparing the opinions of wives of migrants and non-migrants in age groups 15-24 and 25-34 were carried out. When the mean number of children ever born and the total number of children desired were compared, they were not found to be significantly different. With respect to whether women desired the same, more or fewer children than women of their mother's generation, differences also lacked significance across the two groups of wives considered. With regard to responses to a question on who was responsible for deciding how many children a couple would have, the overwhelming response (51 per cent) was that God was responsible. Expecting that the migration experience of husbands might reduce the prevalence of such traditional views, differences between women with and without migrant husbands were examined. Surprisingly, the only difference found was that, among women aged 15-24, significantly more (at a $p < 0.02$ level) wives of out-migrants believed that God was responsible, while among those aged 25-34, significantly more wives of non-migrants said that the couple was responsible. Thus, the hypothesis that the attitudes of the wives of migrants might be less traditional than those of the wives of non-migrants received no support.

Given the low educational level of cane workers, the fact that they may be poorer than non-migrants in ways not controlled for, the very low status accorded to their occupation (D'Incão, 1976) and the fact that many live in cloistered company barracks while away from home, it is perhaps unrealistic to expect them to change their traditional views as a result of their migration experience. Certainly, such changes were not detectable at an aggregate level in the Jequitinhonha Valley.

F. CONCLUSION

The picture that has emerged from this examination of the social and economic consequences of the temporary out-migration of male heads of household from the Jequitinhonha Valley of Brazil is not a very optimistic one: the persons left behind not only experience the psychological stress of being out of touch with husbands or fathers but also face numerous practical difficulties during such absences.

This study documents how the wives of migrants assume responsibility for some of the domestic tasks that used to be carried out by their absent husbands. Indirect evidence suggests that children also help to fill the labour void and in the process may sacrifice their already meagre educational opportunities. Although the wives of migrants become the de facto head of household and take control over the additional tasks associated with that position, it appears that such changes lead to few, if any, long-term social or economic gains for them. The region's rigid division of labour by gender, which leaves few opportunities for women to work outside the home, is doubtless partially responsible for that outcome.

It addition, most families of out-migrants fail to experience upward mobility as a result of the circular out-migration of men. Even when migrants send remittances on a regular basis, as all but 14 per cent did, most of the cash obtained is used either for immediate consumption or to pay debts accumulated because of earlier consumption (which perhaps prompted out-migration).

Socially, the women left behind also appear to experience few, if any, gains as a result of the circular migration of their husbands. They continue to espouse traditional attitudes about child-bearing, seeming to be even more conservative than the wives of non-migrants. The relative isolation in which married women in the valley live doubtless contributes to that outcome. To the extent that men who migrate to the state of São Paulo acquire other views, the "knowledge gap" between husbands and wives may increase and further reinforce the subordinate position of women in the valley.

The primary purpose of circular migration is to permit households to remain in the valley where their families have lived for generations (Goza and Rios-Neto, 1990). In this regard, migration is a success, for it permits semi-proletarian families to maintain their access to land and defer their permanent relocation to urban areas. In general, however, the family as a whole gains little from circular out-migration over the long term and very few of the married women left behind experience enhancements in their social or economic status.

ANNEX

List of variables

Variable	Definition
AGE	Wife's age divided by 100.
AGE2	Wife's age squared divided by 100.
EDUCATION2	Wife's years of schooling squared and divided by 10.
KIDSLT5	Number of children under age 5.
DEBT	Dummy variable: equals one if the household incurred any debts during the 12 months prior to interview.
DROUGHT	Dummy variable: equals one if the household suffered any loss due to drought during the 12 months prior to the interview.
LIGHTS	Dummy variable: equals one if the household has electricity.
URBAN	Dummy variable: equals one if the household is located in an urban area.
MIGRANT87	Dummy variable: equals one if the head of household participated in circular migration in 1987.
MOVESTO87	Number of times the head of household undertook circular migration up to 1987.
RETIRED	Dummy variable: equals one if the head of household was not a temporary out-migrant during the 10 years preceding the interview.

References

Anker, Richard (1980). *Research on Women's Roles and Demographic Change: Survey Questionnaires for Households, Women, Men, and Communities with Background Explanations*. Geneva: International Labour Office.

_____ (1983). Female labour force participation in developing countries: a critique of current definitions and data collection methods. *International Labour Review* (Geneva), vol. 122, No. 6 (November-December), pp. 709-723.

_____, M. E. Khan and R. Gupta (1988). *Women's Participation in the Labour Force: A Methods Test in India for Improving its Measurement*. Women, Work and Development Series, No. 16. Geneva: International Labour Office.

Becker, Gary (1965). A theory of the allocation of time. *Economic Journal* (London), vol. 75, No. 299 (September), pp. 493-517.

_____ (1981). *A Treatise on the Family*. Cambridge, Massachusetts: Harvard University Press.

Bisilliat, Jeanne, and Michèle Fiéloux (1987). *Women of the Third World: Work and Daily Life*. Enne Amman and Peter Amman, trans. Cranbury, New Jersey: Associated University Presses, Inc.; and Rutherford, New Jersey: Fairleigh Dickinson University Press.

Brazil (1970). *Censo Demografico, 1970*, vol. III. Rio de Janeiro: Instituto Brasileiro de Geografia e Estatística.

_____ (1982). *Censo Demografico, 1980*, vol. III. Rio de Janeiro: Instituto Brasileiro de Geografia e Estatística.

Connell, John (1984). Status or subjugation? Women, migration and development in the South Pacific. *International Migration Review* (Staten Island, New York), vol. 18, No. 4 (Winter), pp. 964-983.

Cliffe, Lionel (1978). Labour migration and peasant differentiation: Zambian experience. *Journal of Peasant Studies* (London), vol. 5, No. 3 (April), pp. 326-346.

Deere, Carmen Diana, and Magdalena León de Leal (1982). *Women in Andean Agriculture: Peasant Production and Rural Wage Employment in Colombia and Peru*. Women, Work and Development Series, No. 4. Geneva: International Labour Office.

Deere, Carmen Diana, Jane Humphries and Magdalena León de Leal (1982). Class and historical analysis for the study of women and economic change. In *Women's Roles and Population Trends in the Third World*, Richard Anker, Mayra Buvinic and Nadia H. Youssef, eds. London: Croom Helm.

D'Incão, Maria (1976). *O Bóia fria: accumulação e miséria*. Petrópolis: Editora Vozes, Ltda.

Evenson, Robert, Barry M. Popkin and Elizabeth King-Quizon (1980). Nutrition, work, and demographic behaviour in rural Philippine households: a synopsis of several Laguna household studies. In *Rural Household Studies in Asia*, Hans P. Binswanger and others, eds. Singapore: Singapore University Press.

Findley, Sally E., and Linda Williams (1991). *Women Who Go and Women Who Stay: Reflections of Family Migration Processes in a Changing World*. Population and Labour Policies Programme, Working Paper No. 176. Geneva: International Labour Office.

Goza, Franklin (1992). Causes and consequences of migration in the Jequitinhonha Valley of Minas Gerais. *Sociological Inquiry* (Austin, Texas), vol. 62, No. 2 (Spring), pp. 147-168.

_____, and Eduardo Rios-Neto (1988). O Contraste de experiências migratorias em quatro municípios do Vale do Jequitinhonha. *Anais VI Encontro da Associação Brasileira de Estudos Populacionais* (Porto Alegre, Brazil), vol. 6, No. 2, pp. 503-536.

_____ (1990). *The Labour Process among Temporary Workers in the São Paulo Sugar Industry*. Texto para discussão, No. 56. Belo Horizonte, Brazil: Centro de Desenvolvimento e Planejamento Regional.

Gronau, R. (1977). Leisure, home production and work: the theory of the allocation of time revisited. *Journal of Political Economy* (Chicago, Illinois), vol. 85, No. 6, pp. 1099-1124.

Hugo, Graeme J. (1985). Structural change and labour mobility in rural Java. In *Labour Circulation and the Labour Process*, Guy Standing, ed. Kent, United Kingdom; and Sydney, Australia: Croom Helm.

Mascarenhas-Keyes, S. (1990). Migration, 'progressive motherhood' and female autonomy: Catholic women in Goa. In *Structures and Strategies: Women, Work and the Family*, Leela Dube and Rajni Palriwala, eds. New Delhi: Sage.

Margolies, Luise, and María Matilde Suarez (1978). The peasant family in the Venezuelan Andes. In *Family and Kinship in Middle America and the Caribbean*, Arnaud F. Marks and Raymond A. Römer, eds. Curaçao and Leiden: Curaçao University of the Netherlands Antilles.

Mincer, Jacob (1962). Labor force participation of married women: a study of labor supply. In *Aspects of Labor Economics*, H. G. Lewis, ed. Report of the Universities-National Bureau Committee for Economic Research. Princeton, New Jersey: Princeton University Press.

Mitchell, J. Clyde (1961). Wage labour and African population movements in Central Africa. In *Essays on African Population*, Kenneth Michael Barbour and R. Mansell Prothero, eds. London: Routledge and Kegan Paul.

_____ (1985). Towards a situational sociology of wage-labour circulation. In *Circulation in Third World Countries*, R. Mansell Prothero and Murray Chapman, eds. London: Routledge and Kegan Paul.

Moura, M. (1988). *Os Deserdados da terra: a lógica costumeira e judicial dos processos de expulsão e invasão da terra camponesa no sertão de Minas Gerais*. Rio de Janeiro: Editora Bertrand Brasil S.A.

_____, S. Lacerda and S. Eigenheer (1980). *A Reprodução do pequeno produtor do Vale do Jequitinhonha mineiro*. Belo Horizonte: Fundação Getúlio Vargas.

Palmer, I., S. Subhadhira and W. Grisanaputi (1985). *The Northeast Rainfed Agricultural Development Project in Thailand: A Baseline Survey of Women's Roles and Household Resource Allocation for a Farming Systems Approach*. Population Studies for Planners, Case Study No. 3. New York: The Population Council.

Rios-Neto, Eduardo, and Paula M. R. P. Vieira (1990). Mulheres de migrantes sazonais no Vale do Jequitinhonha, Minas Gerais. In *Contradições do desenvolvimento agrícola em Minas Gerais: uma perspectiva regional*, M. R. Nabuco, ed. Ensaios Econômicos CEDEPLAR, No. 4. Belo Horizonte, Brazil: Centro de Desenvolvimento e Planejamento Regional.

_____ (1991). Temporary circular migration in the Jequitinhonha Valley, Brazil: life-cycle and structural aspects. Paper presented at the Annual Meeting of the Population Association of America, Washington, D.C., 21-23 March.

_____ (1992). The effects of seasonality, migration and life-cycle on the labour force participation of married women: a case study of the Jequitinhonha Valley, Brazil. In *Proceedings of the Conference on The Peopling of the Americas*, vol. 3. Veracruz, Mexico: International Union for the Scientific Study of Population.

Safilios-Rothschild, Constantina (1985). The persistence of women's invisibility in agriculture: theoretical and policy lessons from Lesotho and Sierra Leone. *Economic Development and Cultural Change* (Chicago, Illinois), vol. 33, No. 2 (January), pp. 299-317.

Siegel, James T. (1969). *The Rope of God*. Berkeley and Los Angeles, California: University of California Press.

Silva, N. (1988). Vale do Jequitinhonha: incorporação e transformações estruturais. Belo Horizonte, Brazil: Centro de Desenvolvimento e Planejamento Regional. Mimeographed.

_____ (1992). Vale do Jequitinhonha: transformações estruturais e intensificação do êxodo no pós-sessenta. Unpublished Master's thesis. Minas Gerais, Brazil: Federal University of Minas Gerais, Department of Demography.

_____, and L. Silva (1986). Vale do Jequitinhonha: invasão de capital versus evasão de população. *Indicadores de Conjuntura Minas Gerais* (Minas Gerais, Brazil), vol. 8, No. 2, pp. 194-213.

Standing, Guy (1984). Income transfers and remittances. In *Migration Surveys in Low-income Countries: Guidelines for Survey and Questionnaire Design*, Richard E. Bilsborrow, A. S. Oberai and Guy Standing, eds. Beckenham, United Kingdom; and Sydney, Australia: Croom Helm.

von Braun, J. (1989). *The Importance of Non-agricultural Income Sources for the Rural Poor in Africa and Implications for Food and Nutrition Policy*. Reprint No. 189. Washington, D.C.: International Food Policy Research Institute.

Part Seven

FEMALE MIGRATION, DEVELOPMENT AND POLICY ISSUES

XVIII. THE ROLE OF FEMALE MIGRATION IN DEVELOPMENT

Gavin W. Jones*

The term "development" is not easy to define, but it is taken here to refer to the process whereby the economic and social well-being of people is improved by a rise in income levels, improved education and health, and a range of other trends that include a more balanced income distribution and a more accountable Government. Improvements in the status of women are an important element in development. Since development has both economic and social dimensions, both are relevant to the improvement of women's situation.

Migration has the potential of improving the status of women on both the economic and social fronts. On the economic front, women's productive activities are crucial and migration can enable women to gain access to better job opportunities or to more productive activities. On the social front, migration can lead to changes in norms and values that significantly modify the roles and behaviour of migrant women. Whether these positive outcomes are realized, however, will vary across societies, depending upon such factors as the strength of norms restricting female autonomy, the occupational structure and the degree of sex segregation by occupation.

In many societies, the status of women is subordinate to that of men with respect to decision-making power within the household, freedom to move outside the home, freedom to engage in economic activity and freedom to be active in political and community affairs. Modern societies that impose restrictions on women's freedom include those of Muslim countries in Southern and Western Asia, such as Pakistan and Saudi Arabia. Youssef (1974) notes that despite the similarities in economic structure between Latin American and Western Asian countries, among every 100 workers engaged in non-agricultural activities, women constituted more than one third in Latin America but only one eleventh in Western Asia. Women are almost non-existent among sales workers in Afghanistan, Bangladesh and most Western Asian countries, whereas they constitute the majority in some Latin American and South-eastern Asian countries (Anker and Hein, 1986). The situation of women is again different in sub-Saharan Africa, where they typically carry the double burden of performing most of the agricultural work and handling all child-rearing and household management tasks (Thadani, 1985; Momsen and Townsend, 1987).

Although women's labour force participation is generally understated (Benería, 1982; Anker, 1983; Anker, Khan and Gupta, 1987), even after adjustment the participation of women generally remains relatively low, especially in Muslim countries. Given that women constitute roughly half of the working-age population, it is reasonable to hypothesize that in countries where their participation is low, economic development is significantly hindered. It is also precisely in societies that place severe restrictions on women's freedom that the educational attainment of women is low. The evidence indicates that uneducated women are ill-equipped either to improve the well-being of their children or to aid them in making their way in a competitive and technically sophisticated environment.

Even in societies where women's status is considered to be reasonably high (as in developed countries or in some South-eastern Asian countries), many deficiencies remain, as has been emphasized by the women's movement in developed countries over the past two or three decades and by objective evaluations of women's position in Latin America or South-eastern Asia (see, for instance, Youssef, 1974; Adams and others, 1960; Thomson, 1990; Thailand, 1987).

This study of the role of women's migration in development is based on the premise that in all societ-

---

*Professor of Demography; and Coordinator, Demography Program, The Australian National University, Canberra, Australia. The author wishes to acknowledge the valuable research assistance of Pat Quiggin.

ies women face greater or lesser barriers to their full participation in all aspects of social and economic life. The "developmental" role of women's migration can then be assessed in relation to the economic and social development of society as a whole, to the improved welfare of women's immediate families or to the enhanced status and welfare of individual women.

A. EFFECT OF NORMS AND VALUES CONCERNING WOMEN'S ROLES AND BEHAVIOUR ON FEMALE MIGRATION PATTERNS AND THEIR OUTCOMES

This section outlines key linkages between women's roles and their migration patterns. It is necessary to consider those linkages because the types of migration in which women are involved and the activities in which they engage once they have migrated will depend strongly upon the roles assigned to women in society and the expectations that the society and the family have about female roles and behaviour.

One very important migration stream in developing countries is that to metropolitan areas. The data available on the sex ratios of both metropolitan populations and net migration to metropolitan areas for different regions of the world are strikingly consistent at the regional level (Hugo, 1993). One possible explanation of such consistency within regions is that there are certain economic commonalities within regions that determine the observed patterns of male and female differentials in migration streams. That argument is not very convincing because both economic structures and the pace of economic development vary widely within regions. An alternative explanation is that cultural commonalities that determine the roles and status of women are the main factors influencing the relative participation of men and women in migration as a response to the economic pressures and opportunities facing individuals and families. The latter argument conforms with the observed fact that women predominate in migration flows to metropolitan areas in regions where female status is relatively high (Latin America and most of South-eastern Asia), and men predominate in such flows in regions where women's status is low (Southern and Western Asia). Further light is shed on this issue by examining below the sex ratios within certain occupations which are female-dominated in countries of high female autonomy but male-dominated in countries of low female autonomy.

It is not possible to identify unique female migration patterns for each region of the world, in part because of insufficient evidence, in part because there are considerable intercountry variations within regions and in part because patterns of female migration often differ widely between flows to large metropolitan areas, smaller urban areas and rural areas. Even so, there is some consistency in patterns within regions that is reviewed below together with the cultural values and norms underlying them.

In Southern and Western Asia, patriarchal structures conditioned by Muslim and Hindu beliefs give high priority to the preservation of family honour by ensuring that women are virgins at marriage. Such a goal is usually achieved by protecting pubescent women from contact with the opposite sex (except for close family members) and marrying them off as soon as possible after menarche. After marriage, women are to serve their husbands and raise their children (Srinivas, 1984; Cain, Khanam and Nahar, 1979; Chaudhury and Nilufer, 1980; Shah, 1986; Youssef, 1974). The conventions of female seclusion (purdah) ensure that throughout their married life, women shall have very little contact with male strangers. Although the extreme form of purdah is breaking down to some degree in many countries, the attitudes underlying it are sufficient to explain the great reluctance to educate daughters, especially at the secondary-school level, still present in some countries (e.g., Pakistan) and the very low labour force participation rates among women throughout Southern and Western Asia (although they seem to be somewhat higher in the Northern African Arab States, where 17 per cent of Moroccan women aged 15 or over were economically active in 1982 and 22 per cent of Tunisian women in the same age group were economically active in 1984).

In such circumstances, women mainly engage in migration to get married (usually after a marriage has been arranged by close relatives) or to accompany or join other family members (Joshi and Joshi, 1976). In countries like India, the custom of village exogamy and patrilocal residence generates a substantial volume of female rural-rural migration. Indeed, in India and Bangladesh, not only is rural-rural migration the dominant form of migration but it is heavily female-dominated (Skeldon, 1985; Premi, 1982). In Pakistan, rural-rural migration accounts for approximately one third of all internal migration; and although it shows a slight predominance of males, it is the least male-dominated stream in the country (Shah, 1986). In contrast, rural-urban migration is heavily male-dominated in Bangladesh and Pakistan and less female-dominated than migration to rural areas in India (United Nations Secretariat, 1993). The male share of migration tends to increase the larger the size of the city of destination (Skeldon, 1985) and in India, at least, to decrease with duration of residence (Singh, A. M., 1984; Premi and Tom, 1985).

In sub-Saharan Africa, Boserup (1985) argues, the economic position of women is deteriorating. In traditional African societies women had access to land and could support themselves and their children by subsistence agriculture. Boserup states:

"Both under formal land reforms and when land has been privatised through change of custom, women's cultivation rights have been overlooked or eliminated. Men have become owners of the land, either as individuals or as heads of families, and women no longer have any claim to the land if the men want to dispose of it or if they become widowed, divorced, or abandoned." (1985, p. 389)

Even where women have access to land for cultivation, their economic position has often deteriorated, thus reinforcing their interest in having more children, because they are increasingly dependent upon both child labour and support from adult children later in life (Boserup, 1985).

Africa is too large and varied a continent about which to generalize safely. For example, in parts of Western Africa women are very active in trade which is a major activity of women that migrate to towns, either permanently or temporarily as circular migrants (Sudarkasa, 1977). But women are apparently less active in trade in Eastern and Southern Africa. The relative autonomy that some women have in trading activities in Western Africa, however, should not be allowed to obscure the fact that they remain subordinate to and dependent upon their husbands in major respects, including their lack of access to the resources required to accumulate capital (Afonja, 1990).

Although men appear to outnumber women in rural-urban migration in Africa (Hugo, 1993), women have been prominent in certain African rural-urban migration flows, not only as accompanying family members but as primary migrants; and they appear to have played an increasing part in such migrations in recent times (Caldwell, 1969; Sudarkasa, 1977; Stichter, 1985; Russell, Jacobsen and Stanley, 1990; Peil, 1984). Although most African women move in association with or to join other family members, large numbers also migrate independently for economic reasons. The latter group includes not only single women but those migrating because they lack male support as a result of divorce, desertion, widowhood or unhappy marriages (Stichter, 1985; Peil, 1984; Little, 1973; Tienda and Booth, 1988).

In Eastern and South-eastern Asia, there are great cultural and religious differences between and even within countries, with Islam predominating in Indonesia and Malaysia; Buddhism in Cambodia, the Lao People's Democratic Republic, Myanmar and Thailand; and Christianity in the Philippines. Women's autonomy has traditionally been high in the Philippines and Thailand. Islamic societies in South-eastern Asia tolerate greater freedom for women than their counterparts in Southern or Western Asia, and in recent decades the migration of young women to cities in the region has grown considerably (Fawcett, Khoo and Smith, 1984). This upsurge in female migration to the cities has been associated with the rapid pace of economic development and changes in the employment structure that have favoured women's employment. Malaysia, for example, has become one of the world's leading producers of electronics, particularly semiconductors, an industry in which women are preferred as workers (Salih and Young, 1989).

Patterns of female labour force participation differ greatly between the large cities of Eastern and South-eastern Asia, not only in overall levels but also in age patterns (Jones, 1984). In the Republic of Korea, for instance, female labour force participation rates in urban areas are relatively low, particularly for women in their mid-twenties to late twenties and their thirties, whereas at Bangkok and Manila, rates are considerably higher and there is no drop-off in the late twenties or thirties. At Jakarta, the pattern is similar to Bangkok and Manila but the level of female labour force participation is lower. These differences are no doubt influenced by the work opportunities available, but they appear to relate even more strongly to conventions about women's participation in the labour force. In Japan and the Republic of Korea, once a woman marries she normally withdraws from the workforce, even if she does not yet have children, whereas in sinitic cultures, it is the arrival of children that normally entails the need to stay at home. Yet, in the Philippines and Thailand, even the arrival of children does not necessarily lead to withdrawal from the labour force. In Indonesia and among Malays in Malaysia, Muslim norms have traditionally discouraged unmarried women from working outside the home, but increasing age at marriage and rising educational attainment have led to significant attitude changes in favour of employment.

Both the availability of jobs for women in urban areas and attitudes to female employment influence migration patterns. In Thailand, male predominance in rural-urban migration declined between the late 1950s and the late 1960s, and by the late 1970s women became predominant. Over the same period, the sex distribution of migration to Bangkok changed from being balanced to exhibiting increasing female preponderance (Fuller, 1990; Goldstein and Goldstein, 1986; Arnold and Piampiti, 1984). In Malaysia, the sex ratio of recent migrants fell from 112 in the 1960s to 102 in the 1970s.[1] Women predominated when migration took place over short distances (intrastate), while men were more numerous than women in migration flows over longer distances (interstate). In the 1980s, women accounted for more than half of the migrants aged 15-24 in Malaysia (Hugo, Lim and Narayan, 1989).

In most Latin American countries, women have usually accounted for more than half of all rural-urban migrants (Elizaga, 1965; Jelin, 1977). This female predominance may appear inconsistent with the often stressed "importance of such Latin cultural traditions as machismo, a high degree of male control over women, and women's lack of autonomy outside the family" (Jelin, 1977, p. 131). However, because the participation of women in agriculture and other economic activities in rural areas is low and domestic activities cannot fully occupy both the mother and her older daughters in rural households, young single women often move to towns where employment opportunities are better, especially in domestic service (Boserup, 1970). The sex selectivity of rural outmigration in the region can be explained by taking into account the roles of rural women and the socio-economic dynamics of rural communities, concentrating particularly on changes in family structure and the labour requirements of different rural socio-economic groups. A case-study carried out in Mexico showed that the monetization of the peasant economy and the demise of domestic manufacturing made women more redundant in the rural economy but also more employable than men in the cities (Young, 1982). According to Arizpe (1984), the monetization of the peasant economy often leads to strategies of "relay" migration in which the father, daughters and sons in the household take turns in moving to the city. Young women usually leave at a marriageable age (18-20) or when their marriage prospects in the village are beginning to look doubtful (between ages 22 and 25). Patterns of female migration are not so regular in households dependent upon other economic activities—craft producers or households engaged in intensive cash-crop production, for example, where the labour of daughters may be crucial.

With a high proportion of the Latin American population currently living in urban areas, the traditional emphasis on rural-urban migration of young women, primarily into domestic service, is beginning to look dated. Thus, migration from metropolitan areas to fast-growing medium-sized cities has now become an important stream (Recchini de Lattes and Mychaszula, 1993), and female migrants to smaller cities differ in important respects from those to large metropolitan areas. A study of migration to a medium-sized city in Argentina showed that whereas the characteristics of female migrants moving over short distances matched the stereotype (they were largely young, single and worked in the informal sector, especially in domestic service), migrants that moved over longer distances, especially those originating in large metropolitan areas, were older, better-educated and occupied a varied set of better-paid occupations (Recchini de Lattes and Mychaszula, 1993).

In the Caribbean, the main causes of female migration include unequal ownership of land by sex, population pressure on rural areas and the restriction of women to subsistence agriculture so that they cannot profit from shifts to cash crops. Younger and older women tend to migrate on their own to cities to become domestic servants (especially if young), street or market vendors or industrial workers. Women in the intermediate ages (25-40) generally migrate in the company of husbands or mates (Despradel, 1984).

B. Effects of development on female migration

Theoretical background

Given the important role of economic factors in influencing female migration—even when it is described as "associational" since it is generally related to the economically motivated migration of other family members—the relation between development and migration needs to be examined according to the most prominent theories of economic development. In the dualistic theory popularized by Lewis (1955) and by Fei and Ranis (1964), the key element in development is the expansion of employment in the "industrial" sector to absorb surplus labour from the "agricultural" sector until labour shortages develop and wages are driven up, thus providing strong incentives for labour-saving technological change. This theory implies a considerable volume of rural-urban migration related to the sectoral shifts in economic structure. In the human resource development approach, which seeks to link the productive role of human resources in the human capital model with the consumption role of human resources embodied in the literature on quality of life, rewarded participation in economic activity plays a bridging role, providing simultaneously to people the incentive to invest in human capital and the means to improve their quality of life (Corner, 1991). Migration may be necessary either to secure the means to upgrade health or education or to gain access to satisfactory work once the necessary investment in human capital has been made.

Education is crucial in leading to new roles for women in the development process, especially where migration is involved. Through education women acquire skills and credentials that, being marketable, facilitate their integration into the labour-market. Since modern-sector jobs tend to be geographically concentrated, especially in the cities, educated women are likely to move to those places. In addition, education increases women's bargaining power within the household. Indeed, the very fact that women are allowed to attain a certain educational level indicates in many cultures that the older generation recognizes their worth beyond the household. Consequently, expanded educational opportunities for women are likely to be associated both with increasingly autonomous female migration and with higher levels of participation in modern-sector jobs by those that migrate as accompanying family members.

The fact that women migrating in the company of husbands, parents or siblings frequently engage in economic activity at the place of destination has major significance. When family units move to take advantage of new opportunities, all members become potential economic actors. The question is whether women that have moved, for whatever reason, are then more or less likely to be economically active and in what types of activities. Does participation in economic activity have a positive or negative influence on their status, both within the family and in the wider society? Only by considering such broad implications of female migration can one really begin to identify adequately the role of female migration in development.

Modes of development, effects on employment structure, demand for female labour and patterns of female migration

For the types of female migration in which economic motivations are important, a simple model can be outlined giving priority to the two factors expected to play the greatest role in influencing female migration: economic needs and opportunities; and cultural factors restricting or facilitating women's ability to avail themselves of those opportunities.

Over the course of development, the decline in the share of agriculture in total production is offset by a rising share of manufactures and services. The effect on the structure of employment is somewhat muted, because productivity tends to rise less rapidly in agriculture than in other sectors. Even so, the share of non-agricultural activities in total employment rises steadily. The rise in non-agricultural industries translates into faster employment growth in some occupations than in others. The location of new employment opportunities is a key determinant of migration patterns, and the extent to which new jobs can be filled by women will strongly influence both patterns of independent female migration and the extent to which women migrating for "associational" reasons enter the labour-market.

The evolution of the economy during the course of development is unlikely to be gender-neutral in terms of the occupations that grow more or less rapidly. The initial set of occupations in any country will include some in which women predominate and others in which men do. Over time, women's employment may increase rapidly if the evolution of the economy favours "women's jobs" or if sex segregation by occupation changes through modifications in norms that determine what is "women's work" and what is not, thus giving women increased chances to enter occupations previously dominated by men in urban areas. At the same time, women's job opportunities in rural areas can diminish as men increasingly control the lucrative cash-crop production (as in sub-Saharan Africa) or as technological change removes traditional female activities (e.g., agricultural mechanization in sub-Saharan Africa, rice harvesting and pounding in a number of Asian countries).

The extent to which a response to new work opportunities will involve migration will depend upon the location of job opportunities in relation to the geographical distribution of potential workers. The typical pattern is one in which a disproportionate share of new job opportunities is found in urban areas, particularly metropolitan areas, requiring the migration of those that want to avail themselves of them. Both men and women will move from rural areas seeking the higher incomes potentially available in urban areas, though the importance of family migration means that women's movement is determined by factors other than simply job opportunities for women. At the margin, however, whether women will be more prominent in this movement than men will depend upon both the mix of urban job opportunities and also, to some extent, upon how disadvantaged the situation of women is in rural areas. To the extent that women in rural areas lack power over resources, the promise of income from informal sector work in the cities will be more appealing for them than for men.

An occupation with a predictable evolution over the course of economic development is domestic service.

In poor countries where there is a labour surplus and women are relatively free to work outside the home, sending daughters to work in domestic service is often a strategy used by families to avoid the burden of supporting them. Frequently, entry into domestic service requires a move to the city, where incomes are higher and more people can afford to hire servants. The gender balance of domestic service employment varies widely between cultures and can also change sharply over time. In areas of high female autonomy, such as Latin America and South-eastern Asia, women dominate in the domestic services sector, whereas in countries favouring female seclusion, such as Southern Asia, men tend to predominate.[2] In the rich oil-producing countries of Western Asia, labour shortages at all levels have contributed to making foreign women acceptable as domestic servants. In Africa, men predominated among domestic workers during the colonial era, but domestic work has become increasingly feminized. Thus, a study of a middle-income African area of Nairobi in 1979 found that 95 per cent of the domestic servants were women, most of them between the ages of 15 and 20 (Stichter, 1985). In South Africa, women have long dominated the domestic service sector, constituting 79 per cent of all domestic servants in 1970.

In poor countries with wide income inequalities, domestic service typically comprises a very significant share of the total female labour force in urban areas. For example, in 1970, domestic service employed 29 per cent of all working women in both Jakarta and Manila, 20 per cent in Seoul, 14 per cent in Singapore, 10 per cent in Bangkok and 8 per cent in Hong Kong (Jones, 1984). In South Africa, 37 per cent of the economically active women in 1970 were in the service sector, which consists mainly of domestic workers (Stichter, 1985); the equivalent figures in the urban areas of Ecuador and Honduras in 1974 were 35 and 36 per cent, respectively, and in urban Panama in 1980, 29 per cent. Work in domestic service is therefore a prime objective of many women migrating to the cities. Indeed, in most countries, women already working as domestic servants help fuel further migration by recruiting relatives or friends from their village of origin whenever new positions become available.

As the economy develops, the importance of domestic service in urban employment for women tends to decline. This was the case in European countries. In

England, for instance, domestic service was a key occupation for young women migrating to the cities in the nineteenth century but it declined rapidly in importance during the twentieth century (Ebery and Preston, 1976). Similarly, but more recently, in cities like Seoul, Singapore and Taipei, where economic growth has been rapid for several decades, domestic service declined dramatically during the 1970s. In those cities, not only the proportion but the absolute numbers employed in domestic service declined: in Singapore, from 22,000 to 16,000 between 1970 and 1980; and in Seoul, from 90,000 to 45,000 over the same period (Jones, 1984).

Occupational groupings that tend to grow faster than average in a developing economy include professional and clerical occupations and production workers in growing manufacturing industries. Professional and clerical occupations tend to be particularly important for women, who represent a high proportion of teachers, nurses and, increasingly, secretarial and clerical workers (Anker and Hein, 1986; Stichter, 1985). However, such occupations may not attract many female migrants from rural areas if their levels of education are low. Thus, women frequently migrate first to urban areas to obtain the necessary training (Trager, 1984). In contrast, some production occupations in growing industries have exercised a strong attraction for female migrants, particularly textiles and electronics, as in Malaysia, Thailand and the northern border areas of Mexico (Maex, 1983; Zlotnik, 1993).

A model of female work-related migration, then, might stress such factors as needs (mainly affecting the poor) and opportunities (mainly affecting the educated middle class) in the context of the evolution of the occupational structure of the economy. The extent to which women's migration is directly affected by changes in the structure of job opportunities will depend to a great extent upon underlying cultural and normative factors that restrict or facilitate women's access to certain jobs. However, those two types of factors are themselves subject to change as a result of pressures exerted by the changing socio-economic structure.

If women are increasingly educated and trained in fields in which job opportunities are available, it becomes difficult to deny them entry. If, in addition, convention favours the participation of women in certain growing occupations, pressures to allow them to enter those occupations in large numbers will rise and their migration may be necessary to fill the jobs available. It must be underscored that the necessary expansion of women's education to produce adequate candidates for the jobs available will also help undermine traditional restrictions on women's activities (Caldwell, 1980). Once families and society at large have made the decision to educate girls in large numbers, the increasing independence and mobility of women is generally a foregone conclusion. Societies favouring female seclusion recognize such linkage and therefore vehemently oppose the access of women to education, particularly at the secondary and higher levels.

C. IMPLICATIONS OF FEMALE MIGRATION FOR DEVELOPMENT

Female migration as a mechanism to redistribute labour

In many countries, a substantial proportion of the female labour force is constituted by migrants; consequently, migration may have effects on average productivity, total production and wage levels in different sectors. Neoclassical economics tends to view migration as an equilibrating mechanism, balancing the supply of human resources with the labour needs of different regions, with generally positive effects. However, to the extent that women are generally not free to make independent decisions about where or when to migrate, given that they frequently move to accompany other family members, their migration is circumscribed and does not respond directly to market signals with regard to their own employment prospects. Therefore, the migration of women may not necessarily contribute to the achievement of equilibrium and may instead perpetuate a suboptimal use of labour.

To the extent that women move as associational migrants, their migration is unlikely to be determined mostly by their own employment prospects, but it is nevertheless important to consider that, whatever their motivation for migration, female migrants are likely to become part of the labour force in the place of destination (Thadani and Todaro, 1984). In any event, an examination of the changed circumstances of migrants as documented in a large number of migration surveys indicates that they tend to improve their welfare and economic circumstances. However, this evidence overlooks two important points. One is that surveys of migrants at the place of destination miss those that have returned, many of whom presumably did so because of failure or disappointment with the conditions at the place of destination. The second is that the migration of individuals has effects on others at the places both of origin and of destination, as well as economy-wide effects, so that the gains and losses of the migrants themselves are only part of the evidence that must be considered in evaluating the developmental effects of migration (Bilsborrow, Oberai and Standing, 1984; Hugo, 1987).[3] It is important to avoid evaluating the effects of migration from the purely individual perspective, especially when individuals migrate as part of a household strategy to improve a family's welfare.

Contribution of female migration to the change of norms and values concerning the roles and behaviour of women

In many developing countries, norms and values concerning women's roles and behaviour hinder a more effective contribution by women to the development process. Should migration serve to modify these norms and values, it would facilitate a greater contribution by women to development. Because many migrant women face a change in environment as a result of migration, they have to undergo a process of adaptation that involves changes in their roles and behaviour. Adaptation takes place irrespective of whether women move independently or as part of a family. In fact, women that have moved as children are more likely to adapt fully to the new environment. A key developmental issue is whether migrants adapt to the lower fertility norms and patterns that tend to characterize the areas of destination when rural-urban migration is involved, another is the impact of migration on women's economic activities and yet another is its impact on women's chances to participate fully in community activities.

Since rural-urban migration also increases the linkages between rural and urban areas, migration can also have an impact on the norms and values of the communities of origin through the visits of migrants, exchanges of information initiated by them or their eventual return. The "demonstration effect" of remittances can also bring about changes as non-migrants become aware of the advantages of migrating to urban areas.

The effect of migration on female status and independence will depend very much upon the context in which migration takes place and its modality. For instance, marriage migration at the behest of parents to play a subservient role in the prospective husband's household, as required by Indian tradition, can in no sense be considered to increase female independence, although it may improve the social mobility of those women whose parents manage to arrange an advantageous match. In contrast, the migration of young single women who have received a secondary-school education to secure jobs in the place of destination that are not available in the place of origin will, in all likelihood, serve to foster their independence. However, the separation from husband and family faced by married Javanese women who engage in circular and other forms of internal migration should probably be viewed less in relation to status and autonomy than as a reaction to the harsh realities of poverty in the area of origin (Hetler, 1986).

The degree of autonomy of female migrants varies widely. Autonomy is likely to be least in marriage migration arranged by parents, though not in marriage migration based on self-choice of spouse. In developing a conceptual framework for female migration, Thadani and Todaro (1984) have given considerable prominence to "mobility migration", including much marriage migration. Moving to get married can improve the status of women if marriage is seen as a means of social mobility. Autonomy is likely to be limited when women move passively as "accompanying family members". Indeed, where traditions of purdah are strong, the degree of women's independence may be even more restricted after they have migrated with their husbands to urban areas than if they had stayed in their villages of origin, because by having fewer social ties in the city and less knowledge about urban life, women are likely to view their new surroundings as dangerous and to remain secluded at home (Singh, 1978).

Autonomy in the case of women migrating to work will vary according to their degree of independence in decision-making. If the move results from a family decision-making process and the migrant is closely controlled by the family in the place of destination (by, for example, staying with relatives), she may gain little in terms of autonomy. Sending young women to become de facto servants in the households of wealthier urban relatives is common in many cultures, including those of Java, the Philippines and parts of Latin America. However, if the migrant has some choice with regard to her place of residence at destination and the amount of remittances to send home, she may gain greater autonomy than that which is traditionally sanctioned. A study in Malaysia showed that among young women moving to urban areas the desire to gain some independence from the restrictive kampong environment and from parental supervision was the second most important reason for migrating after job-related reasons (Hugo, Lim and Narayan, 1989).

Greater autonomy, however, may occasionally come at a cost, particularly for women raised under protective and restrictive conditions. In India, for example, in comparison with the situation in the place of origin, female migrants may experience a higher degree of physical and social isolation in the place of destination and freedom to mix more easily with the opposite sex may result in unwanted pregnancy outside marriage, a problem rarely faced by rural non-migrants (Singh, 1978, 1980).

Discussion of particular cases

The developmental implications of changing patterns of female migration, whether viewed from a purely economic perspective or from the perspective of changing women's roles and status in society, are complex. Such complexity can perhaps best be illustrated by presenting a series of vignettes on the role of women's migration in a number of countries or regions.

India

In India, where women constitute a very high proportion of rural-rural migrants (United Nations Secretariat, 1993), it is incorrect to assume that they migrate only because of marriage or other forms of associational migration. Independent female labour migration is also important, though difficult to quantify.

During the slack season, some women seek casual employment in irrigation, road and other public works programmes (Singh, A. M., 1984); female migrant labour plays an important role in sugar-cane harvesting in Maharashtra and Gujarat, in paddy cultivation in the Punjab and Haryana, and in plantation labour in northeastern and southern India (Selvaratnam, 1988).

Migration streams to the cities of northern India tend to be male-dominated, particularly when the distance is longer. Although "associational migration" (moving with family members) is the main form of female migration in this region, there may be a strong economic motive even for this type of female migration (Singh, J. P., 1984), evidenced by the fact that migrant women are more likely to work than non-migrant women. Regardless of whether migrant women intended to work before they migrated, many of them end up joining the labour force at the place of destination. Migration may thus affect their propensity to work by exposing them to increased employment opportunities, forcing them to adjust to new circumstances and become more flexible in their individual interpretation of societal norms, making them adopt new standards and work towards achieving them and providing them with better means to be productive (for instance, by improving their access to education). In Kerala, where women are better educated and have more autonomy than in other parts of India, they are more likely than those in northern India to accompany their husbands in migration or to migrate while still single (Singh, J. P., 1986). In Indian cities, between 20 and 35 per cent of all adult low-income migrant women are the sole providers for their households, "either because they are alone (widowed, divorced, deserted, or single) or because their husbands or other male adults in the household are unemployed, ill, handicapped, or simply irresponsible with their income" (Singh, A. M., 1984, p. 101).

While uneducated women moving to Indian slums may find work as unskilled labourers, domestic servants or in petty trade, there is a dearth of jobs for women with a moderate amount of education. Those that do find work are often restricted to low-paying jobs, where they earn lower wages than men in similar jobs and have fewer promotion prospects (Papola, 1986). Indian women may therefore see few advantages in educating their daughters or becoming literate themselves. Thus, age at marriage remains low among migrants in urban areas and the domestic and child-care responsibilities of daughters are heavier than in rural areas because of the high employment rate of slum women and the tendency to leave the older generation behind in the village.

Malaysia

In Malaysia, the context of female migration has changed dramatically. In the past, both migration because of marriage and after divorce was important, though most brides did not move from their village of origin after marriage and where movement did occur it was over short distances (Tan and Jones, 1990). In traditional Malay culture, the activities of single women were restricted and closely monitored. That system began to break down in the 1960s and 1970s when employment opportunities in the export industry led to the large-scale migration of single Malay women to urban areas. Parents abdicated their rights to control the movement of unmarried daughters to an extent that would have been unthinkable only two decades earlier. The reasons for that change are uncertain, but both the erosion of the authority of uneducated parents to control the behaviour of their better educated daughters and the possibility of receiving remittances from migrant daughters played a part (Jones, 1980).

Given the prevailing occupational segregation by sex, the mode of economic growth pursued by Malaysia during the 1970s and 1980s favoured the employment of women and contributed to the modification of traditional values. Women were considered desirable workers for the electronics industry because of their "nimble fingers" and greater docility (Lim, 1984). In addition, a range of clerical and secretarial jobs opened up because of the rapid growth of the public sector, commerce and industry, thus providing job opportunities for women with secondary and tertiary education, whose numbers were growing rapidly. Consequently, female migration to urban areas played an important role in facilitating the rapid industrial and commercial development in Malaysia, albeit one fraught with role conflicts and exploitation of various kinds (Hugo, Lim and Narayan, 1989).

Thailand

In Thailand, traditional restrictions on the migration of women had never applied, although, as noted by Tongudai (1984), parents in rural areas were happier if a job and suitable accommodation were guaranteed in advance of a daughter's migration. During the 1970s, an increasingly feminine migration flow was generated by the wide range of job opportunities that opened up in urban areas, especially at Bangkok. Female migrants to the capital were young (57 per cent were under 20 years of age when they moved), single and had moved on their own[4] (Arnold and Piampiti, 1984). The strong growth of the Thai economy since 1960 had opened a wide range of jobs, including factory work, retail trade, and clerical and domestic service, although the relative importance of the last-named was declining. Tourism was more prominent in Thailand than perhaps in any other major developing country in South-eastern Asia and generated a wide range of service sector jobs for women.

Not only because of tourism but also because of the integral role of the sex industry in Thai society, that industry in all its manifestations played an important role in providing jobs for female rural-urban migrants, possibly employing as many as 7-9 per cent of all working women at Bangkok (Jones, 1984). To evaluate the developmental role of the sex industry is not easy, both because of the tendency to condemn prostitution out of hand on moral grounds and because the freedom of choice among young women entering the industry varies enormously: cases range from those of young girls sold to brothels by their parents to relieve debt to those of women that deliberately choose to work as a bar girl or masseuse because those occupations yield more pay for less work than does a factory job. Because of the tolerant attitudes prevailing in much of Thailand—particularly, it would appear, among northern villagers—young women who have worked in the sex industry for a period can marry and settle down in their home village without stigma. Consequently, the role of the sex industry in raising the incomes of rural families, enabling them to educate their children and, in some cases, even building capital for investment cannot be disregarded.

Indonesia

In the urban areas of Indonesia, sales work, largely in the informal sector, and production activities have been the main female occupations, with domestic services a distant third and teaching the fourth. Women constitute 43 per cent of all sales workers in Indonesia, 89 per cent of the domestic servants and 45 per cent of the teachers. Although they only constitute 26 per cent of all production workers, in certain industries they account for over half of the workforce (unpublished data, 1985 Intercensal Survey). But a particular feature of the Indonesian (especially Javanese) scene has been the temporary (often, circular) migration of both women and men engaged in trade and other occupations in nearby cities and towns.

A study of Jakarta based on the 1971 census (Jones, 1977) showed that migrant women had higher labour force participation rates than locally born women, though those rates fell with duration of residence. A study based on the 1985 Intercensal Survey produced a similar result, although the relationship did not hold for those with secondary and higher education (Widarti, 1991). The study based on the 1971 census indicated that migrant women were more heavily concentrated in services (particularly domestic service) and trade than the locally born. Domestic service was particularly the preserve of young, recent migrants, whereas women in trade were generally older and longer term migrants. Locally born women were more widely spread across the occupational spectrum. Such census-based studies fail to reflect most of the temporary or circular migrants, but other studies (Jellinek, 1978; Hetler, 1986, 1989) indicate that those migrants are also heavily concentrated in informal sector trade and service activities.

Philippines

In the Philippines, economic growth has been slower than in other market economies of South-eastern Asia, and although the export-oriented industry has attracted significant numbers of female migrants, the informal sector and domestic service continue to be the main employers of female migrant labour. Thus, in 1975, among working women in urban areas, 53 per cent of migrant women were in domestic service, compared with 18 per cent of non-migrants; among employed single women, 61 per cent of migrants were in domestic service compared with 29 per cent of non-migrants (Engracia and Herrin, 1984; see also Eviota and Smith, 1984). The sex industry has also been an important employer of young female migrants in the Philippines.

Latin America

In Latin America, where patterns of rural-urban migration are influenced by deeply embedded structural inequalities, studies of female migration rightly emphasize its structural determinants (Arizpe, 1984). As in other developing countries, women in the region migrate to take advantage of expanding job opportunities as clerical workers, teachers, nurses or factory workers. However, the low rates of economic growth that characterized most Latin American countries during the past 20 years and particularly during the 1980s have negatively affected the growth of job opportunities in the formal sector of urban areas. Consequently, domestic service continues to play a major role as an employer of female labour, especially of migrant women. It has been argued that by being an important source of employment for women with low levels of schooling, domestic service has led to the preponderance of women in the migration flows from rural to urban areas (Schultz, 1971).[5] There is a striking correlation between employment in domestic service and migration status: in metropolitan Buenos Aires, among economically active females in 1970, 52 per cent of the recent internal migrants and 63 per cent of the recent migrants from neighbouring countries worked as domestic servants, while 35 per cent of the earlier migrants and only 5 per cent of the locally-born did so.[6] Data for Santiago and Bogotá showed a similar pattern (Jelin, 1977; Martine, 1975).

Arizpe (1984) notes that peasant families in need of additional income set aside their moral and religious objections to sending young women to the city. Such objections are reduced when young women can be entrusted to the care and protection of an urban matron for whom they work as servants (see also Jelin, 1977). Female migration for domestic service is then both an economic strategy of a peasant household and a social strategy that preserves the "femininity" and marriageability of the young migrant.

D. DEVELOPMENT POLICIES, PLANS AND IMPLICATIONS FOR FEMALE MIGRATION

Development plans vary greatly in their treatment and, in general, lack of treatment of women's issues. In some cases, there is almost no mention of women's issues, as in the five-year plans of Malaysia and Thailand. In other countries, such issues are mentioned but in almost rote fashion, with the obligatory references to integrating women into development but with little specific content. Occasionally, the content even reinforces traditional notions of restricted women's roles. In Indonesia, for instance, the official policy on women in development, as spelled out in the Applied Family Welfare Programme initiated in 1973, argued that the most basic development programmes must begin at the family level where a woman is to play five major roles: loyal backstop and supporter of her husband; caretaker of the household; producer of future generations; the family's prime socializer; and Indonesian citizen. As Sullivan notes: "Women's place is ever more strictly in the home, but now the home has been redefined in vague idealistic terms as a crucial arena of national development" (1983, p. 169). By the time of the Third Five-year Plan (1980-84), however, women's roles rated a half-chapter in the Plan, a practice that has been maintained in the two subsequent Five-year Plans. Those chapters put more emphasis on women's work and community roles than did the Applied Family Welfare Programme of 1973.

In some countries where women are especially disadvantaged, recent development plans give surprisingly detailed attention to women's issues. Thus, the Saudi Arabian Fourth Development Plan of 1985-1990 recognizes the issues posed by the rapid growth of educational attainment among women and the need to find adequate "employment in accordance with the Sharia". Similarly, in Bangladesh, the Third Five-Year Plan (1985-1990) gives considerable attention to women's development, spelling out clear objectives and strategies, and including a number of specific programmes, such as the establishment of women's cooperatives, mothers' centres and vocational training programmes for women (Ahmed and Mabud, 1989). In Pakistan, the Sixth Five-Year Plan (1983-1988) states: "The Plan candidly recognizes that no society can ever develop half-liberated and half-shackled. It provides in each sector of economic activity development programmes to integrate women and their concerns in the mainstream of social and economic life" (p. 19). Goals related to women's development were set in the health sector, training and government employment. Special attention was given to the need of increasing the school enrolment of girls, particularly in rural areas, a development that, as the Plan recognized, would require overcoming the conservatism of rural families. The Seventh Plan (1988-1993), in evaluating the achievements of the Sixth Plan, recognized that such conservatism had proved to be a stumbling-block in raising female enrolment rates. The Seventh Plan added women's cooperatives and legal aid societies to the Sixth Plan programmes directed to women's development.

Examination of development plans for a number of developing countries shows that although certain trends which reflect the consequences of migration (notably the rapid growth of urban populations) are given prominence, little attention is given to migration patterns *per se* or to the policies needed to modify them where they are seen to be inconsistent with developmental goals. Even less frequently is attention given to the gender balance in migration flows. It is probable that development planners, by ignoring patterns of migration and gender differences, formulate policies that frequently exacerbate the problems of female migrants. In particular, in many countries there seems to be little recognition of the fact that female migrants include not only "accompanying family members" but also single women and female heads of household (if not at the time of the move, frequently soon after the move).

In developing countries, the pattern of urbanization favoured in most development plans favours diversion of growth from the largest city or cities to smaller cities. Specific programmes to achieve such an end, however, typically lack muscle and are usually overwhelmed by the unplanned spatial impacts of the broad macroeconomic and sectoral policies adopted (Fuchs, Jones and Pernia, 1987). The latter policies typically foster high levels of urban primacy. Policies specifically seeking to influence migration include land settlement schemes, the imposition of residence permits for those wishing to relocate to urban areas and tax holidays or subsidized input for businesses locating outside the main urban centres. Policies with no explicit intention to influence migration but which nevertheless have important indirect effects on the flows of migrants include: centralized administration systems;

which provide an incentive for businesses to establish themselves in the capital city where decisions are made; import substitution industrialization policies; and overvalued exchange rates. With regard to female migration, the establishment of export-processing zones specializing in such products as electronics or textiles has had important indirect effects on the movement of women.

The type of urban development pursued is likely to affect the gender balance of migration flows, though the outcome will be country-specific. In India, for instance, where the male share of migration flows tends to increase with the distance involved and with the size of the city of destination,[7] a more dispersed pattern of urbanization may result in greater opportunities for women to migrate to cities.

Because of the limited impact of many migration-specific policies, complementary social and economic policies will be needed both to facilitate the flows that the migration-specific policies seek to foster and to promote the welfare of female migrants. For example, low-income working women, many of whom are migrants, need access to low-cost housing near their place of work, access to credit at reasonable terms, a sympathetic attitude when they work in the informal sector and legislation to protect their rights. Governments could take measures to satisfy those needs.

A balanced approach to the developmental aspects of women's migration would require a clear assessment of the effects of women's migration (and, indeed, of their non-migration) on their own welfare as individuals, on that of their families and on the wider community. Assessment of those effects is likely to differ from one society to another and the planners' assessments may differ from those of the actors themselves. For example, in societies where women have traditionally had little freedom of movement, the ideology of the planners could well dictate more attention to the issues of protection of women's physical and moral well-being, and less to the need for increased female autonomy and income, than the women themselves would assign to those issues.

Class structures also intrude on policy to the detriment of migrants, including female migrants. For example, migrants eking out a living in the urban informal sector by engaging in street hawking, pavement vending, scavenging and trishaw pedalling are frequently harassed for breaking rules which are mostly designed to keep order or prevent chaos in pedestrian or vehicular traffic, but some of which are intended to present a modern face to the world by denying the existence of poverty. Even when planners have come to accept the need for the urban informal sector both as a provider of employment and sometimes as a valuable training-ground and means of entry into the urban economy, police and lower level city officials frequently harass those engaging in informal sector activities (Jones, 1988), in part because it is the task of those officials to combat the less savoury forms of informal sector activity, such as begging, pickpocketing or streetwalking, but also because fines provide them with a valuable income supplement. Women are often particularly vulnerable to such harassment (Tongudai, 1984).

A hard-headed approach is needed to evaluate which policies really work in the interest of female migrants. For example, some policies that seek to protect women, such as regulations in Indonesia forbidding night-shift work for women and requiring the provision of one day's menstruation leave each month (Jones, 1984) or generous maternity leave provisions in Zambia or minimum wage policies designed to protect the living standards of workers as a whole, may deter the employment of women (Schultz, 1990; Bardouille, 1986).

The services needed by female migrants differ according to their characteristics. Factory workers need adequate working conditions, freedom to unionize, the provision of dormitory accommodation if single and counselling to prevent stress. Vendors need credit, a suitable place to trade and freedom from harassment by police and city functionaries. Working mothers need child-care services. Female heads of household need special access to a number of services and facilities since they are likely to have little free time and few financial resources. Sex workers need medical check-ups and protection from exploitative arrangements with brothel owners. Although some of these needs apply to women in general, it can be argued that they are especially important for migrants, particularly those from rural areas, because their lack of familiarity with the urban environment makes them much more vulnerable.

E. The main sectors of development planning and female migration

Through what mechanisms are development policies most likely to affect significantly the patterns and levels of female migration? Policies adopted in the various sectors that are normally considered separately in development plans are discussed below in terms of how they are likely to affect the determinants and consequences of female migration.

Agricultural and rural development

With respect to agricultural and rural development, some writers have claimed that planning frequently exacerbates the problems faced by rural women by, for example, introducing technologies that deprive women of their traditional employment, by giving men control over activities that were traditionally women's domain or by disregarding the needs of women in agricultural training programmes (Tinker, 1973). Rogers claims that "much development planning has an adverse effect by depriving women of important resources and intensifying their work-load, while reducing their control over their own work-patterns" (1980, p. 175). If such claims are true, the neglect documented undoubtedly affects female migration because the situation of women in rural areas is a key determinant of their migration.

It is easy to say that rural development policies should be sensitive to the particularities of women's situation, but difficult to identify just what policies are needed to benefit women. The starting-point must be to base rural development policy on an appreciation of the roles that women play in agriculture and other rural economic activities. Frequently, those roles are more important than is recognized, in part because women's work is so devalued by society that their contribution to agriculture tends to be ignored by respondents answering census or survey questions. Women's roles in agriculture, however, vary by region and consequently, their implications for development planning differ. In Africa, for instance, women and children have traditionally been responsible for cultivating and growing foodstuffs which have been eliminated in recent years in many areas (Boserup, 1985). In Latin America, women had traditionally less of a role in agriculture and are becoming increasingly redundant in rural areas.

In Indonesia, developments in both agriculture and manufacturing during the 1970s and 1980s probably affected women's employment in rural areas more adversely than that of men. New harvesting practices and the introduction of mechanical rice hullers displaced female labour, although the effect may have been less severe than many observers believe (Manning, 1988). The development of modern textile and plastics factories undercut women's cottage production of textiles, mats and basketry. Mechanized rice milling also affected the employment of rural women in Bangladesh and India (Ahmed, 1987), and a somewhat comparable case was documented in Mexico (Young, 1982). The appropriate policy response to such developments is surely not to slow technological change but rather to be responsive to the needs of female workers by providing them with viable employment alternatives.

Better job opportunities for women in rural areas are likely to reduce rural out-migration, although it is still a subject of debate whether rural development *per se* or particular aspects of it reduce out-migration (Rhoda, 1980). It is also debatable whether the reduction of migration should be a major goal, since in many parts of the world, women's chances to improve their status appear to be better in urban areas. For instance, Vatuk's study of urban neighbourhoods in a city of northern India (1972) indicates that married women are tending to be less attached to their husbands' kin networks than to their own natal kin, a pattern opposite to that typical in traditional rural areas and that undermines the isolation to which young married women are usually subject. It seems unlikely that such changes, with their positive connotations for raising the welfare of Indian women, would have taken place so rapidly in rural areas.

Industrialization policy

Industrialization policy is probably the most likely to have important impacts on migration and, particularly, on female migration. Its goal is usually to raise the manufacturing industry's share in GDP and thereby to increase economic growth rates. In recent years, the issue of the labour intensity of manufacturing has become crucial throughout much of the developing world which is faced with the problem of absorbing a rapidly growing labour force. Where traditional cottage and small-scale industry dominates employment, modern, capital-intensive plants can displace large numbers of workers in such industries as textiles, packaging materials, food and cigarettes (for Indonesia, see Jones and Manning, 1991). Often, women are the main workers displaced. The new jobs may also be concentrated in fewer locations than those displaced, giving the workers little option but to migrate in search of work.

The gender composition of the workforce in growing industries depends upon the type of industrialization being fostered. In Malaysia in the 1970s, the growing electronics and textile industries favoured female workers, with marked effects, albeit unintentional, on rural-urban migration by sex and on the traditional place of women within the Malay family. The proportion of women among production workers also increased in other countries, some of which had established export-processing zones, including the Dominican Republic, Mexico, the Philippines and the Republic of Korea (Anker and Hein, 1986; Zlotnik, 1993). But in many other countries, including most of Latin America, the share of women among production workers has been declining, supporting Boserup's (1970) hypothesis that development would push women out of their traditional handicraft type of occupations when factories, employing mainly men, were established to produce similar goods.

Education

Education has major effects on the roles and status of women and, consequently, affects all aspects of migration.[8] In many countries, parents treat educated children of either sex differently, expecting less work from them during their period of studies than they would from other children and being willing to spend more money on them (Caldwell, 1980). Such attitudinal changes are maintained over the years. Parents are more likely to tolerate, indeed to expect, attitudes and aspirations among educated daughters that conflict with traditional norms. Educated women are also treated differently by other members of society. Since men are used to "marrying down", well-educated women may find that their choice of husband is restricted and this factor, along with their interest in pursuing a career, is likely to delay marriage significantly.

Because education affects the roles and status of women, it also affects their labour force participation and their needs and opportunities to migrate. In most of the developing world, parents' willingness to educate women beyond junior secondary school implies the parents' acceptance of the possibility that women may pursue a career. In some countries, like India in recent times, the better education of daughters has become necessary for them to secure the well-educated husbands that their parents desire (Caldwell, Reddy and Caldwell, 1985). The empirical evidence on the relation between female education and labour force participation is usually U-shaped, with high rates of labour force participation among those with low and high educational levels and low rates among women with intermediate levels (lower secondary). Such outcome is related, at least in part, to status considerations and the nature of the job opportunities open to women with intermediate levels of education (Standing, 1981; Jones, 1986). However, as lower secondary education ceases to be the preserve of the middle classes, its association with low levels of labour force participation may change (Jones and Manning, 1991).

Both the effects of education on women's status and labour-market considerations may influence the relation between education and migration. Available evidence shows that women with more education are more likely to migrate autonomously. In Trengganu, a conservative state in Malaysia, young women with secondary education were the pace-setters in moving to cities and avoiding arranged marriages (Strange, 1981).

The connection often found between education or skills and migration has led to the conclusion that educational programmes have the unintended consequence of encouraging migration (Findley, 1977). In many countries with inadequate educational facilities in rural areas, the connection is quite direct: a major cause of female rural-urban migration has been the need to move to town to attend secondary school. Although the move was usually seen as temporary, many young women did not return home once their schooling was completed or if they did, they soon returned to the city in search of suitable employment. The expansion of secondary schools in small towns (which is currently under way in countries like Indonesia or Thailand) is seen as a way of stemming this tide. Sometimes, however, it is the educational content and the status of being a secondary-school graduate, rather than the urban location of the school *per se*, that results in out-migration from rural areas. Therefore, aside from setting secondary schools in small towns, the provision of adequate job opportunities locally is also necessary to reduce migration pressures.

Health services

The expansion of both health services and educational services has important implications for women in terms of employment opportunities. Women are heavily represented among teachers (especially primary-school teachers) and health workers (especially nurses and midwives) in most developing countries. The location of those services will therefore influence female migration patterns, though the number of women affected is likely to be small. However, given their relatively high level of skills, the migration of those women can have important implications for the community involved. Thus, when young women from small towns or rural areas who are trained as teachers, nurses or physicians either stay in their home area or return to it after training in the city, they are likely to have an important impact on the well-being of the community as a whole.

In general, an expansion of health services that contributes to improve the health status of the population in general and of women in particular is to be pursued. The provision of family planning information and services is especially important because by enabling couples to control their fertility, it can reduce the child-bearing and child-rearing responsibilities of women and thus make them better able to respond to the economic and educational opportunities that may be open for them, whether by migrating or not.

Tourism

In some countries, the expansion of tourism has been fostered as a potentially lucrative foreign-exchange earner and engine of growth. In Thailand, for instance, it is now a more important foreign-exchange earner than agriculture. Tourism has important implications for women's employment and migration. The tourist industry typically offers more job opportunities for women than men, and employment in tourism is typically more dispersed than that in the modern manufacturing industry, so that work in that sector often involves migration. To the extent that tourism involves the sex industry, female migrants may be preferred both because they are likely to have greater economic need and because they may be better able to maintain their anonymity.

This discussion has shown that female migration can play a positive developmental role. It would be unwise, however, to place too much emphasis on migration as a means of increasing women's autonomy and welfare, because its role in improving the status of women will depend upon whether women's situation is improved in other ways: by raising their educational attainment; by removing the legal barriers that prevent them from being autonomous economic actors; by improving their access to jobs and occupations that offer some prospects of occupational mobility; and by combating norms and customs that validate their subordinate position within the family or in society at large. The main issue, therefore, is to remove all barriers to women's full participation in economic, social and political life. In a context where women are being brought increasingly into the mainstream, migration is likely to have positive synergistic effects. It is in such a context that specific policies—for example, to provide accommodation to recently arrived female migrants in the cities, to counter sexual harassment in the workplace and to provide child-care facilities and labour-market information—are likely to have the most favourable impact.

Notes

[1] Recent migrants are all those that moved to a different locality during the five years immediately preceding the 1970 census or during the 10 years preceding the 1980 census.

[2] Census data for Latin American and Western Asian countries do not usually distinguish persons in domestic service from service workers as a whole. Yet, during the 1960s, women constituted about 70 per cent of all service workers in Latin American countries but only 16 per cent in Western Asian countries (Youssef, 1974). These percentages do not appear to have changed much during the 1970s. In the Philippines, women constituted 82 per cent of domestic servants in 1975 (Palabrica-Costello, 1984). In Pakistan in 1984, women constituted only 5 per cent

of workers in "personal and household services". In Bangladesh, in 1974, women accounted for 26 per cent of service workers in "community, social and personal services", most of whom would be domestic servants. In urban areas of India in 1981, 66 per cent of those working as "cooks, waiters, bartenders and related workers" or "maids and related housekeeping service workers" were men. Although "butlers, bearers and waiters" constituted more than one third of the former group, many of those included in the group would have been employed in institutions rather than households. Focusing only on "maids and related housekeeping service workers", the great majority of whom were classified as domestic servants, men constituted 42 per cent of the group at the national level but 65 per cent of it at Delhi. Furthermore, the proportion of women in those groups was higher at ages 30 or over than at younger ages. It is likely that the real proportion of women among domestic servants in Bangladesh, Pakistan or the urban areas of India is understated by the figures cited above, because many servants are young female relatives from rural areas who live in urban households and who would probably not be reported as servants in censuses or surveys.

[3] At a general level, the most frequently cited effects are the positive effects of human capital flows on areas of destination and the negative brain-drain and age-structure effects on areas of origin. But migration can affect wages, employment, incomes and income distribution, technological change and indeed fertility in quite complex ways. It is therefore not easy to evaluate the net effect of migration on economic development, let alone social development.

[4] Among all female migrants to Bangkok aged 15 or over, 70 per cent were reported to be single by the 1978 Survey of Migration to Bangkok Metropolis. That distribution contrasted sharply with the one characterizing all female migrants in Thailand (including intraprovincial migrants) which, according to the 1970 census, showed that 62 per cent of female migrants were married (Arnold and Piampiti, 1984).

[5] Unfortunately, the author has been unable to determine whether domestic service grew in relative terms in those Latin American countries whose economic situation deteriorated during the 1970s and 1980s.

[6] Similar differences were observed in Neuquén, a medium-sized city in Argentina, in 1980, although they were not as wide (see Recchini de Lattes and Mychaszula, 1993). Such differences are undoubtedly influenced by the migrants' stage in the life cycle and comparisons need to be carried out controlling by age.

[7] In 1971, the sex ratio of lifetime migrants was 138 in cities with more than 1,000,000 population, 111 for cities with 500,000-1,000,000 population, 113 for cities with 200,000-500,000 inhabitants and 98 for cities with 100,000-200,000 (Premi and Tom, 1985). The sex ratios were higher among recent migrants and there was less variation according to size of city (from 140 to 160).

[8] Even in Saudi Arabia, where the expansion of female education has taken place within the context of careful separation, not only of boys and girls, but even of ministerial responsibility for the male and female education systems, the Fourth Development Plan publicly airs the dilemmas of integrating the rapidly growing numbers of educated Saudi women into the workforce in accordance with the requirements of the shariah (Saudi Arabia, 1985). Hope is expressed that developments in computer applications will enable women to work from home, and that in such areas as process control, laboratories and teaching, women will be able to find work in accordance with the shariah (presumably meaning work that will not bring them into contact with men). Frustration by educated women at the severe restrictions placed on their employment opportunities is likely to provide the greatest challenge to the preservation of the Saudi family and social system, and it may be exacerbated by the presence in Saudi Arabia of migrant women from other Arab countries where restrictions on employment of educated women are not as tight.

REFERENCES

Adams, Richard N., and others (1960). *Social Change in Latin America Today*. New York: Harper.

Afonja, Simi (1990). Changing patterns of gender stratification in West Africa. In *Persistent Inequalities: Women and World Development*, Irene Tinker, ed. New York: Oxford University Press.

Ahmed, Ashraf Uddin, and Mohamed Abdul Mabud (1989). Population, health, education and women's status in Bangladesh. In *Frameworks for Population Development Integration*, vol. 2, *Bangladesh, Nepal, Philippines, Thailand*. Asian Population Studies Series, No. 93. Bangkok: United Nations Economic and Social Commission for Asia and the Pacific.

Ahmed, Iflikhar (1987). Technology, production linkages and women's employment in South Asia. *International Labour Review* (Geneva), vol. 126, No. 1 (January-February), pp. 21-40.

Anker, Richard (1983). Female labour force participation in developing countries: a critique of current definitions and data collection methods. *International Labour Review* (Geneva), vol. 122, No. 6 (November-December), pp. 709-723.

_____, and Catherine Hein (1986). Sex inequalities in third world employment: statistical evidence. In *Sex Inequalities in Urban Employment in the Third World*, Richard Anker and Catherine Hein, eds. Essex, United Kingdom: Macmillan Press.

Anker, Richard, M. E. Khan and R. B. Gupta (1987). Biases in measuring the labour force: results of a methods test survey in Uttar Pradesh, India. *International Labour Review* (Geneva), vol. 126, No. 2 (March-April), pp. 151-167.

Arizpe, Lourdes (1984). Agrarian change and the dynamics of women's rural out-migration in Latin America. In *Women on the Move: Contemporary Changes in Family and Society*. Paris: United Nations Educational, Scientific and Cultural Organization.

Arnold, Fred, and Suwanlee Piampiti (1984). Female migration in Thailand. In *Women in the Cities of Asia: Migration and Urban Adaptation*, James T. Fawcett, Siew-Ean Khoo and Peter C. Smith, eds. Boulder, Colorado: Westview Press.

Bardouille, R. (1986). Integration of Zambian women in national development: analysis of constraints and prospects. In *Women in Development: Perspectives from the Nairobi Conference*. IDRCMR137e. Ottawa, Canada: International Development Research Centre.

Benería, Lourdes (1982). Accounting for women's work. In *Women and Development: The Sexual Division of Labor in Rural Societies*, Lourdes Benería, ed. New York: Praeger.

Bilsborrow, Richard E., A. S. Oberai and Guy Standing (1984). *Migration Surveys in Low-Income Countries: Guidelines for Survey and Questionnaire Design*. Beckenham, United Kingdom; and Sydney, Australia: Croom Helm.

Boserup, Ester (1970). *Women's Role in Economic Development*. London: Allen and Unwin; and New York: St. Martin's Press.

_____ (1985). Economic and demographic interrelationships in sub-Saharan Africa. *Population and Development Review* (New York), vol. 11, No. 3 (September), pp. 383-397.

Cain, Mead, Syeda R. Khanam and Shamsun Nahar (1979). Class, patriarchy and women's work in Bangladesh. *Population and Development Review* (New York), vol. 5, No. 3 (September), pp. 405-438.

Caldwell, John C. (1969). *African Rural-Urban Migration: The Movement to Ghana's Towns*. Canberra, Australia: The Australian National University Press.

_____ (1980). Mass education as a determinant of the timing of the fertility decline. *Population and Development Review* (New York), vol. 6, No. 2 (June), pp. 225-255.

_____, P. H. Reddy and Pat Caldwell (1985). Educational transition in rural South India. *Population and Development Review* (New York), vol. 11, No. 1 (January), pp. 29-51.

Chaudhury, R. H., and R. Ahmed Nilufer (1980). *Female Status in Bangladesh*. Dhaka: Bangladesh Institute of Development Studies.

Corner, L. (1991). *Guidelines to an Integrated Approach to Human Resource Development, Policy-making, Planning and Programming*. ST/ESCAP/997. New York: United Nations.

Despradel, Lil (1984). Internal migration of rural women in the Caribbean and its effects on their status. In *Women on the Move: Contemporary Changes in Family and Society*. Paris: United Nations Educational, Scientific and Cultural Organization.

Ebery, Mark, and Brian Preston (1976). *Domestic Service in Late Victorian and Edwardian England, 1871-1914*. Geographical Papers. Department of Geography, University of Reading.

Elizaga, Juan C. (1965). Internal migrations in Latin America. In "Components of Population Change in Latin America", Clyde V. Kiser, ed. *The Milbank Memorial Fund Quarterly* (New York), vol. 43, No. 4, part 2 (October) pp. 144-165.

Engracia, Luisa, and Alejandro Herrin (1984). Employment structure of female migrants to the cities in the Philippines. In *Women in the Labour and Industrial Workforce: Southeast and East Asia*, Gavin W. Jones, ed. Development Studies Centre, Monograph No. 33. Canberra: The Australian National University.

Eviota, Elizabeth U., and Peter C. Smith (1984). The migration of women in the Philippines. In *Women in the Cities of Asia: Migration and Urban Adaptation*, James T. Fawcett, Siew-Ean Khoo and Peter C. Smith, eds. Boulder, Colorado: Westview Press.

Fawcett, James T., Siew-Ean Khoo and Peter C. Smith, eds. (1984). *Women in the Cities of Asia: Migration and Urban Adaptation*. Boulder, Colorado: Westview Press.

Fei, John C. H., and Gustav Ranis (1964). *Development of the Labour Surplus Economy: Theory and Practice*. Homewood, Illinois: Irwin Press.

Findley, Sally Evans (1977). *Planning for Internal Migration: A Review of the Issues and Policies in Developing Countries*. International Statistical Programs Center, Research Document No. 4. Washington, D.C.: United States Bureau of the Census.

Fuchs, Richard J., Gavin W. Jones and Ernesto M. Pernia, eds. (1987). *Urbanization and Urban Policies in Pacific Asia*. Boulder, Colorado: Westview Press.

Fuller, Theodore D. (1990). Thailand. In *International Handbook on Internal Migration*, Charich B. Nam, William J. Serow and David F. Sly, eds. Westport, Connecticut: Greenwood Press.

Goldstein, Sidney, and Alice Goldstein (1986). *Migration in Thailand: A Twentyfive Year Review*. Papers of the East-West Population Institute, No. 100. Honolulu: East-West Center.

Hetler, Carol (1986). Female-headed households in a circular migration village in Central Java, Indonesia. Unpublished doctoral dissertation. Canberra: The Australian National University.

_____ (1989). The impact of circular migration on a village economy. *Bulletin of Indonesian Economic Studies* (Canberra), vol. 25, No. 1 (April), pp. 53-75.

Hugo, Graeme J. (1987). Demographic and welfare implications of urbanization: direct and indirect effects on sending and receiving areas. In *Urbanization and Urban Policies in Pacific Asia*, Roland J. Fuchs, Gavin W. Jones and Ernesto M. Pernia, eds. Boulder, Colorado: Westview Press.

_____ (1993). Migrant women in developing countries. Chapter III in the present volume.

_____, Lin Lean Lim and S. Narayan (1989). Malaysian Human Resources Development Planning Project Module II: Labour Supply and Processes. Study No. 4, Labour mobility. First draft of final report. Adelaide: Flinders University of South Australia, School of Social Sciences.

Jelin, Elizabeth (1977). Migration and labor force participation of Latin American women: the domestic servants in the cities. *Signs* (Chicago, Illinois), vol. 3, No. 1 (Autumn), pp. 129-141.

Jellinek, Lea (1978). The pondok system and circular migration. In *The Life of the Poor in Indonesian Cities*, Lea Jellinek, C. Manning and Gavin Jones, eds. Melbourne, Australia: Monash University, Centre of Southeast Asia Studies.

Jones, Gavin W. (1977). Factors affecting labour force participation of females in Jakarta. *Kajian Ekonomi Malaysia/Malaysia Economic Studies* (Kuala Lumpur), vol. 14, No. 2 (December), pp. 71-93.

_____ (1980). Trends in marriage and divorce in Peninsular Malaysia. *Population Studies* (London), vol. 34, No. 2 (July), pp. 279-292.

_____, ed. (1984). *Women in the Urban and Industrial Workforce, Southeast and East Asia*. Development Studies Centre, Monograph No. 33. Canberra: The Australian National University.

_____ (1986). Differentials in female labour force participation rates in Indonesia: reflection of economic needs and opportunities, culture or bad data? *Majalah Demografi Indonesia/Indonesian Journal of Demography* (Jakarta), vol. 13, No. 26 (December), pp. 1-28.

_____ (1988). Urbanization trends in Southeast Asia: some issues for policy. *Journal of Southeast Asian Studies* (Singapore), vol. 19, No. 1 (March), pp. 137-154.

_____, and Chris Manning (1992). Labour force and employment during the 1980s. In *The Oil Boom and After: Indonesian Economic Policy and Performance in the Soeharto Era*, Anne Booth, ed. Singapore and New York: Oxford University Press.

Joshi, Heather, and Vijay Joshi (1976). *Surplus Labour and the City: A Study of Bombay*. New Delhi: Oxford University Press.

Lewis, William Arthur (1955). *The Theory of Economic Growth*. London: Allen and Unwin.

Lim, Lin Lean (1984). Towards meeting the needs of urban female factory workers in Peninsular Malaysia. In *Women in the Urban and Industrial Workforce: Southeast and East Asia*, Gavin W. Jones, ed. Development Studies Centre, Monograph No. 33. Canberra: The Australian National University.

Little, Kenneth Lindsay (1973). *African Women in Towns: An Aspect of Africa's Social Revolution*. London and New York: Cambridge University Press.

Maex, Rudy (1983). *Employment and Multinationals in Asian Export Processing Zones*. Multinational Enterprises Programme, Working Paper No. 26. Geneva: International Labour Office.

Manning, Chris (1988). Rural employment creation in Java: lessons from the green revolution and oil boom. *Population and Development Review* (New York), vol. 14, No. 1 (March), pp. 47-80.

Martine, George (1975). Volume, characteristics and consequences of internal migration in Colombia. *Demography* (Washington, D.C.), vol. 12, No. 2 (May), pp. 193-208.

Momsen, Janet Henshall, and Janet Townsend, eds. (1987). *Geography of Gender in the Third World*. London: Century Hutchinson Ltd.; and Albany, New York: State University of New York Press.

Palabrica-Costello, Marilou (1984). Female domestic service in Cagayan de Oro, Philippines: social and economic implications of employment in a 'premodern' occupational role. In *Women in the Urban and Industrial Workforce: Southeast and East Asia*, Gavin W. Jones, ed. Development Studies Centre, Monograph No. 33. Canberra: The Australian National University.

Papola, T. S. (1986). Women workers in the formal sector of Lucknow, India. In *Sex Inequalities in Urban Employment in the Third World*, Richard Anker and Catherine Hein, eds. London: Macmillan Press.

Peil, Margaret, with Pius O. Sada (1984). *African Urban Society*. Chichester, United Kingdom; and New York: John Wiley and Sons.

Premi, Mahendra K. (1982). *The Demographic Situation in India*. Papers of the East-West Population Institute, No. 80. Honolulu: East-West Center.

_____, and Judith Ann L. Tom (1985). *City Characteristics, Migration and Urban Development Policies in India*. Papers of the East-West Population Institute, No. 92. Honolulu: East-West Center.

Recchini de Lattes, Zulma, and Sonia María Mychaszula (1993). Female migration and labour force participation in a medium-sized city of a highly urbanized country. Chapter VIII in the present volume.

Rhoda, Richard E. (1980). Development activities and rural-urban migration. *Development Digest* (Washington, D.C.), vol. 18, No. 4 (October), pp. 3-21.

Rogers, Barbara (1980). *The Domestication of Women: Discrimination in Developing Countries*. London: Kegan Paul; and New York: St. Martin's Press.

Russell, Sharon Stanton, Karen Jacobsen and William Deane Stanley (1990). *International Migration and Development in Sub-Saharan Africa*, vol. 1, *Overview*. World Bank Discussion Paper, No. 101. Washington, D.C.: The World Bank.

Salih, K., and M. L. Young (1989). Changing conditions of labour in the semiconductor industry in Malaysia. *Labour and Society* (Geneva), vol. 14, Special issue on High Tech and Labour in Asia, pp. 5980.

Saudi Arabia (1985). *Fourth Development Plan*. Riyadh: Ministry of Planning.

Schultz, T. Paul (1971). Rural-urban migration in Colombia. *Review of Economics and Statistics* (Cambridge, Massachusetts), vol. 53, No. 2 (May), pp. 157-163.

_____ (1990). Women's changing participation in the labor force: a world perspective. *Economic Development and Cultural Change* (Chicago, Illinois), vol. 38, No. 3 (April), pp. 457-488.

Selvaratnam, S. (1988). Population change and women's development. In *Frameworks for Population and Development Integration*, vol. 1, *ESCAP Regional Perspectives*. Proceedings of the Regional Seminar on Frameworks for Population and Development Planning, Bangkok, 6-10 June 1988. Asian Population Studies Series, No. 92. Bangkok: Economic and Social Commission for Asia and the Pacific.

Shah, Nasra M. (1986). *Pakistani Women: A Socioeconomic and Demographic Profile*, Nasra M. Shah, ed. Islamabad: Pakistan Institute of Development Economics; and Honolulu, Hawaii, East-West Center.

Singh, Andrea Menefee (1978). Rural-urban migration of women among the urban poor in India: causes and consequences. *Social Action* (New Delhi), vol. 28, No. 4 (October-December), pp. 326-356.

_____ (1980). The impact of migration on women and the family: research, policy and programme issues in developing countries. *Social Action* (New Delhi), vol. 30, No. 2 (April-June), pp. 181-200.

_____ (1984). Rural-to-urban migration of women in India: patterns and implications. In *Women in the Cities of Asia: Migration and Urban Adaptation*, James T. Fawcett, Siew-Ean Khoo and Peter C. Smith, eds. Boulder, Colorado: Westview Press.

Singh, J. P. (1984). A comparative analysis of rural-urban migration in three states of India: Bihar, West Bengal and Kerala. Unpublished doctoral dissertation. Canberra: The Australian National University, Department of Demography.

_____ (1986). *Patterns of Rural-Urban Migration in India*. New Delhi: Inter-India Publications.

Skeldon, Ronald (1985). Migration in South Asia: an overview. In *Population Redistribution and Development in South Asia*, Leszek A. Kosinski and K. Maudood Elahi, eds. Dordrecht, Netherlands: D. Reidel.

Srinivas, M. N. (1984). *Social Change in India and Changing Position of Women in Developing Countries*. New Delhi: Centre for Women's Development Studies.

Standing, Guy (1981). *Labour Force Participation and Development*. 2nd ed. Geneva: International Labour Office.

Stichter, Sharon (1985). *Migrant Laborers*. Cambridge, United Kingdom: Cambridge University Press.

Strange, Heather (1981). *Rural Malay Women in Tradition and Transition*. New York: Praeger.

Sullivan, Norma (1983). Indonesian women in development: state theory and urban kampung practice. In *Women's Work and Women's Roles: Economics and Everyday Life in Indonesia, Malaysia and Singapore*, Lenore Manderson, ed. Development Studies Centre, Monograph No. 32. Canberra: The Australian National University.

Sudarkasa, Niara (1977). Women and migration in contemporary West Africa. *Signs* (Chicago, Illinois), vol. 3, No. 1 (Autumn), pp. 178-189.

Tan, P. C., and G. W. Jones (1990). Malay divorce in Peninsular Malaysia: the near-disappearance of an institution. *Southeast Asian Journal of Social Sciences* (Singapore), vol. 18, No. 2, pp. 85-114.

Thadani, Veena N. (1985). Social relations and geographic mobility: male and female migration in Kenya. In *Labour Circulation and the Labour Process*, Guy Standing, ed. Beckenham, United Kingdom; and Sydney, Australia: Croom Helm.

_____, and Michael P. Todaro (1984). Female migration: a conceptual framework. In *Women in the Cities of Asia: Migration and Urban Adaptation*, James T. Fawcett, Siew-Ean Khoo and Peter C. Smith, eds. Boulder, Colorado: Westview Press.

Thailand, National Commission on Women's Affairs (1987). *Identification of Issues Concerning Women and their Consideration in Development Planning*. Bangkok: National Commission on Women's Affairs and the United Nations Educational, Scientific and Cultural Organization.

Thomson, S. (1990). Gender issues in Thailand development. Paper prepared for the United Nations Development Programme. Bangkok: Gender and Development Research Institute.

Tienda, Marta, and Karen Booth (1988). Migration, gender and social change: a review and reformulation. *Conference on Women's Position and Demographic Change in the Course of Development, Oslo, 1988: Solicited Papers*. Liège: International Union for the Scientific Study of Population.

Tinker, Irene (1973). Women in development. *International Development Review* (Rome), vol. 2, pp. 39-43.

Tongudai, Pawadee (1984). Women migrants in Bangkok: an economic analysis of their employment and earnings. In *Women in the Urban and Industrial Workforce: Southeast and East Asia*, Gavin W. Jones, ed. Development Studies Centre, Monograph No. 33. Canberra: The Australian National University.

Trager, Lillian (1984). Family strategies and the migration of women: migrants to Dagupan City, Philippines. *International Migration Review* (Staten Island, New York), vol. 18, No. 4 (Winter), pp. 1264-1278.

United Nations Secretariat (1993). Types of female migration. Chapter V in the present volume.

Vatuk, Sylvia J. (1972). *Kinship and Urbanization: White Collar Migrants in North India*. Berkeley and London: University of California Press.

Widarti, D. (1991). Determinants of female labour force participation and work patterns: the case of Jakarta. Unpublished doctoral dissertation. Adelaide: The Flinders University of South Australia.

Young, Kate (1982). The creation of a relative surplus population: a case study from Mexico. In *Women and Development: The Sexual Division of Labor in Rural Societies*, Lourdes Benería, ed. New York: Praeger.

Youssef, Nadia H. (1976). *Women and Work in Developing Societies*. Westport, Connecticut: Greenwood Press.

Zlotnik, Hania (1993). Women as migrants and workers in developing countries. In "Sociology and social development in a time of economic adversity", James Midgley and Joachim Singelmann, eds. *International Journal of Contemporary Sociology* (Joensuu, Finland), vol. 30, No. 1, special issue, pp. 39-62.

XIX. GOVERNMENT POLICIES, WOMEN AND MIGRATION: A REVIEW OF RESEARCH FINDINGS AND POLICY OPTIONS IN DEVELOPING COUNTRIES

Alan B. Simmons[*]

Although both women and men migrate in the process of social and economic transformation, women have often been viewed as being relatively passive and secondary in the process. It has been argued that in many parts of the developing world women have limited mobility due to traditional gender roles which make them subservient to fathers and husbands (Thadani and Todaro, 1984). In societies with early marriage and high levels of fertility, women's child-care responsibilities restrict their ability to work outside the home, their freedom to commute to work or for marketing and the extent to which they can migrate for employment. In such settings, women are more likely to migrate in order to join their husbands after marriage or to accompany their husbands or fathers when the men decide to move.

Images of female migrants as wives following their husbands or as daughters tied to their families have tended to take them out of the spotlight of research and policy discussion. Yet, this image is increasingly being questioned and the continuing lack of policy attention to the role of female migration in development appears as an anomaly. Recent years have witnessed a major increase in public awareness of women's productive roles, mobility and contributions to development; nevertheless, the interrelations between migration and women's economic roles have received little attention in policy discourse (Hugo, 1993; Zlotnik, 1993). Studies repeatedly document that although women in developing countries are far more active in production than conventional statistics would indicate (Spindel, 1987; World Bank, 1989; Bennett, 1992; Recchini de Lattes and Wainerman, 1981), women tend to benefit less from economic growth than men (Crummett, 1987; Greenhalgh, 1991; Bennett, 1992). Thus, women generally obtain less schooling and receive lower wages than men and they are often disadvantaged in terms of nutrition and access to health care. These disadvantages contribute to the underutilization of women as a development resource. Policies that would improve women's access to schooling, employment and other resources would undoubtedly have important implications for female migration.

Although policy assessments stress the need to reduce the lost economic potential arising from the underinvestment in women, and in so doing to improve gender equity and raise family incomes (World Bank, 1989; Bennett, 1992; Deere and León, 1987), even the most recent in-depth country studies by the World Bank give scant attention to the role that female migration can play in improving women's access to schooling, health care and more productive employment.[1] The single migration-related issue considered extensively by recent policy studies involves the special needs of women who stay in rural areas as de facto heads of household when their close male relatives migrate (World Bank studies cited in footnote 1; Adepoju, 1988; Makinwa-Adebusoye, 1988; Findley and Williams, 1991).

There are strong reasons for examining more carefully the links between government policies and female migration. In most societies today, women cannot be characterized as having only weak and secondary roles in relation to migration or employment. Even in traditional societies, important changes in women's economic roles and migration patterns are taking place (Hugo, 1993; Zlotnik, 1993; Findley and Williams, 1991). Female migration is significant in all parts of the world and is increasingly tied to the employment and income-earning prospects of women. Yet, the role of government policies in affecting those trends remains largely to be elucidated. It is important to establish what role, if any, policies may have in ensuring that female migration shall help women to improve their life and prospects.

---

[*]Centre for Research on Latin America and the Caribbean, York University, Toronto, Canada.

Given that there has been almost no systematic research on the topic at hand, the first objective here is to identify hypotheses on the ways in which Government policies can affect female migration and development outcomes for women. A second objective is to review the scattered research findings on those hypotheses and identify gaps that ought to be addressed in future studies, and a third is to provide a preliminary assessment of promising policy options in this field.

Before reviewing specific hypotheses, the existence of an important research gap should be mentioned. That is the gap between the study of population distribution policies, on the one hand, and that of female migration on the other. Although a great deal is known about the impact of different types of Government policies on broad migration and population distribution patterns,[2] the literature on that topic scarcely touches gender issues. On the other hand, most studies on female migration have failed to give adequate consideration to the role of Government policies in shaping female migration and its consequences.[3]

Taking into account the few studies that address directly the influence of Government policies on female migration and those which provide other useful insights from which to make inferences, a number of preliminary conclusions and guidelines for further research and policy development can be drawn. Support for those conclusions varies, because the relevant studies cover some topics better than others and some studies refer only to a single country or case. Furthermore, because the range of potential topics is large, many topics are scarcely covered. Hugo (1993) notes that virtually all aspects of Government policy—education, recruitment for government service, social welfare, employment, occupational licensing, training, landownership, land settlement or access to government housing—are relevant to migration patterns and outcomes for women, but he identifies these more as matters for which there is much scope for assessment, meaning that they must be researched further.

A. Conceptual approach

The hypotheses presented here are largely based on the human resources approach to the understanding of migration and development, giving particular attention to female migration. This perspective emphasizes the inherent interdependence between spatial mobility, schooling, health, labour force participation, technological innovation and rising productivity for both women and men. Within this perspective, spatial mobility is viewed as a key mechanism to increase the access of women and men to schooling and economic opportunities. Spatial mobility can take various forms (daily commuting, seasonal migration, circulation, long-term migration etc.), so that it can be adapted to different circumstances that lead people to take advantage of existing opportunities. Because the forces that limit female mobility are closely linked to those limiting their schooling, their acquisition of job skills and their labour force participation, policies that combat existing limitations in any area are likely to have favourable implications for other areas of women's lives.

The human resources approach views mobility as a type of lubricant which helps individuals and households adapt to changing circumstances and in so doing reallocates human resources more efficiently. This view implies that more lubricant would make the national economic machinery work better. Therefore, measures that increase the mobility of women (and that of men) would lead to higher average national incomes than would have been reached otherwise. This general view, however, needs to be qualified in some important respects.

The human resources approach to migration and development may be understood as a hypothesis largely consistent with a neoclassical, two-sector development model (Lewis, 1963; Fei and Ranis, 1964) which is compatible with neoclassical models of migration (Massey, 1988; Harris and Todaro, 1970). Yet, neoclassical models suffer from important limitations (Cohen, 1987). In particular, the implications of neoclassical models are formulated almost exclusively at the macrolevel and thus involve only average outcomes. Thus, in the neoclassical approach, migration—particularly rural-urban migration—is viewed as a mechanism facilitating the rise of average national productivity and income. Yet, average outcomes do not necessarily reflect those experienced by particular groups of people. Even when the overall economy is growing, certain groups, such as the less educated, ethnic minorities or women, may experience few gains.

A related criticism is that neoclassical models are restricted to the economic realm and thus disregard institutional and cultural forces. To understand how unequal outcomes arise in the development process one must take account of such forces. Cultural values and class structures, among other factors, shape national markets and influence the way in which women, minority groups, less privileged social classes and others participate in development and the rewards they obtain from it. Historical-structural approaches, including those stressing gender and class inequalities in development, have generally given more attention to such power issues (Cohen, 1987; Benería and Roldán, 1987; Peek and Standing, 1982).

When the benefits of development are equally shared, the average outcome would not be very different from that experienced by individuals, whether men or women. In most cases, however, the average experience may hide large disparities between communities and social classes or between men and women. Such inequalities may be viewed as accidental but inevitable outcomes of development (this is typically the neoclassical view) or as the result of cultural power (e.g., patriarchy) and institutional power (e.g., social and political élites) affecting both development strategies and their outcomes, a fundamental assumption in historical-structural studies.

Consequently, the best approach to study the relation between Government policies and female migration is to take account of both macro- and micro-perspectives. That is, both policies that affect the relation of female migration to economic growth and those that ensure an equitable distribution of the benefits of development, particularly where women are concerned, must be considered. Thus, both economic policies affecting the access of female migrants to jobs, land, credit and other productive resources, and social policies influencing female migration by changing the skills that women bring to the economy and the institutional and cultural constraints that limit their involvement in productive activity should be the object of analysis.

Government policies affecting internal migration can be classified into three broad areas:

(a) *Sectoral development policies*. These policies affect migration indirectly by altering the distribution of employment and economic opportunities. The two major sectors are agriculture (rural) and industry (urban). Policies affecting the operation of those sectors typically have major impacts on the employment and migration of both women and men. Their implications for migration and its outcomes, however, can be quite different for women and men, depending upon the context and the specific policies pursued. In countries where industry employs mostly men, policies that promote industrial expansion will generate male-led migration to the cities or other sites where industry is located. If, in contrast, commercial and service activities or certain kinds of manufacturing that tend to employ women are expanded, female migration is likely to increase. Alternatively, agricultural development policies that promote the productive roles of women in rural areas would increase the incomes of peasant households and slow out-migration.

(b) *Social development policies*. These policies govern access to land, employment, education, health care and other resources and have a strong potential to change cultural values. Changes in laws on property ownership and inheritance that ensure that women shall have equal rights as men to own or inherit land, policies that open new fields of schooling or training for women and those which increase their job opportunities can simultaneously expand the resources available to women and shift perceptions about what women can do. Those changes are likely to influence women's spatial mobility, since many will have to commute to nearby towns or cities to study or work and others may have to move to places where their skills are in demand. Similarly, the provision of maternal and child health services that encompass family planning can facilitate migration by allowing women to delay child-bearing or to limit their family size and thus reduce their child-care responsibilities;

(c) *Population distribution policies*. Policies directed to modifying migration trends or patterns, or the regional distribution of the population, do not, in general, attempt explicitly to affect the sex balance of migration. Some, however, may have sex-selective effects in so far as they influence the employment generation and social policy dimensions of population distribution plans.

B. RESEARCH FINDINGS ON GOVERNMENT POLICIES

Agricultural and rural development policies

Changing employment and income opportunities in rural areas clearly have an impact on female migration (Zlotnik, 1993). Rural women migrate for seasonal agricultural work in Africa, Asia and Latin America (Findley and Williams, 1991). They also migrate as members of farm households being relocated as part of rural colonization schemes (Henriques, 1985). When rural opportunities diminish in relative terms, women migrate to towns and cities (Greenhalgh, 1991; Crummett, 1987). Such movements vary considerably from one country to another, in response to different economic, social and cultural patterns (Findley and Williams, 1991).

In many cases, the role of agricultural and other rural development policies in affecting female migration patterns is difficult to assess, in part because Government policies are only one determining factor whose effects may be overriden by the operation of international markets or of national economic and cultural forces. In addition, other sectoral and macroeconomic policies, such as those governing international currency exchange rates and industrial subsidies or protections, may distort or even cancel the effects of rural development policies (Lipton, 1976).

Although research findings are uneven, they point to three common (or at least well-documented) patterns of migration outcomes affecting women. Each of these patterns seems to be associated, at least in part, with development policies, their successes or failures. The three patterns are: *(a)* mixed outcomes associated with female rural-urban migration; *(b)* poor outcomes for women associated with rural-rural migration or with the out-migration of men in a context of economic stagnation; and *(c)* positive outcomes for women in the context of successful rural development and male labour circulation.

Mixed outcomes from Government policies accelerating female rural-urban migration

A review of women's employment prospects and the expansion of informal enterprises leads to the conclusion that in the cases of Ghana, India and Thailand, Government policies favouring urban enterprises have reduced women's economic opportunities in rural areas while increasing those of men in urban areas (Greenhalgh, 1991). Women lost not only the productive roles that they had in rural areas but also other resources: Ghanaian women, for instance, no longer had control over conjugal income and Thai women who had inherited land lost control over it. Migrant women became more dependent upon their husbands, who were more likely than themselves to find wage employment in the city. To earn some income, women had little choice but to turn to the urban informal sector, mostly to street vending, a form of insecure and poorly paid self-employment (Greenhalgh, 1991). Although Greenhalgh notes that these negative changes in the status of women were reinforced by the low educational levels of the women concerned, she does not discuss in detail the particular macroeconomic policies that led to those outcomes nor how those policies affected the migration and well-being of women other than those coming from small farms.

Studies of how Government policies have modified rural and urban economic opportunities in Latin America tend to support the findings detailed above and provide more information on the role of Government policies and on how their outcomes vary for different categories of rural women and female migrants. Research on Latin America spans the 1960s and 1970s, a period when most countries in the region adopted policies to promote industrialization directed to import-substitution. More recent studies focus on the effects of structural adjustment and the export-oriented growth policies adopted in the region during the 1980s. In discussing these two different development strategies, the accent is generally put on the urban and industrial sectors, although those strategies also include important rural development policy dimensions.

Over the 1960s and 1970s, Latin American Governments tended to subsidize and protect national industry in order to satisfy the national consumer market. Subsidies were paid for by the export of raw agricultural products, forestry products and minerals, and by international borrowing. Two types of rural development policies typically emerged in this context. The dominant set of policies promoted more efficient export agriculture by encouraging farm mechanization and modernization. A subordinate set of policies sought to protect small farmers by promoting rural credit, cooperative marketing and land reform. The subordinate policies either failed (land reform efforts were abandoned after partial implementation) or were not implemented (de Janvry, 1981).

The mix of policies described above had a major impact on internal migration patterns, leading to specific female migration trends. Small landowners generally were affected negatively by the rural transformation brought about by the dominant policy thrusts (Shaw, 1974; de Janvry, 1981; Peek and Standing, 1982). Markets for small farmers declined as more efficient large-scale producers took over or as tariff protection dropped and foreign producers undercut their prices. Valuable land held by peasants and small farmers was taken over by large export-oriented producers. Peasants had little voice in the land transfers, either because their poverty forced them to sell at desperation prices or because they were renters and sharecroppers living on estates from which they could be evicted. Credit went mostly to large farmers who could guarantee repayment of loans. Depending upon the country, variable numbers of small farmers have survived by combining seasonal wage employment with peasant farming; others have lost their land but continue to live in rural areas as agricultural workers; many others have moved to the cities, contributing to the high levels of urbanization in the region. Violent class and regional struggles in rural Peru, El Salvador and other countries derive in large part from the declining prospects for peasant agriculture, land shortages and the expansion of large-scale farming (North and CAPA, 1990).

The effect of these trends on female migration in Latin America was notable. Women have generally outnumbered men in migration to cities, while men outnumbered women in seasonal migration to rural areas and resettlement in frontier regions (Recchini de Lattes, 1988; Crummett, 1987). Women left the rural areas because they were particularly disadvantaged by the rural transformation and the Government policies that lay behind it (Crummett, 1987). In families with land, women were least likely to hold the title. If women farmed, they had difficulty getting credit and technical assistance. Women also faced more restricted opportunities in paid agricultural work (with some exceptions, as noted by Lago, 1987) and they were often left semi-abandoned by migrant husbands and other migrant family members. As a result of these factors, women of all ages left rural areas. Younger unmarried women were especially prone to migrate because they were less tied to family responsibilities in the place of origin and were in demand as maids in urban households (Crummett, 1987) and as workers in offshore manufacturing (Carrillo-Huerta, 1990; Szasz, 1993; Gabayet and Lailson, 1990).

Given the context described above, it is not surprising that the Latin American literature has stressed mixed, often negative, outcomes for small farmers, migrant women, men and households. Migrant women, many of whom work in domestic service, face poor wages, abuse and exploitation by the owners of the homes in which they work, as well as loss of freedom and mobility: six-day work weeks for live-in maids are common (Crummett, 1987; Zlotnik, 1993). Others drift into prostitution or street vending. Housing and sanitation conditions for the migrants may be dreadful, leading to epidemics of major diseases: witness the recent outbreak of cholera in the slums of Lima where a high proportion of rural-urban migrants live.

Beginning in the late 1970s, industrial import-substitution policies were abandoned in Latin America (Griffin, 1989) and policies directed to promoting export-oriented development were adopted. To increase export competitiveness, protective industrial tariffs and subsidies to national industry have been reduced or eliminated. Policies favouring traditional exports of agricultural goods, forest products and minerals have been maintained. However, the shift from import-substitution to export-oriented development coincided with a major recession in the region, which produced a 10 per cent decline in average household incomes during the 1980s (IDB, 1988-1991) and whose effects on migration cannot be separated from those attributable to the new development policies. Industrial production and employment in the region shrank dramatically during the 1980s. The more industrialized countries of the region, such as Brazil or Mexico, appear to have experienced a major decline in net migration to their largest cities. Thus, growth in Mexico City slowed to a trickle in the 1980s (Graizbord and Mina, 1993), while the share of São

Paulo in the national population declined (Pacheco, 1993). In the case of Brazil, the 1980s witnessed large flows of male migrants to rural frontier areas (Pacheco, 1993) and a significant outflow of poor women and their children from the inner part of the city of São Paulo to slums in its rural periphery (Bogus, 1993; Pasternak Taschner, 1993). Lack of control over speculative land-pricing appears to have been one of the factors forcing the poor to abandon the city's core.

It is important, however, to qualify the general picture presented above. Female migration is characterized by diversity, since it involves different classes of people and various types of migration streams. In Chile, for example, female migrants were found to have a wide range of educational attainment levels and occupational skills (Herold, 1979). Although poor women from rural areas found only poorly paid work when they moved to the cities, women from more affluent rural families often migrated to intermediate cities to finish their schooling and were thus more likely to secure better jobs. Adepoju (1991) argues that rising levels of female migration from rural areas to the cities of Africa may be linked to rising educational levels among women.

In rural Argentina, women engage in all types of migration, including short-term circulation, longer term migration on their own or accompanied by other family members, migration within rural areas, migration to small or intermediate cities in the vicinity of their village of origin or migration to the city of Buenos Aires (Forni and Benencia, 1988; Forni, Benencia and Neiman, 1991). Recchini de Lattes and Mychaszula (1993) document the diversity of female migrants in the intermediate city of Neuquén, Argentina in terms of educational attainment, occupation and region of origin. Because female migrants originating in Buenos Aires tend to be better educated than those from the areas neighbouring Neuquén, the authors suggest that the former group may benefit more from migration than the latter.

Diversity also characterizes women migrating to the rapidly growing towns of northern Mexico. As in many other streams, female migrants tend to cluster in the categories with relatively high and relatively low levels of schooling, even though, on average, they have higher levels of schooling than women in the regions of origin (Carrillo-Huerta, 1990; Szasz, 1993). Such heterogeneity in migration flows is likely to be associated with the particular mix of policies that the Goverment has in place to promote agriculture, industry or education. However, much remains to be understood about how such policies interact and which policies have the greatest impact on female migration and its characteristics.

Poor outcomes for women associated with rural-rural migration or with male out-migration in a context of economic stagnation

The preceding discussion indicates that rural-urban migration can be at least a survival mechanism and in many cases a beneficial move for rural women when rural income opportunities decline. In contexts of economic stagnation, however, rural women often lack the wherewithal to migrate to urban areas where, in any case, wage-earning opportunities may also be scarce. In such contexts, women often stay behind in rural areas when men migrate or migrate within rural areas in search of work.

The rural-rural migration of women often holds little promise for improving their well-being. Zlotnik (1993) describes this type of movement as a "dead end" for most women, as in the case of women working as unskilled agricultural workers in such countries as Argentina (Forni and Benencia, 1991), Kenya (Addo, 1981), Pakistan (World Bank, 1989) or the United Republic of Tanzania (Bernstein, 1981). The income women earn as unskilled seasonal workers barely allows their survival and that of their families, and their work experience is unlikely to lead to better wages, new job skills or other development benefits. Exceptions may arise when rural work for women becomes more skilled, as seems to have happened in relation to the agricultural export industry in Chile (Lago, 1987).

A common pattern is for women to remain behind in rural areas while the men in their households out-migrate either seasonally or for longer periods. The plight of such women depends mostly upon two factors: the amount of remittances the men send back; and the extent to which women are able to carry out productive activities in the rural areas of origin. The income of migrant men will be influenced by Government policies in the sectors where they find employment, including industry, commerce or mining. The productive and income-earning activities of women in rural areas will be influenced by Government policies related to the technical training of women in rural areas, their access to credit and the possibilities of marketing the goods that they can produce in the absence of men. If women have access to land, their success may also depend upon whether they can hire labour for certain periods (Makinwa-Adebusoye, 1988).

Various studies in Southern and Eastern Africa and in certain countries of Western Africa (such as Ghana) have documented a common pattern of rural-urban male migration, low levels of remittances and a high number of female-headed households in rural areas that lack productive resources and access to income-generating activities (Adepoju, 1988; Makinwa-Adebusoye, 1988; Lloyd and Brandon, 1991; Findley and Williams, 1991). In those circumstances, rural women and their families remain caught in a web of development stagnation and inadequate policy response. Some of those women, particularly those without family responsibilities, engage in circulation to cities or mining towns where they work in marginal jobs or engage in prostitution. Male migrants in the cities, mines and plantations, being isolated from their wives and girlfriends, commonly consort with prostitutes, many of whom are female migrants that have been forced to leave their villages because of deteriorating conditions. Venereal disease is rampant in some areas of high migration (Ross, 1991) and the open genital sores that often result from venereal infections facilitate the spread of HIV infection. There is an urgent need for policies directed to the prevention of HIV infection in a context of highly mobile people pressed by poverty to engage in risky behaviour.

Positive outcomes for women in the context of successful rural development and male labour circulation

Various studies suggest that rural women do not necessarily have to migrate in order to improve their condition. Women benefit particularly from male seasonal migration if they can take on expanded roles in production. Dandler and Medeiros (1988) note that in rural Bolivia male out-migration has had various benefits: overall family income increased because of remittances, commercial contacts between rural and urban areas expanded, new markets were created for the family's farm and handicraft products, and the children of migrants became exposed to new ideas and information. Similarly, during the 1960s and 1970s, when farming in the cash-crop regions of Côte d'Ivoire and Nigeria was viable, women benefited from the out-migration of men because they could maintain farm productivity by hiring workers (labour force was plentiful because of immigration from the Sahel) and by being closely involved in the marketing of produce (Makinwa-Adebusoye, 1988). Women thus gained status and expanded their roles in production and commerce.

In India, contrary to common belief, expanding agricultural production through irrigation and mechanization created new wage-employment opportunities for rural women (Bennett, 1992). It is not clear, however, whether the wages women earned were high enough to ensure improved nutrition, better housing or improved access to health care for the women concerned and their families. As is the case of many of the topics covered in this chapter, the available research is suggestive but inconclusive.

Studies by Colfer (1985) and Stivens (1985) on Indonesia and Malaysia, respectively, provide further evidence that policies and development strategies leading to male circulation can be positive for the women that remain behind, provided they belong to households having some land holdings and local circumstances permit women to have an expanded role in farm production when the men are away. Both cases involve changes in agricultural technology (in part driven by Government policies) and how these have affected migration in general and rural women in particular. In Kalimantan, Indonesia, rural women in a particular village benefited from the rise in labour circulation involving their husbands and other family members (Colfer, 1985). Men, who had traditionally done the plowing, were displaced from agriculture by the introduction of tractors and had to engage in seasonal migration to replace their lost income. Women carried on with farming, relying upon their own male relatives when they were at home or upon hired labour. Thus, women's productive roles were strengthened, their power in family decision-making rose and their control over income expanded. In the more prosperous parts of rural Indonesia, as incomes and aspirations rose, younger generations increasingly withdrew from agriculture and went on to pursue an education. However, these studies fail to document just how much the positive outcomes mentioned depend upon the magnitude of male remittances.

In Chile, Government policies favouring fruit exports have been successful in providing wage employment for rural women that work seasonally picking fruit—a traditional job for men and women—and packing it for exportation—an expanding occupation for women (Lago, 1987). Packing requires greater skill and brings some prestige to the women concerned. Country-specific studies of this type are useful in generating hypotheses that need to be examined in other settings.

Unfortunately, none of the studies cited above analyses the role of Government policies either in depth or systematically. One may nevertheless infer that general development circumstances and Government policies play a joint role in determining the favourable outcomes experienced by rural women, whether they remain in their villages of origin or circulate as seasonal workers. In the period covered by these studies (mostly the 1970s or early 1980s), profits from oil exports in Indonesia and Nigeria, tropical forest products in Côte d'Ivoire and Indonesia, plantation crops in Côte d'Ivoire or wheat in Argentina created opportunities that did not necessarily exist elsewhere. Most of those countries had rising levels of living; and in the case of Côte d'Ivoire or Nigeria, policies favouring higher internal food prices were implemented to provide income supports for farmers and vendors. Hypotheses on the role that Government policies played in benefiting the women affected by migration need more careful scrutiny in those cases.

The only strong hypothesis that can be derived from the research reviewed above is that Government policies can play a key role in improving the production and incomes of farms run by women. Policies can include those which raise the incomes of male migrants and therefore have a positive effect on remittance levels, as well as those which provide technology, credit and marketing support to female farmers. With such supports, rural women may not need to migrate in order to benefit from development.

Urban and industrial policies

In recent years, the thrust towards industrialization in developing countries has been increasingly based on policies favouring export-oriented manufacturing. Interest in this approach stems from the experience of the newly industrializing economies of Eastern and South-eastern Asia, namely, Hong Kong, Malaysia, the Republic of Korea, Singapore, Taiwan Province of China and Thailand. Other countries are trying to emulate their example by adopting various policies intended to encourage foreign direct investment and the expansion of manufacturing, including the creation of export-processing zones and the use of subcontracting and other forms of production that rely heavily upon female labour. When effective, such policies shift the gender composition of employment by involving more women in industrial and informal sector jobs. They affect households through their impact on the relative employment and income of men and women, and they affect migration patterns through their differential impact on employment opportunities for men and women.

Newly industrializing economies of Eastern and South-eastern Asia

The six countries or areas identified above have experienced very significant economic growth in recent decades under forms of government and policy administrations that may be described as limited democracy because they combine authoritarian control with democratic practices, typically by restricting which candidates can run in elections. This type of political system has been successful in maintaining the cheap and pliant labour force desired by manufacturing interests. Thus, union activity is controlled, strikes and wage demands are discouraged and political parties that respond more favourably to the demands of labour are controlled or suppressed (Griffin, 1989). Yet, Government policies in the countries or areas concerned have tended to promote the acquisition of skills among workers and to improve worker productivity by ensuring universal primary education and strengthening secondary, post-secondary and technical training for both women and men. Such policies have tended to raise both productivity and incomes while promoting at the same time a greater degree of income equality than is generally found in developing countries (Griffin, 1989).

The levels of rural-urban migration in Malaysia, the Republic of Korea, Taiwan Province of China and Thailand have been high, accelerated by the growth of manufacturing and commerce in the larger cities and by the concentration of technical schools, hospitals, airports, government services and so on in the major urban centres (Simmons, 1981). In particular, all countries have experienced the rapid growth of their capital cities. In Malaysia and the Republic of Korea, both political will and sufficient resources have been available to bring about limited forms of planned urban and industrial decentralization by creating industrial belts near Kuala Lumpur, for instance, or by locating industry outside of Seoul though still within its immediate vicinity. For the most part, however, decentralization policies have had limited effects, especially in terms of their impact on migration to major urban centres (Simmons, 1979).

Studies of female migration and households affected by migration in these newly industrializing economies show that outcomes for migrants follow those for families and workers more generally. Thus, migrant women interviewed at Seoul, Republic of Korea, reported many job-related hardships, poor living conditions, loneliness and other negative outcomes associated both with economic transformation and with their status as migrants (Hong, 1984). Yet, they also reported that their earnings and purchasing power had improved, so that they enjoyed a higher level of living. Women that were disadvantaged before migration tended to continue being disadvantaged after it, but even they may view the outcomes of migration as positive, particularly when they are able to assure through their remittances the survival of the families that they have left behind.

Export-processing zones

Many developing countries have established export-processing zones, that is, industrial sites that operate under special legislation allowing the duty-free import of raw materials for the assembly and manufacture of goods which are primarily destined for exportation (Zlotnik, 1993). Export-processing zones are meant to attract foreign direct investment by offering low production costs, especially with respect to labour. In 1986, there were 176 export-processing zones operating in 47 developing countries (Zlotnik, 1993). One distinct feature of export-processing zones is the high percentage of women working in them (Mitter, 1986; Zlotnik, 1993; Nash and Fernández-Kelly, 1983). Unfortunately, existing studies on female workers in export-processing zones do not generally distinguish migrant from non-migrant women, though it is often recognized that migrant women constitute significant proportions of the female labour force in these zones, even if they did not migrate specifically to work in them (Zlotnik, 1993).

In some countries, export-processing zones have been intentionally located near labour sources. Thus, in Malaysia, several Japanese electronics firms have established themselves in zones near villages so that female workers can be transported from and to their homes every day, a cheaper strategy than offering them dormitories away from home and one that satisfies local concerns about control over young women's activities (Ong, 1987). Although these practices tend to reduce female migration, their effects on women and their families are often similar to those involving migration. Thus, the increasing income-earning opportunities of young women reinforce positively those values favouring female education and employment, and contribute to change the roles of women.

Studies of export-processing zones have tended to draw attention to the positive outcomes, largely in terms of higher profits, for owners and managers, nearly all of whom are men, and the negative outcomes for workers, a majority of whom are women, often migrants (Mitter, 1986; Nash and Fernández-Kelly, 1983). Thus, female workers are typically paid less than men for equivalent work, may lose their jobs if they protest or attempt to organize in any way and in some instances are subject to significant health risks (Fuentes and Ehrenreich, 1983). That women accept to work under such poor conditions is taken as proof that no other alternatives are available.

Those who are most critical of export-processing zones argue that they reinforce traditional forms of patriarchy by adding a new layer of capitalist patriarchal practices that subordinate women to men (Mitter, 1986). However, detailed studies in Malaysia and Mexico show that work in export-processing zones may simultaneously reinforce some aspects of patriarchy while undermining or threatening others. In the case of Malaysia, young women are encouraged by their families to work in the zones, not so much because their wages are indispensable but rather because they need to accumulate a dowry and thus improve their marriage prospects, especially in a context where rural and manual work is increasingly losing appeal (Ong, 1987). Young women work for low wages in jobs that tax their eyesight and stamina but receive strong support from community traditions and emerging values. Factory work thus becomes part of the culture and of women's socialization, without changing women's subordinate position within the family. Traditional and capitalist patriarchy thus reinforce each other. Yet, at the same time, by earning a wage, women gain some degree of independence. Their tendency to wear new types of clothing and to acquire various consumer durables is viewed with great ambivalence by the community, because their emerging independence threatens Islamic controls over women's economic activities, sexuality and reproduction (Ong, 1987).

Maquiladora plants in the northern part of Mexico have also been criticized for offering low wages and poor working conditions and contributing to the subordination of women (Nash and Fernández-Kelly, 1983). However, some studies indicate that working in the *maquiladoras* can provide women with opportunities for upward mobility. In the state of Guadalajara, migrant women working in the *maquiladoras* have somewhat higher levels of educational attainment than women from the villages from which they originate (Gabayet and Lailson, 1990). Most are married and their employment is essential to a family strategy for upward mobility. When the men in their households are unemployed or have recently migrated to the United States, the women's wages support the household at a minimal level. When the men send remittances, the women's income goes to "extras", including investment in improved housing and savings for the education of children. Women thus feel that they gain important advantages from their work and do not wish to stop working even when their husbands earn a sufficient income.

Subcontracting and piece-work at home

Because large numbers of persons are willing to work for low wages in the cities of developing countries, private investors, often backed by Government policies favouring the expansion of manufacturing, have developed new forms of labour-intensive production. In Mexico, for instance, the plastic components needed to produce toys come from high technology factories, but sorting, assembling and packaging the toys can be done less expensively by women doing piece-work at home (Benería and Roldán, 1987). The women are hired by subcontractors, who deliver the components and pick up the packaged toys. Diverse products are manufactured in this or similar ways, by subcontracting individual women or employing them in small informal sector shops. The apex of the productive system often involves large corporations which produce for both domestic and international markets.

Urban piece-work at home and subcontracting constitute an indirect bridge between policy, migration and its outcomes for women. These forms of production are not intentionally planned by Governments; they are rather the indirect outcome of general development circumstances and macroeconomic policies that favour low-cost manufacturing as a vehicle to attract investment and promote economic growth. In countries where advanced technology is not affordable or where the low levels of education of the labour force make high technology unviable, low-cost manufacturing is equivalent to low-wage manufacturing. Both male and female workers are affected by these practices, but the position of women is more precarious: they tend to work at home for the lowest wages and are poorly placed to organize protests or form unions to protect their interests. Their bargaining position is weak not only because they work in relative isolation but because they fear losing their jobs to other women. Both migrant and non-migrant women are involved, but migrant women of rural backgrounds are particularly vulnerable because of their low educational levels and lack of job skills.

Social development policies

Social policies relevant to migration cover a broad range and include access to housing, health care and schooling. Of these, perhaps the most important is schooling, because higher educational attainment tends to lead to better income prospects and improved access to housing and health care. Schooling is also closely tied to migration, particularly because men and women from rural areas or small towns often need to migrate in order to have access to higher levels of schooling. The content of schooling can shape the expectations of men and women about the occupations appropriate to each sex and can thus assist or prevent a transformation of those cultural values which limit female spatial mobility and occupational opportunities. The relation between female migration and schooling has been noted in a number of studies. The following observations are based on research findings for particular settings and it is not clear to what extent they can be generalized. Nevertheless, they indicate possible hypotheses for further research.

Rural-urban migration often includes a significant number of adolescent men and women that migrate to towns and cities in order to continue their schooling. Some of these young men and women have relatives in the place of destination, others move to boarding-schools and yet others move with their entire families or with some close relatives. In Western Africa, families often put children in the hands of "tutors" (generally relatives) who have the responsibility of educating the children and helping them find a job (Antoine, 1991). In Senegal, boys appear to predominate among children sent to Dakar and they are more likely than girls to speak French (the language of schooling and commerce). In Peru, girls are less likely to commute to school when it is far away and are more likely to drop out when the cost of schooling rises (Gill, 1991). Migration itself is not discussed in the case of Peru but, by implication, girls or young women are less likely to be sent to urban areas to continue their studies than are boys or young men.

Adult women may also migrate to get schooling or training. Oppong (1991) mentions the case of a West African woman who, after bearing three children, "ran away" from an unpromising marriage to complete her education. That example suggests that in some societies schooling and migration are not only out of bounds for women but also that by breaking the barriers in one domain it may be easier to break those in another.

In many migration streams, women with higher levels of educational attainment tend to be overrepresented with respect either to the population of the place of origin or to that of the place of destination (Adepoju, 1991; Recchini de Lattes and Mychaszula, 1991; López, Izazola and Gómez de León, 1993). Women with higher levels of schooling are also likely to have more resources at their command so that for them distance is less of a barrier. Often, therefore, they are overrepresented in migration over long distances. The educational attainment of women in general and of migrant women in particular is closely related to their job prospects. Women with high qualifications are likely to have more options and to act on them when migration is involved.

Diverse findings on the relations between female migration, educational attainment and employment, such as those cited above, can be interpreted from the human capital perspective to mean that parents invest in the migration and education of their children in direct proportion to the anticipated economic returns to such investment. If labour-markets produce greater returns to the schooling of men, then parents will invest in the schooling of their sons more than in that of their daughters (Gill, 1991). When acquiring the necessary schooling implies that offspring have to live elsewhere, families that have the means will invest in that relocation as well.

Government expenditures in education have a direct impact on the educational attainment of men and women. A higher investment in schools and teachers allows the system to accommodate more students. The costs of distributing schools more widely over a country's territory reduce the expenses falling on parents and encourage them to keep their sons and daughters in school longer. By allocating more funds to primary schooling in relative terms, a more universal coverage of basic education is likely to be achieved.

A study relating to Peru, based on the relations between migration, educational attainment and employment, argues that increasing the schooling of women will raise their human capital, make them more responsive to training and job opportunities elsewhere and thus increase their spatial mobility (Gill, 1991). Since investments on female education are often not perceived by parents as producing high returns to investment, any policies that lower the costs that parents have to bear (by locating schools in the communities concerned or lowering fees, for instance) will have significant effects in equalizing the educational attainment of men and women. That is, because women begin at a disadvantaged position, they will benefit disproportionately from such policies. It is clear that the impact of such policies cannot be separated from broader social and cultural practices with respect to the employment of men and women. In the case of Peru, the returns on the schooling of men are not only generally higher than those on the schooling of women, but are particularly high in the industrial sector. The benefits of the schooling of women are higher with respect to urban services. Therefore, an effective way to increase the share of women among highly paid workers is to reduce the costs of schooling in general and to institute other policies that favour the growth of the service sector, particularly with regard to occupations that offer women well-paid employment. Thus, Gill (1991) concludes that policies favouring investment in urban services would be advantageous since they would promote urbanization, female rural-urban migration, the schooling of women and an increase of female wages. These conclusions contrast with those of most development studies, which argue for investment in the industrial rather than in the service sector. The advantage of Gill's approach is that it balances equity (promoting increased opportunities for women) and economic growth, rather than ignoring the former to focus only on the latter.

C. POLICY OPTIONS

This review suggests that any policy that makes available new resources to poor women or their immediate families—such as land reform, credit to small farms (especially those run by women), new job opportunities, better wages or subsidized housing for female migrants—will improve the outcomes of migration for women. Better jobs and incomes for migrant men that send back remittances will also benefit the women left behind in terms of their level of income or nutrition, although they may not necessarily change the prevailing pattern of women's subordination to men.

In so far as migration is mostly an intervening process in resource distribution, the question is not just how to promote migration patterns that will allow women to access new resources but also the extent to which new resources can be redistributed or generated for distribution through policy measures. Whether people have to move in order to access those resources is also an important, though secondary, question. If, for reasons of efficiency or location-specific advantages, new opportunities are best created elsewhere, then women's access to them will be mediated through migration. If new opportunities can be created locally, positive outcomes will arise without recourse to migration. Such a conclusion is consistent with the findings in this chapter but it may not be sufficiently specific to provide guidance to those interested in addressing the impact of migration on women.

One needs to examine those policies which have a particularly strong potential of improving migration outcomes for women. Such policies must be attractive development strategies in their own right. A good starting-point for their formulation is to examine whether the dominant development policies currently pursued by Governments can be modified, expanded or reshaped to improve the migration outcomes for women.

Agricultural exports

In many cases, migrant and non-migrant women in rural areas are involved in agricultural production for exportation, primarily as poorly paid labourers working during peak production periods or sometimes contracted along with their husbands (e.g., the case of Brazil in Spindel, 1987; the case of the Dominican Republic in Mones and Grant, 1987). Those women, if migrants, rarely benefit from their migration except to the extent that it may assure their survival. However, there are cases where female agricultural workers are paid as well as, if not better than, men, mostly because they specialize in fruit packing, a skilled task contributing considerably to the value of the final product (see the case of Chile in Lago, 1987). Thus, policies that promote the acquisition of skills by women so that they can carry out specialized work in agro-industrial operations will tend to benefit those migrating to take up jobs in that sector.

Industrial exports and export-processing zones

Since women are so central in the production process carried out in export-processing zones, it is important to consider whether the implications of their working in the zones can be improved and whether that type of production can be expanded to involve larger numbers of women under favourable conditions. These are difficult issues, particularly because the prospects for improving the conditions of work in export-processing zones are dim. Developing countries are hesitant to impose improved wage and working standards on offshore industry lest that industry relocate elsewhere. Given the limited nature of foreign direct investment and the growing competition between developing countries to attract it, working standards are unlikely to improve in the near future.

Several studies (le Bideau, 1993; Mouhoud, 1993; Bailey and Parisotto, 1993) point out that over the 1980s many developed countries and international firms withdrew capital and productive capacity from developing countries. The reasons for that withdrawal are complex and include rising automation in developed countries, the use of new inventory practices (fast turn-around), and shifts in consumer tastes (towards higher quality goods). According to those studies, continuing investments in offshore production have been heavily concentrated in some countries of South-eastern Asia and Mexico, areas with particular advantages. South-eastern Asia combines relatively low-cost labour (though labour costs have been rising) with technological advances in production. Mexico offers a cheap labour force and is located near the Northern American market. Mexico is trying to attract modern and highly productive industry instead of continuing the expansion of labour-intensive assembly plants. As in Hong Kong and Singapore, where the introduction of robots and the training of workers is raising productivity and wages, Mexico wishes to foster high-technology production that will reinvigorate its economy more than the *maquiladoras*, which have remained poorly integrated into the rest of Mexican industry. Only a few developing countries can compete with the advantages offered by the newly industrializing countries in Eastern and South-eastern Asia or by Mexico. Africa, for example, gains little advantage from its low-cost labour force, because its production capacity and technology are so poor.

One of the few avenues for improving the working conditions of women in offshore processing plants has been the inclusion of stipulations on minimum working conditions in bilateral trade agreements and the General Agreement on Tariffs and Trade (GATT) arrangements (Mouhoud, 1993). The ILO and other bodies have promoted such policies, but they have often been resisted by the developing countries themselves, which see those proposals as protectionist measures on the part of developed countries. Fearful of losing investment in their export-processing zones, Governments of developing countries resist any measures that would increase production costs. In the power triangle involving workers, managers of international corporations and government officials, workers are isolated and relatively weak. When the workers are non-unionized women in poor countries, their bargaining position is particularly feeble. The resulting power juggernaut that favours international corporations can be broken most effectively through international trade and other agreements that assure certain benefits and guarantees to the Governments of developing countries and thus override their concerns about enforcing better working conditions in their industrial plants. Since such benefits and guarantees will represent an extra cost for developed countries, the key issue is whether those countries can be convinced to adopt the proposed policies.

Education and other social development policies

Improving women's opportunities to continue their studies is an effective way to increase their responsiveness to changes in job opportunities and therefore to foster their spatial mobility in ways that improve the functioning of internal markets. Schooling increases the value that women add to production by allowing them to undertake skilled work. Other social policies, such as widely distributed public-health services that include family planning services, can also affect women's mobility and economic roles. Although research on the interrelations between educational attainment, health and migration is scarce, it is likely that women with higher educational attainment may be more prone to migrate and be economically active because they are healthier and have smaller families. Consequently, any policy that improves health and lowers fertility is likely to foster female spatial mobility and employment. Similarly, any policy that facilitates the provision of adequate housing and other services to female migrants will enhance the overall flexibility of the economy by facilitating female mobility in response to economic incentives.

Addressing the needs of vulnerable women

In cases where development circumstances and policies have created particularly damaging and dangerous outcomes for female migrants or for women affected by the migration of close family members, the most pressing need is for immediate damage control, especially in the form of social assistance and health protection programmes. Women in need of special protection and support include: *(a)* poor female heads of rural households, whose male relatives have migrated and who need food and income support in the short term, as well as appropriate technology, credit and marketing services over the longer term; *(b)* poor rural-urban female migrants in need of public health and nutritional education programmes to assist them in overcoming the problems that they face in the urban environment; *(c)* female migrants working in places where they are exposed to toxic substances and other health hazards, whose protection can be assured through the adoption and enforcement of adequate safety standards in the workplace; and *(d)* women engaging in prostitution, many of whom are migrants, who need health care and counselling services.

The preceding policy suggestions are offered cautiously, since policies to combat the negative outcomes of migration for women have been rarely studied in depth to date. Similarly, the arguments supporting strategies to increase the mobility of women through a combination of economic and social development policies are based on inferences from a variety of studies focusing on a limited number of cases. Some of the more important issues, such as the consideration of mechanisms to involve women more effectively in organizations that would increase their voice in the formulation of local, regional and national policies affecting how migration outcomes impact on them and their families, have not even been covered in existing research. It is clear that a concerted effort to link migration outcomes to particular policy mixes is still necessary, especially where women are concerned.

NOTES

[1] The World Bank is preparing a number of detailed country-level assessments of ways to improve opportunities for women and their contributions to development. These studies rely heavily upon household survey data and provide an exceptional opportunity for evaluating the problems facing women and the policy options that would address those problems. Currently available reports on India (Bennett, 1992), Pakistan (World Bank, 1989) and Peru (Herz and Khandker, 1991) provide extensive reviews of the problems facing rural and urban women, but they either fail to mention migration (e.g., India and Pakistan) or deal with it only briefly (e.g., Peru). Thus, the report on Peru only takes into account migration to correct possible biases in a model of income returns to schooling (Gill, 1991).

[2] See, for instance, Simmons (1981, 1984), United Nations (1981, 1984), Bilsborrow and Geores (1992), and Peek and Standing (1982).

[3] Important review papers on female migration include Oliveira (1984, on Mexico), Chaney (1985, on the Caribbean), Crummett (1987, on Latin America), De Vos (1987, on Latin America), Lim (1988, theoretical), Makinwa-Abusoye (1988, on Africa), Recchini de Lattes (1988, on Latin America), Tienda and Booth (1988, theoretical), Findley and Williams (1991, global), Hugo (1993, global), Szasz (1993, on Mexico) and Zlotnik (1993, on female migration and employment).

REFERENCES

Addo, N. O. (1981). The impact of public policies on migration and development in Ghana with special reference to the Asutsuare sugar area. Population and Labour Policies Programme, Working Paper No. 110. Geneva: International Labour Office.

Adepoju, A. (1988). An overview of rural migration and agricultural labour force structure in Africa. *Etudes de la population africaine/ African Population Studies* (Dakar, Senegal), vol. 1.

_____ (1991). Population and the planning of large cities in Africa. *Etudes de la population africaine/African Population Studies* (Dakar, Senegal), vol. 6.

Antoine, Philippe (1991). Croissance urbaine et insertion des migrants dans les villes africaines. *Etudes de la population africaine/African Population Studies* (Dakar, Senegal), vol. 6, pp. 72-94.

Bailey, Paul J., and Aurelio Parisotto (1993). Multinational enterprises: what role can they play in employment generation in developing countries? In *The Changing Course of International Migration*. Paris: Organisation for Economic Co-operation and Development

Benería, Lourdes, and Martha Roldán (1987). *The Crossroads of Class and Gender: Industrial Homework, Subcontracting, and Household Dynamics in Mexico City*. Chicago, Illinois: The University of Chicago Press.

Bennett, Lynn (1992). *Women, Poverty, and Productivity in India*. Economic Development Institute Seminar Paper, No. 43. Washington, D.C.: The World Bank.

Bernstein, Henry (1981). *Pattern of migration in Tanzania*. Population and Labour Policies Programme, Working Paper No. 101. Geneva: International Labour Office.

Bilsborrow, Richard E., and M. Geores (1992). *Rural Population Dynamics and Agricultural Development*. Ithaca, New York: Cornell Population and Development Program and the Cornell International Institute for Food, Agriculture and Development.

Bogus, L. M. Machado (1993). Processos migratorios e transição demografica: o caso da metropole paulista. In *IV Conferencia Latinoamericana de Población: La Transición Demográfica en América Latina y el Caribe, Mexico City, 23-26 March 1993*, vol. II. Mexico: Instituto Nacional de Estadística e Informática—Instituto de Investigaciones Sociales de la Universidad Nacional Autónoma de México.

Carrillo Huerta, M. M. (1990). The impact of *maquiladoras* on migration in Mexico. Working Paper No. 51. Washington, D.C.: Commission for the Study of International Migration and Cooperative Economic Development.

Chaney, Elsa M. (1985). *Migration from the Caribbean Region: Determinants and Effects of Current Movements*. Hemispheric Migration Project, Occasional Paper Series. Washington, D.C.: Georgetown University, Center for Immigration Policy and Refugee Assistance.

Cohen, Robin (1987). *The New Helots: Migrants in the International Division of Labour*. Brookfield, Vermont: Gower.

Colfer, Carol (1985). On circular migration: from the distaff side. In *Labour Circulation and the Labour Process*, Guy Standing, ed. Beckenham, United Kingdom; and Sydney, Australia: Croom Helm.

Crummett, María de los Angeles (1987). Rural women and migration in Latin America. In *Rural Women and State Policy: Feminist Perspectives on Latin American Agricultural Development*, Carmen Diana Deere and Magdalena León, eds. Boulder, Colorado; and London: Westview Press.

Dandler, Jorge, and Carmen Medeiros (1988). Temporary migration from Cochabamba, Bolivia to Argentina: patterns and impacts in sending areas. In *When Borders Don't Divide: Labor Migration and Refugee Movements in the Americas*, Patricia R. Pessar, ed. New York: Center for Migration Studies.

de Janvry, Alain (1981). *The Agrarian Question and Reformism in Latin America*. Baltimore, Maryland: The Johns Hopkins University Press.

De Vos, Susan (1987). Latin American households in comparative perspective. *Population Studies* (London), vol. 41, No. 4 (November), pp. 501-517.

Deere, Carmen Diana, and Magdalena León, eds. (1987). *Rural Women and State Policy: Feminist Perspectives on Latin American Agricultural Development*. Boulder, Colorado: Westview Press.

Fei, John C. H., and Gustav Ranis (1964). *Development of the Labour Surplus Economy*. Homewood, Illinois: Richard Unwin.

Findley, Sally E., and Linda Williams (1991). *Women Who Go and Women Who Stay: Reflections of Family Migration Processes in a Changing World*. Population and Labour Policies Programme, Working Paper No. 176. Geneva: International Labour Office.

Forni, F., and R. Benencia (1988). Demographic strategies in an underdeveloped region of a modern country: the case of Santiago del Estero, Argentina. In *Impact of Modernization on Development and Demographic Behavior*, C. Vlassoff and Barkat-e-Khuda, eds. Ottawa: International Development Research Centre.

Forni, F., R. Benencia and G. Neiman (1991). *Empleo, estrategias de vía y reproducción: hogares rurales en Santiago del Estero*. Buenos Aires: Bibliotecas Universitarias, Centro Editor de América Latina.

Fuentes, Annette, and Barbara Ehrenreich (1983). *Women in the Global Factory*. New York: Institute for New Communications; and Boston, Massachusettes: South End Press.

Gabayet, L., and S. Lailson (1990). The role of female wage earners in male migration in Guadalajara. Working Paper No. 50. Washington, D.C.: Commission for the Study of International Migration and Cooperative Economic Development.

Gill, I. (1991). Does the structure of production affect demand for schooling in Peru? In *Women's Work, Education, and Family Welfare in Peru*, Barbara K. Herz and Shahidur K. Khandker, eds. Discussion Paper, No. 116. Washington, D.C.: The World Bank.

Graizbord, B., and A. Mina (1993). Cambios en la relación población-territorio en Mexico. In *IV Conferencia Latinoamericana de Población: La Transición Demográfica en América Latina y el Caribe, Mexico City, 23-26 March 1993*, vol. II. Mexico: Instituto Nacional de Estadística e Informática—Instituto de Investigaciones Sociales de la Universidad Nacional Autónoma de México.

Greenhalgh, Susan (1991). *Women in the Informal Enterprise: Empowerment or Exploitation?* Population Council Working Papers, No. 33. New York: The Population Council.

Griffin, Keith (1989). *Alternative Strategies for Economic Development*. Basingstoke, United Kingdom: Macmillan.

Harris, John R., and Michael P. Todaro (1970). Migration, unemployment and development: a two-sector analysis. *American Economic Review* (Nashville, Tennessee), vol. 60, No. 1 (March), pp. 126-142.

Henriques, M. H. (1985). The demographic dynamics of a frontier area: the state of Rondonia, Brazil. In *Impact of Rural Development Projects on Demographic Behavior*, Richard E. Bilsborrow and Pamela F. DeLargy, eds. Policy Studies, No. 9. New York: United Nations Fund for Population Activities.

Herold, Joan M. (1979). Female migration in Chile: types of moves and socioeconomic characteristics. *Demography* (Washington, D.C.), vol. 16, No. 2 (May), pp. 257-278.

Herz, Barbara K., and Shahidur E. Khandker (1991). *Women's Work, Education, and Family Welfare in Peru*. Discussion Paper, No. 116. Washington, D.C.: The World Bank.

Hong, Sawon (1984). Urban migrant women in the Republic of Korea. In *Women in the Cities of Asia: Migration and Urban Adaptation*, James T. Fawcett, Siew-Ean Khoo and Peter C. Smith, eds. Boulder, Colorado: Westview Press.

Hugo, Graeme J. (1993). Migrant women in developing countries. Chapter III in the present volume.

Inter-American Development Bank (1988). *Economic and Social Progress in Latin America*. Washington, D.C.: Inter-American Development Bank.

Lago, María Soledad (1987). Rural women and the neo-liberal model in Chile. In *Rural Women and State Policy: Feminist Perspectives on Latin American Agricultural Development*, Carmen Diana Deere and Magdalena León, eds. Boulder, Colorado; and London: Westview Press.

Le Bideau, J.-L. (1993). The economic climate for foreign direct investment. In *The Changing Course of International Migration*. Paris: Organisation for Economic Co-operation and Development.

Lewis, William Arthur (1963). Economic development with unlimited supplies of labour. In *The Economics of Underdevelopment*, A. N. Agarwala and S. P. Singh, eds. London and New York: Oxford University Press.

Lim, Lin Lean (1988). Effects of women's position on migration. In *Conference on Women's Position and Demographic Change in the Course of Development, Oslo, 1988: Solicited Papers*. Liège: International Union for the Scientific Study of Population.

Lipton, Michael (1976). *Why Poor People Stay Poor: Urban Bias in World Development*. Cambridge, Massachusetts: Harvard University Press.

Lloyd, Cynthia, and Anastasia J. Gage-Brandon (1991). *Women's Role in Maintaining Households: Poverty and Gender Inequality in Ghana*. Working Papers, No. 25. New York: The Population Council.

López, María de la Paz, Haydea Izazola and Jose Gómez de Léon (1993). The characteristics of female migrants according to the 1990 census of Mexico. Chapter VII in the present volume.

Makinwa-Adebusoye, Paulina (1988). Labour migration and female-headed households. In *Conference on Women's Position and Demographic Change in the Course of Development, Oslo, 1988: Solicited Papers*. Liège: International Union for the Scientific Study of Population.

Massey, Douglas S. (1988). Economic development and international migration in comparative perspective. *Population and Development Review* (New York), vol. 14, No. 3 (September), pp. 383-414.

Mitter, Swasti (1986). *Common Fate, Common Bond: Women in the Global Economy*. London; and Wolfeboro, New Hampshire: Pluto Press.

Mones, Belkis, and Lydia Grant (1987). Agricultural development, the economic crisis, and rural women in the Dominican Republic. In

Rural Women and State Policy: Feminist Perspectives on Latin American Agricultural Development, Carmen Diana Deere and Magdalena León, eds. Boulder, Colorado; and London: Westview Press.

Mouhoud, El Mouhoub (1993). Enterprise relocation, north-south economic relations and the dynamics of employment. In *The Changing Course of International Migration*. Paris: Organisation for Economic Co-operation and Development.

Nash, June, and María Patricia Fernández-Kelly (1983). *Women, Men and the New International Division of Labour*. Albany, New York: State University of New York Press.

North, Liisa, and Canadian-Caribbean-Central America Policy Alternatives (CAPA) (1990). *Between War and Peace in Central America: Choices for Canada*. Toronto: Between the Lines.

Oliveira, Orlandina de (1984). Migración femenina, organización familiar y mercados laborales en México. *Comercio Exterior* (Mexico), vol. 34, No. 7, pp. 676-687.

Ong, Aihwa (1987). *Spirits of Resistance and Capitalist Discipline: Factory Women in Malaysia*. Albany: State University of New York Press.

Oppong, Christine (1991). Modernizing mothers: analysis of Ghanaian focused biographies. *Etudes de la population africaine/African Population Studies* (Dakar, Senegal), vol. 6.

Pacheco, C. A. (1993). Evolução recente da urbanização e da questão regional no Brasil. In *IV Conferencia Latinoamericana de Población: La Transición Demográfica en América Latina y el Caribe, Mexico City, 23-26 March 1993*, vol. II. Mexico: Instituto Nacional de Estadística e Informática—Instituto de Investigaciones Sociales de la Universidad Nacional Autónoma de México.

Pasternak Taschner, Susana (1993). Dinámica demográfica y transición en el área metropolitana de São Paulo. In *IV Conferencia Latinoamericana de Población: La Transición Demográfica en América Latina y el Caribe, Mexico City, 23-26 March 1993*, vol. II. Mexico: Instituto Nacional de Estadística e Informática—Instituto de Investigaciones Sociales de la Universidad Nacional Autónoma de México.

Peek, Peter, and Guy Standing, eds. (1982). *State Policies and Migration: Studies in Latin America and the Caribbean*. London; and Canberra, Australia: Croom Helm.

Recchini de Lattes, Zulma (1988). Las mujeres en las migraciones internas e internacionales, con especial referencia a América Latina. *Cuaderno del CENEP* (Buenos Aires), vol. 40.

_____, and Sonia María Mychaszula (1993). Female migration and labour force participation in a medium-sized city of a highly urbanized country. Chapter VIII in the present volume.

_____, and Catalina H. Wainerman (1981). *El trabajo femenino en el banquillo de los acusados: la medición censal en América Latina*. Colección Economía y Sociedad. Mexico: The Population Council/Editorial Terra Nova.

Ross, O. (1991). Aids in Africa. *Globe and Mail Newspaper* (Toronto), 20 August, pp. D1 and D4.

Shaw, R. Paul (1974). Land tenure and the rural exodus in Latin America. *Economic Development and Cultural Change* (Chicago, Illinois), vol. 23, No. 1 (October), pp. 123-132.

Simmons, Alan B. (1979). Slowing metropolitan city growth in Asia: a review of policies, programs and results. *Population and Development Review* (New York), vol. 5, No. 1 (March), pp. 87-104.

_____ (1981). A review and evaluation of attempts to constrain migration to selected urban centres and regions. In *Population Distribution Policies in Development Planning*. Papers of the United Nations/UNFPA Workshop on Population Distribution Policies in Development Planning, Bangkok, 4-13 September 1979. Population Studies, No. 75. Sales No. E.81.XIII.5. New York: United Nations.

_____ (1984). Migration and rural development: conceptual approaches, research findings and policy issues. In *Population Distribution, Migration and Development*. Proceedings of the Expert Group on Population Distribution, Migration and Development, Hammamet, Tunisia, 21-25 March 1983. Sales No. E.83.XIII.3. New York: United Nations.

Spindel, Cheywa R. (1987). The social invisibility of women's work in Brazilian agriculture. In *Rural Women and State Policy: Feminist Perspectives on Latin American Agricultural Development*, Carmen Diana Deere and Magdalena León, eds. Boulder, Colorado; and London: Westview Press.

Stivens, Maila (1985). The fate of women's land rights: Gender, matriliny, and capitalism in Rembau, Negeri Sembilan, Malaysia. In *Women, Work and Ideology in the Third World*, Haleh Ashfar, ed. New York: Tavistock Publications.

Szasz, I. (1993). Migración feminina y transición demográfica: algunas reflexiones desde la perspectiva de género. Paper presented at the IV Conferencia Latinoamericana de Población. Mexico: Colegio de México. Mimeographed.

Thadani, Veena N., and Michael P. Todaro (1984). Female migration: a conceptual framework. In *Women in the Cities of Asia: Migration and Urban Adaptation*, James T. Fawcett, Siew-Ean Khoo and Peter C. Smith, eds. Boulder, Colorado: Westview Press.

Tienda, Marta, and Karen Booth (1988). Migration, gender and social change: a review and reformulation. In *Conference on Women's Position and Demographic Change in the Course of Development, Oslo, 1988: Solicited Papers*. Liège: International Union for the Scientific Study of Population.

United Nations (1981). *Population Distribution Policies in Development Planning*. Papers of the United Nations/UNFPA Workshop on Population Distribution Policies in Development Planning, Bangkok, 4-13 September 1979. Population Studies, No. 75. Sales No. E.81.XIII.5. New York: United Nations.

_____ (1984). *Population Distribution, Migration and Development*. Proceedings of the Expert Group on Population Distribution, Migration and Development, Hammamet, Tunisia, 21-25 March 1983. Sales No. E.83.XIII.3. New York: United Nations.

World Bank (1989). *Women in Pakistan: An Economic and Social Strategy*. Washington, D.C.

Zlotnik, Hania (1993). Women as migrants and workers in developing countries. In "Sociology and social development in a time of economic adversity", James Midgley and Joachim Singelmann, eds. *International Journal of Contemporary Sociology* (Joensuu, Finland), vol. 30, No. 1, special issue, pp. 39-62.

كيفية الحصول على منشورات الأمم المتحدة

يمكن الحصول على منشورات الأمم المتحدة من المكتبات ودور التوزيع في جميع أنحاء العالم. استعلم عنها من المكتبة التي تتعامل معها أو اكتب إلى: الأمم المتحدة، قسم البيع في نيويورك أو في جنيف.

如何购取联合国出版物

联合国出版物在全世界各地的书店和经售处均有发售。请向书店询问或写信到纽约或日内瓦的联合国销售组。

HOW TO OBTAIN UNITED NATIONS PUBLICATIONS

United Nations publications may be obtained from bookstores and distributors throughout the world. Consult your bookstore or write to: United Nations, Sales Section, New York or Geneva.

COMMENT SE PROCURER LES PUBLICATIONS DES NATIONS UNIES

Les publications des Nations Unies sont en vente dans les librairies et les agences dépositaires du monde entier. Informez-vous auprès de votre libraire ou adressez-vous à : Nations Unies, Section des ventes, New York ou Genève.

КАК ПОЛУЧИТЬ ИЗДАНИЯ ОРГАНИЗАЦИИ ОБЪЕДИНЕННЫХ НАЦИЙ

Издания Организации Объединенных Наций можно купить в книжных магазинах и агентствах во всех районах мира. Наводите справки об изданиях в вашем книжном магазине или пишите по адресу: Организация Объединенных Наций, Секция по продаже изданий, Нью-Йорк или Женева.

COMO CONSEGUIR PUBLICACIONES DE LAS NACIONES UNIDAS

Las publicaciones de las Naciones Unidas están en venta en librerías y casas distribuidoras en todas partes del mundo. Consulte a su librero o diríjase a: Naciones Unidas, Sección de Ventas, Nueva York o Ginebra.

Litho in United Nations, New York
93-55706—November 1993—5,075
ISBN 92-1-151260-3

United Nations publication
Sales No. E.94.XIII.3
ST/ESA/SER.R/127